Texas

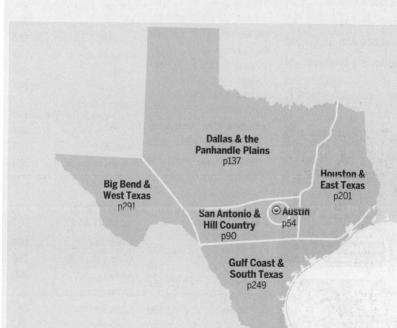

Dallas & the Panhandle Plains
p137

Houston & East Texas
p201

Big Bend & West Texas
p291

San Antonio & Hill Country
p90

◉ **Austin**
p54

Gulf Coast & South Texas
p249

Amy C Balfour, Stephen Lioy, Ryan Ver Berkmoes

Contents

BLUEBONNET
WILDFLOWERS P359

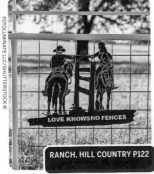

LOVE KNOWS NO FENCES

RANCH, HILL COUNTRY P122

Contents

SPECIAL FEATURES

Welcome to Texas

Bigger than a whole heap of countries, Texas is vast, diverse and welcoming: from big-city lights to small-town simplicity, white-sand beaches to high-country hikes.

Now That's Country

'Country' is as much about a way of life as a place. Slowing down, taking the rural, farm-to-market back roads; steppin' out in polished boots and starched blue jeans for a Saturday-night dance under the stars; doin' nothing more on a Sunday afternoon than floating down a lazy river... Life in the country lopes along. Even if most Texans now live in urban areas, they're influenced by the state's agricultural, roping-and-riding heritage – and they escape to the country just as often as they can.

Fun & Delicious Food

There's just something about eating a big pile of brisket off a butcher-paper 'plate.' Don't dare ask for a fork; the best BBQ is for fingers only. And great barbecue is not the state's only fun food. At festivals, rodeos and fairs much of your meal can be served on a stick, from corny dogs to fried PB&J sandwiches. In Austin and other cities the food truck phenomenon continues. And we haven't even dug into the ubiquitous Mexican food, Dallas' fine upscale dining or the foodie-fave restaurants around Houston.

Cities & Towns

Big cities in Texas? Fun-loving, vibrant and friendly. And delightfully flashy on occasion – this is oil country, after all. Dallas and Houston boast rich arts and culture districts to explore by day, as well as active nightlife. For partying, Austin is the place, with its endless live-music concerts and an outdoorsy, alternative vibe. San Antonio has pockets of bustling activity during the day, and there's a fiesta every night on the River Walk. Beyond the cities, Texas also has countless small towns with courthouse squares, landmark cafes and eclectic antiques and boutiques to explore at a slower pace.

The Great Big Outdoors

We know you've heard, but Texas is big... really BIG. More than 261,000 sq miles, in fact: that's larger than Germany, England, Scotland, Ireland, Northern Ireland, Belgium and the Netherlands combined. And it ain't all just tumblin' tumbleweeds. Barrier islands with windswept dunes and public beaches stretch down 367 miles of coastline. In the west, three mountain ranges top more than 7000ft, and Big Bend National Park is the state's premier trekking and primary rafting destination. And to the northeast, soaring pine forests and sinuous, cypress-lined bayous are perfect for hiking and kayaking.

Why I Love Texas

By Amy C Balfour, Writer

What do I love most? That's easy. It's the people. Texas is a social place, and folks will organize a get-together on the flimsiest of excuses. Texans may have political and cultural differences, but they tend to coexist like one extended family. An underlying pride of place ties them all together. Otherwise, there's not much I don't love: hiking on the Lost Mine Trail in Big Bend, seeing what's doing at Gruene Hall, getting messy with brisket in Lockhart and sipping wine outdoors with friends in the Hill Country. And whoa, those West Texas sunsets!

For more about our writers, see p384

Above: Lost Mine Trail (p296), Big Bend National Park

Texas

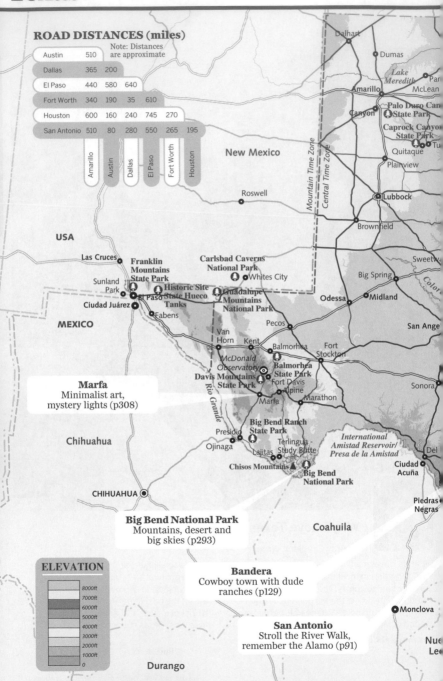

ROAD DISTANCES (miles)

Note: Distances are approximate

	Amarillo	Austin	Dallas	El Paso	Fort Worth	Houston
Austin	510					
Dallas	365	200				
El Paso	440	580	640			
Fort Worth	340	190	35	610		
Houston	600	160	240	745	270	
San Antonio	510	80	280	550	265	195

Marfa
Minimalist art, mystery lights (p308)

Big Bend National Park
Mountains, desert and big skies (p293)

Bandera
Cowboy town with dude ranches (p129)

San Antonio
Stroll the River Walk, remember the Alamo (p91)

ELEVATION

8000ft
7000ft
6000ft
5000ft
4000ft
3000ft
2000ft
1000ft
0

N
0 | 200 km
0 | 120 miles

Fort Worth
Historic Stockyards, great museum district (p158)

Arkansas

Arkansas River

OKLAHOMA CITY

Texola

Lawton

S Canadian River

Eufaula Lake

Conway

Hot Springs National Park

LITTLE ROCK

Pine Bluff

hildress

Red River

Vernon

Oklahoma

Jefferson
Historic, haunted riverboat town (p244)

Wichita Falls

Lake Texoma

Galnesville

Sherman

Paris

Denton

Commerce

Texarkana

Mount Pleasant

Sulphur Springs

Jefferson

Louisiana

Stamford

Fort Worth

Dallas

Longview

Shreveport

Abilene

Weatherford

Ennis

Tyler

Carthage

Austin
Live music, fun town (p54)

Stephenville

Hillsboro

Corsicana

Jacksonville

Palestine

Coleman

Mexia

Nacogdoches

Brownwood

Waco

Lufkin

Angelina National Forest

Sabine National Forest

Brady

Killeen

Davy Crockett National Forest

Temple

Lake Livingston

Houston
Houston Museums and parks galore (p204)

Enchanted Rock State Natural Area

Lampasas

Lake Travis

Bryan

Huntsville

Livingston

Fredericksburg

Johnson City

College Station

Sam Houston National Forest

Beaumont

Luckenbach

AUSTIN

Brenham

Conroe

Orange

ost Maples State Park

Kerrville

San Marcos

Lockhart

Liberty

Port Arthur

Gruene

Luling

Houston

La Porte

Bandera

Gonzales

Shiner

Clear Lake

High Island

Uvalde

San Antonio

Florcsville

Wharton

Galveston

Pleasanton

Edna

Galveston
Southern charm, sunny beaches (p255)

Carrizo Springs

Victoria

Port Lavaca

Beeville

Rockport

Aransas National Wildlife Refuge

Lockhart
BBQ capital of Texas (p79)

Sinton

Matagorda Island

Port Aransas

Alice

Corpus Christi

Mustang Island

Gulf of Mexico

uevo redo

Laredo

Kingsville

North Padre Island

Aransas National Wildlife Refuge
Superb bird-watching (p264)

Padre Island National Seashore

Rio Grande City

Weslaco

Harlingen

Padre Island National Seashore
Brilliant beaches (p277)

McAllen

South Padre Island

Reynosa

Port Isabel

Nuevo Progreso

Palo Alto Battlefield National Historical Site

Brownsville

Rio Grande

Texas'
Top 25

1

Live Music in Austin

1 In the airport, at the grocery store, in a record shop or at an actual bar or nightclub – a concert might take place anywhere. To say that Austin is the 'live-music capital of Texas' is to promote truth in advertising. Austin country classics such as Dale Watson or Kelly Willis are some of our favorites, but you can also rock out, get the blues, go punk, dig rockabilly or turn alternative. You name it, you can hear it here. Where to start? You'll never go wrong at the Continental Club.

Below left: Anderson Paak performs at South by Southwest (p70)

The Alamo

2 A small chapel and a long barrack don't seem quite sufficient for remembering the Alamo , but that doesn't deter more than 1.4 million visitors from paying homage annually. Never mind the tacky tourist attractions nearby and the fact that the site is now dwarfed by its big-city surrounds. A few hundred Texas freedom fighters battled and died here during the 13-day siege by Mexican forces of this fortified mission, a fact that still stirs the feisty independent spirit of locals and underdog-lovers alike.

STOCK-P-OTO_WORLD/SHUTTERSTOCK ©

BRANDON SEIDEL/SHUTTERSTOCK ©

Big Bend National Park

3 You knew Texas was big, but did you know that it has a national park (p293) larger than Rhode Island? Out in way-far-west Texas, the Chisos Mountains (7825ft) provide an excellent place to take a hike. But then so, too, does the Chihuahuan desert or the Rio Grande Valley. Having three distinct ecosystems in one vast and remote parkland provides something for everyone. Make sure to plan ahead, though – the mountaintop lodge has limited accommodations, and campgrounds fill up quickly in spring and fall.

Sixth Floor Museum, Dallas

4 The 6th floor of the old Texas School Book Depository, looking down on Dealey Plaza: Lee Harvey Oswald stood here almost 55 years ago and fired the shots that killed John F Kennedy. Or did he? This museum (p140) investigates the dark ambiguities that swirl at the heart of the tragedy. Through video, audio clips and interactive exhibits, you'll relive moment by moment the events that transpired on that day, as well as looking into the lead-up to them. History – powerful and tragic – is alive here.

Austin's South Congress Avenue

5 The now-iconic mural on the wall of Jo's Coffee (p76; at the corner of W James St) says it all: 'I love you so much.' A heady mishmash of everything we love about the town, South Congress is lined with funky thrift stores and boutiques, locally owned restaurants, cool food trailers, lively bars and a hip couple of hotels – without a single Chili's or Starbucks in sight. In the surrounding residential area, the neomodern environmental-standard homes and the arts-and-crafts bungalows – one or two turned B&B – add heaps of charm to the neighborhood.

State Fair of Texas

6 When the weather finally cools down in October, it's festival season around the state – and no event is more iconic than the State Fair of Texas (p148). Although Big Tex, the 50ft-tall cowboy that welcomed fairgoers starting in 1952, burned down in 2012, there's still the state's largest Ferris wheel (pictured right), a midway full of carnival rides, livestock and other animal shows – plus all those crazy fair foods to try. The corny dog debuted here, as did fried butter. Our favorite? Deep-fried Oreos.

JAMES KIRKIKIS/SHUTTERSTOCK ©

Houston Museum District

7 Sure, the world-class Museum of Fine Arts Houston and the Houston Museum of Natural Science (with its stunning pale-ontology hall; pictured below) make their home here. And there are smaller, more specialized museums focusing on topics such as the weather and the Holocaust. The new themed gardens and viewing hill at Hermann Park are also worth a stroll. But the star of the neighborhood really is the Menil Collection (p208) – one of the country's top private holdings–based museums, the complex contains everything from 10,000-year-old antiquities to abstract art.

Padre Island National Seashore

8 A narrow ridge of sand dunes backs the 70-mile-long protected coastline at Padre Island National Seashore (p277). To say this place is windswept is an understatement: Bird Island Basin, on the lagoon side of the park's barrier-island home, is a mecca for windsurfers. While the first mile or so of beach south of the visitor center is usually busy, it doesn't take long to walk away from the crowds. If you have a 4WD vehicle, 60 miles of beach is open for you to explore.

San Antonio River Walk

9 Now stretching all the way to the museum district to the north and the missions to the south, the River Walk (p93) is earning a newfound reputation as an adventure mecca, with hiking, paddling and cycling. Downtown, it remains a mighty entertaining experience: located below street level, stone footpaths following the riverbank are lined with places to eat and drink, while outdoor stages host frequent events and there are hotels aplenty. Take a cruise along the canal or a tour during Christmas-light season to get the full festive effect.

Hill Country

10 Slow down and take a scenic country drive. Meander through the green rolling hills (p122) covered in live oaks, climb up to a vista and cruise down a curve. In spring the roadsides and fields are colored with Indian paintbrushes and Texas bluebonnets. But all year you'll find a tiny old Texas town, a tranquil ranch, a pretty vineyard or a friendly dance hall around the next bend. Stop to sit in a river or enjoy a pie in an old cafe. This is small-town Texas life at its best.

High School & College Football

11 How to sum up Texans' affection for football? 'Obsession' might just cover it. At the corner cafe on a Saturday morning you'll hear 'em hotly debating the stats and stars of last night's game – and they're talking about the local *high* school. College rivalries are even more heated, whether you're chanting on your feet as the '12th man' for the Texas A&M team or signaling 'hook 'em horns' for the University of Texas (p57). Game day is party time, whether at home or on a tailgate in the stadium parking lot.

Barbecue

12 The best beef brisket has a visible pink smoke ring around the edge, testament to the fact that it takes hours and hours of cooking under precise conditions to produce the juiciest cuts. From Tyler to Temple, Texans know their barbecue. They eat it at home, at famous hole-in-the-walls or bought from a roadside smoker. It's in central Texas that you'll find the state's unofficial BBQ capital, Lockhart (p79), with several of the most lauded meat market–style joints in the state. Below left: Kreuz Market (p79), Lockhart

Aransas National Wildlife Refuge

13 The South Texas coast is known worldwide for its excellent bird-watching. Herons and egrets, shore and seabirds – hundreds of species congregate along the marshy coastal plains. But the premier site is Aransas National Wildlife Refuge (p264), home to the only naturally migrating flock of whooping cranes in the United States. These 5ft-tall white birds with its red crowns would be noteworthy anyway, but what's incredible is that the population has risen to more than 250 from its lowest point in 1941, when just 15 birds remained. Below right: Whooping crane

JIM ENGELBRECHT/DANITADELIMONT.COM/ALAMY ©

Fort Worth Stockyards

14 Wander into the Old West at the Fort Worth Stockyards (p159), where you can drink at the saloon bar after a mini cattle drive comes through town. The old steam train that was once used to take the herds north now offers tourist rides. It sure is fun to watch the kids (and some adults) get their pennies flattened on the wheelhouse rail. In addition to Western shops, there are several in-theme restaurants and bars. Conquer both the mechanical bull and the two-step at Billy Bob's, one of the world's largest honky-tonks.

Luckenbach

15 With a permanent population of three, you can't really call Luckenbach (p129) a town. What remains today is a cluster of Old West–era buildings that typify Texas country charm. Grab a Shiner Bock beer and listen to guitar pickers and singers under the giant live oak tree. In colder weather, musicians move inside the general store, which is also the post office and a saloon. If you're lucky there will be a Friday-night dance on at the 1880s hall. And yes, Willie and Waylon have played here.

RAULUMINATE/GETTY IMAGES ©

Galveston

16 Repeated hurricanes have not been able to destroy Galveston (p255), a beguiling bit of the Old South on the Gulf Coast. Victorian neighborhoods still stand, and shops and restaurants have come back to the century-old downtown Strand District. Tour an 1800s tall ship, and learn about the town's heyday from local films. On the flip side of the island, sandy stretches beckon residents from nearby Houston. Surf-bum bars and condo rentals make kicking back at the beach all the easier. When little ones get bored, entertain them at mid-island amusement parks.

Texas Bluebonnets

17 Every March, the roadsides of Texas erupt with color: red Indian paintbrushes, yellow and red Indian blankets, pink evening primrose, yellow brown-eyed Susans. But the bluebonnet is Texas' state flower, and easily the star. Entire fields turn a vibrant bluish-purple for a couple of weeks, sending families flocking to take pictures among the blooms. Hill Country (p122) and Washington County are the usual picture-taking sites, but you can also find 2ft-tall bluebonnets in Big Bend and fields full of flowers as far north as Dallas.

Bandera Dude Ranches

18 Finding places to indulge your inner cowpoke is surprisingly difficult in Texas. Not so if you head for Hill Country. The area around Bandera (p129) hosts more than a dozen dude (or guest) ranches. Don't expect cattle drives; do expect daily horseback rides, hay wagons, swimming holes, rodeos and at least one chuckwagon breakfast or outdoor barbecue per stay. Although everything's included in the experience, be sure to take time to trot into town, where there are daily activities and two of the best cowboy bars around.

Route 66

19 OK, so the Texas stretch of the Mother Road (p199) doesn't amount to much, considering it's only 178 miles long. But Amarillo is a worthy guardian of the route, with timeless roadside attractions such as the Big Texan Steak Ranch and Cadillac Ranch, a series of old spray-painted Caddies planted nose down in the dirt. There's also the McLean Devil's Rope barbed-wire museum, which produces a detailed map of the road's Texas attractions. The best part may be riding through the region's pancake-flat plains – the epitome of an open road.

Marfa

20 Mysterious lights, an obsession with the classic film *Giant,* and modern-art installations: Marfa (p308) is nothing if not out there. This West Texas desert outpost attracts a mix of artists and rugged individualists; the number of New Yorkers here may surprise you, but then so might the replica Prada store in the middle of nowhere. Sleep in a tipi, a modernist cube or the Hotel Paisano, where James Dean and Elizabeth Taylor once stayed. A midnight drive to the lonely lights-viewing platform will rattle even the staunchest skeptic. Bottom: El Cosmico (p309)

NASA's Space Center Houston

21 Cape Canaveral may be where rockets launch, but the trip-planning and astronaut training take place outside Houston in Clear Lake. The Johnson Space Center's official visitor center and museum, Space Center Houston (p230), lets you learn about NASA's history through films and exhibits; you can then try your hand at key astronaut skills. A tram tour leads you through some of the actual working parts of the complex, including space-walk labs and the original mission control. Upgrade your tour and you can even eat with the astronauts.

Lazy Rivers & Natural Pools

22 Texans beat the heat by heading to the nearest river or swimming hole (often formed by cold springs). So pack your swimsuit if you're visiting the Lone Star State in summer. You'll find popular pools in Austin, Dripping Springs and Wimberley, but for a full-on embrace of sweet summer laziness in the east, head to the Guadalupe River in New Braunfels for a day of tubing. In the west, there are springs south of Marfa, as well as a spring-fed pool at beloved Balmorhea State Park (p307) – a true desert oasis. Bottom: Tubing on the Guadalupe River (p117)

JIM ENGELBRECHT / DANITADELIMONT.COM/ALAMY ©

WILLIAM SILVER/SHUTTERSTOCK ©

World Birding Center

23 More than nine splendid bird-watching sites roost under the umbrella organization in the Rio Grande Valley. Texas' position on the central migratory flyway and the valley's southern locale make this both a stopover and wintering grounds for transient species. The 760-acre Bentsen-Rio Grande Valley State Park (p289) acts as the center headquarters for sites along the border all the way to to South Padre Island. Pick up maps and a bird-watching list, and then test yourself. How many of the more than 600 reported species can you spot? Above left: Audubon's oriole

Dance Halls

24 Built by German, Czech and Polish immigrants as community gathering places in the mid 1800s, many Texas dance halls today are famed for their great live music, singer-songwriter nights and two-stepping masses. You'll find busy dance halls in and around Austin and San Antonio, but you won't fully realize their role in community-building until you head to the Hill Country and central Texas, where they anchor small towns there. At Gruene Hall (p120; pictured top right), check out the photographs of past performers, sip a Shiner, then try two-stepping. It's pretty darn fun.

Guadalupe Mountains National Park

25 The ruins of the old Butterfield stage-coach station look right at home in the high-country scrub of the Guadalupe Mountains (8749ft) in West Texas. The place hasn't changed much over the centuries – part of the appeal at this national park (p328), which may be one of the state's best-kept secrets just because it's so darn far away from anywhere. (Carlsbad Caverns in New Mexico is the closest neighbor.) Make the journey and your reward is stunning upland hikes, scenic drives and excellent fall color, especially in Mc-Kittrick Canyon.

Need to Know

For more information, see Survival Guide (p361)

Currency
US dollar ($)

Language
English

Visas
Visas are not required for citizens of Visa Waiver Program (VWP) countries, but you must request travel authorization from ESTA (p367) at least 72 hours in advance.

Money
ATMs are widely available. Credit cards are widely accepted, and generally required for reservations and car rentals. Tipping is essential – not optional.

Cell Phones
Network reception can be spotty in rural areas. Only foreign phones that operate on tri- or quad-band frequencies will work in the USA.

Time
All but two far-west Texas counties are in the US Central Time Zone (GMT/UTC minus five hours).

When to Go

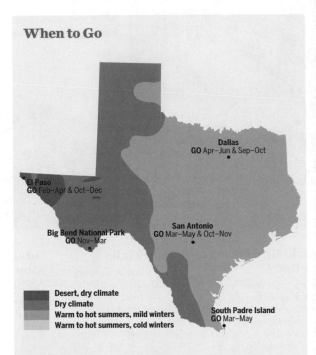

Dallas
GO Apr–Jun & Sep–Oct

El Paso
GO Feb–Apr & Oct–Dec

Big Bend National Park
GO Nov–Mar

San Antonio
GO Mar–May & Oct–Nov

South Padre Island
GO Mar–May

- Desert, dry climate
- Dry climate
- Warm to hot summers, mild winters
- Warm to hot summers, cold winters

High Season (Jun–Aug)

➡ Kids are out of school, so attractions are busiest.

➡ Temperatures will be stiflingly hot outside, but everywhere inside has air-con.

➡ Prime time for beaches, lakes and rivers.

Shoulder (late Mar–May & Sep–early Nov)

➡ Best time of year to travel: the weather is less intense, everything is open.

➡ Spring is when most festival planners throw events, including rodeos.

➡ Head to West Texas and parts of the Hill Country in fall for leaf-peeping.

Low Season (Dec–Feb)

➡ Some theme parks are closed for the season.

➡ North Texas occasionally freezes; South Texas rarely does.

➡ Christmastime festivities statewide.

Useful Websites

Travel Texas (www.traveltexas.com) Official state tourism website, where you can request the huge *Texas Travel Guide* and search through tons of info.

Texas Monthly (www.texasmonthly.com) Glossy mag with great writing about Texas, dining and shopping guides; all available online.

Lonely Planet (www.lonelyplanet.com) Destination information, hotel bookings, traveler forum and more.

Texas Highways (www.texashighways.com) Travel magazine with extensive festival and event listings.

Texas Parks & Wildlife (www.tpwd.texas.gov) A complete guide to Texas' outdoor recreation and environment.

Important Numbers

Most, but not all, numbers require you to dial the area code, even when you are within the city.

Country code	✆1
International dialing code	✆011
Emergency (ambulance, police & fire)	✆911
Directory assistance	✆411

Exchange Rates

Australia	A$1	$0.75
Canada	C$1	$0.74
Euro zone	€1	$1.09
Japan	¥100	$0.90
NZ	NZ$1	$0.69
UK	£1	$1.29

For current exchange rates, see www.xe.com.

Daily Costs

Budget: Less than $120

➡ Campground or dorm bed: $15–25

➡ Basic motel room: $70

➡ Pizza or takeout: $6–10

➡ Car rental and fuel: $40

Midrange: $200–300

➡ B&B or better quality motel: $100–170

➡ Restaurant meals and food-truck takeout: $40–60

➡ Car rental and fuel: $40–60

➡ Museums and sight entry: $15

Top End: Over $350

➡ Upscale hotel: $250–400

➡ Restaurant meals and fine dining: $100–140

➡ Car rental and fuel: $40–80

➡ Museums, shows, major attractions, theme parks: $40–60

Opening Hours

Individual opening hours are listed in reviews; below are generalities. Sight and activity hours vary throughout the year and may decrease during the shoulder and low seasons.

Banks 9am–5pm Monday to Friday

Cafes 7am–8pm

Nightclubs 8pm–2am

Restaurants 11am–2pm and 5pm–10pm, or often all day

Shops 9am–6pm Monday to Saturday, 11am–6pm Sunday

Arriving in Texas

Austin-Bergstrom International Airport (p368) Taxis to town (20 minutes) cost $25 to $30, shared-ride shuttles $14; the limited bus service is only $1.

Dallas-Fort Worth International Airport (p368) Taxis to central Dallas (25 minutes) cost $40 to $60, shared-ride shuttles $17; the Trinity Express train from downtown, and shuttle to the terminal, costs $2.50, but doesn't run weekends.

George Bush Intercontinental Airport, Houston (p368) Taxis cost about $50 to downtown Houston (30 minutes), shared-ride shuttles $25; the Metro runs a limited bus service ($1.25) to downtown, but it takes an hour or more.

Hobby Airport, Houston (p368) Taxis to downtown (20 minutes) cost around $30, shared-ride shuttles $19; the Metro runs a limited bus service ($1.25) to downtown, but it takes an hour.

San Antonio International Airport (p368) A taxi ride to downtown (15 minutes) costs $25 to $30, a shared-ride shuttle is a few bucks cheaper. Via runs a regular bus to downtown (35 minutes) for $1.20.

Getting Around

Unless you plan to stay exclusively in central Dallas, downtown in San Antonio or Austin, or along the light-rail corridor in Houston, you really need a car to get around efficiently.

Car Easy to rent at any airport, at in-town locations and even in suburbia.

Public Transportation Extremely limited outside big cities; not comprehensive even within.

For much more on **getting around**, see p369

If You Like...

Beaches

Few beaches along the Texas coast are organized. Mostly you'll find undeveloped acres, where you're allowed to drive. (Yes, drive. The 'roads' near the tide line even have speed limits.)

Matagorda Island Thirty-eight miles of wonderfully deserted, white-sand beaches waiting for you to venture out and stake your claim. (p263)

South Padre Island Spring break central: there are 23 beach access points within this city's limits. (p279)

East Beach Live concerts and revelry on the weekends on the hard-packed sand of this fun beach. (p258)

Padre Island National Seashore Wild and windswept, most of the protected beach is accessible only by 4WD. (p277)

Port Aransas Stop here for a laid-back version of South Padre Island. (p273)

Bird-Watching

Aransas National Wildlife Refuge The last remaining wild flock of whooping cranes (250-plus strong) winters here. (p264)

South Padre Island Birding & Nature Center Shorebirds make themselves right at home among the sand dunes. (p280)

Laguna Atascosa National Wildlife Refuge On the US–Mexican border, this refuge shelters 100,000 shorebirds. (p279)

Anahuac National Wildlife Refuge Snow geese, whistling ducks and other waterfowl winter here by the hundreds – sometimes thousands. (p253)

Bentsen-Rio Grande Valley State Park Headquarters of the World Birding Center in the Rio Grande Valley. (p289)

Davis Mountains State Park Look for the Montezuma quail year-round and the threatened common black hawk from March to September. (p305)

Cowboy Culture

Dude Ranches Cowboy up and learn to rope and ride at one of many local dude ranches near Hill Country State Natural Area. (p130)

Fort Worth Stockyards National Historic District Watch a miniature recreation of a longhorn cattle drive down main street in the historic stockyards. (p159)

King Ranch Tour a small portion of one of the world's largest ranches (it's bigger than Rhode Island). (p278)

Houston Livestock Show & Rodeo Three weeks' worth of nightly barrel-racing, bronc-busting, bull-riding action. (p211)

Cowboy Poetry Gathering Get back to the days when cowboys entertained themselves with poetry and ate chuck wagon breakfasts. (p312)

Briscoe Western Art Museum Learn about ranching life, listen to cowboy songs and check out the spur collection beside the River Walk. (p93)

Cowboys on Main Saturdays, the little false-front town of Bandera hosts Western entertainment on the square. (p129)

Dance Halls & Honky Tonks

You'll find most old dance halls on some rural route in central Texas, but honkytonks can be anywhere there's music, a bar and sand for the dance floor.

John T Floore Country Store You can't beat Floore's for atmosphere. Willie Nelson played here regularly back in the 1950s – sometimes still does. (p113)

Gruene Hall Texas' 'oldest' dance hall and still one of the most popular. On weekend

nights the dance floor is always packed. (p120)

Billy Bob's Texas Think *Rhinestone Cowboy:* barn-size dance floor, numerous bars and live, indoor bull-riding weekends. (p168)

Broken Spoke George Strait used to swing from the wagon-wheel chandeliers here. Chow down at the restaurant, then boot-scoot in the hall. (p83)

Arkey Blue's Silver Dollar Saloon This darn tiny basement club has been entertainin' folks since the 1940s. (p131)

Luckenbach Dance Hall An 1850s German *tanzhalle* that helped put Luckenbach on the map when outlaw country stars played here in the 1970s. (p129)

Museums

Bob Bullock Texas State History Museum Fancy, high-tech displays and theatrical exhibits tell the story of Texas. (p61)

Sixth Floor Museum Relive the day President John F Kennedy died, inside the building he was shot from. (p140)

National Museum of the Pacific War Explosions will grab your attention during battle reenactments at the revamped Pacific Combat Zone. (p125)

Menil Collection One of the best private collections in the country; strong on modernists. (p208)

Perot Museum of Nature & Science Check out the earth-friendly architecture and interactive exhibits. (p145)

Museum of Fine Arts Houston Impressive permanent exhibits and world-class rotating shows. (p210)

Top: John T Floore Country Store (p113), San Antonio
Bottom: Longhorn cattledrive, Fort Worth Stockyards (p159)

National & State Parks

Big Bend National Park Both the Chisos Mountains and Chihuahuan desert are located in this 1252-sq-mile park. (p293)

Padre Island National Seashore The 70 miles of sandy coastline are a haven for more than 350 bird species. (p277)

Big Thicket National Preserve Cypress swamps, desert sands, hardwood forests and coastal plains together in one amazing area. (p253)

Enchanted Rock State Natural Area A pink granite dome rising 425ft just calls out to be climbed. (p126)

Palo Duro Canyon State Park Second in size only to the Grand Canyon, Palo Duro is quite a surprise on the Panhandle Plains. (p194)

Guadalupe Mountains National Park High-country hiking in far-northwest Texas; fall colors in McKittrick Canyon are stunning. (p328)

Scenic Drives

Galveston to Corpus Christi, TX 35 Cruise through small towns and across marshland and bays. (p267)

River Road, Big Bend Snake along the edge of the Rio Grande. (p305)

Washington County Take the rural route, past bucolic ranches and, in spring, bluebonnets. (p233)

Fort Davis Ascend into the Davis Mountains amid gorgeous, rocky scenery. (p306)

Small Towns

Jefferson Take a riverboat ride and tour a haunted house (or two) in this Southern Belle of an East Texas town. (p244)

Waxahachie The historic downtown district here is filled with early-Victorian, Queen Anne and Greek Revival beauties. (p174)

Gruene Shop in late-1800s wooden buildings, step out on the state's oldest dance floor, then sleep in a historic house inn. (p119)

Brenham You scream, I scream, we all scream for Blue Bell ice cream! Tour the factory and the town's fun-and-funky shops. (p233)

Fort Davis A scenic route leads to this mountain town, a base for hiking, star-gazing and Old West museums. (p305)

Nacogdoches Follow the azalea trail through stately neighborhoods and around the red-brick buildings of the historic courthouse square. (p240)

Texas History

Texas was once a republic of its own, and it has a good number of sites linked to the independence period.

Alamo Heard of this little fortified mission? Davy Crockett and about 150 other Texas independence fighters died defending it. (p92)

Mission Trail Before US settlers arrived, the Spanish colonized the territory of Tejas. Tour four 18th-century missions built south of San Antonio. (p101)

Goliad The battle at Goliad preceded the siege at the Alamo; today you can visit the Spanish mission, fort and battlefield. (p266)

San Jacinto Battleground State Historic Site Learn about the last battle in the Texas war for independence, then take an elevator up to view the site. (p231)

Palo Alto Battlefield National Historic Site The first battle of the Mexican War is compellingly and thoroughly explored at the excellent visitor center. (p287)

Washington-on-the-Brazos Tour the site where the declaration of Texas independence was signed and experience an 1850s living history farm. (p237)

The Offbeat

Orange Show for Visionary Art A wacky art-car parade, a beer-can-covered home and a mazelike orange house curated by visionaries in Houston. (p205)

Museum of the Weird Shrunken heads, a Fiji merman and the mysterious Minnesota Ice Man, plus a live show with incredible stunts, in Austin. (p57)

International Bowling Museum Crazy-colored shoes, pitchers of beers, strikes and spares are celebrated here. (p174)

Chicken-Shit Bingo Really. Beer-swilling country folk bet on where the poop will land while listening to live music. (p82)

Stonehenge II Stone monoliths and Easter Island–like statues stand outside the Hill Country Arts Foundation in Ingram. (p136)

National Museum of Funeral History Brush up on your embalming tricks and celebrate the Day of the Dead. (p210)

Buckhorn Saloon & Museum A kitschy monument to old Texas ways and taxidermy; look for the two-headed calf. (p93)

Bluebonnet and Indian paintbrush wildflowers (p359)

Wildflowers & Garden Trails

Blooming seasons start from south to north; roughly expect bluebonnets from late February into April, azaleas late March through April and roses beginning in May.

Lady Bird Johnson Wildflower Center Get a primer on wildflowers at a botanical garden named for the First Lady who beautified state highways with them. (p65)

Wildseed Farms You're guaranteed to see gorgeous fields in full bloom come spring at this garden center and show farm. (p126)

Azalea Trail Follow set routes through leafy neighborhoods bursting with azaleas during Nacogdoches' annual festival. (p240)

Tyler The Rose Capital of Texas has a 14-acre municipal garden and puts on a heck of a rose festival. (p242)

Wineries

Sandy soil and cool nights make the Lubbock area the state's most conducive to grape growth. But in recent years cottage wine industries have popped up everywhere.

La Diosa Cellars This wine bar in Lubbock sells its own, and other Texas wines. (p190)

Becker Vineyards A much-decorated winery with an impressive underground cellar in Hill Country. (p126)

Pleasant Hill Winery Frequent hosted events attract the locals from nearby Brenham to this east-central vineyard. (p233)

Hawk's Shadow Winery For Hill Country views and a friendly afternoon of wine sipping not far from Austin, head to this small winery in Dripping Springs. (p123)

Month by Month

February

Rodeo season starts in big and small towns across the state. Cool, not cold, weather in Big Bend means it's a great time to hike.

☆ Houston Livestock Show & Rodeo

Starting in late February or early March, the three-week event attracts about 2.6 million visitors. Tour the animal shows, shop for Western gear, see the cowboys rope and ride – then watch a different top-name singer perform nightly (think Brad Paisley or Demi Lovato). (p211)

⚒ Mardi Gras

For 12 days every February Galveston does its best New Orleans imitation, hosting two dozen parades, even more concerts and several masked balls. Events are admittedly a bit tamer here: the first Sunday is usually coined 'Family Gras.' (p259)

March

Spring wildflowers bloom, spreading from south to north. The weather across the state is mild, making this a great time to stop by.

☆ South by Southwest

One of the music industry's biggest annual events. A couple thousand musicians and a few *hundred* thousand visitors besiege the city for five days. The fun doesn't stop there: a concurrent film festival and techie show stretch the festivities to two weeks. (p70)

☆ Cowboy Poetry Gathering

Relive the cattle-drive days out in the far-west Texas town of Alpine. Start the morning with a chuckwagon breakfast and watch the old hands twirl their six-shooters and recite witty, trail-inspired verse. (p312)

☆ Spring Break

The spring break weeks vary across Texas, but they all fall in the month of March.

South Padre Island is the biggest party, by far. But other beaches, like those in Galveston, also host events.

⚒ Nacogdoches Azalea Trail

Each spring the historic east Texas town of Nacogdoches outlines more than 25 miles of routes through the brilliantly blooming azaleas of the region. (p240)

April

Bluebonnets generally peak in Hill Country from mid-March to mid-April, so take a rural Sunday drive. Several towns around the state host festivals while it's still cool enough.

⚒ Fiesta

Mariachi music, parades, live concerts, dance performances, carnivals, food and craft shows... San Antonio knows how to throw one mammoth, multicultural party. It lasts 11 days every April and benefits area nonprofits. (p104)

⚒ Main Street Arts Festival

The visual arts, including fiber arts, sculpture, mixed media, leatherwork and painting, are at the heart of this four-day festival in Fort

Worth, but the performing and culinary arts aren't forgotten. Stop at the Wine Experience tent to sample Texas' finest. (p164)

May

★☆ Buccaneer Days Festival

Arrr! Everyone loves the pirate's life! In early May, head to Corpus Christi, the alleged hideout of pirate Jean Lafitte. Beside the bay, the festival features music, rides and merriment. (p269)

☆ Kerrville Folk Festival

An 18-day-long folk-music festival kicks off every May in Kerrville. More than 100 songwriters perform during the event. Camp at the ranch site and you'll be privy to many more private pickin'-and-singin' circles. (p135)

☆ Houston Art Car Parade

The self-billed 'largest art parade in the world' is also Houston's largest free event. Imagine giant sharks and Dr Seuss mobiles motoring down the road and you have an idea of all the wacky fun. (p211)

July

Independence Day celebrations abound. Even if you don't attend formal firework displays, you may see some: many counties allow private fireworks.

☆ Shakespeare at Winedale

For four long weekends starting in July, the University of Texas hosts a Shakespeare festival at the open-air historical complex outside tiny Round Top. The Bard's comedies and dramas are well represented. (p235)

☆ Marfa Film Festival

In mid-July, watch new features and shorts at various spots around Marfa, then head outside to watch a classic movie under the west-Texas sky. Only one movie is shown at a time, so folks have plenty of time to socialize. (p309)

September

Labor Day marks the official end of summer high season, but things aren't really cooling off yet – the heat lingers until October everywhere but in the mountains.

October

Finally some temperature relief. Toward the end of the month, Halloween takes over with theme events and haunted houses. Amusement parks reopen to host fright-nights.

★☆ State Fair of Texas

Having a corny dog in Dallas is a rite of passage for Texans. Fun foods (deep-fried PB&J, cheesecake on a stick) are a big attraction, but so is the largest Ferris wheel in Texas, carnival rides and livestock exhibits. (p148)

☆ Austin City Limits

Locals much prefer this two-weekend music festival in Zilker Park to the insanity of SXSW. Though lower key, the more than 110 musical acts that take the stage are still pretty darn impressive. (p70)

☆ Oktoberfest

Residents of Fredericksburg celebrate their town's German heritage in a big way one long weekend every October. Polka bands play, schnitzel and sausage are served and there's plenty of beer – more than 65 varieties are available. (p127)

★☆ Sand Castle Days

(www.sandcastledays.com) For more than 25 years artists have been turning sand into sculpture on South Padre Island. Events take place over a long weekend in October and include concerts, arts-and-crafts sales and a juried sandcastle-building contest. (p246)

December

Almost all of December is a festive season: Christmas light shows, town festivals and decorated hotel events all say that Santa is on his way.

★☆ Dickens on the Strand

One weekend every December, Galveston transforms into Victorian London during its annual Christmas festival. Costumed performers, vendors and even 'the Queen' show up to celebrate. (p259)

Itineraries

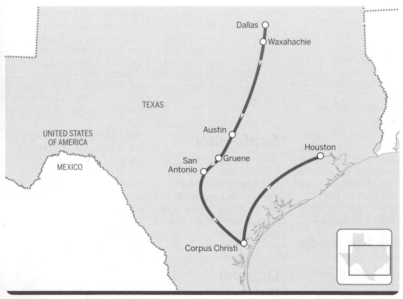

 2 WEEKS **Texas' Greatest Hits**

So you want to do it all but are short on time? Start with three days in **Dallas**. See the JFK assassination sites downtown and eat in trendy Uptown, then the next day take a trip out to the historic Fort Worth Stockyards. Heading south out of town on day three, stop in cute little **Waxahachie** for a bite before spending two nights in **Austin** listening to live music and watching the bats fly.

Stop for a night in the Old West–era town of **Gruene** to dance at one of the state's oldest halls, then continue on to **San Antonio**. In two days there you can explore the Alamo and River Walk. From there **Corpus Christi** is just a three-hour drive south; it's a good base to kick back for a couple of nights and hit the beach at Padre Island National Seashore or Port Aransas.

Afterwards it's time to turn north for three nights in **Houston**. NASA's Space Center Houston is a don't-miss attraction, as is the museum district. For a third day's excursion, hikers could trek out to Big Thicket National Preserve; history and sunshine lovers should see Galveston.

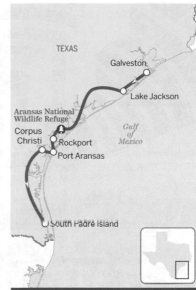

 Austin, Hill Country & San Antonio
10 DAYS

Start your Hill Country adventure with two days in **Austin**. Don't miss the Texas State History Museum, a splash in Barton Springs Pool or eating along quirky South Congress Ave before club-hopping.

Next, head west to the countryside to spend one night in **Dripping Springs**, home of microbreweries, distilleries and cool Hamilton Pool. Then, continue west to the German town of **Fredericksburg**; area activities include a visit to the Texas wine country, a climb up Enchanted Rock or a musical pilgrimage to Luckenbach.

Enjoy the road, and wildflowers in spring, as you meander south. Skirt the Guadalupe River and lunch in **Kerrville** before overnighting in the cowboy town of **Bandera**. A trail ride at a local dude ranch and a drink at the 11th Street Cowboy Bar are must-dos.

Take time to go antique hunting (or caving) in **Boerne** on your way to three nights in **San Antonio**. There you can follow the Mission Trail and eat Mexican food to your heart's content. One night make sure to catch a live local act outside of town at John T Floore's Country Store in Helotes or at Gruene Hall near New Braunfels – now that's country.

 Coastal Texas
1 WEEK

Trade the cities for sunny beaches, small museums, historical towns and some of the state's best bird-watching. Begin in **Galveston**, spending two days admiring the turn-of-the-20th-century mansions, exploring the state park, and dining and shopping on the Strand.

Follow the coast south, stopping at the fun little Sea Center Texas aquarium and hatcheries in **Lake Jackson**. Then make your way down to **Aransas National Wildlife Refuge**, the best bird-watching site on the Texas coast. Stay a night nearby in the seaside town of **Rockport**; in season, boat tours depart from here for the endangered whooping crane's feeding grounds.

Spend a couple of nights at the coastal fishing town of **Port Aransas**, near the outlet to Corpus Christi Bay, and explore **Corpus Christi** or Padre Island National Seashore – or just laze on a local beach.

Four more hours south finds you for the last two nights in **South Padre Island**. Be sure to stop at the Birding & Nature Center there, as well as trying beachfront horseback riding or water sports.

KELLY VANDELLEN/SHUTTERSTOCK ©

Top: Galleria megamall, Dallas (p140)

Bottom: Mission Espada (p102), San Antonio

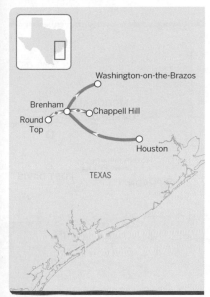

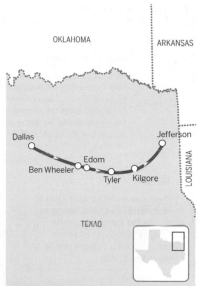

Houston & East-Central Texas
5 DAYS

Ah, big-city life. Spend three days immersed in culture and fine food around **Houston**. Check out some of the many arts and sciences exhibits in the Museum District, then prowl the eclectic Montrose neighborhood for your evening meal. While in town don't miss catching a show in the Theater District or have a night out clubbing on Washington Ave. After you've eaten, sipped and shopped yourself silly, escape to the country for a few days.

Book into a B&B and spend the next two nights in the small town of **Brenham**, home of Blue Bell ice cream (yes, you should tour the factory). From there you can explore the tiny towns of the region, stopping at famous Royer's Cafe in **Round Top** or checking out the lavender farm in **Chappell Hill**. To the north are the historical site and museums at **Washington-on-the-Brazos**, where the Texas Declaration of Independence was signed. While you're in the area, don't forget to eat some of the Czech-resident-inspired *kolaches* (sweet-bread pastries stuffed with savory or sweet filling).

Dallas & Northeast Texas
1 WEEK

Spend two days museum-hopping in **Dallas**. Be sure to take a break for shopping and dining in the Bishop Arts District, or for braving the huge Galleria megamall.

Then it's time to head east for small-town pleasures among the pine forests. Be sure to detour down FM 279: the 8-mile stretch of road from **Ben Wheeler** to **Edom** has a surprising number of cafes, artisan shops and live music in the evenings. You can spend the night in nearby **Tyler**, which is an especially good idea if it's spring and the azaleas are in bloom...or if you want to see a tiger sanctuary.

From there continue east, pausing for lunch and to see the Rangerette Showcase & Museum and the old oil derricks in the little town of **Kilgore**. Spending three nights in **Jefferson** allows you to peruse the historic town and take excursions. Choose from a canoe ride or a swamp-boat nature trip on sinuous Caddo Lake or a drive to Tex Ritter's hometown Texas Country Music Hall of Fame in Carthage.

Off the Beaten Track: Texas

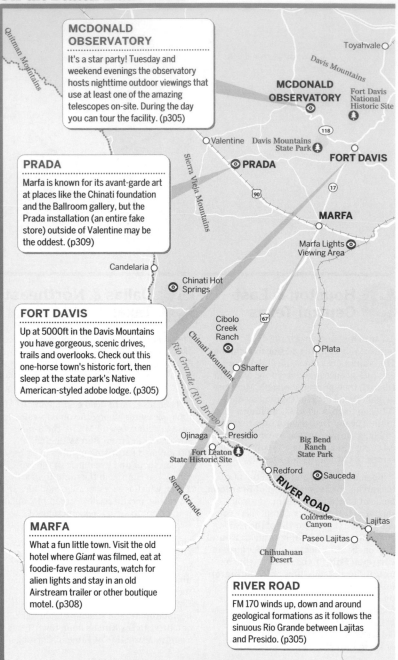

MCDONALD OBSERVATORY

It's a star party! Tuesday and weekend evenings the observatory hosts nighttime outdoor viewings that use at least one of the amazing telescopes on-site. During the day you can tour the facility. (p305)

PRADA

Marfa is known for its avant-garde art at places like the Chinati foundation and the Ballroom gallery, but the Prada installation (an entire fake store) outside of Valentine may be the oddest. (p309)

FORT DAVIS

Up at 5000ft in the Davis Mountains you have gorgeous, scenic drives, trails and overlooks. Check out this one-horse town's historic fort, then sleep at the state park's Native American-styled adobe lodge. (p305)

MARFA

What a fun little town. Visit the old hotel where *Giant* was filmed, eat at foodie-fave restaurants, watch for alien lights and stay in an old Airstream trailer or other boutique motel. (p308)

RIVER ROAD

FM 170 winds up, down and around geological formations as it follows the sinuous Rio Grande between Lajitas and Presido. (p305)

Toyahvale

Quitman Mountains

Davis Mountains

MCDONALD OBSERVATORY

Fort Davis National Historic Site

118

Valentine   Davis Mountains State Park

FORT DAVIS

PRADA

Sierra Vieja Mountains

90   17

MARFA

Marfa Lights Viewing Area

Candelaria

Chinati Hot Springs

Cibolo Creek Ranch

67

Rio Grande (Rio Bravo)

Chinati Mountains

Shafter

Plata

Ojinaga   Presidio

Fort Leaton State Historic Site

Big Bend Ranch State Park

Redford   Sauceda

RIVER ROAD

Sierra Grande

Colorado Canyon

Lajitas

Paseo Lajitas

Chihuahuan Desert

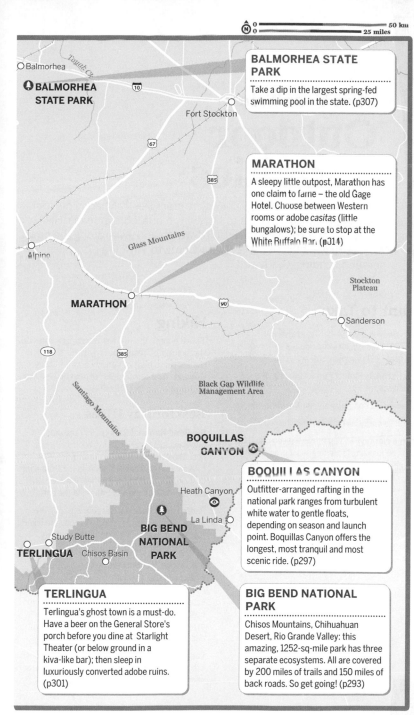

N 0 _____ 50 km
   0 _____ 25 miles

O Balmorhea

Touah Ch

BALMORHEA STATE PARK

BALMORHEA STATE PARK

Take a dip in the largest spring-fed swimming pool in the state. (p307)

10

Fort Stockton

67

385

Glass Mountains

Alpine

MARATHON

A sleepy little outpost, Marathon has one claim to fame – the old Gage Hotel. Choose between Western rooms or adobe *casitas* (little bungalows); be sure to stop at the White Buffalo Bar. (p314)

Stockton Plateau

MARATHON

90

O Sanderson

118

385

Santiago Mountains

Black Gap Wildlife Management Area

BOQUILLAS CANYON

Heath Canyon

La Linda

Study Butte

TERLINGUA Chisos Basin

BIG BEND NATIONAL PARK

BOQUILLAS CANYON

Outfitter-arranged rafting in the national park ranges from turbulent white water to gentle floats, depending on season and launch point. Boquillas Canyon offers the longest, most tranquil and most scenic ride. (p297)

TERLINGUA

Terlingua's ghost town is a must-do. Have a beer on the General Store's porch before you dine at Starlight Theater (or below ground in a kiva-like bar); then sleep in luxuriously converted adobe ruins. (p301)

BIG BEND NATIONAL PARK

Chisos Mountains, Chihuahuan Desert, Rio Grande Valley: this amazing, 1252-sq-mile park has three separate ecosystems. All are covered by 200 miles of trails and 150 miles of back roads. So get going! (p293)

Plan Your Trip

Outdoor Activities

You may not need to sleep under the stars like trail hands did, but there are plenty of reasons to want to go outdoors in Texas. Hike and camp at the state's parks, bird-watch and swim along the coast. And if you want those new cowboy boots to fulfill their purpose, go horseback riding. Giddy-up!

What to Take

Long-sleeved shirt Some areas leave you exposed to the sun for hours; wear a button-down shirt made out of vented, sun-protectant material.

Water sandals Protect your feet during river adventures.

Sunscreen & sunglasses A must in the outdoors.

Mosquito spray Hiking and along the coast.

Orange clothing We can't say we recommend it, but if you're hiking in hunting season, embrace this universal symbol for 'I am not a game animal so please do not shoot me.'

Hiking

There is perhaps no better way to appreciate the beauty of Texas than by trail. Note that the extreme heat of summer, at late May through mid-September, is not the best time to follow your foot's desire.

Best for Day Hikes

Big Bend National Park (p293) The most popular trails here, including Window View and Lost Mine, are in the Chisos Mountains. But Chihuahuan desert hikes such as the Grapevine trail are not to be missed either (if the weather's cool). Over 200 miles of trails lace the park.

Padre Island National Seashore (p277) The entire 70-mile-long coastal park is open to hikers; hardy souls (with a 4WD) favor the sparsely visited southern 60 miles.

Big Thicket National Preserve (☑409-951-6700; www.nps.gov/bith; 6102 FM 420, Kountze; ☺9am-5pm) At the intersection of Texas ecosystems, the Kirby Nature Loop can take you past soaring pine and hardwood forests, over cypress swamps and through sandy dunes with desert cacti.

Lady Bird Lake (p69) One of the state's prettiest urban hike-and-bike trails skirts the town lake for nearly 10 miles.

Lost Maples State Natural Area (p130) Hiking trails here take you into rugged limestone canyons and through prairielike grasslands.

Palo Duro Canyon State Park (p194) Follow the steep and rugged Upper Canyon Trail past the canyon cliffs and bluffs.

Davis Mountains State Park (p305) Trails climb to crisp views of surrounding mountains and plains, plus one linking to a path to a historic military fort.

Treading Lightly

Backcountry areas are composed of fragile environments and cannot support an inundation of human activity, especially insensitive and careless activity. Treat the backcountry like you would your own backyard – minus the barbecue pit.

Most conservation organizations and hikers' manuals have their own set of backcountry codes, all of which outline the same important principles: minimizing the human impact on the land, leaving no trace, and taking nothing but photographs and memories. Above all, stay on the main trail, stay on the main trail and, finally, even if it means walking through mud or crossing a patch of snow, *stay on the main trail.*

Bird-Watching

Texas has more than 600 documented bird species – over 75% of all species reported in the US. The **Audubon Texas** (☑214-370-9735; http://tx.audubon.org) website has loads of additional information on birding in the state, as does **Texas Parks & Wildlife** (☑800-792-1112, 512-389-4800; www.tpwd.texas.gov). The latter publishes full-color, interpretive guide–like 'Great Texas Wildlife Trails' maps, which are available from their website and some park ranger stations and visitor bureaus. The *Coastal Birding Trails* maps are the best, but all of the regional series note local avian species.

West Texas Keep your binoculars peeled for peregrine falcons, golden eagles, cactus wren and roadrunners at Guadalupe National Park (p328) and Davis Mountains State Park (p305). In the Chisos Mountains of Big Bend National Park (p293) you may spot the rare Colima warbler in its only US nesting site.

Rio Grande Valley The preeminent winter bird-watching location. Headquartered in the Bentsen-Rio Grande Valley State Park (p289), the World

PLAN YOUR TRIP OUTDOOR ACTIVITIES

WILDERNESS HIKING & CAMPING

To get far off the beaten path, you'll need to be prepared. Longer hikes require GPS or the appropriate United States Geological Survey (USGS) Quadrangles, also known as 7.5-minute maps, which are available through http://topomaps.usgs.gov. Remember to take plenty of water and tread lightly; pack out anything you pack in.

Texas' preeminent wilderness experiences are at Big Bend and Guadalupe Mountains National Parks, both in the state's western half. You can go far at Padre Island National Seashore too, but remember there is no shade and no freshwater available. Whenever heading into the backcountry, map out your route and be ready to show it to park rangers. Permit requirements are as follows.

Big Bend National Park (p293)

➡ Available in-person only, at all visitor centers
➡ $12 for overnight, use at designated sites only
➡ 14 consecutive nights possible

Guadalupe Mountains National Park (p328)

➡ Available from Pine Springs Visitor Center
➡ Free
➡ Two consecutive nights allowed per campground

Padre Island National Seashore (p277)

➡ Available from Malaquite Campground, Bird Island Basin and at South Beach
➡ No fee on North or South Beach
➡ 14-day permits

Chisos Mountains loom over Chisos Basin Campground (p298), Big Bend National Par

Birding Center has nine different locations across the valley and on the far southern coast.

Lower Gulf Coast Shore- and seabirds such as herons, egrets and roseate spoonbills inhabit the Gulf Coast year-round. Migratory species, including numerous waterfowl, overwinter here as well as in the valley. Laguna Atascosa (p279) is a highlight, as are the many small World Birding Centers properties within easy reach from here.

Upper Gulf Coast The area from Port Arthur to Corpus Christi attracts water-related species. Aransas National Wildlife Refuge (p264), a breeding ground to the endangered whooping cranes, is undoubtedly the star site. Don't discount smaller reserves like Anahuac National Wildlife Refuge (p253), however, as they also have plenty of species in often remote and beautiful surroundings.

Camping & State Parks

Texas' state parks are by far your best bet for camping. More than 60 of the 95 parks have campgrounds with electrical and water hook-ups; many even have wi-fi. Some parks also, or only, have walk- or hike-in tent sites – one has a canoe-in site.

Booking ahead is always recommended. Campground fees range from $10 to $25 per night; cabins cost anywhere from $45 to $200. To make reservations online, log onto http://texas.reserveworld.com. Each park holds its own individual attraction; following is a list of some of the best.

➡ To be riverside, try Guadalupe River (p117) or Caddo Lake (p246).

➡ For a mountain high, Davis Mountains (p306).

➡ Sleep by the sea at Mustang Island (p276).

➡ Looking for leafy? Lost Maples (p130).

➡ Go remote in Palo Duro (p194).

➡ Love bird-watching? Bentsen-Rio Grande Valley (p289) is for you.

➡ Snooze in the bayou at Brazos Bend State Park (p262).

➡ Caddo Lake (p246), Davis Mountains (p306), Balmorhea (p307) and **Bastrop** (⌨512-321-2101; www.tpwd.texas.gov; Hwy 21, Bastrop; adult/under 13yr $5/free) are among the parks that have Civilian Conservation Corps (CCC)–built cabins or lodging.

Cycling & Mountain Biking

Car-crazy Texas is only friendly to road cyclists in some places. Cities such as Austin and Fort Worth have developed good bike trails, but in many instances road riders will be sharing space with street traffic and extreme caution is necessary. B-cycle bike-share bikes and stations can be found in Austin and San Antonio.

For urban excursions, Austin has a number of good trails, including those in Zilker Park (p64) and at Lady Bird Lake (p69). In Fort Worth, Trinity Trails (p162) run riverside for 35 miles. Katy Trail (p148) is only 3.5 miles, but passes through some nice neighborhoods in Dallas. McAllister Park (p103) will give you a taste of Hill Country cycling but is only 7 miles from downtown San Antonio. In Houston, you can explore the new Buffalo Bayou Park (p204), which borders Buffalo Bayou west from downtown.

In West Texas you'll find a good variety of road cycling under not-too-crowded conditions, especially around Fort Davis. The Davis Mountains State Park (p305) also has mountain biking. Big Bend Ranch State Park (p303) has the only 'Epic' ride, as categorized by the International Mountain Biking Association.

In the Panhandle Plains, the 64-mile Caprock Canyons Trailways (p192) is an excellent multiple-use trail with many bridges, fenced railroad trestles and a 1000ft tunnel.

For more on cycling and mountain biking, check out the Activities page at Texas Parks & Wildlife (p35).

neither has horses available for hire. If you bring your own, do some route planning before you get the required permits at the respective visitor centers.

Best Places for Riding

Bandera (p130) Several of the more than dozen guest ranches in Bandera offer day rides. If you want to reenact your own version of *City Slickers*, sign up for a multiday, all-inclusive dude-ranch experience, which includes horseback rides, hay rides, cowhand activities, meals and lodging (from $120 per person, per day). Some of the places have natural swimming holes, creeks or swimming pools to cool off in.

Old West Stables (p194) Take an hour-long trot through stunning Palo Duro Canyon.

South Padre Island Adventures (p280) A morning or a sunset ride on the beach is a great way to start or end a day.

Big Bend & Lajitas Stables (p302) Trail rides take you not through the national park but through the similar West Texas terrain around Terlingua.

Hot-Air Ballooning

Floating above the state in a wicker gondola has its attractions, given the scenery, but it's not cheap: one-hour flights for two people typically cost $225 to $275 or more per person. Most flights leave at dawn or at sunset and rise 1000ft to 2000ft above the ground. Generally speaking there's ballooning in every major city. The best place to check for balloonists in a given area is at the local convention and visitor bureau or at the airport.

Horseback Riding

Few images are more iconic than a cowboy on horseback riding across an open plain, but in this big ol' state you can also gallop seaside, in the mountains or at a full-fledged dude ranch. Rides typically last one to two hours (from $35/60), but longer tours are often available.

Note that while both of Texas' national parks (Big Bend and Guadalupe Mountains) have trails that allow horseback riding,

Rock Climbing

Rock climbing has become increasingly popular around the state. Perhaps the best Texas rock climbing is at Hueco Tanks State Historical Park (p317), although access is curbed to preserve the prehistoric rock art. Also in West Texas, Franklin Mountains State Park (p316) has 17 mapped climbing routes. The Hill Country west of Austin is another popular area, especially Enchanted Rock State Natural Area (p126) north of Fredericksburg. Indoor climbing gyms can be found in most major Texas cities; they are a good place to learn before attempting to climb real rock outdoors. The **Texas Mountaineers** (www.texas mountaineers.org) website lists climbing sites and classes.

Water Sports
Boating & Jet Skiing

Texas actually has a *lotta* water and locals love to get out onto area lakes, rivers, bays and the Gulf by motorboat and Jet Ski. Rental options are a bit limited, but they can still be found. Boats and Jet Skis both start at $85 to $90 for the first hour, but the rate goes down for additional time.

Clear Lake Outside Houston, the marinas of Clear Lake act as the city's water recreation central. Rent Jet Skis from Pinky's Kayak Rental (p230), charter a sailboat with **Windsong** (☑832-905-6994; www.thewindsongchartercompany.com; 800 Mariners Dr; cruises from $160) or take a ride on the Beast at Kemah Boardwalk (p231).

Corpus Christi Buzz around the relatively protected bay. Rent Jet Skis and boats at places such as **CC Fun Time Rentals** (☑361-443-0707; http://funtimerental.tripod.com; 400 N Shoreline Blvd at Lawrence St T-Head; ⊙10am-7pm Mar-Sep).

Port Aransas Off the northern tip of Mustang Island, outside Corpus, you can get into some serous Gulf swell. Rent three-seater Jet Skis at Woody's Sports Center (p274).

South Padre Island Numerous water-sport outfitters rent both boats and Jet Skis. Beachside concession stands also offer banana-boat inner-tube rides.

Lake Travis Rent a boat from **Lakeway** (☑512-261-6600; www.lakewayresortandspa.com; 101 Lakeway Dr, Austin; r from $249; P@🔊🕿) and explore one of the richest coasts in Texas. After admiring the Austinites' mansions, find a marina restaurant to stop at for refreshment.

Fishing

Towns all along the coast provide access to charter fishing in the Gulf of Mexico; here anglers hunt for everything from red snapper and wahoo to shark and big-game marlin. From the piers and jetties along the coast you can catch redfish, flounder, and speckled and sand trout.

Best Places to Fish

Port Aransas Fishing is big business here. Hire a four- to eight-hour charter from outfitters such as Woody's Sports Center (p274).

(North) Padre Island Shore fishing is popular among Corpus Christi locals.

South Padre Island Wander the docks and talk to the skippers along the piers on the lagoon side of South Padre: you'll soon find one who offers the boat charter of your dreams.

Rockport Look for fishing boat charters along Rockport Harbor (p264).

Galveston Charter-fishing outfits line up along Pier 19 on the bay side of Galveston Island.

Licenses

A fishing license is required for all anglers older than 17. A one-day, all-water license is $11 for Texas residents, $16 for non-residents; an entire year costs residents $47 and nonresidents $68. Texas Parks & Wildlife licenses are sold online at http://tpwd.texas.gov and at sporting-goods stores, at bait-and-tackle shops and at some park offices.

Kayaking & Canoeing

Texas' estuaries, streams and rivers are ripe for exploration by canoe or kayak, and numerous parks make good bases from which to set off. The lagoons and canals of the long Intracoastal Waterway system are ideal for sea kayaking.

If a place has good kayaking and canoe-ing conditions, there is usually some savvy entrepreneur around to rent you the gear. Prices tend to run from $31 to $60 a day. For more on paddling activities in state parks, check out Texas Parks & Wildlife (p35).

Best Places to Kayak & Canoe

Caddo Lake (p246) Mist-shrouded waters, Spanish moss draped from every cypress tree: Caddo Lake is a moody and beautiful place to weave in and out of narrow bayous, around islands and through swamps.

Rockport & Fulton (p264) The coastal estuaries are prime paddling territory. Several local companies also offer kayak ecotours.

South Padre Island (p279) Sea-kayaking action off the coast of the state's prettiest beaches.

New Braunfels (p117) Inner-tubing down the Guadalupe River (with cooler in tow) may be the most popular way to go, but kayak and canoe rentals are also available.

Goose Island State Park (p267) Kayaking along the calm inlets of this marshy island allows access to Aransas Pass National Wildlife Refuge.

Bastrop State Park (p36) Paddle a calm section of the Colorado River.

Surfing

For many, 'Texas surfing' is an oxymoron. But local aficionados will argue that it is not as bad as surfers from elsewhere have heard. Longboard surfers, in fact, will have a fun time here on most days; the longer the board, the more rideable the Gulf's mush (3ft or lower). The key to riding little waves is timing, luck and patience. When a hurricane warning sounds, local surfers run toward the water instead of away from it.

The coastline south from Port Aransas is all somewhat surfable. The best surf is found furthest south, at South Padre Island, where there's a chance of catching some waves with good groundswell. Board rentals are readily available in Port A, Corpus Christi and South Padre. Mustang Island State Park, on Padre Island near Corpus Christi, is an especially popular surfing spot

In Corpus Christi you can learn more about Lone Star surfing at the Texas Surf Museum (361-882-2364; www.texas surfmuseum.org; 309 N Water St; ⊙11am-7pm Mon-Sat, to 5pm Sun) FREE, while the folks at Wind & Wave Watersports (p269) down the coast can rent you a board.

Tubing & Rafting

From the classic Rio Grande white-water trips at Big Bend to lazy tubing on the Guadalupe River near New Braunfels, Texas offers both wild and mild river adventure. The extensive Texas section

online at RiverFacts (www.riverfacts. com) outlines all the white-water paddling in the state.

Rio Grande Rapids up to Class IV alternate with calm stretches on the Rio Grande in the five canyons of Big Bend National Park (p293). A river trip here can last from several hours to several days, traversing the impressive Boquillas Canyon. Outfitters offer complete row, eat and sleep tours. Some also have multisport tours that also include hiking or biking. Early spring and autumn usually have the best weather and water conditions.

Guadalupe River One of our favorite things in the world is floating down the Guadalupe (or the Frio, or the San Marcos) in an inner tube, cold beer in hand. You can rent tubes in New Braunfels (p117) or at Kerrville-Schreiner Park (p135). The former has frequent return shuttles. Outfitters will even rent you tubes with reinforced bottoms to put your cooler in.

San Marcos River This spring-fed river is always cool, but not always flowing much. When it is, rent tubes from the Lion's Club (p121) in San Marcos.

Colorado River The Bastrop River Company (512-321-4661; www.bastropivercompany.com; 601 Chestnut St, Bastrop; paddle trips year-round per hr $45, tube rental May-Sep $15; ⊙daily summer, by appointment winter) rents tubes and provides return shuttles for two- to eight-hour floats on the Colorado.

Windsurfing

If Texas' waves are unreliable, the wind is not. Constant coastal breezes, coupled with shallow bodies of water sheltered by the barrier islands, make for great windsurfing conditions. Rentals will usually run you between $65 and $75 per day. Top spots, with rentals:

Padre Island National Seashore (p277) Bird Island Basin, off the Laguna Madre, ranks as one of the top windsurfing spots in the US. Lessons available locally.

South Padre Island (p280) The lagoon side of the island is popular with windsurfers, and rightly so. Numerous outfitters provide gear and instruction.

Plan Your Trip

Travel with Children

With beaches for building sandcastles, state and national parks for outdoor exploring, museums for fun and learning – and amusement parks for when your child needs a little more action – Texas is an ideal family destination. Locals love little cowpokes, so expect a warm welcome here.

Best Regions for Kids

San Antonio & Hill Country

Historic sites with activity books, plus theme parks, make San Antonio especially family-friendly. In Hill Country, Kerrville and New Braunfels serve as launch points for river inner-tubing.

Gulf Coast & South Texas

Beaches line the southern Gulf Coast: some have diversions, some simply star nature herself. Galveston Island, with its organized beaches, pleasure pier, water park and amusements, offers much fun. Corpus Christi is home to the USS *Lexington* Museum, the huge Texas State Aquarium and a lovely bayfront promenade.

Houston

The Houston Museum of Natural Science has popular hands-on exhibits on chemistry, energy and other science disciplines.

Dallas & the Panhandle Plains

Nearby in Arlington, a theme park and water park don't hurt either.

Texas for Kids

There's not too much to worry about when traveling in Texas with your kids – as long as you keep them covered in sunblock.

Necessities

Dining It's more than fine to bring kids along to casual restaurants, which often have high chairs and children's menus. Many places break out paper placemats and crayons for drawing.

Lodging Most motels and hotels offer rooms with two double beds, which are ideal for families. Some also have roll-away beds or cribs that can be brought into the room for an extra charge. Some hotels offer 'kids stay free' programs for children up to 18 years old. Note that most B&Bs do not allow children under 12 to stay.

Supplies Baby food, formula, soy and cow's milk, disposable diapers (nappies) and other necessities are widely available in drugstores and supermarkets. Breastfeeding in public is accepted when done discreetly. Many public toilets have a baby-changing table, and gender-neutral 'family' bathrooms may be available at airports, museums etc.

Health & Safety

Though hopefully not needed, medical services and facilities in Texas are of a high standard. Urgent Care facilities can handle

Houston Museum of Natural Science (p205)

minor emergencies and cost much less than hospital emergency rooms.

For automobiles, Texas law requires that children under the age of eight, or under the height of 4ft 9in, ride in a federally approved child safety seat. Every car-rental agency should be able to provide one (usually $10 per day) if you request it when booking in advance.

Note that while Texas' beaches are great, many allow driving on the beach and children will need to be monitored closely.

Discounts

Children's discounts are available for everything from museum admission to movie tickets. The definition of a 'child' varies, but usually means those between two and 12. Under two is generally free.

Domestic airlines don't charge for children under two who are carried on your lap. Others must have a seat. Southwest Airlines is one of the few that have discounted fares for children.

Children's Highlights

The four main cities – San Antonio, Austin, Dallas and Houston – each have children's museums, public parks and many other attractions. See individual city sections for more options.

Museums

Houston Museum of Natural Science, Houston (p205) A giant new dinosaur hall, hands-on chemistry experiments, butterfly house and planetarium.

Dallas World Aquarium, Dallas (☑214-720-2224; www.dwazoo.com; 1801 N Griffin St; adult/child $21/15; ⊙9am-5pm; ☷) Fourteen different watery ecosystems brought to life.

Perot Museum of Nature and Science, Dallas (p145) Loads of interactive fun: travel through space or design your own robot in Dallas' Arts District.

San Antonio Children's Museum, San Antonio (p97) Two floors of dress-up, crawl-around, role-playing fun.

USS Lexington Museum, Corpus Christi (p269) Tour a retired aircraft carrier, complete with foldable airplanes, in Corpus Christi.

Moody Gardens, Galveston (p258) Three glass pyramids contain a greenhouse, an aquarium and science exhibits in Galveston. Outside there's a beach and a boat ride.

Parks & Rivers

Big Bend National Park, West Texas (p293) Junior rangers have extensive trail choices here, but it's far from anything else.

Guadalupe River, New Braunfels Take a family float down the river, then splash things up at the Schlitterbahn Waterpark (p118).

Hermann Park, Houston (p205) Ride paddle boats on the lake and a train around this big park; also home to the city zoo.

Barton Springs, Austin (p68) Cool off in a spring-fed pool in the center of town.

Amusements

Six Flags Over Texas, Arlington (p173) Thirteen roller coasters are only a small sampling of rides at the state's largest amusement park; outside Dallas.

Schlitterbahn, New Braunfels (p118) This Texas-size water park has four locations: South Padre Island, Galveston, Corpus Christi and this original in New Braunfels.

Splashtown, San Antonio (p103) Beat the Hill Country heat in Texas' biggest wave pool at this kids' favorite on the edge of San Antonio.

Planning
When to Go

Be warned: most of Texas gets quite hot in summer, and sights and amusements will be crowded. Spring has much nicer weather. Texas schools' spring breaks cover all the weeks in March, so book ahead during that time or – even better – avoid it completely.

What to Pack

Don't forget the sunscreen. Many of Texas' best activities for children are outdoors, and the sun can be brutal here. Count on needing mosquito spray at some point as well. If you're going to a beach or a river, be sure to bring water shoes to protect sensitive little feet .

Useful Resources

For all-round information and advice, check out Lonely Planet's *Travel with Children*.

Family Travel Files (www.thefamilytravelfiles. com/locations/texas) Vacation-planning articles, tips and discounts.

Travel Texas (www.traveltex.com/trip-ideas.aspx) Tourist-board trip planner with family-friendly ideas.

Classic barbecue fare at Franklin Barbecue (p77), Austin

Texas BBQ & Cuisine

If American cooking could be summed up as combining generous portions of homegrown foods with foreign sensibilities and techniques, Texas spins this into a cuisine that is uniquely its own. Highlights include Texas-style barbecue, authentic Mexican fare, creative Tex-Mex dishes, down-home Southern comfort food and Gulf Coast seafood.

Tastes Born in Texas

Corny Dogs

Cornbread-batter-dipped-and-fried hot dogs on a stick were created in 1948 by Neil Fletcher for the State Fair of Texas. Fletcher's still sells 'em there; they're now available with jalapeño cornbread, too.

Shiner Bock

The state's favorite amber ale came to be when Kosmos Spoetzl brought Bavarian brewing to Shiner, Texas, in 1914. Available countrywide, Shiner Bock is still brewed at Spoetzl Brewery.

Chicken-Fried Bacon

You may have heard of steak coated and deep-fried like chicken, but the taste (and heart-attack factor) was taken to new heights when Sodolak's, near Bryan-College Station, started cooking bacon the same way in the early 1990s.

Dr Pepper

A pharmacist in a Waco drugstore–soda shop invented this aromatic cola in the 1880s. Taste the original sugarcane formula at the first bottling plant, Dublin Dr Pepper.

Big Red

Invented in Waco in 1937 by Grover C Thomsen and RH Roark, this super-sweet red cream soda has a dedicated following and is a favorite with kids.

Barbecue

Make no bones about it – Texas barbecue is an obsession. It's the subject of countless newspaper and magazine articles, from national press (including the *New York Times)* to regional favorite *Texas Monthly.* Some of central Texas' smaller towns – Lockhart and Elgin, to name only two – maintain perennial reputations for their smokehouse cultures, and routinely draw dedicated pilgrims from miles around.

No self-respecting Texan would agree with another about who has the best barbecue, since that would take the fun out of it.

But most do see eye-to-eye on a few things: brisket is where a pit master proves his or her reputation; seasoning is rarely much more than salt, pepper and something spicy; and if there's a sauce, it's probably made from ketchup, vinegar and the drippings of the wood-smoked meat.

The best Texas barbecue often comes from famous family dynasties that have been dishing up the same crowd-pleasing recipes for generations. Telltale signs that you've located an authentic barbecue joint include zero decor, smoke-blackened ceilings and laid-back table manners (silverware optional). At most places, you can order a combination plate or ask for specific meats to be sliced by the pound right in front of you. Of course, there are variations on this nowadays, but in Texas, where barbecue baiting is a bit of a pastime, some swear this down-home style is the only way.

However you like it – sliced thick onto butcher paper, slapped on picnic plates, doused with a tangy sauce or eaten naturally flavorful right out of the smokehouse barbecue pit – be sure to savor it...and then argue to the death that *your* way is the best way. Like a true Texan.

History

The origins of central Texas barbecue can be traced to 19th-century Czech and German settlers, many of whom were butchers. These settlers pioneered methods of smoking meat, both to preserve it (before the advent of refrigeration) and also to tenderize cuts that might otherwise be wasted.

Credit also goes to Mexican *vaqueros* (Spanish-speaking cowboys), especially in Texas' southern and western borderland regions, who dug the first barbecue pits in about the 16th century, then grilled spicy meats over mesquite wood. African Americans who migrated to Texas brought with them recipes for a 'wet' style of barbecue, which involved thick marinades, sweet sauces and juicier meats.

Somewhere along the way, slow-smoked barbecue crossed the line from simple eating pleasure to statewide obsession. Maybe it's the primal joy of gnawing tender, tasty meat directly from the bone, or the simplistic, sloppy appeal of the hands-on eating experience. Whatever the reason, dedicated barbecue eaters demonstrate nearly religious devotion by worshipping at the pits of Texas' renowned smokehouses.

Ingredients

In today's Texas, barbecue recipes are as varied as central Texas summers are long. Most folks agree on the basics: slow cooking over a low-heat fire. A cooking time of up to 12 or 16 hours isn't unheard of – anything less and you're just too darn impatient. It allows the meat to be infused with a smoky flavor of usually hickory or pecan in the eastern part of the state, oak in central Texas and mesquite out west. (Mesquite was considered all but a weed until someone realized how nice a flavor it lent to wood chips.)

The Meat

Texas barbecue leans heavily toward beef – a logical outgrowth of the state's cattle industry – and most signature dishes come straight from the sacred cow. The most common is beef brisket, a cut often used for corned beef. With a combination of patience, experience and skill, a seasoned pit boss can transform this notoriously tough meat into a perfectly smoked, tender slab of heaven. Even tougher cuts of meat enter the smokehouse and emerge hours later, deeply flavorful and tender to the tooth. Sliced thin and internally moistened by natural fat, a well-smoked brisket falls apart with the slightest touch and can rival more expensive cuts for butter-smooth consistency.

Carnivores seeking a more toothy challenge can indulge in beef ribs – huge meaty racks that would do Fred Flintstone proud – or relax with a saucy chopped-beef sandwich. Word to the wise: If you need to stay presentable, think twice about ribs, which tend to be a full-contact eating experience (even as part of a three-meat sampler plate).

Lone Star cattle worship stops short of excluding other meats from the pit. The noble pig makes appearances in the form of succulent ribs, thick buttery chops and perfect slices of loin so tender they melt on the tongue. In recent years, chicken has shown up on the menu boards, mainly to provide beginners with a nonhoofed barnyard option. Traditionalists, however, stick with the good stuff – red meat and plenty of it.

Every self-respecting barbecue joint will also serve sausage. Texas hot links, the peppery sausage of regional renown, is created with ground pork and beef combined with pungent spices. Although it's not technically in the barbecue family, sausage is cooked over the same fire so has the same smoky flavor. If nothing else it makes

Texas ribs

an excellent meat side dish to go alongside your meaty main dish.

The Rub

Everyone knows that the word 'barbecue' is usually followed by the word 'sauce.' But not so fast, there. Good barbecue is more than just meat and sauce. The other key component is the rub, which is how the meat is seasoned before it's cooked.

There are wet rubs and dry rubs. A dry rub is a mixture of salt, pepper, herbs and spices sprinkled over or painstakingly rubbed into the meat before cooking. A wet rub is created by adding liquid, which usually means oil, but also possibly vinegar, lemon juice or even mustard. Applied like a paste, a wet rub seals in the meat's natural juices before cooking. This key step is just as important as the slow cooking in getting the flavor just right.

The Sauce

Wisdom about barbecue sauce varies widely from region to region and sometimes joint to joint. There's huge debate over what kind, how much or whether you need it at all. In Lockhart, Kreuz Market's (p79) meat is served without any sauce at all, and it's so naturally juicy and tender you'll agree it's not necessary. But excellent, sauce-heavy barbecue is divine as well. We'll leave it up to you to make up your own mind.

Texas barbecue sauce has a different flavor from other types – that's why it's Texas barbecue, y'all. It's not as sweet as the kind you'll find gracing the tables of barbecue joints in Kansas City and Memphis – more a blend of spicy and slightly sweet. There are thousands of variations and no two sauces are exactly alike, but recipes are usually tomato based with vinegar, brown sugar, chili powder, onion, garlic and other seasonings.

The Sides

Side dishes naturally take second place to the platters of smoked meat. Restaurant-style sides usually include pinto beans, potato salad or coleslaw, while markets sometimes opt for simpler accompaniments like onion slices, dill pickles, cheese slices or whole tomatoes. (Not to worry, if your meat is served on butcher paper, the sides will come in a bowl or on a plate.)

Cook-Offs

There are people who will travel the entire state of Texas to sample all the various permutations of barbecue. But if your time's more limited, you can always try one of the many organized cook-offs around the state. Amateurs and pros alike come together for the noble joint cause of barbecue perfection and, if they're lucky, bragging rights. Cook-offs generally start on Friday afternoon so the pit masters have plenty of time to get their meat just right before the judging on Saturday, even if it means staying up all night. (You can't rush these things.) Once the judging is complete, the public is invited to swoop in and judge for themselves.

One of the largest events is the **Taylor International Barbecue Cook-off** (www.taylorchamber.org; ⊗Jun), held in early June in Taylor (northeast of Austin), with up to 100 contestants competing in divisions like beef, ribs, pork, poultry, lamb, seafood and wild game. If you can't make that one, a quick search on www.tourtexas.com will lead you to events, such as the **Good Times Barbecue Cook-off** in Amarillo.

Otherwise, check out the calendar on the **Central Texas Barbecue Association** (www.ctbabbq.com) website, where you can also read the detailed rules that competitions must follow ('CTBA recommends the use of a Styrofoam tray with a hinged lid

Texas barbecues grilling smoked meats

and without dividers or the best readily available judging container that is approximately 9 inches square on the bottom half').

Barbecue Etiquette

The first question that comes to most people's mind is, 'How do I eat this without making a mess?' You don't. Accepting the fact early on that barbecue is a messy, messy venture will give you the attitude you need to enjoy your meal. One coping mechanism is to make a drop cloth of your napkin. Bibs haven't exactly caught on in the barbecue world – this is a manly meal, after all – but tucking your napkin into your shirt is never frowned upon, especially if you didn't come dressed for it.

Which leads to another question: how does one dress for barbecue? First off, don't wear white. Or yellow, or pink, or anything that won't camouflage or coordinate with red. At 99% of barbecue restaurants (the exception being uppity nouveau 'cue) you will see the most casual of casual attire, including jeans (harder to stain) and shorts, and maybe even some trucker hats.

Whether you eat with your hands or a fork depends on the cut of the meat. Brisket and sausage are fork dishes, while ribs are eaten prehistoric-style. (It also depends on the restaurant. Kreuz Market (p79) doesn't offer forks. As the owner famously says, 'God put two of them at the end of your arms.')

If you're eating with your hands, grab extra napkins. Ah, heck, grab extras anyway. You might also be provided with a small packet containing a moist towelette, which will at least get you clean enough to head to the restrooms to wash up.

A final thought on etiquette: if you're at a restaurant that uses a dry rub and you don't see any sauce, it's probably best not to ask. It would be a bit like asking for ketchup to put on your steak.

Best Places to Try Barbecue

West Texas & Panhandle

➡ **KD's Bar-B-Q** (p179)
➡ **Rib Hut** (p323)
➡ **DB's Rustic Iron BBQ** (p303)

Central Texas

➡ **Franklin Barbecue** (p77)
➡ **Cooper's Old Time Pit Bar-B-Cue** (p74)
➡ **Black's Barbecue** (p79)
➡ **County Line Smokehouse** (p108)
➡ **Kreuz Market** (p79)
➡ **Lamberts** (p75)
➡ **Salt Lick** (p123)
➡ **Smoke** (p153)
➡ **Vitek's BBQ** (p177)

East Texas

➡ **Country Tavern** (p244)
➡ **Joseph's Riverport Barbecue** (p246)
➡ **New Zion Missionary Baptist Church** (p232)

Gulf Coast

➡ **Goode Co BBQ** (p222)

PLAN YOUR TRIP TEXAS BBQ & CUISINE

Texas BBQ

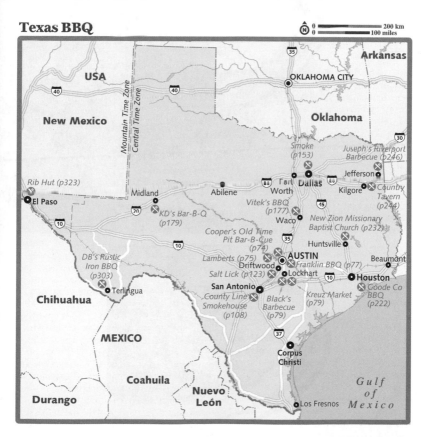

MOLPIX/SHUTTERSTOCK ©

Top: Huevos rancheros

Bottom: Barbecue pork

COBBLER OR PIE?

You're full already? Well, just let your belt out a notch, because you've got to try the dessert. You might be off the hook if the restaurant doesn't serve sweets, but nothing follows a plate of barbecue like some peach or blackberry cobbler with a scoop of ice cream. (If you're feeling dainty, you can just go for the ice cream.) If you're not familiar with cobbler, picture a deconstructed fruit pie without a bottom crust. Fruit and sugar are cooked together on the stovetop then layered into a baking dish with dough on top.

Of course, a pie always works, especially if it's a pecan pie made from locally grown pecans, and chocolate cake would not be frowned upon either, but cobblers are a classic. As a bonus, since they're seldom mass-produced, you're likely to get something made fresh in-house.

Mexican & Tex-Mex
What's the Difference?

A regional variation on Mexican food, Tex-Mex includes Americanized versions of Mexican dishes, as well as American dishes with a Mexican twist. Don't spend too much effort trying to sort the two: there's a lot of overlap and, unless you're eating at a restaurant that serves 'authentic' or 'interior Mexico' dishes, you're probably going to have some Tex sneak into your Mex.

Mexican and Tex-Mex staples are often variations on a theme: take some sort of tortilla, whether soft or deep-fried, and put meat on it or in it, whether chicken, beef, pork or seafood. Then top it with cheese, whether melted or not, and maybe some lettuce, sour cream, salsa and guacamole. The result? Burritos, tacos, enchiladas, nachos, fajitas and tostadas. Almost universally, a Tex-Mex main dish will be served with beans and rice on the side.

Mexican Dishes

➡ **Breakfast burritos** Eggs and either refried beans or bacon rolled in a soft tortilla

➡ **Migas** Eggs scrambled with broken tortilla strips and cheese

➡ **Huevos rancheros** Fried eggs on tortillas, covered in salsa

➡ **Chile relleno** A mild pepper stuffed with a ground-beef mixture and then fried

➡ **Empanada** A small pastry with savory or sweet fillings

➡ **Tamales** Corn dough stuffed with meat, beans, cheese, chilies or nothing at all, wrapped in cornhusks and steamed

➡ **Gorditas** Fried corn dough filled with refried beans and topped with sour cream, cheese and lettuce

➡ **Salsa** Spanish for 'sauce' – made with chopped tomatoes, onions, cilantro and chilies

➡ **Menudo** A heady stew of jalapeños, hominy and tripe (beef stomach), and a traditional Mexican hangover cure

Vegetarians & Vegans

Vegetarianism has caught on big time in the USA, even in cattle country like Texas. Austin in particular is bursting with vegetarian- and vegan-friendly eateries. Like any major city, San Antonio also has plenty of options for vegetarians. In rural areas, though, it can be more difficult, with meat playing a key role in most Southern cooking. Ask twice if something contains meat – some people don't consider things like sausage seasoning or bacon bits to be meat, and you may hear tell of someone serving 'beef for everyone, and chicken for the vegetarians.' Also inquire about cooking with lard, which many restaurants do even with so-called 'vegetarian' menu items.

Otherwise, salad bars are a good way to stave off hunger, and many restaurants serve large salads as main courses. Even at barbecue joints, you can often cobble together a decent meal with a number of 'sides' (side dishes) such as potato salad, beans (make sure there's no pork added), corn bread and banana pudding for dessert. Throughout this book, we've mentioned good vegetarian options in restaurant reviews wherever possible.

CapRock Winery (p19.

Drinking

The quasi-official soft drink of Texas is iced tea – almost always served unsweetened. If you want *hot* tea, specify that or you'll wind up with iced tea instead. Soft drinks are the same as everywhere in the world, but a local favorite is Dr Pepper, invented in Waco. Big Red, also invented in Waco, is a sweet, red cream soda. Bottled drinking water is widely available, although tap water in Texas is usually fine to drink.

The strictly enforced drinking age in Texas is 21, and it's illegal to drive with a blood-alcohol level over .08%. Carry a driver's license or passport as proof of age. Minors are not allowed in bars and pubs, even to order nonalcoholic beverages.

Beer

Texas was a little slow in building up its microbrew culture – maybe folks were satisfied with the excellent and widely available commercial brand, Shiner, produced in Texas. Today, you'll find microbreweries opening their doors across the state. You'll also find a good selection of out-of-state craft and and specialty brews in larger cities, where pubs routinely have dozens of beers available. If a bar advertises 'longnecks,' that's just a standard 12oz beer served in a bottle with a longer neck.

Wine

Texas has two major viticulture areas, which are home to the state's most celebrated wineries: the High Plains surrounding Lubbock, and the Hill Country west of Austin and San Antonio. Popular varietals are Cabernet Sauvignon, Merlot, Chardonnay and Pinot Noir.

Liquor

Tequila is the most popular poison around these parts, if for no other reason than it's the main ingredient in margaritas. The unofficial state cocktail, margaritas are made with tequila, lime juice and triple sec, then served either on the rocks or frozen, in a glass with a salted rim. A few restaurants stake their reputations on specialty flavors, such as mango or watermelon. Don't knock 'em 'til you've downed at least one.

Distilleries are popular too, and often offer tours and tastings. If you're in Austin or the Hill Country, head to Dripping Springs, where there are several new distilleries.

Regions at a Glance

In a vast and varied place like the Lone Star State, it should come as no surprise that you can have just about any experience your little ol' heart desires. If you're looking for outdoor adventure, the Gulf Coast and West Texas have it in spades. Dallas and Houston are your ticket to big-city culture. Simpler, small-town pleasures await outside metro areas everywhere, especially in northeast Texas, Hill Country and east-central Washington County If you want to eat, drink and be entertained, San Antonio and Austin have you covered. The only trouble may be deciding exactly what you want to do.

Austin

Music
Outdoors
Food

Live Performances

Fun and funky Austin has something going on every day of the week. Live music runs the gamut from local country to alternative and avant-garde.

Zilker Park

Take a dip in a natural spring pool, hike and bike along Lady Bird Lake or rent canoes or kayaks in Zilker Park. A big part of Austin's attraction is to be found outdoors.

South Congress Ave

Explore Austin's 'weird' side on South Congress Ave, where you can stay at an upscale Zen motel; eat at wonderfully independent cafes and food trailers; and shop for vintage clothes or get a new tattoo.

p54

San Antonio & Hill Country

Culture
History
Small Towns

Hispanic Heritage

The state's Hispanic roots run deep in San Antonio, and the culture thrives here today. Munch Mexican food to your heart's content before you tour the *mercado* (market) or listen to mariachis on the River Walk.

The Alamo

Although small, the site of the historic siege of the Alamo should top any visitor's list. Four more old Spanish missions (built between 1720 and 1756) lie south of the city along the Mission Trail.

The Hill Country

Winding roads and rivers lead past old towns set among the rolling hills. In the spring, brilliant wildflowers carpet the hills and dales.

p90

Dallas & the Panhandle Plains

Dallas & Fort Worth

These neighboring cities have incredible museums and arts districts. But they also have low-ball fun such as fried cheesecake and mechanical-bull rides.

President John F Kennedy

The stellar Sixth Floor Museum examines the facts and theories surrounding the assassination of President John F Kennedy. Other JFK-related sights include Dealey Plaza and the Kennedy Memorial.

Panhandle Scenery

Amarillo's classic Mother Road (Route 66) stops include the Big Texan Steak Ranch and Cadillac Ranch. South of town, Palo Duro Canyon is the only break in the pancake-flat Panhandle Plains.

p137

Houston & East Texas

Houston Art Enclaves

Houston has several world-class art museums. The Museum of Fine Art is certainly not to be discounted, but the modern-leaning Menil Collection is one of a kind.

Culinary Diversity in the City

The food scene in Houston is hot. You might dine on inspired organic creations at Haven, French-Tex fusion at Philippe's or see what chef Monica Pope is up to at Sparrow Bar & Cookshop.

Northeast Texas

Leave the city to explore the Southern-belle towns set among soaring pine forests up in the northeast. Tyler is the rose capital of Texas, Nacogdoches the oldest (maybe), and Jefferson boasts the most ghosts.

p201

Gulf Coast & South Texas

Seaside Wanderings

Towns such as Matagorda, Rockport and Port Aransas may all be home to harbors and shrimp-fishing fleets, but you'll also find sea-themed shops, boat tours and quaint accommodation.

South Padre Island & Around

The largest of Texas' barrier islands, Padre Island stretches 113 miles. In the north near Corpus Christi, commercial and residential areas with beaches give way to the pristine, 70-mile-long Padre Island National Seashore.

World Birding Center

Nine individual sites scattered along the Rio Grande Valley make up the incomparable World Birding Center. Interesting year-round, though winter is when the most birds come to roost.

p249

Big Bend & West Texas

Big Bend National Park

The more than 200 miles of trails at Big Bend National Park are the highlight of Texas hiking. Tromp up mountains, trace riverside trails or explore the Chihuahuan desert.

Davis Mountains

Though not as tall as neighboring ranges, the Davis Mountains provide an excellent opportunity for scenic driving. Wind your way up to the McDonald Observatory for the most comprehensive views.

Quirky West Texas

Each quirky little west-Texas town has an individual claim to fame: Fort Davis is Old West-inspired; Marfa's a funky artist's escape; and Terlingua is a repopulated ghost town.

p291

On the Road

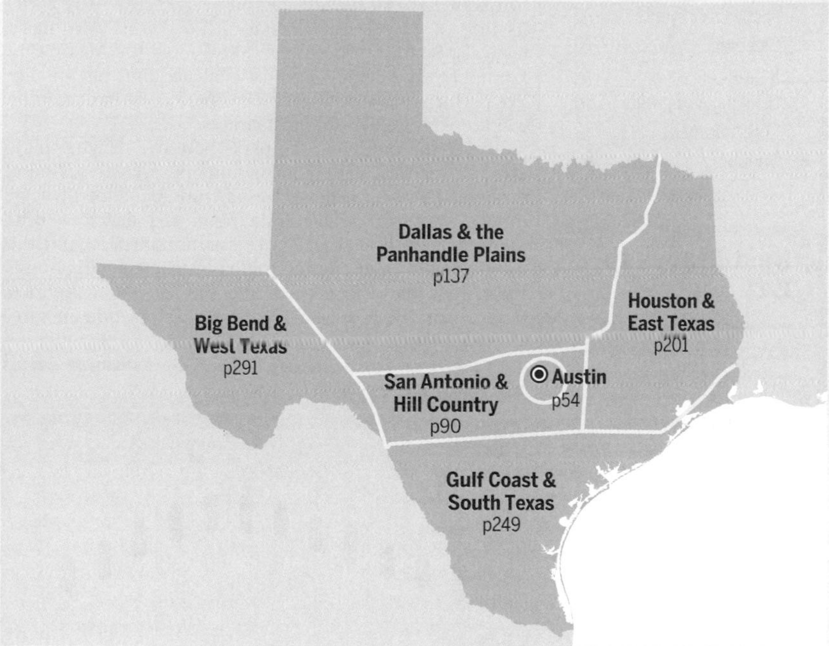

Dallas & the Panhandle Plains
p137

Big Bend & West Texas
p291

Houston & East Texas
p201

San Antonio & Hill Country
p90

⊙ **Austin**
p54

Gulf Coast & South Texas
p249

Austin

POP 820,611 / 512

Best Places to Eat

➡ Franklin Barbecue (p77)

➡ Amy's Ice Creams (p80)

➡ Uchiko (p79)

➡ Dai Due (p78)

➡ Veracruz All Natural (p78)

➡ Hopdoddy Burger Bar (p76)

Best Places to Sleep

➡ Hotel Van Zandt (p71)

➡ Driskill Hotel (p71)

➡ Heywood Hotel (p73)

➡ Austin Motel (p73)

➡ Hotel San José (p73)

Why Go?

A big city with a small-town heart, Austin earns the love through great music, fantastic parks, culinary prowess, cool murals, whip-smart locals and a sociable streak impossible to resist. Let's start with the music. The city easily earns its title of 'Live Music Capital of the World.' Two music festivals, South by Southwest (SXSW) and the Austin City Limits Festival, enjoy international acclaim, but quality live performances go down every single night in one of the countless clubs, bars and restaurants.

As for the outdoors, the parks here are thriving playgrounds packed with hikers, runners, cyclists and dog walkers. All reward themselves at world-class food trucks, innovative farm-to-table restaurants and delicious BBQ joints. But the best part? The communal spirit. Despite the rapid growth (and terrible traffic), Austin remains hospitable. Just join a food truck line and ask about the food Vscene. You'll kick-start a passionate conversation for sure.

When to Go
Austin

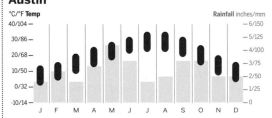

Mar & Apr Wildflowers and mild weather make this the perfect time of year to visit.

May & Jun The weather is hot but bearable, and everything is still green for the most part.

Sep & Oct You won't see any fall foliage, but temperatures will have cooled by now.

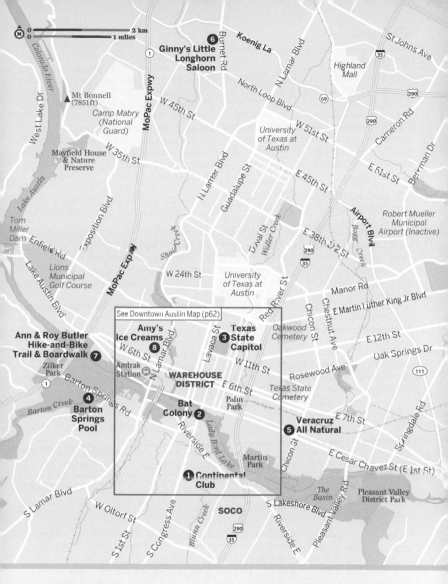

Austin Highlights

1 **Continental Club** (p83) Catching a band at this iconic club or one of Austin's hundreds of other music venues.

2 **Bat Colony** (p56) Watching the nightly exodus of America's largest urban bat colony in summer.

3 **Texas State Capitol** (p56) Gazing up at the Texas star 266ft above you!

4 **Barton Springs Pool** (p68) Jumping into the icy waters for instant relief from the Texas heat.

5 **Veracruz All Natural** (p78) Savoring tacos at what some say is the best food truck in the city.

6 **Ginny's Little Longhorn Saloon** (p82) Honky-tonkin' and playing chicken shit bingo.

7 **Ann & Roy Butler Hike-and-Bike Trail & Boardwalk** (p65) Pausing on your lakeside stroll on the boardwalk for awesome skyline views.

8 **Amy's Ice Creams** (p80) Creating a perfect blend of ice cream and toppings.

⊙ Sights

⊙ Downtown

Downtown Austin is an orderly grid. The main north–south artery is Congress Ave, with Cesar Chavez St running east–west. Most downtown streets are one way, including 6th St, a major westbound thoroughfare, and southbound Guadalupe St (pronounced *guad*-ah-loop locally, despite what you might have learned in Spanish class).

★**Texas State Capitol**   HISTORIC BUILDING
(Map p62; ☑ 512-463-5495, tours 512-463-0063; cnr 11th St & Congress Ave; ⊙ 7am-10pm Mon-Fri, 9am-8pm Sat & Sun; 🚻) FREE Built in 1888 from sunset-red granite, this state capitol is the largest in the US, backing up the ubiquitous claim that everything is bigger in Texas. If nothing else, take a peek at the lovely rotunda – be sure to look up at the dome – and try out the whispering gallery created by its curved ceiling.

Self-guided-tour brochures of the capitol building and grounds are available inside the tour guide office on the ground floor. From here you can also take one of the interesting 40-minute guided tours offered daily (schedules vary; call first or show up and try your luck). Stop by the gift shop for Texas-themed gifts. The green sprawl of the capitol grounds and its monuments are worth a stroll before or after your tour. You'll also find an exhibit about the capitol building in the freestanding visitor center.

Want to see government in action? Take a seat in the 3rd-floor **visitors balconies** overlooking the House of Representatives and Senate chamber galleries, which are open to the public when the state legislature is in session (odd-numbered years from mid-January through May or June).

Free two-hour parking is available inside the Capitol Visitors Parking Garage, entered from either 12th St or 13th St, off San Jacinto Blvd.

★**Bat Colony Under Congress Avenue Bridge**   BRIDGE
(Map p62; Congress Ave; ⊙ sunset Apr-Nov) Every year up to 1.5 million Mexican free-tailed bats make their home upon a platform beneath the Congress Ave Bridge, forming the largest urban bat colony in North America. It's become an Austin tradition to sit on the grassy banks of Lady Bird Lake and watch the bats swarm out to feed on an estimated 30,000lbs (13,500kg) of insects per night. it looks a lot like a fast-moving, black, chittering river.

AUSTIN IN...

One Day
Start your day with gingerbread pancakes at the **Bob Bullock Texas State History Museum** (p61) then pop into the **Blanton Museum of Art** (p61) across the street. In the afternoon, cool off at **Barton Springs** (p68), where you can work up an appetite for Tex-Mex at **Trudy's Texas Star** (p75). After dark, sip craft beer on the patio at **Easy Tiger** (p80) then plug into Austin's live-music scene with club-hopping along Red River.

Two Days
On day two, explore the **Texas State Capitol** (p56), then head to South Congress for lunch at **Güero's** (p77) followed by shopping and people-watching. If it's summer, make your way toward the **Congress Avenue Bridge** (p56) to witness the nightly exodus of America's largest urban bat colony. End with Texas two-stepping at the **Broken Spoke** (p83).

Three Days
On day three, it's time for a road trip. Head out of town to Lockhart (p79) for Texas-style barbecue. From here, drive south to Gruene (p119) for antique shopping, Texas wine tasting and an evening at Texas' oldest dance hall.

Four Days
The next day, check out the smaller museums around town - whatever strikes your fancy – then enjoy outdoor time by exploring **Mt Bonnell** (p67), **Lady Bird Lake** (p69) or the **Lady Bird Johnson Wildflower Center** (p65). Make dinner a moveable feast by roaming the food trucks. End with live music at the **Continental Club** (p83).

Don't miss this nightly show; best viewing in August.

The colony is made up entirely of female and young animals. Such is the bat-density that bat-radars have detected bat-columns up to 10,000 bat-feet (3,050m) high. In June, each female gives birth to one pup, and every night at dusk the families take to the skies in search of food. Capitol Cruises, behind the Hyatt Hotel, offers bat-watching cruises on Town Lake below the bridge.

Bat Conservation International has volunteers on hand and holds programs throughout the bat season. Congress Ave Bridge crosses the Colorado at the southern end of downtown.

Mexic-Arte Museum   MUSEUM
(Map p62; 512-480-9373; www.mexic-arte museum.org; 419 Congress Ave; adult/child under 12yr/student $5/1/4; 10am-6pm Mon-Thu, to 5pm Fri & Sat, noon-5pm Sun) This wonderful, eclectic downtown museum features works from Mexican and Mexican American artists in exhibitions that rotate every two months. The museum's holdings include carved wooden masks, modern Latin American paintings, historic photographs and contemporary art. Don't miss the back gallery, where new and experimental talent is shown. Admission is free on Sundays.

The museum's gift shop is another draw, with killer Mexican stuff that's pricey if you're heading south of the border but reasonable if you're not.

Museum of the Weird   MUSEUM
(Map p62; 512-476-5493; www.museumof theweird.com; 412 E 6th St; adult/child $12/8; 10am-midnight) Pay the entrance fee, walk through the gift shop and then step inside Austin's version of a cabinet of curiosities. Or perhaps we should say hallway of curiosities, one lined with shrunken heads, malformed mammals and a range of unusual artifacts. The show stealer? The legendary Minnesota Ice Man – is that a frozen prehistoric man under all that ice? Step up to see for yourself then grab a seat for a live show of amazing physical derring-do.

Contemporary Austin   MUSEUM
(Map p62; 512-453-5312; www.thecontemporary austin.org; 700 Congress Ave; adult/child under 18yr $5/free; 11am-7pm Tue-Sat, noon-5pm Sun) This two-site museum has a new name and a freshly renovated downtown space. Downtown, the Jones Gallery features rotating exhibits representing new voices. Don't miss the view

THE SWARM
....

Looking very much like a special effect from a B movie, a funnel cloud of up to 1.5 million Mexican free-tailed bats swarms from under the **Congress Avenue Bridge** nightly from late March to early November. Turns out, Austin isn't just the live-music capital of the world; it's also home to the largest urban bat population in North America.

Austinites have embraced the winged mammals – figuratively speaking, of course – and gather to watch the bats' nightly exodus right around dusk as they leave for their evening meal. (Not to worry: they're looking for insects, and they mostly stay out of your hair.)

There's lots of standing room around parking lots and on the bridge itself, but if you want a more leisurely bat-watching experience, try **Lone Star Riverboat** (p70) or **Capital Cruises** (p69) for **bat-watching tours**.

of the city from the new Moody Rooftop, an open-air event space. You'll also find temporary exhibits at the museum's original home at Laguna Gloria (3809 W 35th St).

Located on the shores of Lake Austin, Laguna Gloria is an Italianate villa built in 1916 – the former home of Texas legend Clara Driscoll. The grounds hold an engaging sculpture park.

UT & Central Austin
Several top-notch museums can be found at UT. They are arranged in two clusters on opposite sides of campus, so check a map before setting out to maximize your time – and to keep your feet happy. Most of the museums focus on some aspect of Texas-related history, but a few art-minded spaces add some appreciated scenery. The well-stocked studio of an acclaimed Texas sculptor is a short drive north from campus.

University of Texas at Austin   UNIVERSITY
(Map p58; www.utexas.edu; cnr University Ave & 24 Ave) Whatever you do, don't call it 'Texas University' – them's fightin' words, usually used derisively by Texas A&M students to take their rivals down a notch. Sorry, A&M, but the main campus of the University of Texas is kind of a big deal. Established in 1883, UT

Austin

N

0   1 mile
0   2 km

Country Line (1mi);
Highland Lakes (9mi)

Capitol City
Comedy Club (1mi)

Colorado River

Lake Austin

Tom
Miller
Dam

Mt Bonnell Park

Mt Bonnell
(785ft)

Camp Mabry
(National Guard)

Mayfield
House &
Nature Preserve

West Lake Dr

Balcones Dr

Shoal Creek

Northland Dr

Hancock Dr

Perry La

W 35th St

Exposition Blvd

Enfield Rd

Windsor Rd

N Lamar Blvd

Kerbey La

Burnet Rd

Koenig La

North Loop Blvd

N Lamar Blvd

Justin La

Waller Creek

Airport Blvd

St Johns Ave

Middle Fiskville Rd

Highland Mall

Greyhound
Bus Station

W 53rd St

W 51st St

Avenue H

W 45th St

W 44th St

E 43rd St

Avenue G

Avenue D

W 38th St

King St

Rio Grande St

W 30th St

W 29th St

Duval St

Red River St

E 45th St

E 41st St

E 38th St

E 38th 1/2 St

University of Texas
at Austin

E Anderson La

Berkman Dr

Cameron Rd

Bartholomew District Park

Robert Mueller
Municipal Airport
(inactive)

Airport Blvd

35
290

2222

1

1

35

111

8
60
58
7
41
38
57
34
46
50
67
24 2
39
71
30
12
73
49
52 72
62

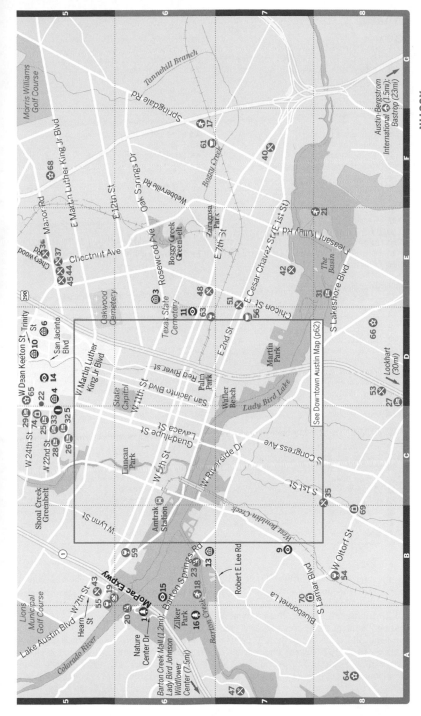

Morris Williams Golf Course

Tannehill Branch

Springdale Rd

Austin-Bergstrom International (1.5mi); Bastrop (23mi)

68

Manor Rd

E Martin Luther King Jr Blvd

E 12th St

Oak Springs Dr

Webberville Rd

Boggy Creek

61

17

40

Chestnut Ave

Chestnut Rd

37

Rosewood Ave

Boggy Creek Greenbelt

Zaragosa Park

E 7th St

E Cesar Chavez St (E 1st St)

Chicon St

21

Pleasant Valley Rd

45 44

Oakwood Cemetery

Texas State Cemetery

3

48

51

42

The Basin

E 2nd St

56

31

S Lakeshore Blvd

W Dean Keeton St Trinity St

10

6

San Jacinto Blvd

11

63

Martin Park

66

Lockhart (30mi)

W Martin Luther King Jr Blvd

65

22

4 14

State Capitol

W 11th St

San Jacinto Blvd

Red River St

Palm Park

Waller Beach

Lady Bird Lake

53

27

W 24th St

29

74

25

28

33

26

32

5

Guadalupe St

Lavaca St

S Congress Ave

See Downtown Austin Map (p62)

Lincoln Park

W 5th St

W Riverside Dr

W Lynn St

S 1st St

35

69

Amtrak Station

West Bouldin Creek

Shoal Creek Greenbelt

590

W 7th St

Hearn St

55

43

59

Barton Springs Rd

23

13

Robert E Lee Rd

9

W Oltorf St

54

70

S Lamar Blvd

Bluebonnet La

Lions Municipal Golf Course

Lake Austin Blvd

20

19

1

15

18

16

Zilker Park

Barton Creek

Mopac Expwy

Nature Center Dr

Barton Creek Mall (1.2mi); Lady Bird Johnson Wildflower Center (7.5mi)

Colorado River

1

47

64

Austin

has the largest enrollment in the state, with over 50,000 students.

Notable buildings on campus include four excellent museums and the Texas Memorial Stadium, home of the Texas Longhorns football team. But none define the UT campus as much as the **UT Tower**. Standing 307ft high, with a clock over 12ft in diameter, the tower looms large, both as a campus landmark and in Austin history as the perch that shooter Charles Whitman used during a 1966 shooting spree. On a more cheerful note, it now serves as a beacon of victory when it's lit orange to celebrate a Longhorn win or other achievement.

The tower's observation deck is accessible only by guided tours (p69), which are offered frequently in summer but only on weekends during the school year. Advance reservations are recommended, although standby tickets may be available at the Texas Union's front desk.

Want to see some Big 12 football or other college athletics while you're in town? The UT Box Office (p88) is your source for all things Longhorn.

Lyndon Baines Johnson (LBJ) Library & Museum   MUSEUM
(Map p58; ☑512-721-0200; www.lbjlibrary.org; 2313 Red River St; adult/child 13-17yr/senior $8/3/5; ⊙9am-5pm) A major renovation has brought the museum into the new millennium with interactive exhibits and audiovisual displays. Fortunately, they didn't lose the hokey, animatronic LBJ that regales visitors with the president's recorded stories – although they did stir some controversy when they changed him out of his ranch duds into a suit much more befitting an animatronic of his stature.

There are some fascinating mementos from the 00th US president, including his presidential limo and gifts from heads of state (including two terracotta horseback riders from Chiang Kai-shek). The museum also provides insight into the events of the 1960s, including the Vietnam War, the Cuban Missile Crisis and the Kennedy assassination. Don't miss the 8th floor for a look at a replica of Johnson's Oval Office, and an exhibit on Lady Bird Johnson, the president's wife.

Blanton Museum of Art   MUSEUM
(Map p62; ☑512 471-5482; www.blantonmuseum. org; 200 E Martin Luther King Jr Blvd; adult/child $9/free; ⊙10am-5pm Tue-Fri, 11am-5pm Sat, 1-5pm Sun) A big university with a big endowment is bound to have a big art collection, and now, finally, it has a suitable building to show it off properly. With one of the best university art collections in the USA, the Blanton showcases a variety of styles. It doesn't go very in-depth into any of them, but then again you're bound to find something of interest.

Especially striking is the permanent installation of *Missão/Missões (How to Build Cathedrals)* – which involves 600,000 pennies, 800 communion wafers and 2000 cattle bones.

Harry Ransom Humanities Research Center   MUSEUM
(Map p58; ☑512-471-8944; www.hrc.utexas.edu; 300 W 21st St; ⊙10am-5pm Mon-Wed & Fri, to 7pm Thu, noon-5pm Sat & Sun) FREE The fascinating Ransom Center is a major repository of historic manuscripts, photography, books, film, TV, music and more. Highlights include a complete copy of the Gutenberg Bible (one of only five in the USA) and what is thought to be the first photograph ever taken, from 1826.

Check the website for special online-only exhibitions and the center's busy events calendar of author readings, live music, lectures and more.

Bob Bullock Texas State History Museum   MUSEUM
(Map p62; ☑512-936-8746; www.thestoryoftexas. com; 1800 Congress Ave; adult/child $13/9; ⊙9am-5pm Mon-Sat, noon-5pm Sun) This is no dusty historical museum. Big and glitzy, it shows off the Lone Star State's history, from when it used to be part of Mexico up to the present, with high-tech interactive exhibits and fun theatrics. A new permanent exhibit on the 1st floor showcases the history – and the recovered hull – of the *La Belle*, a French ship that sank off the Gulf Coast in the 1680s, changing the course of the Texas region's story. Allow a few hours for your visit.

Upstairs, visitors trace the revolutionary years of the Republic of Texas, its rise to statehood and its economic expansion into oil drilling and space exploration; you can even explore Western movies and home-grown music from Bob Wills to Buddy Holly to the Big Bopper.

The museum also houses Austin's first **IMAX theater** (check website for listings; adult/child four to 17 years $9/7) and the **Texas Spirit Theater** (adult/child four to 17 years $5/4), both of which offer discounted combination tickets when bought with a museum admission. The Texas Spirit Theater is where you can see *The Star of Destiny*, a 15-minute special-effects film that's simultaneously high-tech and hokey fun.

Museum parking is $8.

Hi, How Are You Mural   PUBLIC ART
(Map p58; 21st St & Guadalupe) Created by songwriter and artist Daniel Johnston, this bug-eyed frog greets passersby near the University of Texas. The mural, also known as *Jeremiah the Innocent,* covers the south wall of a Thai restaurant known as Thai, How Are You – which changed its name from the less punny Thai Spice.

Elisabet Ney Museum   MUSEUM
(Map p58; ☑512-974-1625; www.austintexas.gov/ department/elisabet-ney-museum; 304 E 44th St; donations welcome; ⊙noon-5pm Wed-Sun) A German-born sculptor and spirited trailblazer, Elisabet Ney lived in Austin in the early 1880s, and her former studio is now one of the oldest museums in Texas. Filled with more than 100 works of art, including busts and statues of political figures, the castlelike

AUSTIN

Downtown Austin

0   500 m
0   0.25 miles

CLARKESVILLE

MARKET DISTRICT

WAREHOUSE DISTRICT

DOWNTOWN

EAST AUSTIN

Oakwood Cemetery

University of Texas at Austin

Interregional Hwy

Interregional Hwy

E Martin Luther King Jr Blvd

Texas State Capitol

Capitol Visitors Center

Waterloo Park

Pease District Park

House Park

Duncan Park

Shoal Creek

Shoal Creek Greenbelt

Republic Square

Amtrak Station

Brush Park

Austin Visitor Information Center

Shoal Beach

Capital Metro Transit Store

Capital Metro

W Lynn St
W 10th St
W 13th St
W 12th St
W 10th St
W 9th St
Highland Ave
Oakland Ave
Pressler St
W 9th St
W 5th St
Castle Hill St
Enfield Rd
Blanco St
Baylor St
Parkway
N Lamar Blvd
West Ave
Rio Grande St
Nueces St
San Antonio St
Guadalupe St
W 9th St
W 10th St
W 11th St
W 12th St
W 13th St
W 14th St
W 15th St
W 16th St
W 17th St
Guadalupe St
Lavaca St
Colorado St
N Congress Ave
Brazos St
Brazos St
Colorado St
Congress Ave
San Jacinto Blvd
Trinity St
Neches St
Red River St
Sabine St
San Marcos St
E 7th St
E 6th St
E 6th St
E 7th St
E 8th St
E 9th St
E 10th St
E 11th St
E 12th St
E 11th St
E 12th St
E 14th St
E 15th St
San Jacinto Blvd
Red River St
Walter Creek
Bowie St
W 3rd St
W Cesar Chavez St (W 1st St)
W 5th St
E 3rd St
E 4th St
W 5th St
W 6th St
W 7th St
W 8th St
W 9th St
W 10th St
W 11th St

3
2
4
17
59
63
73
36
45
55
12
33
53
68
11
61
62
22
20
69
71
5
56
58
64
67
34
10
40
41
16
21
48
52
8
80
30
51
76
66
19

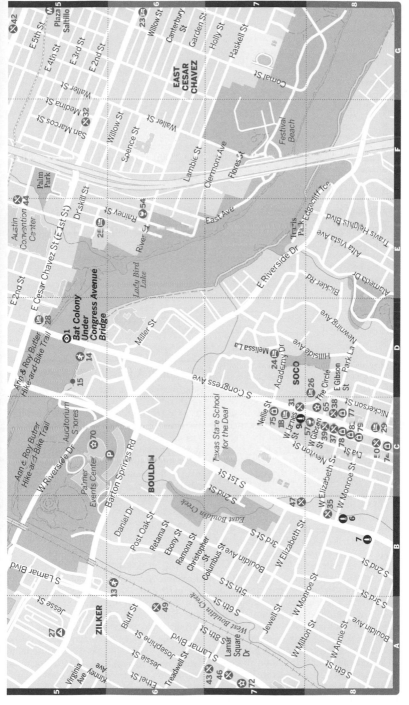

AUSTIN

Downtown Austin

building made from rough-hewn stone is reason enough to visit. Look for the hidden door on the 2nd floor.

Three of Ney's better-known works reside in the state capitol, but the artist considered her greatest legacy to be a sculpture of Lady Macbeth. The Smithsonian owns the original, but you can see a replica of it here.

Texas Memorial Museum MUSEUM
(Map p58; ☑ 512-471-1604; www.tmm.utexas.edu; 2400 Trinity St; adult/child $4/3; ☺ 9am-5pm Tue-Sat; 🚻) We all know how kids feel about dinosaurs, and this natural history museum is the perfect place for them to indulge their fascination. Look up to see the swooping skeleton of the Texas Pterosaur – one of the most famous dino finds ever. This impressively humongous Cretaceous-era flying reptile has a wingspan of 40ft and was recovered at Big Bend in 1971. There are other exhibits, too, focusing on anthropology, natural history, geology and biodiversity.

Upstairs, you can glimpse a Texas horned lizard in a jar, a preserved prairie rattlesnake and a taxidermied American bison and other critters, but most of the exhibits are like something you'd find in an eccentric's attic.

◉ South Austin

South Austin is an offbeat and oh-so-Austin neighborhood that was pretty marginal just 25 or so years ago. Today this quirky but festive area – especially along S Congress Ave – is the city's soul. Tourism types nicknamed it SoCo, which has somewhat stuck, but the locals mostly still call it South Congress. The road is the main thoroughfare through the neighborhood and the epicenter of the action; most of the rest is residential. S 1st St has been been seeing more action in recent years with the openings of several restaurants and coffee shops.

Zilker Park PARK
(Map p58; ☑ 512-974-6700; www.austintexas.gov/department/zilker-metropolitan-park; 2100 Barton Springs Rd; ☺ 5am-10pm; 🚻) This 350-acre park is a slice of green heaven, lined with hiking and biking trails. The park also provides access to the famed Barton Springs natural swimming pool (p68) and Barton Creek Greenbelt (p68). Find boat rentals, a miniature train, a playground and a botanical garden, too. On weekends from April to early

September, admission is $5 per car. The park celebrated its centennial in 2017.

Ann & Roy Butler Hike-and-Bike
Trail & Boardwalk   VIEWPOINT, ARCHITECTURE

(Map p58; www.austintexas.gov; 1820 Lakeshore Blvd; ⊙5am-midnight; 🚻 🐕) You can gaze at the downtown skyline from a series of photogenic boardwalks on this scenic 10-mile trail, which loops around Lady Bird Lake. Shorten the loop by crossing the lake on one of several bridges. You'll find restrooms, water fountains and waste bags for your pet along the way. Check the city's Parks & Recreation webpage (www.austintexas.gov/department/parks-and-recreation) for parking lots and trail access points. ADA accessible. Austin old-timers may refer to the trail as the Lady Bird Trail or the Town Lake Trail.

I Love You So Much Mural   PUBLIC ART

(Map p62; 1300 S Congress Ave) This simple expression of devotion draws legions of photo-taking lovebirds. Spray-painted on the side of Jo's Coffee on South Congress, it now joins the Austin Motel sign and the patio at Guero's as an iconic symbol of the neighborhood. Eagle-eyed visitors may spot funny spin-offs of the mural around town.

Greetings from Austin Mural   PUBLIC ART

(Map p62; 1720 S 1st St) Well of course you're going to pull over and take a photo in front of this wall-sized postcard. It's awesome. The eye-catching mural adorns the southside of the Roadhouse Relics building.

Lady Bird Johnson
Wildflower Center   GARDENS

(📞512-232-0100; www.wildflower.org; 4801 La Crosse Ave; adult/child 5-17yr/student & senior $10/4/8; ⊙9am-5pm Tue-Sun) Anyone with an interest in Texas' flora and fauna should make the 20-minute drive to the wonderful gardens of the Lady Bird Johnson Wildflower Center, southwest of downtown Austin. The center, founded in 1982 with the assistance of Texas' beloved former first lady, has a display garden featuring every type of wildflower and plant that grows in Texas, separated by geographical region, with an emphasis on Hill Country flora. Spring is the best time to visit, but there's something in bloom all year.

DON'T MISS

AUSTIN'S MURALS

The city is dotted with eye-catching murals, and even has its own **outdoor graffiti gallery**. For a list of the best wall art, with addresses, check out www.austintexas.org/visit/austin-murals.

The Wildflower Center hosts a variety of events during National Wildlflower Week in May.

SouthPop CULTURAL CENTER

(South Austin Popular Cultural Center; Map p58; ☑512-440-8318; www.southpop.org; 1516-B S Lamar Ave; ⊙1-6pm Thu-Sun) **FREE** Pop into this South Austin gallery for rotating exhibits that spotlight Austin's live music and entertainment scenes, from the 1960s to the present. One recent exhibit celebrated the city's punk rock bands.

Dazed and Confused Mural PUBLIC ART

(Map p62; S 1st St, near Monroe St) Alright, alright, alright. Fans of Matthew McConaughey and *Dazed and Confused* can pay their respects to Wooderson – the unrepentant admirer of high school girls – at this eye-catching mural a short walk south from Monroe St, near the food truck park.

Zilker Botanical Garden GARDENS

(Map p58; ☑512-477-8672; www.zilkergarden.org; 2220 Barton Springs Rd; adult/child $3/1; ⊙9am-5pm, to 7pm during daylight saving time) These lush gardens cover 31 acres on the south bank of the Colorado River, with displays including natural grottoes, a Japanese garden and a fragrant herb garden. You'll also find interesting historical artifacts sprinkled about the site – kind of like an outdoor architectural museum – including a 19th-century pioneer cabin, a cupola that once sat atop a local schoolhouse, and a footbridge moved from Congress Ave.

Cash or check only for the entrance fee.

Umlauf Sculpture Garden MUSEUM

(Map p58; ☑512-445-5582; www.umlaufsculpture.org; 605 Robert E Lee Rd; adult/child under 12yr/student $5/free/1; ⊙10am-4pm Tue-Fri, noon-4pm Sat & Sun) If the weather's just too perfect to be inside a climate-controlled building, stroll the open-air Umlauf Sculpture Garden, located in the south end of Zilker Park. Within the sculpture garden and the indoor **museum**, there are more than 130 works by 20th-century American sculptor Charles Umlauf, who was an art professor at UT for 40 years.

Austin Nature & Science Center PARK

(Map p58; ☑512-974-3888; www.austintexas.gov/department/austin-nature-science-center; 301 Nature Center Dr; donations requested; ⊙9am-5pm Mon-Sat, noon-5pm Sun) In the northwestern area of Zilker Park, this center has exhibitions of native Texan mammals, birds, reptiles, amphibians and arthropods that have been injured and nursed back to health here, but cannot be released back into the wild. There are also outdoor nature trails lined with native plants, where you'll see bats, butterflies and birds.

Cathedral of Junk SCULPTURE

(☑512-299-7413; 4422 Lareina Dr; requested donation per group $10; ⊙by appointment) An ongoing (and climbable!) backyard sculpture that turns one man's trash into everyone's treasure. Visitation is by appointment, by phone. Owner Vince Hanneman doesn't always get to his voicemail, so keep trying until he answers. He'll fill you in on parking. Note that you can't really see the cathedral from a drive-by.

◉ East Austin

The state cemetery here is filled with historic notables. Got the kids? An innovative children's museum recently relocated to the neighborhood. Another museum traces the accomplishments and history of area African Americans, with an informative kids' exhibit spotlighting African-American scientists and inventors.

George Washington Carver Museum MUSEUM

(Map p58; www.austintexas.gov; 1165 Angelina St; ⊙10am-6pm Mon-Wed, to 9pm Thu, to 5pm Fri, to 4pm Sat; ⛟) **FREE** On 19 June 1865, slaves in Texas were freed pursuant to the Emancipation Proclamation – 2½ years after it was signed by President Lincoln. This day is now honored as Juneteenth, and an exhibit at this small museum examines its history. The museum also holds a few personal items of African American botanist and inventor George Washington Carver.

The Children's Gallery introduces children to African American inventors, while another exhibit shares the stories of prominent African American families in Austin.

Thinkery MUSEUM

(Map p58; ☑512-469-6200; www.thinkeryaustin.org; 1830 Simond Ave; $10, child under 2 yrs free; ⊙10am-5pm Tue, Thu & Fri, to 8pm Wed, to 6pm Sat

& Sun; 🖼) This huge 40,000-sq-ft space north of downtown is an inspiring place for young minds, with hands-on activities in the realms of science, technology and the arts. Kids can get wet learning about fluid dynamics, build LED light structures and explore chemical reactions in the Kitchen Lab, among many other attractions. There's also an outdoor play area with nets and climbing toys. Closed Monday except for Baby Bloomers and other special events.

Texas State Cemetery CEMETERY
(Map p58; ☑512-463-0605; 909 Navasota St; ⊙8am-5pm daily, visitor center 8am-5pm Mon-Fri) Revitalized in the 1990s, the state's official cemetery is the final resting place of key figures from Texan history. Interred here are luminaries including Stephen F Austin, Miriam 'Ma' Ferguson (the state's first female governor), writer James Michener and Lone Star State flag designer Joanna Troutman, along with thousands of soldiers who died in the Civil War, plus more than 100 leaders of the Republic of Texas who were exhumed from other sites and reburied here. Self-guided-tour brochures usually available from the visitor center. The cemetery is just north of E 7th St.

⊙ Market District, Clarksville & North Austin

Heavily residential and commercial, you won't find many cultural attractions – although chicken shit bingo might just qualify. An outdoor graffiti park does keep the scene artistically interesting.

Hope Outdoor Gallery GALLERY
(Grafitti Park at Castle Hill; Map p62; http://hope-campaign.org; 11th St & Baylor St; ⊙9am-7pm) For a wild collision of colors and art, make your way to this sprawling collection of graffiti that's been spray-painted across multilevel concrete ruins. The on-site open-air gallery here is run by the HOPE Foundation, a collection of creatives who support education. To add your own art, email murals@hopecampaign.org for a permit. Note that the property could be closed or repurposed at any time, so get there now.

⊙ West Austin

Austin has numerous beautiful parks in and around downtown, but if you really want to escape the urban grind, head west. A couple of

WHAT THE...? MOONLIGHT TOWERS

Keep an eye out for Austin's **moonlight towers**. All the rage in the late 1800s, these 165ft-tall street lamps were designed to give off the light of a full moon. Austin is the only city in which these historic triangular metal towers topped by a halo of six large bulbs still operate. There are 17 of them remaining around the city: how many can you spot?

scenic parks border Lake Austin, and there's a gorgeous creek-fed pool further west in Dripping Springs.

Mt Bonnell PARK
(Covert Park; Map p58; ☑512-974-6700; www.austintexas.gov; 3800 Mt Bonnell Rd) On the weekend, you might find yourself tiptoeing around a wedding ceremony at Mt Bonnell, the highest point in the city at 775ft. This pretty overlook has impressed day-trippers since the 1830s. At sunset, climb the short but steep stairway for broad views of Lake Austin (a section of the Colorado River) and the homes along the nearby hillsides.

From the summit, follow the trail both left and right for a variety of views.

No parking from 10pm to 5am.

Mayfield House & Nature Preserve PARK
(Map p58; ☑512-974-6700; www.austintexas.gov; 3805 W 35th St; 🖼) FREE Did somebody say peacocks? Kids will love gawking at these showy birds while exploring the riverside trails and grounds at this low-key park beside Lake Austin. The park is a nice companion to Mt Bonnell, just up the road, if you want to do a bit more hiking and exploring. It's a good place to let younger kids run a little bit wild. No pets.

🏃 Activities

Austin has quite a few places to play outside, including Zilker Park, Lady Bird Lake, and creekside parks and greenbelts throughout the city. You can get just about any information you might need from the City of Austin Parks & Recreation Department (www.austintexas.gov/department/parks-and-recreation). Check the website to find everything from municipal golf courses to tennis complexes to cemeteries.

🏃 Downtown

Mellow Johnny's Bike Shop   CYCLING
(Map p62; 📞512-473-0222; www.mellowjohnnys. com; 400 Nueces St; day use adult $20-50; ⊙7am-7pm Mon-Fri, 7am-6pm Sat, 8am-5pm Sun) Say what you will about Lance Armstrong, you can still count on him to find you a pretty good bike. Located right downtown, Mellow Johnny's is co-owned by the disgraced seven-time Tour de France winner. It rents high-performance bikes as well as commuter bikes, and offers free guided bike rides (check the website for a schedule).

🏃 South Austin

Barton Springs Pool   SWIMMING
(Map p58; 📞512-867-3080; 2201 Barton Springs Rd; adult/child $8/3; ⊙5am-10pm) Hot? Not for long. Even when the temperature hits 100, you'll be shivering in a jiff after you jump into this icy-cold natural-spring pool. Draped with century-old pecan trees, the area around the pool is a social scene in itself, and the place gets packed on hot summer days.

Barton Creek Greenbelt   PARK
(Map p58; www.austintexas.gov; 3753 S Capital of Texas Hwy) From Zilker Park, this refreshing multiuse path unfurls for more than 8 miles along Barton Creek. Hike, bike and splash around. There are several access points, including the entry path near 1601 Spyglass Rd. Leashed dogs OK.

Bicycle Sport Shop   CYCLING
(Map p62; 📞512-477-3472; www.bicyclesport shop.com; 517 S Lamar Blvd; per 2hr from $16; ⊙10am-7pm Mon-Fri, 9am-6pm Sat, 11am-5pm Sun) The great thing about Bicycle Sport Shop is its proximity to Zilker Park, Barton Springs and the Lady Bird Lake bike paths, all of which are within a few blocks. Rentals range from $16 for a two-hour cruise on a standard bike, to $62 for a full day on a top-end full-suspension model. On weekends and holidays, advance reservations are advised.

Veloway Track   CYCLING
(www.veloway.com; 4900 La Crosse Ave; ⊙dawn-dusk) FREE Plan some extra time to ride or skate the great 3.1-mile Veloway track, near the Lady Bird Johnson Wildflower Center. The track runs clockwise, and no walking or running is permitted.

Zilker Zephyr   RAIL
(Map p58; 📞512-478-8286; 2201 Barton Springs Rd; adult/child $3/2; ⊙10am-5pm) Trains on the Zilker Zephyr miniature railroad make the 25-minute, 2-mile ride along Barton Creek and Town Lake year-round. They leave the depot near the playground every hour on the hour weekdays and every 30 to 40 minutes on weekends. Cash only.

Zilker Park Boat Rentals   CANOEING
(Map p58; 📞512-478-3852; www.zilkerboats. com; 2101 Andrew Zilker Rd; per hr/day $15/45; ⊙10am-dusk) This outfit rents 17ft canoes and open-deck ocean kayaks. It also has maps and will describe the best routes. The price includes paddles and life jackets; arrive early on the weekends before the boats are all gone.

To find the rental facility, turn left immediately after entering the park from Barton Springs Rd. The canoes are below the parking lot, on the shore of the creek. Look for the 'Canoe Rental is Open' banner.

Roy G Guerrero Disc Golf Course   GOLF
(Map p58; 517 S Pleasant Valley Rd; ⊙sunrise-sunset) FREE A newer course with 18 holes suitable for beginners and skilled players alike.

🏃 East Austin

Austin Bouldering Project CLIMBING
(Map p58; ☑512-645-4633; www.austinboul
deringproject.com; 979 Springdale Rd; day pass
adult/child $16/12; shoe rental $4; ⊗6am-11pm
Mon-Fri, 9am-10pm Sat & Sun) If a fear of ropes
and harnesses has kept you from rock
climbing, give bouldering a try at this new
facility in East Austin. The climbing heights
are typically 13 to 15ft, with a few stretching
higher. A thick floor pad will cushion your
fall. Bright and airy, the complex has a 2nd-
floor viewing area, and the place has a posi-
tive and communal vibe.

After a workout, you can socialize over a
bento box and kombucha, both sold on-site.
Shoe rental is free on your first visit.

🏃 West Austin

Lady Bird Lake CANOEING
(Map p58; ☑512-459-0999; www.rowingdock.com;
2418 Stratford Dr; ⊗9am-6pm) Named after former first lady 'Lady Bird' Johnson, Lady Bird
Lake looks like a river. And no wonder: it's
actually a dammed-off section of the Colorado River that divides Austin into north
and south. Get on the water at the rowing
dock, which rents kayaks, canoes and stand-
up paddle boards from $10 to $20 per hour
Monday to Thursday, with higher prices on
weekends and during major events.

Deep Eddy Pool SWIMMING
(Map p58; ☑512-974-1189; www.deepeddy.org;
401 Deep Eddy Ave, adult/child under 11yr/junior
$8/3/4; ⊗9am-7:30pm Mon-Fri, 9am-7pm Sat &
Sun) With its vintage 1930s bathhouse built
as part of the Works Progress Administration,
Texas' oldest swimming pool is fed by cold
springs and surrounded by cottonwood trees.
There are separate areas for waders and lap
swimmers.

👉 Tours

Texpert Tours TOURS
(☑512-383-8989; www.texperttours.com; per hr
from $100) For an interesting alternative to
your stereotypical, run-of-the-mill bus and
van tour, try Texpert Tours, led by affable
public-radio host Howie Richey (aka the
'Texas Back Roads Scholar'). Historical anecdotes, natural history and environmental
tips are all part of the educational experience. A three-hour tour of central Austin
takes visitors to the state capitol, the Governor's Mansion and the top of Mt Bonnell.

👉 Downtown

Historic Walking Tours WALKING
(Map p62; ☑512-474-5171; www.tspb.state.tx.us/
plan/tours/tours.html; ⊗9am Tue & Thu-Sat, 11am &
1pm Sun) FREE One of the best deals around
are the free Historic Walking Tours of downtown Austin, which leave from the capitol's
south steps. Tours last between 60 and 90
minutes. Make reservations at least 48 hours
in advance either online or by phone through
the visitor center.

Austin Duck Adventures BOATING
(Map p62; ☑512-477-5274; www.austinducks.com;
adult/child 3-12yr/senior & student $28/18/26;
⊗check website for schedule) Utilizes amphib-
ious British Alvis Stalwarts, which start at
the Visitors Center, parade around the state
capitol, roll down Congress Ave and 6th St,
then splash into Lake Austin. Tour guides
provide a few entertaining historical tidbits
along the way.

Austin Ghost Tours WALKING
(Map p62; ☑512-853-9826; www.austinghost
tours.com; adult $20; ⊗Fri & Sat) Austin Ghost
Tours take visitors on tours of haunted
buildings and streets in areas including the
Old Pecan St District or Warehouse District.
Downtown ghost tours last 90 minutes. On
Saturday night, the Historic District tour
departs from the Moonshine Patio Bar &
Grill on Red River St.

👉 UT & Central Austin

UT Tower Tours TOURS
(Map p58; ☑512-475-6636; http://tower.utexas.
edu; $6; ⊗hours vary seasonally) Student escorts
accompany visitors to the observation deck
of the landmark tower, where they provide a
bit of information about its history and background. Guests can then walk around the observation deck on their own. The escort takes
the group back down. The tour includes an
elevator ride to the 27th floor followed by a
climb up three short flights of stairs (auxilia-
ry elevator available for those with restricted
mobility). Reserve your ticket in advance; pick
it up at the Texas Union.

No bags or purses are permitted. You cannot leave the tour early.

👉 South Austin

Capital Cruises BOATING
(Map p62; ☑512-480-9264; www.capitalcruises.
com; adult/child $10/5) Between March and

November, Capital Cruises offers competitively priced lake excursions and bat-watching trips that depart from a dock near the Hyatt at 208 Barton Springs Rd.

Lone Star Riverboat   BOATING
(Map p62; ☑512-327-1388; www.lonestarriverboat. com; adult/child $10/7; ◷ Mar–mid-Dec) With a dock on the south shore of Lady Bird Lake near the Hyatt, Lone Star Riverboat runs one-hour cruises on its double-decker paddle-wheel riverboat at 3pm each Saturday and Sunday, March through mid-December. The company also offers nightly sunset bat-watching trips on its 32ft electric cruiser from March through October. See its website for parking tips.

⚡ Festivals & Events

South by Southwest   MUSIC, FILM
(SXSW; www.sxsw.com; single festival $825-1325, combo pass $1150-1650; ◷ mid-Mar) One of the American music industry's biggest gatherings has now expanded to include film and interactive media. Austin is absolutely besieged with visitors during this two-week window, and many a new resident first came to the city to hear a little live music.

Eeyore's Birthday Party   CULTURAL
(☑512-448-5160; www.eeyores.com; Pease Park, 1100 Kingsbury St; ◷ late Apr; ⛟) Perhaps no other annual event proves Austin's offbeat flavor so completely. This event, started during the hippy-dippy 1960s, has maypole dancing, live music and even a birthday cake for the name-sake melancholy Winnie-the-Pooh character. You'll feel silly if you *don't* wear a costume.

Austin Pride   PARADE
(www.austinpride.org; ◷ Sep) Austin's gay pride celebration is one of Texas' largest, with block parties, music and a parade.

Austin City Limits Music Festival   MUSIC
(www.aclfestival.com; 1-/3-day pass $100/250; ◷ Oct) What do music lovers do in autumn? The Austin City Limits Festival, which is not as big as SXSW but has been swiftly gaining on it in terms of popularity. The three-day festival held on eight stages in Zilker Park books more than 100 pretty impressive acts and sells out months in advance.

Formula 1 Grand Prix   SPORTS
(www.formula1.com; ◷ late Oct or Nov) In Travis County, just outside of Austin, a high-speed racetrack draws legions of F1 fans during a high-octane weekend in autumn.

Austin Film Festival   FILM
(☑800-310-3378, 512-478-4795; www.austinfilmfestival.com; ◷ mid-Oct) Hollywood and independent filmmakers and screenwriters flock to this multiday event held at various venues.

🛏 Sleeping

There's no shortage of rooms, until major events come to town, such as SXSW, the Formula 1 Grand Prix, the Austin City Limits Festival and the Thanksgiving Day football game between UT and Texas A&M. At these peak times prices skyrocket and rooms are booked

---

MUSIC FESTIVALS: SOUTH BY SOUTHWEST (SXSW) & AUSTIN CITY LIMITS

For five nights in mid-March tens of thousands of record-label reps, musicians, journalists and rabid fans from around the country descend on Austin for **South by Southwest**, a musical extravaganza that attracts a couple thousand groups and solo artists from around the world at more than 100 different Austin venues.

Though SXSW started out as an opportunity for little-known bands and singers to catch the ear of a record-label rep, it has since become a wildly popular industry showcase for already-signed bands. Add to that a hugely popular interactive festival, as well as a more subdued but still well-attended film festival, and you've got a major international draw that takes over the city and sends most of the locals into hiding for two weeks every spring.

You can buy a pass for just one of the three festivals, or go all out and buy a combo pass. However, what you can't do any more is buy a single-day pass. But this is one of those times when preplanning can save you a lot of money: early-bird tickets are on sale through mid-September and they can save you hundreds of dollars; then, the price inches up each month until the walk-up rate takes effect.

Too much hoopla? Come in October for a slightly more mellow experience at the **Austin City Limits Music Festival**, an outdoor festival held over two weekends at Zilker Park.

months in advance. At other times, choose accommodations as close to downtown as you can afford.

Chains border I-35, and while they may not offer the best Austin experience, great deals can be found.

🛏 Downtown

For the most part, downtown hotels come with downtown prices, but they do keep you close to the action. Many cater to tourists and business travelers. Budget travelers will find a great hostel in the thick of the action and one solid budget hotel. The handful of historic and boutique hotels really shine, with cool Texas- and Austin-specific touches adding a homey feel.

Firehouse Hostel   HOSTEL $

(Map p62; ☎ 512-201-2522; www.firehousehostel. com; 605 Brazos St; dm $32-40, r $110-170, ste $130-170; ⊖❄🛜) Open since 2013, this hostel in downtown Austin is pretty darn spiffy. In a former firehouse, it still feels fresh, and the downtown location right across from the historic Driskill Hotel is as perfect as you can get.

The best feature: the stylish lounge, with red walls, flickering candles and bespoke cocktails. The entrance is concealed. Get in via the sliding bookshelf beside the check-in desk.

Extended StayAmerica   BUSINESS HOTEL $$

(Map p62; ☎ 800-398-7829, 512-457-9994; www. extendedstayamerica.com; 600 Guadalupe St; ste $160-200; P⊖❄🛜🐾) This extended-stay hotel has an excellent downtown location, walking distance to tons of bars and restaurants. Suites are a little on the bland side and could use some TLC – but include a kitchenette stocked with utensils. Parking is included in the price. It's all a great excuse to hang out in Austin a while.

Pet fee is $25 per pet per night; up to two allowed. Other locations around town will net you even better rates, if not the same easy proximity to everything you'll love about Austin.

Radisson Hotel & Suites   HOTEL $$

(Map p62; ☎ 512-478-9611, 800-333-3333; www. radisson.com/austintx; 111 E Cesar Chavez St; r from $309; P⊖❄@🛜🐾) Bats? Yes, bats. This is a great place from which to watch their nightly exodus from under the Congress Ave Bridge. It puts you right on the water and upstairs from the hiking and biking trail around Lady Bird Lake.

Parking is $28 per night.

⭐ Hotel Van Zandt   HOTEL $$$

(Map p62; ☎ 512-542-5300; www.hotelvanzandt. com; 605 Davis St; r/ste from $299/499; 🛜❄🐾) Named for Texas singer-songwriter Townes Van Zandt, this Kimpton property impresses with the details. From the French horn chandelier above the lobby to the leather chairs with low-key buckles, these touches give a stylish nod to Austin's cowboy and musical sensibilities. The big-windowed rooms come in a variety of configurations but whatever you do, angle for a view of Lady Bird Lake.

The hotel is in the thick of the late-night Rainey St district, lined with bars and food trucks. If you don't feel like wandering, try dinner and a show at on-site Geraldine's. No pet fee, but parking is $40 per night – spots are rare in the neighborhood.

⭐ Driskill Hotel   HISTORIC HOTEL $$$

(Map p62; ☎ 512-439-1234; www.driskillhotel.com; 604 Brazos St; r/ste from $299/419; P⊖❄@🛜🐾) Every city should have a beautiful historic hotel made out of native stone, preferably built in the late 1800s by a wealthy cattle baron. Although it's now owned by the Hyatt, you'll find no generic hotel decor here; this place is pure Texas, especially the bar with wall-mounted longhorns, leather couches and a stained-glass dome. The elegant rooms are taxidermy free.

A bit of trivia? LBJ and Lady Bird had their first date here. Valet-only parking is $40. The pet fee is $100 per stay, up to six nights.

🛏 UT & Central Austin

This is your best bet for finding a B&B in Austin, with several located near the southwest corner of campus.

Drifter Jack's   HOSTEL $

(Map p58; ☎ 512-243-8410; www.drifterjackshostel. com; 2602 Guadalupe St; dm $29-39; ❄@🛜) Across from the UT campus, Drifter Jack's is a friendly, laid-back place, with mural-covered rooms and a small lounge. The hostel draws mostly a young crowd (though all are welcome) and organizes pub crawls and other outings.

College Houses Cooperatives   HOSTEL $

(Map p58; ☎ 512-476-5678; www.collegehouses. org; r per person $25) During the summer when (most of) the students have gone home, the empty rooms in the seven student coop houses are quite the bargain, and they keep you centrally located near the UT campus. The planning window is short, however: you have to give them 48 hours' notice, and they don't take reservations more than a week in advance.

Star of Texas Inn B&B **$$**

(Map p58; ☎866-472-6700; www.staroftexasinn.com; 611 W 22nd St; r from $120; P ⊖ ❄ ☰) The buttercup-yellow building in the bustling West Campus area started as a private residence, spent some time as a fraternity house, and has now been outfitted with claw-foot tubs and Victorian furnishings. The wraparound porches might sag a bit, but they're a gracious place to sit a spell. Works well for guests who plan to come and go, without needing lots of personal direction.

Solo travelers on a budget should check out Room 17. If the main house is full, they can set you up at Austin Folk House, a sister property just down the street, or in the newly opened but unimaginatively named Building 2, which sits just behind the main house.

Adams House B&B **$$**

(Map p58; ☎512-453-7696; www.theadamshouse.com; 4300 Ave G; r $149-159, ste $179; P ⊖ ❄ ☰) On a quiet corner in historic Hyde Park, the Adams House will have you feeling like a local resident in no time. The welcoming guest rooms have hardwood floors, high ceilings, wooden shutters and antique beds, all the better to make yourself at home.

Although there's no pool on site, it's just down the street from a city pool that's open during the summer months.

Austin's Inn at Pearl Street B&B **$$**

(Map p58; ☎512-478-0051; www.innpearl.com; 809 W Martin Luther King Jr Blvd; r $195-245, ste $265-365; P ⊖ ❄ @ ☰) This is a preservationist's dream come true. The owners picked up this run-down property and completely restored it, decorating the whole place in a plush European style. The rooms come in a variety of flavors and are located in four separate buildings, so check the website to find one that suits.

Austin Folk House B&B **$$**

(Map p58; ☎866-472-6700, 512-472-6700; www.austinfolkhouse.com; 506 W 22nd St; r from $195; P ⊖ ☰) One part gallery, one part B&B, the Austin Folk House has colorful and whimsical folk art in every room and up and down the halls. The rooms are comfortable (though some are a little fussy) and it's right in the bustling West Campus area.

Hotel Ella B&B **$$$**

(Map p58; ☎800-311-1619, 512-495-1800; www.hotelella.com; 1900 Rio Grande St; r $269-409, ste $469; P ⊖ ❄ ☰ ≋) With its wraparound porch, Corinthian columns and commanding perch on Judge's Hill, this stately building is hands-down the most photogenic inn in town. Visually striking Texas modernist artwork adorns the walls in both rooms and common areas, setting this new boutique hotel apart from its competitors. The hotel car service transports guests to destinations within a 3-mile radius.

Prices seem high for the smaller rooms (which may have views of junky college apartments), but the inviting parlor bar will keep you away from the room anyway. Valet-only parking is $25 per night. The pet fee is $150 per stay.

AT&T Executive Education & Conference Center HOTEL **$$$**

(Map p62; ☎512-404-1900; www.meetattexas.com/hotel; 1900 University Ave; r from $229; ⊖ ❄ ☰) This swanky hotel on the UT campus is perfect for alums who want to relive their college days but in much higher style. References to UT abound, but the motif is so subtle that nonalums would never notice – think burnt-orange accent walls, historical campus photos and leather headboards.

Parking is $18 per night.

South Austin

South Austin has lots of unique lodging options, and many of the most unique are boutique properties. The hotels that border Congress Ave keep you close to the S Congress Ave action and plenty close to downtown.

HI – Austin HOSTEL **$**

(Austin Hostel; Map p58; ☎512-444-2294; www.hiusa.org/austin; 2200 S Lakeshore Blvd; dm $34-39, r $65; P ⊖ @ ☰) Just 2.5 miles from downtown, this 47-bed hostel is located on a shady street right on the shore of Lady Bird Lake. Two-story views of the water from the sunny great room – complete with fish tank, guitar and comfy couches – might make even nonhostelers consider a stay.

The facilities are clean, tidy and cheerful. And with 24-hour access you can enjoy it at your leisure – although they do ask that all jam sessions end by 11pm. Rates for nonmembers are slightly higher.

Pecan Grove RV Park CAMPGROUND **$**
(Map p62; ☑ 512-472-1067; 1518 Barton Springs Rd; RV sites with full hookups per day $35-40, per week $220-250; P 🛜) The name says it all. Located in a shady grove of pecan trees, this pleasant RV park is exceedingly well located. It's smack dab in the middle of town and just steps away from the ever-popular Shady Grove Restaurant. Your RV never had it so good. No tent sites.

★**Hotel San José** BOUTIQUE HOTEL **$$**
(Map p62; ☑ 512-852-2350; www.sanjosehotel.com; 1316 S Congress Ave; r $215-360, r without bath $150, ste $335-500; P ⊖ ❄ 🛜 🏊) Local hotelier Liz Lambert has revamped a 1930s-vintage motel into a chic SoCo retreat with minimalist rooms in stucco bungalows, a lovely bamboo-fringed pool and a very Austin-esque hotel bar in the courtyard that's known for its celebrity-spotting potential. South Congress has become quite the scene, and this hotel's location puts you right in the thick of it.

In the early evening you may catch the faint sounds of bands playing in the Continental Club across the street – an utterly pleasing perk.

Best Western Plus – Austin City HOTEL **$$**
(Map p58; ☑ 512-444-0561; www.bestwestern.com; 2200 S IH 35, on highway frontage road; r/ste $157/180; P ⊖ ❄ @ 🛜 🏊) Our favorite detail? The Texas-shaped waffles at the breakfast spread. Bordering I-35, south of Lady Bird Lake, this recently renovated Best Western is close to downtown and South Congress Ave. It's also welcoming and stylish, and the spacious rooms are loaded with amenities, including mini-refrigerators, microwaves and Keurig coffee makers. This top-notch lodging is one of the best deals going in Austin.

If you're easily distracted, try for a 3rd-floor room; the floors can get a bit squeaky. It's $20 per pet, and parking is free.

Austin Motel MOTEL **$$**
(Map p62; ☑ 512-441-1157; www.austinmotel.com; 1220 S Congress Ave; r $95-180, ste $207-225; P ❄ 🛜 🏊) Liz Lambert's Bunkhouse Group recently purchased this budget favorite, long known for its 'garage-sale chic' and wonderfully funky appeal. At press time, its new owners were revamping the property. We hear the new motel will feature design elements inspired by classic 1930s motor courts, with some mid-century modern touches to keep things cool. Unchanged? The excellent location, friendly staff and enticing pool, which will always make this a great choice.

Expect prices to increase minimally, about $35 per room, which is a relief for this rapidly gentrifying street.

South Congress Hotel BOUTIQUE HOTEL **$$$**
(Map p62; www.southcongresshotel.com; 1603 S Congress Ave; r/ste from $352/640; 🛜 🏊 🏊) Austinites take their staycations at this boutique hotel, a smallish property that somehow squeezes four eateries, two bars, several shops and a pool into its stylish footprint. Minimalist rooms feel spacious and inviting (even if they're not warm and cuddly). If you want to be near, but not in, the late-night conviviality of South Congress, this hotel is a pleasant oasis just one block south.

And though the hotel may be starkly hip, the valets do a fine job with Texas hospitality. The pet fee is $125. Parking is a ridiculous $32 per night. If you can find a spot, and don't mind a short walk, park your car overnight on Congress. Electric bikes and Revival motorcycles for rent.

Hotel St Cecilia BOUTIQUE HOTEL **$$$**
(Map p62; ☑ 512-852-2400; www.hotelsaintcecilia.com; 112 Academy Dr; r/ste from $580/655; P ⊖ ❄ 🛜 🏊) The hustle and bustle of South Congress melts away the moment you cross over onto the serene lawn graced by a 300-year-old live oak. Choose from a suite in the Victorian-style house (c 1888) furnished with the perfect blend of modern, vintage and artistic touches, a studio in the main building, or one of the sleek poolside bungalows.

A splurge, to be sure – but if you have the time to stick around and enjoy it, this place really gets under your skin.

Kimber Modern BOUTIQUE HOTEL **$$$**
(Map p62; ☑ 512-912-1046; www.kimbermodern.com; 110 The Circle; r $309-339, ste $419-449; P ⊖ 🛜) Staying in one of the seven rooms at the architecturally adept Kimber is like staying in a minimalist art museum, with lots of white space accented by splashes of color. But the patio – now that's a different story altogether. If the rooms feel sterile, just step outside and relax under the insanely sprawling live oak. Within walking distance of South Congress action.

🛏 East Austin

Heywood Hotel BOUTIQUE HOTEL **$$$**
(Map p62; ☑ 512-271-5522; www.heywoodhotel.com; 1609 E Cesar Chavez St; d $220-310; P ❄ 🛜)

The first boutique hotel in East Austin, the Heywood is a seven-room gem that puts equal emphasis on design and comfort. The contemporary furnishings create a serene and sophisticated oasis, and the rooms are designed for privacy. Adults only.

Market District, Clarksville & North Austin

Emma Long Metropolitan Park CAMPGROUND $
(512-346-1831; www.austintexas.gov; 1706 City Park Rd; tent with hookup $10-20, RV with hookup $20-25, plus entrance fee per car Mon-Thu/Fri-Sun $5/10; gates open 7am-10pm; P) The only Austin city park with overnight camping, 1000-acre Emma Long Metropolitan Park (aka 'City Park') on Lake Austin, 16 miles northwest of downtown, has good swimming, sunbathing, fishing and boating. Get here early as it fills quickly and doesn't take reservations.

Habitat Suites HOTEL $$
(Map p58; 512-467-6000; www.habitatsuites.com; 500 E Highland Mall Blvd; ste $100-160; P@) Locally owned and eco-friendly, this quiet place is tucked away just north of downtown, away from the hustle and bustle. The furnishings may be slightly past their prime, but practical travelers will get a lot for their money here.

The property feels like an apartment complex, both inside and out, which means plenty of room to make yourself at home. You won't go hungry, either: rates include a hot breakfast and hospitality hour, and all suites have full kitchens. Traveling with the family? Spread out in a two-bedroom suite.

Brava House B&B $$
(Map p62; 512-478-5034; www.bravahouse.com; 1108 Blanco St; r/ste $169/189; P) Located right downtown, this B&B has two lovely rooms and three spacious suites, each one with different things to offer: choose a canopy bed in the Moroccan-style Casablanca Room, a claw-foot bathtub in the Garbo Suite and tons of space in the 650-sq-ft Monroe Suite.

Lone Star Court HOTEL $$$
(512-814-2625; www.lonestarcourt.com; 10901 Domain Dr; r $189-209, ste $399; P) Next door to the Domain shopping mall, this new hotel exudes cowboy cool. Spacious rooms feature stylish barn-style doors and retro refrigerators stocked with local brews. In the courtyard, fire pits await your cowboy beans and trail coffee...oh wait, we meant your modern-day s'mores fixin's. The on-site restaurant offers live music regularly and a tasty hot breakfast.

You'll find a food truck beside the parking lot. The mall is across the street. Pet fee is $25 per pet per stay.

Eating

Barbecue and Tex-Mex are the mainstays, but Austin also has many fine-dining restaurants and a broadening array of world cuisines. For hot tips on new restaurants, pick up the free alternative weekly *Austin Chronicle,* published on Thursday. Downtown eateries are a real mixed bag, serving tourists, business folks, politicians, artists and night-owl clubbers. South Austin, Hyde Park and East Austin have lots of interesting choices. Around the UT campus area, prices drop – but often so does quality.

Downtown

Texas Chili Parlor TEX-MEX $
(Map p62; 512-472-2828; 1409 Lavaca St; chili $4-9, mains $5-15; 11am-2am) Ready for an X-rated meal? When ordering your chili, keep in mind that 'X' is mild, 'XX' is spicy and 'XXX' is melt-your-face-off hot at this Austin institution. There's more than just chili on the menu; there's also Frito pie, which is chili over Fritos. Still not feeling it? There's also burgers, enchiladas and, of course, more chili.

Coopers Old Time Pit Bar-B-Cue BARBECUE $$
(Map p62; 512-474-2145; www.coopersbbqaustin.com; 217 Congress Ave; beef ribs & brisket $18 per pound, other meats vary; 11am-10pm) The downtown lunch crowd has discovered this new outpost of beloved Cooper's Bar-B-Cue in Llano. Pick your meat at the counter (paid by the pound) then add sides. We're partial to the jalapeno mac-and-cheese, which you won't want to share. The baked beans and the white bread are always free.

And ladies, we noticed a heavy contingent of men digging in at lunch along the communal tables. If you're lookin', just sayin'...

La Condesa MEXICAN $$
(Map p62; 512-499-0300; www.lacondesa.com; 400 W 2nd St; lunch $11-14, dinner $10-25; 11:30am-2:30pm Mon-Fri, 11am-3pm Sat & Sun, 5-10pm Sun-Wed, to 11pm Thu-Sat) Here in slacky Slackerville, decor is often an afterthought, but La Condesa came along and changed all that with an eye-poppingly gorgeous space that's colorful, supermodern and artsy, with a dazzling mural taking up an entire wall. If you

find the dinners to be a little spendy, come for brunch (in the $9 to $20 range).

Moonshine Patio Bar & Grill AMERICAN **$$**
(Map p62; ☎512-236-9599; www.moonshinegrill.com; 303 Red River St; dinner mains $12-25; ⏲11am-10pm Mon-Thu, to 11pm Fri & Sat, 9am-2pm & 5-10pm Sun) Dating from the mid-1850s, this historic building is a remarkably well preserved homage to Austin's early days. Within its exposed limestone walls, you can enjoy upscale comfort food, half-price appetizers at happy hour or a lavish Sunday brunch buffet ($20). Or, chill on the patio under the shade of pecan trees.

Lamberts BARBECUE **$$$**
(Map p62; ☎512-494-1500; www.lambertsaustin.com; 401 W 2nd St; lunch $12-19, dinner $19-42; ⏲11am-2:30pm Mon-Sat, to 2pm Sun, 5:30-10pm Sun-Wed, to 10:30pm Thu-Sat) Torn between barbecue and fine dining? Lambert's serves intelligent updates of American comfort-food classics – some might call it 'uppity barbecue' – in a historic stone building run by Austin chef Lou Lambert.

Sides are extra, so be prepared to spend. Or come early and nosh on half-price appetizers at happy hour (5pm till 7pm).

Chez Nous FRENCH **$$$**
(Map p62; ☎512-473-2413; www.cheznousaustin.com; 510 Neches St; lunch $8-19, dinner mains $20-37; ⏲11:45am-2pm Tue-Fri, 6-10:30pm Tue-Sun) This classic Parisian-style bistro has been quietly serving excellent food since 1982. Low-key and casual, Chez Nous is as unpretentious as they come, and has made many a French food lover *trés heureux*, especially with its three-course *menu du jour* for $32.50.

UT & Central Austin

Avoid the bland, student-oriented fare that crowds Guadalupe St (aka the Drag). There are still plenty of cheap eats in the UT area. Head north to N Lamar Ave for better choices.

Trudy's Texas Star TEX-MEX **$**
(Map p58; ☎512-477-2935; www.trudys.com; 409 W 30th St; breakfast $6-11, lunch & dinner $8-19; ⏲11am-2am Mon-Fri, from 9am Sat & Sun) Get your Tex-Mex fix here; the menu is consistently good, with several healthier-than-usual options. But we'll let you in on a little secret: this place could serve nothing but beans and dirt and people would still line up for the margaritas, which might very well be the best in Austin.

WORTH A TRIP

TEXAS BARBECUE TRAIL

They call it the **Texas Barbecue Trail** (www.texasbbqtrails.com): 80 artery-clogging miles worth of the best brisket, ribs and sausage Texas has to offer, stretching from Taylor (36 miles northeast of Austin) down to Luling, passing through Elgin and Lockhart along the way. Marketing gimmick? Perhaps. Do our stomachs care? They do not. If your schedule or limited appetite make driving two hours and eating at 12 different barbecue restaurants unfeasible, make a beeline for brisket in Lockhart, or, if it's hot sausage you crave, Elgin is your best bet.

Via 313 PIZZA **$$**
(Map p58; ☎512-358-6193; www.via313.com; 3016 Guadalupe St; pizzas $10-29; ⏲11am-11pm Sun-Thu, to 11pm Fri & Sat) What? Why is my pizza a square? Because it's Detroit-style, baby, meaning it's cooked in a square pan, plus there's caramelized cheese on the crust and sauce layered over the toppings. And after just one bite of one of these rich favorites, we guarantee you'll forget all geometric concerns. Good craft beer selection too.

There's also a Via 313 food truck beside Violet Crown Social Club (p82) in East Austin.

Hyde Park Bar & Grill AMERICAN **$$**
(Map p58; ☎512-458-3168; www.hpbng.com; 4206 Duval St; mains $8-19; ⏲11am-10:30pm Mon-Thu, to 11pm Fri & Sat, 10:30am-10:30pm Sun) Look for the enormous fork out front to guide you to this homey neighborhood haunt. The diverse menu has plenty of options, but no matter what you choose, we insist that you order the batter-dipped French fries, which is what this place is famous for.

South Austin

With more variety than any other neighborhood in the city, South Austin is a sure-fire choice for any appetite. Reservations are recommended for top-end restaurants. There are a lot of good choices on S Congress Ave and on the increasingly popular S 1st St.

★**Amy's Ice Creams - South Austin** ICE CREAM **$**
(Map p62; ☎512-440-7488; www.amysicecreams.com; 1301 S Congress; ice cream $3.25-6; ⏲11:30am-11pm Sun-Thu, to midnight Fri & Sat) The

South Congress location of this beloved local ice-cream chain shares its daily flavors on a chalkboard out front. Pick your favorite add-on, and they'll pound it into your ice-cream choice.

★Hopdoddy Burger Bar   BURGERS $

(Map p62; ☎512-243-7505; www.hopdoddy. com; 1400 S Congress Ave; burgers $7-13; ⊗11am-10pm Sun-Thu, to 11pm Fri & Sat) People line up around the block for the burgers, fries and shakes – and it's not because burgers, fries and shakes are hard to come by in Austin. It's because this place slathers tons of love into everything it makes, from the humanely raised beef to the locally sourced ingredients to the fresh-baked buns. The sleek, modern building is pretty sweet, too.

Ramen Tatsu-ya   RAMEN $

(Map p62; ☎512-893-5561; www.ramen-tatsuya. com; 1234 S Lamar Blvd; ramen $10; ⊗11am-10pm) With its communal tables, loud indie music and hustling efficiency, we wouldn't say this busy ramen joint is a relaxing experience, but darn is it good. Step up to the counter – there will be a line – and take your pick of seven noodle-and-veggie-loaded broths. Like it spicy? Order the Mi-So-Hot. You can also add spicy or sweet 'bombs' to vary the flavor.

Skip the edamame.

FOOD TRAILERS
∙∙

From epicurean Airstreams to regular old taco trucks, food trailers are kind of a big deal in Austin, and wandering from one to another is a fun way to experience the local food scene. Because of their transient nature, we haven't listed any of these rolling restaurants, but since they travel in packs, we can tell you where they tend to congregate.

South Austin Trailer Park and Eatery
This seems to be a rather settled trailer community, with a fence, an official name, a sign and picnic tables.

East Austin This area has its own little enclave, conveniently located right among all the bars on the corner of E 6th and Waller St.

Rainey St A cluster of food trucks is ready to serve the downtown hordes downing beers at nearby bars.

Tacodeli   TEX-MEX $

(Map p58; ☎512-732-0303; www.tacodeli.com; 1500 Spyglass Dr; ⊗7am-3pm Mon-Fri, 8am-3pm Sat & Sun) Oh Tacodeli, how we love your handcrafted tacos – surely blessed with the smiles of angels. From the Tacoloco with its adobo-braised brisket to the Pollo Fantistico with its shredded chicken and crema Mexican, the tacos are fresh, local and a touch gourmet. And you simply can't leave without trying the self-serve creamy dona sauce – it has kick. Order at the counter.

Across the street you can pick up the greenbelt trail for a nice stroll after lunch.

Bouldin Creek Coffee House   VEGETARIAN $

(Map p58; ☎512-416-1601; www.bouldincreek cafe.com; 1900 S 1st St; mains $6-10; ⊗7am-midnight Mon-Fri, 8am-midnight Sat & Sun; 🛜🖉) You can get your veggie chorizo tacos or a potato leek omelet all day long at this buzzing vegan-vegetarian eatery. It's got an eclectic vibe and is a great place for people-watching, finishing a novel or joining a band.

Jo's Coffee   TEX-MEX, SANDWICHES $

(Map p62; ☎512-444-3800; www.joscoffee. com; 1300 S Congress Ave; tacos $3.50, sandwiches $6-9; ⊗7am-9pm; 🛜) Walk-up window, friendly staff, shaded patio, plus great people-watching... Throw in breakfast tacos, gourmet deli sandwiches and coffee drinks. Stick it in the middle of hopping South Congress, and you've got a classic Austin hangout. Don't miss the *I Love You So Much* mural (p65) on the north side.

Home Slice   PIZZA $

(Map p62; ☎512-444-7437; www.homeslicepizza. com; 1415 S Congress Ave; slice $4, pizzas $15-22; ⊗11am-11pm Sun, Mon, Wed & Thu, to midnight Fri & Sat) Everybody knows about Home Slice. And on Saturday night between 6pm and midnight, it seems everybody is in fact here! All of them digging into the New York–style pies.

If you're heading to a show, step into the darkly lit restaurant beforehand for a glass of wine with your pizza. If it's after the show, step up to the to-go window (1421 S Congress St; 11am to 11pm Sunday to Thursday, to 3am Saturday and Sunday) next door.

Torchy's Tacos   TEX-MEX $

(Map p62; ☎512-916-9235; www.torchystacos.com; 1311 S 1st St; tacos $3-5; ⊗7am-10pm Mon-Thu, 7am-11pm Fri, 8am-11pm Sat, 8am-10pm Sun) At the South Austin Trailer Park location, they'll tell you what you should be ordering if they think you're making the wrong choice. We like your initiative Torchy's! This long-time favorite, which now has brick-and-mortar locations across the state, was former President Obama's pick on a 2016 Austin visit. His tacos of choice? The Democrat, the Republican and the Independent, we hear.

Lick ICE CREAM **$**

(Map p62; www.ilikelick.com; 1100 S Lamar Blvd; ⊙12:30-10pm Sun-Thu, to 11:30pm Fri & Sat) We can't help but be wooed by Lick's creative flavor combinations, like coconut and avocado, or roasted beet and fresh mint, all made with local, seasonal ingredients. Dairy-free and vegan options available.

South Austin Trailer Park & Eatery FOOD TRUCK **$**

(Map p62; 1311 S 1st St; ⊙hours vary by food truck) This seems to be a rather settled food truck community, with a fence, an official name, a sign, a small pavilion and a shaded outdoor eating area. The big standout here is Torchy's Tacos.

Whip In INDIAN **$**

(Map p58; ☎512-442-5337; www.whipin.com; 1950 S I-35; breakfast $7-9, brunch, lunch & dinner $9-14; ⊙10am-11pm Sun-Mon, to midnight Tue-Sat) It started as a convenience store on a frontage road. Then the beer and Indian food started to take over. Now it's part Indian restaurant, part bar and part beer store, with a few groceries still hanging around to keep it confusing. Would we mention it if the food (breakfast naan and 'panaani' sandwiches) wasn't awesome? We would not.

★Güero's Taco Bar TEX-MEX **$$**

(Map p62; ☎512-447-7688; www.gueros.com; 1412 S Congress Ave; breakfast $5-7, lunch & dinner $10-34; ⊙11am-10pm Mon-Wed, to 11pm Thu & Fri, 8am-11pm Sat, to 10pm Sun) Set in a former feed-and-seed store from the late 1800s, Güero's is an Austin classic and always draws a crowd. It may not serve the best Tex-Mex in town but with its free chips and salsa, refreshing margaritas and convivial vibe, we can almost guarantee a fantastic time. And the food? Try the homemade corn tortillas and chicken tortilla soup.

Head to the oak-shaded garden for live music (Wednesday through Sunday).

Elizabeth Street Cafe FRENCH, VIETNAMESE **$$**

(Map p62; ☎512-291-2882; www.elizabethstreet cafe.com; 1501 S 1st St; pastries $2-7, breakfast $8-19, lunch & dinner $9-23; ⊙8am-10:30pm Sun-Thu, to 11pm Fri & Sat) We're going to irritate some locals by highlighting this dapper cottage of deliciousness. Pop in for croissants, crepes and a few noodle dishes in the morning, plus the deliciously creamy Vietnamese coffee. And the banh mi? Available all day, these soft baguettes are loaded with bewitchingly tasty fillings. Later in the day look for pho, bun and more Vietnamese house specialties.

Uchi JAPANESE **$$$**

(Map p62; ☎512-916-4808; www.uchiaustin.com; 801 S Lamar Blvd; sushi & small plates $3-22, sushi rolls $10-13; ⊙5-10pm Sun-Thu, to 11pm Fri & Sat) East and West collide beautifully at this top-notch South Austin sushi joint run by owner and executive chef Tyson Cole. The sleek interior would feel right at home in LA, and the sushi is every bit as fresh and imaginative as what you'd get there.

Vespaio ITALIAN **$$$**

(Map p62; ☎512-441-6100; 1610 S Congress Ave; mains $24-34; ⊙5:30-10pm Sun & Mon, to 10:30pm Tue-Fri, 5-10:30pm Sat) This cozy Italian restaurant gets high marks for its fresh, authentic, seasonal menus. You can always go the pizza or pasta route, but the critics' favorites are usually found among the *specialitas della casa*.

✕ East Austin

East Austin's ethnic eateries are worthy of notice, especially if you're already sightseeing in the neighborhood. This area is majorly up-and-coming, especially on 6th and 7th Sts. Look for new bars and restaurants In the blocks just east of I-35. Some of the city's best food trucks are found along the major east–west thoroughfares.

★Franklin Barbecue BARBECUE **$**

(Map p62; ☎512-653-1187; www.franklinbarbecue. com; 900 E 11th St; sandwiches $6-10, ribs/brisket by the pound $17/20; ⊙11am-2pm Tue-Sun) This famous BBQ joint only serves lunch, and only till it runs out – usually well before 2pm. In fact, to avoid missing out, you should join the line – and there will be a line – by 10am (9am on weekends). Just treat it as a tailgating party: bring beer or mimosas to share and make friends. And yes, you do want the fatty brisket.

A few tips? Look for handy fold-out chairs near the front of the line. While you wait, you can buy beer from a cooler-toting server. And when your moment of glory arrives, go for the two-meat plate, or nab all you can for a feast to enjoy later. (Just be quick about it. The people behind you are starving.)

Veracruz All Natural
MEXICAN $

(Map p58; 512-981-1760; www.veracruztacos.com; 1704 E Caser Chavez St; tacos $3-4, mains $8; 7am-3pm) Two sisters from Mexico run this East Austin taco truck (an old bus), which may serve the best tacos in town. Step up to the window, order a *migas* breakfast taco (you must!) then add a quesadilla or torta for variety. Take your buzzer – yep, this food truck has a buzzer – and grab a picnic table.

What's in the famed *migas* taco? Eggs, tortilla chips, avocado, pico de gallo and monterey jack cheese. Don't miss the salsas near the pick-up window.

Thai-Khun at Whisler's
THAI $

(Map p58; 512-719-3332; www.thaikun.com; 1816 E 6th St; mains $7-10; 4pm-1:45am) The beef panang curry is, simply put, amazing. Served from a colorful food truck behind Whisler's cocktail bar, this spicy curry is one of a half-dozen noodle and curry dishes on the menu, all under the oversight of chef Thai Changdong. The food truck was named one of the best new restaurants in America by *Bon Appetit!*

Cenote
CAFE $

(Map p62; 1010 E Cesar Chavez St; mains $8-15; 7am-10pm Mon-Fri, from 8am Sat, 8am-4pm Sun;) One of our favorite cafes in Austin, Cenote uses seasonal, largely organic ingredients in its simple but delicious anytime fare. Come for housemade granola and yogurt with fruit, banh mi sandwiches and couscous curry. The cleverly shaded patio is a fine retreat for a rich coffee or a craft beer (or perhaps a handmade popsicle from Juju).

Mi Madre's
MEXICAN $

(Map p58; 512-322-9721; www.mimadres restaurant.com; 2201 Manor Rd; tacos $3-5, mains $9-14; 6am-2pm Mon & Tue, to 10pm Wed-Sat, 8am-4pm Sun) Barbacoa, chorizo and adobada are just a few of the authentic Mexican specialties here. In fact, it was recommended by a friend who said the barbacoa was just like his grandma used to make. Praise doesn't come much higher than that. Before dinner, enjoy a drink at the brand-new mezcal bar on the roof.

El Chilito
TEX-MEX $

(Map p58; 512-382-3797; www.elchilito.com; 2219 Manor Rd; tacos & burritos $3-9; 7am-10pm Fri, from 8am Sat & Sun) If you want quick, cheap and easy, this walk-up taco stand (with a big deck for your dining pleasure) can't be beat.

You've got to try breakfast tacos while you're in Austin, and this is a good place to get them.

Paperboy
AMERICAN, BREAKFAST $

(Map p62; www.paperboyaustin.com; 1203 E 11th St; mains $7-9; 7am-2pm Tue-Fri, 8am-2pm Sat & Sun) Even the food trucks here are going hyper local, 'curating' menus based on what's available. Breakfast wunderkind Paperboy does this particularly well, luring in-the-know locals with gourmet breakfast sandwiches. A recent menu featured an egg-covered pimien-to cheese and bacon sandwich and a sweet potato hash with braised pork belly and kale.

Licha's Cantina
MEXICAN $$

(Map p62; www.lichascantina.com; 1306 E 6th St; mains $13-27; 4-11pm Tue-Thu, 4pm-midnight Fri, noon-midnight Sat, 11am-3pm Sun) This cozy cottage may lure you in with its $5 drink specials at happy hour (4pm to 6pm Tuesday to Friday), but the interior Mexican dishes will have you sticking around. Eat inside, or out front, or settle in at the bar where the conversations are intriguing and the service top-notch.

Laundrette
MODERN AMERICAN $$

(Map p58; 512-382-1599; 2115 Holly St; mains $18-24; 11am-2:30pm daily, 5-10pm Sun-Thu, to 11pm Fri & Sat) A brilliant repurposing of a former washeteria, Laundrette boasts a stylish, streamlined design that provides a fine backdrop to the delicious Mediterranean-inspired cooking. Among the many hits: crab toast, wood-grilled octopus, brussels sprouts with apple-bacon marmalade, a perfectly rendered brick chicken and whole grilled branzino.

Salty Sow
AMERICAN $$

(Map p58; 512-391-2337; www.saltysow.com; 1917 Manor Rd; small plates $8-12, mains $16-24; 4:30-10pm Sun-Thu, to 11pm Fri & Sat) Behold the porcine wonder! This snout-to-tail restaurant advertising 'swine + wine' offers a thoroughly modern take on down-home cooking, including plenty of choices in the nonpork category.

Once you step inside, the modern farmhouse atmosphere makes you forget it's housed in a dowdy cinder-block building. We love the patio when the weather allows.

★ Dai Due
AMERICAN $$$

(Map p58; 512-719-3332; www.daidue.com; 2406 Manor Rd; breakfast & lunch $13-22, dinner $22-84; 10am-3pm & 5-10pm Tue-Sun) Even your basic eggs-and-sausage breakfast is a meal to remember at this lauded restaurant, where all the ingredients are from farms, rivers and hunting grounds in Texas, as well as the Gulf

WORTH A TRIP

BBQ DETOUR: LOCKHART

In 1999 the Texas Legislature adopted a resolution naming Lockhart the barbecue capital of Texas. Of course, that means it's the barbecue capital of the world. You can eat very well for under $15.

Black's Barbecue (☑ 512-398-2712; www.blacksbbq.com; 215 N Main St; sandwiches $10-13, brisket per pound $16.50; ⊙ 10am-8pm Sun-Thu, to 8:30pm Fri & Sat) A longtime Lockhart favorite since 1932, with sausage so good Lyndon Johnson had them cater a party at the nation's capital.

Kreuz Market (☑ 512-398-2361; www.kreuzmarket.com; 619 N Colorado St; brisket per pound $16.49; ⊙ 10:30am-8pm Mon-Sat, to 6pm Sun) Serving Lockhart since 1900, the barnlike Kreuz Market uses a dry rub, which means you shouldn't insult them by asking for barbecue sauce; they don't serve it, and the meat doesn't need it.

Chisholm Trail Bar-B-Q (☑ 512-398-6027; www.lockhartchisolmtrailbbq.com; 1323 S Colorado St; lunch plates $8-13, brisket per pound $13.50; ⊙ 8am-8pm Sun-Wed, 6am-9pm Thu-Sat) Like Black's and Kreuz, Chisholm Trail has been named one of the top 10 barbecue restaurants in the state by *Texas Monthly* magazine. Has a drive-through if you're in a hurry.

Smitty's Market (☑ 512-398-9344; www.smittysmarket.com; 208 S Commerce St; brisket per pound $14.90; ⊙ 7am-6pm Mon-Fri, to 6:30pm Sat, 9am-6:30pm Sun) The blackened pit room and homely dining room are all original (knives used to be chained to the tables). Ask them to trim off the fat on the brisket if you're particular about that.

of Mexico. Supper Club dinners spotlight limited items like wild game and foraged treats. Like your cut of meat? See if they have a few pounds to-go at the attached butcher shop.

Menus change regularly to reflect what's available.

Justine's   FRENCH $$$
(Map p58; ☑ 512-385-2900; www.justines1937. com; 4710 E 5th St; mains $20-28; ⊙ 6pm-2am Wed-Mon) With a lovely garden setting festooned with fairy lights, Justine's is a top spot for wowing a date. French onion soup, seared scallops and grilled pork chop are standouts on the small, classic brasserie menu. There are also a few more creative changing daily specials like pan-seared quail with parsnip casserole or grilled swordfish with artichokes and cauliflower puree.

✖ Market District, Clarksville & North Austin

Kerbey Lane Café   AMERICAN $
(Map p58; ☑ 512-451-1436; www.kerbeylanecafe. com; 3704 Kerbey Lane; breakfast $6-13, lunch & dinner $9-13; ⊙ 6:30am-11pm Mon-Thu, 24 hr from 6:30am Fri–11pm Sun; 🖋🖰) Kerbey Lane is a longtime Austin favorite, fulfilling round-the-clock cravings for anything from gingerbread pancakes to black-bean tacos to mahimahi. Try the addictive Kerbey Queso while you wait. (They have vegan queso, too!) There are

several other locations around town, but this location located in a homey bungalow is the original and has the most character.

Whole Foods Market   MARKET $
(Map p62; www.wholefoods.com; 525 N Lamar Blvd; sandwiches $6-9, mains $6-15; ⊙ 7am-10pm; 🖰) The flagship of the Austin-founded Whole Foods Market is a gourmet grocery and cafe with restaurant counters and a staggering takeaway buffet, including self-made salads, global mains, deli sandwiches and more. The sushi tuna burritos ($11) from the sushi counter are delicious.

If there's no parking in the lot out front, head to the free underground garage.

Stiles Switch   BARBECUE $
(Map p58; ☑ 512-380-9199; www.stilesswitchbbq. com; 6610 N Lamar Blvd; mains $7-18; ⊙ 11am-9pm Tue-Thu, to 10pm Fri & Sat, to 9pm Sun) With manageable lines, you won't have to suffer to enjoy outstanding brisket, fired up to tender, smoky perfection, at this popular eatery 6 miles north of downtown. Top it off with some ribs, a side of corn casserole and a local microbrew.

★ Uchiko   JAPANESE $$$
(Map p58; ☑ 512-916-4808; www.uchikoaustin.com; 4200 N Lamar Blvd; small plates $4-28, sushi rolls $10-16; ⊙ 5-10pm Sun-Thu, to 11pm Fri & Sat) Not content to rest on his Uchi laurels, chef Tyson Cole opened this restaurant that describes itself as 'Japanese farmhouse dining.' But we're

I SCREAM, YOU SCREAM

Short of jumping into Barton Springs, there's no better way to cool off than at **Amy's Ice Creams** (Map p62; ☑ 512-480-0673; www.amysicecreams.com; 1012 W 6th St; ice cream $3.25-6; ⊙ 11:30am-midnight Sun-Thu, to 1am Fri & Sat). It's not just the ice cream itself, which, by the way, is smooth, creamy and delightful. It's the toppings – pardon us, *crush'ns* they call 'em – that get pounded and blended in, violently but lovingly, by staff wielding a metal scoop in each hand. Mexican vanilla bean with fresh strawberries, dark chocolate with Reese's Peanut Butter Cups, or mango with jelly beans if that's what you're into. With 15 flavors (rotated from their 300 recipes) and dozens of toppings, ranging from cookies and candy, to fruit or nuts, the combinations aren't endless, but they number too high to count. Look for other locations on Guadalupe St north of the UT campus, on South Congress near all the shops, or at the airport for a last-ditch fix.

here to tell you, it's hard to imagine being treated to fantastic, unique delicacies such as these and enjoying this sort of bustling ambience in any Japanese farmhouse. Reservations are highly recommended.

Barley Swine AMERICAN $$$
(Map p58; ☑ 512-394-8150; www.barleyswine.com; 6555 Burnet Rd; small plates $9-30; ⊙ 5-10pm Sun-Thu, to 11pm Fri & Sat) Small plates. Tantalizing flavors. Locally sourced. Changing menus. Snout-to-tail culinary creations. And craft cocktails. All served in a rustically chic setting. Yep, hardcore farm-to-table joints are trending these days, but Barley Swine has a sense of fun often missing from similar establishments. Why yes, I will have the Rotating Obligatory Tiki – only $6 during the Swine Time happy hour (4pm to 7pm Monday to Friday).

Selections vary daily. A recent menu featured lamb sausage, pig-skin noodles with hot sauce, and shiitake pasta.

Wink FUSION $$$
(Map p62; ☑ 512-482-8868; 1014 N Lamar Blvd; mains $17-33; ⊙ 6-9:30pm Mon-Wed, 5:30-9:30pm Thu-Sat) Date night? At this intimate gem hidden behind Whole Earth Provision Co, diners are ushered to tables underneath windows screened with Japanese rice paper, then presented with an exceptional wine list. The chef-inspired fare takes on a nouveau fusion attitude that is equal parts modern French and Asian. For a special splurge, try the five-course ($68) tasting menu.

Fonda San Miguel MEXICAN $$$
(Map p58; ☑ 512-459-4121; 2330 W North Loop Blvd; mains $16-39; ⊙ 5:30-9:30pm Mon-Thu, to 10:30pm Fri & Sat, 11am-2pm Sun) The gorgeous building is drenched in the atmosphere of old Mexico, with folk-inspired art, and this place has been

serving interior Mexican cooking for over 25 years. The Sunday brunch buffet is an impressive event but, at $39 per person, you'd better come hungry. Note that the last seating is one hour before close.

 ## West Austin

Magnolia Cafe TEX-MEX $
(Map p58; ☑ 512-478-8645; www.themagnoliacafe.com; 2304 Lake Austin Blvd; breakfast $5-9, mains $7-16; ⊙ 24hr) In Westlake, opposite Deep Eddy Cabaret, this casual, all-night cafe serves American and Tex-Mex standbys such as *migas*, enchiladas, pancakes and potato scrambles. It gets absurdly crowded on weekends.

❓ Drinking & Nightlife

There are bejillions of bars in Austin. The legendary 6th St bar scene has spilled onto nearby thoroughfares, especially Red River St. Many of the 6th St places are shot bars aimed at college students and tourists, while the Red River establishments retain a harder local edge. A few blocks south, the scene on Rainey St is also jumping, with old bungalows now home to watering holes.

 ## Downtown

Locals refer to the bar-lined strip of 6th St between Congress Ave and the I-35 as Dirty 6th. Home to shot-bars and general party mayhem, this is where college kids and folks who want to relive their college days come to get smashed. There are a few quality bars in the mix, plus a great local cinema, but just be aware you may be surrounded by alcohol-driven craziness.

Easy Tiger BEER GARDEN
(Map p62; www.easytigeraustin.com; 709 E 6th St; ⊙ 11am-2am) The one bar on Dirty 6th that

all locals love? Easy Tiger, an inside-outside beer garden overlooking Waller Creek. The place welcomes all comers with an upbeat communal vibe. Craft beers are listed on the chalkboard. And the artisanal sandwiches? Baked on tasty bread from the bakery upstairs (7am to 2am). The meat is cooked in-house.

Craft Pride BAR
(Map p62; 512-428-5571; www.craftprideaustin. com; 61 Rainey St; 4pm-2am Mon-Fri, 1pm-2am Sat, 1pm-1am Sun) If it ain't brewed in Texas, then it ain't on tap at this cozy bar, which bursts with Lone Star pride. Yep, from the All Call kolsch to the Yellow Rose IPA, all 54 craft beers served here are produced in Texas. Look for it at the southern end of Rainey St.

Garage LOUNGE
(Map p62; 512-369-3490; www.garagetx.com; 503 Colorado St; 5pm-2am Mon-Sat) Hidden inside a parking garage, this cozy, dimly lit lounge draws a hip but not overly precious Austin crowd who give high marks to the first-rate cocktails, handsomely designed space and novel location.

Casino El Camino BAR
(Map p62; 512-469-9330; 517 E 6th St; 11:30am-2am) With a legendary jukebox and even better burgers, this is the spot for serious drinking and late-night carousing. If it's too dark inside, head for the back patio.

Hideout Coffee House & Theatre COFFEE
(Map p62; 512-476-1313; 617 Congress Ave; 7am-10pm Mon-Wed, to midnight Thu & Fri, 8am-noon Sat, 8am-10pm Sun;) Despite its downtown location, it has a near-campus vibe and damn fine brews.

Oilcan Harry's CLUB
(Map p62; 512-320-8823; 211 W 4th St; 2pm-2am Mon-Fri, noon-2am Sat & Sun) Oh, yes, there's dancing. And oh, yes, it's packed. (And how are you supposed to dance with all those people in there?) As much as the girls wish it were a mixed crowd, this scene is all about the boys. Sweaty ones.

 UT & Central Austin

Spider House CAFE
(Map p58; 512-480-9562; 2908 Fruth St; 11am-2am;) Traveling carnival? Haunted house? Or a European cafe with a great patio? North of campus, Spider House has a big, funky outdoor area bedecked with all sorts of oddities. It's open late and also serves beer and wine.

In the afternoon, bring a laptop, sip coffee and use the wi-fi, available until 2am.

Scholz Garten BEER HALL
(Map p62; 512-474-1958; 1607 San Jacinto Blvd; 11am-11pm) This German *biergarten* has been around forever – or at least since 1866 – and its proximity to the capitol building has made it the traditional favorite of politicians. The author O Henry was also a fan.

 South Austin

ABGB BEER GARDEN
(Austin Beer Garden Brewery; Map p58; 512-298-2242; www.theabgb.com; 1305 W Oltorf St; 11:30am-11pm Tue-Thu, 11:30am-midnight Fri, noon-midnight Sat, noon-10pm Sun;) Want a place to meet your friends for beer and conversation? Then settle in at a picnic table inside or out at this convivial brewery and beer garden that's also known for its great food. The boar, tasso and spinach pizza? Oh yes, you do want a slice of this thin-crusted specialty pie ($4). Live music Tuesday and Wednesday, and Friday through Sunday.

Got Fido? He's welcome to join you.

Hotel San José BAR
(Map p62; 512-852-2350; 1316 S Congress Ave; noon-midnight) Transcending the hotel-bar genre, this is actually a cool, Zen-like outdoor patio that attracts a chill crowd, and it's a nice place to hang if you want to actually have a conversation. Service can be leisurely, but maybe that's OK for an oasis?

East Austin

Whisler's COCKTAIL BAR
(Map p58; 512-480-0781; www.whislersatx.com; 1816 E 6th St; 4pm-2am) If vampires walk the streets of East Austin, then this dark and moody cocktail bar is where they congregate before a night of feeding. And we don't quite trust that taxidermied boar overlooking the bar from his lofty perch. Head to the patio for a less intimate scene, as well as live music. There's a fantastic Thai food truck out back.

White Horse HONKY-TONK
(Map p58; 512-553-6756; www.thewhitehorse austin.com; 500 Comal St; 3pm-2am) Ladies, you will be asked to dance at this East Austin honky-tonk, where two-steppers and hipsters mingle like siblings in a diverse but happy family. Play pool, take a dance lesson or step outside to sip a microbrew on the patio. Live music nightly, and whiskey on tap. We like this place.

Sa-Ten Coffee & Eats COFFEE
(Map p58; ☑512-524-1544; www.sa-ten.com; 916 Springdale Rd; ⊙7am-10pm; ☜) If you're on the east side of town and need a caffeine jolt, head to this bright and minimalist box for top-notch coffees and a small menu of Japanese snacks. This busy place is tucked among galleries and studios in the Canopy Austin artist complex. There are outside tables if you need some sunshine.

Flat Track Coffee COFFEE
(Map p58; ☑512-814-6010; www.flattrackcoffee. com; 1619 E Cesar Chavez St; ⊙7am-7pm) This East Austin joint also houses a bicycle repair shop. Or maybe it's the other way around. Either way, this former coffee-catering company is the go-to for coffee aficionados east of the I-35. On weekends, you'll find a food truck out front selling mini-donuts. Cycles also for rent.

Violet Crown Social Club BAR
(Map p62; 1111 E 6th St; ⊙5pm-2am) It's dark. It's loud. At first glance it's not terribly inviting. But damn, the drinks are cheap, making this a popular spot on the East 6th circuit.

🍸 Market District, Clarksville & North Austin

★**Ginny's Little Longhorn Saloon** BAR
(Map p58; ☑512-524-1291; www.thelittlelonghorn-saloon.com; 5434 Burnet Rd; ⊙5pm-midnight Tue & Wed, to 1am Thu-Sat, 2-10pm Sun) This funky little cinder-block building is one of those dive bars that Austinites love so very much – and did even before it became nationally famous for chicken-shit bingo on Sunday night. The place gets so crowded during bingo that you

GAY & LESBIAN AUSTIN

With a thriving gay population – not to mention pretty mellow straight people – Austin is arguably the most gay-friendly city in Texas. The Austin Gay & Lesbian Chamber of Commerce (www.aglcc. org) sponsors the Pride Parade in June, as well as smaller events throughout the year. The *Austin Chronicle* (www. austinchronicle.com) runs the Gay Place, a gay event column among the weekly listings, and the glossy *L Style/G Style* (www.lstylegstyle.com) magazine has a dual gal/guy focus.

Austin's gay and lesbian club scene is mainly in the Warehouse District, though there are outposts elsewhere.

can barely see the darn chicken – but, hey, it's still fun. The overflow crowd is out back.

Mean Eyed Cat BAR
(Map p58; ☑512-920-6645; www.themeaneyed cat.com; 1621 W 5th St; ⊙11am-2am) We're not sure if this watering hole is a legit dive bar or a calculated dive bar (it opened in 2004). Either way, a bar dedicated to Johnny Cash has our utmost respect. Inside, Man in Black album covers, show posters and other knick-knackery adorn the walls of this former chainsaw repair shop. A 300-year-old live oak anchors the lively patio.

🍸 West Austin

Hula Hut BAR
(Map p58; ☑512-476-4852; 3825 Lake Austin Blvd; ⊙11am-10pm Mon-Thu, to 11pm Fri, 10:30am-11pm Sat, to 10pm Sun) The hula theme is so thorough that this restaurant feels like a chain, even though it's not. But the bar's sprawling deck that stretches out over Lake Austin makes it a popular hangout among Austin's nonslackers.

Deep Eddy Cabaret BAR
(Map p58; ☑512-472-0961; 2315 Lake Austin Blvd; ⊙noon-2am) This great little neighborhood bar is known for its excellent jukebox, loaded with almost a thousand tunes in all genres. Yep, it's a dive, but a top-rate one.

Mozart's Coffee Roasters COFFEE
(Map p58; ☑512-477-2900; 3825 Lake Austin Blvd; ⊙7am-midnight Mon-Thu, 7am-1am Fri, 8am-1am Sat, 8am-midnight Sun) Out on Lake Austin, you'll find a great waterfront view and a sinful dessert case.

☆ Entertainment

Austin calls itself the 'Live Music Capital of the World,' and you won't hear any argument from us. Music is the town's leading nighttime attraction, and a major industry as well, with several thousand bands and performers from all over the world plying their trade in the city's clubs and bars. Most bars stay open till 2am, while a few clubs stay hoppin' until 4am.

You can get heaps of information on the city's whole entertainment scene from the *Austin Chronicle*, out on Thursdays, or from the *Austin American-Statesman's* Austin 360 website. The latter has streamlined listings for concerts and nightlife that let you plan your evening's entertainment at a glance, but the *Chronicle's* night-by-night encyclopedia of listings often includes set times (handy if you'd like to hit several venues in one night),

COFFEE CULTURE

Austin's a laid-back kind of town, and there's no better way to cultivate your slacker vibe than hanging out, sipping coffee and watching everyone else doing the same. Most places offer light meals in addition to caffeinated treats. Here are a few of our favorites:

Bouldin Creek Coffee House (p76) Very representative of the South Austin scene, with a great vegetarian menu to boot.

Hideout Coffee House & Theatre (p84) Despite its downtown location, it has a near-campus vibe and damn fine brews.

Sa-Ten Coffee & Eats (p82) In an artists complex in East Austin, you can enjoy Japanese snacks with your latte.

Mozart's Coffee Roasters (p82) Out on Lake Austin you'll find a great waterfront view and a sinful dessert case.

Spider House (p81) North of campus, Spider House has a big, funky patio bedecked with all sorts of oddities. It's open late and also serves beer and wine.

plus music critics' picks and local gossip to really plug you into the scene.

☆ Live Music

Music is a proud tradition in this part of the state, where you can see any kind of musical performance, from a four-piece bluegrass band kicking out jug tunes to a lone DJ spinning the latest trance grooves. The area's unique prominence on the country's musical stage can be traced all the way back to the German settlers who immigrated to the area in the mid-1800s, as well as to the rich musical heritage Texas always shared with Mexico. Austin's modern sound first took shape in the early 1970s at a barnlike venue known as the Armadillo World Headquarters.

Today, most live-music bars and clubs have a mix of local and touring bands. On any given Friday night there are several hundred acts playing in the town's 200 or so venues, and even on an off night (Monday and Tuesday are usually the slowest) you'll have your pick of more than two dozen performances. Often there are two or three bands per venue each night. Cover charges range from $5 for local bands to $15 or more for touring acts. Music shows start late, with the headliner starting anywhere from 9pm to midnight, though a few clubs offer music as early as 4pm, and doors almost always open half an hour to an hour before showtime. Showing up at the last minute or fashionably late may result in not getting in. If you want to get started early, most places have a happy hour (4pm to 7pm).

Although the part of 6th St between I-35 and S Congress Ave has become more of a frat-boy-and-tourist scene, there are still a few venues for dependably great live shows, especially as you head west of Congress. West of Congress Ave, the Warehouse District is more about sexy salsa spots and swanky martini bars, but you'll also find a couple of decent live-music venues.

Many of the venues we recommend are Austin institutions. If you want to experience Austin's music scene but aren't sure where to start, any of these are good bets.

★ Broken Spoke   LIVE MUSIC
(Map p58; www.brokenspokeaustintx.net; 3201 S Lamar Blvd; ⊙ 11am-11:30pm Tue, to midnight Wed & Thu, to 1:30am Fri & Sat) George Strait once hung from the wagon-wheel chandeliers at the wooden-floored Broken Spoke, a true Texas honky-tonk. Not sure of your dance moves? Take a lesson. They're offered from 8pm to 9pm Wednesday through Saturday. As the sign inside says: 'Please do Not!!!! Stand on the Dance Floor.'

★ Continental Club   LIVE MUSIC
(Map p62; ☑ 512-441-2444; www.continentalclub. com; 1315 S Congress Ave; ⊙ 4pm-2am Mon-Sun, from 3pm Sat & Sun) No passive toe-tapping here; this 1950s-era lounge has a dance floor that's always swinging with some of the city's best local acts. On most Monday nights you can catch local legend Dale Watson and his Lone Stars (10:15pm).

Stubb's Bar-B-Q   LIVE MUSIC
(Map p62; ☑ 512-480-8341; www.stubbsaustin. com; 801 Red River St; ⊙ 11am-10pm Mon-Thu, to 11pm Fri & Sat, 10:30am-9pm Sun) Stubb's has live music almost every night, with a great mix of

premier local and touring acts from across the musical spectrum. Many warm-weather shows are held out back along Waller Creek. There are two stages, a smaller stage indoors and a larger backyard venue.

Antone's   LIVE MUSIC
(Map p62; www.facebook.com/antonesnightclub; 305 E 5th St; ☺ showtimes vary) A key player in Austin's musical history, Antone's has attracted the best of the blues and other popular local acts since 1975. All ages, all the time.

Saxon Pub   LIVE MUSIC
(Map p62; ☑ 512-448-2552; www.thesaxonpub.com; 1320 S Lamar Blvd) The super-chill Saxon Pub, presided over by 'Rusty,' a huge knight who sits out the front, has music every night, mostly Texas performers in the blues-rock vein. A great place to kick back, drink a beer and discover a new favorite artist.

Cedar Street Courtyard   LIVE MUSIC
(Map p62; ☑ 512-495-9669; www.cedarstreetaustin.com; 208 W 4th St; ☺ 4pm-2am Mon-Fri, from 6pm Sat & Sun) Forget the dark and crowded club scene; this sophisticated courtyard venue serves martinis along with jazz and swing.

Flamingo Cantina   LIVE MUSIC
(Map p62; ☑ 512-494-9336; www.flamingocantina.com; 515 E 6th St) Called 'the last place with soul on 6th,' Austin's premier reggae joint prides itself on its good rasta vibes and bouncy dance floor. Seat yourself on the carpeted bleachers for good views of the stage.

Elephant Room   LIVE MUSIC
(Map p62; ☑ 512-473-2279; www.elephantroom.com; 315 Congress Ave; ☺ 4pm-2am Mon-Fri, from 8pm Sat & Sun) This intimate, subterranean jazz club has a cool vibe, and live

---

CHICKEN SHIT BINGO
....

We love **Ginny's Little Longhorn Saloon** (p82) any old time, but for a uniquely Austin outing, you've really got to experience the Sunday-night phenomenon known as chicken shit bingo. Beer-swilling patrons throw down their bets of $2 per square and wait to see what number the chicken 'chooses,' with the whole pot going to the winner. The chicken doesn't seem to mind, and most Sundays local favorite Dale Watson keeps everyone entertained while they wait for the results to drop.

---

music almost every night. The cover charge stays low, mostly free except on weekends, and there are happy-hour shows at 6pm weekdays.

Cactus Cafe   LIVE MUSIC
(Map p58; www.cactuscafe.org; Texas Union, cnr 24th & Guadalupe Sts; ☺ showtimes vary) Listen to acoustic up close and personal at this intimate club on the UT campus.

Emo's East   LIVE MUSIC
(Map p58; ☑ tickets 888-512-7469; www.emosaustin.com; 2015 E Riverside Dr; ☺ showtimes vary) For over 20 years, Emo's led the pack in the punk and indie scene in a crowded space on Red River St. Since 2011, it's been enjoying some shiny new digs (and a whole lot more space) out on Riverside.

Skylark Lounge   BLUES
(Map p58; ☑ 512-730-0759; www.skylarkaustin.com; 2039 Airport Blvd; ☺ 5pm-midnight Mon-Fri, to 1am Sat, to 10pm Sun) It's a bit of a drive (2.5 miles northeast of downtown), but well worth the effort to reach this friendly dive bar that serves up live blues – along with fairly priced drinks, free popcorn and a shaded patio.

Donn's Depot   LIVE MUSIC
(Map p62; ☑ 512-478-0336; www.donnsdepot.com; 1600 W 5th St; ☺ 2pm-2am Mon-Fri, from 6pm Sat) Austin loves a dive, and Donn's combines a retro atmosphere inside an old railway car with live music six nights a week, including Donn performing with the Station Masters. A mix of young and old come to Donn's, and the dancefloor sees plenty of action.

☆ Comedy & Improv

Esther's Follies   COMEDY
(Map p62; ☑ 512-320-0553; www.esthersfollies.com; 525 E 6th St; reserved seating/general admission $30/25; ☺ shows 8pm Thu-Sat, plus 10pm Fri & Sat) Drawing from current events and pop culture, this long-running satire show has a vaudevillian slant, thanks to musical numbers and, yep, a magician. Good, harmless fun.

Hideout Coffee House & Theatre   COMEDY
(Map p62; ☑ 512-443-3688; www.hideouttheatre.com; 617 Congress Ave; tickets $5-15; ☺ shows usually Thu-Sun) The hipsters' Hideout is a small coffeehouse–theater space that rubs shoulders with the big theaters on Congress Ave. Shows here feature live improv with plenty of audience participation. The box office usually opens half an hour before showtime.

Performing Arts

Paramount Theatre THEATER
(Map p62; ☑ 512-474-1221; www.austintheatre.org;
713 Congress Ave; ⊙ box office noon-5:30pm Mon-
Fri, 2hr before showtime Sat & Sun) Dating from
1915, this old vaudevillian house has staged
everything from splashy Broadway shows to
stand-up comics to classic film screenings.

**Long Center for the
Performing Arts** PERFORMING ARTS
(Map p62; ☑ 512-457-5100; www.thelongcenter.org;
701 W Riverside Dr) This state-of-the-art theater
opened in late 2008 as part of a waterfront
redevelopment along Lady Bird Lake. The
multistage venue hosts drama, dance, concerts and comedians. Also known for its gorgeous view of the downtown skyline from its
outdoor terrace.

Hyde Park Theatre THEATER
(Map p58; ☑ 512-479-7529; www.fronterafest.org;
511 W 43rd St) This is one of Austin's coolest
small theaters, presenting regional pre-
mieres of off-Broadway hits and recent Obie
(Off-Broadway Theater Awards) winners. Its
annual FronteraFest presents more than 100
works over five weeks at venues around town.

Austin Symphony PERFORMING ARTS
(Map p62; ☑ 512-476-6064; www.austinsym
phony.org; box office 1101 Red River St; tickets
$12-55; ⊙ box office 9am-5pm Mon-Thu, to 4pm
Fri, noon-5pm Sat performance days only, 2hr
before showtime performance days) Founded
in the early 20th century, the city's oldest
performing-arts group plays classical and
pop music at numerous venues throughout
the city. The main performance season runs
from September to April.

Cinema

Alamo Drafthouse Cinema CINEMA
(Map p62; ☑ 512-861-7020; www.drafthouse.com;
320 E 6th St; tickets $12-13) Easily the most fun
you can have at the movies: sing along with
Grease, quote along with *Princess Bride,* or
just enjoy food and drink delivered right to
your seat during first-run films. Check the
website for other locations.

Austin Film Society CINEMA
(AFS; ☑ 512-322-0145; www.austinfilm.org)
Frequent classic and independent film
screenings at venues around town. *Slacker*
director Richard Linklater was an early

promoter and Quentin Tarantino is now on
the board of directors.

☆ Spectator Sports

The whole town turns burnt orange during
University of Texas game weekends, especially
during football season, when the fiercely loyal
Longhorn fans are downright fanatical. For
tickets to any university-sponsored sporting
event, contact the UT box office (p88).

Shopping

Not many folks visit Austin just to shop. That
said, music is a huge industry here and you'll
find heaps of it in Austin's record stores. Employees are usually fairly knowledgeable and
will likely be in a band themselves. The best
stores let you listen to just about anything
before you buy, and will carry the bands you
see around town.

Vintage is a lifestyle, and the city's best
hunting grounds for retro fashions and furnishings are South Austin and Guadalupe St
near UT. For more options, check out www.
vintagearoundtownguide.com.

For a list of art galleries and happenings
around town, visit www.artaustin.org.

Domain MALL
(☑ 512-795-4230; www.simon.com/mall/the do
main; 11410 Century Oaks Tce; ⊙ 10am-9pm Mon-
Sat, noon-6pm Sun) Stores like Apple, Neiman
Marcus and Anthropologie line the streets
of this upscale outdoor shopping center in
far northwest Austin.

Arboretum MALL
(☑ 512-338-4765; 10000 Research Blvd; ⊙ 10am-
9pm Mon-Sat, noon-6pm Sun) About 20 minutes
northwest of downtown, the Arboretum is a
parklike collection of mall stalwarts, including Barnes & Noble, Gap and Pottery Barn.

Downtown

Toy Joy TOYS
(Map p62; ☑ 512-320-0090; www.toyjoy.com; 403
W 2nd St; ⊙ 10am-9pm) This colorful toy store
for grown-ups and big kids is an exuberant
repository that's packed floor to ceiling with
fun.

UT & Central Austin

Antone's Records MUSIC
(Map p58; ☑ 512-322-0660; www.antones
recordshop.com; 2928 Guadalupe St; ⊙ 10am-10pm
Mon-Sat, 11am-8pm Sun) North of UT, legendary Antone's was founded in 1972 and has a

Around Austin

well-respected selection of Austin, Texas and American blues music (with plenty of rare vinyl), plus a bulletin board for musicians, and vintage concert posters for sale.

University Co-op   GIFTS & SOUVENIRS
(Map p58; ☑ 512-476-7211; www.universitycoop. com; 2246 Guadalupe St; ⊗ 9am-8pm Mon-Fri, to 7pm Sat, 10am-6pm Sun) Stock up on souvenirs sporting the Longhorn logo at this store brimming with school spirit. It's amazing the sheer quantity of objects that come in burnt orange and white.

Buffalo Exchange   CLOTHING
(Map p58; ☑ 512-480-9922; 2904 Guadalupe St; ⊗ 10am-9pm Mon-Sat, 11am-8pm Sun) The Austin branch of this nationwide used-clothing chain has an impressive selection of vintage clothes and shoes for men and women, including Texas styles and Western wear.

🏠 South Austin

★Uncommon Objects   VINTAGE
(Map p62; ☑ 512-442-4000; 1512 S Congress Ave; ⊗ 11am-7pm Sun-Thu, to 8pm Fri & Sat) 'Curious oddities' is what they advertise at this quirky antique store that sells all manner of knickknacks, all displayed with an artful eye. More than 20 different vendors scour the state to stock their stalls, so there's plenty to look at.

Big Top Candy Shop   FOOD
(Map p62; www.bigtopcandyshop.tumblr.com; 1706 S Congress Ave; ⊗ 11am-7pm Sun-Thu, 11am-8pm Fri. 10am-9pm Sat; 👪) If you're trying to tame your sweet tooth, don't step into this colorful candy emporium where old-school treats like Squirrel Nut Zippers and Charleston Chews jostle for your attention near tropical gummy bears and caramel coffee truffles. And yes, you can get a malt at the soda fountain.

Austin Art Garage ART

(Map p58; ☑512-351-5934; www.austinartgarage. com; 2200 S Lamar Blvd; ⊙11am-6pm Tue-Sun) This cool independent...well, we hesitate to call it a 'gallery' because that would needlessly scare some people off. Anyway, it features some pretty great artwork by Austin artists. (Hey, Joel Ganucheau: we're fans.) Check the website to catch the vibe, and definitely check out the 'gallery' if you like what you see.

Lucy in Disguise VINTAGE

(Map p62; ☑512-444-2002; www.lucyindisguise. com; 1506 S Congress Ave; ⊙11am-7pm Mon-Sat, noon-6pm Sun) Colorful and over the top, this South Congress staple has been outfitting Austinites for years. You can rent or buy costume pieces, which is this place's specialty, but you can also find everyday vintage duds as well.

Allens Boots FASHION & ACCESSORIES

(Map p62; ☑512-447-1413; 1522 S Congress Ave; ⊙9am-8pm Mon-Sat, noon-6pm Sun) In hip South Austin, family-owned Allens sells rows upon rows of traditional cowboy boots for ladies, gents and kids. A basic pair costs from $100 or so, while somethin' fancy runs a few hundred dollars.

Tesoros Trading Co ARTS & CRAFTS

(Map p62; ☑512-447-7500; 1500 S Congress Ave; ⊙11am-6pm Sun-Fri, 10am-6pm Sat) Browse folk art and crafts from around the world, with a heavy Latin American influence of metalwork, jewelry, colorfully painted handicrafts, the Virgin Mary and Día de los Muertos.

Stag CLOTHING

(Map p62; ☑512-373-7824; www.stagaustin.com; 1423 S Congress Ave; ⊙11am-7pm Mon-Thu, to 8pm Fri & Sat, to 6pm Sun) Embrace the art of manliness at this stylish store that's just for the guys, or for girls who are shopping for guys.

Yard Dog ART

(Map p62; ☑512-912-1613; www.yarddog.com; 1510 S Congress Ave; ⊙11am-5pm Mon-Fri, 11am-6pm Sat, noon-5pm Sun) Stop into this small but scrappy gallery that focuses on folk and outsider art.

Amelia's Retrovogue & Relics VINTAGE

(Map p58; ☑512-442-4446; www.ameliasretro vogue.com; 2213 S 1st St; ⊙noon-5pm Tue-Sat) Austin's queen of vintage high fashion, Amelia's brings together *Vogue*-worthy dresses, retro '50s bathing suits and other old-school

glamour for both men and women. It's a favorite with film-industry folk.

Blackmail CLOTHING

(Map p62; ☑512-804-5881; 1202 S Congress Ave; ⊙11am-7pm Mon-Sat, to 6pm Sun) Black is the new black at this color-challenged store that unites Goths, punks and urban sophisticates. That means gorgeous black dresses and *guayabera* shirts, black-and-silver jewelry, black beaded handbags, black shoes and even minimalist black-and-white home decor.

🅰 Market District, Clarksville & North Austin

Book People Inc BOOKS

(Map p62; ☑512-472-5050; 603 N Lamar Blvd; ⊙9am-11pm) Grab a coffee and browse the shelves of this lively independent bookstore across the street from Waterloo Records. Great travel section. Hosts authors for talks and provides lots of staff picks.

Blue Velvet VINTAGE

(Map p58; ☑512-452-2583; www.bluevelvetaustin. com; 217 W North Loop Blvd; ⊙11am-8pm Mon-Sat, to 7pm Sun) Western wear, vintage T shirts and even oddities such as all-American bowling wear hang on the racks at Blue Velvet, where you'll find an equal number of men and women eyeing the goods. Summer fashions are stocked year-round.

Waterloo Records MUSIC

(Map p62; ☑512-474-2500; www.waterloo records.com; 600 N Lamar Blvd; ⊙10am-11pm Mon-Sat, from 11am Sun) If you want to stock up on music, this is the record store. There are sections reserved just for local bands, and listening stations featuring Texas, indie and alt-country acts.

New Bohemia JEWELRY

(Map p58; ☑512-326-1238; www.facebook.com/ NewBohemiaATX; 4631 Airport Blvd; ⊙noon-9pm) When it comes to retro thrift shops, New Bohemia is the place to look for vintage jewelry and clothing.

🅰 West Austin

Barton Creek Mall MALL

(☑512-327-7041; www.simon.com/mall/barton-creek-square; 2901 S Capital of Texas Hwy; ⊙10am-9pm Mon-Sat, 11am-7pm Sun) This indoor mall in southwest Austin has your standard offerings.

ℹ️ Information

Police (📞512-974-2000, non-emergency 311)

DOWNTOWN

Austin Visitor Information Center (Map p62; 📞512-478-0098; www.austintexas.org; 602 E 4th St; ⊙9am-5pm Mon-Sat, from 10am Sun) Helpful staff, free maps, extensive racks of information brochures and restrooms. You'll also find a fun collection of Austin souvenirs – from bat magnets to T-shirts to art – for sale.

Bank of America (📞512-542-9799; 515 Congress Ave; ⊙9am-4pm Mon-Thu, to 5pm Fri) Bank of America exchanges foreign currency and traveler's checks.

Brackenridge Hospital (📞512-324-7000; www.seton.net/locations/brackenridge; 601 E 15th St) Downtown Austin's central emergency room.

Capital Metro Transit Store (Map p62; www.capmetro.org; 209 W 9th St; ⊙7:30am-5:30pm Mon-Fri) Step into the downtown Capital Metro Transit Store for information.

Capitol Visitors Center (CVC; Map p62; 📞512-305-8400; www.tspb.texas.gov/prop/tcvc/cvc/cvc.html; 112 E 11th St; ⊙9am-5pm Mon-Sat, noon-5pm Sun) Get oriented with self-guided-tour booklets for the state capitol and grounds at this office on its southeast corner. It also has Austin information and state maps.

Downtown Austin Post Office (Map p62; 📞512-473-8334; 823 Congress Ave; ⊙8:30am-5:30pm Mon-Fri) Call 800-275-8777 to locate other branches.

Faulk Central Public Library (📞512-974-7400; https://library.austintexas.gov/faulk-central-library; 800 Guadalupe St; ⊙11am-8pm Mon-Thu, 10am-6pm Fri & Sat, noon-6pm Sun; 📶) Downtown, Faulk Central Public Library has dozens of wired terminals.

UT & CENTRAL AUSTIN

UT Box Office (📞512-471-3333; www.texassports.com; 2139 San Jacinto Blvd, Darrel K Royal-Texas Memorial Stadium) Purchase football game tickets here. See website for other ticket locations.

SOUTH AUSTIN

Emergency Animal Hospital & Clinic (📞Northwest Austin 512-331-6121, South Austin 512-899-0955; www.eahnwa.com)

Seton Kozmetsky Community Medical Center (📞512-324-4940; www.seton.net/locations/kozmetsky; 3706 S 1st St; ⊙9am-6pm Mon-Thu, 9:15am-4:30pm Fri)

EAST AUSTIN

Bennu (📞512-478-4700; www.bennucoffee.com; 2001 E Martin Luther King Jr Blvd; ⊙24hr) For free wi-fi, join the mass of UT students at the 24-hour Bennu.

Seton McCarthy Community Health Care Center (📞512-324-4930; www.seton.net/locations/mccarthy; 2811 E 2nd St; ⊙9am-6pm Mon-Thu, 9:15am-4:30pm Fri) Seton's nonemergency clinic charges on a sliding scale based on family size and income.

MARKET DISTRICT, CLARKSVILLE & NORTH AUSTIN

Seton Medical Center (📞512-324-1000; www.seton.net/locations/smc; 1201 W 38th St) A major hospital near the UT campus.

ℹ️ Getting There & Away

AIR

Opened in 1999, **Austin-Bergstrom International Airport** (AUS; www.austintexas.gov/airport) is about 10 miles southeast of downtown. It's served by Air Canada, Alaska Airlines, Allegiant, American, British Airways, Delta, Frontier, JetBlue, Southwest, United and Virgin America.

A nice welcome to the city, the airport features live music by local acts on some evenings near the center of the departures level. You can also sample food from Austin-based restaurants, including Amy's Ice Creams and Salt Lick Bar-B-Que, or buy some last-minute CDs from the Austin City Limits store. The airport's only big drawback is its lack of lockers, so plan to keep your carry-on bags with you.

Transport Options

Ground transportation from Austin-Bergstrom International Airport can be found on the lower level near baggage claim. A taxi between the airport and downtown costs $25 to $30. Capital Metro runs a limited-stop Airport Flyer (bus 100) service between the airport and downtown and the University of Texas for just $1.25 each way, with departures every 30 minutes. Check with **Capital Metro** (CapMetro; Map p62; 📞512-474-1200, transit store 512-389-7454; www.capmetro.org; transit store 209 W 9th St; ⊙transit store 7:30am-5:30pm Mon-Fri) for exact schedules. It takes at least 20 minutes to get downtown from the airport, and 35 minutes to reach UT.

SuperShuttle (📞800-258-3826; www.supershuttle.com) offers a shared-van service from the airport to downtown hotels for about $14 one way, or a few dollars more to accommodations along N I-35 and near the Arboretum Mall.

You can walk from the terminal to the **rental car facility**. All major rental car agencies are represented.

Shared-ride companies that pick up and drop off passengers at the airport are **Fare** (www.ridefare.com), **Fasten** (www.fasten.com) and the nonprofit **Ride Austin** (www.rideaustin.com), plus a few others. Uber and Lyft are not currently operating in Austin.

BUS

The **Greyhound bus station** (Map p58; ☎ 512-458-4463; 916 E Koenig Lane) is 5 miles north of downtown. Capital Metro bus 10-South First/Red River(www.capmetro.org) will deliver you from the station to downtown. Buses leave from here for other major Texas cities frequently. There is a **Megabus** (Map p62; ☎ 800-256-2757; www.megabus.com; 1500 San Jacinto Blvd) pick-up and drop-off stop at 1500 San Jacinto Blvd on the northeast corner of the state capitol grounds.

CAR & MOTORCYCLE
Road Distances

Austin to Dallas 200 miles, 3½ hours
Austin to Dripping Springs 23 miles, 30 minutes
Austin to Fredericksburg 80 miles, one hour and 40 minutes
Austin to Gruene 45 miles, 55 minutes
Austin to Lockhart 30 miles, 40 minutes
Austin to San Antonio 80 miles, one hour and 20 minutes

TRAIN

The downtown **Amtrak station** (☎ 512-476-5684; www.amtrak.com; 250 N Lamar Blvd) is served by the *Texas Eagle*, which extends from Chicago to Los Angeles. There's free parking and an enclosed waiting area but no staff. Fares vary wildly.

ⓘ Getting Around

BICYCLE

A grand bicycle tour of greater Austin isn't feasible, due to interstate highways and the like, but cycling around downtown, South Congress and the UT campus is totally doable. There are also miles of recreational paths around the city that are ideal for cruisin'. Check https://austintexas.gov/bicycle for a route map. You'll also find routes and maps at www.bicycleaustin.info.

The city also offers bike sharing, with more than 40 **Austin B-cycle** (www.austin.bcycle.com) stations scattered around the city.

CAR & MOTORCYCLE

Getting around Austin is easy enough, but the main consideration for drivers – other than rush-hour gridlock and what people from other towns consider crazy drivers – is where to leave your car.

Downtown, the best deal is at the **Capitol Visitors Parking Garage** (1201 San Jacinto Blvd). It's free for the first two hours, and only $1 per half-hour after that, maxing out at $12. Other downtown garages and lots are fairly abundant. They usually charge $2 to $3 per hour, with a daily maximum of $10 to $18.

Other downtown garages and parking lots typically charge a flat fee of around $7 to $10 or so after dark. People also park for free under I-35 at the east end of 6th St, but you can't depend on it being available (or legal).

Parking meters downtown cost $1.20 per hour. Outside of downtown they usually run about $1 per hour, although rates may vary on the UT campus or within the State Capitol Complex. Gone are the days of free downtown street parking on nights and weekends. To discourage drunk driving after partying downtown, the city implemented the get Home Safe program. You can now prepay at meters that have yellow Next Day buttons. If you forget to prepay, you may have the ticket waived if you complete and email a waiver form stating you took a safe ride home. Your car will not be towed – unless you park on 6th St between Red River and Brazos Sts. Visit www.austintexas.gov/gethomesafe for more parking and safe travel options.

Elsewhere around Austin, you can find free on-street parking, but pay careful attention to posted permit parking and time limits.

Day or night, finding a spot around the UT campus can take a while. Free visitor parking is available outside the LBJ Library in Lot 38, but from there it's a long, hot walk across campus to the UT Tower and other sights. Parking spots on Guadalupe St are both timed and metered. Otherwise, your best bet is to search for free parking in the residential streets west of Guadalupe St.

PUBLIC TRANSPORT

Austin's handy public-transit system is run by **Capital Metro**. Call for directions or stop into the downtown **Capital Metro Transit Store** for information. Regular city buses – not including the more expensive express routes – cost $1.25. Children under six years of age are free. There are bicycle racks (where you can hitch your bike for free) on the front of almost all CapMetro buses, including more than a dozen UT shuttle routes.

RIDE SHARE

Uber and Lyft are not available in Austin. For ride sharing, try **Fare** (www.ridefare.com), **Fasten** (www.fasten.com) or the nonprofit **Ride Austin** (www.rideaustin.com)

TAXI

You'll usually need to call for a cab instead of just flagging one down on the street, except at the airport, at major hotels, around the state capitol and at major entertainment areas. The flag drops at $2.50, then it's $2.40 for each additional mile. Larger companies include **Yellow Cab** (☎ 512-452-9999) and **Austin Cab** (☎ 512-478-2222) .

Human-powered bicycle taxis, or pedicabs, are available downtown on 6th St and around the Warehouse District, usually from about 9pm until after 2am from Wednesday to Saturday evenings. The drivers, typically young students or musicians, work entirely for tips, so please be generous.

San Antonio & Hill Country

🎵 210, 830

Best Places to Eat

➜ Pieous (p123)

➜ Cured (p110)

➜ Vaudeville (p128)

➜ Green Vegetarian Cuisine (p109)

➜ Salt Lick (p123)

➜ Il Sogno Osteria (p110)

Best Places to Sleep

➜ Hotel Emma (p106)

➜ Omni La Mansion del Rio (p105)

➜ Gruene Mansion Inn (p119)

➜ King William Manor (p106)

Why Go?

Tourism has been good to San Antonio and the sprawling city reciprocates with a wide variety of attractions to keep everyone entertained. In addition to its colorful, European-style River Walk lined with cafes and bars, it rewards visitors with a well-rounded menu of museums, theme parks, outdoor activities and historical sites. The Alamo is a stalwart tourist favorite, and the scene of the most famous battle in the fight for Texas' independence from Mexico. You can find four other beautifully preserved Spanish missions within the city limits.

San Antonio also puts you in close proximity to the Hill Country, a naturally beautiful region known for its wildflower-lined roadways, charming small towns, gorgeous wineries and, yes, hills. Fredericksburg is the most touristy Hill Country town, but the area is more about winding roads and stopping along the way than any particular destination.

When to Go
San Antonio

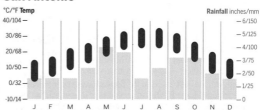

Mar & Apr Hill Country comes alive with bluebonnets, Indian paintbrushes and other wildflowers.

May & Jun The kids are out of school and temperatures are still bearable – mostly.

Dec & Jan Brush off cabin fever: it's warm enough to get outdoors, even if the trees are bare.

SAN ANTONIO

📞 210 / POP 1.4 MILLION

San Antonio's selling point these days? Tourists might say they've come for the Alamo and the River Walk. But locals are touting the city's easy diversity, with all races and cultures truly coexisting and supporting each other. Residents are also excited about the ever-growing Pearl District – it may seem like half the city is here on a sunny Saturday afternoon. And we've never seen a place with so many bicycle-share stations,

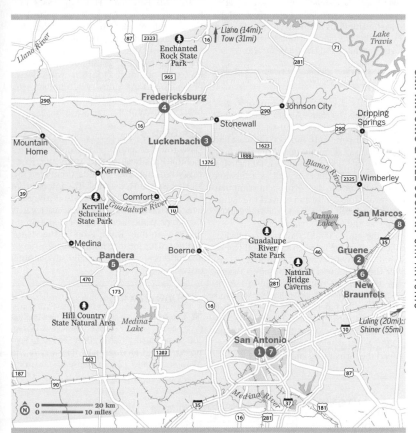

🔘 San Antonio & Hill Country Highlights

❶ **The Alamo** (p92)
Paying your respects at the historic shrine to the men who fought for Texas' independence.

❷ **Gruene Hall** (p120)
Taking a spin around the worn wooden floors at the oldest dance hall in Texas.

❸ **Luckenbach** (p129)
Settling in for a no-stress day of drinking cold beer and listening to live music.

❹ **Fredericksburg** (p125)
Strolling Main St and the museums in the unofficial capital of Hill Country, a town offering a hearty *wilkommen* to all.

❺ **Bandera** (p129)
Saddling up at a dude ranch in Bandera, the Cowboy Capital of Texas.

❻ **New Braunfels** (p117) Floating along the

Guadalupe River, a Texas summertime tradition.

❼ **Pearl Brewery Complex** (p114) Checking out the eateries and shops and the neo-Victorian glamour of the stunning Hotel Emma.

❽ **San Marcos Premium Outlets** (p121) Browsing the shops for the best deals around.

making it easy to explore the Museum Reach and the Mission Reach (the newest sections of the famed River Walk).

The biggest surprise for visitors? The fact that two of the state's most popular destinations – the aforementioned Alamo and River Walk – are smack dab in the middle of downtown, surrounded by historical hotels, tourist attractions and souvenir shops. The rest of the city sprawls out beyond them, never impinging on the tourist trade.

History

Although the area around San Antonio was first populated by Native Americans, the city's official history begins in 1691 when Spanish explorers discovered the area on the feast day of St Anthony of Padua and dubbed it 'San Antonio.' In 1718 the Spanish established a military presidio there, as well as a mission called San Antonio de Valero – a mission that was meant to colonize and convert the native people and that would one day be known simply as 'the Alamo.'

At the time, Texas belonged to Mexico, which in turn belonged to Spain, and things stayed that way for nearly a hundred years after the Alamo was built. But after Mexico won its independence from Spain in 1821, it wasn't long before Texas followed suit and fought for its independence from Mexico. One of the most important battles in the Texas Revolution was the Battle of the Alamo (p336), where patriots fought to the death to defend the former mission.

After Texas won its independence, San Antonio boomed as a cattle town. European settlers moved to the area, including vast numbers of Germans and Czechs, and the Germans built the city's King William area, named for Kaiser Wilhelm I of Prussia.

In 1879 Fort Sam Houston was established by the US Army. It was joined by Kelly Air Force Base in 1917 and then later by Lackland, Randolph and Brooks Air Force bases. Much of San Antonio's 20th-century growth was a result of the military's presence, although tourism will always be an important industry – thanks to the 300-year-old mission that sits right in the heart of downtown.

◉ Sights

Downtown's major north–south arteries include Broadway St and Main Ave. East–west thoroughfares include Commerce St, Market St and Houston St. The intersection of Commerce and Losoya Sts is the very heart of downtown; below street level is the River Walk, a developed canal loop off the San Antonio River. Stop by the visitor center (p115) for discount passes for major attractions – you can usually save a buck or two.

◉ Downtown

★ The Alamo   HISTORIC BUILDING
(Map p98; ☑ 210-225-1391; www.thealamo.org; 300 Alamo Plaza; ⊙ 9am-5:30pm Sep-Feb, to 9pm Mar-Aug) FREE Find out why the story of the Alamo can rouse a Texan's sense of state pride

---

SAN ANTONIO IN...

Two Days

Start your day at the **River Walk**, then take some time to remember the **Alamo**. Check out whatever downtown sights you fancy, perhaps the **Buckhorn Museum** or the new **Briscoe Western Art Museum**. Later, explore the historic homes of the King William District (p96) and plan on dinner anywhere along Alamo St.

On your second day, head north to **Brackenridge Park** (p97). Spend some time at the **San Antonio Botanical Gardens** (p97), then visit the divine **McNay Art Museum** (p100) or the **San Antonio Museum of Art** (p97).

Four Days

On your third day, explore the four missions along the Mission Trail (p101) or take your kids to the **Six Flags** (p101) amusement park, then head over to explore the new development at the old **Pearl Brewery** (p114) and stick around for dinner.

Finally, get out and explore any of the great small towns around San Antonio. Wildflowers (p126) in the **Hill Country**? Outlet malls in San Marcos (p120)? River tubing (p118) in New Braunfels? All are within an hour or two of the city.

like few other things. For many, it's not so much a tourist attraction as a pilgrimage – you might notice some visitors getting downright dewy-eyed at the description of how a few hundred revolutionaries died defending the fort (p336) against thousands of Mexican troops.

The main chapel building is now known as the **Shrine**. From here you can set off for a free history talk in the Cavalry Courtyard, hearing one of many perspectives on the actual events – which are somewhat in dispute – or browse the museum in the **Long Barrack**, which served as a residence for the Spanish priests and later as a hospital for Mexican and Texan troops. There's also a 17-minute film, which not only gives you another perspective on the battle, but is an excellent place to escape the heat.

If you're interested in walking the front perimeter of the old fort, which extends beyond the chapel, and learning more details about the battle and its participants, join the one-hour guided Battlefield Tour ($15 per person). A 33-stop audio tour ($7) is self-guided and takes about 45 minutes. (Visitors taking the guided tour are also given the audio tour, since the Battlefield Tour does not cover all 33 stops.)

★ River Walk   WATERFRONT
(Map p98; www.thesanantonioriverwalk.com) A little slice of Europe in the heart of downtown San Antonio, the 15-mile River Walk is an essential part of the San Antonio experience. This is no ordinary riverfront, but a charming canal and pedestrian street that is the main artery at the heart of San Antonio's tourism efforts. For the best overview, hop on a Rio San Antonio river cruise (p103).

You can meander past landscaped hotel gardens and riverside cafes, and linger on the stone footbridges that stretch over the water. During summer it gets mighty crowded, but at peaceful times (and as you get away from downtown) it's a lovely place to stroll – especially during the holidays, when it's bedecked with twinkling lights.

The River Walk used to be just a downtown thing, but a $358-million project completed in 2013 extended it to the north and south. As part of the 8-mile Mission Reach expansio, you can walk south to the King William District and beyond to the Spanish missions (p101). The new 4-mile **Museum Reach** stretches north to the San Antonio Art Museum, the Pearl Brewery complex and Brackenridge Park.

Feeling athletic? Once out of downtown, cycling to the missions or to the museums via the River Walk is also an option. Check the B-Cycle (p103) website for rental locations.

Briscoe Western Art Museum   MUSEUM
(Map p98; ☎ 210-299-4499; www.briscoemuseum.org; 210 W Market St; adult/child under 13yr $10/free; ⊙ 10am-9pm Tue, to 5pm Wed-Sun) It's quality over quantity at this repository of Western art, which opened its stately doors in 2013. Cowboys, Native Americans, Hispanic settlers and the women of the west all get their due (although we wish the ladies had a few more exhibits). You'll find 1880s photographs of Yosemite National Park, Native American weaponry, Pancho Villa's saddle, recordings of Western songs and plenty of landscapes, spurs and taxidermy. The large diorama depicting the fall of the Alamo is fascinating.

Guided tours are offered at 10:30am on Fridays. Check the online calendar for gallery talks, film series and live music.

Buckhorn Saloon & Museum   MUSEUM
(Map p98; ☎ 210-247-4000; www.buckhornmuseum.com; 318 E Houston St; adult/child 3-11yr $20/15; ⊙ 10am-5pm Sun-Thu, to 6pm Fri & Sat, to 9pm daily late May-early Aug) Waaaay back in 1881, when the original Buckhorn Saloon opened up, the owner promised patrons a free beer or whiskey shot for every pair of deer antlers they brought in. Although the location has changed a couple of times, you can still see the collection – and the bar – at the Buckhorn Saloon & Museum. Admission includes the adjacent **Texas Ranger Museum**.

You don't need a ticket to sip an over-priced beverage in the saloon, which has an impressive number of mounted animals watching over you, including a giraffe, a bear and all manner of horn-wielding mammals. If that doesn't quench your thirst for taxidermy, pony up for a kitsch walk through the attached museum, which includes wildlife from all over the world, as well as oddities such as a two-headed cow and an eight-legged lamb.

There are also other only-in-Texas displays, such as maps of Texas made from rattlesnake rattles and a jaw-dropping collection of Lone Star Beer paraphernalia. In the Texas Ranger Museum you can learn the stories of early rangers and step into a recreated western town.

San Fernando Cathedral   HISTORIC BUILDING
(Map p98; ☎ 210-227-1297; www.sfcathedral.org; 115 W Main Plaza; ⊙ gift shop 9am-5pm Mon-Fri, to 6:30pm Sat, 8:30am-3:30pm Sun) More than just

San Antonio

San Antonio

another pretty church, San Fernando's role in the Battle of the Alamo (p000) makes it an important local landmark. In happier times, future Alamo hero James Bowie was married here. But as Bowie defended the Alamo just across the river, Mexican general Santa Anna took over the church as an observation post and raised a flag of 'no quarter' (meaning he would take no prisoners), which began the deadly siege.

In 1936 some remains were uncovered; since they included charred bones and fragments of uniforms, they were purported to be those of Davy Crockett, William Travis and James Bowie. (Never mind that the Alamo defenders didn't wear uniforms.) Pay your respects to whoever they are at the marble casket at the left entrance to the church.

On most Tuesday, Friday, Saturday and Sunday nights, you can immerse yourself in **San Antonio: The Saga**, a dazzling new sound-and-light show that shares the history of San Antonio on the outside facade of the cathedral. It's free and can be viewed from the Main Plaza (www.mainplaza.org) in front of the church. The 24-minute show starts at 9pm, 9:30pm and 10pm.

Ripley's Alamo Plaza Attractions   MUSEUM
(Map p98; ☑ 210-226-2828; www.ripleys.com/phillips; 329 Alamo Plaza; combination ticket adult/child 3-11yr $30/20; ☉ 10am-11pm Sun-Thu, to midnight Fri & Sat late May–early Sep, to 8pm Sun-Thu, to 11pm Fri & Sat early Sep–late May; ⊕) Time to throw the kids a bone? After touring historical sites all day, you can reward them with a visit to this teen-friendly trio: **Ripley's Haunted Adventure**, **Guinness World Records Museum** and **Tomb Rider 3D**, a theme-park-style ride. It's a little cheesy, and definitely touristy, but

a good antidote to slogging around the missions all day.

One combo admission gets you into all three, or you can pay a reduced admission if you only have time for one or two. There are plenty of discount coupons floating around, too – check brochures at the visitor center or your hotel.

Spanish Governor's Palace   HISTORIC BUILDING
(Map p98; 📞 210-224-0601; www.spanishgovernors palace.org; 105 Plaza de Armas; adult/child 7-13yr $5/3; ☺ 9am-5pm Tue-Sat, 10am-5pm Sun) This low-profile adobe structure that was the seat of Texas' colonial government was already more than 150 years old when City Hall was built in 1889. But it was occupied by commercial tenants – including a saloon, a clothing store and even a pawn shop – until the city realized its historical significance and bought the building back in 1928.

It's now been restored to the way it looked (approximately) back when it was first built, and outfitted with period furnishings. Take a half-hour out of your day to learn the building's fascinating history, and be glad San Antonio discovered what they had before it was torn down to build a parking lot.

La Villita Historic Arts Village   HISTORIC SITE
(Map p98; 📞 210-207-8614; www.getcreativesan antonio.com; 418 Villita St; ☺ 10am-6pm Mon-Sat, 11am-5pm Sun) **FREE** History meets commerce at downtown's La Villita. San Antonio's first neighborhood, this 'little village' of stone and adobe houses dates back to the early 1800s and now contains a collection of touristy shops and galleries. It doesn't exactly offer a portal into the past, but it's worth a stroll, especially if you pause for a **walking tour** that puts the village into the right historical context. (Maps are posted around the village.)

La Villita occupies the space between Paseo de la Villita and Nueva St, and between Alamo and Presa Sts.

Artpace   MUSEUM
(Map p98; 📞 210-212-4900; www.artpace.org; 445 N Main Ave; ☺ noon-5pm Wed-Sun) **FREE** This unique contemporary museum hosts temporary exhibitions by its outstanding artists-in-residence, who are selected from a pool drawn from across Texas, the USA and abroad. Inside a 1920s automobile showroom, the renovated gallery space is inspiring and the works are often experimental. Artpace also schedules special community events, including lectures, films, artist conversations and more.

Institute of Texan Cultures   MUSEUM
(Map p98; 📞 210-458-2300; www.texancultures. com; 801 E César Chavez Blvd, Hemisfair Park; adult/ child 6-17yr $10/8; ☺ 9am-5pm Mon-Sat, from noon Sun) Thirty cultures have made Texas what it is; explore them at the museum of the Institute of Texan Cultures. This Smithsonian affiliate explores the origins of Texas folk traditions and tells the stories of the state's earliest contributors. The Latin American influence is fairly prominent in San Antonio, so this museum can be an eye-opener to visitors learning about Texas' diverse background.

◉ King William District & Southtown

South of downtown on the banks of the San Antonio River, the charming King William District (once nicknamed 'Sauerkraut Bend') was built by wealthy German settlers at the end of the 19th century. The architecture here is mostly Victorian, though there are fine examples of Italianate, colonial-revival, beaux-arts and even art-deco styles. Most of the district's houses have been renovated and are privately owned or run as B&Bs. It's a very pleasant area for a stroll; stop by the King William Association (p115) or the San Antonio Conservation Society (p115) for self-guided walking tour brochures.

Southtown, the adjoining area, has two art walks held each month.

Steves Homestead Museum   HISTORIC BUILDING
(Map p98; 📞 210-227-9160; www.saconservation.org; 509 King William St; adult/child under 12yr $7.50/ free; ☺ 10am-3:30pm, last tour 3pm) Most of the mansions in the King William District can only be appreciated from curbside, but one of them provides **guided tours**: the Steves Homestead. Volunteer docents from the San Antonio Conservation Society (p115) run guided tours through this Italianate villa and French Second Empire–style home that dates from 1876.

Built for Edward Steves, a wealthy lumber merchant, this stately house has been restored to demonstrate the life of the affluent at the end of the 19th century. Incidentally, San Antonio's first indoor swimming pool is on the property.

◉ Brackenridge Park & Around

A couple of miles north of downtown, Brackenridge Park has been a favorite San Antonio getaway spot for more than a century, with boat rentals, playgrounds, rides and gardens. Its main attraction – other than a serene green setting – is that it's the headspring for the San Antonio River. Many of the park's sights are designed for children, but may be equally interesting for adults, such as the impressive Witte Museum.

Witte Museum
MUSEUM

(Map p94; ☑ 210-357-1900; www.wittemuseum. org; 3801 Broadway St; adult/child 4-11yr $10/7; ⊙10am-5pm Mon & Wed-Sat, to 8pm Tue, noon-5pm Sun; ⓘ) Older kids will most enjoy this museum on the eastern edge of Brackenridge Park. The Witte (pronounced 'witty') is educational but engaging, with hands-on explorations of natural history, science and Texas history. At press time, the museum was preparing to open the **New Witte**, the result of a 170,0000-sq-ft expansion project. Look for a dinosaur gallery, a prehistoric peoples exhibit and immersive wildlife dioramas. A replica of the winged Quetzalcoatlus dinosaur will hang above the foyer.

Outside, don't miss the **Science Treehouse**, a high-tech activity center in back of the museum building. It's a hit with all ages, even the really big kids (aka parents). The museum is free on Tuesdays from 3pm to 8pm.

San Antonio Museum of Art
MUSEUM

(SAMA; Map p94; www.samuseum.org; 200 W Jones Ave; adult/child under 13yr $10/free, 4-9pm Tue & 10am-noon Sun free; ⊙10am-5pm Wed, Thu, Sat & Sun, to 9pm Tue & Fri) Housed in the original 1880s **Lone Star Brewery** (a piece of art in itself), the San Antonio Museum of Art is home to an impressive trove of Latin American art, including Spanish Colonial, Mexican and pre-Columbian – one of the most comprehensive collections in the US. Beyond Latin American works, the museum holds a little of everything, from Egyptian antiquities to contemporary abstracts, as well as an impressive Asian wing with a collection of Chinese ceramics, paintings and decorative items.

The museum is off Broadway St just north of downtown.

San Antonio Botanical Gardens
GARDENS

(Map p94; ☑ 210-207-3250; www.sabot.org; 555 Funston Pl; adult/child 3-13yr $10/7; ⊙9am-5pm) This expertly tended, 38-acre garden complex showcases native Texas flora. There's also a rose garden and a wonderful conservatory, with a bit of everything from equatorial rainforest to desert plants. Call or go online for a calendar of special events – from concerts

under the stars and yoga classes to bird walks and summer classes for children.

The strolling garden was designed and created by a 26th-generation gardener and one of Japan's living national treasures from the island of Kyūshū – specifically the city of Kumamoto, which is also home to one of Japan's most revered traditional gardens, Suizenji Park. A few of that famous garden's elements appear here.

DoSeum
MUSEUM

(San Antonio Children's Museum; Map p94; ☑ 210-212-4453; www.thedoseum.org; 2800 Broadway; $12; ⊙10am-5pm Mon-Fri, 9am-5pm Sat, noon-5pm Sun; ⓘ) This place is perfect for the 10-and-under set. Got toddlers? Head to Little Town and its miniature-sized businesses. Older kids will get a kick out of the Spy Academy, where there may or may not be a secret passage leading out of the library. There's a fun treehouse outside, too.

Japanese Tea Garden
GARDENS

(Map p94; ☑ 210-212-4814; www.sanantonio.gov/ ParksAndRec; 3853 N St Marys St; ⊙dawn-dusk) **FREE** Hard to believe that this lovely, tranquil place was just a clever way to hide a hole in the ground. What started out as an eyesore of a quarry nearly 100 years ago was transformed into a Japanese-style strolling garden, with stone bridges, floral displays and a 60ft waterfall. The garden is meant to be enjoyed year-round, but it's especially pretty in spring, when the flowers are in bloom.

Brackenridge Park
PARK

(Map p94; www.brackenridgepark.org; 3700 N St Marys St; ⊙5am-11pm; ⓘ) North of downtown near Trinity University, this 343-acre park is a great place to spend the day with your family. In addition to the **San Antonio Zoo** (Map p94; ☑ 210-734-7184; www.sazoo. org; 3903 N St Marys St; adult/child $14.25/11.25; ⊙9am-5pm Mon-Fri, to 6pm Sat & Sun; ⓘ), you'll find the **Kiddie Amusement Park** (Map p94; ☑ 210-824-4351; www.kiddiepark.com; 3015 Broadway; 1 ticket $2.50, 6 tickets $11.25, day pass

Downtown San Antonio

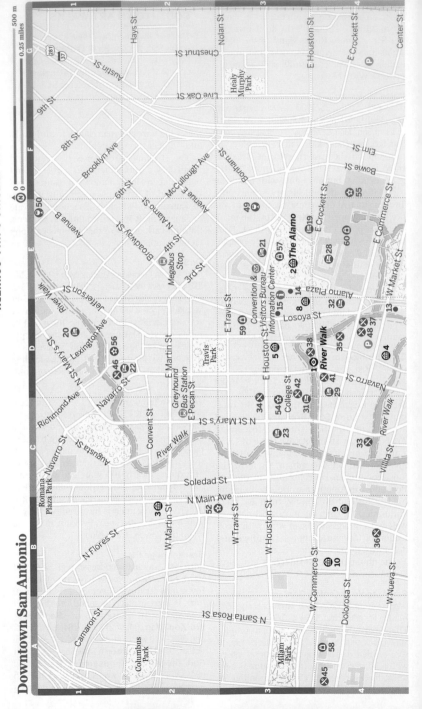

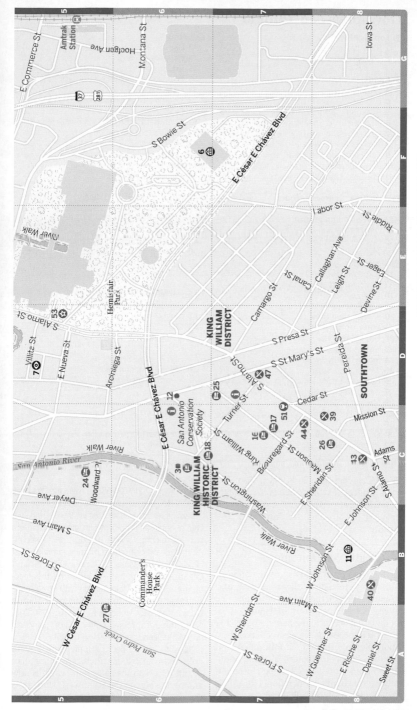

E Commerce St
Amtrak Station
Hochgen Ave
Montana St
S Bowie St
6
E César E Chávez Blvd
Tabor St
Riddle St
Eager St
Canal St
Carrango St
Callaghan Ave
Leigh St
Devine St
River Walk
Hemisfair Park
S Alamo St
53
Villita St
7
E Nueva St
KING WILLIAM DISTRICT
S Presa St
S St Mary's St
Pereida St
SOUTHTOWN
12
San Antonio Conservation Society
E César E Chávez Blvd
Arciniega St
25
S Alamo St
47
Cedar St
51
Mission St
39
Turner St
17
44
26
1
King William St
Beauregard St
Madison St
18
KING WILLIAM HISTORIC DISTRICT
3
Washington St
E Sheridan St
13
Adams St
S Alamo St
E Johnson St
24
Woodward
Dwyer Ave
San Antonio River
River Walk
S Main Ave
11
W Johnson St
S Main Ave
40
Commander's House Park
S Flores St
W Sheridan St
W Guenther St
E Rische St
Daniel St
Sweet St
27
W César E Chávez Blvd
San Pedro Creek
S Flores St

Downtown San Antonio

$13; ◎10am-7pm Wed-Sun Mar-Aug, 10am-7pm Fri-Sun Sep-Feb; ⊞), the *Brackenridge Eagle* miniature train ($3.50), an old-fashioned carousel ($2.50) and the **Japanese Tea Gardens**.

◎ Greater San Antonio

Leaving downtown yields a greater breadth of options, including theme parks and museums. With all the firepower in the area, the city is teeming with military museums. But note that access to the bases is restricted and you'll need to get visitor's passes – obtainable only through certain gates, and even then subject to change – so bring photo ID. Sometimes the bases may be closed entirely except to military personnel and their dependents, so always call ahead.

McNay Art Museum   MUSEUM
(Map p94; ☎210-824-5368; www.mcnayart.org; 6000 N New Braunfels Ave; adult/child $10/free, special exhibits extra; ◎10am-4pm Tue, Wed & Fri, to 9pm Thu, to 5pm Sat, noon-5pm Sun, grounds 7am-7pm Mar-Oct, to 6pm Nov-Feb) In addition to seeing paintings by household names such as Van Gogh, Picasso, Matisse, Renoir, O'Keeffe and Cézanne, half the fun is wandering the spectacular Spanish Colonial revival–style mansion that was the private residence of Marion Koogler McNay. Upon her death in 1950, McNay left her impressive collection of European and American modern art to the city.

It has since been supplemented with even more art: today there are more than 20,000 pieces in the collection, which is now among the best in the Southwest. Don't miss the contemporary works – local artist Kelly

O'Connor's *Magnetic Fields* is an eye-catching look at the dark side of pop-culture classics.

The Stieren Center for Exhibitions was added in June 2008. While it doesn't integrate seamlessly with the original mansion (the center describes itself as a 'translucent two-story box'), it does add 45,000 sq ft of exhibition space for rotating shows.

Six Flags Fiesta Texas　　　AMUSEMENT PARK
(✆ 210-697-5050;　www.sixflags.com/fiestatexas; 17000 IH-10 W, exit 555; adult/child under 48in $75/59; ⊗ hours vary, daily Jun-Aug, Sat & Sun only Sep-May; ⊕) You don't have to be a kid to enjoy Fiesta Texas – this popular theme park has plenty of rides that you must be 'this tall' to enjoy. Of course, there are also more than 25 kids' rides for the vertically challenged, as well as swimming pools and water rides over in the White Water Bay area (open May to mid-September).

The setting – against a limestone quarry that looks similar to the Arizona desert – is dramatic, and there's plenty of music and other live performances. Parking is $20.32.

San Antonio Missions
National Historical Park　　HISTORIC BUILDING
(Map p94; ✆ visitor center 210-932-1001; www.nps. gov/saan; 6701 San José Dr; ⊗ 9am-5pm) Spain's missionary presence can best be felt at the ruins of the four missions south of town: **Concepción** (807 Mission Rd; ⊗ 9am-5pm; 1731), **San José** (1720), **San Juan** (9101 Graf Rd; ⊗ 10am-5pm; 1731) and **Espada** (p102;

1745–56). Religious services are still held in the mission churches and the mariachi Mass at noon on Sunday at San José church is a San Antonio tradition.

From downtown, VIA transit bus 42 goes to Concepción and San José. Bus 36 runs from downtown to Mission San Juan. **Alamo Trolley tours** (www.thealamotrolley.com) visit San José and Concepción. Otherwise, rent a bicycle or drive. From downtown, take St Marys St south until it becomes Mission Rd, then follow the brown signs indicating the direction to the missions

Mission San José　　　HISTORIC BUILDING
(Map p94; ✆ visitor center 210-932-1001; www.nps. gov/saan; 6701 San José Dr; ⊗ 9am-5pm) **FREE** Known in its time as the Queen of the Missions, San José is certainly the largest and arguably the most beautiful of all the sites on the Mission Trail (p101). Because it's a little more remote and pastoral, surrounded by thick stone walls, you can really get a sense of what life was like here in the 18th and 19th centuries. It's also the location of the main **visitor center** for San Antonio Missions National Historical Park, which oversees the four mission sites.

Ranger-led tours (10am, 11am, 2pm and 3pm) cover life in the mission and show up-close the magnificent church and its famous **rose window**, a stunningly carved masterpiece attached to the sacristy. The best time to visit is absolutely on Sundays at noon, when

---

MISSION TRAIL

Spain's missionary presence can best be felt at the ruins of the four missions south of town, all overseen by the National Park Service as part of the **San Antonio Missions National Historical Park**. The main park visitor center is at **Mission San José**, which is the best place to start before exploring the missions. You'll find helpful trip-planning information on the park website.

The San Antonio missions were constructed in the early 18th century as part of an effort to provide way-stations and staging areas for Spanish colonial expansion to the north. The native Coahuiltecans, already under pressure from other nomadic Native American tribes pushing down from the north, showed a willingness to convert to Christianity, and labored for the colonial Spanish priests in order to receive food and protection at the missions.

Constructed in what is now downtown, the first and most impressive mission was what would come to be known as the **Alamo** (p92). With the destruction by war or disease of many East Texas missions, the Spanish quickly built four more missions south of the Alamo, now collectively known as the **Mission Trail**. Religious services are still held in the mission churches.

The new **Mission Reach**, an 8-mile extension of the River Walk, connects downtown with all four missions. South of the Blue Star Arts Complex, the River Walk becomes a pretty walking and cycling trail, open from dawn to dusk.

they hold a **mariachi Mass** (www.missionsan josechurch.org).

Mission San José is the second mission as you head south from downtown.

Mission Espada   HISTORIC BUILDING
(☑ visitor center 210-932-1001; www.nps.gov/ saan; 10040 Espada Rd; ⊘ 10am-5pm) FREE The southernmost mission on the Mission Trail (p101) and part of San Antonio Missions National Historical Park, this site is home to the oldest mission in the east-Texas chain, dating to 1690. The church here was built between 1745 and 1756. This is the best place to check out the historic *acequia* (aqueduct) – the missions' irrigation system that's still in use today and has been designated as a Historic Civil Engineering Landmark.

Fort Sam Houston   HISTORIC SITE
(Map p94; ☑ 210-221-1886; www.facebook.com/pg/ FSHMuseum; ⊘ 10am-4pm Tue-Sat) FREE 'Fort Sam' – as it's known 'round here – is ready to enlist you for a little military history. Its claims to fame? The Apache chief Geronimo was held here for 40 days, and it was also the site of the first military flight in US history, in 1910. And it's home to several historic buildings with designated museums. You'll need a photo ID to enter the grounds of the base.

The oldest building at Fort Sam (and Geronimo's short-term residence) is the **Quadrangle** (Map p94; ☑ 210-221-1232; 1400 E Grayson St; ⊘ 8am-5pm Mon-Fri, noon-6pm Sat & Sun) FREE, built in 1876. Today the Quadrangle is open to the public, and it leads through

---

BUILT ON BEER

San Antonio was once a brewing town, home to two of Texas' largest breweries: the Lone Star Brewery and Pearl Brewery were both established by German settlers in the late 1800s. And while both of them eventually shut down, they left behind two remarkable buildings.

The Lone Star Brewery has provided an impressive setting for the **San Antonio Museum of Art** (p97), which opened in 1981. And the old Pearl Brewery has received a massive face-lift as part of the new **Pearl development** (p114) north of downtown, including shops, cafes, restaurants and the stunning **Hotel Emma** (p106). Looks like beer wasn't the only good thing to come out of these breweries.

---

to a sort of petting zoo: deer have been kept here for more than 100 years, and rabbits, ducks and chickens abound. It's also home to the **Fort Sam Houston Museum**, where you can learn more about the history of the fort and the soldiers once stationed there.

In the northeast section of the grounds, the **US Army Medical Department Museum** (AMEDD; Map p94; ☑ 210-221-6358; www.face book.com/ameddmuseum; Bldg 1046, 3898 Stanley Rd; ⊘ 10am-4pm Tue-Sat) FREE has a display of army medical gear from the US and several other countries, including Germany, the former Soviet Union, Vietnam and China, and a cool collection of restored ambulances, helicopters and a hospital rail car. But what makes it really worth the trip is the collection of Civil War surgical gear, notably the disturbing saws and portable amputation kits.

🏃 Activities

Apart from Brackenridge Park (p97) and the Mission Trail (p101), San Antonio is short on places to enjoy the great outdoors. You've usually got to head into the Hill Country or drive north on I-35 to the aquatic wonderlands of New Braunfels, Gruene and San Marcos, where you can go swimming and tubing to your heart's content on local rivers and at amusement parks. Golfers are in luck here, however.

⛳ Golf

San Antonio is a favorite golf destination, thanks to the region's mild year-round climate. Rates vary from $26 to tote your own bag around a public course to more than $112 to play at a private resort.

Brackenridge Golf Course   GOLF
(Map p94; ☑ 210-226-5612; www.alamocitygolf trail.com; 2315 Ave B; 18 holes Mon-Fri/Sat & Sun $50/60) A municipal golf course north of downtown in Brackenridge Park (p97).

Olmos Basin Golf Course   GOLF
(Map p94; ☑ 210-826-4041; www.alamocitygolf trail.com; 7022 McCullough Ave; 18 holes Mon-Thu/ Fri-Sun $26/31) This popular municipal golf course is located in Olmos Basin Park, about 7 miles north of downtown. Good for all levels of players.

Cedar Creek Golf Course   GOLF
(☑ 210-695-5050; www.alamocitygolftrail.com; 8250 Vista Colina; 18 holes Mon-Fri/Sat & Sun $26/31) The city's most remote municipal course is in far northwest San Antonio.

🏃 Hiking & Cycling

Biking or strolling around Brackenridge Park, along the Mission Trail and along the River Walk makes for a nice outing when the weather is mild. Check www.visitsanantonio.com for a list of suggested cycling routes.

B-Cycle CYCLING
(🖳 210-281-0101; www.sanantonio.bcycle.com; day/monthly pass $10/18) The B-Cycle racks you'll see all around downtown make hopping on a bike convenient – not to mention tempting. It's great for sightseeing outside of downtown; just dock your bike at a station when you're done using it and the meter stops. Come back when you're ready, hop on any bike and go.

You'll find B-Cycle stations at most major tourist destinations, from the northernmost station at the Witte Museum south to the Pearl District, the Alamo, near the River Walk, and all four missions. The River Walk is closed to cycling in the heart of downtown, but you can cycle along the river further out. Download the free B-Cycle smartphone app for route details or ask about routes at the visitor center (p115).

The pricing structure is a little complicated, but it could end up saving you quite a bit of money over an all-day rental. A day pass (which you can pay for online or at one of the stations) allows you a day's worth of unlimited bike trips of up to 60 minutes each (there's a charge of $2 for every 30 minutes beyond that). By returning and checking out a new bike once every hour, you'll pay only the day-pass fee.

Abel's Bicycle Repair & Rental CYCLING
(Map p94; 🖳 210-542-6272; www.abelsbicycleshop.com; 1119 Ada St; bike rental per day $30) If you want to rent a bike for the whole day, try Abel's. They'll even deliver them free of charge to the downtown area.

Friedrich Wilderness Park HIKING
(🖳 210-207-3781; www.sanantonio.gov/parksandrec; 21395 Milsa Rd, north of Loop 1604; ⊙ 5am-11pm) This 600-acre park near Six Flags Fiesta Texas (p101) is just for hikers. It has 10 miles of walking trails in a Hill Country landscape that are especially worth a detour when wildflowers are blooming in spring.

McAllister Park WALKING, CYCLING
(🖳 210-207-7275; www.sanantonio.gov/parksandrec; 13102 Jones Maltsberger Rd; ⊙ 5am-11pm) For a taste of the Hill Country without venturing outside the city limits, head to this 976-acre park. It has about 7 miles of trails for walking and cycling; one of the trails is also wheelchair-accessible. Also has a 1.5-acre dog park.

🏃 Water Sports

Splashtown SWIMMING
(Map p94; 🖳 210-227-1400; www.splashtownsa.com; 3600 N IH-35; adult/child under 48in tall $33/$28, after 4pm $17; ⊙ from 10:30am Jun-Aug; 🚻) San Antonio can get awfully hot and sticky in summer, and one of the best remedies is putting on your swimsuit and heading to the water park. Splashtown is where you'll find Texas' biggest wave pool, plus waterslides galore – grab your inner tube! There are also gentler floating rides and a special 'Kids Kove' for preschoolers.

Call or check the website to find out the schedule before heading out. Rates are slightly lower Monday through Friday.

Mission Reach Paddling Trail CANOEING, KAYAKING
(Map p94; www.tpwd.texas.gov) This brand-new paddling trail stretches 8 miles along the San Antonio River, from **Roosevelt Park**, just south of downtown, to a take-out near Mission Espada, with numerous access points along the way. For kayak rentals and shuttles, try Mission Kayak.

Mission Kayak KAYAKING
(Map p94; www.missionkayak.com; 330 Mission Pkwy, Espada Park; 1hr kayak rental $20, kayak trips $40-70) Rents kayaks at Espada Park's Davis Lake, beside the San Antonio River and the River Walk; also runs shuttles for guided and self-guided paddle trips on the San Antonio River, including a trip on the new Mission Reach Paddling Trail. There's no office – look for the kayak trailer in the parking lot.

🏃 Tours

The downtown visitors center (p115) has information about guided (and other) tours.

Rio San Antonio Cruises CRUISE
(Map p98; 🖳 210-244-5700; www.riosanantonio.com; 706 River Walk; tour $10, river taxi one way $10, 24hr pass from $12; ⊙ 9am-9pm) These 40-minute narrated cruises give you a good visual overview of the river and a light history lesson. You can buy your tickets online or get them on the waterfront at any of the stops. No reservations are necessary and tours leave every 15 to 20 minutes.

You'll find a ticket booth and a boarding point for the cruise at 706 River Walk. Check the website for additional ticket booths and boarding points.

The same company also operates a **river taxi**, stopping at 39 points along the river. You can hail them from the River Walk (look for the Rio Taxi sign). You can now track their location via GPS on the website.

Alamo City Ghost Tours
WALKING

(Map p98; ☑ 210-336-7831; www.alamocityghost tours.com; ⊘ tours 8pm & 8:30pm) Offers two great options: the After Dark Ghost Hunt (8:30pm, adult/children aged 5-12 years $18/13), a 90-minute walk through the historic King William neighborhood; and the Haunted House Tour (8pm, $25), which explores a (supposedly) haunted former residence, now used as a Masonic Lodge. Meet at the corner of S St Marys and King William Sts.

SegCity Ghost Tours
TOURS

(Map p98; ☑ 210-224-0773; www.segcity.com; 124 Losoya St; tours $65) A fun twist on predictable ghost tours? Do it on a Segway. (So it means if you do see a ghost, it'll be easier to outrun it.) Like outlaw history? Take the Wild Bunch Tour through the old Red Light District, where Butch and Sundance spent some time. This company also offers regular old (nonhaunted) tours of downtown.

San Antonio Trolley Tours
TOURS

(Map p98; ☑ 210-492-4144; www.citytoursinc.com; 321 Alamo Plaza; 1hr tour $22, Hopper Pass $24; ⊘ 9:30am-4:30pm) Get a quick overview of the town with a one-hour narrated tour, or spend a few dollars more for a two-day Hopper Pass that lets you get off and on at all the attractions. If you're looking to get out of town, there are also Hill Country tours and wine tours.

✲ Festivals & Events

Fiesta San Antonio
CULTURAL

(☑ 210-227-5191; www.fiesta-sa.org; ⊘ Apr) For over 10 days in late April there are river parades, the Battle of the Flowers (p104) street parade, carnivals, Tejano music, dancing and tons of food in a mammoth, citywide party (p112).

Battle of the Flowers
CULTURAL

(www.battleofflowers.org; ⊘ Apr) This grand parade honors the fallen at the Alamo and celebrates the Texan victory at San Jacinto. Dating back to 1891, today it is part of the Fiesta San

Antonio (p104) celebration and draws more than 350,000 spectators.

San Antonio Stock Show & Rodeo
RODEO

(www.sarodeo.com; ⊘ Feb) Big-name country-music performers like Brad Paisley, Keith Urban and Willie Nelson perform after each night's rodeo; takes place over 16 days in mid-February.

Rodeo events include steer wrestling and tie-down roping in which animals are wrestled to the ground, sometimes causing injury to the animal. Rodeo events such as this are often criticized by animal welfare groups.

Fiesta Noche del Rio
PERFORMING ARTS

(www.fiestanochesa.com; ⊘ May-Sep) All summer long, the Fiesta Noche del Rio brings Latin music to the Arneson River Theater in a series of concerts and dance performances.

🛏 Sleeping

Many hotels are booked solid, with high rates, during major sporting events, city festivals and large conventions. Summer rates are also high.

Budget lodging downtown is scarce, but there's a good selection of midrange motels. Cheaper options cluster near the airport and along the interstates.

B&Bs ensconced in fine old homes in historic and more residential areas of the city (especially the King William District) are generally good value.

Downtown

For many large River Walk properties, you can often find special discounts when you book online. Most will have overnight parking fees.

★ City View Inn & Suites at Sunset Station
MOTEL $$

(Map p94; ☑ 210-222-2220; www.cityviewinnsa.com; 1306 E Commerce St; r $99-109; P ❋ ❋ 🐾) Just beyond I-37, less than a mile from the Alamo, sits a skinny little three-story building full of clean, new rooms. Amenities are few, but if you're just looking for a place to park your bags, this friendly place is great. It's also just two blocks from the Amtrak station – handy if you're arriving by train.

Menger Hotel
HISTORIC HOTEL $$

(Map p98; ☑ 800-345-9285, 210-223-4361; www.mengerhotel.com; 204 Alamo Plaza; r from $176; P ❋ ❋ 🐾 🐾 🐾) Built next to the Alamo just 23 years after the famous battle, this historic hotel has hosted Oscar Wilde, Mae West and

Teddy Roosevelt; at night, you might even see a ghost tour gathered near the lobby. New additions from over the decades make it a bit rambling. Rooms vary in size and decor; 'Victorian lite' best describes the latter.

For more history, pick up a self-guided-tour brochure at the front desk. Valet-only parking is $28 per day; the pet fee is $125 per stay.

Crockett Hotel
HOTEL $$
(Map p98; ☑ 210-225-6500; www.crocketthotel. com; 320 Bonham St; r $189-219, ste $299; P ⊛ ❄ 🖵 🐾) No wonder pictures of the Alamo are always tightly cropped: pull back and you can see the Crockett's sign hovering just behind the fort. (In Texas, they call that 'spittin' distance.') Rooms are basic but stylish and pleasant. There's an outdoor pool and Jacuzzi, plus a great complimentary breakfast buffet. Self-parking and valet parking are both $24 per day. The pet fee is $60 per pet per stay.

Emily Morgan Hotel
BOUTIQUE HOTEL $$
(Map p98; ☑ 210-225-5100; www.emilymorgan hotel.com; 705 E Houston St; r $219-239, ste $249-750; P ⊛ ❄ 🖵 🐾) The name sounds as though it should be awash in floral prints and lace, but this historic hotel right behind the Alamo is actually pretty stylish, and is now a Hilton property. The boutique-style rooms are clean, large and enjoy all the luxury amenities.

(The names are similar, but note that the Emily Morgan Hotel is not the Hotel Emma (p106), which recently opened in the Pearl District.) Parking is valet-only and is $35 per day. The pet fee per stay is $50.

Riverwalk Vista
B&B $$
(Map p98; ☑ 210-223-3200, 866-898-4782; www. riverwalkvista.com; 262 Losoya St; r from $174; ⊖ ⊛ @) Soaring ceilings, enormous windows, exposed brick walls, crisp, white bedding – this is simplicity done right. And just because the decor is simple doesn't mean they don't pamper: there are still plenty of niceties, like flat-screen TVs, leather chairs and feather blankets. Enjoy a complimentary glass of wine in the early evening. Breakfast included.

Parking is at a nearby garage with rates of $12 to $16 per day.

Hotel Havana
HOTEL $$
(Map p98; ☑ 210-222-2008; www.havanasan antonio.com; 1015 Navarro St; r $115-280; P ⊖ ⊛ @ ❄ 🐾) Texas design guru and hotelier Liz Lambert has turned her sights on revamping a few lucky properties such as this one, judiciously adding eclectic touches – a retro pink refrigerator, for example – to her clean,

elegant designs. We'd love more electrical outlets and more lighting in the rooms, but the Texas goodies in the fridge? Thumbs up.

The bar-restaurant Ocho (p107), set in a glassed-in conservatory overlooking the river, is a great spot for a happy-hour drink or a bite. Parking is $17 per night; pet fee is $25 per visit.

El Tropicano Hotel
HOTEL $$
(Map p98; ☑ 877-214-9768, 210-223-9461; www. eltropicanohotel.com; 110 Lexington Ave; r $159-179, ste $199; P ⊖ ⊛ ❄ 🖵 🐾) At El Tropicano, the retro-tropical vibe is a little old-school Vegas, a little Miami Beach – the only thing missing is the tiki bar. But even though this breezy hotel originally opened in 1962, a fresh, mid-century modern lobby and updated rooms make it feel fun instead of old. (The $18 daily parking fee, however, can dampen the fun.)

Valet parking is $21 per day. The pet fee is $50 per stay.

Inn on the Riverwalk
B&B $$
(Map p98; ☑ 210-225-6333, 800-730-0019; www. innontheriverwalksa.com; 129 Woodward Pl; r $189-339; P ⊖ ⊛ ❄) Presided over by a venerable pecan tree, this B&B is in a beautiful, peaceful setting by the river. Each cheery room has its own private bath, with the more expensive digs equipped with a Jacuzzi, private porch or balcony. Full made-to-order breakfast (included) is offered in the morning. *Migas*, anyone?

La Quinta Inn & Suites – Downtown
HOTEL $$
(Map p98; ☑ 210-212-5400; www.lq.com; 100 W César Chavez Blvd; r from $129; P ⊛ @ ❄ 🖵) It's just over a 1-mile walk to the Alamo from this all-suites La Quinta, where rooms preen with a touch of modern style (we're looking at you, hip green chair by the closet with nothing to do but look cool). The location gets points for its proximity to a well-stocked H-E-B minimarket and free on-site parking. Breakfast included.

Omni La Mansion del Rio
HISTORIC HOTEL $$$
(Map p98; ☑ 210-518-1000; www.lamansion. com; 112 College St; r/ste from $269/799; P ⊖ ⊛ @ 🖵 🐾) This fabulous downtown property was born out of 19th-century religious school buildings in the Spanish-Mexican hacienda style. It's on a quiet stretch of the River Walk and its discreet oasis attracts stars and other notables. Enjoy in-room spa services, swim in the outdoor heated pool or unwind at the hotel's exceptional restaurant, **Las Canarias** (Map p98; ☑ 210-518-1063; www.omnihotels.com;

112 College St; mains breakfast $11-19, lunch $12-21, dinner $27-49; ☺ 6:30am-2pm Mon-Sat, 6:30-10am & 11am-2:30pm Sun, 5:30-10pm daily).

Valet-only parking is $39 per night. The pet fee is $50 per stay.

Mokara Hotel & Spa HOTEL $$$
(Map p98; ☑ 210-396-5800, 866-605-1212; www.mokarahotels.com; 212 W Crockett St; r $349-429, ste $999; ☺ ✳ @ 🔊 ≋ 🛏) If you really want to go all out, this luxurious hotel (formerly the Watermark) is a good place to get pampered, with top-of-the-line amenities and an on-site spa. Its serenity stands in stark contrast to the tourist scene waiting just downstairs – perfect for anyone who wants to just draw the blinds and enjoy some relaxation.

The pet fee is $50 per stay.

Hotel Valencia BOUTIQUE HOTEL $$$
(Map p98; ☑ 210-227-9700; www.hotelvalencia-riverwalk.com; 150 E Houston St; r $199-339, ste $469; P ☺ ✳ 🔊) Faux-mink throws, molded concrete, light shining through perforated metal – this place is all about texture. It could have been transported from New York City, both for its minimalist-chic style and the size of some of the smaller rooms – a hip option for those who eschew chains and historic hotels.

Parking is valet-only and $34 per night.

🛏 King William District

This historic district is known for its beautiful homes, so it's no surprise that the majority of offerings here are B&Bs.

★ King William Manor B&B $$
(Map p98; ☑ 210-222-0144; www.kingwilliammanor.com; 1037 S Alamo St; r $129-165; P ☺ ✳ 🔊 ≋) In a neighborhood known for beautiful old houses and B&Bs, this grand, Greek Revival mansion occupying a large corner lot still manages to stand out. Maybe it's the columns, the sprawling lawn or perhaps the wraparound porches. The inside lives up to the exterior, with understatedly elegant rooms, some of which are enormous.

A Yellow Rose Inn B&B $$
(Map p98; ☑ 210-229-9903; www.ayellowrose.com; 229 Madison St; r $100-200; P ☺ ✳ 🔊) True to its name, this butterscotch-colored house is a beauty. Spacious rooms are tastefully furnished, with well-thought-out amenities like fresh flowers, snacks, sodas and juice. We love their flexible breakfast policy, which allows you to take your breakfast in your room or skip it altogether and pay a little less.

Brackenridge House B&B B&B $$
(Map p98; ☑ 210-271-3442; www.brackenridgehouse.com; 230 Madison St; r $159-174, ste $164-179; P ☺ ✳ 🔊) This hospitable B&B serves up a gourmet three-course breakfast (included). The rooms are of the frilly sort, with quilts, floral prints and lace, but they're also practical, with bar fridges and microwaves.

Ogé House B&B $$$
(Map p98; ☑ 210-223-2353; www.nobleinns.com; 209 Washington St; r $199-259, ste $299-359; ✳ 🔊) Ogé Inn epitomizes the antebellum southern mansion: expansive, gazebo-graced grounds slope down to the riverfront, ancient pecan trees shade the lawns and rose gardens bloom in the sun. This is definitely the most stately of lodgings in the King William district. No children under 13 allowed. The property is managed by Noble Inns, which also runs **Carriage House** (Map p98; ☑ 210-223-2353; www.nobleinns.com; 202 Washington St; r/ste $169/229; P ☺ ✳ 🔊 ≋) and **Jackson House** (Map p98; ☑ 210-223-2353; www.nobleinns.com; 107 Madison St; r $159-199, ste $219; P ☺ ✳ 🔊).

Afternoon snacks and evening aperitifs hint at the genteel age in which this house was constructed (c 1857). Velvet drapes and crystal chandeliers hang in the formal dining room; you can eat there, or you might also take your complimentary breakfast at the wrought-iron tables on the terrace. (At the odd hour that something is not being served, you can help yourself to the honor bar in the parlor.) Toile and floral patterns decorate the luxurious linens in large guest rooms and suites, while French revival and other imperial antiques are de rigueur throughout.

🛏 Brackenridge Park & Around

This neighborhood offers relief from downtown prices, but still keeps you close to the action.

★ Hotel Emma BOUTIQUE HOTEL $$$
(Map p94; ☑ 210-448-8300; www.thehotelemma.com; 136 E Grayson St; r/ste from $395/895; P ✳ 🔊 ≋) Is steampunk-glam a thing? We hope so. By this new Pearl District hotel, we hope so. Common areas impress with a striking mix of Victoria-era decor and bold industrial fixtures, which trace to the building's days as a 19th-century brewhouse. Rooms evoke the charms of a stylish but understated Texas

ranch. The nicest amenity? The guests-only library, home to 3700 books.

With three on-site eateries, a rooftop pool and rooms with terrace fireplaces, you'll never want to leave the grounds. And everyone looks good in the sultry confines of the **Sternewirth Bar**, where you can squeeze into an old beer tank for cocktails and camaraderie. The hotel is named for Emma Koehler, who ran the brewery in the early 1900s.

Greater San Antonio

Admiralty RV Resort
CAMPGROUND **$**
(☑ 210-647-7878, 877-236-4715; www.admiraltyv resort.com; 1485 N Ellison Dr; RV sites regular $50-60, luxury $70; P 🛜 🍃 ♿ 🐾) On the western edge of town, this top-notch RV park with a large swimming pool and plenty of shade is convenient to SeaWorld, which runs a free shuttle service to the campground during summer. Rental cottages ($120) are also on site. Discounts are available for weekly stays and association memberships (including AARP). No tents permitted.

Travelodge Inn & Suites –
San Antonio Airport
MOTEL **$**
(Map p94; ☑ 210-599-4204; www.travelodge.com; 2383 NE Loop 410; r/ste from $79/89; P ♿ ❄ 🛜 ♿) Just north of downtown, this anachronistic place feels like it belongs in the Hill Country more than off an interstate, with cabin-style rooms, ranch-style porches and country-style furnishings. With its playground and picnic tables, it's great for families. Breakfast included.

Hyatt Place Northwest
HOTEL **$$**
(☑ 210-561-0099; www.sanantonionorthwest.place. hyatt.com; 4303 Hyatt Place Dr; r $139-144; P ♿ ❄ @ 🛜 🍃 ♿) Almost everything out near Six Flags (p101) is a chain, but this awesome little Hyatt Place is one of the best. It's clean and fresh, with spacious rooms and a smartly modern decor, and it's just 6 miles from the park. Flat-screen TVs, continental breakfast included and free computer access and printing make it a bargain.

Westin La Cantera Resort
RESORT **$$$**
(☑ 210-558-6500, 855-499-2960; www.destination hotels.com; 16641 La Cantera Pkwy; r/ste from $399/599; P ♿ ❄ @ 🛜 🍃) Standard rooms are elegant but on the small side, so you'll enjoy this resort most if you're willing to get out and take advantage of the five pools, several hot tubs, golf course, tennis courts, health club and spa. It's almost outside of town, and the

overwhelming offerings might upstage your other sightseeing activities.

This place must be trying to break the world record for most hospitality awards ever. *Condé Nast Traveler, Golf Digest* and *AAA Four Diamond* are among those that have recognized the destination property.

Resort fee is $32 per day.

🍴 Eating

A location along the pretty River Walk (p93) gives any restaurant instant atmosphere – especially when there's a patio involved. Prices are typically high. The Pearl District is packed tight with both high-end and midrange restaurants. Hip eateries in Southtown tend to be inexpensive, and north of downtown around Brackenridge Park are tons of budget dining options.

Naturally, some of the best cooking in town is Tex-Mex and Mexican.

🍴 Downtown

Schilo's German Delicatessen
DELI **$**
(Map p98; ☑ 210-223-6692; www.schilos.com; 424 E Commerce St; mains breakfast $6-8, lunch & dinner $6-9; ⏰ 7am-8:30pm Mon-Sat) Schilo's has certainly earned its ambience: this German restaurant has been around since 1917 and looks the part, down to the wooden booths and the elaborate pattern of the hexagonal floor tiles. Specialties include wonderful split-pea soup, baked goods, fresh pumpernickel bread, German beer and homemade root beer.

Justin's Ice Cream Company
ICE CREAM **$**
(Map p98; ☑ 210-222-2707; 245 E Commerce St, River Walk, small/large serving $4/6; ⏰ 11am-11pm) Ready to stop and rest for a bit? Cool off with a dish of house-made Italian-style ice cream, gelato or sorbet at a table overlooking the river. Look for it across the river from the Mansion del Rio Hotel.

Candy's Old Fashioned Burgers
BURGERS **$**
(Map p98; ☑ 210-222-9659; www.candysburgers. com; 115 S Flores St; mains $5-11; ⏰ 10am-3pm Mon & Tue, to 8pm Wed-Fri) This little place across from the Bexar County Courthouse has a tiny dining room with a nostalgic, small-town feel. If that sounds a bit quaint, wait till you see the whoppin' burgers and big fried-catfish platters it serves up.

Ocho at Hotel Havana
CUBAN **$$**
(Map p98; ☑ 210-222-2008; www.havanasan antonio.com; 1015 Navarro St; mains breakfast $14-16, lunch & dinner $10-25; ⏰ 7am-10pm Sun-Thu,

to midnight Fri & Sat; 🕾) You're never going to stumble across Ocho while roaming the River Walk or checking out the King William District, but this hidden-away lounge next to Hotel Havana is worth seeking out. The Cuban-inspired menu is not extensive, but it's excellent, serving everything from breakfast to late-night cocktails.

A glassed-in conservatory that looks onto the northern stretch of the River Walk has been outfitted with chandeliers and velvet furnishings for an eclectic-chic decor that's become hotelier Liz Lambert's trademark. Besides, you came for the ambience, right? If it's a nice evening, you can get there by strolling along the River Walk about 20 minutes north of the main hub.

Mi Tierra Cafe & Bakery
TEX-MEX $$
(Map p98; ☑ 210-225-1262; www.mitierracafe. com; 218 Produce Row; mains $9-29; ⊙24hr) Strands of Christmas lights keep things festive year-round at Mi Tierra, which has been dishing out traditional Mexican food since 1941. This 500-seat behemoth in Market Square sprawls across several dining areas, giving the busy wait staff and strolling mariachis quite a workout. It's also open 24 hours, making it ideal for 3am enchilada cravings.

County Line Smokehouse
BARBECUE $$
(Map p98; ☑ 210-229-1941; www.countyline.com; 111 W Crockett St, River Walk; platters $15-26; ⊙11am-10pm Sun-Thu, to 11pm Fri & Sat) San Antonio isn't known for its barbecues – it's clearly more of a Tex-Mex kind of town – but this outpost of the Austin chain scratches the itch nicely with heaping dishes of brisket, ribs and sausages.

Casa Rio
MEXICAN $$
(Map p98; ☑ 210-225-6718; www.casa-rio.com; 430 E Commerce St, River Walk; mains $9-19; ⊙11am-10pm Sun-Thu, to 11pm Fri & Sat) One of San Antonio's oldest Mexican restaurants, Casa Rio has been around since 1946, and the building itself is a Spanish hacienda that dates back to the colonial period of Texas history. Overall, it's a cheerful (and affordable) place to soak up the River Walk ambience while noshing on tacos, tamales and enchiladas.

Boudro's
TEX-MEX $$$
(Map p98; ☑ 210-224-8484; www.boudros.com; 421 E Commerce St, River Walk; lunch mains $11-18, dinner $22-42; ⊙11am-11pm Sun-Thu, to midnight Fri & Sat) This brightly colored waterside restaurant is hugely popular with locals. Fresh guacamole is made right at your table. The upscale Tex-Mex menu reveals some gourmet surprises,

such as jumbo shrimp and gulf crab enchiladas, mesquite-grilled quail stuffed with wild mushrooms, and achiote-spiced lamb chops. For a lighter option at lunch, the blackened ahi tuna salad is quite nice.

You'll also find first-rate cocktails (try a prickly-pear margarita) and an extensive wine list.

Biga on the Banks
AMERICAN $$$
(Map p98; ☑ 210-225-0722; www.biga.com; 203 S St Marys St, River Walk; mains $19-65; ⊙5:30-10pm Sun-Thu, to 11pm Fri & Sat) This is one of the most justifiably praised restaurants in town, run by chef Bruce Auden. The menu is a wonderful mix of European, Tex-Mex, American and Asian influences and dishes that probably don't cost as much as they should (and certainly not what they could). It's stylish yet welcoming, and the wine list is impressive.

Bohanan's
STEAK $$$
(Map p98; ☑ 210-472-2277; www.bohanans.com; 219 E Houston St; steaks from $45; ⊙5-10pm Mon-Thu, to 11pm Fri & Sat, to 9pm Sun) These people take their steaks seriously – at these prices, so should you. Many people can appreciate a great steak, but you'll treasure the experience even more if you're the type of person who throws around terms such as 'Akaushi beef.' These cows were raised in a humane and healthy fashion, and possibly given pedicures too, from the sound of it.

✕ King William District & Southtown

Lots of fun new places are springing up just a few minutes south of downtown, especially along Alamo St.

Madhatters Tea House & Café
CAFE $
(Map p98; ☑ 210-212-4832; www.madhatterstea. com; 320 Beauregard St; breakfast mains $3-7, sandwiches $7-9, salads $9-12; ⊙7am-6pm Mon-Thu, to 9pm Fri, 8am-9pm Sat, 9am-3pm Sun; 🕾🥤) A cute neighborhood cafe located in a former house, Madhatters is a pleasingly homey place to stop when you're feeling peckish. Breakfast during the week, brunch on the weekends, and soups, sandwiches and great big salads to refuel during the day. Or stop by for an afternoon tea party for two, complete with scones and petit fours ($20).

Guenther House
CAFE $
(Map p98; ☑ 210-227-1061; www.guentherhouse. com; 205 E Guenther St; mains $6-9; ⊙7am-3pm) Located in the Pioneer Flour Mill complex,

this is the kind of place you'd choose if you were meeting up with the gals or taking your mom out to lunch. Their specialty is the champagne chicken enchiladas, but they also serve yummy sandwiches and all-day breakfast.

Liberty Bar   AMERICAN $$
(Map p98; ☑ 210-227-1187; www.liberty-bar.com; 1111 S Alamo St; mains $8-26; ⊙11am-midnight Mon-Fri, from 9am Sat & Sun) The building itself is spectacular: an 1883 home that became a Benedictine convent in 1939 and has now been painted circus-peanut orange. Inside, soaring ceilings and big windows lend an airy vibe, and the menu includes a nice selection of salads, sandwiches and full mains.

In the evening, you can finish your meal with a trip up to the full bar on the 2nd floor.

Rosario's Mexican Cafe   TEX-MEX $$
(Map p98; ☑ 210-223-1806; www.rosariossa.com; 910 S Alamo St; mains lunch $8-11, dinner $10-23; ⊙11am-10pm Mon-Thu, to 11pm Fri & Sat, to 9pm Sun) This lively restaurant is always hopping, with huge windows that let in natural light and wistful glances from hungry onlookers. The Tex-Mex–style food is solid, and the complimentary basket of chips and salsa that show up at your table are better than most.

Feast   TAPAS $$$
(Map p98; ☑ 210-354-1024; www.feastsa.com; 1024 S Alamo St; small plates $7-22, brunch $8-16; ⊙5-10pm Tue-Thu, to 11pm Fri & Sat, 10:30am-2:30pm Sun) The seasonally inspired tapas dishes are solid, but the atmosphere alone is worth the trip to the King William District: clear Lucite chairs, sparkly pendant lights and faux taxidermy come together to provide a whimsically modern feel. The front patio is even more enticing, with twinkling lights beneath a big, shady tree and a gardenlike backdrop.

🍴 Brackenridge Park & Around

This area has some of the best-value eateries in the city. If you have a car, take advantage of the lower prices; most of these restaurants are just five to 10 minutes' drive from downtown. The Pearl District (p114) has tons of great choices.

Cove   AMERICAN $
(Map p94; ☑ 210-227-2683; www.thecove.us; 606 W Cypress St; tacos $4-5, burgers $8-12; ⊙11am-10pm Tue-Thu, to 11pm Fri & Sat, to 8pm Sun; 🐾) This weird, wonderful place is a restaurant, bar, laundromat and car wash. As casual as the restaurant is, the food is top-notch, made

from organic, sustainable meat and produce. Sure, it's just tacos, burgers, salads and appetizers but the food is made with love.

There's even a playground for the kids so you can reward them for all their hard work washing your car.

Green Vegetarian Cuisine   VEGETARIAN $
(Map p94; ☑ 210-320-5865; www.eatatgreen.com; 200 E Grayson St; mains breakfast $4-8, lunch & dinner $8-12; ⊙8am-9pm Mon-Thu, to 8pm Fri, 9am-9pm, closed Sat; 🐾) 🌱 Vegetarians rejoice: San Antonio's first vegetarian restaurant has an appealing location in the Pearl Brewery complex. With dishes like a portabella burger, 'fishless' fish and chips, and enchiladas, it's the kind of place even a meat-eater can enjoy. Not only is it 100% vegetarian, it's also 100% kosher and any meal can be made vegan.

Bakery Lorraine   BAKERY, CAFE $
(Map p94; ☑ 210-862-5582; www.bakerylorraine. com; 306 Pearl Pkwy; pastries $3-6, salads & sandwiches $7-10; ⊙7am-8pm) There's a reason everybody strolling around the Pearl District is carrying a small box labeled Bakery Lorraine – its pastries are delicious. Macaroons. Tarts. Cookies. You won't walk away from this bright place's bakery counter empty-handed. Gourmet sandwiches and a few salads are available at lunch. The patio tables are a pleasant spot on a spring afternoon.

Chris Madrid's   BURGERS $
(Map p94; ☑ 210-735-3552; www.chrismadrids.com; 1900 Blanco Rd; mains $7-10; ⊙11am-10pm Mon-Sat) Two words: tostada burgers. Topping a burger with tortilla chips and refried beans sounds weird, but it works, combining two of our favorite meals into one deliciously unholy alliance. Throw some jalapeños on for a memorable meal.

Pearl District Farmers Market   MARKET $
(Map p94; www.atpearl.com.farmers-market; 312 Pearl Pkwy; ⊙9am-1pm Sat, 10am-2pm Sun) The 40+ food producers and artisans at this bustling market are all based within 150 miles of San Antonio.

Adelante Mexican Food   MEXICAN $
(Map p94; ☑ 210-822-7681; 21 Brees Blvd; mains $7-10; ⊙11am-9pm Tue-Fri, to 4pm Sat; 🐾) This cute Mexican diner is a nice little secret. Located in a strip mall near the McNay Art Museum, it would be easy to overlook, but the inside has the feel of a Mexican *mercado,* with colorful handicrafts right down to the painted

furniture. Plus, the food seems a little lighter than most and doesn't leave you wanting a siesta.

Cash or checks only.

Earl Abel's
AMERICAN $$

(Map p94; ☑ 210-822-3358; www.earlabelsa.com; 1201 Austin Hwy; mains breakfast $6-19, lunch & dinner $8-25; ☺ 7am-9pm Sun-Thu, to 10pm Fri & Sat) Earl Abel's has been feeding San Antonians since 1933. This isn't the original location, but it keeps the tradition alive, with photos and memorabilia from the original. More importantly, the home-style meals (many less than $10) are deliciously satisfying, with breakfast staples served all day.

Josephine Street Cafe
AMERICAN $$

(Map p94; ☑ 210-224-6169; www.josephinestreet.com; 400 E Josephine St; mains $9-23; ☺ 11am-10pm Mon-Thu, to 11pm Fri & Sat, to 9pm Sun) The neon signs in the window advertise 'steak' and 'whisky.' There's a tree growing up through the floor and out the ceiling of the dining room. And the creaky hardwood floors slant more than a little. This isn't the place for fussy foodies – it's for anyone who wants good steak and seafood, hold the fine-dining ambience and prices.

Paloma Blanca
MEXICAN $$

(Map p94; ☑ 210-822-6151; www.palomablanca.net; 5800 Broadway St, Alamo Heights; lunch $8-12, dinner $9-26; ☺ 11am-9pm Mon-Wed, to 10pm Thu & Fri, 10am-10pm Sat, 10am-9pm Sun) There are oodles of great Mexican choices around, but this place sets itself apart with a sleek and stylish ambience – think dim lighting, exposed brick walls and oversize artwork – and outstanding traditional cooking (enchiladas, chiles rellenos, quesadillas).

The downside: it's a long drive (4.5 miles) from downtown.

★ Cured
AMERICAN $$$

(Map p94; ☑ 210-314-3929; www.curedatpearl.com; 306 Pearl Pkwy; lunch $12-28, dinner $13-35; ☺ 11am-3pm & 5-11pm Mon-Fri, 5-11pm Sat, 10am-3pm Sun) Slabs of meat hang smack-dab in the center of the dining room at new-on-the-scene Cured, where the charcuterie platters ($18 to $36) are loaded with meats, spreads, pickles and crackers. At lunch, look for the daily gourmet po'boys and a few salads and sandwiches. Dinner is a carnivore's delight, with pork cheeks, roasted bone marrow, spiced quail and more.

Il Sogno Osteria
ITALIAN $$$

(Map p94; ☑ 210-223-3900; 200 E Grayson St; mains breakfast $8-16, lunch & dinner $13-45; ☺ 7:30am-10am & 11:30am-2pm Tue-Fri, 6-9:30pm Tue-Sat, 9:30am-3pm Sun) This stylish former warehouse space in the Pearl complex is frequently packed with people vying for a shot at the fresh, house-made pastas. Best for groups of four or less, since space is at a premium. If you can swing it, get a front-row seat for the action in the open kitchen by sitting at the bar.

 ## Drinking & Nightlife

Downtown is packed with watering holes, but more interesting choices abound in Southtown, which has more independent-minded nightlife. Most bars stay open until 2am, while a few clubs stay hoppin' until 3am.

San Antonio doesn't have a real club scene, but some dance clubs are huge. Check the local papers about schedules and drop-in classes for tango, salsa, folk and country two-stepping.

 ## Downtown

There's no shortage of beverages of the adult variety around the River Walk. For the best atmosphere, stick to the local and independent bars and avoid the national chains that have also claimed prime downtown real estate.

VFW Post 76
BAR

(Map p94; ☑ 210-223-4581; 10 10th St; ☺ 4-10:30pm Mon-Thu, to 2am Fri & Sat, noon-10:30pm Sun) We're giving this hidden-away joint near the Pearl development a medal for outstanding service in being a dive bar. But don't get us wrong – it's one of the classiest dives you'll ever visit, where hipsters and old-timers chug longnecks side by side in a two-story Victorian that serves as the oldest Veterans of Foreign Wars post in Texas.

Brooklynite
COCKTAIL BAR

(Map p98; ☑ 212-444-0707; www.thebrooklynitesa.com; 516 Brooklyn Ave; ☺ 5pm-2am) Beer and wine are easy to come by in San Antonio, but head here for a creative, handcrafted cocktail. Vintage wallpaper and wingback chairs give the place a dark, Victorian-esque vibe. Sip away your cares with a gin-based 'Photo Booth Kisses,' with hints of raspberry and rose petals, or a classic old-fashioned – all in a fittingly dignified atmosphere.

GAY & LESBIAN SAN ANTONIO

Despite the city's conservative outlook, there's definitely a vibrant LGBT community here. In addition to June's **PrideFest San Antonio**, one of the best times to visit is during **Fiesta San Antonio** (p104).

➡ The River City's gay nightlife scene is concentrated along Main and San Pedro Aves, just north of downtown. (Venues change, but the strips remain the same.)

➡ San Antonio's **LGBT Chamber of Commerce** (www.sagaychamber.com) provides lists of gay-owned and gay-friendly bars, clubs, businesses and other services.

➡ There's nothing low-key about the **Bonham Exchange** (p112): this enormous dance club is dark, loud and packed on weekends.

➡ **Heat** (Map p94; ☑ 210-227-2600; www.heatsa.com; 1500 N Main Ave; before 11pm free; ☺ from 10pm Wed, from 9pm Thu-Sun), an 18-and-up club, is frequently open after hours, catering to a late-night crowd which comes for the huge dancefloor, techno music, theme nights and drag shows.

Menger Bar BAR
(Map p98; ☑ 210-223-4361; www.mengerhotel.com; 204 Alamo Pl; ☺ 11am-midnight Mon-Fri, from noon Sat & Sun) More than 100 years ago, Teddy Roosevelt recruited Rough Riders from this bar – which, incidentally, was a replica of the House of Lords Pub in London. To complete the image, picture a mounted moose head, scant lighting and lots of wood. There probably won't be a local in sight, but the history alone makes it a worthwhile stop.

♀ King William District & Southtown

Refreshingly unpretentious is what you'll find just south of downtown. Several of the restaurants in this neighborhood double as bars, including Liberty Bar (p109) and Rosario's (p100).

★ Friendly Spot Ice House BAR
(Map p98; ☑ 210-224-2337; www.thefriendlyspot. com; 943 S Alamo St; ☺ 3pm-midnight Mon-Fri, from 11am Sat & Sun; ⊞ ☜) This place feels like a big neighborhood party where everyone is getting along. And what could be more inviting than a pecan tree–shaded yard filled with colorful metal lawn chairs? Friends (and their dogs) gather to knock back longnecks while the kids amuse themselves in the playground area. More than 250 bottled beers and 76 on tap.

On a sunny Sunday afternoon there might be a DJ spinning tunes in the back.

La Tuna Ice House BAR
(Map p94; ☑ 210-224-8862; www.latunagrill. com; 100 Probandt St; ☺ 4pm-midnight Mon-Wed, 2pm-midnight Thu-Sun) When the sun starts to set over Southtown, scoot down by the railroad tracks to this beloved watering hole for a few cold beers and nostalgic, school-size snacks. Locals, even families, crowd around outdoor tables until well after dark, especially on weekends when there's live music.

Blue Star Brewing Company BREWERY
(Map p94; ☑ 210-212-5506; www.bluestar brewing.com; 1414 S Alamo St; ☺ 11am-9pm Sun, to 10pm Mon, to 11pm Tue-Thu, to midnight Fri & Sat) See those great big brewing tanks behind the bar? That's your craft beer being made. The people-watching, the relaxed vibe and the location inside the Blue Star Arts Complex all invite you to linger.

Halcyon CAFE
(Map p94; ☑ 210-277-7045; www.halcyoncoffee bar.com; 1414 S Alamo St; ☺ 7am-2am Mon-Fri, from 8am Sat & Sun; ☜) With excellent coffees, creative cocktails and an inviting coffeehouse vibe (with outdoor seating as well), Halcyon makes a fine destination after a bike ride along the river. There's plenty of good snacking and dining choices, and even make-your-own s'mores for the pyrotechnically inclined. Occasional live music.

♀ Brackenridge Park & Around

Southerleigh BREWERY
(Map p94; ☑ 210-455-5701; www.southerleigh. com; 136 E Grayson St; ☺ 11am-midnight Mon-Fri, 2pm-1am Sat) The setting for this Pearl District hotspot is vintage industrial chic: this was once the historical Pearl Brewery. Today, excellent and varied house brews are once again flowing through the 19th-century complex. Also worth a try is the seasonal,

farm-to-table comfort fare (dinner mains $21 to $38) – think mac 'n' cheese with crab, or cornmeal-crusted catfish.

Greater San Antonio

Flying Saucer Draught Emporium　　BAR
(📞 210-696-5080; www.beerknurd.com; 11255 Huebner Rd; ⊘11am-1am Mon-Thu, to 2am Fri & Sat, noon-midnight Sun) More than 300 kinds of beer (from Abita Abbey Ale to Young's Double Chocolate Stout) make this place a beer-lover's paradise, as does the casual beer-garden vibe. It's a bit of a schlep from downtown – around a 15- to 20-minute drive – but it's a good way to unwind after a (child-free) visit to Six Flags.

Bonham Exchange　　BAR
(Map p98; 📞 210-224-9219; www.bonhamex change.com; 411 Bonham St; ⊘8pm-2am Sun, Wed & Thu, to 3am Fri & Sat) There's plenty of room for everyone at the Bonham: although it's predominantly a gay bar, the sheer size of the place attracts a mixed crowd with drinking and dancing on their mind. Located in an imposing Victorian edifice built in 1892, it has huge dancefloors and five bars spread over three levels.

☆ Entertainment

Although the live music scene isn't as jumping as in Austin, there's still plenty of entertainment in San Antonio. Check the *San Antonio Current* or the calendar section of the *San Antonio Express-News* for upcoming concerts. Both publications also have comprehensive listings of art exhibitions and openings, touring shows, theater, classical music and cinema.

☆ Live Music

Olmos Pharmacy　　LIVE MUSIC
(Map p94; 📞 210-822-1188; www.olmosrx.com; 3902 McCullough Ave; ⊘8am-11pm Mon-Fri, to midnight Sat, to 9pm Sun) This former pharmacy, built in 1938, will cure what ails you with wine, beer and live music seven nights a week. Grab a seat at the old-fashioned soda fountain and enjoy a little jazz, an open-mic night or even a Celtic music jam. Stop by during the day for a meal or a milkshake – it's also a restaurant.

Sam's Burger Joint　　LIVE MUSIC
(Map p94; 📞 210-223-2830; www.samsburger joint.com; 330 E Grayson St; ⊘shows Wed-Mon) More than just a burger joint, Sam's also has a hoppin' live-music venue with a full schedule of bands playing every night except Tuesday. Check online to see who's playing. Monday night brings Swing Nite, with a jazz band and dance lessons.

Martini Club　　LIVE MUSIC
(Martini's; Map p94; 📞 210-344-4747; www.the martiniclubsatx.com; 8507 McCullough Ave; ⊘4pm-2am Mon-Fri, 8pm-2am Sat) Singer/guitarist/trumpeter/saxophonist Wayne Harper

---

FIESTA SAN ANTONIO

In late April, hundreds of thousands of partygoers throng the streets of San Antonio for **Fiesta San Antonio** (p104). A 10-day series of riotous events makes for the city's biggest celebration, with general mayhem, fairs, races and a whole lot of music and dancing. Going strong after more than 125 years, the festival is the high point of the River City's calendar.

Fiesta San Antonio dates back to 1891, when local women paraded on horseback in front of the Alamo and threw flowers at each other, all meant to honor the heroes of the Alamo and the Battle of San Jacinto. Today's **Battle of the Flowers** (p104) is only a small piece of Fiesta, which has grown into an enormous party involving 75,000 volunteers, millions of spectators and 150 or so events.

At the beginning of Fiesta week, the **Texas Cavaliers' River Parade** kicks off with decorated floats drifting along the San Antonio River and a pilgrimage to the Alamo. On the final Saturday night, **Fiesta Flambeau** (which claims to be the largest lighted parade in the USA) sees marchers carrying candles, sparklers, flashlights, torches and anything else illuminated they can find.

But locals' top pick of Fiesta week is **A Night in Old San Antonio** (aka 'NIOSA'), which runs for four nights, during which a small army of women volunteers transform **La Villita** (p96) into a multiethnic bazaar of food, music, dancing, arts and much, much more.

recently sold his kitsch lounge bar – a taste of Las Vegas in the heart of San Antonio. But this fun-loving place rolls on most nights of the week, with a music jam on Tuesdays, live music on Wednesdays, Fridays and Saturdays, and karaoke on Thursdays.

Located in a strip mall next to the Avon shop, the only indication of the bar's existence is a small brass plaque reading 'Martini's' screwed to the wall next to the entrance.

Carmen's de la Calle Café　　　LIVE MUSIC
(Map p98; ☑ 210-281-4349; www.carmensdela calle.com; 320 N Flores St; ⊙ 5-11pm Thu, to midnight Fri & Sat, 11:30am-2:30pm 1st Sun) Indulge in a little Spanish culture with tapas and sangria and live jazz, flamenco and world music.

John T Floore Country Store　　　DANCE
(☑ 210-695-8827; www.liveatfloores.com; 14492 Old Bandera Rd, Helotes; ⊙ 11am-midnight Fri & Sat, to 10pm Sun) Northwest of San Antonio in Helotes, this dance hall celebrated its 75th birthday in 2017. The space hosts plenty of country-and-western concerts: Willie Nelson, Bob Wills, Lyle Lovett, Patsy Cline and Elvis have all performed here. Sunday is family night, with free admission and dancing after 6pm.

☆ Cinema

Alamo Drafthouse　　　CINEMA
(☑ 210-677-8500; www.drafthouse.com; 1255 SW Loop 410; tickets $12) It's a bit of a drive from downtown, but you can catch both dinner and a movie at this theater that surprisingly has nothing to do with the Alamo at all. (It actually started in Austin. Go figure.) It serves a full menu (including beer and wine) that's brought right to your seat to enjoy during the first-run films.

Check the website for other locations around town.

San Antonio IMAX Alamo Theatre　　　CINEMA
(Map p98; ☑ 210-247-4629; www.amctheatres. com; Rivercenter Mall, 849 E Commerce St; adult/ child 2-12yr $16/13) Films shown here include the 45-minute award-winning film *Alamo: The Price of Freedom*, about guess what. If you've never seen a film on a six-story-tall screen in six-track surround sound, you'll want to go to one of the several movies they show in IMAX format – it's worth the admission price just for the experience.

☆ Spectator Sports

San Antonio Spurs　　　BASKETBALL
(Map p94; www.nba.com/spurs; ⊙ Oct–mid-Mar) The big news in town is the San Antonio Spurs, currently one of the top NBA teams in the country. The city is understandably proud, so you'll forgive them if they indulge in a little Spurs mania seven or eight months out of the year. Games held at the **AT&T Center** (Map p94; ☑ tickets 210-444-5000; www. attcenter.com; 1 AT&T Center Pkwy) are exciting, action-packed spectacles.

Buy your tickets on the Spurs' website or through **Ticketmaster** (www.ticketmaster.com).

San Antonio Missions　　　BASEBALL
(☑ 210-675-7275; www.samissions.com; 5757 US 90 W; tickets $10-14; ⊙ regular season Apr-Aug) Winners of the Texas League championships in 2003, 2007 and 2013, the San Antonio Missions, a minor-league baseball affiliate of the San Diego Padres, play at **Nelson Wolff Municipal Stadium**, a short drive west of downtown. Seating on the grass berm beside left field is $5.

☆ Performing Arts

**Tobin Center for the
Performing Arts**　　　THEATER
(Map p98; ☑ 210-223-8624; www.tobincenter.org; 100 Auditorium Circle; ⊙ box office 10am-6pm Mon-Fri, to 2pm Sat, plus 1hr before showtime) On the River Walk, San Antonio's performance hall underwent a seven-year renovation project and now hosts performances by **Ballet San Antonio** (www.balletsanantonio.org) and the San Antonio Symphony (p114). The cutting-edge theater company **Attic Rep** (www.atticrep. org), in residence here, produces shows that are edgy, compelling and current.

A fun way to arrive? On a river taxi (p103).

Majestic Theatre　　　THEATER
(Map p98; ☑ 210-226-5700, box office 210-226-3333; www.majesticempire.com; 224 E Houston St; ⊙ box office 10am-5pm Mon-Fri, hours vary Sat) Head to the historic Majestic Theatre downtown for musical concerts, touring Broadway shows and other live events year-round.

Magik Children's Theatre　　　THEATER
(Map p98; ☑ 210-227-2751; www.magiktheatre.org; 420 S Alamo St; adult/child 2-17yr $15/12; ⊙ box office 9am-5pm Mon-Fri, 10am-7pm Sat, 10am-3pm Sun; ⊕) This merry theater troupe stages adaptations of favorite children's books, hilarious original musicals and modern retellings

of Texas legends and classic fairy tales, such as the witty (and bilingual!) *La Cinderella*. The theater's regular season starts in September and runs through August, and includes a contemporary play series for adults, too.

San Antonio Symphony PERFORMING ARTS
(Map p98; ☑ 210-223-8624; www.sasymphony.org; tickets from $15) The symphony performs a wide range of classical concerts, operas and ballets at different venues around town, including the newly revamped Tobin Center for the Performing Arts (p113) and the spectacular Majestic Theatre (p113). Tickets (which wildly range in price) can be bought from the symphony's box office or from Ticketmaster outlets.

🛍 Shopping

Don't overlook San Antonio's museum gift shops, especially those at the San Antonio Museum of Art (p97) and the McNay Art Museum (p100), which can be exceptional. Popular attractions such as the Alamo (p92), Buckhorn Saloon (p93) and Guenther House (p108) also make for unique souvenir shopping. If you forget to get gifts until the last minute, Texas-made goods are sold at stores in both terminals of San Antonio's airport.

For mall offerings such as Macy's, Gap and Bath & Body Works, try **Ingram Park Mall** (☑ 210-523-1228; www.simon.com/mall/ingram-park-mall; 6301 NW Loop 410, at Ingram Rd; ⊙ 10am-9pm Mon-Sat, noon-6pm Sun) or **North Star Mall** (Map p94; ☑ 210-340-6627; www.northstarmall.com; 7400 San Pedro Ave, Loop 410; ⊙ 10am-9pm Mon-Sat, noon-6pm Sun).

Pearl Brewery Complex SHOPPING CENTER
(Map p94; www.atpearl.com; 200 E Grayson St) The old Pearl Brewery has received a massive face-lift as part of the new Pearl development north of downtown, including shops, cafes and restaurants. The stylish Hotel Emma (p106) has taken over the brewery site and now anchors the neighborhood. The **Culinary Institute of America** also has a campus on the grounds.

Twig Book Shop BOOKS
(Map p94; ☑ 210-826-6411; www.thetwig.com; 306 Pearl Pkwy; ⊙ 10am-6pm) For biographies, fiction, children's books and Texas-related titles, step inside this indie bookstore in the Pearl District. Traveling with young kids? Stop by for Miss Anastasia's Storytime every Friday at 10:30am.

Paris Hatters FASHION & ACCESSORIES
(Map p98; ☑ 210-223-3453; www.parishatters.com; 119 Broadway St; ⊙ 10am-6:30pm Mon-Sat, noon-5pm Sun) Despite the name, this is no French haberdashery, but a purveyor of fine cowboy hats, established in 1917. You'll walk out looking like a real cowboy with a hat that's been shaped and fitted to your very own noggin. It's one of the best places in the state to get a Stetson, or any other type of lid you like.

Dave Little's Boots SHOES
(Map p94; ☑ 210-923-2221; www.littlesboots.com; 110 Division Ave; ⊙ 9am-5pm Tue-Fri, to 1pm Sat) This high-quality bootmaker's shop, established in 1915, now caters to country music stars, actors and locals alike. Get your custom pair with a belt to match – made from calf, crocodile, 'gator, lizard, eel, ostrich or even kangaroo skin. Allow a few months for delivery.

Adelante Boutique CLOTHING, JEWELRY
(Map p94; ☑ 210-826-6770; www.adelanteboutique.com; Suite 107, 303 Pearl Pkwy; ⊙ 10am-6pm Mon-Sat, to 5pm Sun) Like a romantic breath of fresh air, this shop has mix-and-match pieces in vibrant prints and fabrics you won't find anywhere else, along with designer jewelry imports. It's in a new location in the Pearl complex.

Cavender's Boot City CLOTHING, SHOES
(☑ 210-520-2668; www.cavenders.com; 5075 NW Loop 410; ⊙ 9am-9pm Mon-Sat, 11am-6pm Sun) Cavender's Boot City is an affordably priced Western-wear chain around town. There are two other locations in San Antonio (303 NW Loop 410 and 8640 Four Winds Dr), and many more across the state.

San Angel Folk Art Gallery ARTS & CRAFTS
(Map p94; ☑ 210-226-6688; www.sanangelfolkart.com; 110 Blue Star; ⊙ 11am-5pm Mon-Sat, to 3pm Sun) Located inside the Blue Star Arts Complex, this store has a fabulous collection of colorful and whimsical folk art, and is a good place to start when exploring the shops and galleries.

Melissa Guerra HOMEWARES
(Map p94; ☑ 210-293-3983; www.melissaguerra.com; 303 Pearl Pkwy; ⊙ 10am-6pm Mon-Fri, 9am-6:30pm Sat, 10am-4pm Sun) San Antonio's answer to Williams Sonoma, Melissa Guerra has upscale kitchen implements and table settings with a Latin flavor, layered in with Mexican craft items such as *lotería* jewelry and painted pottery.

Alamo Gift Shop & Bookstore BOOKS
(Map p98; ☑ext 141 210-225-1391; www.thealamo.
org; 300 Alamo Plaza; ☉9am-5:30pm Sep-Feb, to
8pm Mar-Aug) You'll find an amazing array of
area history books in this busy shop that is
part of the Alamo (p92) complex. Don't miss
the diorama depicting the famous battle.

Papa Jim's Botanica GIFTS & SOUVENIRS
(Map p94; ☑210-922-6665; www.papajimsbo
tanica.com; 5630 S Flores St; ☉9am-6pm Mon-Fri,
to 5pm Sat) Embracing more than a couple
of belief systems, Papa Jim's Botanica offers
help from above or help from the beyond
for a wide variety of problems. It's basically
a religious and Santeria superstore (mixed
with a bit of voodoo), selling items to rid you
of the problem of your choice: Get-Rich candles, Do-As-I-Say floor wash, Jinx Removal
air freshener, Run Devil Run and Get-out-
of-Jail oil, and Stop-Gossip soap, all for a few
dollars apiece.

Located in the southern part of the city,
the store also has books, herbal teas, incense,
good-luck charms and other items related to
Santeria, a synthesis of Catholicism and the
Nigerian Yoruba folk beliefs of slaves brought
to the Caribbean. Papa Jim's motto is 'Whatever Works,' and obviously it works for some:
the botanica has been around since 1980.

Alamo Quarry Market MALL
(Map p94; ☑210-824-8885; www.quarrymarket.
com; 255 E Basse Rd; ☉10am-9pm Mon-Sat, noon-
6pm Sun) Making use of a 19th-century cement
plant, this outdoor mall has plenty of top-
brand stores, a multiplex cinema and restaurants. A few Austin-based chains here include
Whole Foods Market (great for groceries if
you're self-catering), Amy's Ice Creams and
the outdoors outfitter Whole Earth Provision
Co. Cinema and restaurant hours vary.

Hogwild Records MUSIC
(Map p94; ☑210-733-5354; www.facebook.com/
hogwildrecords; 1824 N Main Ave; ☉10am-9pm
Mon-Sat, noon-8pm Sun) Featuring an expert selection of vinyl, Hogwild also sells tapes and
CDs. If you're after alt-country, punk zines or
rare drum 'n' bass records, this independent
music store is the place. Just look for the front
door, plastered with band flyers and deep layers of stickers.

Rivercenter Mall MALL
(Map p98; ☑210-225-0000; www.shoprivercenter.
com; 849 E Commerce St; ☉10am-9pm Mon-
Sat, noon-6pm Sun) It's the most accessible
megamall in town, and its setting on the River

Walk isn't bad at all. Thanks to the cinemas,
IMAX theater, comedy club, restaurants and
dozens of shops, you'll probably end up here
at some point during your stay.

Market Square MARKET
(Map p98; ☑210-207-8600; www.getcreativesan
antonio.com; 514 W Commerce St; ☉10am-6pm) A
little bit of Mexico in downtown San Antonio, Market Square is a fair approximation
of a trip south of the border, with Mexican
food, mariachi bands and store after store
filled with Mexican wares. A big chunk of the
square is taken up by El Mercado, the largest
Mexican marketplace outside of Mexico.

The market has historical roots – it goes
back to the 1890s – but it can feel like a bit
of a tourist trap at times. You can find some
beautiful handicrafts if you take time to sort
through the mass-produced sombreros and
serapes. Wander the booths and stock up
on Mexican doodads such as paper flowers, colorful pottery, maracas, *papel picado*
(elaborate cut-paper designs), onyx figurines
and the Virgin Mary reproduced in every
conceivable medium.

ℹ Information

Baptist Medical Center (☑210-297-7000; www.
baptisthealthsystem.com; 111 Dallas St; ☉24hr)
A central hospital, just east of Navarro and
Soledad Sts. 24hr emergency room.

**Convention & Visitors Bureau Information
Center** (Map p98; ☑800-447-3372; www.visit
sanantonio.com; 317 Alamo Plaza; ☉9am-5pm)
Well stocked with maps and brochures; their
website has loads of information for preplanning.
Staff can answer questions and also sell tour and
VIA bus/streetcar passes. Opposite the Alamo.

King William Association (Map p98; ☑210-227-
8786; www.ourkwa.org; 122 Madison St; ☉9am-
3pm Mon-Fri) Stop by to pick up a walking-tour
map for the King William District. (If the office
is closed, there should be a few maps in the box
out front.)

Metropolitan Methodist Hospital (☑210-757-
2200; www.sahealth.com; 1310 McCullough Ave;
☉24hr) Just north of downtown.

Post Office (USPS; Map p98; ☑210-212-8046;
www.usps.com; 615 E Houston St, enter off
Alamo St; ☉9am-2:30pm & 3:30-5pm Mon-Fri)
Near the Alamo. Call 800-275-8777 to locate
other branches.

San Antonio Conservation Society (Map p98;
☑210-224-6163; www.saconservation.org; 107
King William St; ☉8:30am-4:30pm Mon-Fri) Has
brochures for self-guided walking tours of the
King William District (also downloadable from the
website).

San Antonio Public Library (Central Branch)
(☑ 210-207-2500; www.mysapl.org; 600 Soledad St; ◷ 9am-9pm Mon-Thu, to 5pm Fri & Sat, 11am-5pm Sun; ☎) The central branch and all satellite locations provide free wi-fi and computer internet access. You'll need a library card or a guest pass to use a computer (bring photo ID). Basic printing services also available ($0.20 per page for B&W prints).

❶ Getting There & Away

Air

San Antonio International Airport (SAT; ☑ 210-207-3433; www.sanantonio.gov/sat; 9800 Airport Blvd) is about 8 miles north of downtown, just north of the intersection of Loop 410 and US 281. It's served by taxis, public transportation, shuttles and ride services, including Uber and Lyft.

The airport offers frequent flights to destinations in Texas and the rest of the USA, and there are also direct or connecting air services to Mexico. Southwest Airlines is the best airline for short-hop flights around Texas.

Transport Options

VIA bus 5 runs at least hourly between the airport and downtown from around 5:30am (6am on weekends) until 9:30pm or so. The regular service costs $1.30; the journey takes about 40 minutes. The VIA stop is on the Lower Roadway at Arrivals/Baggage Claim. Walk to the outer curb; the stop is at the far west end of Terminal B.

Major downtown hotels have free airport courtesy shuttles; be sure to ask when booking. A taxi ride from the airport to downtown costs from $29 for up to four people. If you're traveling solo, you can save a few bucks and take a shuttle with **San Antonio Super Shuttle** (☑ 210-281-9900; www.citytoursinc.com; one way to/from airport $19).

All of the major rental-car agencies have outlets at San Antonio International Airport.

Bus

Greyhound (Map p98; ☑ 210-270-5868; www.greyhound.com; 500 N St Marys St) has a terminal downtown. **Megabus** (Map p98; ☑ 877-462-6342; www.usmegabus.com; cnr 4th & Broadway Sts) stops downtown and connects to Houston and Austin.

Car & Motorcycle

Downtown San Antonio is bordered by I-35, I-10 and I-37, with concentric rings of highways around the center. I-35 connects Austin and San Antonio, and I-10 connects San Antonio with Houston to the east and El Paso to the west.

To get to the Hill Country, take I-10 north to Fredericksburg and Kerrville, or US 281, which is the northbound continuation of I-37, to Johnson City.

All major rental-car agencies have outlets at **San Antonio International Airport**, and some have outlets downtown as well.

Train

Squeezed between Sunset Station and the Alamodome, the **Amtrak station** (☑ 800-872-7245; www.amtrak.com; 350 Hoefgen Ave) is served by the *Sunset Limited* and *Texas Eagle* train services.

❶ Getting Around

Bicycle

Citywide, San Antonio is becoming more bike friendly, but cycling between downtown attractions on busy urban streets with your kids might not be a relaxing experience. Check www.visitsanantonio.com for route maps for five separate routes between top sights in and around downtown.

There are numerous **B-Cycle** (p103) bike-share stations scattered across downtown. You'll also find them beside most major tourist attractions.

Downtown you cannot ride a bike on the River Walk and must ride on surrounding streets. Once you get out of downtown, however, you can ride your bike on long stretches of the River Walk. Beyond Lexington Ave, follow the River Walk north to the Pearl Brewery complex and the Brackenridge Park area's attractions (the Museum Reach). South of downtown, from Nueva St, you can cycle to the historic missions (the Mission Reach), with a walk-your-bike section near the Blue Star Brewery Complex. Before setting out, confirm the cycling start points with the visitor center and obey current signage so you don't get a ticket. The website www.sanantonioriver.org also has helpful maps.

Car & Motorcycle

When visiting downtown, you'll definitely want to ditch your car, but street parking is hard to find. There are plenty of public parking lots downtown, including with most of the major hotels; the lots generally cost $3 per hour, or $5 to $10 for 24 hours. Here are some alternatives:

➡ Park on the street for free in the residential King William District or Southtown, then take the 11 VIA bus (dubbed 'the Culture Route').

➡ Park for free at **VIA Ellis Alley Park & Ride** (212 Chestnut St, btwn E Crockett & Center Sts) then pay $2.60 round-trip to ride downtown.

➡ Park inexpensively at **Market Square** (612 W Commerce St; parking flat rate $10-11), then walk 15 minutes to the Alamo.

➡ Park at **Riverbend Garage** (210 N Presa; daily parking $2-16; ◷ 24hr), which is a little more expensive but puts you right in the heart of things.

Public Transport

San Antonio's public-transport network, **VIA Metropolitan Transit** (☑ 210-362-2020; www.viainfo.

net; ride/day pass $1.30/2.75), operates numerous regular bus routes. VIA passes, bus schedules and route maps are available at VIA's downtown **information center** (☑ general 210-362-2020, info center 210-475-9008; www.viainfo.net; 211 W Commerce St; ☺ 7am-6pm Mon-Fri, 9am-2pm Sat).

Local VIA bus fares are $1.30 (15¢ for a transfer), and exact change is required. VIA express buses, which use interstate highways and include buses to theme parks, cost $2.60. Discount fares are available for children, seniors and the mobility-impaired. Otherwise, a $2.75 pass allows a full day of unlimited rides on all VIA buses.

There are three VIA routes that link top attractions: Route 11 (major museums, the Pearl District, Southtown), Route 40 (the Alamo and the missions) and Route 301 (the Alamo, Tobin Center and Market Square).

Taxi & Ride-Share

Taxi stands are found at major downtown hotels, the Greyhound and Amtrak stations and the airport. Otherwise you'll probably need to call for one. Rates are $2.50 at flag fall ($3.50 between 9pm and 5am), then $2.45 for each additional mile. Fares to downtown start at about $29.

AAA Taxi (☑ 210-599-9999; www.etaxisa.com)

San Antonio Taxis (☑ 210-444-2222; www.sataxis.com)

Yellow Cab (☑ 210-222-2222; www.yellowcabsa.com)

Car services such as **Uber** (www.uber.com), **Lyft** (www.lyft.com) and the new **GetMe** (www.getme.com), which is headquartered in Austin, also operate in San Antonio.

AROUND SAN ANTONIO

The area directly north of San Antonio is known primarily as a haven for shoppers, who stream by the hundreds of thousands into the factory outlet malls in the cities of San Marcos and New Braunfels, off I-35. It's definitely something every bargain-shopper should put on his or her itinerary. But these towns are also great destinations for outdoor recreation on local rivers – perfect for families or anyone else who needs to cool off on a hot summer's day.

On an extended visit, the region also makes a great central base for exploring Austin, San Antonio and the Hill Country.

Natural Bridge Caverns

Natural Bridge Caverns   CAVE
(☑ 210-651-6101; www.naturalbridgecaverns.com; 26495 Natural Bridge Caverns Rd, San Antonio;

adult/3-11yr $22/14; ☺ 9am-4pm, extended hours summer; ⛟) About halfway between San Antonio and New Braunfels, this national landmark cave is one of the state's largest underground formations. Its name comes from the 60ft **limestone bridge** that spans the entrance. Inside, where it's always 70°F (21°C), are simply phenomenal formations, including the **Watchtower**, a 50ft pedestal that looks like a crystallized flower.

You can only see the caverns as part of a guided tour, which includes the family-friendly Discovery Tour, the Hidden Passages Illuminations Tour, or the more challenging Adventure Tours. Attached is the **Natural Caverns Wildlife Park**, a small zoo with rare animals.

From downtown San Antonio, take I-37 N to I-35 N, following the latter 10.5 miles to exit 175 for Hwy 3009 N. Follow Hwy 3009 for just over 8 miles to the caverns.

Guadalupe River State Park

Guadalupe River State Park   PARK
(☑ 830-438-2656; www.tpwd.texas.gov; 3350 Park Rd 31; adult/under 13yr $7/free, campsites $15-24; ☺ 8am-10pm) Thirty miles north of San Antonio, this exceptionally beautiful state park straddles a 9-mile stretch of the clear, bald-cypress-tree-lined Guadalupe River, and it's great for canoeing and tubing. There are hiking, biking and equestrian trails through the park's almost 2000 acres.

Two-hour guided tours of the nearby **Honey Creek State Natural Area** are included in the price of admission. Honey Creek is home to a wide variety of plants, animals and geology. The tours leave at 9am on Saturday from the Rust House, which will be on the right as you drive from Guadalupe River State Park's entrance gate toward the camping area.

New Braunfels

☑ 830 / POP 70,543

Tucked between the ever-expanding monoliths Austin and San Antonio on the I-35 corridor, New Braunfels was the second-fastest growing city in the US in 2015–16. The richly historic town (named for its Prussian founder, Prince Carl of Solms-Braunfels) was the first German settlement in Texas. Today, residents from Austin and San Antonio flock to New Braunfels in summer for its main attraction: the cool and easy-flowing waters of the Guadalupe and Comal Rivers – perfect for tubing and lazy days on the water.

◉ Sights

McKenna Children's Museum MUSEUM
(📞830-606-9525; www.mckennakids.org; 801 W San Antonio St; $7.50; ☺10am-5pm Mon-Sat) Looking for family fun on dry land? Kids can experience everything from outer space to dude ranches at the McKenna Children's Museum. The outdoor climber, with its ropes and launch pads, should satisfy energetic tykes who like a lofty challenge.

Dry Comal Creek Winery & Vineyards WINERY
(📞830-885-4076; www.drycomalcreek.com; 1741 Herbelin Rd, off Hwy 46; tasting fee $10-18; ☺noon-5pm) Proprietor Franklin Houser gives his own tours around the tiny winery, which is constructed of stone and cedar trees. The Dry Spanish wine is made entirely from Texas grapes. The vineyard is 7 miles west of New Braunfels.

🏃 Activities

Landa Park PARK
(📞830-221-4350; www.nbtexas.org; 164 Landa Park Dr; ☺park 6am-midnight) If you don't have a full day but still want to splash around a little, head to this scenic community park just west of Schlitterbahn. The park has an Olympic-size **swimming pool** (350 Aquatic Circle, summer only, adult/child 3-12yr $4/3), an 18-hole **mini-golf course** ($3), a **miniature railroad** ($3), **paddleboats** ($3 per person) and shady picnic facilities. All have different opening hours, so call first.

Schlitterbahn Waterpark Resort SWIMMING
(📞830-625-2351; www.schlitterbahn.com; 400 N Liberty Ave; all-day pass adult/child $51/39; ☺10am-8pm late May–mid-Aug; ♿) For an exhilarating experience, try Texas' largest water park, featuring about 40 different slides and water pools all using water from the Comal River. It's one of the best places to be with kids on a hot day. Hours vary from April through mid-May, and from mid-August through mid-September – check the online calendar for specific opening dates and times.

City Tube Chute WATER SPORTS
(📞830-608-2165; www.nbtexas.org; 100 Leibscher Dr; admission $5, tube rental $7; ☺noon-7pm Mon, 10am-7pm Tue-Sun Jun–mid-Aug, 10am-7pm Sat & Sun only May & mid-Aug–early Sep) In Prince Solms Park, the City Tube Chute is like a water slide for your inner tube that shoots you

around a dam on the Comal River. Cash or check only. Parking costs $10 June through August.

Rockin' R River Rides WATER SPORTS
(📞830-629-9999; www.rockinr.com; 1405 Gruene Rd; tube rental $20) This popular outfit offers inner-tube rides for a scenic float along the Guadalupe River.

Gruene River Company WATER SPORTS
(📞830-625-2800; www.gruenerivercompany.com; 1404 Gruene Rd; tube rental $20; ☺10am-2pm Sep-May, 9am-4pm Jun-Aug) Floating down the Guadalupe in an inner tube is a Texas summer tradition. This outfitter buses you upstream and you float the three to four hours back to base. Put a plastic cooler full of beverages (no glass bottles) in a bottom-fortified tube next to you and you have a day. You can also rent kayaks.

When the river is high, GRC offers white-water rafting trips.

🛏 Sleeping

Faust Hotel HISTORIC HOTEL $$
(📞830-625-7791; www.fausthotel.com; 240 S Seguin Ave; r $99-159, ste $199) Built in the 1920s as a travelers' hotel, the Faust retains its old-fashioned charm – while the rooms have been updated, there's still plenty of evidence of the hotel's historic roots. The cheapest rooms are rather small but they're a great deal, all things considered.

🍴 Eating

Uwe's Bakery & Deli BAKERY, DELI $
(📞830-632-6585; www.facebook.com/uwesbakery deli; 1024 W San Antonio St; sandwiches $8-10; ☺7am-4pm) Get your streusels, danishes and pretzels here, as well as sandwiches, wraps, soup and daily specials. It's not all German specialties here, but they've got 'em if you want 'em. Nice service, too.

Faust Brewing Co PUB FOOD $
(📞830-625-7791; www.faustbrewing.co; 240 S Seguin Ave; mains $7-12; ☺11am-midnight Sun-Fri, to 1am Sat) Located in the Faust Hotel (p118), this convivial pub compliments its microbrews with bar food with a German twist – perfectly befitting its setting in this oh-so-German of towns. They're especially known for their German Nachos: house-made potato chips topped with brats, sauerkraut and beer-cheese sauce.

Naegelin's Bakery BAKERY $
(📞830-625-5722; www.naegelins.com; 129 S Seguin Ave; pastries under $5; ☺6:30am-5:30pm Mon-Fri,

WORTH A TRIP

LULING

Luling trumpets that it's the 'crossroads to everywhere.' But the main reasons to stop here these days as you whiz through on the way to Shiner? To dig into the famed barbecue at **City Market** (☑830-875-9019; 633 E Davis, Luling; brisket/sausage per pound $13/2.30; ☺7am-6pm Mon-Sat) – oh, that succulent brisket! – and to see the annual **Luling Watermelon Thump** (☑830-875-3214; www.watermelonthump.com; 421 E Davis St, Luling; ☺Jun), which has been covered in *People* magazine and the *New York Times*. The famous fruit-growing contest, complete with a crowned queen, takes place the last full weekend of June. (Incidentally, Luling is also the two-time holder of the world watermelon-seed-spitting championship, as documented in the *Guinness Book of World Records*.)

Luling was founded as the western end of the Sunset branch of the Southern Pacific Railroad in 1874, and in 1922 oil was discovered beneath it. The downtown **Luling Oil Museum** (☑830-875-1922; www.lulingoilmuseum.org; 421 E Davis St, Luling; by donation; ☺9am-noon & 1-4pm Mon-Fri, 10am-2pm Sat) is dedicated to Luling's history and heritage. In the same building, the Luling **Chamber of Commerce** (☑830-875-3214; www.lulingcc.org; 421 E Davis St, Luling; ☺9am-1pm Mon-Fri, 10am-2pm Sat) has more information on the area, including its antique shops.

Luling is on US 183 where it meets Hwys 80 and 90, just north of I-10; it's about an hour's drive from San Antonio or Austin, and is served by **Greyhound** (p129).

to 5pm Sat) More than just a great place to pick up German strudels and Czech kolaches, Naegelin's is also the oldest bakery in Texas; having opened in 1868, it's got nearly 150 years under its baking belt. If you're nice, they might just toss an extra cookie into your bag when you're not looking.

Huisache Grill & Wine Bar   AMERICAN $$
(☑830-620-9001; www.huisache.com; 303 W San Antonio St; mains $10-25; ☺11am-10pm) Located in a former home, this cozy, stylish eatery breaks with local tradition by not being even remotely German. An impressively lengthy wine list is one of the draws, as is the variety of choices on the menu – everything from sandwiches to seafood and steaks.

Friesenhaus   GERMAN $$
(☑830-214-0055; www.friesenhausnb.com; 1050 S Seguin Ave; mains $9-23; ☺11am-10pm Mon-Sat, to 9pm Sun; ⊞🐾) Schnitzel, *leberkäse* and *sauerbraten* are among the specialties you can expect at this German restaurant and bakery. (They also serve several fish dishes.) On Friday and Saturday nights, you can enjoy your meal to the tune of German accordion music. Dogs are welcome in the lively biergarten.

❶ Information

Chamber of Commerce (☑830-625-2385; www.nbcham.org; 390 S Seguin Ave; ☺8am-5pm Mon-Fri)

New Braunfels Visitors Center (☑830-625-7973; www.innewbraunfels.com; 237 IH 35 N; ☺9am-5pm Mon-Sat, 11am-3pm Sun)

Gruene
☑830

The charming and historic town of Gruene (pronounced 'green') is just 4 miles northeast of New Braunfels. It's close to the Guadalupe River tubing outfitters and loaded with antiques and crafts shops. **Old Gruene Market Days** are held the third weekend of the month from February through November.

The town is best known for Gruene Hall (p120), a dance hall open since 1878. Antique stores and specialty shops line Hunter Rd, which is anchored by the dance hall. The whole town can be explored in an hour or two, just before the evening show.

🛏 Sleeping & Eating

Gruene River Inn   INN $$
(☑830-627-1600; www.grueneriverinn.com; 1111 Gruene Rd; r incl breakfast $200; 🅿🛜) Rooms are old-school B&B-style – with quilts and antiques – but the real draw is the private decks overlooking the Guadalupe River. Great views.

Gruene Mansion Inn   INN $$$
(☑830-629-2641; www.gruenemansioninn.com; 1275 Gruene Rd; r incl breakfast from $225; 🅿❄🛜) This cluster of buildings is practically its own village, with rooms in the mansion, a former

WORTH A TRIP

SHINER

For some it's a detour, for others a pilgrimage. But a trip to Shiner to visit the **Spoetzl Brewery** (☑ 361-594-3852; www.shiner.com; 603 E Brewery St, Shiner; ⊙ tours 11am & 1:30pm Mon-Fri year-round, plus 10am & 2:30pm Jun-Aug) FREE is a must-do for any self-respecting lover of Texas' favorite microbrew, Shiner Bock.

Longing for a taste of the old country, Czech and German settlers founded the brewery over 100 years ago and hired brewmaster Kosmos Spoetzl (*shpet*-zul) to create a traditional German-style Bock. Today the brewery still produces the beloved Shiner Bock, as well as a honey wheat, blonde and winter ale – all of which you can sample for free right after the tour (which is also free).

By car from San Antonio, take I-10 past Luling to US 95 and go south to get to Spoetzl Brewery. From Austin, take US 183 south through Luling to Gonzales, then turn east and follow US 90A, which brings you to the center of town; cross the railroad tracks and make a left turn on US 95.

carriage house and the old barns. Richly decorated in a style the owners call 'rustic Victorian elegance,' the rooms feature lots of wood, floral prints and pressed-tin ceiling tiles. The hot breakfast buffet is fantastic. Gruene Hall (p120) is next door. Two-night minimum.

★ **Gristmill Restaurant** AMERICAN $$
(☑ 830-606-1287; www.gristmillrestaurant.com; 1287 Gruene Rd; mains $10-24; ⊙ 11am-9pm Sun-Thu, to 10pm Fri & Sat, closes 1hr later summer) Conscientious service and juicy steaks topped with lemon-butter are highlights here, where a preshow dinner (it's behind Gruene Hall) transforms into a memorably pleasant experience. Right under the water tower, the restaurant is located within the brick remnants of a long-gone gristmill. Indoor seating affords a rustic ambience, while outdoor tables get a view of the river.

🍸 Drinking & Nightlife

★ **Gruene Hall** DANCE HALL
(☑ 830-606-1281; www.gruenehall.com; 1280 Gruene Rd; ⊙ 11am-midnight Mon-Fri, 10am-1am Sat, 10am-9pm Sun) Folks have been congregating here since 1878, making it one of Texas' oldest dance halls and the oldest continually operating one. Toss back a longneck, two-step to live music on the wellworn wooden dance floor, check out the photos of past performers (love that 'do, Lyle Lovett!) or play horseshoes out in the yard. Music nightly.

There's only a cover on weekend nights and when big acts are playing, so at least stroll through and soak up the vibe.

Grapevine WINE BAR
(☑ 830-606-0093; www.grapevinegruene.com; 1612 Hunter Rd; ⊙ 10am-9pm year-round, until

10pm Fri & Sat summer) Wine tastings are complimentary at this amiable place, where all the samples are from Texas wineries. Prefer a glass or a bottle? You'll find more Texas wines, plus a few selections from California, Germany and Italy. The patio is a pretty spot to while away the afternoon before the music starts at Gruene Hall.

San Marcos

☑ 512 / POP 60,684

Around central Texas, San Marcos is practically synonymous with outlet malls. But the town is also home to Texas State University, as well as both natural and tourist attractions. Tucked between Austin and San Antonio, it's also one of the fastest growing regions in the country, working well as an affordable and small-townish home base for workers in either city.

⊙ Sights

Wittliff Collections GALLERY
(☑ 512-245-2313; www.thewittliffcollections.txstate. edu; Alkek Library, 601 University Dr, TSU Campus; ⊙ 8am-5pm Mon-Fri, 11am-5pm Sat, noon-5pm Sun) FREE Screenwriter/photographer Bill Wittliff founded this repository of literary and photographic archives on the campus of Texas State University. Stop here for the excellent photography exhibits. The museum's 6600 sq ft of gallery space is room enough for several exhibitions, including the permanent *Lonesome Dove* Collection. (Wittliff wrote the screenplay for the popular TV miniseries based on Larry McMurtry's novel about two aging cowboys on a cross-country cattle drive.) The collection shares costumes and artifacts from the shoot.

The Wittliff Collection is located on the 7th floor of the Alkek Library. Directions are available on their website. Call ahead to confirm hours.

🏃 Activities

San Marcos Lions Club
Tube Rental WATER SPORTS
(📞512-396-5466; www.tubesanmarcos.com; tube rental $10; ⊙10am-7pm Jun-Aug, 10am-7pm Sat & Sun May) Just south of the Meadows Center, the Lions Club rents tubes in City Park (next to the Texas National Guard Armory) to tackle the usually docile stretch of the San Marcos River. The last shuttle pickup from Rio Vista Dam is at 6:30pm. Rental includes unlimited shuttle rides.

Wonder World CAVING
(📞512-392-3760; www.wonderworldpark.com; 1000 Prospect St; combination tickets adult/youth 6-12yr/child 3-5yr $25/18/10; ⊙9am-5pm Mon-Fri, 8am-8pm Sat & Sun Jun–mid-Sep, hours vary rest of the year; 🚻) A mini-theme park has been built around this earthquake-created cave – the most visited cave in Texas. Take a 1½-hour tour through the Balcones Fault Line Cave, where you can look at the Edwards Aquifer up close; tours leave every 25 minutes year-round. Outside, in the 110ft **Tejas Observation Tower**, you can make out the fault line itself.

Other attractions include a petting park filled with Texas animals, a train ride around the park and the quaint 'Anti-Gravity House,' a holdover from family vacations of yesteryear. There's a picnic area on the grounds.

In fall and winter, they are closed most weekdays, except during the winter holiday season (mid-December to early January).

Meadows Center for Water & the Environment OUTDOORS
(Aquarena Springs; 📞512-245-9200; www.meadows center.txstate.edu; 201 San Marcos Springs Dr; ⊙10am-4pm; 🚻) **FREE** Famed for its glass-bottom boat tours over **Spring Lake**, the headwaters of the San Marcos River, this enjoyable place is home to family-oriented exhibitions on ecology, history and archaeology, and includes the ruins of a Spanish mission founded here on the Feast of San Marcos. You'll also find trails and a wetlands boardwalk.

Boat tours (adult/child 3-12yr $10/6) last 30 minutes and let visitors peep beneath the surface of the lake formed by the town's namesake springs, which gush forth 1.5 million gallons of artesian water every day. Parking is $3.

🍴 Eating

Head downtown for indie restaurants with good food and small-town hospitality.

Railyard Bar & Grill AMERICAN $
(📞512-392-7555; www.railyardbarandgrill.com; 116 S Edward Gary St; mains $8-10; ⊙11am-2am Tue-Sat, to midnight Sun & Mon) Grab some fried pickles and play a game of ping-pong, or enjoy a burger and beer while watching a game of horseshoes out on the patio. No surprise the Railyard is a popular hangout for college students: the vibe is easy and casual, and there's plenty to keep you entertained.

Root Cellar Cafe CAFE $$
(📞512-392-5158; www.rootcellarcafe.com; 215 N LBJ Dr; mains breakfast & lunch $4-12, dinner $11-29; ⊙7am-10pm Tue-Sun) This intimate cafe sits a few steps below street level and has rock walls, but that's where the comparison to an actual root cellar ends. The atmosphere is on the cozy side of upscale, with local art adorning the small dining rooms. Numerous tempting menu choices make it a no-brainer when you're looking for a grown-up meal. Welcoming staff, too.

⭐ Entertainment

Cheatham St Warehouse LIVE MUSIC
(📞512-353-3777; www.cheathamstreet.com; 119 Cheatham St; ⊙3pm-2am Mon-Fri, 4pm-2am Sat) Down by the railroad tracks, in an old warehouse covered in corrugated tin, sits this 1970s-era honky-tonk that has helped launch many a career, including those of George Strait and Stevie Ray Vaughan, who both had regular gigs there in the early days. Their signature event is the Songwriters Circle (8pm) on Wednesday nights.

You can catch free shows during happy hour every weekday between 5:30pm and 7pm. San Marcos hasn't banned smoking, so don't be surprised if some enthusiastic smokers are sitting next to you.

🔒 Shopping

San Marcos Premium Outlets MALL
(📞512-396-2200; www.premiumoutlets.com; 3939 S IH-35, exit 200; ⊙10am-9pm Mon-Sat, to 7pm Sun) There are 145 name-brand factory-outlet stores at this enormous – and enormously popular – shopping complex. Outlet shops at the mall offer at least a 30% discount on regular retail prices and sometimes as much

as 75% off brands. Stores include Last Call by Neiman Marcus, Tory Burch, Calvin Klein, J Crew and Coach, just to name a few.

The Premium Outlets are next door to the Tanger Outlets, which sit just south along I-35.

Tanger Outlets MALL
(✔ 512-396-7446; www.tangeroutlet.com/sanmar cos; 4015 S IH-35, exit 200; ⊙ 9am-9pm Mon-Sat, 10am-7pm Sun) What? You're not exhausted from shopping in San Marcos yet? You still have money left to spend? Just south of the Premium Outlets (p121) is the Tanger Outlets center – if you weren't paying attention, you might – not even notice it's a separate mall.

Stores include a few big names, but for the most part they're not as high-end as they are across the street. Think Forever 21, H&M, Reebok and such.

ⓘ Information

San Marcos Tourist Information Center
(✔ 512-393-5930; www.toursanmarcos.com; 617 N IH-35, exit 204B/205; ⊙ 9am-5pm Mon-Sat, 10am-4pm Sun) The San Marcos Tourist Information Center has maps and brochures.

ⓘ Transport

Train Station (✔ 800-872-7245; www.amtrak. com; 338 S Guadalupe St) Trains stop here on the *Texas Eagle* route between San Antonio and Chicago.

HILL COUNTRY

New York has the Hamptons, San Francisco has the wine country, and Texas has the Hill Country. Just an hour or two's drive from both Austin and San Antonio, the area is an easy day trip or weekend getaway, and its natural beauty paired with its easygoing nature has inspired more than a few early retirements.

Thanks to former First Lady Claudia Taylor Johnson – around here everyone calls her Lady Bird – each spring the highways are lined with stunning wildflowers that stretch for miles, planted as part of her Highway Beautification Act.

In addition to the bluebonnets, Indian paintbrushes and black-eyed Susans, the Hill Country shirks Texas' reputation for being dry and flat, with rolling hills, oak trees, spring-fed creeks and flowing rivers. Those hills abound with small wineries, stylish B&Bs, lively dance halls and Instagram-ready geological wonders, from caverns to a grand granite dome. Gorgeous back roads connect them all.

ⓘ Orientation

Ask 10 people the boundaries of the Hill Country and you'll get 11 different answers but, generally speaking, the Hill Country is an area west of the I-35 corridor between Austin and San Antonio, with Fredericksburg and Kerrville being the westernmost points and largest towns. Some people consider San Marcos, New Braunfels and Gruene to be part of the Hill Country, but you really have to leave the Interstate to get the effect.

Dripping Springs
✔ 512 / POP 1,788

Simply put, Dripping Springs is fun. Long seen as a quiet rural community minding its manners, Drip has become a bit of a party girl, while retaining her charm and graciousness. Why the transformation? Ever-growing Austin is just 25 miles east, and Dripping Springs is now a popular bedroom community for those seeking a respite from urban life. Regulations for breweries and distilleries in surrounding Hays County are also looser than in Austin, we hear, so craft brewers and distillers are popping up everywhere. Wineries are widespread too.

The small historic district along Mercer St, just north of Hwy 290, stays lively with its come-one-come-all atmosphere, especially at the Mercer Street Dance Hall. Other charms include Hamilton Pool, a pretty box canyon favored by swimmers and nature lovers.

⊙ Sights

Hamilton Pool Preserve WATERFALL
(✔ 512-264-2740; https://parks.traviscountytx. gov; 24300 Hamilton Pool Rd; per vehicle $15; ⊙ 9am-6pm; reservations required May-Sep; 🅿) How gorgeous is the pool beneath Hamilton Creek, which spills over limestone outcroppings just upstream from the Pedernales River? Let's just say reservations are needed to visit this lush box canyon and waterfall-fed swimming hole from late spring through early fall. The special spot sits within a 30,428-acre preserve, which is also home to the endangered gold-cheeked warbler, a striking yellow-crowned bird.

The preserve can also fill up on winter weekends, before the spring and summer busy season, so get there early if the weather is looking nice.

🛏 Sleeping

There is only one hotel in Dripping Springs, but the community is dotted with B&Bs, cabins and cottages, many of them catering to wedding parties and small groups.

Hill Country Casitas   COTTAGE **$$**
(☑ 512-809-4958; www.hillcountrycasitas.com; 7400 McGregor Ave; 1-bedroom casita $125-185, 2 bedrooms $250; P ✳ 🎝 🐕) The 10 casitas at this new hillside lodging 8 miles north of Dripping Springs make a stylish but comfortable base camp for exploring Austin and the Hill Country. Each stone cottage has a kitchenette and covered patio, and a few have outdoor fireplaces.

🍴 Eating

★ **Pieous**   PIZZA **$**
(☑ 512-394-7041; www.facebook.com/pieous; 12005 W Hwy 290; pizzas $10-15; ⊙ 11am-2pm & 4-9pm Tue-Fri, 11am-9pm Sat, to 8pm Sun) Holy moly, this is good pie. Open a mere four years, this wood-fired pizza joint has earned kudos left and right. The motto here is 'food is our religion,' which gives a nod to the name of the place and to their focus on using fresh and homemade ingredients. The beloved pastrami is cooked in a BBQ smoker out back.

★ **Salt Lick**   BARBECUE **$$**
(☑ 512-858-4959; www.saltlickbbq.com; 18300 FM 1826, Driftwood; mains $10-22; ⊙ 11am-10pm; ⊕) It's worth the 20-mile drive out of town just to see the massive outdoor barbecue pits at this parklike place off US 290. It's a bit of a tourist fave, but the crowd-filled experience still gets our nod. Hungry? Choose the family-style all-you-can-eat option (adult/child $25/9). Cash only and BYOB.

Homespun   AMERICAN **$$**
(☑ 512-829-4064; www.homespunkitchenandbar.com; 131 E Mercer St; lunch mains $12-17, dinner mains $17-45; ⊙ 11am-9pm Tue-Thu, to 10pm Fri & Sat, 10am-8pm Sun) Settle into this cozy but convivial spot in the historic district for Southern comfort food with the occasional fancy twist, like deviled eggs tarted up with pickled jalapeños and bacon. The chopped brisket mac 'n' cheese is served in a cast-iron skillet. Live music is offered most nights.

🍸 Drinking & Nightlife

★ **Jester King Brewery**   MICROBREWERY
(www.jesterkingbrewery.com; 13187 Fitzhugh Rd; ⊙ 4-10pm Fri, noon-10pm Sat, noon-7pm Sun) Jester

---

King may be the perfect country brewery. In a rural setting with picnic tables, cornhole games, shady oaks and a barn-style brewery, the backdrop is mighty picturesque, especially as the sun goes down. The long beer menu, with a focus on sour brews, is fun to sample. Hours may vary seasonally.

Hungry? Grab a delicious gourmet pie ($12 to $16) at Stanley's Farmhouse Pizza next door. The bathrooms for both establishments are inside the airstream trailer, if you're looking.

Treaty Oak Distilling   DISTILLERY
(☑ 512-599-0335; www.treatyoakdistilling.com; 16604 Fitzhugh Rd; ⊙ 3-9pm Fri, noon-9pm Sat, noon-6pm Sun) This destination distillery is the perfect host: fun, friendly and a master when it comes to cocktails. Sample their spirits in the tasting room then head to one of the bars for a fine mixed drink. You can supplement your sipping with snacks, a burger or a sandwich from the on-site **Ghost Hill Restaurant** (snacks $2 to $10, mains $6 to $7).

Lawn games await outside. You might catch live music on the weekends

Hawk's Shadow Winery   WINERY
(☑ 512-587-9085; www.hawksshadow.com; 7500 McGregor Ln; tasting per person $10; ⊙ noon-6pm Sat, by appointment Wed-Fri & Sun; 🐕) This family-run winery is the full package: Texas hospitality, sweet views of the Hill Country from the patio and small-batch reds infused with Texas terroir – and that means easy drinking. Budding geologists can step into the cellar for a look at fossils found in the limestone here.

Hawk's Shadow is a popular road trip for Austinites. If you can't make it on Saturday, don't be afraid to call for an appointment.

Mazama Coffee Co   COFFEE
(☑ 512-200-6472; www.mazamacoffee.com; 301 Mercer St; ⊙ 6:30am-6pm Mon-Fri, 8am-5pm Sat, 8am-1pm Sun; 🖥) Vacationing in Dripping

Springs? You'll likely find yourself returning day after day to this amiable coffee shop in the historic district. There's likely to be a line in the morning, but staff keeps it moving. If there are any breakfast tacos left on the menu when you get there, nab them. Pleasant courtyard too.

☆ Entertainment

Mercer Street Dance Hall LIVE MUSIC
(☑ 512-858-4314; www.mercerstreetdancehall.com; 332 Mercer St; tickets $7-15, free on Thu; ⊙ 6-11pm Thu, 7pm-midnight Fri, 7pm-1am Sat) For live country music, plenty of ice-cold beer and lots of two-stepping (single ladies, you will be asked to dance), head on over to this convivial place anchoring the historic district. Dance lessons are offered at 7:30pm Saturday. Bands start at 8:30pm and it's open from 3pm to 6pm on the second Sunday of the month.

❶ Information

Dripping Springs Chamber of Commerce & Visitors Bureau (☑ 512-858-4740; www.destinationdrippingsprings.com; 509 W Mercer St; ⊙ 9am-4pm Mon-Fri) Stop here for brochures and local information. Good website too.

❶ Getting There & Around

Drippery Tours (☑ 512-872-7883; www.thedripperytours.com) Provides rides for groups in your choice of vehicles – car, SUV, limo or shuttle – to wineries, breweries and distilleries in the Dripping Springs area.

Johnson City & Stonewall

☑ 830 / POP 1738

You might assume Johnson City was named after President Lyndon Baines Johnson, who lived here as a child and had a ranch nearby where he spent most of his life. But the bragging rights go to James Polk Johnson, a town settler back in the late 1800s. The fact that James Johnson's grandson went on to become the 36th president of the United States was just pure luck.

You'll find a few antiques stores and restaurants in Johnson City today, but the big draws are Johnson's Boyhood Home and the visitor center for the Lyndon B Johnson National Historical Park. The LBJ Ranch, also part of the national park, is 14 miles west in Stonewall.

B&Bs and wineries are scattered across the area.

◉ Sights

Johnson's Boyhood Home HISTORIC BUILDING
(☑ 830-868-7128; www.nps.gov/lyjo; 200 E Elm St, Johnson City; ⊙ tours half-hourly 9am-noon & 1-4:30pm) FREE Lyndon B Johnson himself had this house restored for personal posterity. Park rangers from the neighboring visitor center, where you can find local information and exhibits on the former President and First Lady, offer free guided tours every half-hour that meet on the front porch of the house. On the surface, it's just an old Texas house, but it's fascinating when you think about the boy who grew up there.

LBJ Ranch HISTORIC SITE
(☑ national park visitor center 830-868-7128, state park visitor center 830-644-2252; www.nps.gov/lyjo; Hwy 290, Stonewall; tour adult/child under 18yr $3/free; ⊙ ranch grounds 9am-5:30pm, house tours 10am-4:30pm) In Stonewall, 14 miles west of Johnson City, you'll find the LBJ Ranch, now part of the Lyndon B Johnson National Historical Park. Stop by the state-run visitor center nearby (as opposed to the national park visitor center in Johnson City) to get your free park driving permit and a map of the expansive grounds; admission is only charged if you take the half-hour tour of the Johnson home. Tour tickets are purchased in the airplane hangar beside the home.

The park is a beautiful piece of Texas land where LBJ was born, lived and died. It includes the former President's birthplace, the one-room schoolhouse he briefly attended and a neighboring farm that now serves as a living history museum. The centerpiece of the park is the ranch house where LBJ and his wife Lady Bird lived, and where he spent so much time during his presidency that it became known as the 'Texas White House.'

You can also see the airfield used by Johnson and foreign dignitaries, the private jet he used as president and the Johnson family cemetery, where LBJ and Lady Bird are buried under sprawling oak trees. Though the state and national park systems operate different sections of the complex, it all flows together fairly seamlessly.

⌷ Sleeping & Eating

Chantilly Lace Country Inn B&B $$
(☑ 830-660-2621; www.chantillylacesoaps.com; 625 Nugent Ave, Johnson City; ste $140-179; ⊙ ⌗ 🛜) The Chantilly Lace Country Inn offers Texas-style rooms that aren't as lacy and

countrified as its name would imply. They also make and sell goat's milk soap.

Rose Hill Manor   B&B $$$
([phone] 830-644-2247; www.rose-hill.com; 2614 Upper Albert Rd, Stonewall; ste $250-279; [icons]) This exquisite B&B offers top-notch accommodation, with beautifully appointed suites and cottages. A three-course hot breakfast is served. If you like sunlight views early or late, choose either the Sunrise Suite or the Sunset Suite on the 2nd floor of the main house, both with access to the upstairs verandah. Some packages include a tasting at the winery next door.

There's wi-fi in most rooms and the common areas. It's in Stonewall, 14 miles west of Johnson City.

Pecan Street Brewing   PUB FOOD $
([phone] 830-868-2500; www.pecanstreetbrewing.com; 106 E Pecan Dr, Johnson City; mains $9-15; [time] 11am-9pm Tue-Sun) A friendly neighborhood brew pub that serves up a variety of dishes alongside its own microbrews in a casual, friendly environment. It usually has live music on Saturday nights, which means it doubles as nightlife.

🛍 Shopping

Pieces of the Past   ANTIQUES
([phone] 830-868-2890; www.pieces-of-the-past.com; 104 Hwy 281 S, Johnson City; [time] 9am-3pm Mon & Thu, 10am-5pm Fri & Sat, noon-5pm Sun) Salvaged doors, metal sign letters, movie theater lights...you never know what you'll find wandering around the yard at this place specializing in architectural salvage, but it sure is fun to hunt.

ℹ Information

Lyndon B Johnson National Historical Park Visitor Center ([phone] 830-868-7128; www.nps.gov/lyjo; 100 E Ladybird Lane, cnr E Ladybird Lane & Ave G, Johnson City; [time] 9am-5pm) Next to Johnson's Boyhood Home.

Lyndon B Johnson State Park and Historic Site Visitor Center ([phone] 830-644-2252; www.tpwd.texas.gov; Hwy 290, Stonewall; [time] 8am-5pm) Across the Pedernales River from the LBJ Ranch, you can pick up free self-guided driving permits here before entering the ranch grounds. You can also find information about the visitor center on the national park website at www.nps.gov/lyjo.

It's in Stonewall, 14 miles west of Johnson City.

Fredericksburg
📞 830 / POP 10,530

Although we highly recommend meandering through the Hill Country, if you're only going to see one town, make it this one. The 19th-century German settlement packs a lot of charm into a relatively small amount of space. There is a boggling array of welcoming inns and B&Bs, and a main street lined with historic buildings that house German restaurants, beer gardens, antique stores and shops. The downtown museums are interesting too.

Many of the shops are typical tourist-town offerings (think T-shirts, fudge and faux-quaint painted signs), but there are enough unique stores to make it fun to wander. Plus, the town is a great base for checking out the surrounding peach orchards, vineyards and getaways, such as Enchanted Rock and Johnson City, as well as little Luckenbach, just 10 miles away.

⊙ Sights

National Museum of the Pacific War   MUSEUM
([phone] 830-997-8600; www.pacificwarmuseum.org; 340 E Main St; adult/child $14/7; [time] 9am-5pm) This museum complex consists of three war-centric galleries: the **Admiral Nimitz Museum**, chronicling the life and career of Fredericksburg's most famous son; the **George HW Bush Gallery of the Pacific War**, a large, impressive building housing artifacts and an expansive chronicle of WWII's Pacific campaign; and the revamped **Pacific Combat Zone**, a 2-acre indoor/outdoor exhibit, which spotlights PT (Patrol Torpedo) boats and military vehicles.

The combat zone also offers reenactments – with landing craft and explosions –

U-R-B-A-N P-L-A-N-N-I-N-G

Street names in Fredericksburg appear to be a mishmash of trees, Texan towns and former US presidents. But they were actually named so their initials spell out secret codes – which support the town's reputation for hospitality. The streets crossing Main St to the east of Courthouse Sq and Marktplatz are Adams, Llano, Lincoln, Washington, Elk, Lee, Columbus, Olive, Mesquite and Eagle. And the streets to the west are Crockett, Orange, Milam, Edison, Bowie, Acorn, Cherry and Kay.

SCENIC DRIVE: WILDFLOWER TRAILS

You know spring has arrived in Texas when you see cars pulling up roadside and families climbing out to take the requisite picture of their kids surrounded by bluebonnets – Texas' state flower. From March to April in Hill Country, orange Indian paintbrushes, deep-purple wine-cups and white-to-blue bluebonnets are at their peak.

To see vast cultivated fields of color, there's **Wildseed Farms** (☑830-990-1393; www.wildseedfarms.com; 100 Legacy Dr; ⊙9:30am-5pm) **FREE**, which is 7 miles east of Fredericksburg on US 290.

For a more do-it-yourself experience, check with the Texas Department of Transportation (TXDOT) **Wildflower Hotline** (☑800-452-9292) to find out what's blooming where. Taking Rte 16 and FM 1323, north from Fredericksburg and east to Willow City, is usually a good route. Then again you might just set to wandering – most back roads host their own shows daily. At visitor centers, look for the *Texas Wildflowers* pamphlet from *Texas Highways* magazine. It identifies Lone Star flowers and provides routes for scenic wildflower drives.

on scheduled weekends ($10). Check online calendar for dates.

For a respite from the violent stories, stroll the **Japanese Peace Garden** beside the Bush Gallery. Overall, history buffs can learn about (or refresh their memories on) the many battles conducted in the Pacific, and kids will be awed by the enormous vehicles. Tickets are good for two days – there is a lot to see and contemplate. Admission is free for WWII veterans.

★ **Enchanted Rock State Natural Area** PARK
(☑830-685-3636; www.tpwd.texas.gov; 16710 Ranch Rd 965; adult/child under 13yr $7/free; ⊙8am-10pm) What's so enchanting about a rock? Well, when you see the pink granite dome dating from the Proterozoic era rising 425ft above ground – one of the largest batholiths in the US – you'll know you're not looking at any old rock. (And remember, that's just the part you can see; most of the rock formation is underground.) The dome heats up during the day and cools off at night, making a crackling noise that the Tonkawa people believed were ghost fires.

Two of the most popular activities at this much-visited park are hiking and rock climbing. The one-way Summit Trail to the top of the dome is 0.67 mile. The pleasant walk-in tent camping sites, with a picnic table and barbecue, are $18 per night, while primitive sites are $14 per night.

Enchanted Rock is 18 miles north of Fredericksburg off RR 965 and 24 miles south of Llano. It gets crowded on weekends, spring break and holidays, so get there early during peak times (by 11am at the latest). The park will close the gate and

not allow anyone else to enter when the park is full.

Pioneer Museum HISTORIC SITE
(☑830-990-8441; www.pioneermuseum.net; 325 W Main St; adult/child 6-17yr $5/3; ⊙10am-5pm Mon-Sat) Find out what life was like for the town's early inhabitants as you wander the 10 historic buildings at the Pioneer Museum. Short audio interpretations begin as you step into each building. If nothing else, this collection of restored homes and businesses from the late 1800s will help you appreciate the modern conveniences awaiting you at your guesthouse.

Vereins Kirche HISTORIC BUILDING
(☑830-990-8441; Marktplatz, 100 W Main St; ⊙10am-4:30pm Tue-Sat) **FREE** The city's Vereins Kirche was the original town church, meeting hall and school. The tiny building anchoring the town square – the Marktplatz – contains archival photos and historical artifacts that can be interesting for history buffs and, if you're lucky, you'll get a great docent who will really bring the stories to life.

Becker Vineyards WINERY
(☑830-644-2681; www.beckervineyards.com; 464 Becker Farms Rd; tasting $15; ⊙10am-5pm Mon-Thu, to 6pm Fri & Sat, noon-6pm Sun) Located 10 miles east of Fredericksburg, just off US 290, this is one of the state's most decorated wine producers. Its vineyard has 36 acres of vines and allegedly Texas' largest underground wine cellar. The tasting room is housed in a beautiful old stone barn, with plenty of outdoor seating on the patio.

Pioneer Public Library LIBRARY
(📞830-997-6513; 115 W Main St; ⊘9am-6pm Mon-Thu, to 2pm Fri & Sat) **FREE** Check out the enormous tapestry on the 2nd floor of the beautiful library building. About 8ft by 16ft, the mixed-media tapestry highlights many of Fredericksburg's landmarks.

🏃 Activities

Old Tunnel Wildlife Management Area WILDLIFE WATCHING
(📞866-978-2287; http://tpwd.texas.gov/state-parks/old-tunnel; 10619 Old San Antonio Rd; ⊘sunrise-5pm, after 5pm Thu-Sun May-Oct) Right around dusk from May to October, you can watch a colony of bats emerging from an abandoned railroad tunnel for their nightly meal. Over three million Mexican free-tailed bats make their home here.

The **upper-deck viewing area** is open daily. It's free, but has limited capacity. The park will close it when full, at 250 visitors. The **lower viewing area**, which is open Thursday to Sunday and has a $5 charge per person, affords an up-close view that is decidedly more impactful. Exact payment required for bat viewing (no change available). No pets.

🎉 Festivals & Events

Oktoberfest CULTURAL
(📞830-997-4810; www.oktoberfestinfbg.com; Marktplatz, 100 W Main St; adult/child 7-12yr $8/1; ⊘Oct) Every October, Fredericksburg celebrates its German heritage in a big way with Texas' largest Oktoberfest. Families crowd around the Vereins Kirche, the original town church, for oompah bands, endless kegs of German beer, and schnitzels and pretzels galore. On the Saturday, join hands for the Chicken Dance!

🛏 Sleeping

Lady Bird Johnson Municipal Park CAMPGROUND $
(📞830-997-4202; www.fbgtx.org; 432 Lady Bird Drive, off Hwy 16; campsites/RV sites $10/40; P🛜🐾) This pretty country park sits 3 miles south of town on the Pedernales River. There are plenty of RV hookups but no tent sites per se, just a big field behind the park's headquarters.

Dietzel Motel MOTEL $
(📞830-997-3330; www.dietzelmotel.com; 1141 W US 290; r $99; P❄🛜🐾🐾) This simple, family-run motel is a great budget option

located at the west end of town away from the hustle and bustle. Some rooms have wi-fi, and some are pet friendly. Rates are higher during special events, but all in all, it's a good deal.

Pets are $25 each per night.

Cotton Gin Village CABIN $$
(📞830-990-8381; www.cottonginlodging.com; 2805 S Hwy 16; cabins incl breakfast $229; P🛜) Rustic on the outside, posh on the inside. Oh yes, we like it here. Just south of town, this cluster of stone-and-timber cabins offers guests a supremely private stay away from both the crowds and the other guests. Cabins come with a stone wood-burning fireplace. Romantic getaway? Start packing.

The three-bedroom Big House ($499 per night) works well for groups. Cabernet Grill restaurant, serving steaks and Southern fare (mains $21 to $38), is on site.

Fredericksburg Inn & Suites MOTEL $$
(📞830-997-0202; www.fredericksburg-inn.com; 201 S Washington St; r incl breakfast $199-219, ste incl breakfast $249; P❄🛜🐾🐾) Tops in the mid-priced-motel category, this place was built to look like the historic house it sits behind, and it succeeds. Property features include a fabulously inviting pool with a water slide, a spacious hot tub, and clean and updated rooms. It's within walking distance of Main St.

Pets are $50 per stay.

Hangar Hotel INN $$
(📞830-997-9990; www.hangarhotel.com; 155 Airport Rd; r $189; P🛜) If you didn't know better, you'd think this rounded, barnlike structure right on the tarmac of the Gillespie County Airport was a converted hangar from the 1940s, but it's actually a new building with a fun aviation shtick. All rooms have king beds and the front desk is welcoming. No children under 18 years old.

PEACH PICKING

Fredericksburg is known throughout the state for its peaches, and for good reason. They're fat, juicy and nothing like what you'll find in your local produce department. Mid-May through June is peach-pickin' season around town. You can get them straight from the farm, and some will let you pick your own. For a list of more than 20 local peach farms, visit www.texaspeaches.com.

SAN ANTONIO & HILL COUNTRY FREDERICKSBURG

✖ Eating

Tubby's Ice House AMERICAN, MEXICAN $
(☎830-307-3026; www.tubbysfbg.com; 318 E Austin St; mains $5-11; ⊙11am-9pm Sun-Thu, to midnight Fri & Sat) One block from tourist-lined Main St, Tubby's draws a laid-back, mostly local crowd, who come for plates of pulled pork, tacos, burgers and other snacks, plus a fine selection of microbrews. The setting: colorful outdoor picnic tables; and there's a bocce court.

Hondo's on Main AMERICAN $
(☎830-997-1633; www.hondosonmain.com; 312 W Main St; mains $8-15; ⊙11am-10:30pm Wed, Thu & Sun, to midnight Fri & Sat) Named after local legend Hondo Crouch, this hoppin' place caters to your need for both food and fun, with live music on the patio five nights a week. It's famous for its 'doughnut burger,' which has more to do with the way the patty is formed than the actual ingredients.

**Old German Bakery &
Restaurant** GERMAN, AMERICAN $
(☎830-997-9084; www.oldgermanbakeryand restaurant.com; 225 W Main St; breakfast mains $6-10, lunch mains $7-17; ⊙7am-3pm) For a solid German meal, try this busy and loud Main St stand-by. You'll find German pancakes as well as omelets on the breakfast menu, served all day, with schnitzels, bratwurst and a sausage plate. Burgers and sandwiches are available at lunch.

They may close at 2pm depending on how busy they are.

★ Vaudeville CAFE $$
(☎830-992-3234; www.vaudeville-living.com; 230 E Main St; lunch mains $15-17, dinner mains $16-36; ⊙10am-4pm Mon, Wed, Thu & Sun, to 9pm Fri & Sat) This dapper underground bistro looks like a soda fountain gone posh. The folks lunching here are as stylish as the decor, but don't worry, you'll find welcoming Hill Country hospitality in these hip digs. The gourmet salads and sandwiches are top notch – and you do want the pork belly taco. Desserts, coffees, teas and craft beer are also offered.

Aesthetically, the restaurant is an extension of the home furnishings and decor showroom upstairs, a fun place to browse after lunch. The bistro's logo will keep you pondering all through lunch. Is it a 'V,' a steer skull or Vaudevillian acrobats? Hmm, let me order another salted caramel cookie and think it over.

Hill Top Café AMERICAN $$
(☎830-997-8922; www.hilltopcafe.com; 10661 N Hwy 87; lunch mains $8-19, dinner mains $16-34; ⊙11am-2pm Tue-Sun & 5-9pm Tue-Thu, to 10pm Fri & Sat, to 8pm Sun) Located 10 miles north of town in a renovated 1950s gas station, this cozy roadhouse serves up satisfying meals and Hill Country ambience at its best. Look for a few Cajun dishes on the menu. Reservations are recommended.

Check the online calendar for live music from the owner, Johnny Nicholas, a former member of the West Coast swing band Asleep at the Wheel.

Silver Creek Restaurant AMERICAN $$
(☎830-990-4949; www.silvercreekfbg.com; 310 E Main St; lunch mains $15-32; ⊙11am-4pm & 5-9pm Wed-Mon) A great compromise when only some of you want schnitzel, this place serves both American and German dishes, mostly under $20, though the steaks can get a little spendy. The shady patio is a great place to hang out, especially Mondays at lunch when they host live music. It's one of the *only* places to go on a Monday night.

Navajo Grill AMERICAN $$$
(☎830-990-8288; www.navajogrill.com; 803 E Main St; mains $25-39; ⊙5:30-8:30pm Sun-Thu, to 9:30pm Fri & Sat) For something more upmarket, head straight to the Navajo Grill, which boasts a lovely patio, creative Southern cuisine and a list of about 40 different wines by the glass, and more by the bottle. Reservations recommended on weekends, especially in the spring.

🔒 Shopping

FarmHaus ANTIQUES
(☎830-468-5212; www.farmhausstore.com; 211 W Main St; ⊙10am-5pm Mon-Sat, from noon Sun) It's hard to leave this antique and home furnishings store empty handed. It's filled with decor for the modern cabin or cottage, plus items for your patio and garden.

ℹ Information

Broadway National Bank (☎830-997-7691; www.broadway.bank; 204 W Main St; ⊙9am-4pm Mon-Fri) Has a 24-hour ATM.

Fredericksburg Visitor Information Center (☎830-997-6523, 888-997-3600; www.visit fredericksburgtx.com; 302 E Austin St; ⊙9am-5pm Mon-Sat, 11am-3pm Sun; 🖥) Has friendly staff and an attractive building a block off Main St, close to the Pacific War Museum. Lot's of parking too if you can't find anything on Main St.

Hill Country Memorial Hospital (☑ 830-997-4353; www.hillcountrymemorial.org; 1020 Hwy 16 via S Adams St) Has 24-hour emergency services.

❶ Getting There & Around

Heading west from Austin, US 290 becomes Fredericksburg's Main St. Hwy 16, which runs between Fredericksburg and Kerrville, is S Adams St in town. It isn't easy to get to Fredericksburg without a car; the closest bus station is at Kerrville, but **Greyhound** (☑ 800-231-2222; www.greyhound.com) will drop you off or pick you up at the **Stripes Shell Station** (2204 Hwy 16 S) located 2½ miles southwest of downtown.

You can get a shuttle service from the San Antonio Airport through **Stagecoach Taxi and Shuttle** (☑ 830-385-7722; www.stagecoachtaxiandshuttle.com); the cost is $95 each way for up to four people. However, since driving around the Hill Country is half the fun, your best bet is to drive yourself.

When in town, you can rent bicycles at **Hill Country Bicycle Works** (☑ 830-990-2609; www.hillcountrybicycle.com; 702 E Main St; rental per day $30-45; ☺10am-6pm Mon, Tue, Thu & Fri, to 4pm Sat).

Luckenbach

☑ 830 / POP 3

As small as Luckenbach is – there are only three permanent residents, not counting the cat – it's big on Texas charm. You won't find a more laid-back place. The main activity is sitting at a picnic table under an old oak tree with a cold bottle of Shiner Bock beer and listening to guitar pickers, who are often accompanied by roosters.

☆ Entertainment

Luckenbach Dance Hall   LIVE MUSIC
(☑ 830-997-3224; www.luckenbachtexas.com; Luckenbach Town Loop) There are usually live-music events on the weekends in the old dance hall. The 4th of July and Labor Day weekends see a deluge of visitors for concerts.

❶ Information

Luckenbach General Store (☑ 830-997-3224, www.luckenbachtexas.com; 412 Luckenbach Town Loop; ☺9am-11pm Sun-Thu, to midnight Fri, to 1am Sat) The heart of the, er, action is the old trading post established back in 1849 – now the Luckenbach General Store, which also serves as the local post office, saloon and community center.

Bandera

☑ 830 / POP 857

It's not always easy finding real, live cowboys in Texas, but the pickin's are easy in Bandera, which has branded itself the Cowboy Capital of Texas. There are certainly lots of dude ranches around, and rodeos and horseback riding are easy to come by. Another great reason to come to Bandera? Drinking beer and dancing in one of the many hole-in-the-wall cowboy bars and honky-tonk clubs, where you'll find friendly locals, good live music and a rich atmosphere. Giddy up!

THE STORY BEHIND THE SONG

A famous saying in Luckenbach goes something like this: 'We have discovered that, on the globe, Luckenbach is at the center of the world.' And while today's casual visitor may question that logic over a cold beer and a lazy afternoon, not so in 1977, when the town was at the center of the world – or at least the country music world. Waylon Jennings and Willie Nelson's hit song 'Luckenbach, Texas (Back to the Basics of Love)' stayed at number one on the country music charts for nearly the entire summer.

What's odd about one of the most catchy country tunes ever recorded is that it was written by Bobby Emmons and Chips Moman, two Nashville producers who'd never been to Luckenbach. Even Jennings couldn't say he'd actually set foot in any one of the three buildings in town until the first and only time he made the trip, in 1997, 20 years after the song's original release. Still, 'Luckenbach, Texas' was and remains a well-loved tribute to the Hill Country hamlet, partly because Nelson is a Texas fixture and has held his famous 4th of July Picnic here off and on for years. Also, since Jennings' death in 2002, Luckenbach has thrown an annual mid-July tribute party to the musician, giving the town's regulars (and its three permanent residents) one more reason to call Luckenbach the center of the world.

HILL COUNTRY WINERIES

When most people think of Texas, they think of cowboys, cactus and Cadillacs – not grapes. But the Lone Star State is a major wine producer, and the Hill Country, with its robust Provence-like limestone and hot South African–style climate, has become the state's most productive wine-making region. Today, these rolling hills are home to more than 50 wineries, with the largest concentration of vineyards found around Fredericksburg, primarily along Hwy 290.

Most larger wineries are open daily for tastings and tours. Many also host special events, such as grape stompings and annual wine and food feasts. Smaller wineries are typically open during set hours on weekends, but by appointment on weekdays. Local visitor bureaus stock the handy *Texas Hill Country Wineries Guide & Map*, which summarizes the wineries and pinpoints their locations (or visit www.texaswinetrail.com).

You could leave the driving to someone else with **Fredericksburg Limo & Wine Tours** (830-992-0696; www.texaswinelimos.com; tours per person $109-149), which offers limo tours or more affordable shuttle van tours. For a list of tour operators, check www.wineroad290.com, which covers wineries along US 290 and provides a map of their locations.

Sights

Frontier Times Museum MUSEUM
(830-796-3864; www.frontiertimesmuseum.org; 510 13th St; adult/child 6-17yr/senior $6/2/4; 10am-4:30pm Mon-Sat) To get some historical perspective, stop by this museum's display of Western art, cowboy tchotchkes such as guns, branding irons and cowboy gear, and 'curiosities' collected by the museum's founder, J Marvin Hunter – including the famous two-headed goat.

Lost Maples State Natural Area PARK
(830-966-3413, reservations 512-389-8900; www.tpwd.texas.gov; 37221 FM 187; adult/child under 13yr $6/free, primitive camping $10, tent & RV sites $20) The foliage spectacle in October and November at Lost Maples is as colorful as any in New England. In fall, big-tooth maple trees turn shocking golds, reds, yellows and oranges. In the summertime there's good swimming in the Sabinal River. Hiking trails take visitors into rugged limestone canyons and prairielike grasslands populated by bobcats, javelinas and gray foxes.

Bird-watching is another popular attraction at Lost Maples due to green kingfishers, who take up residence in the park year-round. Also throughout the year, campers will find back-country areas where they can pitch a tent, as well as more convenient sites supplied with water, electricity and nearby showers.

The park can close for up to three hours in the fall if the parking lots are full. It's located 5 miles north of Vanderpool and 40 miles west of Bandera.

Activities

A dozen or so dude ranches are scattered in and around town, where you can horseback ride for around $35 to $50 an hour. (Note that according to Texas law riders must not weigh more than 240lb.) Some offer packages that include meals in the price, and many take advantage of the **Hill Country State Natural Area**, a park with over 5000 acres. Most of the ranches are within 10 miles of Bandera.

If you'd like to stay longer, these dude ranches offer all-inclusive experiences with horseback riding, meals and a place to hang your hat for the night. Some ranches offer unique features to set themselves apart, but you can generally expect enormous ranch houses set on hundreds of acres. Other cowboy amenities might include hayrides, campfires and barbecues.

Silver Spur Guest Ranch HORSEBACK RIDING
(830-796-3037; www.silverspur-ranch.com; 9266 Bandera Creek Rd; horseback riding non-guests 1hr/2hr $45/80) Day visitors can enjoy one- or two-hour rides, and can throw in lunch or dinner for a small extra fee. For overnight guests, after a long day on the dusty trails, Silver Spur's junior Olympic pool provides a good way to cool off. Also offers hayrides, fossil digging and nightly campfires. Overnight rates ($150) include two horseback rides and three meals daily, plus use of ranch amenities. Also offers a lower rate ($120 per night) for those who don't want to horseback ride.

Flying L Guest Ranch HORSEBACK RIDING

(☑ 800-292-5134; www.flyingl.com; 566 Flying L Dr; nonguest 2hr horseback ride per person $100) As much a resort as a dude ranch, the Flying L includes a water park and golf course. Horseback rides and meals are available a la carte, as are various activities.

The villas are $255 to $329 per night and suites are $339 to $349. Horseback riding and meal packages can be arranged for guests.

Twin Elm Guest Ranch HORSEBACK RIDING

(☑ 830-796-3628; www.twinelmranch.com; 810 FM 470; horseback riding nonguests per hour $35) Provides lots of family-friendly activities, including horseback riding and tubing on the Medina River.

The price for lodging only is $120 for a room and $145 for a cabin, while primitive tent camping is $10 and RV sites are $135. For guests to enjoy the package, with two horseback rides plus meals, it's an extra $90 per adult and $70 per child.

🛏 Sleeping

River Front Motel CABIN $

(☑ 800-870-5671, 830-460-3690; www.theriver frontmotel.com; 1103 Maple St; cabins $99, ste $159-179; P ✳ 🛜 🐾) This friendly, family-run motel on the south side of town offers 11 cabins by the river, each with a fridge, a coffeemaker and cable TV. It's your best bet for the money. Pet fee is $15 per night.

Mayan Ranch RANCH $$

(☑ 830-796-3312; www.mayanranch.com; 350 Mayan Ranch Rd; adult $165, child $80-100; P 🛜 🐾) With activities such as horseback riding, tubing on the river, tennis and nightly programs, Mayan has tons to do for both adults and kids. Room rates include three meals per day and two horseback rides per day. No rides on Sunday. Wi-fi available in rooms in the main lodge.

Dixie Dude Ranch RANCH $$

(☑ 800-375-9255, 830-796-7771; www.dixiedude ranch.com; 833 Dixie Dude Ranch Rd; adult $165, child $55-105; P 🛜 🐾) This working stock ranch founded in 1901 has an authentic Western feel and 725 acres. Three meals and two horseback rides are included in the price, plus ranch activities. Some rooms have kitchenettes. Wi-fi is available at the main ranch, but may not be speedy.

🍴 Eating

Sid's Main Street BBQ BARBECUE $

(☑ 830-796-4227; www.sidsmainstreetbbq.com; 702 Main St; sandwiches $7-10, mains $9-15; ⊙ 11am-8pm Mon-Sat, to 3pm Sun) Head to Sid's for your barbecue fix. It serves smoky, succulent meat dishes in a former gas station.

OST Restaurant AMERICAN $

(☑ 830-796-3836; 311 Main St; mains $8-17; ⊙ 6am-9pm Mon-Sat, from 7am Sun) It should come as no surprise that cowboy cuisine is the dominant theme around these parts. The OST (which stands for Old Spanish Trail) serves up hearty chuckwagon-style breakfasts, along with Tex Mex and the ubiquitous chicken-fried steaks at dinner. The decor includes wagon-wheel chandeliers, saddle seats at the bar, and an entire wall devoted to John Wayne.

🍺 Drinking & Nightlife

If it's honky-tonkin' and beer drinkin' you're looking for, you've come to the right place. Head downtown for dancing.

11th Street Cowboy Bar BAR

(☑ 830-796-4849; www.11thstreetcowboybar.com; 307 11th St; ⊙ 10am-2am Tue-Sat, from noon Sun & Mon) This not-to-be-missed spot just north of Cypress St is the 'Biggest Little Bar in Texas.' The quirky main room features dozens of liberated ladies' undergarments and is a great place to enjoy some local color. Out back, the huge outdoor space hosts big-name acts and special events such as grill-your-own steak night. Check the website for a schedule of events.

☆ Entertainment

Arkey Blue's Silver Dollar Saloon LIVE MUSIC

(☑ 830-796-8826; 308 Main St; ⊙ 10am-midnight) At this small but atmospheric basement music space, join cowboy-hat-wearing folk for live music throughout the week. The building dates to the late 1800s and the honky-tonk, opened in 1968, is nearing its 50th birthday. Look for Hank Williams Sr's carved signature in one of the wooden tables. There's a $5 cover per person on Saturdays but otherwise it's free.

ℹ Information

Bandera County Convention & Visitors Bureau

(CVB; ☑ 830-796-3045; www.banderacowboy capital.com; 126 Hwy 16; ⊙ 9am-5pm Mon-Fri, 10am-3pm Sat) Offers helpful information and friendly advice. A half block off Main St.

SAN ANTONIO & HILL COUNTRY BANDERA

Boerne

📞 830 / POP 13,674

The bustling little center of Boerne (pronounced 'Bernie') was settled by German immigrants in 1849. The town, which clings strongly to its German roots, is less overrun with tourists than Fredericksburg and is a pleasant place to spend a few hours.

Main St focuses on antique stores, most of which stock a handy leaflet that will help you navigate around the plethora of shops. The Cibolo Creek Trail, a paved path stretching 1.75 miles along scenic Cibolo Creek on the outskirts of downtown, is especially nice in the late afternoon and before sunset. Boerne is also a good launchpad for exploring regional cave systems.

◉ Sights

Cave Without a Name   CAVE
(📞 830-537-4212; www.cavewithoutaname.com; 325 Kreutzberg Rd; adult/child 6-12yr $20/10; ⊙ 9am-6pm Jun-Aug, to 5pm Sep-May; 🅿) If your tour pauses while descending the 126 steps that lead into this cave, don't lean back. You might bump a sleeping bat! But no worries, they're harmless and just one of the many fascinating sights on the one-hour tour through six rooms. You'll see stalactites, stalagmites and formations named after food, including popcorn, grapes, eggs and bacon. It's quite amazing.

Moonshiners probably used the cave during Prohibition, but three brave kids in the 1930s were the first to explore the chambers and share their discovery – after climbing down by rope and ladders! One of them was Mary McGrath Curry, about six years old at the time, who went on to become a successful hand mathematician (she used a slide rule and formulas) for the US space program in the 1950s.

The woodsy area near the cave is open for tent camping and RVs (tent/RV $15/25). The last cave tour starts one hour before close.

From downtown follow E Blanco Rd east. Turn left onto Ranch Road 474 and follow it just over 5 miles north to Kreutzberg Rd. Turn right onto Kreutzberg Rd and follow it 3.5 miles to the entrance road to the cave.

Cascade Caverns   CAVE
(📞 830-755-8080; www.cascadecaverns.com; 226 Cascade Caverns Rd; adult/child 4-11yr $18/12; ⊙ 9am-5pm, tours on the hour 10am-4pm; 🅿) The popular Cascade Caverns include a 140ft-deep cave featuring giant stalagmites and stalactites and a 100ft waterfall, which you can see by taking the one-hour tour. The caverns are about 3 miles south of Boerne; take exit 543 off the I-10. Hours vary, so check the website for details.

🛏 Sleeping

Ye Kendall Inn   HISTORIC HOTEL $$
(📞 830-249-2138; www.yekendallinn.com; 128 W Blanco Rd; r $159-179, cabins & cottages $199; 🅿 🛜) A National Historic Landmark dating from 1859, this is the nicest place to stay in Boerne. The creekside main house is made of hand-cut limestone and features a two-story, 200ft-long front porch. The hotel also has three cabins and a church, all dating from the 1800s and relocated from around the state (the stunning Enchanted Cabin was built near Enchanted Rock).

Note that some rooms in the main house share space with in-room bathroom facilities, including a claw-foot tub. These rooms are quaint for sure, if not for everyone, and you'll have fantastic sunset views from the 2nd-floor porch.

The pretty Cibolo Creek Trail starts beside the inn.

🍴 Eating

Mary's Tacos   MEXICAN $
(📞 830-249-7474; 518 E Blanco St; tacos $3; ⊙ 6am-1:30pm Mon-Fri, 7am-1pm Sun) Everybody in town recommends Mary's, where the tortillas are homemade. The drill? Step up to the counter. Order a breakfast taco and a Big Red. Grab a table. Squeeze some hot sauce from the container. Take a bite. And call it a very good day. They close early – so don't mess around!

Bear Moon Bakery & Cafe   CAFE $
(📞 830-816-2327; www.facebook.com/bearmoon bakery; 401 S Main St; breakfast buffet adult/child $14/6, sandwiches $7-9; ⊙ 6am-5pm Tue-Sat, 8am-4pm Sun) For a fresh, delicious breakfast buffet, look no further than Bear Moon Bakery & Cafe. On weekends, be sure to arrive early – it's always packed. There are plenty of home-baked goodies to tempt you as well, along with fresh soups, salads and sandwiches for lunch.

Po Po Family Restaurant   AMERICAN $$
(📞 830-537-4194; www.poporestaurant.com; 829 FM 289, off the I-10; breakfast mains $5-11, lunch mains $9-12, dinner mains $11-30; ⊙ 7-10:30am daily, 11am-8:30pm Sun-Thu, to 9:30pm Fri & Sat) Seven miles north of town, this hospitable restaurant

serves steaks and seafood – including hard-to-find frogs' legs – but the main reason to come is to see the absolutely astounding collection of souvenir plates: more than 2000 of them cover almost every inch of wall space. They now serve breakfast too.

Drinking & Nightlife

Peggy's on the Green BAR
(✆830-572-5000; www.peggysonthegreen.com; 128 W Blanco Rd; ⊙11am-2pm & 5-10pm Tue-Sun) This clubby and intimate cocktail bar inside Ye Kendall Inn is the perfect spot for a cozy tête-à-tête.

Dodging Duck Brewhaus MICROBREWERY
(✆830-248-3825; www.dodgingduck.com; 402 River Rd; mains $9-25; ⊙11am-9pm Mon-Thu, to 10pm Sat & Sun) This small brewpub offers tasty homemade beers in an eclectic atmosphere across from Cibolo Creek. It also serves Mexican and German dishes and plenty of shareable bar snacks.

Daily Grind CAFE
(✆830-249-4677; 143 S Main St; ⊙7am-4pm) A prime choice for early-morning coffee and tea, this cute little spot is right on the main strip.

❶ Information

Boerne Convention & Visitors Bureau
(✆830-249-7277; www.visitboerne.org; 1407 S Main St; ⊙9am-5pm Mon-Fri, 10am-2pm Sat) Has brochures covering historical markers around town.

Wimberley

✆512 / POP 2626
It's not really on the way to or from anywhere else, so, as the locals like to say, 'You have to mean to visit Wimberley.' A popular weekend spot for Austinites, this artists' community gets absolutely jam-packed during summer weekends – especially on the first Saturday of each month from March to December, when local art galleries, shops and craftspeople set up booths for Wimberley Market Days (p134). The event fills Lion's Field with a bustling collection of live music, food and more than 475 vendors.

Even on weekends when there's no market, there are plenty of shops to visit, stocked with antiques, gifts, and local arts and crafts. You can also taste olive oil in one of the state's few commercial olive orchards, eat

expertly baked homemade pies or kick back at the creekside lodgings.

Sights

Bella Vista Ranch PLANTATION
(✆512-847-6514; www.texasolivoil.com; 3101 Mt Sharp Rd, off CR 182; tours per person $15; ⊙noon-4:30pm Fri & Sat, to 3:30pm Sun, tours 1pm Sat & noon Sun) This ranch is home to more than 1200 olive-producing trees. It has a gift shop with free tastings, and runs a tour that takes in the orchard, the olive press and the winery.

🏃 Activities

Devil's Backbone SCENIC DRIVE
For excellent scenic views of Wimberley's surrounding limestone hills, take a drive on FM 32, otherwise known as the Devil's Backbone. From Wimberley, head south on RR 12 to FM 32, and turn right toward Fischer and Canyon Lake. The road gets steeper, then winds out onto a craggy ridge (the 'backbone') with a 360-degree vista.

Blue Hole SWIMMING
(✆512-660-9111; www.cityofwimberley.com; 100 Blue Hole Lane; adult/child 4-12yr/under 4 $9/5/free; ⊙park 8am-dusk, swimming area 10am-6pm Sat & Sun May, daily Jun-Aug) One of the Hill Country's best swimming holes, this city-run spot is found in the calm, shady and crystal-clear waters of Cypress Creek. To get here from Wimberley, follow Old Kyle Rd northeast from the town square for about 350yd then turn left onto Blue Hole Lane.

🛏 Sleeping

There are dozens of B&Bs and cottages in Wimberley; call the Wimberley Convention & Visitors Bureau (p134) or visit its website for more information.

Hotel Flora and Fauna BOUTIQUE HOTEL $$
(✆512-842-9110; www.hotelfloraandfauna.com; 400 River Road; r incl breakfast $179; 🅿🐾♿) The wildlife mural adorning the front

privacy wall will pull you in for a closer look, but the gracious service, inviting courtyard and stylish rooms – with record players and retro albums – will have you sticking around at this new property a short walk from downtown. All rooms are king studios with kitchenettes. Local art, inside and out, is a highlight.

Pet fee is $10 per night.

Wimberley Inn MOTEL $$
(☑512-847-3750; www.wimberleyinn.com; 200 RM 3237; r $135-199; ❋☎) Close to the action, just a quarter-mile east of the square, this motel has large rooms at a fair price. Standard rooms are inexpensive and simple, deluxe rooms step it up a notch. At press time the property was under new management and room remodeling was under way. The oak-shaded grounds are lovely, and a home-cooked breakfast is included at weekends.

✖ Eating

Wimberley Pie Company DESSERTS $
(☑512-847-9462; www.wimberleypie.com; 13619 RR12; slice $3.25, pie $10-17; ⊙10am-5pm Tue-Sat, noon-4pm Sun) You haven't eaten until you've wrapped your mouth around a pie from this small but popular bakery, which supplies many of the area's restaurants (and a few in Austin) with every kind of pie and cheesecake you can imagine, and then some. It's about a quarter-mile east of the square.

Leaning Pear AMERICAN $
(☑512-847-7327; www.leaningpear.com; 111 River Rd; lunch mains $7-13, dinner mains $11-24; ⊙11am-9pm Tue-Sat, to 3pm Sun) Get out of the crowded downtown area for a relaxed lunch. This cafe exudes Hill Country charm like a cool glass of iced tea, with salads and sandwiches served in a restored stone house.

🍷 Drinking & Nightlife

Devil's Backbone Tavern BAR
(☑830-964-2544; 4041 FM 32, Fischer; ⊙noon-midnight) Devil's Backbone Tavern is a perfectly tattered and dusty beer joint with a country-music jukebox, dollar bills stuck to the wall and a Thursday-night music jam from 8pm. And some say there's also a ghost.

🛍 Shopping

Art galleries, antique shops and craft stores surround **Wimberley Square**, located where Ranch Rd 12 crosses Cypress Creek and bends into an 'S.'

Wimberley Market Days MARKET
(www.shopmarketdays.com; 601 FM 2325; admission free, parking $5; ⊙7am-4pm 1st Sat Mar-Dec) Local art galleries, shops and craftspeople set up booths for Wimberley Market Days, a bustling collection of live music, food and more than 475 vendors at Lion's Field. It takes place on the first Saturday of the month, and closes at 3pm in summer.

ⓘ Information

Wimberley Convention & Visitors Bureau
(CVB; ☑512-847-2201; www.wimberley.org; 14100 RR 12; ⊙9am-4pm Mon-Sat, from 1pm Sun) Contact them for information on market days and other happenings around town.

Kerrville
☑830 / POP 23,136

Kerrville makes a good base for exploring the Hill Country if you're looking for a city that's not too fussy or overdone with B&B-style cuteness. What it might lack in historic charm, it makes up for in size, offering plenty of services for travelers as well as easy access to kayaking, canoeing and swimming on the Guadalupe River. A beautiful new walking and cycling trail links parks along the river. The city is also home to an engaging museum of cowboy life, a jam-packed springtime folk festival and a historic district around Main St. It may not turn on the charm, but it's a welcome relief for anyone trying to avoid excessive quaintness.

⊙ Sights

Louise Hays City Park PARK
(☑830-257-7300; www.kerrvilletx.gov; 202 Thompson Dr; ⊙dawn-11pm; ⊛) FREE This 60-acre park may not be Kerrville's largest, but it's free and offers river access, shaded picnic tables, sports courts and barbecue pits. Also, as part of a $1.4 million renovation project completed in 2015, the city connected Louise Hays to Lehmann-Monroe Park for an additional 27 acres. The latter is home to a kiddie 'sprayground' and a dog park.

Museum of Western Art MUSEUM
(☑830-896-2553; www.museumofwesternart.com; 1550 Bandera Hwy; adult/student/child under 8yr $7/5/free; ⊙10am-4pm Tue-Sat) This is a nonprofit showcase of Western Americana. The quality and detail of the work, mostly paintings and bronze sculptures, is astounding; all depict scenes of cowboy and Western

life, the landscape or vignettes of Native American life.

Kerrville-Schreiner Park
PARK

(☑830-257-5300; www.kerrvilletx.gov; 2385 Bandera Hwy; adult/child 3-12yr/senior $4/1/2; ☉office 8am-5pm, day use to 10pm) Three miles southeast of town, this 517-acre park is a beautiful place for cycling, hiking, canoeing, tubing and camping. For lazy floats along the Guadalupe River, rent kayaks, canoes, paddle boards and inner tubes at Kerrville Kayak & Canoe on site.

Riverside Nature Center
PARK

(☑830-257-4837; www.riversidenaturecenter.org; 150 Francisco Lemos St; ☉10am-6pm Mon-Sat) FREE Near the river, at the south end of downtown, the center has walking trails, a wildflower meadow and Guadalupe River access.

Kerr Arts & Cultural Center
ARTS CENTER

(☑830-895-2911; www.kacckerrville.com; 228 Earl Garrett St; admission free; ☉10am-4pm Tue-Sat, from 1pm Sun) FREE Step inside to catch the pulse of the Hill Country art scene. Located in the old post office, it frequently changes exhibits, which could include anything from quilts to watercolors to gourd art.

🏃 Activities

River Trail
WALKING, CYCLING

(www.kerrvilletx.gov; ☉dawn-dusk; 🏵) This new trail unfurls beside the Guadalupe River, stretching east from the Riverside Nature Center to Kerrville-Schreiner Park, about 4 miles away. Open to pedestrians, dog walkers and cyclists, this paved path is a pretty addition to the city.

Kerrville Kayak & Canoe Rentals
KAYAKING

(☑830-459-2122; www.paddlekerrville.com; 1617 Broadway; per hr $10-15; ☉10am-5pm Tue-Sat) This outfit rents out watercraft by the hour. They sometimes open daily, with later hours, in late spring and summer, and they have satellite locations at Kerrville-Schreiner Park and Louise Hays City Park, with varying hours. You can save money with half- or full-day rentals.

🎉 Festivals & Events

Kerrville Fall Music Festival
MUSIC

(☑830-257-3600; www.kerrville-music.com; 3876 Medina Hwy; ☉Labor Day weekend) A three-day miniversion of Kerrville's spring folk festival, with an added focus on Texas wine and beers.

Kerrville Folk Festival
MUSIC

(☑830-257-3600; www.kerrville-music.com; 3876 Medina Hwy; ☉late May-early Jun) The Quiet Valley Ranch turns up the volume each spring. This 18-day musical extravaganza starts right around Memorial Day and features music by national touring acts and local musicians. One-day tickets cost $20 to $45; check the website for information about camping at the ranch.

🛏 Sleeping

Inn of the Hills Resort & Conference Center
HOTEL $

(☑830-895-5000; www.innofthehills.com; 1001 Junction Hwy; d $77-104; ⊛❄🛜❄) The renovated lower-level cabana rooms opening onto the pool are a lovely surprise; with stone walls and stylish decor, they were among the nicest we saw in town. All rooms come with microwaves and mini-fridges. The common areas are nice enough, although the restaurant is a little countrified. The inn's best feature? The beautiful Olympic-style pool surrounded by shade trees.

Kerrville-Schreiner Park Campground
CAMPGROUND $

(☑830-257-5392; www.kerrvilletx.gov; 2385 Bandera Hwy; day use adult/child 3-12yr/senior $4/1/2, tent sites $15, RV sites $23-28, cabins $50 110; 🏵) This is a beautiful park set right on the river. Pitch a tent or hook up your RV in one of the well-tended campsites, then go enjoy the 500 acres.

WHAT THE...? STONEHENGE II

So **Stonehenge II** isn't the real Stonehenge. We're not real druids, so there you go. This second-string henge has much less mysterious origins than the ancient megalithic structure near Salisbury, England. Two locals built the 60%-scale model out of concrete and threw in some Easter Island statues for good measure.

Just a few years back you could find it out in a field on a country road, but alas, the property changed hands and the new owners weren't interested in maintaining the henge's important cultural legacy. Luckily, the installation has been saved by the **Hill Country Arts Foundation** (p136), whose lawn it now graces.

Eating

★ Taco to Go
MEXICAN $

(☎ 830-896-8226; www.tacotogokerrville.com; 428 Sidney Baker St; mains $3-9; ⏱ 6am-2pm Mon-Sat, from 7am Sun) You can take your tacos to-go or eat inside this tiny joint beside Walgreens, but don't miss out on the excellent soft tacos – including breakfast tacos served all day – made with homemade tortillas and salsa. Friendly folks.

Hill Country Cafe
CAFE $

(☎ 830-257-6665; www.hill-country-cafe.com; 806 Main St; mains $5-11; ⏱ 6am-2pm Mon-Fri, to 11am Sat) The waitress might just call you 'hon' at this tiny hole-in-the-wall diner near the historic district, which serves up hearty home cooking in heaped portions. You'll find just about everything you could want for breakfast. Later in the day look for sandwiches and lunch plates, including chicken fried steak. Cash and local checks only.

Classics Burgers & 'Moore'
BURGERS $

(☎ 830-257-8866; www.classicsburgers.net; 448 Sidney Baker St; mains $4-10; ⏱ 11am-3pm & 5-8pm Mon-Fri, 11am-3pm Sat) This burger joint does have sort of a classic quality to it, and its burgers and fries blow the fast-food chains out of the water. Order at the register. Cash and local checks only.

Rails: A Cafe at the Depot
AMERICAN $$

(☎ 830-257-3877; www.railscafe.com; 615 E Schreiner; meals $9-32; ⏱ 11am-9pm Mon-Sat) This warm and intimate cafe in the old train depot downtown is awfully pleasant. Make a lunch of panini or salad, or splurge a bit with the osso buco (a Milanese specialty of cross-cut veal shanks braised with vegetables) or beef tenderloin.

Francisco's
AMERICAN $$$

(☎ 830-257-2995; www.franciscos-restaurant.com; 201 Earl Garrett St; lunch mains $7.25-10, dinner mains $13-38; ⏱ 11am-3pm Mon-Sat & 5:30-9pm Thu-Sat) Colorful, bright and airy, this bistro and sidewalk cafe is housed in an old limestone building in the historic district. It's packed at lunch, and is one of the swankiest places in town for a weekend dinner.

☆ Entertainment

Hill Country Arts Foundation ARTS CENTER (☎ 830-367-5121; www.hcaf.com; 120 Point Theatre Road S, Ingram) Runs the Point Theater, which hosts performances year-round (on indoor and outdoor stages). Also the home of the concrete Stonehenge II (p135).

ℹ Information

Bank of America (☎ 830-792-0430; www.bankofamerica.com; 601 Main St; ⏱ 9am-4pm Mon-Fri, to noon Sat) You can change money at the bank, which has an ATM.

Butt-Holdsworth Memorial Library (☎ 830-257-8422; www.kerrvilletx.gov; 505 Water St; ⏱ 10am-6pm Mon, Wed & Sat, to 8pm Tue & Thu, 1-5pm Sun; 🛜) Provides free wi-fi and 30-day internet access on a library computer for $8.

Peterson Regional Medical Center (☎ 830-896-4200; www.petersonrmc.com; 551 Hill Country Dr) Has a new facility and 24-hour emergency services.

Visitor Center (☎ 830-792-3535, 800-221-7958; www.kerrvilletexascvb.com; 2108 Sidney Baker St; ⏱ 8:30am-5pm Mon-Fri, 9am-3pm Sat, 10am-3pm Sun) Kerrville's excellent visitor center has everything you'll need to get out and about in the Hill Country, including heaps of brochures and coupon books for accommodations.

ℹ Getting There & Away

Kerrville is half an hour south of Fredericksburg on Hwy 16, or just over an hour northwest from San Antonio on I-10. In town, Hwy 16 becomes Sidney Baker St, and Hwy 27 (aka Junction Hwy) becomes Main St.

By car from Austin, take US 290 west to Fredericksburg, then turn south onto Hwy 16, which meets Kerrville south of I-10. From San Antonio, take I-10 north to Hwy 16, then head south. Greyhound runs between Kerrville and San Antonio, as well as Fredericksburg.

In town, **Bicycle Works** (☎ 830-896-6864; www.hillcountrybicycle.com; 141 W Water St; day rental $30-45; ⏱ 10am-6pm Mon-Fri, to 4pm Sat) rents out bikes.

Dallas & the Panhandle Plains

Best Places to Eat

➜ Javier's (p153)

➜ Lonesome Dove Western Bistro (p167)

➜ Big Texan Steak Ranch (p198)

➜ West Table (p190)

➜ Peasant Village Restaurant (p183)

Best Places to Sleep

➜ Adolphus (p149)

➜ Hotel Settles (p180)

➜ Overton Hotel (p189)

➜ Hotel Belmont (p149)

➜ Stockyards Hotel (p164)

Why Go?

Dallas and Fort Worth may be next-door neighbors, but they're hardly twins – or even kissing cousins. Long regarded as being divergent as an Escalade-driving sophisticate and a rancher in a dusty pickup truck, these two cities have starkly different facades. Beyond appearances, however, they share a love of high (and low) culture and good old-fashioned Texan fun. In the surrounding area is a plethora of fabulous small towns worthy of a road trip, including Waxahachie and McKinney.

Leave the big smoke behind and you'll find that the Panhandle and Central Plains may be the part of Texas that most typifies the state to outsiders. This is a land of sprawling cattle ranches, where people can still make a living on horseback. The landscape appears endlessly flat, punctuated only by utility poles and windmills, until a vast canyon materializes and seems to plunge into another world.

When to Go
Dallas

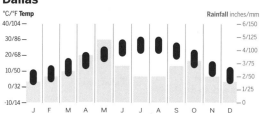

Mar–May Spring comes early to Texas and the wildflowers stage a grand show.

Jun–Aug It's hot! But air-conditioning and swimming in watering holes will cool you down.

Sep & Oct Forget winter – balmy fall days are the best.

Dallas & the Panhandle Plains Highlights

1 Sixth Floor Museum (p140) Reliving the tragic day of JFK's assassination at Dallas' Dealey Plaza.

2 Waxahachie (p174) Wandering this beautifully preserved town dating to the 1870s.

3 Texas Hwy 70 (p190) Meandering through forgotten small towns, lush ranches and evocative wide open spaces.

4 Big Texan Steak Ranch (p198) Being foolhardy and taking the challenge in Amarillo to eat a huge steak and sides in under an hour.

5 San Angelo (p181) Exploring the old streets and beautiful river trails, then having an excellent meal or perhaps a craft-brewed pint of beer.

6 Palo Duro Canyon (p193) Taking in America's amazing, colorful and, yes, grand second-largest canyon.

7 Billy Bob's Texas (p168) Bull-riding and two-steppin' at the biggest honky-tonk on earth in Fort Worth's cow-scented Stockyards.

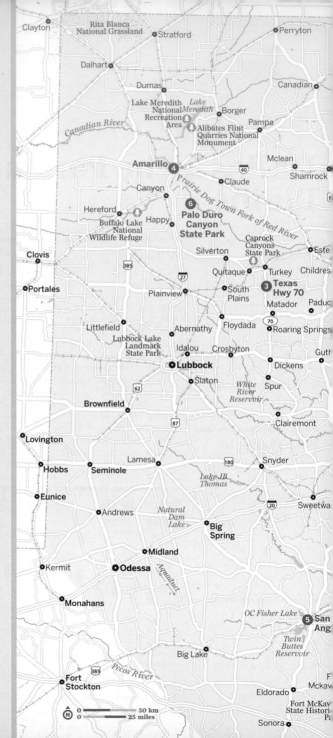

DALLAS

📞 214, 469, 972 / POP 1,300,000

Dallas is Texas' most mythical city, with a past and present rich in the stuff that American legends are made of. The 'Big D' is famous for its contributions to popular culture – notably the Cowboys and their cheerleaders, and *Dallas,* the TV series that once was a worldwide symbol of the USA. An upscale ethos makes for a vaunted dining and shopping scene, where the more conspicuous your consumption, the better.

The museums are not only excellent, but unique – history buffs should not miss the memorials to President John F Kennedy's assassination. The most impressive addition to Dallas' cultural landscape in recent years is the massive 68-acre Arts District.

Pick a neighborhood like Deep Ellum, Lower Greenville or the Bishop Arts District and stake out a space on a patio with a cold beer for the quintessential Dallas experience.

History

In 1839 John Neely Bryan, a Tennessee lawyer and Indian trader, stumbled onto the three forks of the Trinity River, a site he thought had the makings of a good trading post. Dallas County was created in 1846, and both county and town were probably named for George Mifflin Dallas, US vice president under James K Polk; the two were elected on a platform favoring Texas statehood.

Dallas grew slowly for 30 years, though from the start the city had a flair for self-promotion: Bryan saw to it that Dallas was placed on maps even before there was much of a town. In the 1870s the state decided Dallas would be the junction of the north–south Missouri, Kansas and Texas Railroad and the east–west Texas and Pacific Railroad. It worked like magic: merchants from New York, Chicago, Boston and St Louis invested heavily in the city.

Cotton created another boom. In 1885 farmland sold for $15 an acre. By 1920, with cotton prices soaring, land values had risen to $300 an acre. And when the East Texas Oil Field was struck 100 miles east of town in 1930, Dallas became the financial center of the oil industry.

Post-WWII Dallas continued to build on its reputation as a citadel of commerce. But its image took a dive when President John F Kennedy was assassinated during a November 1963 visit to the city. This tragic incident, coupled with the ensuing turmoil of the 1960s, badly battered Dallas' self-esteem. Gradually, however, the city reclaimed its Texas swagger with help from a few new chest-thumping sources of civic pride: the Dallas Cowboys won the first of five Super Bowl titles in 1972. And then there was that little ol' TV show, the top-rated series in the US from 1980 to '82. Dallas was back, louder and prouder than ever – a roll it's been on with hardly a bump in the road since.

○ Sights

Many of Dallas' major sights are blissfully compact, which you'll appreciate given the local sprawl. Downtown museums and Arts District attractions are in areas easily traversed by either walking or taking the McKinney Ave trolley – in fact, there's no reason to drive between them.

Fair Park attractions can be reached by light rail, but for everything else you'll need to jump in a car.

◎ Downtown

★ **Sixth Floor Museum** MUSEUM
(Map p150; 📞 214-747-6660; www.jfk.org; Book Depository, 411 Elm St; adult/child $16/13; ⊗ 10am-6pm Tue-Sun, noon-6pm Mon; light rail West End)
No city wants the distinction of being the site of an assassination – especially if the victim happens to be President John F Kennedy. But rather than downplay the events that sent the city reeling in 1963, Dallas gives visitors a unique opportunity to delve into the world-altering events unleashed by an assassin in the former Texas School Book Depository. Fascinating multimedia exhibits (plus the included audioguide) give an excellent historical context of JFK's time, as well as his life and legacy.

And while any museum dedicated to the subject could have reconstructed the historical event using footage, audio clips and eyewitness accounts, this museum offers you a goosebump-raising view through the exact window from which Lee Harvey Oswald fired upon the motorcade. (If that last statement raises your hackles, not to worry: the displays don't shy away from conspiracy theories, either.) Note just how close Kennedy's limo was to Oswald's gun – the shooting distance was fairly short.

The museum also offers an interesting self-guided Cell Phone Walking Tour (one hour; $2.50) of Dealey Plaza and other JFK assassination sites.

Dealey Plaza & the Grassy Knoll PARK
(Map p150; light rail West End) Now a National Historic Landmark, this rectangular park is south of the former Book Depository. Dealey Plaza was named in 1935 for George Bannerman Dealey, a longtime Dallas journalist, historian and philanthropist. Just steps from here, John F Kennedy was assassinated in November 1963.

The grassy knoll is the hillock that rises from the north side of Elm St to the edge of the picket fence separating Dealey Plaza from the railroad yards. While some witnesses to the assassination claim shots came from this area, investigators found only cigarette butts and footprints on the knoll after the shooting. The House Select Committee on Assassinations, investigating from 1976 to 1978, concluded via acoustical analysis that a sniper did fire from behind the picket fence but missed. That bolstered the belief that Kennedy's assassination was part of a conspiracy. We may never know the truth.

★ Pioneer Plaza SQUARE
(Map p150; cnr S Griffin & Young Sts) For a Texas-sized photo op or just a sight of the largest bronze monument on earth, head to Pioneer Plaza. Its showpiece is a collection of 40 bronze larger-than-life longhorns, amassed as if they were on a cattle drive. There is an unmistakable and compelling power to the tableau.

Old Red Museum MUSEUM
(Map p150; ☑ 214-745-1100; www.oldred.org; 100 S Houston St; adult/child $10/7; ⊗ 9am-5pm) The 1892 Old Red Courthouse that houses this museum is almost as interesting as the museum's interactive exhibits on Dallas county history. Entry includes a building tour (daily, check for times).

Thanks-Giving Square SQUARE
(Map p150; ☑ 214-969-1977; www.thanksgiving.org; bounded by Bryan St, Pacific Ave & Ervay St; ⊗ garden 5am-11pm, chapel 1-3pm Mon & 11am-3pm Wed-Sun; light rail St Paul) **FREE** For all its din, drive and shopping malls, Dallas has a surprisingly quiet side – a triangular piece of prime downtown real estate set aside for spiritual renewal and reflection. Thanks-Giving Square was established by the Thanks-Giving Foundation as a 'place where people can use gratitude as a basis for dialogue, mutual understanding and healing.'

Designed by Philip Johnson, the tranquil center includes a meditation garden, a Wall of Praise, an interdenominational Chapel of Thanksgiving and a museum of gratitude.

Dallas Heritage Village HISTORIC SITE
(Map p150; ☑ 214-421-5141; www.dallasheritage village.org; 1515 S Harwood St; adult/child $9/5; ⊗ 10am-4pm Tue-Sat, noon-4pm Sun; light rail Cedars) This 13-acre museum of history and architecture, set on a wooded property south of downtown, shows what it was like to live in North Texas from about 1840 to 1910. The modern skyline makes for a striking

A DARK DAY IN NOVEMBER

In the early 1960s, the USA was fascinated with its young president, his little children at play in the Oval Office and his regal wife. They seemed the perfect family, and the USA – still awash in postwar prosperity – considered itself a place where justice and amity prevailed.

But beneath the glossy surface, the USA was heading into its most divisive decade since the Civil War. By no means universally popular, John F Kennedy had won the election over Richard Nixon by fewer than 120,000 votes from among 69 million cast. His 1961 Bay of Pigs invasion of Cuba was a foreign-policy disaster.

In the eyes of many, Kennedy redeemed his presidency in the fall of 1962, when he stood up to Soviet premier Nikita Khrushchev after US intelligence services discovered Soviet offensive-missile sites in Cuba. Yet in the nine months prior to his Dallas appearance, Kennedy had received more than 400 death threats, from critics on both the left, who felt him guilty of warmongering during the Cuban missile crisis, and the right, who felt him soft on communism. The president's advisers were seriously concerned about the trip to Dallas, where right-wing groups, including the John Birch Society and the Indignant White Citizens Council, held powerful sway. Yet nearly a quarter-million people lined the streets on November 22, 1963, to greet him.

Greater Dallas

0   1 mile
0   2 km

Dallas Love Field Airport

Marsh La

HIGHLAND PARK

Lemmon Ave

Cedars Springs Rd

W Mockingbird La

Denton Dr

Inwood/ Love Field

26 ❌

Inwood Rd

Southwest Medical District/Parkland

Market Center

Medical/Market Center

Dallas North Tollway

32 🅿
36 🏨

Oak Lawn Ave

14 🏨

47 🏛

Dallas Country Club

Lovers La

17 ❌

13 🏨

NorthPark Center (.5mi)

5 🏛

7 🏛

Lovers Lane

Skillman St

41 ❤

Mockingbird

E Mockingbird La

White Rock Greenbelt

White Rock Lake

Dallas Arboretum & Botanical Gardens (0.75m)

LAKEWOOD

40 ✪

E Garland Ave

Gaston Ave

La Vista Dr

38 ✪

29 🅿

33 🏨

46 🏨

Goodwin Ave

10 🏨

Henderson Ave

Fitzhugh Ave

20 ❌

48 🏨
19 ❌ 15 🏨

27 ❌
34 🏨

McKinney Ave

N Central Expwy

Hillcrest Ave

Cityplace/ Uptown

22 ❌

White Rock

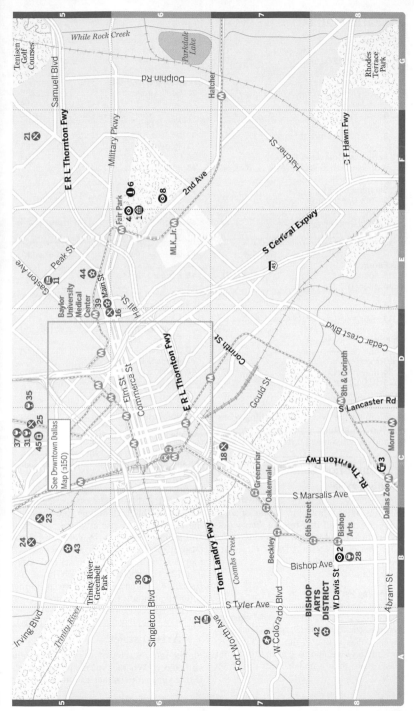

DALLAS & THE PANHANDLE PLAINS

Tenison Golf Courses

While Rock Creek

Parkdale Lake

Rhodes Terrace Park

Samuell Blvd

Dolphin Rd

Hatcher

Hatcher St

E R L Thornton Fwy

Military Pkwy

C F Hawn Fwy

21 ✗

2nd Ave

MLK Jr.

6

8

4

1

Fair Park

Peak St

S Central Expwy

45

Gaston Ave

11

44

Baylor University Medical Center

Main St

Hall St

39

16

Elm St

Commerce St

E R L Thornton Fwy

Corinth St

Cedar Crest Blvd

8th & Corinth

S Lancaster Rd

Gould St

See Downtown Dallas Map (p150)

37

31

45

25

35

Morrel

18 ✗

Greenbriar

Oakenwald

S Marsalis Ave

RL Thornton Fwy

3

Dallas Zoo

23 ✗

24 ✗

43

Trinity River Greenbelt Park

30

Tom Landry Fwy

Coombs Creek

6th Street

Bishop Arts

Beckley

S Marsalis Ave

Irving Blvd

Trinity River

Singleton Blvd

12

W Colorado Blvd

Fort Worth Ave

S Tyler Ave

Bishop Ave

2

28

9

42

BISHOP ARTS DISTRICT

W Davis St

Abram St

Greater Dallas

◎ Sights
1 African American Museum	E6
2 Bishop Arts District	B8
3 Dallas Zoo	C8
4 Fair Park	E6
5 George W. Bush Presidential Library & Museum	E2
6 Hall of State	F6
7 Meadows Museum	D2
8 Texas Discovery Gardens	F6

◐ Activities, Courses & Tours
9 Stevens Park Golf Course	A7

⊜ Sleeping
10 Abby Guest House	E3
11 Corinthian B&B	E5
12 Hotel Belmont	A6
13 Hotel Lumen	D2
14 Rosewood Mansion on Turtle Creek	C4

⊗ Eating
15 Abacus	D3
16 AllGood Café	D5
17 Bubba's Cooks Country	D1
18 Fuel City	C7
19 Highland Park Soda Shop	D3
20 Javier's	D3
21 Kalachandji's	F5
22 Keller's Drive-In	F1
23 Meddlesome Moth	B5
24 Rodeo Goat	B5
25 S&D Oyster Company	C5

Smoke	(see 12)
26 Sonny Bryan's Smokehouse	A3
27 Velvet Taco	D3

◉ Drinking & Nightlife
28 Boulevardier	B8
29 Cosmo's	F4
30 Four Corners Brewing Co	B6
31 Ginger Man	C5
32 JR's Bar & Grill	C4
33 Mudsmith	E3
34 Old Monk Pub	C5
35 Parliament	D5
36 Sue Ellen's	C4
37 Two Corks and a Bottle	C5

✪ Entertainment
38 Balcony Club	F4
39 Dallas Comedy House	E5
40 Goat	G4
41 Granada Theater	E2
42 Kessler Theater	A8
43 Kitchen Dog Theater	B5
44 Sons of Hermann Hall	E5

⊜ Shopping
45 David Dike Fine Art	C5
Deep Vellum Books	(see 39)
Froggie's 5 & 10	(see 19)
46 Good Records	E4
47 Highland Park Village	C2
48 Nest	D3

(side margin) DALLAS & THE PANHANDLE PLAINS DALLAS

backdrop for the living history exhibits comprised of 38 historic structures, including a tipi and a Civil War–era farm.

◉ Convention Center & Reunion Area

Come evening, if it seems like downtown Dallas is full of roaming businesspeople looking to burn off the stress of their workday but not entirely sure where to go, you're right. Everything's a short walk from either DART Rail's Convention Center Station or Union Station.

Kay Bailey Hutchison
Convention Center Dallas   NOTABLE BUILDING
(Map p150; ☎214-939-2750; www.dallasconventioncenter.com; 650 S Griffin St; light rail Convention Center) Dallas is one of the world's biggest convention cities, and its convention center boasts more than a million sq ft of exhibit space.

Reunion Tower   LANDMARK
(Map p150; ☎214-712-7040; www.reuniontower.com; 300 Reunion Blvd E; adult/child from $17/8; ⊙hours vary by season; light rail Union Station) What's 50 stories high and has a three-level spherical dome with 260 flashing lights? It's Reunion Tower, the unofficial symbol of Dallas. Take the 68-second elevator ride up for a pricey sky-high panoramic view. Or enjoy the view from the celebrity-chef restaurant and lounge **Five Sixty by Wolfgang Puck** (Map p150; ☎214-571-5784; www.wolfgangpuck.com; Reunion Tower, 300 E Reunion Blvd; mains from $25; ⊙restaurant 5-10pm Mon-Thu, to 11pm Fri-Sun). An underground pedestrian tunnel connects Reunion Tower with Union Station and the Hyatt Regency Dallas.

◉ Arts District

Plunge into 68 acres of arts, entertainment and culture. Whether you're an opera fanatic or go gaga for abstract sculpture, the Arts

District (www.thedallasartsdistrict.org) has something for you.

★ **Perot Museum of Nature & Science**   MUSEUM
(Map p150; ☑ 214-428-5555; www.perotmuseum. org; 2201 N Field St; adult/child from $20/13; ⊙10am-5pm Mon-Sat, noon-5pm Sun; ⬛; light rail St Paul) A sizable star of the Arts District, this striking museum opened to much acclaim in 2012. It wows both on the outside (thanks to award-winning architect Thom Mayne) and on the inside (there are six floors of wonder). Most of the exhibits are interactive: visitors can design their own bird, journey through the solar system, command robots, commune with dinosaurs and much more.

The building is designed to be environmentally sound, and this feature is explained in detail. It also has a 3D theater with ever-changing movies.

Dallas Museum of Art   MUSEUM
(Map p150; www.dallasmuseumofart.org; 1717 N Harwood St; ⊙11am-5pm Tue-Sun, to 9pm Thu; ⬛; light rail St Paul) FREE This museum is a high-caliber world tour of decorative and fine art. Among the many treasures are Edward Hopper's enigmatic *Lighthouse Hill*, Frederic Church's lush masterpiece *The Icebergs* and Rodin's *Sculptor and his Muse*. Other highlights include exquisite pre-Colombian pottery, carvings and tapestries from Oceania, and a villa modeled on Coco Chanel's Mediterranean mansion (where you can see paintings by statesman Winston Churchill).

Thursday nights feature live jazz in the atrium and cocktails in the DMA Cafe. Kids (and parents) will appreciate the Young Learners Gallery, with fun projects for budding artists.

Crow Collection of Asian Art   MUSEUM
(Map p150; ☑ 214-979-6430; www.crowcollec tion.com; 2010 Flora St; ⊙10am-9pm Tue-Thu, to 6pmFri&Sat,noon-6pmSun;lightrailStPaul) FREE Enter another world in this calm, pagoda-like oasis of a museum that's nearly as remarkable for its ambience as for its rich collection of artworks from China, Japan, India and Southeast Asia, dating from 3500 BC to the early 20th century. Don't miss the gorgeous sandstone facade from North India. There are free guided tours at 1pm on Saturdays.

DALLAS ARCHITECTURE

The Dallas skyline has long been one of the most vibrant in the USA, and it's getting more interesting all the time. Sleek contemporary designs mix with buildings inspired by French neoclassicism. Some buildings to look out for include the following:

Magnolia Petroleum Company Building (Map p150; 1401 Commerce St) The red neon **Pegasus** (p146) became a symbol of Dallas when it first flew atop this building in 1934. It disappeared for decades before reemerging on the newly renovated building, now a hotel, in 1999. Then it flew off again.

Bank of America Plaza (Map p150, 901 Main St) The tallest building in Dallas, this 72-story modernist skyscraper is outlined each night in cool green argon tubing which plays well with all the other colored-by-night buildings downtown.

Nasher Sculpture Center   MUSEUM
(Map p150; ☑ 214-242-5100; www.nashersculpture center.org; 2001 Flora St; adult/child $10/free; ⊙11am-5pm Tue-Sun; light rail St Paul) Modern-art installations shine at the fabulous glass-and-steel Nasher Sculpture Center. The Nashers accumulated what might be one of the greatest privately held sculpture collections in the world, with works by Calder, de Kooning, Rodin, Serra and Miro. The divine sculpture garden is one of the best in the country.

Check the calendar for gallery talks, hands-on art days for kids, and free evening concerts and film screenings in the garden. Even the Renzo Piano–designed wing is a work of art.

Klyde Warren Park   PARK
(Map p150; ☑ 214-716-4500; www.klydewarren park.org; 2012 Woodall Rodgers Fwy, btwn Pearl & St Paul Sts; ⊙6am-11pm; ⬛) FREE This innovative 5.2-acre park is an urban green space built over the recessed Woodall Rodgers Freeway. It has its own programming and, besides outdoor areas for chess, yoga, croquet and other activities, it offers performances and many more special events. It gets very crowded with families on weekends.

Fair Park

Created for the Texas Independence–themed 1936 Centennial Exposition, the art-deco buildings of **Fair Park** (Map p142; ☑214-426-3400; www.fairpark.org; 1300 Robert B Cullum Blvd; light rail Fair Park) today contain several interesting museums. While the grounds themselves are safe, the surrounding area – particularly to the east and south – can have safety issues.

Don't miss **Big Tex**, the 55ft-tall icon who greets visitors to the State Fair of Texas (p148). The current version debuted in 2013, replacing a previous Tex who burst into flames in 2012. The loss of his mug was widely mourned and he was quickly rebuilt.

Hall of State   MONUMENT
(Map p142; 3939 Grand Ave, Fair Park; ⊙9am-5pm Tue-Sat, 1-5pm Sun; light rail Fair Park) **FREE** Fair Park is full of superb 1930s art-deco architecture, none of it quite as inspired as this tribute to all things Texan. The **Hall of Heroes** pays homage to such luminaries as Stephen F Austin and Samuel Houston; the **Great Hall of Texas** features huge murals depicting episodes in Texas history from the 16th century on.

As you leave the Hall of State, stop by the reflecting pool outside of the entrance: the golden Greek-inspired statues will thrill art-deco buffs.

Texas Discovery Gardens   GARDENS
(Map p142; ☑214-428-7476; www.texasdiscovery gardens.org; 3601 Martin Luther King Jr Blvd, Fair Park; butterfly house & garden adult/child $8/4; ⊙outdoor gardens 24hr, indoor gardens 10am-5pm; light rail Fair Park) These pretty indoor-outdoor gardens include a tropical conservatory, a fragrance garden and a butterfly garden. Don't miss the native Texas plants.

African American Museum   MUSEUM
(Map p142; ☑214-565-9026; www.aamdallas.org; 3536 Grand Ave, Fair Park; admission free, tours $5; ⊙11am-5pm Tue-Fri, 10am-5pm Sat) This museum has exhibits of more than 1000 objects that richly detail the art and history of African American people from precolonial Africa through the present. Its folk-art collection is one of the best nationwide.

Elsewhere in Dallas

★**Dallas Arboretum & Botanical Gardens**   GARDENS
(☑214-515-6615; www.dallasarboretum.org; 8525 Garland Rd; adult/child $15/10; ⊙9am-5pm) On the shores of White Rock Lake, this gorgeous 66-acre arboretum showcases plants and flowers in theme gardens such as the Sunken Garden and the Woman's Garden. Expect to see a lot of wedding parties posing for pictures amid the posies. During the spring wildflower season it gets so mobbed that nearby streets are closed.

Pegasus Sign   LANDMARK
(Map p150; cnr Young St & S Lamar St) The red neon Pegasus became a symbol of Dallas during the decades when it flew atop Magnolia Building, starting in 1934. After a couple of moves and a stint in storage, the proud neon winged horse had now been restored and mounted on a (too short) pedestal in front of the Omni Dallas Hotel.

George W. Bush Presidential Library & Museum   MUSEUM
(Map p142; ☑214-346-1650; www.georgew bushlibrary.smu.edu; 2943 SMU Blvd; adult/child $19/13; ⊙9am-5pm Mon-Sat, noon-5pm Sun; light rail Mockingbird) This vast $300-million facility documents the presidency of George W Bush. Like other presidential libraries it has two missions: to allow research and to present a record of the president to the public. Exhibits include all manner of gifts Bush received while president. Its take on the 43rd president is especially glossy compared to other presidential libraries. Don't look for extended discussions on Bush-era controversies such as the Iraq war or the bungled response to Hurricane Katrina.

Its most interactive feature is the Decision Points Theater, which allows you to see how Bush made decisions around events such as 9/11 and the invasion of Iraq. Needless to say, the process tends to vindicate the Bush administration. Although Bush had no connection to Southern Methodist University, the university outbid others to host the facility. (Bush's father George HW Bush went through the same process when he located his presidential library at Texas A&M, a school where he had no previous connection.) Overall, given the size and cost of the facility, the exhibit area is fairly small and most people finish their visit in under an hour. There is a good cafe and the grounds have beautiful gardens.

Meadows Museum   MUSEUM
(Map p142; ☑214-768-2516; www.meadows museumdallas.org; 5900 Bishop Blvd, Southern Methodist University; adult/child/studentchild $12/4/free; ⊙10am-5pm Tue-Sat, to 9pm Thu, 1-5pm Sun; light rail Mockingbird) Located on the

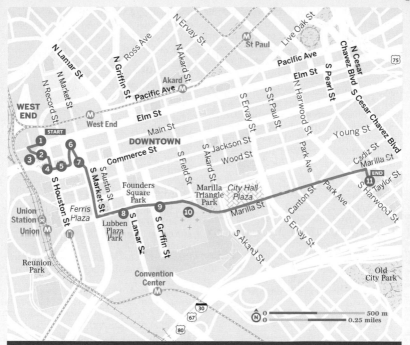

Walking Tour
Downtown Dallas

START SIXTH FLOOR MUSEUM
END DALLAS FARMERS MARKET
LENGTH 1 4 MILES; THREE HOURS

Begin your walk indoors at the **1 Sixth Floor Museum** (p140), where you can learn all about the events of November 22, 1963 when President John F Kennedy was shot by Lee Harvey Oswald from this building. Notice just how close the fateful window is to the X painted on Elm St where the bullets struck Kennedy.

Now go outside to **2 Dealey Plaza** (p141). You can't help but be struck by how small it is. All the images from that day make it seem like one vast expanse, rather than the intimate park that it really is. Note how close the **3 Grassy Knoll** is to the X.

Should you want to discuss theories about what happened that day, there are always conspiracy theorists and others with books to sell ready to share their views.

Otherwise, walk south along the top of the plaza, past the restored **4 fountains**. Turn east on Commerce St and get a dose of Dallas' other history at the **5 Old Red Museum**

(p141). Cut across **6 Founders Plaza**, where a much-moved and much-restored 1850s cedar cabin gives a little idea of how the early pioneers lived. Better yet, prance through the water jets in the pavement for a cooling splash.

Head south across Main St to the enigmatic **7 John F Kennedy Memorial**). Read the signs explaining the design and see if it makes sense to you. Walk south on S Market St for three blocks and turn east on Young St. You can't miss the **8 Pegasus Sign** (p146), a red neon icon for Dallas that has ended up on a rather stumpy pedestal (it used to be on a skyscraper).

Continue on Young St for a block and you'll see a herd of bronze longhorns looming down on you at **9 Pioneer Plaza** (p141). Wander uphill through the naturalistic setting and pause among the old trees and older tombstones of the **10 Pioneer Cemetery**.

Keep going west for five blocks along Marilla St for a final reward: the shops, food and refreshments of the **11 Dallas Farmers Market** (p157).

Southern Methodist University campus, this museum exhibits perhaps the best and most comprehensive collection of Spanish art outside of Spain, including masterpieces by Velázquez, El Greco, Goya, Picasso and Miró.

Bishop Arts District AREA
(Map p142; www.bishopartsdistrict.com; W Davis St & N Bishop Ave) For quirky and one-of-a-kind objects, like vintage Fiestaware plates, funky chandeliers and DIY crafts, head to the Bishop Arts District. Check the website for periodic festivals where local artists showcase their wares, such as the Oak Cliff Art Crawl held in April.

Dallas Zoo ZOO
(Map p142; ☑469-554-7500; www.dallaszoo.com; 650 S RL Thornton Fwy/I-35E; adult/child $15/12; ◉9am-5pm; ⊕) Africa is the focus of this urban zoo, which is just 3 miles south of downtown. It has gorilla and chimpanzee habitats and an entire exhibit called Giants of the Savanna. Kids like the Children's Zoo with its winsome, furry critters and the Koala Walkabout.

🏃 Activities

★**Katy Trail** WALKING
(☑214-303-1180; www.katytraildallas.org; ◉5am-midnight) For see-and-be-seen running and cycling, hit the tree-lined Katy Trail that runs 3.5 miles from the American Airlines center downtown almost all the way to SMU, passing through interesting neighborhoods along the way. The old railway route is tree-lined and at times feels like the country. Planned extensions will link it to other walking routes.

Stevens Park Golf Course GOLF
(Map p142; ☑214-670-7506; www.stevenspark golf.com; 1005 N Montclair Dr; 18 holes weekday/weekend $43/50; ◉6am-8pm) In a city with no shortage of tony golf clubs and high profile PGA tour events, this municipal course stands out for its location close to downtown, affordable green fees and well-maintained rolling hills with views of the Dallas skyline. One of the oldest of the city-owned courses, it went through a top-to-bottom makeover in 2011.

Koffee Day Spa SPA
(Map p150; ☑214-428-9696; www.koffeeday spa.com; 1118 S Akard St; 1hr massage from $80; ◉10am-6pm Tue-Sat or by appointment; light rail Akard) This day spa is by far the best trade-off for convenience (close to downtown)

and quality of service (high). The staff here are friendly: don't pass over the signature Koffee wrap. Make an appointment first: through the website or by phoning.

👉 Tours

Dallas Arts District Architectural Tours WALKING
(☑214-744-6642; www.thedallasartsdistrict.org; adult/child/senior & student $10/free/5; ◉10am 1st & 3rd Sat of each month) Walking tours of the arts district, sponsored by the Dallas Center for Architecture. Advance online reservations required.

🎉 Festivals & Events

Martin Luther King Jr Parade PARADE
(◉Jan) For the last 30 years Dallas has hosted one of the largest events in the country commemorating Dr King's life. In mid-January, the parade, a festive mix of floats and marching bands, goes from MLK Blvd and Lamar to Fair Park.

Deep Ellum Arts Festival ART, PERFORMING ARTS
(☑214-855-1881; www.deepellumartsfestival.com; Main St, Deep Ellum; ◉Apr) To experience Dallas at its most bohemian, diverse and relaxed, head down to the live-music stages and eclectic arts booths in early April.

★**State Fair of Texas** FAIR
(www.bigtex.com; Fair Park, 1300 Cullum Blvd; adult/child $18/14; ◉late Sep–mid-Oct) This massive fair is the fall highlight for many a Texan. Come ride one of the tallest Ferris wheels in North America, eat corn dogs (it's claimed that this is where they were invented), and browse the prize-winning cows, sheep and quilts.

🛏 Sleeping

Staying uptown is pricey, but you're closest to restaurants and nightlife. Otherwise, you'll find all manner of chains for all manner of budgets along the highways, especially US 75 and to the west and north of the center.

Abby Guest House GUESTHOUSE $
(Map p142; ☑214-264-4804; www.airbnb.com/rooms/7273; 5417 Goodwin Ave; cottages from $70; ▣❀@ 🀆) This bright and cheerful garden cottage is within walking distance of great cafes and bars on Upper Greenville Ave (about 5 miles northeast of downtown). With a full kitchen and sunny private patio, it's a great deal although often booked. Two-night minimum. Book through Airbnb.

★Hotel Belmont
BOUTIQUE HOTEL $$

(Map p142; ☑ 866-870-8010; www.belmontdallas. com; 901 Fort Worth Ave; r $95-180; ⓟ✿@🛜🏊) Just 2 miles west of downtown, this stylish 1940s bungalow hotel is a fabulously low-key antidote to Dallas' flashier digs, with a touch of mid-century-modern design and more than its share of soul. The garden rooms – with soaking tubs, Moroccan-blue tile work, kilim rugs and some city views – are tops.

Magnolia Hotel
BOUTIQUE HOTEL $$

(Map p150; ☑ 214-915-6500; www.magnolia hotels.com; 1401 Commerce St; r from $200; ➡✿@🛜🏊) Housed in the 1922, 29-story Magnolia Petroleum Company Building, this gracious hotel offers a sumptuous stay. Rooms have period details including wooden blinds and retro furniture. The commodious rooms have fridges, while the suites have kitchenettes.

Corinthian B&B
GUESTHOUSE $$

(Map p142; ☑ 214-818-0400; www.corinthian bandb.com; 4125 Junius St; r $150-210; ⓟ✿🛜) Once a boarding house for young ladies, this beautifully restored 1905 mansion has attractive rooms, set with antique furnishings and original details. A lovely backyard, a stately parlor and kind hosts (not to mention the tasty cooked breakfasts) make the Corinthian good value. It's about 1.5 miles northeast of downtown.

★Hotel Lumen
HOTEL $$$

(Map p142; ☑ 214-219-2400; www.hotellumen.com; 6101 Hillcrest Ave; r $240-380; ⓟ➡@🛜🏊) This ultramodern concrete hotel across from SMU doesn't completely live up to the hype. Yet we love the parade of poodles and shih tzus through the lobby, the video library and the strong coffee in the morning. It has a breezy rooftop lounge.

★Adolphus
HISTORIC HOTEL $$$

(Map p150; ☑ 214-742-8200; www.hoteladol phus.com; 1321 Commerce St; d $270-370; ➡✿@🛜🏊; light rail Akard) Feel like royalty (yes, Queen Elizabeth has stayed here) the old-fashioned way. The 422-room Adolphus takes us back to the days when gentlemen wore ties and hotels were truly grand, not bastions of ascetic minimalism. Just exploring the 22 floors is an adventure in the 1912 labyrinth. Note that room sizes vary widely. It's part of the Marriott empire.

Rosewood Mansion on Turtle Creek
LUXURY HOTEL $$$

(Map p142; ☑ 214-559-2100; www.rosewood hotels.com; 2821 Turtle Creek Blvd; r from $400; ✿@🛜🏊🍽) Step into a life of ease, where for every two guests there's one staff member attending. This is the definitive five-star Dallas hotel, and a worthy splurge. Rooms have fresh flowers and hand-carved European furnishings, and dinner is served in the original, marble-clad, 1925 Italianate villa.

🍴 Eating

Dining in Dallas sprawls with options much like the city itself. There are several areas worthy of your attention: Deep Ellum, just east of downtown, is your choice for eclectic eats. This area, 'deep' up Elm St, gets its name from the Southern-drawl pronunciation of 'Elm.'

Heading uptown offers myriad choices, especially in the Lower Greenfield neighborhood with its walkable blocks. To the west, the Arts District, University Park and uptown are among the neighborhoods worth exploring for a bite.

Southwest, the Bishop Arts District is dotted with interesting places to eat and drink. It merges hipster and funky – walk off your vittles by window-shopping the boutiques.

★Fuel City
MEXICAN $

(Map p142; ☑ 214-426-0011; www.fuelcity.com; 801 S Riverfront Blvd; tacos from $2; ⊗24hr) A short drive from downtown, Fuel City serves up some of Dallas' best tacos in one of its most idiosyncratic locations (it's also a gas station and car wash). Sit out on picnic tables munching on roast pork and steak-filled tortillas – and do order *elotes* (cup filled with corn, cheese and paprika) from an adjoining food stand. It's about 1.5 miles south of Dealey Plaza. Check out the friendly donkeys near the parking lot.

★Sonny Bryan's Smokehouse
BARBECUE $

(Map p142; ☑ 214-357-7120; www.sonnybryans. com; 2202 Inwood Rd; mains $6-19; ⊗24hr) You cannot beat the original location of this Dallas classic. Where some barbecue places serve up their fare for only a few hours a day, this one can sate your smoky fantasies around the clock.

★AllGood Café
TEX-MEX $

(Map p142; ☑ 214-742-5362; www.allgoodcafe. com; 2934 Main St; mains $5-9; ☑) A postmodern Deep Ellum cafe with Tex-Mex

Downtown Dallas

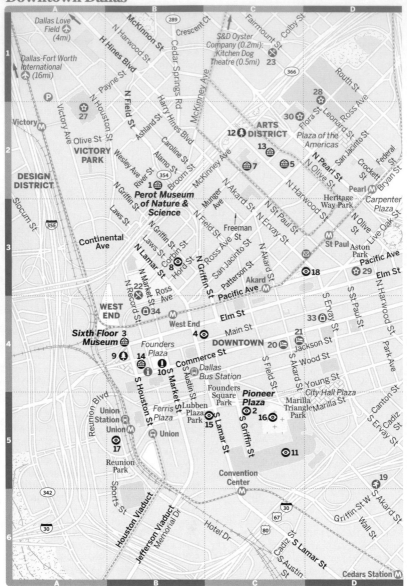

grace notes and tattooed waitresses, the AllGood is cozy as all get out. Families and rocker types all chow down on King Ranch chicken casserole and other comfort foods. The suppliers are local and listed by name.

Keller's Drive-In   FAST FOOD **$**
(Map p142; ☐ 214-368-1209; 6537 E Northwest Hwy; mains $4-8; ⏰ 10:30am-10pm) You supply the dining room – your car – at this long-running classic, true, drive-in. The waitresses (yes, all women) have seen it

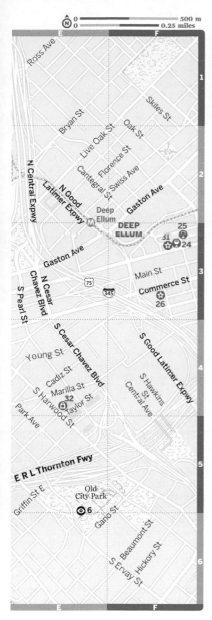

Bubba's Cooks Country   AMERICAN $
(Map p142; 📞214-373-6527; http://bubbas
dallas.com; 6617 Hillcrest Ave; mains $6-15;
⊘6:30am-10pm) Great American breakfasts
and true Texas fare make this a must-stop
for anyone who wants to have the full local
culinary experience. Portions are big and the
iced teas never stop coming in this diner out
of central casting.

Rodeo Goat   BURGERS $
(Map p142; 📞214-741-4628; www.rodeogoat.
com/dallas; 1926 Market Center Blvd; mains $9-
12; ⊘10am-11pm Sun-Thu, to midnight Fri & Sat;
📶) Rodeo Goat is located on an unpromis-
ing stretch of roadway on the outskirts of
the Design District and, from the outside,
looks like a low-key strip club. Stepping inside the Rodeo is a revelation, though. The
smoky scent of sizzling burgers (oodles of
varieties are on the menu) wafts from the
open-air kitchen grill. There are craft brews
and creative cocktails.

The large open-plan space is usually
crowded with the after-work crowd – more
of a party vibe on weekend nights – and
it's a great spot for catching sports on TV.
Outdoors, in back, there's a great space with
picnic table and heat lamps.

Sammy's BBQ   BARBECUE $
(Map p150; 📞214-880-9064; http://sammysbar
beque.com; 2126 Leonard St; mains $8-15; ⊘11am-
3pm Mon-Sat; 📶) The line of regular lunch-
goers, most clad in business casual, shuffles
along quickly for plate-swamping portions
of smoked brisket and other meats at this
long-running institution. Sandwiches, plates
and by-the-pound orders are complemented
with sides, even spinach for those experienc-
ing vegetable withdrawal.

Highland Park Soda Shop   AMERICAN $
(Map p142; 📞214-521-2126; www.highlandparksoda
fountain.com; 3229 Knox St; mains $4-8; ⊘7am-
6pm Mon-Fri, from 8am Sat, 10am-5pm Sun; 📶)
Since 1912, this classic soda fountain has
been serving up vanilla malts and comfort
fare such as grilled-cheese sandwiches to
generations of diners. When in doubt, get
the root-beer float. It's in Highland Park,
about 4 miles north of downtown.

Velvet Taco   MEXICAN $
(Map p142; 📞214-823-8358; www.velvettaco.
com; 3012 N Henderson Ave; mains from $4;
⊘10am-2am Sun-Thu, to 5am Fri & Sat) An
immensely popular hipster taqueria with
globally accented tacos, including wagyu

all but still hustle out to take your order as
soon as you park. The burgers are remarkably juicy and come with myriad options.
The onion rings are a cut above.

Downtown Dallas

brisket and tikka chicken. Despite its freeway-side location, the outdoor patio with heat lamps and fans (ready for all weather eventualities) is a great spot. The taqueria makes its own tortillas fresh daily.

Ellen's Southern Kitchen   AMERICAN $
(Map p150; ☑469-206-3339; www.ellenssouthern kitchen.com; 1790 N Record St; mains $9-15; ⊙7am-9pm; 🐾; light rail West End) In the center of historic West End, Ellen's serves up American comfort fare in a slightly up-scale diner setting (think wild wallpaper, elegant light fixtures, dark wood furniture). Fluffy pancakes, Cajun shrimp and grits, blackened catfish and pulled-pork tacos are among the many temptations. Breakfast served all day. Full bar and outside seating.

★Gabriela & Sofia's Tex-Mex   TEX-MEX $$
(☑214-647-1033; www.gabriela-sofias.com; 10455 N Central Expy; mains $9-20; ⊙11am-9:30pm Sun-Thu, to 10:30pm Fri & Sat; 🐾) The interior here is just acceptable: dark and roomy. But that's good as it doesn't get in the way of the beauty you'll find on your plate. Regional Mexican and Tex-Mex dishes are cooked with attitude and authority. Any of the fajitas are mem-orable and will make you forget any other

version you've had. The owners constantly circulate making certain patrons are happy. The amazing guacamole is made tableside.

★Meddlesome Moth   MODERN AMERICAN $$
(Map p142; ☑214-628-7900; www.mothinthe.net; 1621 Oak Lawn Ave; lunch mains $10-15, dinner mains $10-20; ⊙11am-midnight Mon-Sat, 10am-10pm Sun) In the Design District, this buzz-ing gastropub draws small groups of friends who linger over Belgian-style mussels, shrimp and homestead grits, great burgers and beautifully turned out sharing plates. You'll find good cocktails and a superb and rotating selection of craft brews (including 40 on draft). The menu changes by season.

It's around 2 miles northwest of downtown.

★Zodiac   AMERICAN $$
(Map p150; ☑214-573-5800; www.neimanmarcus. com; 1618 Main St, Neiman Marcus; mains $14-25; ⊙11am-3pm Mon-Sat) This classic downtown lunch spot, which has been tucked into Nei-man Marcus for more than 50 years, evokes old-school Dallas. Attentive waiters bus-tle about, soothing and pampering diners with hot chicken consommé, popovers with strawberry butter and elegant salads. You may share space with a bridesmaids party.

Smoke
BARBECUE $$

(Map p142; ☑ 214-393-4141; www.smokerestau
rant.com; 901 Fort Worth Ave, Belmont Hotel; mains
$10-40; ⊙ 8am-10pm Sun-Thu, to 11pm Fri & Sat) A
barbecue joint that grows its own veggies and
smokes its own meats gets enough street cred
to claim the motto 'Raisin' Hell from Scratch.'
The style of the dining room matches the
style of the excellent food. Besides barbecue,
it is famous for its bacon-cheeseburgers and
fine steaks.

Kalachandji's
VEGETARIAN $$

(Map p142; ☑ 214 821 1048; www.kalachandjis.
com; 5430 Gurley Ave; buffet lunch/dinner $12/15;
⊙ 11:30am-2pm & 5:30-9pm Tue-Sun; ☑) Inside
a lavishly decorated Hare Krishna temple,
you'll find a small but varied buffet serving
basmati rice, curries, mustard greens, *pap-
padums* and chutneys, *pakora*, tamarind
tea and other changing daily specials. It's
a fine counterpoint to Texas' many meaty
temptations. You can dine in the peaceful,
plant-filled courtyard. It's located about 4
miles east of downtown.

S&D Oyster Company
SEAFOOD $$

(Map p142; ☑ 214-880-0111; www.sdoyster.com;
2701 McKinney Ave; mains $15-25; ⊙ 11am-10pm
Mon-Sat; 🖶) An uptown staple for years (com-
plete with red-and-white checked tablecloths
and old-time jazz playing overhead), S&D has
earned many fans for its fresh oysters, broiled
flounder, barbecue shrimp and other Gulf
Coast hits. Waitstaff wear classic red aprons.
Service is excellent.

★ Javier's
MEXICAN $$$

(Map p142; ☑ 214-521-4211; www.javiers.net; 4912
Cole Ave; mains $20-35; ⊙ 5:30-10pm Sun-Thu,
to 11pm Fri & Sat) Discard any ideas you have
about Tex-Mex at this deeply cultured restaurant which takes the gentrified food of
old Mexico City to new levels. The setting
is dark, leathery and quiet. The food meaty
and piquant. Steaks come with a range of
Mexican flavors that bring out the best in
beef. Get a table under the stars.

It's in Highland Park, about 4 miles north
of downtown.

Abacus
AMERICAN $$$

(Map p142; ☑ 214-559-3111; http://abacus-
restaurant.com; 4511 McKinney Ave; mains $35-60,
tasting menus from $65; ⊙ 6-10pm Mon-Sat; 🐾)
Too many steakhouses in Dallas are part of
chains. For the real deal with a contempo-
rary twist, Abacus delivers the beef. Start
with sushi or the wildly popular lobster

shooters and then make your way through
a menu of small, seasonal plates. Then feast
on simply superb steaks. The bar is excellent.

🍷 Drinking & Nightlife

Those seeking a mix of high and low culture
will dig the numerous pubs (usually with
outdoor patios) that line Greenville Ave
and Knox-Henderson. Deep Ellum is dive-
bar central, but it's also the edgiest neigh-
borhood and prime territory for hitting the
streets and making your own discoveries.

Watch for beers from local legends like 903,
Community and Deep Ellum Brewing Co.

★ Four Corners Brewing Co
BREWERY

(Map p142; ☑ 214-748-2739; www.fcbrewing.com;
423 Singleton Blvd; ⊙ 5-10pm Mon-Fri, noon-10pm
Sat, 2-8pm Sun) A great local microbrewery lo-
cated just west of downtown, over the Trin-
ity River. All the usual styles are here (IPAs,
oatmeal stout, saison etc). The staff in the
small ale room are passionate about their
brews and you should be too.

★ Mudsmith
CAFE

(Map p142; ☑ 214-370-9535; www.mudsmith
coffee.com; 2114 Greenville Ave; ⊙ 6:30am-11pm; 🛜)
A hipster vibe reigns at this boho-style coffee
shop on the Lower Greenville Ave strip – think
ironic antelope heads, Western-themed paint-
ings and apothecary elements as decor. Plenty
of outlets, big work tables and good espresso
drinks make this a good place to catch up on
work or lounge outside with a beer or wine.

★ Green Room
BAR

(Map p150; ☑ 214-748-7666; www.dallasgreen
room.com; 2715 Elm St; ⊙ 4pm-2am Tue-Sun) In
bar-lined Deep Ellum, the Green Room is a
go-to spot for rooftop cocktails, a fun crowd
and excellent food, from snacks to meals
(tacos, burgers, poutine). Pick from three
bar areas.

★ Two Corks and a Bottle
LOUNGE

(Map p142; ☑ 214-871-9463; www.twocorksanda
bottle.com; 2800 Routh St; ⊙ noon-7pm Sun & Tue, to
10pm Wed-Thu, to 11pm Fri & Sat) Creative owners
make all the difference and the pair behind
this cork-sized little uptown wine bar prove it.
Besides a fine selection of vino, it has frequent
diversions such as acoustic, blues or jazz. That
it's romantic is a bonus. Wine flights let you
sample widely from the wine list.

★ Ginger Man
PUB

(Map p142; ☑ 214-754-8771; www.thegingerman.
com/uptown; 2718 Boll St; ⊙ 1pm-2am) An

appropriately spice-colored house is home to this always-busy neighborhood pub. It has multilevel patios and porches, out front and back, plus one of the best beer menus in the city. Great bartenders.

Parliament   COCKTAIL BAR

(Map p142; ☑469-804-4321; www.parliament dallas.com; 2418 Allen St; ⊙5pm-2am Mon-Sat) This upscale bar captures the city's gilded vibe perfectly. Outside is an auto enthusiast's collection of patron's parked cars. Inside, the cocktails are exquisite, although you may overhear a poser chattering about their new $4200 watch. Finely dressed Uptown denizens browse the 30-page drinks menu while waitstaff in minimalist black proffer suggestions.

Cosmo's   BAR

(Map p142; ☑214-826-4200; www.cosmosbar. net; 1212 Skillman St; ⊙5pm-2am) A mishmash of colorful vintage lamps, worn thrift-store-esque furniture and a faux fireplace set the scene for a fun evening of drinking (martinis, cosmos), while listening to old-school hits on the jukebox. Fight hunger with pizza and sandwiches. It's in Lakewood, about 4 miles northeast of downtown.

Reno's Chop Shop Saloon   BAR

(Map p150; ☑214-742-7366; 210 N Crowdus St; ⊙2pm-2am Mon-Fri, noon-2am Sat & Sun) Slightly off Deep Ellum's Elm St artery, this is where you'll find Dallas' friendliest bikers. Hogs

---

GAY & LESBIAN DALLAS

You've got to love that the top gay and lesbian bars in Dallas are named JR's and Sue Ellen's, respectively, after the two lead characters in *Dallas*. Both are 3 miles north of downtown in Oak Lawn.

JR's Bar & Grill (Map p142; ☑214-528-1004; www.jrsdallas.com; 3923 Cedar Springs Rd; ⊙11am-2am Mon-Sat, from noon Sun) One of the busiest bars in Texas, JR's serves lunch daily and boasts a variety of fun entertainment at night. From the patio you can cheer on Dallas' modest cruising scene. Many Mondays have drag shows.

Sue Ellen's (Map p142; ☑214-559-0707; www.sueellensdallas.com; 3014 Throckmorton St; ⊙4pm-2am) Chill out in the 'lipstick lounge' or on the dance floor at Dallas' favorite lesbian bar. Good back garden.

---

line the front while a jovial crowd parties inside. The rear patio has great tables with umbrellas, along with the odd band. There's lots of leather in the collective wardrobe.

Boulevardier   WINE BAR

(Map p142; ☑214-942-1828; www.dallasboulevar dier.com; 408 N Bishop Ave; ⊙4:30-11pm Tue-Fri, 11am-11pm Sat, 11am-10pm Sun) A fine French bistro, this culturally inspired local hangout has a vast selection of wines by the glass. Enjoy top global vintages, possibly with a plate of housemade charcuterie.

Old Monk Pub   PUB

(Map p142; ☑214-821-1880; www.oldmonkdallas. com; 2847 N Henderson Ave; ⊙3pm-2am Mon-Thu, from 11:30am Fri-Sun) The dimly lit patio on a starry night! The perfect cheese plate! The Belgian beers! Add in upscale pub food and outdoor seating and you may not leave. Hang in the dark bar, or sunlit courtyard.

It's in Knox-Henderson, 4 miles north of downtown.

☆ Entertainment

High culture, low culture, country culture... Dallas has it in spades.

☆ Live Music

★ Kessler Theater   LIVE MUSIC

(Map p142; ☑214-272-8346; http://thekessler.org; 1230 W Davis St; ⊙6pm-midnight) Let the aqua neon outside catch your eye and draw you in to this Oak Cliff landmark. The one-time neighborhood movie house has been transformed into a fairly intimate live music venue. Drink prices are friendly, the bands and acts are good (drag shows!) and the vibe is down-home fun.

★ Sons of Hermann Hall   LIVE MUSIC

(Map p142; ☑214-747-4422; www.sonsofhermann. com; 3414 Elm St; ⊙7pm-midnight Wed & Thu, to 2am Fri & Sat) For almost 100 years, this classic Texas dancehall has been a chameleon: equal parts pickup bar, live-music venue, honky-tonk and swing-dancing club. A Deep Ellum stalwart. The opening hours can vary; call to find out what's on. Come here and plunge deep into the heart of full-on Big D.

★ Goat   BLUES

(Map p142; ☑214-317-8119; www.thegoatdallas. com; 7248 Gaston Ave, Lakewood; ⊙7am-2am Mon-Sat, noon-2am Sun) Open at the crack of dawn for those impromptu morning pub crawls, the Goat's a divey neighborhood bar with live blues three nights a week plus live music other nights. Beware of karaoke nights. Note the opening time!

★**Granada Theater**   LIVE MUSIC
(Map p142; ☑214-824-9933; www.granadatheater. com; 3524 Greenville Ave) This converted movie theater, often praised as the best live-music venue in town, books popular rock and country bands. It's the anchor of Lower Greenwood. Check the website for what's on.

Balcony Club   LIVE MUSIC
(Map p142; ☑214-826-8104; www.balconyclub. com; 1825 Abrams Rd; ⊙bar 5pm-2am) This mysterious upstairs hideaway feels like a secret, even though it's not. With emerald walls, a tiny stage and a cozy patio nook above the Landmark Theater, this spot draw all ages for nightly live music – mostly jazz – and sassy drinks such as moonlight martinis and three-way tropical punch.

Trees Dallas   LIVE MUSIC
(Map p150; ☑214-741-1122; http://treesdallas. com; 2709 Elm St) This famous Deep Ellum club has top musical acts and bands several nights a week. Regulars love it for its compact, sweaty size; band members often hang at the bar after shows.

Adair's Saloon   LIVE MUSIC
(Map p150; ☑214-939-9900; www.adairssaloon. com; 2624 Commerce St; ⊙11am-2am) The regulars call it 'Aayy-dares.' Down-to-earth patrons and infectious country and redneck rock bands go down well with cheap beer and shuffleboard.

☆ **Sports**

Dallas Mavericks   BASKETBALL
(www.mavs.com; single game $50-1000) The local NBA team is very popular and has had some success on the courts. Games typically sell out in advance. The owner is Mark Cuban, who has had his own reality TV show. Games are played at the **American Airlines Center** (Map p150; ☑214-222-3687; www.americanair linescenter.com; 2500 Victory Ave; light rail Victory).

☆ **Classical Music & Dance**

Morton H Meyerson Symphony Center   CONCERT VENUE
(Map p150; ☑214-670-3600; www.mydso.com; 2301 Flora St) Renowned architect IM Pei designed the Morton H Meyerson Symphony Center where the **Dallas Symphony**

Orchestra (☑214-692-0203; www.dallas symphony.com) performs.

AT&T Performing Arts Center   THEATER
(Map p150; ☑214-880-0202; www.attpac.org; 2403 Flora St; light rail Pearl/Arts District) Four architecturally noteworthy performance venues are located here, including the 2000-seat **Winspear Opera House**, home to the **Dallas Opera** (☑214-443-1043; www.dallasopera.org; tickets $20-200); the 1500-seat **Wyly Theatre**; and **Strauss Square**, an open-air stage.

The vertically stacked, 12-story Wyly Theatre broke the architectural mold by challenging traditional theater designs. It's worth seeing just for the building. It is the headquarters of the **Dallas Theater Center**, a major American regional theatre, producing classic dramas, musicals and edgy new works.

☆ **Theater & Comedy**

Kitchen Dog Theater   THEATER
(Map p142; ☑214-953-1055; www.kitchendog theater.org; 161 Riveredge Dr; $15-30) You'll get professional theater with attitude from Kitchen Dog. This razor-sharp company specializes in performing plays with a message. Some shows are staged at the AT&T Performing Arts Center. (p155)

Majestic Theatre   THEATER
(Map p150; ☑214-670-3687; http://dallasculture. org; 1925 Elm St; light rail St Paul) This grand 1700-seat downtown theater presents a year-round schedule of touring Broadway musicals.

Dallas Comedy House   COMEDY
(Map p142; ☑214-741-4440; www.dallascomedy house.com; 3025 Main St; free-$25; ⊙7pm-2am Tue-Sat) Following in the footsteps of New York's UCB or LA's the Groundlings, this is Dallas' best place for improv comedy (and lessons). On student nights, the hilarity is free.

🛍 **Shopping**

★**Deep Vellum Books**   BOOKS
(Map p142; ☑214-638-7741; http://deepvellum. com; 3000 Commerce St; ⊙11am-6pm Sun, Tue & Wed, to 8pm Thu-Sat) Dallas is not a good town for bookstores, except for this one. Of course it's in Deep Vellum and of course it's run by some passionate local publishers. Expect the offbeat, the unheralded, the wonderful, the acclaimed and much more. Great regular author events.

Dallas–Fort Worth Metroplex

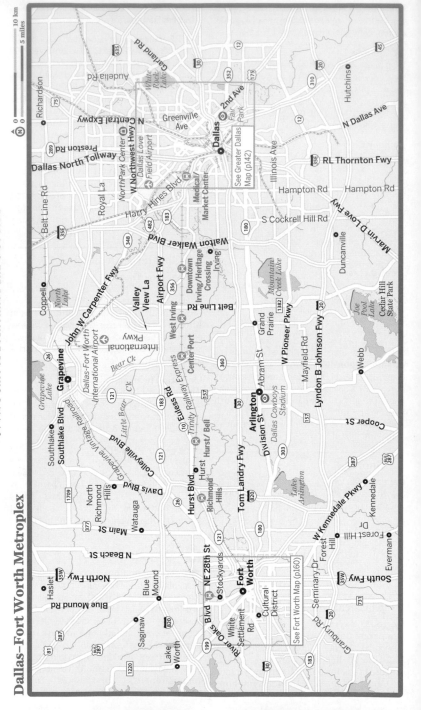

10 km
5 miles

Richardson

935

Garland Rd

Audelia Rd

30

75

12

352

175

45

N Central Expwy

Preston Rd

289

Dallas North Tollway

NorthPark Center
W Northwest Hwy

Greenville
Ave

Dallas Love
Field Airport

White
Rock
Lake

Fair
Park

2nd Ave

Dallas

310

20

12

N Dallas Ave

Hutchins

Belt Line Rd

35E

Royal La

Harry Hines Blvd

Medical/
Market Center

See Greater Dallas
Map (p142)

RL Thornton Fwy

35E

Illinois Ave

Hampton Rd   Hampton Rd

482

183

180

S Cockrell Hill Rd

Marvin D Love Fwy

348

Walton Walker Blvd

Duncanville

John W Carpenter Fwy

North
Lake

Coppell

Valley
View La

356

Downtown
Irving/Heritage
Crossing

Irving

Mountain
Creek Lake

Joe
Pool
Lake

Cedar Hill
State Park

Airport Fwy

Belt Line Rd

West Irving

1382

Grand
Prairie

W Pioneer Pkwy

Webb

20

Grapevine
Lake

Grapevine

26

Dallas–Fort Worth
International Airport

International
Pkwy

Bear Ck

Center Port

360

Abram St

Mayfield Rd

Lyndon B Johnson Fwy

157

Cooper St

Southlake

Southlake Blvd

Little Bear Ck

121

Grapevine Vintage Railroad

183

Euless Rd

10

Trinity Railway Express

157

Arlington

Division St

Dallas Cowboys
Stadium

30

303

Lake
Arlington

North
Richmond
Hills

1709

Davis Blvd

Colleyville Blvd

121

121

Hurst Blvd

Hurst/ Bell

Richmond
Hills

Tom Landry Fwy

820

180

287

W Kennedale Pkwy

Forest Hill

Forest Hill Dr

Kennedale

Watauga

377

Main St

N Beach St

26

Haslet

35W

North Fwy

Blue Mound Rd

Blue
Mound

Saginaw

287

81

820

Lake
Worth

1220

199

River Oaks Blvd

NE 28th St

Stockyards

Fort
Worth

White Settlement
Rd

Cultural
District

See Fort Worth Map (p160)

30

183

20

35W

South Fwy

Seminary Dr

731

Granbury Rd

287
US
287

Everman

★**Wild Bill's Western Store**   CLOTHING
(Map p150; ☑214-954-1050; www.wildbills
western.com; 311 N Market St; ⊙10am-7pm Mon
& Tue, to 9pm Wed-Sat, noon-6pm Sun; light rail
West End) Wild Bill's is a West End treasure
chest of Western wear. You'll find Stetsons,
snakeskin boots, oilskin jackets, oversize
belt buckles, rhinestone-covered T-shirts,
fun kitschy souvenirs, popguns and other
toys, country-music CDs and much more.
Enjoy a cold beer while you shop.

★**Dallas Farmers Market**   MARKET
(Map p150; ☑214-664-9110; http://dallasfarmers
market.org; 920 S Harwood St; ⊙10am-6pm
Sat Thu, to 8pm Fri; light rail St Paul) Buy pro-
duce directly from the many excellent local
growers, or shop for flowers and antiques
at this multibarn market. It's at its best
Thursday to Saturday. Eateries include
Taqueria La Ventana, which sells Mexico
City–style tacos.

**Nasher Sculpture
Center Store**   GIFTS & SOUVENIRS
(Map p150; ☑214-241-5110; www.store/nasher
sculpturecenter.org; 2001 Flora St; ⊙11am-5pm
Tue-Sun) This shop in the Nasher Sculpture
Center (p145) sells handcrafted jewelry,
books, design items and other accessories by
local and nationally renowned artisans.

Good Records   MUSIC
(Map p142; ☑214-752-4663; www.goodrecords.
com; 1808 Lower Greenville Ave; ⊙10am-11pm
Mon-Thu, to midnight Fri & Sat, 11am-9pm Sun)
Greenville Ave is home to one of Dallas's only
indie record stores. According to the store
philosophy, it carries whatever's 'good.'

Neiman Marcus   DEPARTMENT STORE
(Map p150; ☑214-741-6911; www.neimanmarcus.
com; 1618 Main St; ⊙10am-6pm Mon-Sat, to 7pm
Thu; light rail Akard) A downtown landmark,
this six-story veteran was the first Neiman
Marcus store. Today it's still a wonderful
place to enjoy a timeless high-end shopping
experience. You may feel the urge to don
white gloves.

Nest   ARTS & CRAFTS
(Map p142; ☑214-373-4444; www.nestdallas.
com; 4524 McKinney Ave; ⊙10am-6pm Mon-Sat)
Located in the Knox-Henderson neighborhood, this eclectically stocked boutique
sells everything from quirky ceramic gifts,
like a buffalo door light and a deer jewelry
holder, to high-end design and chic home
accessories and furniture.

METROPLEX
....
The roots of using 'Metroplex' to describe
the whole Dallas–Fort Worth region are
obscure. Some evidence links the term
to the early 1970s when the two cities
were joining together to build DFW airport. Boosters wanted something snazzy
that promoted the entire region.

   Regardless, the word stuck, sort of.
While you'll hear it used around the
Metroplex, it's not a word locals use
outside the region. Rare is the local
who says they are from the Metroplex.
Texas Monthly summed up the term as
a 'grotesque word that means nothing.'

Dallas Cowboys Pro Shop   SPORTS & OUTDOORS
(☑972 661 1111; www.shopcowboys.com; Dallas
Pkwy, Galleria Mall; ⊙10am-9pm Mon-Sat, midday-
6pm Sun) The place to get all the Cowboys
gear you could want. One of many outlets in
the region.

Froggie's 5 & 10   TOYS
(Map p142; ☑214-522-5867; www.froggies
5and10.com; 3211 Knox St; ⊙10am-9pm Mon-
Sat, noon-6pm Sun; ☻) Kids will adore this
old-fashioned uptown toy store with a
smart-alecky edge: wash-off tattoos, retro
candy, books and silly stuff.

David Dike Fine Art   ART
(Map p142; ☑214-720-4044; www.daviddikefine
art.com; 2613 Fairmount St; ⊙10am-5pm Mon-Fri,
11am-4pm Sat) A long-established gallery that
reps some of the best Texas painters of the
last 100 years. An anchor of the uptown arts
scene.

🔒 **Malls**

★**Highland Park Village**   MALL
(Map p142; ☑214-443-9898; www.hpvillage.com;
Preston Rd & Mockingbird Lane; ⊙hours vary by
store) For an eye-rolling, gasp-inducing and
credit-card-maxing experience, head to
Spanish Mission–style Highland Park Village
in upper-crust Highland Park, which claims
to be the oldest suburban shopping center in
the world. If Jimmy Choo and Carolina Her-
rera are among your intimate acquaintances,
you'll feel at home.

   If they're not, it's still worth a look around
to see Dallas money in action (or just to see
who wins when an Escalade and a Jaguar
face off for a prime parking spot).

NorthPark Center   MALL

(🎦 214-363-7441; www.northparkcenter.com; 8687 N Central Expwy; ⏱ 10am-9pm Mon-Sat, noon-6pm Sun) Almost 2 million sq ft of retail space, NorthPark's major stores include Neiman Marcus, Nordstrom and Macy's. It has hundreds of other retailers, including most upscale brands. Despite its size, it gets jammed and parking on a Saturday afternoon can be a pain.

ℹ Information

Dallas Visitor's Center (Map p150; 🎦 214-571-1316; www.visitdallas.com; Old Red Courthouse, 100 S Houston St; ⏱ 9am-5pm; 🎦) Centrally located, this useful office can answer questions and distribute myriad local guides.

Downtown Post Office (Map p150; 🎦 800-275-8778; 400 N Ervay St; ⏱ 8:30am-5pm Mon-Fri) A useful location.

Prima Care (🎦 888-286-4603; www.primacare.com; 6350 E Mockingbird Lane, Lakewood; ⏱ 8am-8pm Mon-Fri, to 5pm Sat & Sun) Ten locations treat walk-in patients with minor illnesses and injuries; travel medicine services, too.

ℹ Getting There & Away

Dallas-Fort Worth International Airport (DFW; 🎦 972-973-3112; www.dfwairport.com; 2400 Aviation Dr), 16 miles northwest of the city via I-35 E, is a hub for American Airlines. Major airlines provide extensive domestic and international service.

Dallas Love Field Airport (DAL; Map p142; 🎦 214-670-6080; www.dallas-lovefield.com; 8008 Herb Kelleher Way), just northwest of downtown, is a hub for Southwest Airlines and has extensive domestic service.

Greyhound buses (www.greyhound.com) make runs to major cities in the region from the **Dallas Bus Station** (Map p150; 🎦 214-849-6831; 205 S Lamar St).

The **Amtrak** (www.amtrak.com) San Antonio–Chicago *Texas Eagle* train stops at downtown's **Union Station** (🎦 800-872-7245; www.unionstationdallas.com; 400 S Houston St; light rail Union Station), which is also a hub for local transit.

ℹ Getting Around

DART (Dallas Area Rapid Transit; 🎦 214-979-1111; www.dart.org; 2-hour ticket $2.50, daypass $5) operates buses and an extensive light-rail system that connects downtown with outlying areas. Tickets are sold on board buses and from vending machines at rail stops. It also operates the Dallas Streetcar, which runs to the southwest from downtown, where it links to bus 723 that serves the Bishop Arts District.

Travel from downtown to uptown on the historic and free **M-Line Trolley** (🎦 214-855-0006; www.mata.org; ⏱ 7am-10pm Mon-Thu, to 11pm Fri, 10am-midnight Sat, to 10pm Sun), which runs from the St Paul DART station via the Arts District and up McKinney Ave to City Place/Uptown Station.

Trinity Railway Express (TRE; 🎦 info 214-979-1111; www.trinityrailwayexpress.org; single ride 1/2 zones $2.50/5, daypass 1/2 zones $5/10; ⏱ half-hourly 5am-1am Mon-Sat) trains run between Dallas **Union Station** and Fort Worth (one hour), with a stop at CenterPort/DFW Airport where there is a shuttle-bus connection to the airport.

FORT WORTH

🎦 682, 817 / POP 795,000

Oft-called 'Where the West Begins,' Fort Worth definitely has the cowboy feel.

The city first became famous during the great open-range cattle drives of the late 19th century, when more than 10 million head of cattle tramped through the city on the Chisholm Trail. Today you can see a mini-cattle drive in the morning and a rodeo on Saturday night.

Don't forget to scoot into Billy Bob's, the world's biggest honky-tonk. Down in the Cultural District, tour the Cowgirl Museum and three amazing art collections. Then, after you've meditated on minimalism, Sundance Sq's restaurants and bars call you to the kick-up-your-heels downtown.

Whatever you do, don't mistake Fort Worth for being Dallas' sidekick. This city's got a headstrong spirit of its own, and it's a lot more user friendly than Dallas (not to mention greener and cleaner). Bottom line? There's a lot to do here – without a whole lot of pretense.

History

Fort Worth got its start in 1849 as Camp Worth, one of a string of military forts on the Texas frontier, and later found fame during the great open-range cattle drives, which lasted from the 1860s to the 1880s. Millions of cattle trooped through the city on the Chisholm Trail. Most of the time, the herds moved on to the end of the trail in Kansas. Yet after the railroad arrived in 1873 and stockyards were established at Fort Worth, many drovers chose to end their trek here.

The late 19th and early 20th centuries saw rampant lawlessness in Fort Worth. Robert LeRoy Parker and Harry Longabaugh (better known as Butch Cassidy and the Sundance Kid) spent a lot of time hiding out in a part of downtown known as Hell's Half Acre, and Depression-era holdup artists Bonnie Parker and Clyde Barrow also kicked around the city.

Yet most of the mayhem in Fort Worth came not from celebrity ne'er-do-wells but from rank-and-file cowboys with too much pent-up energy from the trail. They were the ones who boozed and brawled their way down Exchange Ave, giving Fort Worth a far different image than that of Dallas.

Museums put the city on the high-culture map back in 1892 when the Kimbell became the first museum in Texas. Since then, the nationally renowned Cultural District has continued to expand, and Sundance Sq has become one of the more successful downtown-revitalization projects in the US. All this pretty much solidifies Fort Worth's claim to the somewhat paradoxical title 'City of Cowboys and Culture.'

○ Sights

The Stockyards are cowboy central, while most of the area's museums call the leafy Cultural District home. Between these two areas and downtown, you can easily spend a couple of days savoring Fort Worth.

○ Stockyards National Historic District

★ Stockyards   HISTORIC SITE
(Map p163; ☑ 817-624-4741; www.fortworthstock yards.org; Exchange Ave) Western-wear stores and knickknack shops, saloons and steakhouses occupy the Old West–era buildings of the Stockyards. Don't miss the twice-daily cattle drive with the Fort Worth Herd when cowboys drive a small herd of longhorn up Exchange Ave. Start your visit getting info at the Fort Worth Stockyards Visitor Center (p169). It can seem touristy at times but there is a genuine authenticity here.

There's a lot to see and do in the area. You can explore the past at the **Stockyards Museum** (Map p163; ☑ 817-625-5082; www.stock yardsmuseum.org; 131 E Exchange Ave, Livestock Exchange Bldg; adult/child $2/free; ☺10am-5pm Mon-Sat year-round, noon-5pm Sun Jun-Aug) and the **Texas Cowboy Hall of Fame** (Map p163; ☑ 817-626-7131; www.texascowboyhalloffame.org; 128 E Exchange Ave; adult/child $6/3; ☺9am-5pm

Mon-Thu, 10am-7pm Fri & Sat, 11am-5pm Sun). Learn more on a Stockyards Guided Walking Tour (p162). You can watch a Wild West show or take in a **rodeo** (Map p163; ☑ 817-625-1025; www. stockyardsrodeo.com; 121 E Exchange Ave, Cowtown Coliseum; adult/child rodeo from $22.50/13.50, Wild West Show $18.50/11.50; ☺8pm Fri & Sat). Note that concerns about animal treatment are always present at rodeos.

★ Fort Worth Herd   HISTORIC SITE
(Map p163; ☑ 817-336-4373; www.fortworth.com/ the-herd; 131 E Exchange Ave; ☺cattle drive 11:30am & 4pm) See the cows for real out behind the Livestock Exchange Building: the Fort Worth Herd are the longhorns that parade down E Exchange Ave in a recreated cattle drive daily. You can see them in their corral from a viewing area which comes complete with picture-portraits of each – see if you can match names to critter

○ Cultural District

Fort Worth has some of the best museums of any city in Texas. Plus, it's easy to museum-hop around the parklike Cultural District on Camp Bowie Blvd, west of downtown.

★ Kimbell Art Museum   MUSEUM
(Map p160; ☑ 817-332-8451; www.kimbellart.org; 3333 Camp Bowie Blvd; ☺10am-5pm Tue-Thu & Sat, noon-8pm Fri, noon-5pm Sun) **FREE** Welcome to one of America's best small museums, with European masterpieces by Caravaggio, El Greco and Cézanne, as well as Michelangelo's first painting, *The Torment of St Anthony*.

STOCKYARDS NATIONAL HISTORIC DISTRICT

Sure, you'll spot cowboys on horseback roaming around, but wander the dusty streets of the Stockyards and you'll be mingling with a mix of families, curious international tourists and the odd freelance guitar player. This place puts fun first, with equal parts authentic history and camera-ready tourism, but it never crosses the line and becomes hokey, despite petting zoos and other gimcrackery.

At night, the area's focus moves on to its restaurants, nightspots and the legendary **Billy Bob's Texas** (p168).

Most parking lots offer $5 all-day parking, otherwise park on E Exchange Ave, or in the free lot to the northeast of Stockyards Station.

Fort Worth

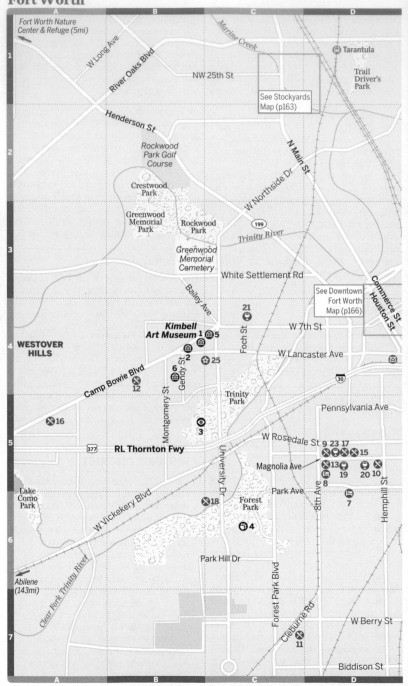

Fort Worth Nature Center & Refuge (5mi)

W Long Ave

River Oaks Blvd

Marine Creek

Tarantula

Trail Driver's Park

NW 25th St

See Stockyards Map (p163)

Henderson St

Rockwood Park Golf Course

N Main St

W Northside Dr

Crestwood Park

Greenwood Memorial Park

Rockwood Park

199

Trinity River

Greenwood Memorial Cemetery

White Settlement Rd

Bailey Ave

Commerce St

Houston St

See Downtown Fort Worth Map (p166)

W 7th St

21

Kimbell Art Museum 1 5

Foch St

W Lancaster Ave

WESTOVER HILLS

2

6

Gendy St

25

30

12

Camp Bowie Blvd

Montgomery St

Trinity Park

Pennsylvania Ave

16

3

377

RL Thornton Fwy

University Dr

W Rosedale St 9 23 17

15

Magnolia Ave

13

19

20 10

8th Ave

8

Lake Como Park

W Vickekery Blvd

Park Ave

7

Hemphill St

18

Forest Park

4

Abilene (143mi)

Clear Fork Trinity River

Park Hill Dr

Forest Park Blvd

W Berry St

Cleburne Rd

11

Biddison St

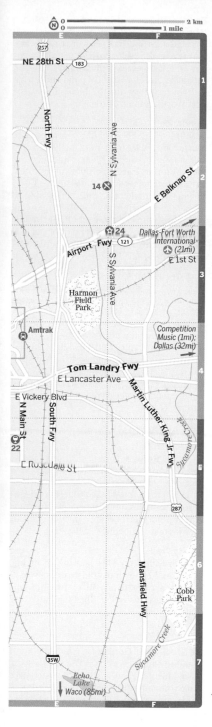

The architecture is no less stunning. Galleries are spread between an original Louis Kahn building and a more recent edition, designed by celebrated architect Renzo Piano. Special exhibitions charge admission.

Take your time: the stunning architecture lets in natural light that allows visitors to see paintings from antiquity to the 20th century the way the artists originally intended.

Modern Art Museum of Fort Worth MUSEUM
(Map p160; ☑817-738-9215; www.themodern.org; 3200 Darnell St; adult/child $10/free; ☺10am-5pm Wed, Thu, Sat & Sun, to 8pm Fri, to 7pm Tue) In a stunning, soaring space, this museum houses provocative works by luminaries such as Mark Rothko and Picasso.

Can't-miss pieces include Anselm Kiefer's *Book with Wings*, Martin Puryear's *Ladder for Booker T Washington* and Andy Warhol's *Twenty-Five Colored Marilyns*. The

DON'T MISS

SHOW ME THE MONEY

Watch millions roll off the presses at one of two places in the nation where 'In God We Trust' and Ben Franklin's face are legally printed on oh-so-hard-to-find paper: Fort Worth's **Bureau of Engraving and Printing** (🖊 817-231-4000; www.money factory.gov; 9000 Blue Mound Rd; ⊙ 8:30am-5:30pm Tue-Fri) FREE. This US Treasury facility produces currency not just for the US but for the scores of other nations around the world (such as Panama) that use US dollars. Learn how the money's design is ever-shifting in an effort to stay ahead of high-tech counterfeiters. It's 7 miles north of the Stockyards.

museum's artful restaurant, Café Modern, seems to float on the water of the surrounding reflective pools.

Amon Carter Museum of American Art
MUSEUM

(Map p160; 🖊 817-738-1933; www.cartermuseum. org; 3501 Camp Bowie Blvd; ⊙ 10am-5pm Tue, Wed, Fri & Sat, to 8pm Thu, noon-5pm Sun) FREE Pre-1945 American art shines at this museum, including iconic works by John Singer Sargent, Winslow Homer and Alexander Calder, as well as an impressive collection of works depicting the American West by artists Frederic Remington and Charles M Russell.

There's also an extensive photography collection. Walking through the exhibits is like taking a visual tour of the US – from Yosemite National Park with Albert Bierstadt to New Mexico with Georgia O'Keeffe.

National Cowgirl Museum
MUSEUM

(Map p160; 🖊 817-336-4475; www.cowgirl.net; 1720 Gendy St; adult/child $10/8; ⊙ 10am-5pm Tue-Sat, noon-5pm Sun) This airy, impressive museum explores the myth and the reality of cowgirls in American culture. From rhinestone costumes to rare film footage, this is a fun and educational ride: by the time you walk out, you'll have a whole new appreciation for these tough workers.

◉ Downtown & Around

Chisholm Trail Mural
PUBLIC ART

(Map p166; Sundance Sq) Overlooking Sundance Sq (p162), the iconic Chisholm Trail Mural commemorates the local segment of the Chisholm Trail cattle drives of 1867–75.

Fort Worth Botanic Garden
GARDENS

(Map p160; 🖊 817-871-7686; www.fwbg.org; 3220 Botanic Garden Blvd, Trinity Park; main garden free, Japanese Garden adult/child $7/4; ⊙ main garden 8am-8pm, Japanese Garden 9am-7pm) FREE A Japanese garden with a koi pond and a tropical conservatory are the highlights at the Fort Worth Botanic Garden.

Sundance Square
AREA

(Map p166; 🖊 817-255-5700; www.sundance square.com; 201 Main St) You can stroll yourself happy in the 14-block Sundance Sq, near Main and 3rd Sts. Colorful architecture, art galleries and a host of bars and restaurants make this one 'hood not to miss. The big, spurting fountain and cafe tables are fine spots to cool off. The iconic Chisholm Trail Mural commemorates the local segment of the Chisholm Trail cattle drives of 1867–75.

Fort Worth Zoo
ZOO

(Map p160; 🖊 817-759-7555; www.fortworthzoo. com; 1989 Colonial Pkwy, Forest Park off S University Dr; adult/child $14/10; ⊙ 10am-5pm; 🚻) A highly regarded American zoo (and the second-most-popular attraction in the state), it's home to about 5000 inhabitants representing 650 species, many of them endangered. Check out the Komodo dragons and the Great Barrier Reef exhibit. Other noted inhabitants include elephants and gorillas. Parking is $5.

🏃 Activities

Fort Worth Nature Center & Refuge
NATURE RESERVE

(🖊 817-237-1111; www.fwnaturecenter.org; 9601 Fossil Ridge Rd; adult/child $5/2; ⊙ 7am-5pm Mon-Fri, to 7pm Sat & Sun May-Sep, 8am-5pm Oct-Mar) Explore 25 miles of hiking and nature trails and an interpretive center. Includes forests, prairies and wetlands.

Trinity Trails
HIKING

(www.trinitytrails.org) This network of hiking, biking and equestrian trails covers over 40 miles along the Trinity River, by 21 of Fort Worth's parks as well as the Stockyards and downtown.

☞ Tours

★ Stockyards Guided Walking Tour
WALKING

(Map p163; 🖊 817-625-9715; http://stockyards station.com/attractions/historical-walking-tours/; Stockyards Station, 140 E Exchange Ave; adult/child

Stockyards

Stockyards

from $7/5; ⊘ daily) A great way to learn about the history of the Stockyards. There are two different walks offered.

⭐ Festivals & Events

Fort Worth Stock Show & Rodeo RODEO (www.fwssr.com; ⊘ mid-Jan–early Feb) Catch the rodeo with nearly a million other people. Started in 1896, it's held for several weeks each year at **Will Rogers Memorial Center** (Map p160; ☑817-392-7469; 3401 W Lancaster Ave) in the Cultural District. Rodeo events include steer wrestling and tie-down roping, sometimes causing injury to the animal. Rodeo events such as this are often criticized by animal welfare groups.

Main Street Arts Festival ART
(www.mainstreetartsfest.org; ⊘mid-Apr) One of the Southwest's biggest arts festivals, this spring event turns Sundance Sq into a center of live music, art shows and food booths.

🛏 Sleeping

Budget motels cluster near highway interchanges and along the Jacksboro Hwy (Hwy 199), northwest of downtown. You'll find decent chains along S University Dr, near the Cultural District. Staying near the Stockyards puts you close to the fun night and day.

Hotel Texas INN $
(Map p163; ☑817-624-2224; www.magnuson hotels.com/hotel/hotel-texas-fort-worth; 2415 Ellis Ave; r $75-100; ☺※☜) This 1939 'cattleman's home away from home' is a good deal, smack in the center of the Stockyards action. Although the service can be gruff and rooms very basic, it's hard to fault the prices of these simple, clean rooms decorated with framed Western art. Cash only.

★Rosen House Inn INN $$
(Map p160; ☑888-791-4850; www.rosenhouse inn.com; 1714 S Henderson St; r $105-165; ※☜☒) Enjoy the outdoor pool in the garden of this beautiful Craftsman-style house in a historic neighborhood south of the center. The three rooms are very well appointed with furniture appropriate to the house. Some rooms have claw-foot tubs.

★Stockyards Hotel HISTORIC HOTEL $$
(Map p163; ☑817-625-6427; www.stockyards hotel.com; 109 E Exchange Ave; r $150-300; ※☜) First opened in 1907, this 52-room place clings to its cowboy past with Western-themed art, cowboy-inspired rooms and a grand Old West lobby with lots of leather. Hide out in the Bonnie and Clyde room, where the outlaw pair actually stayed while on the lam in 1933 (the faux bullet holes and Bonnie's .38 revolver only add to the mystique).

Hyatt Place Fort Worth
Historic Stockyards HOTEL $$
(Map p163; ☑817-626-6000; www.hyatt.com; 132 E Exchange Ave; r $120-200; ※☜☒) A surprisingly good-value chain hotel in the heart of the Stockyards. The 101 rooms are very well appointed and are good-sized with work areas. The decor is vaguely Mission-style, the pool is outside.

Miss Molly's Hotel B&B $$
(Map p163; ☑817-626-1522; www.missmollys hotel.com; 109 W Exchange Ave; r $100-175; ※☜) Set in the heart of the Stockyards, eight-room Miss Molly's occupies a former bordello. Its heavily atmospheric vibe will feel authentic to some (Miss Josie's room still looks like madame's boudoir), eerie to others (they say it's haunted...), but probably at least a little charming either way. Look for cheap deals during the week.

Etta's Place INN $$
(Map p166; ☑817-255-5760; www.ettas-place.com; 200 W 3rd St; r $150-250; ※☜) A grand piano, a comfy library and quilts galore are among the cozy pleasures at this Sundance Sq inn. Breakfast can be taken on the airy patio. The 10 rooms are large; suites have kitchenettes. The inn takes its name from Etta Place, the rumored paramour of the Sundance Kid.

Texas White House B&B $$
(Map p160; ☑817-923-3597; www.texaswhite house.com; 1417 8th Ave; r $180-250; ※☜) A large historic home with contemporary Texas style near downtown. The five rooms are well equipped and uniquely designed (many have claw-foot tubs). Top picks include the Tejas room (with Mexican pottery and folk art), the Lonestar (with antique furniture and cowboy gear) and the Treehouse suite (with private balcony, dry sauna and Jacuzzi tub). Breakfasts have Mexican flair.

Ashton Hotel BOUTIQUE HOTEL $$
(Map p166; ☑817-332-0100; www.theashton hotel.com; 610 Main St; r $180-290; ※☜☒) This 39-room six-story boutique hotel in a turn-of-the-century building off Sundance Sq offers hush-hush elegance without an ounce of snootiness. Turndown service comes with cookies and each room has a gourmet coffeemaker. There's a free wine happy hour on weekends.

🍴 Eating

Downtown offers options around Sundance Sq. The Stockyards are rich with feed possibilities. Prowl W Magnolia Ave for innovative and diverse choices. Many of the museums, such as the Kimbell, also have excellent cafes. PS: you're in Fort Worth – have a steak.

★**Heim Barbecue** BARBECUE $
(Map p160; ☑817-882-6970; http://heimbbq.
com; 1109 W Magnolia Ave; mains $8-18; ⊙11am-
10pm Wed-Mon) Barbecue for a new age, the
family behind this joint brings knowledge
and passion to the cause. Sausage, brisket
(of course!), turkey, pulled pork and more
are smoky and delectable. Note that the
meats sell out, so don't delay. It's probably
not going to happen, but try to save room
for the banana pudding.

★**Enchiladas Ole** TEX-MEX $
(Map p160; ☑817-984-1360; www.enchiladasole.
com; 901 N Sylvania Ave; mains $8-13; ⊙11am-
3pm Mon-Wed, to 8pm Thu, 10am-9pm Fri & Sat)
The antidote to same-seeming Tex-Mex.
Yep, the dining room is dead simple and
the menu a familiar litany of enchiladas, quesadillas and guacamole. But here
everything is just that much better. The
enchiladas will give you new respect for a
dish you thought you knew. Prepare for the
salsas.

★**Curly's Frozen Custard** ICE CREAM $
(Map p160; ☑817-763-8700; www.curlysfrozen
custard.com; 4017 Camp Bowie Blvd; treats from
$3; ⊙11am-10pm) Creamy frozen custard
which you can customize with all sorts of
mix-ins to make a 'concrete'. Good any day
the temp is above freezing. The patio has a
cute fountain.

★**Kincaid's** BURGERS $
(Map p160; ☑817-732-2881; www.kincaidsham
burgers.com; 4901 Camp Bowie Blvd; mains $5-8;
⊙11am-8pm Mon-Sat, to 3pm Sun) Sit on picnic tables amid disused grocery shelves at
this local institution (never mind the sickly
green walls) and wolf down some of the
best burgers in the region. They are thick,
juicy and come covered in condiments.

Benito's MEXICAN $
(Map p160; ☑817-332-8633; http://benitosmex
ican.com; 1415 W Magnolia Ave; meals $6-14;
⊙11am-9pm Mon-Thu, to 2am Fri & Sat, 10am-
9pm Sun) The welcoming Gonzalez family
has been here for more than three decades,
offering a good mix of familiar and adventurous items, like Mexican-style pork chops
and *tamal oaxaqueno* (cornmeal baked in a
banana leaf with chicken and red mole). We
like the Spanish lesson on the menu, so you
can say '*Mas cerveza por favor*' (more beer
please) with aplomb.

RODEO CLOWNS
....
While it sounds like a particularly cruel
cowboy insult, it's an actual profes-
sion, and one of the most notoriously
dangerous in the rodeo industry. As
a performer who works in bull-riding
events, a rodeo clown's function is to
protect a rider from being gored by the
bull should they fall off the horse. But
how? By distracting the bull, of course,
which accounts for their colorful
clothes. Sometimes the clowns jump in
and out of a barrel, which offers mini-
mal protection but requires even more
agility, and sometimes the clowns
entertain the crowd between events.
Through it all, this remains a job for the
wily and fleet-footed: the bulls never
laugh.

Carshon's Deli DELI $
(Map p160; ☑817-923-1907; www.carshonsdeli.
com; 3133 Cleburne Rd; mains $7-12; ⊙9am-
3pm Mon-Sat) Since 1928 Fort Worth's only
kosher deli has served up classic New York
sandwiches. Half the fun's in watching local
movers and shakers make and break deals
in between bites of pastrami on rye.

Love Shack BURGERS $
(Map p163; ☑817-740-8812; www.loveburger
shack.com; 110 E Exchange Ave; mains $5-10;
⊙11am-8pm Sun-Wed, to 9pm Thu, to midnight Fri
& Sat) Enjoy a gourmet burger (the signature
Dirty Love has bacon, cheese and a fried
quail egg) at this Stockyards joint owned by
Texas-born TV chef Tim Love. Don't miss the
home-cut fries or Parmesan chips. Local singers take the stage from Wednesday through
Sunday.

Spiral Diner & Bakery CAFE $
(Map p160; ☑817-332-8834; http://spiraldiner.
com; 1314 W Magnolia Ave; mains $8-12; ⊙11am-
10pm Tue-Fri, 9am-10pm Sat & Sun; ☑⛾) One
of the most inventive organic vegan restaurants in Texas, this retro-feel diner serves up
fresh juices, smoothies, salads and a whole
bevy of delicious dishes (fig and fennel sandwich, anyone?). Breakfast is served all day.
The bakery is famous for cakes. Craft brews
and organic wines round out the menu.
There's a great shade tree over the sidewalk
picnic table.

Downtown Fort Worth

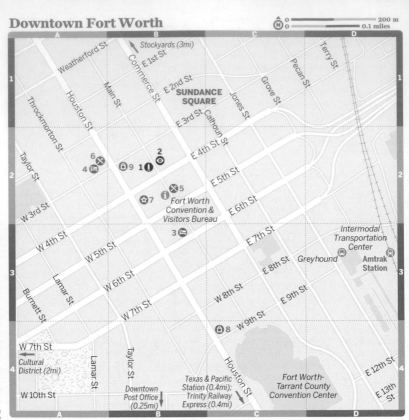

Downtown Fort Worth

◉ Sights

🛏 Sleeping

✗ Eating

✪ Entertainment

🛍 Shopping

★ **Ellerbe Fine Foods**   INTERNATIONAL **$$**
(Map p160; ☎817-926-3663; www.ellerbefine
foods.com; 1501 W Magnolia Ave; lunch mains $10-
18, dinner mains $23-32; ⊘11am-2pm & 5.30-9pm

Tue-Thu, 11am-2pm & 5.30-10pm Fri, 5.30-10pm Sat)
Fresh, seasonal and local are the keywords
in this serene, light-filled cafe. The farm-to-
table ethos is a religion here and the seasonal
menus always reflect what's fresh now from
the best local producers. Count on good
steaks and seafood at dinner. The relaxed el-
egance here almost hides the art-deco lines
of this old gas station. Lovely seating outside.

★ **Joe T Garcia's**   MEXICAN **$$**
(Map p163; ☎817-626-4356; www.joets.com; 2201
N Commerce St; mains $8-16; ⊘11am-2:30pm &
5-10pm Mon-Thu, 11am-11pm Fri & Sat, to 10pm Sun)
The most famous restaurant in Fort Worth,
this fourth-generation place takes up a city
block. Dining in the walled courtyard is a
magical experience (and can entail long
waits for a table), as Mexican-tile fountains
bubble among the acres of tropical foliage.
On weekends the line (no reservations!) often stretches around the block.

Brewed
MODERN AMERICAN **$$**

(Map p160; ☑ 817-945-1545; www.brewedfw.com; 801 W Magnolia Ave; mains $6 20; ☺ 8am-10pm Tue & Wed, to 11pm Thu-Sat, 9:30am-2:30pm Sun; ☎) Brewed is an easygoing spot with exposed brick walls, mismatched tables and chairs, taxidermy and friendly waitstaff. With great coffee, 60 craft brews and an appealing food menu, it's a good anytime spot. Start the day with chicken and waffles or housemade granola. Later, feast on a fiery shrimp, bacon mac 'n' cheese, or a burger and duck-fat fries

Woodshed Smokehouse
BARBECUE **$$**

(Map p160; ☑ 817-877-4545; www.woodshed smokehouse.com; 3201 Riverfront Dr; mains $10-28; ☺ 10am-10pm Mon-Thu, 10am-11pm Fri, 8am-11pm Sat, 8am-10pm Sun; ☺) ✒ A star of the Trinity River area, this hugely successful riverside barbecue joint packs 'em in. Texas celebrity chef Tim Love serves up gourmet barbecue. The lack of air-conditioning, which the airy location and building design negates the need for, is an eco-nod. Enjoy live bluegrass on the vast terrace Wednesday to Sunday. Dog and kid friendly.

There's a 'Dining with Friends' menu if you're coming with a group of meat-lovers and are ready for some big platters.

Reata
AMERICAN **$$**

(Map p166; ☑ 817-336-1009; www.reata.net; 310 Houston St; mains $12-42; ☺ 11am-2.30pm & 5-10pm) The proprietors also own their own cattle ranch, so the sizable steaks are worth their weight. But you might also try the Texas specialties such as tenderloin tamales and jalapeño-cheddar grits. The chicken-fried steak regularly makes bests lists. The rooftop has fabulous views over downtown. The restaurant is named for the ranch at the center of the iconic west Texas movie *Giant*.

★Lonesome Dove Western Bistro
AMERICAN **$$$**

(Map p163; ☑ 817-740-8810; www.lonesome dovebistro.com; 2406 N Main St; mains $10-50; ☺ 11:30am-2:30pm Tue-Sat, 5-10pm Mon-Thu, to 11pm Fri & Sat; ☎) At Tim Love's mod-Western Stockyards dining experience, even the chefs wear cowboy hats. It's Southern fusion, with the traditional flavors of the region enlivened by all manner of influences. Roasted meats and grilled steaks take prime place on the menu. Stick someone else with the bill for the $115 Wagyu Tomahawk Ribeye. The wine list is superb.

Grace
AMERICAN **$$$**

(Map p166; ☑ 817-877-3388; http://gracefort worth.com; 777 Main St; mains $18-45; ☺ 5:30-9:30pm) At downtown's Grace, local luminaries hold court (and martinis) on the couch-strewn outdoor patio. In the stunning dining room with its temp-controlled wall of wine, a seasonal menu features fresh and inventive fare. Regularly changing tasting menus are $85 (with wine parings add $50). Steaks get a place of honor.

🍷 Drinking & Nightlife

★Chimera
BREWERY

(Map p160; ☑ 817-923-8000; www.chimerabrew. com; 1001 W Magnolia Ave; ☺ 11:30am-midnight Mon-Fri, from 10am Sat, 10am-10pm Sun; ☎) Fort Worth's top brewery keeps a rotating range of eight beers on tap. The lineup changes regularly. Watch for the bacon special and the wet hop sour among others. Hungry? The pizza is thin-crust Italian and comes in a dozen varieties. Enjoy in the exposed brick dining area or outside on the patio.

★Lola's Saloon
BAR

(Map p160; ☑ 817-877-0666; www.lolassaloon.com; 2736 W 6th St; ☺ 2pm-2am Mon-Fri, noon-2am Sat & Sun) Dive into this dive bar for a fairly intimate music experience. Bands (rock, honky-tonk, bluegrass) play many nights to a fun, eclectic crowd. Catch your breath on the small outside patio. On non-show nights, there's a jukebox that's addictive. Regularly voted a favorite bar by readers of *Fort Worth Weekly*.

★Usual Bar
COCKTAIL BAR

(Map p160; ☑ 817-810-0114; www.facebook.com/ theusualbar/; 1408 W Magnolia Ave; ☺ 4pm-2am Mon-Fri, from 6pm Sat & Sun) Craft-cocktail lust packs hipsters in nightly at this bar that serves up debonair drinks such as the 'Maximillian-aire' and 'the Parlor.' Of course you can be ironic and just have a well-poured Sidecar. Great terrace.

Chat Room
BAR

(Map p160; ☑ 817-922-8319; www.thechatroom pub.com; 1263 W Magnolia Ave; ☺ 2pm-2am; ☎) Cheap drinks, a great jukebox and a pool table are among the lures of this dive-champ, which happily bills itself as 'easily Fort Worth's eighth best bar'. The patio is really some picnic tables on the sidewalk. A favored spot for last call.

Rahr & Sons Brewing Co   BREWERY

(Map p160; ☑817-810-9266; http://rahrbrewing.com; 701 Galveston Ave, at S Main St; $10; ⏱5-7:30pm Wed, 1-3pm Sat) Keep the pint glass after sampling some Ugly Pug dark beer or Mr Wiggles double IPA as you burp your way through this fun tour. Watch for its beers around town.

☆ Entertainment

Toward the weekend, you'll hear live country music wafting from the Stockyards District. Otherwise, you'll find good venues for country tunes scattered about town.

★Stagecoach Ballroom   LIVE MUSIC

(Map p160; ☑817-831-2261; http://stageroachball room.com; 2516 E Belknap St) By day it looks like it could be a plumbing-supply warehouse but by night, this nondescript building shakes to hundreds of dancers moving in rhythm on the 3500-sq-ft dance floor. It gets a top lineup of local and touring acts.

★Pearls Dance Hall   LIVE MUSIC

(Map p163; ☑817-624-2800; www.pearlsdancehall. corn; 302 W Exchange Ave; ⏱6pm-2am Wed, from 7pm Fri & Sat) On the edge of the stockyards, this raucous old brothel once owned by Buffalo Bill Cody is an atmospheric place to hear traditional country music with an edge. Texas luminaries are known to rock out here to the strains of the slide guitar and fiddle. Two-steppers hit the floor many nights.

Scat Jazz Lounge   JAZZ

(Map p166; ☑817-870-9100; www.scatjazzlounge. com; 111 W 4th St; ⏱7pm-2am Sun & Tue-Thu, 5pm-2am Fri, from 6pm Sat) Tucked into a downtown alley, this subterranean jazz spot is low-key, with just a touch of smoky glamor. There is live music most nights.

Billy Bob's Texas   LIVE MUSIC

(Map p163; ☑817-624-7117; www.billybobstexas. com; 2520 Rodeo Plaza; cover Sun-Thu $2-5, Fri & Sat varies; ⏱11am-10pm Mon-Wed, to 2am Thu-Sat, noon-10pm Sun) The 100,000-sq-ft building that is now the world's largest honky-tonk was once a barn housing prize cattle during the Fort Worth Stock Show. Now after a stint as a department store, Billy Bob's can hold more than 6000 people and has 40 bars to serve the thirsty masses. Don't miss the mechanical bull-riding competitions at 9pm and 10pm Friday and Saturday.

The most bottled beer sold in one night was 16,000 bottles, during a 1985 Hank Williams Jr concert. Top country-and-western stars, house bands and country DJs play on two stages. Pool tables and games help make this a family place; under 18s are welcome with a parent.

White Elephant Saloon   LIVE MUSIC

(Map p163; www.whiteelephantsaloon.com; 106 E Exchange Ave; cover free-$10; ⏱noon-midnight Sun-Thu, to 2am Fri & Sat) Stockyards cowboys have been bellying up to this bar since 1887 (now owned by the ubiquitous Tim Love). Local singers and songwriters are showcased nightly. Most nights there's no cover.

Texas Motor Speedway   SPECTATOR SPORT

(☑817-215-8500; www.texasmotorspeedway.com; cnr Hwy 114 & I-35, exit 72; tours adult/child $10/8; ⏱9am-5pm Mon-Fri, 10am-5pm Sat, noon-5pm Sun) Have yourself a full-on NASCAR experience. The annual stock-car race is in November, but there are races through the year. You can go for a ride with a racer (from $125). The speedway is 20 miles north of downtown, on I-35 W.

🔒 Shopping

Head to the Stockyards for Western gear and over-the-top Texas kitsch. Downtown has some veteran Western-wear sellers.

★Peters Bros Hats   HATS

(Map p166; ☑817-335-1715; www.pbhats.com; 909 Houston St; ⏱10am-5pm Mon-Sat) Get your Stetson on at this downtown hat shop, in business since 1911. Enjoy the wall of fame – famous folks wearing their hats.

ML Leddy's   CLOTHING

(Map p163; ☑817-624-3149; www.leddys.com; 2455 N Main St; ⏱10am-6pm Mon-Sat) Ah, the smell of leather that unmistakably says 'new boots.' Check out the bank ledgers, which contain the foot measurements of rock stars and presidents. If you still don't feel like kicking up your heels, the selection of hats, buckles and clothes might fit the bill.

Retro Cowboy   CLOTHING

(Map p166; ☑817-338-1194; http://retrocowboy. com; 406 Houston St; ⏱10am-7pm Mon-Thu, to 10pm Fri & Sat, noon-5pm Sun) Cool cowboy-themed stuff that screams 'perfect Fort Worth souvenir!' Look hard and you'll find the elusive jackalope.

Competition Music   MUSICAL INSTRUMENTS

(☑817-535-2040; www.competitionmusic.net; 3136 E Lancaster Ave; ⏱10am-6pm Mon-Sat) If Fort Worth's incredible music scene has you thinking you want to join in, this is the shop to get gear. It's one of the region's best indie dealers of musical instruments.

❶ Information

Downtown Post Office (Map p160; ☑ 817-870-8128; www.usps.com; 251 W Lancaster Ave; ☺ 9am-6pm Mon-Fri, 8am-4pm Sat)

Fort Worth Convention & Visitors Bureau (Map p166; ☑ 800-433-5747; www.fortworth. com; 508 Main St; ☺ 10am-6pm Mon-Thu, to 7pm Fri & Sat) A solid tourist office with region-wide info. Very helpful and right Downtown.

Fort Worth Stockyards Visitor Center (Map p163; ☑ 817-624-4741; www.fortworthstockyards.org; 130 E Exchange Ave; ☺ 9am-5pm) The place for all details on the Fort Worth Stockyards National Historic District.

❶ Getting There & Away

Dallas-Fort Worth International Airport (p158) is 17 miles east of Fort Worth.

Buses and trains in Fort Worth share the **Intermodal Transportation Center** (1001 Jones St), easing transfers.

The **Amtrak** (☑ 800-872-7245; www.amtrak. com; 1001 Jones St) *Texas Eagle* stops in Fort Worth en route to San Antonio and Chicago. The *Heartland Flyer* serves Oklahoma City.

Trinity Railway Express (p158) trains run between Fort Worth and Dallas Union Station (one hour), with a stop at CenterPort/DFW Airport where there is a shuttle-bus connection to the airport.

Several **Greyhound** (Map p166; www.grey hound.com; 1001 Jones St) buses a day make the trip ($8 to $10, 45 minutes to one hour) from downtown Fort Worth to Dallas. There's also service to other major Texas cities.

❶ Getting Around

Fort Worth is fairly compact and easy to drive around; I-30 runs east–west through downtown, and I-35 W runs to the south.

The T (Fort Worth Transit Authority; ☑ 817-215-8600; www.the-t.com; single ride/day pass $1.75/3.50) runs buses 12 and 15 to the Stockyards from downtown and bus 2 to the Cultural District. Stops include the **Intermodal Transportation Center**. All of these lines run well into the evening.

A useful and free bus route, deceptively called **Molly the Trolley** (☑ 817-204-0302; www.molly thetrolley.com; ☺ 10am-10pm), shuttles around downtown every 10 minutes on two routes.

Fort Worth B-Cycle (http://fortworth.bcycle. com; 24hr/3 days $8/15; ☺ 24hr) lets you pick up a bike at one of dozens of self-checkout stations around Fort Worth. After purchasing a pass, you have unlimited trips of up to 30 minutes each use

before additional charges are incurred. Use the app to check availability and pickup locations.

NORTH OF DALLAS & FORT WORTH

Much of the region's phenomenal growth is north of Dallas. Quaint little towns such as McKinney are now enveloped by the Metroplex. Towns such as Grapevine, however, have their own inherent charms and you can – eventually – go far enough north that you leave all the urban hubbub far behind.

Grapevine

☑ 214, 469, 972 / POP 50,200

Although it's right next to DFW Airport, Grapevine is as quaint a town as you'll find in the Metroplex. Its classic Main St oozes history and appeal, and begs a stroll. Thanks to the airport fees, its myriad civic attractions are well funded.

◉ Sights & Activities

With the exception of its large mall, everything listed here is in the walkable, compact historic downtown area called the Cotton Belt Railroad District.

Grapevine Historical Society MUSEUM
(☑ 817-488-0235; www.grapevinehistory.org; 206 W Hudgins St; ☺ 10am-4pm Tue-Sat, 11am-4pm Sun) **FREE** This well-funded museum has impressive quarters in the 1940 Grapevine Ice Company building next to the Visitor Information Center. It has excellent displays covering just who settled in Grapevine and why.

Delaney Winery & Vineyards WINERY
(☑ 817-481-5668; www.delaneyvineyards.com; 2000 Champagne Blvd; tour & tasting $10; ☺ noon-5pm Wed-Sat) This north Texas winery has an attractive tasting room. Learn about winemaking on tours, then sample five wines while you hear the roar of jets at DFW Airport just to the east. The winery is 5 miles south of the Cotton Belt district.

Grapevine Blacksmith Shop HISTORIC SITE
(☑ 940-435-1684; www.facebook.com/The-Black smith-Shop; 707 S Main St; ☺ 10am-5pm Thu-Sun) **FREE** Just east of the historic Cotton Belt train station, this is a fascinating place to watch genial blacksmiths demonstrate their craft.

★ **Grapevine Vintage Railroad**   RAIL
(☑ 817-410-3185; www.gvrr.com; 636 S Main St; adult/child from $15/10; ⊙ departs 1pm Fri-Sun Jun-Aug, plus other dates year-round) Grapevine's own historic railroad runs tourist trains to and from Fort Worth's Stockyards. The ride takes 90 minutes one-way and you have about 90 minutes in Fort Worth. Extra cash gets you air-conditioning in 1st class or a ride in the caboose. Some runs have a steam engine. Trains leave from the restored Cotton Belt depot.

✕ Eating & Drinking

Weinberger's Delicatessen   DELI $
(☑ 817-416-5577; www.weinbergersdeli.com; 601 S Main St; mains $7-15; ⊙ 10am-7pm Mon-Sat, 11am-5pm Sun; 🖰) This Chicago-style deli is a transplant from the Windy City and has a bevy of local fans. Thick-cut sandwiches and dripping Italian beefs are among the 100 items on the menu. Daily specials can be excellent; there's a kids menu. It's close to the Cotton Belt Railroad District.

Su Vino Winery   WINE BAR
(☑ 817-416-9333; www.suvinowinery.com; 120 S Main St; ⊙ noon-7pm Tue-Sat, 1-5pm Sun) Look out your window at the right moment as you fly into DFW and you might spot the vineyards of one of Grapevine's several wineries. Su Vino is one of the best. Right downtown, you can sample its range of wine and enjoy light snacks.

🔒 Shopping

Grapevine Mills Shopping Center   MALL
(☑ 972-724-4900; www.simon.com/mall/grapevine-mills; 3000 Grapevine Mills Pkwy at I-635 & TX 121; ⊙ 10am-9:30pm Mon-Sat, 11am-7pm Sun; 🖰) Almost as big as Minnesota's Mall of America, the Grapevine Mills Shopping Center is an outlet mall with over 200 stores selling off-price goods by famous brands and labels. Bored? It has a 30-screen movie theater. Kids can enjoy a small Legoland with a big admission price ($21, discounts online).

ℹ Information

Visitor Information Center (☑ 817-410-3185; www.grapevinetexasusa.com; 636 S Main St; ⊙ 8am-5pm Mon-Fri, 10am-6:30pm Sat, noon-5pm Sun) Housed in a lavish brick edifice downtown, this center brims with useful information and helpful staff. It also has a free gallery with rotating exhibits.

ℹ Getting There & Away

Grapevine Visitors Shuttle (☑ 817-410-8185; www.grapevinetexasusa.com/shuttle; day pass individual/family $5/10; ⊙ 10am-10pm Mon-Sat, 11am-7pm Sun) Unlike many other Metroplex cities, Grapevine has a visitor shuttle that links the airport, Grapevine Mills, the historic downtown and some hotels.

Frisco

☑ 214, 469, 972 / POP 138,600

Frisco has arrived! Regularly named America's fastest growing city, its population was a mere 1000 as recently as 1990. This means that the city is trying to define itself even as new multilane roads are plowed through in all directions.

The city has been working to secure high-profile attractions, many of them sports related.

⊙ Sights

Star   SPORTS GROUND
(☑ 972-497-4800; www.thestarinfrisco.com; One Cowboys Way; tours adult/child $33/28; ⊙ hours vary) Only the Dallas Cowboys could find a way to turn their training facility into a money-making machine. Thanks to a generous gift of land and subsidies by boosters in Frisco, the NFL football team has built a vast facility here. Opened in phases beginning in 2016, it includes a 12,000-seat indoor stadium where the public can buy tickets to watch the team practice. There will also be a mall with upscale chain restaurants and much more.

Museum of the American Railroad   MUSEUM
(☑ 214-428-0101; www.museumoftheamerican railroad.org; 8004 Dallas Pkwy, Frisco; adult/child $8/4; ⊙ hours vary) One of the best collections of historic railroad locomotives and cars in the country moved to Frisco in 2013. Some famous locomotives and train cars are on display outside; however, visits can require some advance planning. Due to museum construction, at times you can't self-guide your way around the site and instead have to go on a guided tour, which may only happen a few times per week. Check details in advance.

When you can get in, the huge collection includes a Union Pacific Big Boy, one of the very largest steam locomotives ever built. Note that tours may depart from the Frisco Heritage Museum (6455 Page St), which is about half a mile north of the trains and which has a small exhibit about the museum's holdings.

McKinney

📍 214, 469, 972 / POP 149,200

Visitors to McKinney will find no shortage of reminders that the historic town was once named one of the best places to live in the US. Certainly, compared to the created-from-scratch vibe of nearby Frisco, it has a real patina of authenticity.

Even as the Metroplex eddies around its edges, McKinney has lovely small-town streets lined with restored Queen Anne and Victorian houses that exude charm. And the town's center is easily the most vibrant downtown of any historic town in north Texas. Shops, boutiques, cafes and bistros around the main square buzz with action. You can easily spend a half day or more enjoying the charms of McKinney.

◉ Sights

**Chestnut Square
Historic Village** HISTORIC SITE
(📞972-562-8790; www.chestnutsquare.org; 315 S Chestnut St; adult/child $10/7; ⊙tours 11am Thu & Sat) A collection of old buildings from around McKinney. Highlights include the Faires House, an 1854 house made from wood. Other buildings date from the 1870s and the early 20th century. You can wander around around anytime, take the tour to get inside.

🛏 Sleeping & Eating

Grand Hotel HISTORIC HOTEL $$
(📞214-726-9250; www.grandhotelmckinney.com; 114 W Louisiana St; r $120-200; ❇🅿🛜) In an 1880 building that once was McKinney's opera house, this inn has 45 plush, modern rooms set amid exposed bricks and other small luxurious details. It's right on the main square.

★**Patina Green Home and Market** CAFE $$
(📞972-548-9141; www.patinagreenhomeandmarket.com; 116 N Tennessee St; mains from $12; ⊙store 10am-6pm Mon-Sat, 11am-3pm Sun, lunch 11am-3pm) 🌱 For most of the day, Patina Green is an attractive shop with creative and tasteful housewares plus a deli section with some of the best local prepared foods and cheeses. But at lunchtime, a line often forms for the exquisite soups, salads and sandwiches the chef makes each day. The emphasis is on sustainability and seasonality.

Several nights a month it creates a seasonal menu (from $85, beer and wine pairing $35).

★**Farmers Market** MARKET
(📞972-562-8790; www.chestnutsquare.org; 315 S Chestnut St, Chestnut Square Historic Village; ⊙8am-noon Sat Apr-Oct; 🅿) 🌱 Features the best organic vendors and food producers in the region. There's a big selection of food vendors offering ready-to-eat items like tamales.

Denton

📍 940 / POP 123,200

A bastion of college cool and indie cred, Denton has a good music scene. Home to the University of North Texas and its renowned arts programs, the fast-growing city rightfully claims the title as the most musical city in the region. The downtown, centered on Courthouse Sq, boasts a plethora of music venues, music shops and instrument stores (www.dentonmainstreet.org).

Denton has one of the state's most walkable small-town downtowns day and night.

◉ Sights

**Courthouse on the
Square Museum** MUSEUM
(📞940-349-2850; http://dentoncounty.com; 110 W Hickory St; ⊙10am-4:30pm Mon-Fri, 11am-3pm Sat) FREE By day, pop into the Courthouse on the Square Museum inside the grandiose 1896 former courthouse for local lore and an amazing display of art created with pecans. It's nuts! Outside, check out the 1918 Confederate War Memorial which has been modified with apologetic disclaimers.

🍽 Eating

★**Tex Tapas** TAPAS $
(📞940-218-6577; www.textapas.com; 109 Industrial St; mains $5-15; ⊙11am-11pm Tue-Sat, to 10pm Sun) Unusual and good tapas include green curry meatballs and grilled vegetable rellenos plus constantly changing seasonal specials. There are artworks inside and outside the restored vintage building. The cocktail list is as interesting as the food and the art.

West Oak Coffee Bar CAFE $
(📞940-218-2666; www.westoakcoffeebar.com; 114 W Oak St; mains from $5; ⊙7:30am-10:30pm; 🛜🅿) Unusual and inventive coffee drinks and interesting baked goods are available through the day. Sandwiches are served until 3pm. There's a bare-brick vibe, tables outside and plenty of outlets for your gear.

★**Ranchman's Ponder**
Steakhouse AMERICAN $$
(☏940-479-2221; www.ranchman.com; 110 W Bailey St, Ponder; mains $7-35; ⏰11am-9pm Sun-Thu, to 10pm Fri & Sat) Given its size, this famous cafe is almost all there is to pint-sized Ponder. The chicken fried steak has drawn TV coverage. The steaks are the kind that even beef ranchers can respect. A key to quality here: even often-humdrum sides like green beans are fresh and inventive. Save room (!) for the pies. It's only 10 miles west of Denton.

 Drinking & Nightlife

★**Dan's Silver Leaf** LIVE MUSIC
(☏940-320-2000; www.danssilverleaf.com; 103 Industrial St; cover free-$5; ⏰4pm-2am) For music, this top venue has a revered owner who books top bands but doesn't gouge on drink prices. Top regional bands are booked near nightly. Chill out on the back patio.

Harvest House BAR
(☏940-218-6148; www.dentonharvesthouse.com; 331 E Hickory St; ⏰noon-2am) A huge wraparound patio nearly encircles the stylish bar. There are dozens of craft brews from the region as well as a long cocktail list. This is the kind of place you can hang out at with friends for hours on end. There's usually live music at least three nights a week.

 Shopping

★**Recycled Books Records CDs** MUSIC
(☏940-566-5688; www.recycledbooks.com; 200 N Locust St; ⏰9am-9pm) Lose track of time browsing aisle after aisle of intriguing old titles and hard-to-find tunes.

ℹ **Getting There & Away**

A-Train (☏940-243-0077; www.dcta.net; 604 E Hickory St, Eulene Brock Downtown Denton Transit Center (DDTC); ⏰5:30am-8pm Mon-Fri, 9am-11pm Sat) Operates commuter trains that connect to Dallas from Denton (adult/child $5/1.25). Trains run every half-hour Monday to Friday and every two hours on Saturday. To reach Dallas, change from the A-Train to the DART light rail Green Line at the Trinity Mills Station. The total transit time is about 90 minutes.

Decatur

📞940 / POP 6300

For 20 years beginning in the late 1860s, Decatur was an important waypoint on the Chisholm Trail, the legendary cowboy route along which millions of heads of Texas cattle were driven north to markets. As the beef went one way, the state's first fortunes came south with the the first cattle barons. Today you'll most likely stop in Decatur on your way to the Panhandle.

Surrounding the courthouse square where State and Main Sts meet are lively shops and cafes.

 Sights

Wise County Courthouse HISTORIC BUILDING
(101 N Trinity St) Decatur's 1896 Wise County Courthouse is a marvel in pink granite. It cost $110,000, which sparked an outcry among tax-hating voters who promptly voted out of office the responsible public officials. Some things never change.

SOUTHFORK RANCH

Seen by billions of glossy TV soap fans worldwide, **Southfork Ranch** (☏972-442-7800; www.southfork.com; 3700 Hogge Rd/FM 2551; adult/child $15/9; ⏰10am-5pm) is the real-world mansion that posed as the home of JR Ewing and company on *Dallas*. Built as a rich family's home in 1970, the ranch was chosen to be the Ewing Ranch when *Dallas* hit the airwaves in 1978. From then on it was used for certain exterior shots for the series until 1989.

The ranch was called back to duty for reunion movies over the years and then for the return of the series for two years in 2012. In the meantime, fans kept coming by to see the mansion and by the 1990s it had been converted into a conference center hosting corporate events, Tea Party rallies and a memorial for actor Larry Hagman (who played JR in *Dallas*) after his death in 2012.

Southfork is still popular with *Dallas* fans. While it does have some old props from the show (like the gun that shot JR), don't expect to see Miss Ellie's kitchen or JR's bedroom, as interior shots of the ranch were filmed on a Hollywood set. It's 20 miles northwest of Dallas, near Parker.

Eating

Cakes by Leisha BAKERY $
(📞940-626-4783; 103 S Trinity St; treats from $2; ⊙10am-5pm Tue-Fri, to noon Sat) This irresistible bakery creates treats which you can enjoy here or on your onward journey.

Sweetie Pie's Ribeyes SOUTHERN US $$
(📞940-626-4555; www.sweetiepiesribeyes.com; 201 W Main St; mains $12-30; ⊙11am-9pm; 🛜) Serves up Texas menu stalwarts with color and flair. Steaks come with a huge choice of sides.

SOUTH OF DALLAS & FORT WORTH

From the big attractions in Arlington to the prehistoric sights in Glen Rose, the lands south of Dallas and Fort Worth are diverse. Enjoy Waxahachie, one of the state's best small towns, and feel the bliss of wide open spaces as you head southwest.

Arlington

📞682, 817 / POP 380,000
For once the hype is real: Arlington really is the home of sports and thrills. Blockbuster attractions, the Dallas Cowboys and the Texas Rangers draw people from far and wide to icons of today's Texas, such as the gargantuan AT&T Stadium.

🏃 Activities

★ **Six Flags over Texas** AMUSEMENT PARK
(📞817-530-6000; www.sixflags.com/overtexas; 2201 Road to Six Flags, I-30 & Hwy 360; admission $60-75, parking from $23; ⊙hours vary by season; ♿) The most popular attraction in the state and only 20 minutes' drive from the downtowns of Dallas and Fort Worth, this amusement park can be a blast. Roller coasters rule: there are 13 of them, including two of the old-fashioned (wooden) kind.

Plan ahead to avoid the worst crowds (weekends, midday in summer). Hit the most popular rides either first thing in the morning or in the evening, when lines are shortest. Aside from the mighty, scream-inducing roller coasters such as Batman the Ride, Mr Freeze, and Shock Wave (once the world's tallest coaster), other reliable thrills include the adrenaline-charged Superman: Tower of Power, which shoots brave souls up into the sky at 45mph (cape not included), and La

Vibora, a bobsled ride that gives riders a fun taste of the Olympic sport. The Texas Sky-Screamer whisks you around 400ft from the ground. Other highlights are the legendary Texas Giant, which has the steepest drop (79 degrees) of any wooden coaster in the world.

Loony Tunes Land is populated by Warner Bros cartoon characters and caters to kids.

To ease your visit, stow valuables and bags in lockers at the entry mall just inside the park gate, where you can also rent strollers and wheelchairs, or board your pets ($10). Remember that height restrictions vary per ride and range from 42in to 54in.

Purchase tickets online for discounts. Unfortunately there is no public transportation to Six Flags; however, some local hotels are linked via the Arlington Trolley. The hours vary, but in June and July the park is open daily. Opening hours and days vary from March to May and August to December.

Six Flags Hurricane Harbor WATER PARK
(📞817-265-3356; www.sixflags.com/hurricanehar bortexas; 1800 E Lamar Blvd, off I-30; adult/child $37/32, parking from $24; ⊙hours vary by season) You can get soaked at Six Flags Hurricane Harbor, an over-the-top water park with a good mix of thrills, chills and family-friendly rides. The adventurous can surf at the Surf Rider, free-fall six stories on the Geronimo, or brave the dubiously named Mega Wedgie (no explanation needed).

Of course, nothing beats just chilling out in the Surf Lagoon (a pool with 4ft-high waves) or gliding on an inner tube down the Lazy River. For kids, the Hook's Lagoon Treehouse is loads of fun. Hours vary, but the park is open daily in June and July. Days and opening hours vary in May, August and September; check the online calendar.

🛏 Sleeping

At first Arlington may seem like a showplace for every sleeping chain in America – and it is (especially with hotels and motels). Look for ones linked by the Arlington Trolley to avoid event-related traffic jams.

Wingate by Wyndham HOTEL $$
(📞817-640-8686; www.wyndhamhotels.com; 1024 Brookhollow Plaza Dr; r from $80; ❄🛜🏊) This tidy, good-value hotel has 92 large, well-appointed rooms (fridges, microwaves and large work areas) spread over four floors. Bonuses include an indoor Jacuzzi and an outdoor pool. It's on the bus system

WHAT THE...? INTERNATIONAL BOWLING MUSEUM

It's not just the strikes at Rangers Ballpark that are celebrated in Arlington, the strikes of bowling get their dues as well at the **International Bowling Museum** (☑817-385-8215; www.bowlingmuseum.com; 621 Six Flags Dr; adult/child $9.50/7.50; ☺9am-5pm Tue-Sat, noon-6pm Sun). All facets of the game of big balls, garish shoes and pitchers of beer are celebrated. You might just want to spare a moment for a visit.

linking area hotels with Arlington's major attractions.

Eating

You can find some excellent indie restaurants amid the chains; Arlington has a surprising number of top-notch Vietnamese places.

★**Pho Pasteur Restaurant** VIETNAMESE $
(☑817-274-6232; http://phopasteurarlington.com; 100 W Pioneer Pkwy; mains $7-10; ☺9am-9:30pm Mon-Sat, 8am-8.30pm Sun) Southwest of the stadiums and parks, this Vietnamese restaurant specializes in pho, the iconic beef soup. Steaming bowls are served from pots that have been simmering for 12 hours or more. Patrons also love the *bánh bot loc* (traditional cold dumplings with fillings wrapped in chewy tapioca sheets).

Damian's Cajun Soul Cafe CAJUN $$
(☑817-649-7770; http://damians.letseat.at; 185 S Watson Rd, at TX 360 & E Abram St; mains $8-15; ☺11am-4pm Tue-Sat) It's not much to look at from the outside (ie it's a dive), but at Damian's it's what's inside that counts. The Cajun fare is good and spicy. Many drive miles just for the pork chops, catfish and macaroni and cheese. It pays to visit early as popular items sell out.

☆ Entertainment

★**Texas Rangers** BASEBALL
(☑817-273-5222; http://texas.rangers.mlb.com; 1000 Ballpark Way, at I-30 exits 28 or 30; tickets $18-214) From April to October the Texas Rangers play at the vintage-ballpark–inspired Globe Life Park, which features replicas of the Fenway Park scoreboard and the right-field home-run porch from Tiger Stadium. **Guided tours** (☑817-273-5098; http://m.mlb.

com/rangers/tickets/tours/index; 1000 Ballpark Way; adult/child $15/8; ☺off-season 10am-4pm Tue-Sat, on-season 9am-2pm Mon-Sat, from 11am Sun) are better off-season: they include a peek into the ballplayers' inner sanctum. With over 49,000 seats, you can usually get tickets to weekday games on short notice.

Dallas Cowboys FOOTBALL
(☑817-892-4000; http://stadium.dallascowboys.com; AT&T Stadium, 1 Legends Way, off I-30 exits 28 & 29; tours adult/child from $18/15; ☺tours 10am-4:30pm Sat, 11am-3:30pm Sun) The Dallas Cowboys gave themselves the nickname 'America's Team' after it had great success (with cheerleaders and otherwise) in the 1970s. Although the team's fortunes have been modest of late (no Super Bowl wins since 1996), it still has swagger, as shown in its enormous, retractable-roof home – the AT&T Stadium, located 18 miles west of Dallas in Arlington.

If you want to see the spectacle that is a Dallas Cowboys home game, you'll need to find tickets on the secondary market as the games are always sold out. There are many other events in the stadium during the year, including college-football bowl games, high-school football championships, truck exhibitions and concerts. Tours of the stadium depart from Entry A.

❶ Getting Around

Arlington Trolley (☑817-504-9744; http://arlingtontrolley.com; free for hotel guests; ☺hours vary) A network of buses disguised to look like trolleys link Arlington's chain hotels with the major attractions: Six Flags Over Texas, Six Flags Hurricane Harbor, Globe Life Park, AT&T Stadium and downtown Arlington.

Waxahachie

☑214, 469, 972 / POP 31,600
With sensational Victorian, Greek Revival and Queen Anne architecture lining its main square, Waxahachie is easily one of the most beautiful small towns in Texas. That it has a real vibrancy only adds to its appeal.

◉ Sights

★**Ellis County Courthouse** HISTORIC BUILDING
(☑972-825-5000; Courthouse Square, 101 W Main St; ☺9am-5pm Mon-Fri) This stunner of a courthouse (1895) uses every Romanesque trick in the book to awe you. The pink granite and red limestone are magnificent and a recent restoration has only added sheen to the splendor. On weekdays

you can wander the compact interior and look into the wood-trimmed courtroom.

Webb Gallery GALLERY
(☑972-938-8085; www.webbartgallery.com; 209-211 W Franklin St; ☉1-5pm Sat & Sun) Inside this ornate brick building (1902) is an eclectic and intriguing gallery which showcases works by dozens of very talented local artists. The ground floor is open and airy, a great place to ponder what's on show. Antiques and unusual books are also on sale.

Ellis County Museum MUSEUM
(☑972-937-0681; 201 S College St; ☉10am-5pm Mon-Sat) FREE Housed in the 1893 Masonic Lodge, this well-curated museum gives a good sense of the history of the area. Don't miss the details on all the shenanigans behind the construction of the courthouse.

✖ Eating

Vault Smokehouse BARBECUE $
(☑469-672-4637; www.thevaultsmokehouse.com; 305 W Madison St; mains $7-20; ☉11am-7pm Wed-Sat, noon-3pm Sun; 🐾) Great family-run barbecue joint right downtown. As always, you can't go wrong with the Texas-style sliced beef brisket. But go on, have yourself a sausage too (or pork ribs, chicken etc). Grab a table outside or stay inside, where it's even easier to keep the iced-tea refills coming.

Glen Rose
☑254 / POP 2500
Some 100 million years ago dinosaurs wandered this part of Texas, feasting on the lush primeval vegetation (not knowing that someday they'd be part of the oil that would make a not-yet-existing species rich – and dependent).

Evidence of these dinosaurs has survived in fossil form and today fuels a thriving prehistoric-tourism industry that includes an appealing park and various commercial sights.

◉ Sights

Dinosaur Valley State Park PARK
(☑254-897-4588; http://tpwd.texas.gov/state-parks/dinosaur-valley; 1629 Park Rd 59, off FM 205; adult/child $7/free; ☉7am-10pm) See actual tracks left by a *Tyrannosaurus rex* in a riverbed in this sylvan park. There are also 20 miles of trails.

Dinosaur World AMUSEMENT PARK
(☑254-898-1526; www.dinosaurworld.com; FM 205 at Park Rd 59; adult/child $13/10; ☉9am-5pm) Has huge statues of dinosaurs set on 22 acres. In comparison to the animated dinosaurs in films such as *Jurassic Park*, those here seem all the more, well, static. It's near the Dinosaur Valley State Park entrance.

Fossil Rim Wildlife Center ZOO
(☑254-897-2960; www.fossilrim.org; off US 67, 2299 Co Rd 2008; adult/child weekday $22/16, weekend $26/20; ☉9:30am-5:30pm mid-Mar-Oct, 10am-4:30 Nov–mid-Mar) Drive a nearly 10 mile course through an open-air zoo that's home to over 60 animal species, including cheetahs, rhinoceroses and giraffes.

Waco
☑214 469 972 / POP 130 400
Don't feel bad if you associate this unassuming town with its unlucky past: it's probably best known for the infamous 1993 'Waco Siege' that took place nearby and 2015's big biker shootout that left nine dead and hundreds arrested. Notoriety aside, this is a pleasant little city with a few diversions (Dr Pepper, woolly mammoths, anyone?).

Waco is home to the world's largest Baptist university (Baylor University); college legend claims that students can ostensibly attend a different area Baptist church every weekend during their four years. (It's true – there are almost 100 of them.)

◉ Sights
Spend the morning checking out Waco's unique museums, then take a leisurely stroll through Cameron Park.

Make sure to visit the stately 475ft pedestrian-only **Waco Suspension Bridge**, built from 1868 to 1870 and the first to cross the Brazos.

★Waco Mammoth National Monument HISTORIC SITE
(☑254-750-7946; www.nps.gov/waco; 6220 Steinbeck Bend Rd; tours adult/child $5/3; ☉9am-5pm) In 1978 two Waco arrowhead hunters found a bone in a ravine. It turned out to belong to a Columbian mammoth that had perished there about 68,000 years ago. Now open to the public after over 30 years of excavation, the site features the nation's only recorded discovery of a herd of Pleistocene mammoths that includes young ones. In 2015 it was added to the National

Park System, which has brought added funding and prominence.

It's generally thought that the herd was trapped and drowned by fast-rising floodwaters of the Bosque River.

Dr Pepper Museum   MUSEUM

(☑254-757-1024; www.drpeppermuseum.com; 300 S 5th St; adult/child $10/6; ☺10am-5:30pm Mon-Sat, noon-5:30pm Sun; 🐾) The Dr Pepper soft drink was invented by Waco pharmacist Charles C Alderton in 1885. This museum celebrates his creation and is housed in a stately brick building that was one of the company's first facilities. There is a small, old-style soda fountain (admission fee not required) where you can get sodas and other treats.

The collection is vast and offers a fascinating look at one of the few companies (including Coca-Cola!) to survive from the days when pharmacists created hundreds of soft drinks nationwide. Note that the attached 'Free Enterprise Institute' is an advocacy area for conservative dogma about the perceived evils of government regulation.

Dublin Bottling Works   TOUR

(☑888-398-1024; www.olddocs.com; 105 E Elm St, Dublin; museum free, tours adult/child $5/4; ☺10am-5pm Tue-Sat, 1-5pm Sun) Taste original sugarcane-formulated sodas at the first bottling plant for Dr Pepper, which now produces its own line of drinks and has no connection to the current brand. The WP Kloster Museum covers the history of fizzy drinks. It's 90 miles west of Waco.

Armstrong Browning Library   MUSEUM

(☑254-710-3566; www.browninglibrary.org; 710 Speight Ave; ☺9am-5pm Mon-Fri, 10am-2pm Sat) **FREE** On the Baylor campus, this peaceful refuge of a museum houses a beautiful collection of stained glass, as well as the world's largest collection of original manuscripts and personal effects of the Romantic English poets Robert and Elizabeth Barrett Browning. Don't miss the 'sunrise/sunset' windows in the gorgeous Foyer of Meditation.

Texas Sports Hall of Fame   MUSEUM

(☑254-756-1633; www.tshof.org; 1108 S University Parks Dr; adult/child $7/3; ☺9am-5pm Mon-Sat) All manner of Texas sports legends, including golfer Byron Nelson, boxer and pitchman

---

BRANCH DAVIDIANS & THE WACO SIEGE

For more than two decades Waco has been associated with the Branch Davidians and the standoff that ended in the fiery deaths of dozens on live television. The after-effects of this event are still felt locally.

The Branch Davidians were an offshoot of a radical sect of Seventh Day Adventists. The original group, the Davidians, set up shop in Waco in 1935 but moved outside the city in 1959 to establish a compound called New Mt Carmel, near the town of Elk. Fighting between internal factions led to splits and drama, and in 1987 Vernon Howell, who had joined the group in 1981, took control and changed his name to David Koresh.

Koresh's platform involved, among other things, arming the compound to defend it against the apocalyptic nightmare the world would become after the second coming of Christ. Believing that Koresh was buying, selling and storing illegal weapons, the federal Bureau of Alcohol, Tobacco and Firearms (ATF) staged a disastrous raid that a 1993 US Treasury report deemed 'tragically wrong.' The agents were fired on; four ATF agents and five cult members were killed in the ensuing firefight. The resulting standoff lasted 51 days.

As local authorities and FBI hostage negotiators surrounded the compound with hundreds of police cars and even a tank, the standoff became a media sensation; viewers around the world were treated to deadly scenes from the original raid plus the day-to-day drama of the situation.

The standoff ended on April 19, 1993, when federal agents fired tear gas bombs into the compound. Within hours, the buildings were completely engulfed in flames fueled by the ignition of the tear-gas canisters. Some 76 Branch Dividians died, including Koresh and many children. Nine cult members survived. The government's handling of the incident is still the subject of controversy and conspiracy theories. (Timothy McVeigh said the Waco siege was his primary motivation for bombing the federal building in Oklahoma City in 1995.)

For more information on the siege, including interviews and photos, PBS has an excellent website: www.pbs.org/wgbh/pages/frontline/waco.

George Foreman and pitcher Nolan Ryan, are saluted here.

🛏 Sleeping

Rooms get scarce during Baylor University events such as fall football weekends. You'll find plenty of chain motels and hotels along I-35.

Super 8 Waco
MOTEL $

(📞 254-754-1023; 1320 Jack Kultgen Fwy; r $45-120; ❄ 🛜 🐾) A standard Super 8 (three stories, 78 rooms with inside corridors), this well-located motel is close to downtown and Baylor. Most rooms have fridges and microwaves. Just north of I-35 exit 334 on the east frontage road.

Hotel Indigo Waco
HOTEL $$

(📞 254 754 7000; www.ihg.com, 211 Clay Ave, r $125-200; ❄ 🛜 🐾) This somewhat bland corporate hotel has the advantage of being newer than Waco's many other bland corporate hotels. Rooms are large. If you see lots of people with huge shopping bags in the elevator, it's because the Magnolia Market (p177) is only three blocks away.

Cotton Palace
B&B $$

(📞 254-753-7294; www.thecottonpalace.com; 1910 Austin Ave; r from $130; ❄ 🛜) Find big breakfasts and a lovely sunporch at this genteel 1910 arts-and-crafts style house. The six rooms have a luxurious, frilly and doodad decor.

🍴 Eating

★ Lolita's Tortilleria & Restaurant
MEXICAN $

(📞 254-755-7301; 1911 Franklin Ave; mains $4-10; ⏱ 7am-2pm Tue-Sun) Lolita's exudes that family-run, small-town spirit that can't be manufactured. The hugely popular all-day breakfast menu includes tacos, huevos rancheros, *migas* (a signature Texas dish of eggs scrambled with corn tortillas, onions, tomatoes, peppers and often cheese) and the 'elephante,' a massive breakfast burrito with six fillings. Savor the fresh salsa and *queso* (cheese).

Dubl-R Old Fashioned Hamburgers
BURGERS $

(📞 254-753-1603; www.dubl-r.com; 1810 Herring Ave; mains $3-6; ⏱ 10am-6:30pm Mon-Fri, to 2pm Sat) Chargrilled burgers with grilled onions and all the usual toppings are the thing at this near-shack local legend. Have a shake, maybe some tots and scarf down pure Americana.

World Cup Cafe
CAFE $

(📞 254-757-1748; www.worldcupcafe.org; 1321 N 15th St; mains $3-8; ⏱ 7am-2pm Mon-Fri, from 8am Sat, 11am-2pm Sun, 🌐) Fair-trade coffees are brewed at this simple cafe and served with breakfasts and sandwiches. Income goes to community development.

★ Vitek's BBQ
BARBECUE $$

(📞 254-752-7591; www.viteksbbq.com; 1600 Speight Ave; mains $5-13; ⏱ 10:30am-3pm Tue-Thu, to 9pm Fri-Sat) Since 1915 Vitek's has drawn the hungry crowds. Whatever your carnivorous pleasure, it's all homemade and excellent. Big appetite? Order the legendary Gut Pak, a monster of a sandwich with Fritos, cheese, chopped beef, beans, sausage, pickles, onions and jalapeños. Great beer selection; enjoy on the covered outside area.

🍷 Drinking & Nightlife

★ Dancing Bear
BAR

(📞 254 753 0026; 1117 Speight Ave; ⏱ 4pm-midnight Sun-Fri, noon-1am Sat) A few blocks from the Baylor campus, you'll find over a dozen microbrews on tap, along with helpful advice and beer samples for neophytes and connoisseurs alike. Over 100 bottles of craft beers round out the superlative selection. Enjoy a frosty one on the back terrace.

Cricket's Grill & Draft House
BAR

(📞 254-754-4677; www.cricketsgrill.com; 221 Mary Ave; mains $6-12; ⏱ 11am-2am) A cavernous beer hall and garden with fine pizzas, lots of craft beers on tap and tons of games, including darts, pool and shuffleboard.

🛍 Shopping

★ Magnolia Market at the Silos
HOMEWARES

(📞 254-235-6111; http://magnoliamarket.com; 601 Webster Ave; ⏱ 9am-6pm Mon-Sat) Fans of the

DALLAS & THE PANHANDLE PLAINS WACO

Home & Garden Television (HGTV) show *Fixer Upper* flock to this sprawling retail compound. Chip and Joanna Gaines have created this empire (real estate, retail et al) based on their show where the plot has them helping home-buyers find a cheap house and then remodel it into a stylish showplace. Their trademark (and much copied) faux distressed, whitewashed look is on full display here.

The compound, set at some artfully rusty old silos, also features a demonstration garden (behold the lavender!) which has a number of food trucks from local restaurants. There is also an on-site cupcake-peddling bakery.

ⓘ Information

Waco Tourist Information Center (☑254-750-8696; www.wacocvb.com; 106 Texas Ranger Trail; ⊗8am-5pm Mon-Sat, noon-4pm Sun) At the western end of Fort Fisher Park. It has free coffee and friendly staff who offer advice.

ⓘ Getting There & Away

Waco is easy to reach by car: it's right on I-35, halfway between Dallas–Fort Worth and Austin, about two hours from either.

Greyhound buses (☑254-753-4534; www.greyhound.com; 301 S 8th St) run between Waco and Dallas ($22, 2½ hours, four daily) and Waco and Austin ($24, 1¾ hours, five daily).

PANHANDLE PLAINS

The vast open stretch of the Texas Panhandle and Plains is a region of long drives on lonely two-laners. Its cities are few and small. The scope and scale make this a place where people tend to think big, but some of the area's purest pleasures are in its details: the scent of sage after rainfall, a flint quarry plied by humans thousands of years ago, or the wistful love songs written by young troubadours whose legacies ultimately reached far beyond the Plains.

And it's not all tumbleweeds. Midland is at the heart of the Texas energy boom, Lubbock embodies the region's rich music heritage with its favorite son, Buddy Holly, and Amarillo keeps cattle king of the Panhandle. Natural wonders include America's second-largest canyon, Palo Duro, where the Comanche fought on long after other tribes gave in. But the region's greatest assets are the tiny towns seemingly lost in the past.

Midland

☑432 / POP 110,900

Compared to Odessa, Midland is the more dudelike of the twin cities, a sprawling series of middle class, white-collar subdivisions, with mirrored high-rises towering above a nearly lifeless downtown.

The recent boom in oil production has definitely cooled off and Midland no longer sports signs everywhere begging for workers. Still, you'll see plenty of evidence of the industry and this is a good place to learn about it.

⊙ Sights

★Permian Basin Petroleum Museum   MUSEUM

(☑432-683-4403; www.petroleummuseum.org; 1500 I-20 W exit 136, north side; adult/child $12/8; ⊗10am-5pm Mon-Sat, 2-5pm Sun) This museum is worth a stop even if you're not utterly fascinated with the oil business, for it's as much a history and geology museum as a shrine to the prominent local industry (it has a hall of fame and an ironically entertaining 1970s sensibility). Follow the steps needed to discover oil and see a small collection of Chaparral race cars.

Outside is a big collection of antique oil-drilling equipment. Inside, interactive exhibits include one in which players can drill their own wells and another that simulates the roar of a blowout, an oil well gone wild.

George W Bush Childhood Home   HISTORIC SITE

(☑432-685-1112; www.bushchildhoodhome.com; 1412 W Ohio Ave; adult/child $5/3; ⊗10am-5pm Tue-Sat, 2-5pm Sun) George and Barbara Bush moved to west Texas from patrician New England in 1948. A growing family, the Bushes lived in this house from 1952 to 1956, when their son George W was aged five to nine.

What's most surprising about this modest house is that even a rising oil exec like George HW didn't live in the 1950s equivalent of a McMansion. There's plenty of material on the life of W that may delight fans and irritate others, but all will find this well-curated museum within a perfectly restored house to be a fascinating look at life in a simpler era.

The museum gift shop has pretty much every book about W by aids and acolytes you can imagine, plus material on W's wife, Laura, who writes about growing up in Midland in *Spoken from the Heart*. There's also an earlier Bush house in Odessa.

Museum of the Southwest MUSEUM
(📞 432-683-2882; www.museumsw.org; 1705 W Missouri Ave; adult/child $5/3, Sun free; ⊙10am-5pm Tue-Sat, 2-5pm Sun; ♿) Housed in the 1937 Turner Mansion, itself a work of art, this museum has an art gallery, planetarium and a children's museum. Larger-than-life sculptures from the permanent collection dot the tree-shaded grounds, which were built by oil baron Fred Turner.

🛏 Sleeping

Midland offers more options than Odessa, even if they're all chains. Budget choices are north of I-20 exit 134; more upscale brands can be found on the TX 250 Loop where it meets TX 158 west of the center.

Super 8 MOTEL $
(📞 432 680 0822; www.super8.com, 3828 W Wall St; r $60-120; ❄🐕♿) A tidy two-story version of the ubiquitous budget chain. The neighborhood is charmless except for other cheap motels – and industry. It's north of I-20 exit 134, off Midkiff Rd. Most rooms have fridges and microwaves.

Residence Inn Midland HOTEL $$
(📞 432-689-3511; www.residenceinn.marriott.com; 5509 Deauville Blvd; r $90-250; ❄@🛜🐕🏊) Amid a plethora of brightly lit franchise restaurants, this extended-stay hotel has 131 units in an attractive, if generic, complex. All come with kitchen facilities and are ideal for families.

🍴 Eating & Drinking

⭐**KD's Bar-B-Q** BARBECUE $$
(📞 432-683-4013; www.facebook.com/KDsBBQ/; 3109 Garden City Hwy/TX 158; mains $9-25; ⊙11am-8pm Tue-Thu, to 9pm Fri & Sat) If you had to go to one Texas 'cue joint, this would do. Line your platter with wax paper and tell the cook what to pile on (the brisket is divine, and the pork ribs almost candied). Add sides such as potato salad, then head to the amazing 'bean bar' where you can get beans, pickles and an ocean of sauces.

And the peach cobbler? Dang! This rambling place is east of town, just off I-20 at exit 138.

Basin Burger House BURGERS $$
(📞 432-687-5696; www.basinburgerhouse.com; 607 N Colorado St; mains $11-21; ⊙7am-9pm Mon-Thu, to 11pm Fri, 11am-11pm Sat, 9am-2pm Sun; 🐕) It looks so sprightly from the outside that this upscale burger joint could be a chain, but it's

not. All retro chrome inside, its burgers are excellent and come in myriad forms (including a great salmon burger). Zippy touches abound, such as serving aioli with the onion rings. There's a variety of excellent salads and some fine veggie options.

Garlic Press BISTRO $$$
(📞 432-570-4020; www.thegarlicpress.net; 2200 W Wadley Ave; mains $17-35; ⊙11am-2pm & 5-9:30pm Tue-Fri, 5-10pm Sat) In an upscale little shopping plaza north of town, the Garlic Press is one of the more stylish places in town. Med-style fare is best enjoyed outside under the shady trees. There's an array of prime steaks with a variety of preparations and, yes, there's warm bread served with roasted garlic and housemade butter.

Midland Beer Garden BEER GARDEN
(📞 432-558-0772; www.midlandbeergarden.com; 7112 W Hwy 80; ⊙4pm-midnight Mon-Thu, 11am-2am Fri & Sat, noon-8pm Sun) A constantly rotating selection of over 50 domestic, craft and imported beers on tap would be draw enough, but this place ups the ante with its great indoor-outdoor atmosphere of tents, gardens and beer halls. There is excellent food (the kitchen closes one hour before the bar). Brats, burgers and some really sinful jalapeño poppers are among the delights.

ℹ Information

Midland Visitors Center (📞 432-683-3381; www.visitmidlandtexas.com; 1406 W I-20, northside frontage road; ⊙9am-5pm Mon-Sat) Near the Permian Basin Petroleum Museum and I-20 exit 136, this large facility is filled with genial volunteers and useful information.

ℹ Getting There & Away

Midland International Air & Space Port (MAF; 📞 432-560-2200; www.flymaf.com; 9506 La Force Blvd) The airport sits midway between Midland and Odessa near exit 126 on I-20 and TX 191. Despite its grandiose name, service at the airport is much more mundane: American Eagle to Dallas–Fort Worth, United Express to Houston and Denver plus Southwest to Dallas, Houston and Las Vegas.

Odessa

📞 432 / POP 110,900

In contrast to its somewhat prim neighbor Midland, hardscrabble Odessa has a downbeat feel. It's the classic split between management and workers, with the latter making their homes here. The low-rise downtown has some barely perceptible glories left over from the original boom; most notably, however, it has a very big rabbit.

⊙ Sights

White-Pool House   HISTORIC SITE
(✐432-333-4072; www.whitepoolhouse.org; 112 E Murphy St; ⊙10am-3pm Fri & Sat) FREE Built in 1887, this is the oldest existing house in Ector County. It had just two owners for nearly a century when in 1973 the Pool family deeded it to the county for preservation. It shows the change in local fortunes from ranching in the 1880s to the oil boom of the 1920s.

Presidential Archives & Leadership Library   MUSEUM
(✐432-363-7737; http://shepperdinstitute.com/presidential-archives/; 4919 E University Ave, University of Texas of the Permian Basin; ⊙8am-5pm Mon-Fri, from 10am Sat) FREE This much-lauded museum has an interesting collection of items and info on all the presidents. It includes folk art, campaign materials and memorabilia. Out back is the very modest 1948 home of the Bush family, which was moved here and restored.

✕ Eating

Norma's Restaurant   CAFE $
(✐432-335-0304; 111 E 5th St; mains $5-9; ⊙6:30am-1:30pm Mon-Fri) The menu couldn't be simpler: eggs for breakfast, sandwiches and chicken-fried steak for lunch, but everything is prepared with care. Quality is tops as are the pies. The biggest problem here? Limited hours (but let's not overwork Norma).

Whitehouse Meat Market   BURGERS $
(✐432-367-9531; www.whitehousemeatmarket.com; 200 E 52nd St; mains from $7; ⊙7am-6pm Tue-Sat) Hidden among some industrial buildings north of the center, this is the place to get a great burger, cooked or

uncooked. Besides fine Texas beef in deli cases, it serves up fab burgers in simple surrounds. Get a double and make new friends at the communal tables.

❶ Getting There & Away

Greyhound (✐432-332-5711; www.greyhound.com; 2624 E 8th St) Runs two buses daily along the I-20 corridor between El Paso ($40, 5¼ hours) and Fort Worth ($50, six hours).

Big Spring
✐432 / POP 28,200

The relentlessly flat Permian Basin landscape starts to show signs of a change 40 miles east of Midland. Big Spring is on the edge of the Edwards Plateau Caprock Escarpment, the defining topographical feature of the Texas Panhandle.

⊙ Sights

Big Spring State Park   PARK
(✐432-263-4931; http://tpwd.texas.gov/state-parks/big-spring; 1 State Park Rd; ⊙dawn-dusk) FREE The 380-acre Big Spring State Park has a fine nature trail with labels describing the hearty plants, such as the spiky argarita bush. A short drive around the top of the park has sweeping views out across the basin and plateau.

Comanche Trail Park   PARK
(100 Whipkey Dr) The spring for which the town is named sits in Comanche Trail Park, a cute little park just south of the center.

⏢ Sleeping

★Hotel Settles   HISTORIC HOTEL $$
(✐432-267-7500; www.hotelsettles.com; 200 E 3rd St; r $130-300; ⊛🖥🐾) This 15-story hotel is a classic Texas story: born during a 1930s boom, it eventually closed, leaving a humungous corpse looming over an otherwise tiny town. Enter Brint Ryan, a local boy who made zillions helping corporations avoid taxes. He bought the Settles' remains and millions of dollars later it reopened in 2013 as a luxury hotel.

The Settles definitely looms large locally and although public areas have been restored to period glory, the suites and smaller guest rooms are modern and lavish. There's a top-end restaurant and a sumptuous bar, perfect for sipping bourbon and telling lies.

WHAT THE...? JACKRABBIT
....

Odessa claims to have the world's largest **jackrabbit statue** (cnr N Sam Houston Ave & 8th St). This 8ft-tall rabbit was the product of a local booster in 1962. Now a popular photo op, it reflects local attitudes about varmints in that a plaque lists a recipe for 'jackrabbit and dumplings'.

FRIDAY NIGHT LIGHTS

In 1990 the book *Friday Night Lights*, by journalist HG 'Buzz' Bissinger, was published to much critical acclaim. It follows the Panthers football team of **Permian High School** (☑432-456-0039; www.permianpanthersfootball.com; 1800 W 42nd St) during the team's 1988 season. No fawning bit of fluff, the book delves deeply into the lives of the young players and their coaches. It displays teenage angst and portrays a community where academic excellence is ridiculed in favor of success on the playing field. Many locals were horrified at its exposure of racism and other social ills in Odessa. The book was adapted into a 2004 movie and used as the basis for the popular TV series that ran from 2006 to 2011.

The huge Ratliff Stadium, which seats nearly 20,000, is next to the school. Signs, emblazoned with the nickname 'Mojo,' show the team's long history of victory, which coincidentally went into decline when the book was published. (Archrival Midland Lee High School has been doing much better.) But fall Friday nights here under the lights are still *the* place in Texas to watch high-school football. See www.mojoland.net for more info.

☆ Entertainment

Stampede   LIVE MUSIC
(☑432-267-2060; 1610 E Hwy 350) There are few west Texas dancehalls more authentic than the Stampede, a bare-bones, early-1950s affair 1.5 miles northeast of Big Spring. If you're real lucky you'll catch Jody Nix and the Cowboys (www.jodynix.com), a legendary family band that has been fueling two-steppers for years. Stampede schedules, however, are sporadic.

San Angelo

☑325 / POP 97,600

Situated on the fringes of the Hill Country, San Angelo is the kind of place where non-poser men in suits ride motorcycles, while women in pickups look like they could wrestle a bull and then hit the catwalk. It's a purely Western town with an appealing overlay of gentility amid real historic authenticity. The Concho River, which scenically runs through the town, offers numerous walks along its wild, lush banks.

San Angelo is worth a detour just to enjoy time here.

◉ Sights

★**Presidio de San Sabá**   HISTORIC SITE
(☑325-396-4789; www.presidiodesansaba.com; off US 190, 191 Presidio Rd, Menard; ⊙8am-5pm) **FREE** What was once the largest Spanish fort in Texas has been beautifully restored. Presidio de San Sabá dates to 1757 and is close to the town of Menard, some 21 miles northeast of Fort McKavett. The site is great for wandering, especially when it's just you, bird calls and the buzz of cicadas.

★**Fort McKavett State Historical Park**   HISTORIC SITE
(☑325-396-2358; www.thc.texas.gov/historic-sites/fort-mckavett-state-historic-site; 7066 FM 864, Fort McKavett; adult/child $4/3; ⊙8am-5pm) General William Tecumseh Sherman once called this fort along the San Saba River 'the prettiest post in Texas.' Today, Fort McKavett State Historical Park, about 65 miles southeast of San Angelo, preserves the striking ruins of a once-important fort.

Fort McKavett was established by the Eighth Infantry of the US Army in 1852 as a bulwark against Comanche and Apache raids. The fort saw its peak in the mid-1870s, when it housed more than 400 troops and many civilians. Some of the 25 buildings have been restored; the grounds are alive with wildflowers for much of the year. Check out the boiled-turnips recipe in the excellent museum.

★**Fort Concho National Historic Landmark**   HISTORIC SITE
(☑325-481-2646; www.fortconcho.com; 630 S Oakes St; adult/child $3/1.50; ⊙9am-5pm Mon-Sat, 1-4:30pm Sun) No matter how many forts you've seen in your Texas travels, this one is likely to be a highlight. Many folks claim it's the best-preserved Western frontier fort in the US, and much of it has been restored by the city over the decades.

Designed to protect settlers and people moving west on the overland trails, the fort went up in 1867 on the fringes of the Texas frontier and saw service until 1889. Among its highlights are the Headquarters Building, which includes the Fort Concho Museum, and the Post Hospital.

**Concho Avenue
Historic District** HISTORIC SITE
(Concho Ave) At the heart of downtown, the Concho Avenue Historic District is a good place to stroll – be sure to pick up a historic walking-tour brochure at the Visitor Center. The most interesting section, known as Historic Block One, is between Chadbourne and Oakes Sts. Don't miss the elegant and restored lobby of the 14-story 1929 **Cactus Hotel** (☑ 325-655-5000; http://cactushotel.net; 36 E Twohig Ave).

Miss Hattie's Bordello Museum MUSEUM
(☑ 325-653-0112; http://misshatties.com; 18 E Concho Ave; tours adult/child $6/free; ⊙ tours 2pm & 4pm Tue-Thu, 1pm, 2pm, 3pm & 4pm Fri & Sat) Few can resist the come-on of Miss Hattie's Bordello Museum, which operated as a downtown house of pleasure from 1896 until the Texas Rangers shut it down in 1946. Rooms re-create the plush velvet look considered essential back in the day, but the best feature is the stories of the women and their clients. Confirm tour times.

Meet at Legend Jewelers (p184) next door.

San Angelo State Park PARK
(☑ 325-949-4757; http://tpwd.texas.gov/state-parks/san-angelo; 3900-2 Mercedes Rd; adult/child $4/free; ⊙ dawn-dusk) This state park is on the western outskirts of town, accessible via FM 2288 (Loop 2288) off W Ave N (which becomes Arden Rd west of downtown), US 87 or US 67. The 7600-acre park surrounds the 1950s reservoir, OC Fisher Lake. More than 50 miles of trails are popular with animal- and bird-watchers.

Producers Livestock Auction MARKET
(☑ 325-653-3371; www.producersandcargile.com; 1131 N Bell St; ⊙ 9am Tue & Thu) `FREE` No one has a baaad time at the largest sheep auction in the USA, the Producer's Livestock Auction. Sheep are sold on Tuesday and cattle on Thursday. The auctioneers' banter is the most fascinating aspect of the whole deal – it's totally incomprehensible.

Railway Museum of San Angelo MUSEUM
(☑ 325-486-2140; www.railwaymuseumsanangelo. homestead.com; 703 S Chadbourne St; adult/ child $5/3; ⊙ 10am-4pm Sat) The beautifully renovated Santa Fe Depot is home to much railroad nostalgia. The station, on the El Paseo, is the main attraction. Inside, the museum has models of 1920s San Angelo and old rail cars.

🏃 Activities

⭐ **El Paseo de Santa Angela** WALKING
(Concho River Walk; 🚶) The El Paseo is a family-friendly, pleasure-filled stroll that is part of the 4½-mile-long river walk that follows the Concho, from just west of downtown heading east to Bell St. **Celebration Bridge** links San Angelo's main street, Concho Ave, to the main attractions south of the river, which include a collection of historic buildings along Orient St.

Santa Angela was San Angelo's original name, and the El Paseo de Santa Angela marks the route that soldiers stationed at Fort Concho once used to visit the wanton town in its heyday. In 1870 the post surgeon at the fort wrote that 'the village across the Concho...is attaining an unenviable distinction from the numerous murders committed there... Over 100 murders have taken place in the radius of 10 miles.' And then there were the 35 bordellos and saloons that lined Santa Angela's sidewalks.

🎉 Festivals & Events

San Angelo Stock Show & Rodeo RODEO
(☑ 325-481-0261; www.sanangelorodeo.com; 50 E 43rd St, San Angelo Coliseum Fairground; ⊙ Feb) The big annual San Angelo Stock Show & Rodeo Cowboys Association Rodeo runs over two weeks in February. It is one of the largest in the Southwest. Note that animal treatment is always an issue around rodeos. Some viewers may be disturbed.

🛏 Sleeping

Most motels are situated on the major highways on the periphery of town. There are a growing number of appealing inns and B&Bs in the center.

**San Angelo State Park
Campground** CAMPGROUND $
(☑ 325-949-4757; www.tpwd.state.tx.us; 3900-2 Mercedes Rd; campsites $10-20, cabins from $50) San Angelo State Park has beautifully located backpackers tent sites; the sites with hookups have some shade. Basic cabins with air-conditioning, fridges and microwaves are also available.

⭐ **Inn at the Art Center** B&B $$
(☑ 325-659-3836; www.innattheartcenter.com; 2503 Martin Luther King Blvd, Old Chicken Farm Art Center; r $100-165; ⊖❄🛜) Funky is an understatement for this four-room B&B at the back of the bohemian Chicken Farm Art

Center. Rooms are as artful as you'd expect at a 1970s chicken farm turned artists co-op. The Ponderosa Room has some beautiful floors made from pecan wood. The adjoining restaurant Silo House is excellent for lunch and dinner.

Flamingo Flatts
INN $$

(☑ 325-653-0437; www.flamingoflatts.com; 204 S Oakes St; r $100-200; ❄ 🛜) This inn is housed in a much-restored historic antebellum hotel from 1908. The three beach-themed suites have vintage seashore decor. It's very comfortable and well located.

Inn of the Conchos
MOTEL $$

(☑ 325-658-2811; www.inn-of-the-conchos.com; 2021 N Bryant Blvd; r $60-120; ❄ 🛜 🐾) On the northwest edge of downtown US 87, this is an older, modest 125-room motel that hangs on in the face of the chains. Excellent service, an included hot breakfast buffet, plus microwaves and fridges in the rooms are its ammo.

✖ Eating

Los Gallos Bakery
BAKERY $

(☑ 325-212-1894; 2029 Armstrong St; treats from $2; ⏱ 5am-7pm) Right downtown, this Mexican bakery is one of the region's best. It's dead simple from the outside, but head on in and grab some tongs and pile up your tray with treats. There are breakfast burritos and other typical hot foods like tamales through the day.

Packsaddle Bar-B-Q
BARBECUE $

(☑ 325-949-0616; www.packsaddlebarbque.com; 6007 Knickerbocker Rd; mains $6-13; ⏱ 10am-9pm Wed-Mon) Don't let the downmarket location in a strip mall 6 miles southwest of the center put you off – the brisket here is among the finest you'll find anywhere in these parts (and beyond). It's bone-simple here but it has diverting Nascar displays and plush booths. There's cold beer.

★ Peasant Village Restaurant
DELI, BISTRO $$

(☑ 325-655-4811; 23 S Park St; lunch mains from $9, dinner mains $25-35; ⏱ 11am-1:30pm Mon-Fri, 6-9:30pm Tue-Sat; 🐾) Casual for lunch, luxe for dinner. Located in a beautiful 1920s house near downtown, this refined restaurant is just the place if you'd like some fine wine to go with a meal from a menu that changes with the seasons. Creative mains of steak and seafood are always listed and there's a touch of Med throughout. The desserts are fab.

Jason Helfer, the talented chef, also assembles the best deli sandwiches and salads in town at lunch. With the many pastries on offer, you can have a splendid picnic across the street in beautiful rose gardens.

Silo House
AMERICAN $$

(☑ 325-658-3333; www.silohouse.net; 2503 Martin Luther King Blvd, Inn at the Art House; lunch mains $9-15, dinner mains $28-33; ⏱ 11am-2pm Mon-Sat, 6-10pm Thu-Sat) A lovely restaurant run by the same creative folks as the Inn at the Art Center. Lunches feature a changing menu of salads, soups, quiches, sandwiches etc. Dinners are much more complex, with a seasonal menu that features local ingredients. It's BYOB, so do your best.

Miss Hattie's Café & Saloon
SOUTHERN US $$

(☑ 325-653-0570; www.misshattiesrestaurant.com; 26 E Concho Ave; mains $8-25; ⏱ 11am-10pm Mon-Sat; 🐾) This place tips its hat to the bordello museum up the block, with early 20th-century decor featuring tapestries and gilt-edged picture frames. However, the tasty meat is the main attraction, especially the hunk of seasoned beef grilled into a hamburger and finished with an array of yummy toppings. The vintage-style bar is as alluring as the drinks.

🍷 Drinking & Nightlife

SoCo Taphouse
PUB

(☑ 325-703-6218; www.socotaphouse.com; 113 E Concho Ave; ⏱ 3pm-midnight Mon-Fri, noon-1am Sat) Kind of an ideal pub: sit outside in a very relaxed setting and enjoy house-brewed beers plus other great ones from around the region.

🛍 Shopping

Chicken Farm Art Center
ARTS & CRAFTS

(☑ 325-653-4936; www.chickenfarmartcenter.com; 2502 Martin Luther King Blvd; ⏱ 10am-5pm Tue-Sat) More than 20 artists create and display their works in studios in this old chicken farm. Many further tend to their nests by also living here.

JL Mercer & Son
CLOTHING

(☑ 325-658-7634; www.mercerboots.com; 224 S Chadbourne St; ⏱ 10am-5pm Mon-Sat) Noted for its custom boots, spurs and other Western gear. Texas legends such as Lyndon Johnson got their boots here (as did on-screen cowboy John Wayne). Custom boots start at $600, but with options (there are many!) you can scoot past $2000 without breaking stride.

Cactus Book Shop   BOOKS
(☑ 325-659-3788; www.cactusbookshop.com; 6 E Concho Ave; ◷ 10am-5pm Tue-Sat) Right downtown, it carries new and used books plus a good selection of Texana titles.

Legend Jewelers   JEWELRY
(☑ 325-653-0112; 18 E Concho Ave; ◷ 10am-5pm Mon-Sat) Family jewelers, the best place to shop for Concho River pearls.

Eggemeyer's General Store   GIFTS & SOUVENIRS
(☑ 325-655-1166; www.eggemeyers.com; 35 E Concho Ave; ◷ 10am-6pm Mon-Sat) This old-style place has penny candy and lots of gift-item nonsense.

❶ Information

San Angelo Visitor Center (☑ 325-655-4136; www.visitsanangelo.org; 418 W Ave B; ◷ 9am-5pm Mon-Fri, to 4pm Sat, noon-4pm Sun) This helpful center has a stunning location on the Concho River, near downtown. A pedestrian bridge links to a groovy kids playground.

Junction
☑ 325 / POP 2550
Winding through the lush and beautiful South Llano River valley, US 377 is light on traffic but big on vistas on its 100-mile route southwest from the pretty little town of Junction toward the border and Del Rio.

◉ Sights

South Llano River State Park   PARK
(☑ 325-446-3994; http://tpwd.texas.gov/state-parks/south-llano-river; 1927 Park Rd 73, off US 377; adult/child $5/free; ◷ 24hr) Junction proper has a few places where you can get organized for a rafting trip on the river. Or you can go hiking (18 miles of trails) and spot deer, squirrels and the iconic Rio Grande turkey in South Llano River State Park. It's also ideal for a picnic, a swim or a stroll. One great reason to camp here: the park has been designated an International Dark Sky Park, which means it's a spectacular site for stargazing.

✖ Eating

Lum's   BARBECUE $
(☑ 325-446-3541; www.facebook.com/pg/lumsbq; 2031 Main St; mains $8-15; ◷ 8am-9pm Sun-Thu, to 11pm Fri & Sat) An old gas station is home to one of the region's best barbecue joints. Lum's has the requisite dining area cluttered with high-school team pennants and Bud signs. Amid a classic menu, the ribs,

brisket, jalapeño sausage and potato salad earn raves and are served up on wax paper.

Plumley's Country Store   AMERICAN $
(☑ 325-446-3986; http://plumleyscountrystore.com; 2341 N Main St; mains $6-8; ◷ 8am-5pm Mon-Sat) An antidote to generic freeway convenience stores. Fresh pecans, baked goods, local fruit and much more are for sale. The restaurant has tasty burgers, baked potatoes, Mexican dishes and more.

Abilene
☑ 325 / POP 122,300
Abilene is frequently called the 'buckle of the Bible Belt,' and not without reason (it has three bible colleges, for one). This is a buttoned-down town where nonconformists can feel seriously out of place. About 150 miles from either Midland or Fort Worth, the cow-dotted plains barely seem to yield to the city. However, Abilene makes for a good stop owing to one mighty fine museum and some traditional places to eat that will have you happy that modernity seems in short supply.

◉ Sights

Most sights, except for the zoo, are within a few blocks of each other downtown. Treadway Blvd (Business Route 83D) is the main north–south street running through downtown; it is marked by little of architectural interest.

★ Frontier Texas!   MUSEUM
(☑ 325-437-2800; www.frontiertexas.com; 625 N 1st St; adult/child $10/5; ◷ 9am-6pm Mon-Sat, 1-5pm Sun; 🅿) Reason enough to stop if you're any place near Abilene, Frontier Texas! makes 100 years of frontier history (1780–1880) possibly more interesting than the real thing. The museum also serves as the main visitor information center for the region.

Life-size holograms and other special effects take you inside a buffalo stampede, next to a conniving card shark and at home on a firefly-filled range. Hairs will raise on your arms at the appearance of Comanche chief Esihabitu. New exhibits include a video overview of the collection and a detailed look at the natural landscape before the arrival of humans.

Grace Museum   MUSEUM
(☑ 325-673-4587; www.thegracemuseum.org; 102 Cypress St; adult/child $6/3; ◷ 10am-5pm Tue-Sat, to 8pm Thu; 🅿) This fine museum complex includes three distinct collections housed

in the former Grace Hotel (1909), once the grandest in Abilene. It features periodically changing art exhibitions and displays on Abilene's history from 1900 through 1950 with artifacts and photographs.

It's heavy on railroad and military memorabilia plus what home life was like in a simpler time. An on-site children's museum has fun science experiments, including one where you can ponder gravity.

Fort Phantom Hill   HISTORIC SITE
(FM 600; ☉dawn-dusk) Boredom rather than combat doomed this 1851 fort along the clear fork of the Brazos River. Fort Phantom Hill was among the outposts constructed to protect settlers on the Texas frontier; it was abandoned just three years later after droves of bored soldiers left it (and the service). Today, visitors will find only a handful of buildings and about a dozen chimneys among the windy, lonely ruins. Fort Phantom Hill is on private land but the site is open during daylight hours. The grounds are 11 miles north of I-20 on FM 600 (a total of 14 miles north of Abilene). Nearby Lake Fort Phantom is popular for picnicking.

In the 1800s time and fires took their toll on the fort and the nearby ghost town – by 1880, 546 people had moved to the settlement, but a letter written to the *San Antonio Daily Express* in 1892 indicated the town had dwindled to 'one hotel, one saloon, one general store, one blacksmith shop and 10,000 prairie dogs.'

**National Center for Children's
Illustrated Literature**   MUSEUM
(☑325-673-4586; www.nccil.org; 102 Cedar St; ☉10am-4pm Tue-Sat; ⓐ) **FREE** This small museum has a permanent exhibition of works by William Joyce and other well-known children's book illustrators. The real attractions are the constant special exhibits, which highlight the works of individual artists.

Center for Contemporary Arts   GALLERY
(☑325-677-8389; www.center-arts.com; Grissom Bldg, 220 Cypress St; ☉11am-5pm Tue-Sat, to 9pm Thu) **FREE** This gallery features exhibits by noted artists and is home to 10 working studios. It's a nurturing spot for art.

Paramount Theatre   HISTORIC BUILDING
(☑325-676-9620; www.paramount-abilene.org; 352 Cypress St; admission for self-guided tours free; ☉noon-5pm Mon-Fri) Stars twinkle and clouds drift across the velvet blue ceiling of this magical movie and performing-arts palace.

You can tour the beautifully restored Paramount or take in a movie, concert or other performance many nights.

✯✯ Festivals & Events

Western Heritage Classic   RODEO
(☑325-677-4376; www.westernheritageclassic.com; 1700 Hwy 36, Expo Center of Taylor County; grounds pass adult/child $7/5; ☉2nd weekend in May) A big rodeo featuring working cowboys from ranches across the USA, complete with campfire cook-offs, a Western art show and dances. Rodeo tickets (from $25) include grounds admission. Rodeo events include steer wrestling and tie-down roping in which animals are wrestled to the ground, sometimes causing injury to the animal. Rodeo events such as this are often criticized by animal welfare groups..

🛏 Sleeping

It's chain city in Abilene. Exits 285, 286 and 288 off I-20 are dotted with motels. Older indie operations south of the center on South 1st St are mostly dubious.

Emerald Inn Expo   MOTEL $
(☑325-677-8100; www.emeraldinnexpo.net; 840 E US 80; r $65-90; ✳ 🕸 ⚟ 🐾) This well-managed indie motel has a pool area that goes beyond the puddle-in-a-parking-lot standard elsewhere: it's big and even has shade from a large tree. Rooms have a fridge and microwave, and a better-than-average breakfast is included. There are barbecue facilities.

Antilley Inn   MOTEL $
(☑325-695-3330; www.antilleyinn.com; 6550 US 83/84; r $50-80; ✳ 🕸 ⚟ 🐾) The Antilley offers great value. It's an updated motel, with two stories of rooms and outside walkways. Rooms have fridges and microwaves and a continental breakfast is set out each morning.

**Courtyard by Marriott
Abilene Southwest**   HOTEL $$
(☑325-695-9600; www.marriott.com; 4350 Ridgemont Dr; r $100-200; ✳ @ 🕸 🐾) Within sight of the Mall of Abilene, this corporate hotel is one of many slathered across these flatlands by national franchises. The three-story building has 100 sizable units, some with slivers of balcony-like diversion.

🍴 Eating

Abilene has some decent restaurants that are as casual and timeless as a big-sky sunset on the wide open plains. Many locally owned places are closed Sunday.

DALLAS & THE PANHANDLE PLAINS ABILENE

WORTH A TRIP

FRIO CANYON

Since prehistoric times, humans have been enjoying the beauty of the Frio River and its lovely canyon and valley. The region is lush with trees that provide their own harmonious coloring during the fall. The tiny town of **Leakey** (61 miles south of Junction) is little more than a crossroads, but what a crossroads! US 83 follows the river north and south, while FM 337 runs east and west through wooded hills and secluded little valleys.

El Pulgarcito de America   TEX-MEX $
(☎ 325-670-9292; 2502 S 7th St; mains $5-10; ⊙ 7am-8pm Mon-Sat) The kind of unassuming but excellent Mexican restaurant that pops up like treasure in west Texas. Just try to decide between the green enchiladas and the fajitas.

Belle's Chicken Dinner House   SOUTHERN US $
(☎ 325-677-7100; 2002 N Clack St, off US 83/277; mains $7-13; ⊙ 11am-2pm & 5-9pm Mon-Sat, 10:30am-2pm Sun) Part shack, part steakhouse, this locally loved institution spares you choices. It offers chicken in various forms or chicken-fried steaks. Unlimited sides of mashed potatoes, dumplings, cream corn, greens beans and a basket of rolls are trundled out – just as you'll need to be at the end of the meal. Should dessert happen, have the banana cream pie.

Lucy's Big Burgers   BURGERS
(☎ 325-677-5829; 3110 S 27th St; mains $4-9; ⊙ 11am-9pm Mon-Sat) Specially baked buns and plenty of fixings make these burgers standouts. The decor is old-time West cafe, the tables have checked plastic covers. Definitely save room for dessert: homemade ice cream in several flavors. The coconut will have you doing a U-turn in the parking lot.

Beehive   STEAK $$
(☎ 325-675-0600; www.beehivesaloon.com; 442 Cedar St; mains $8-30; ⊙ 11am-1:30pm Tue-Fri, 5-10pm Tue-Sat) This is the place for a traditional beefy lunch or dinner after the sights downtown. The menu takes supper-house standards such as shrimp cocktail and steaks and does them up just right (the lunchtime burgers are also good). The cocktails are renowned in teetotaling Abilene for not only having alcohol but being generous.

☆ Entertainment

Check to see what's on at the beautiful Paramount Theatre (p185).

★ Big Country Raceway   SPECTATOR SPORT
(☎ 325-673-7223; www.bigcountryraceway.com; 5601 W Stamford St; from $10) Racing cars is a Texas tradition and Abilene's drag strip is open to everyone. Watch dudes in their pickups challenge each other or go nuts and trash your minivan. The track is generally open Friday nights and all day weekends from spring to fall. It's just off I-20 exit 281, Shirley Rd.

🛍 Shopping

Hickory St, between 5th and 8th Sts near downtown Abilene, has a good selection of antique and gift shops selling everything from fudge to stained glass to vintage clothing.

James Leddy Boots   SHOES
(☎ 325-677-7811; www.jamesleddyabilene.com; 1602 N Treadway Blvd; ⊙ 8am-5pm Mon-Fri) A legendary maker of custom boots, this family-run store has prices ranging from $500 to five figures. You can usually get a tour of the shop and work area. Breathe deep.

ℹ Information

Abilene Convention and Visitors Bureau
(☎ 325-676-2556; www.abilenevisitors.com; 1101 N 1st St; ⊙ 8:30am-5pm Mon-Fri) Has its offices in the restored Texas & Pacific Railway Depot. Info also available at Frontier Texas!.

ℹ Getting There & Away

For driverse, Abilene is circled by US 83 on the west side of town, by Loop 322 on the southeast side and I-20 on the northeast.

Greyhound (☎ 325-677-8127; www.greyhound.com; 1657 TX 351, off I-20) is on the northwest side. Abilene is on the I-20 line running west from Fort Worth ($24, 2½ hours, three daily).

Albany
☎ 325 / POP 2030

Albany ranks among the most interesting small towns in Texas. Sitting 35 miles northeast of Abilene, the Shackleford County seat of about 2000 people is a bit off the beaten path on TX 180. It's a worthy 25-mile detour off I-20 or a highlight of one of the loneliest roads in Texas, US 283.

⊙ Sights

★ Fort Griffin
State Historic Site   HISTORIC SITE
(☑325-762-3592; www.visitfortgriffin.com; 1701 N
US 283; adult/child $4/free; ⊙8am-4:30pm) Some
15 miles north of Albany, the Fort Griffin
State Historic Site showcases a handful of
somewhat-restored buildings and the ruins
of a fort that served the frontier during the
Comanche wars from 1867 through 1881.
Today, the park is probably best known as a
principal home of the official Texas longhorn
herd. There's a good visitor center.

Old Jail Art Center   MUSEUM
(☑325-762-2269; www.theoldjailartcenter.org; 201 S
2nd St; ⊙10am-5pm Tue-Sat) FREE A remarkable
facility, the 1877 Old Jail Art Center houses a
surprising collection that includes ancient ter
racotta Chinese tomb figures and art by such
masters as Pablo Picasso, Amedeo Modigliani,
Henry Moore and Grant Wood.

✗ Eating

★ Fort Griffin General
Merchandise Restaurant   AMERICAN $$
(Albany Beehive; ☑325-762-3034; www.beehive
saloon.com; 517 US Hwy 180 W; mains $9-33;
⊙11am-2pm Tue-Fri, 6-10pm Wed-Sat) This
branch of the Abilene original is revered for
its chicken-fried steak. Tender, juicy, crunchy
all at once. Set in historic buildings, it's also
favored for its trad salad bar and excellent
steaks. Full bar.

☆ Entertainment

Fort Griffin Fandangle   THEATER
(☑325-762-3838;   www.fortgriffinfandangle.org;
Prairie Theater, 1490 CR 1084; $10-20; ⊙Fri & Sat
last 2 weeks of Jun) Each June, several hundred
Albany townspeople get together and put on
a show, Fort Griffin Fandangle. This energetic musical tells the story of the area's pioneer
days, complete with a cattle drive, stagecoach
chase and plenty of Old West tomfoolery.
Meals are available before the shows.

Lubbock
☑806 / POP 241,600

'Lubbock or leave it' sing the Dixie Chicks,
but this seemingly characteristic bit of Texas bravado isn't what it seems, as the song
includes sardonic lines such as 'Got more
churches than trees.' And while you'll see
plenty of steeples on the horizon, what will
really strike you about west Texas' liveliest
city is its celebration of life beyond cotton
and cows.

Buddy Holly grew up in Lubbock and the
town celebrates his legacy in both attractions
and an entire entertainment district. It's possible to still find the rockabilly sound that
Holly made famous. The other big sound
happens on fall weekends when the roar of
sport-made fans at Texas Tech football games
can stop a tumbleweed in its tracks.

Lubbock is known as 'Hub City' because
so many major highways meet here.

FUNDAMENTALIST WORRIES

The Mormon Church has spawned many offshoot sects which have broken with the main
church over its disavowal of polygamy. In recent years none has been more notorious than
the Fundamentalist Church of Jesus Christ of Latter Day Saints (FLDS).

Under the auspices of imprisoned sex offender Warren Jeffs, the FLDS has secretive
communities across North America, including Arizona, Utah and British Columbia. In 2003
the sect purchased a ranch 4 miles northeast of Eldorado, in a spot as isolated as any in
Texas (San Angelo, the nearest city, is 40 miles north).

Named the Yearning for Zion Ranch (YFZ Ranch), the property has housed 700 or more
people at various times and is rumored to be the current headquarters of the church. In
2008 the ranch made headlines when the Texas Department of Child Protective Services,
acting on a phone tip claiming that children had been sexually abused at the ranch, removed more than 400 children and placed them in protective custody in San Angelo. A legal
(and media) circus ensued, during which it was established that the original phone call had
been a hoax.

Eventually, most of the children were returned to their mothers, but a number of men at
the ranch have been indicted and convicted of a variety of sex offences with underage girls.
In 2014 the state of Texas took possession of the land and the last church members left.

Visitors to Eldorado today, the namesake of the John Wayne movie, will see little trace of
the once-notorious church.

DALLAS & THE PANHANDLE PLAINS LUBBOCK

⊙ Sights

Buddy Holly's roots in Lubbock are reason enough to visit.

The Texas Tech campus sprawls all over the city's near-northwest side, but is mainly centered between 4th and 19th Sts north and south and University and Quaker Aves east and west. The Depot District, Lubbock's liveliest dining and nightlife area, is centered on Buddy Holly Ave (formerly known as Ave H) and 19th St.

Don't miss Prairie Dog Town in Mackenzie Park.

★**Mackenzie Park**   PARK
(off Parkway Dr; ☉dawn-dusk) **FREE** Located off I-27 at Broadway St and Ave A, 248-acre Mackenzie Park has two dynamite highlights amid what's otherwise a mundane urban park.

Prairie dogs are the stars of **Prairie Dog Town**, a hugely popular 7-acre habitat for the winsome rodents who keep busy excavating their 'town' and watching for groundskeepers.

The irresistibly named **Joyland** (☑806-763-2719; www.joylandpark.com; 500 Canyon Lake Dr, Mackenzie Park; $6-21; ☉varies mid-Mar–Oct, to 10pm Jun-Aug) has three roller coasters, 30 other rides and an array of carnival arcades and games that are little changed from Holly's time.

★**National Ranching Heritage Center**   MUSEUM
(☑806-742-0498; www.depts.ttu.edu/nrhc/; 3121 4th St; ☉10am-5pm Mon-Sat, 1-5pm Sun) **FREE** A real Lubbock gem, this open-air museum, part of the Texas Tech museum complex, tells a detailed story of what life was like on the Texas High Plains from the late 1700s until the Dust Bowl era of the 1930s. Nearly 50 preserved ranch structures are arrayed on 27 acres.

Among the highlights are the gun ports on the 1780 Los Corralitos house, the 2nd-story stronghold on the 1872 Jowell House and the grand 1909 Barton House.

★**Buddy Holly Center**   MUSEUM
(☑806-767-2686; www.buddyhollycenter.org; 1801 Crickets Ave; adult/child $8/5; ☉10am-5pm Tue-Sat, from 1pm Sun) A huge version of Holly's trademark horn-rims mark the Buddy Holly Center. The center is home to the Buddy Holly Gallery; a room devoted to the man with those glasses and pristine teeth. The gallery includes some of his schoolbooks,

shoes and records, but best of all are Holly's Fender Stratocaster and hallmark glasses.

The collection delves into Holly's life and gives a good idea of all the rock musicians he inspired, including Bob Dylan, the Beatles and the Rolling Stones.

The center also houses a fine-arts gallery, a gift shop, and the Texas Musicians Hall of Fame, which features ever-changing exhibitions on the music and musicians of Texas.

Buddy Holly's Grave   CEMETERY
(2011 E 31st St, E of Martin Luther King Jr Blvd, City of Lubbock Cemetery; ☉dawn-dusk) The headstone in the Lubbock City Cemetery reads 'In Loving Memory of Our Own Buddy Holley. September 7, 1936 to February 3, 1959.' Musical notes and an electric guitar are engraved on the marker too. Some visitors leave guitar picks, coins and other tokens. The cemetery is located on the eastern edge of town. Once inside the gate, turn down the lane to your right.

Buddy Holly Statue & West Texas Walk of Fame   MONUMENT
(1824 Crickets Ave) In front of the Civic Center, a larger-than-life-size statue of Holly is surrounded by plaques honoring him and other west Texans who made it big in arts and entertainment. Honorees include musicians Joe Ely, Roy Orbison, Bob Wills, Tanya Tucker and Mac Davis.

Lubbock Lake National Historic Landmark   HISTORIC SITE
(☑806-742-1116; www.museum.ttu.edu/lll; 2401 Landmark Dr; ☉9am-5pm Tue-Sat, 1-5pm Sun) **FREE** A Tech-run attraction, this site is a sort of time capsule for all the cultures that have inhabited the South Plains for the last 12,000 years. Bones of critters such as wooly mammoths were first unearthed here when agricultural irrigation caused Lubbock Lake's water table to decline in the 1930s, and excavations have gone on here since 1939.

Four miles of trails now wend through the site, where digs are ongoing. A visitor center provides information on long-gone species such as the giant short-faced bear.

To get there, follow Loop 289 to Clovis Rd west of I-27 on the northwest side of town.

American Wind Power Center   MUSEUM
(☑806-747-8734; www.windmill.com; 1701 Canyon Lake Dr; adult/child $7.50/5; ☉10am-5pm Tue-Sat year-round, 2-5pm Sun summer) A squeaky windmill is part of the iconic opening to *Once Upon a Time in the West,* and you can

see more than 90 examples of these Western icons at the American Wind Power Center, located on a 28-acre site at E Broadway St south of MacKenzie Park. Seen together, the windmills form their own compelling sculpture garden.

Museum of Texas Tech University   MUSEUM
(☑ 806-742-2490; www.depts.ttu.edu/museum ttu; 3301 4th St & Indiana Ave; ⊙ 10am-5pm Tue-Sat, 1-5pm Sun) FREE Art, natural history and science are showcased at this campus museum, which has more than five million items in its rather eclectic collection. Special exhibits are usually the highlights.

⭐ Festivals & Events

★ National Cowboy Symposium and Celebration   CULTURAL
(☑ 806-798-7825; www.cowboy.org; ⊙ Sep) September is a big time in Lubbock, with returning Tech students and this huge gathering of cowboys, cowboy wannabes, cowboy scholars, cowboy musicians and cowboy cooks. Yee-haw! There's a huge line-up of entertainment.

🛏 Sleeping

There are several motels on Ave Q just south of US 82. They are close to downtown and a reasonable 1.3-mile walk southeast to the Depot District. There's another cluster of chains south of the center at exit 1 off I-27 and still more scattered along TX 289, the ring road southwest of town.

Super 8 Lubbock
Civic Center North   MOTEL $
(☑ 806-762-8726; www.super8.com; 501 Ave Q; r $50-110; ❋ 🛜 🐾) Across from a Super Wal-Mart, so you have quick access to cheap pizza (which you can heat up in your in-room microwave), the 35 basic rooms here are arranged over two floors, with outside walkways.

Buffalo Springs Lake   CAMPGROUND $
(☑ 806-747-3353; www.buffalospringslake.net; FM 835 & E 50th St; tent sites $25-40; 🛜 🐾) The lake is 5 miles southeast of Lubbock and is big on fun (think ATV trails) as opposed to natural splendor. Sites vary from basic tent-only ones to those with full hookups.

★ Overton Hotel   HOTEL $$
(☑ 806-776-7000; www.overtonhotel.com; 2322 Mac Davis Lane; r $140-350; ❋ @ 🛜) The best place to stay in town, the 15-story independently

owned Overton is downtown and is close to the Tech campus. From the valets to the turndown service, this is a luxurious hotel. Percolate your cares away in the Jacuzzi then unwind in your boldly decorated room.

Arbor Inn & Suites   HOTEL $$
(☑ 806-722-2726; http://arborinnandsuites.com; 5310 Englewood Ave; r $100-180; 🅿 ❋ 🛜 ❄ 🐾) Lavishly furnished and extra-large rooms set this indie hotel apart. There is a full breakfast buffet for guests. The outdoor pool is in a lush garden and even has a waterfall. It's in a suburban setting southwest of the center, off the Hwy 289 loop.

Woodrow House   B&B $$
(☑ 806-793-3330; www.woodrowhouse.com; 2629 19th St; r $105-190; ❋ 🛜 🐾) Right across from Texas Tech, this professionally run B&B offers a range of themed rooms. Up-and-comers may enjoy the sumptuous charms of the Honeymoon Suite while those who prefer to bring up the rear may enjoy the suite in an actual old Sante Fe caboose in the garden. All 10 rooms have individual bathrooms.

🍴 Eating

Good restaurants are scattered around town, although you won't go wrong basing yourself in the Depot District and browsing.

Lubbock Downtown
Farmers Market   MARKET $
(http://lubbockdowntownfarmersmarket.com; cnr Buddy Holly Ave & 19th St; ⊙ 9am-5:30pm Sat Jun-Oct; 🐾) 🍴 This organic farmers market sells the best produce from the region. There are also plenty of ready food vendors.

Picantes   TEX-MEX $
(☑ 806-793-8304; 3814 34th St; mains $6-12; ⊙ 9am-10pm) In an otherwise-nondescript old coffee shop, this hugely popular Tex-Mex stalwart turns out excellent chile rellenos and other standards. On weekends folks settle into the booths for all-you-can-eat menudo, the suitably picante beef soup.

Tom & Bingo's Hickory Pit BBQ   BARBECUE $
(☑ 806-799-1514; 3006 34th St; mains $6-8; ⊙ 10:30am-4pm Mon-Sat) Calling this place a shack is an insult to decrepit buildings everywhere, but appearances are forgotten when you taste the smoked ham and brisket sandwiches (have the latter chopped). Sides are few: use the fries to mop up the tangy, sweet sauce. Open since 1952. It sells out so don't wait much past 2pm.

★ **Crafthouse** GASTROPUB $$
(📞 806-687-1466; www.crafthousepub.com; 3131 34th St; mains $10-24; ⊙11am-10pm Tue-Sat, 10am-2pm Sun; 🅿) Lubbock's most creative restaurant is the work of Jason and Kate Diehl. From the pickled seasonal vegetables on the starter list to inventive seasonal fare, it has something to catch your eye. Mindful of local budgets it serves cheeseburgers, but what burgers they are. The twice-fried fries are sublime. The beer and wine list is lengthy and enticing.

Sunday brunch has comfort food, perfect for a languid start to the day.

★ **West Table** AMERICAN $$$
(📞 806-993-9378; www.thewesttable.com; 1204 Broadway St; lunch mains $12-14, dinner mains $22-44; ⊙11am-2pm Wed-Fri, 5-9pm Wed-Sat, 11am-1pm Sun) One of Lubbock's best restaurants has creative and seasonal dishes on a menu that changes daily. There is a large and spare dining area with polished wood floors. Service is polished. Seafood, pork and beef mains are all excellent; many come with spicy accents. Great wine list.

🍷 Drinking & Nightlife

The Depot District is Lubbock's nightlife HQ (fittingly, the namesake building at the Buddy Holly Center looks hungover), and covers a few blocks adjoining Buddy Holly Ave between 17th and 19th Sts. Otherwise, raucous bars, cheap burrito joints and plasma labs mark the classic college neighborhood where Broadway crosses University Ave into the campus.

★ **La Diosa Cellars** WINE BAR
(📞 806-744-3600; www.ladiosacellars.com; 901 17th St; ⊙11am-11pm Tue-Thu, to midnight Fri & Sat) One of several local wineries, La Diosa uncorks a range of Texas wines beyond its own label in this art-filled space. There are inventive Mediterranean-style snacks and meals as well as a coffee bar. On many nights there's live entertainment. Come for a glass of wine, a snack, a meal or just to get down. A Depot District fave.

Flippers Tavern BAR
(📞 806-701-5130; www.facebook.com/flipstavern lubbock; 1406 Ave Q; ⊙11am-midnight) Good dive bar that takes its name from the vintage pinball machines that line the back room. Serves a dozen creative versions of hot dogs with names like 'French tickler.'

Cricket's Grill & Draft House BAR
(📞 806-744-4677; www.cricketsgrill.com; 2412 Broadway St; ⊙11am-2am; 🅿) A slightly more upscale college joint near the entrance to Texas Tech. It has a huge selection of draft beer and all sorts of fried treats.

Bash Riprock's BAR
(📞 806-762-2274; www.bashriprocks.com; 2419 Main St; ⊙2pm-2am Mon-Sat, 4pm-2am Sun) It's dark and grungy, and the huge beer selection gets a workout during the 4pm-to-7pm happy hour. A classic college bar, it's right near the Texas Tech entrance.

☆ Entertainment

Blue Light LIVE MUSIC
(📞 806-762-3688; www.thebluelightlive.com; 1806 Buddy Holly Ave; ⊙9pm-2am) This legendary club has plenty of live Texas country and rock.

🛍 Shopping

Dollar Western Wear CLOTHING
(📞 806-793-2818; www.dollarwesternwear.com; 5011 Slide Rd; ⊙10am-6pm Mon-Sat) This place is among the biggest of Lubbock's many Western-gear shops.

ℹ Getting There & Away

Lubbock International Airport (LIA; 📞 806-775-3126; www.flylia.com; 5401 N Martin L King Blvd) Situated 7 miles north of town, at exit 8 off of I-27. Airlines include American Eagle (Dallas–Fort Worth), United Express (Houston) and Southwest (Dallas, Houston and Las Vegas).

Greyhound (📞 806-687-4501; www.greyhound.com; 801 Broadway St) Has buses serving most major Texas cities including Dallas ($48, 6½ hours, three daily).

Along Texas Hwy 70

Evocative small towns – some thriving, others nearly gone – are found throughout west Texas. One little burg after another seems ripped from the pages of a Larry McMurty novel. Texas Hwy 70 manages to link a string of these nearly forgotten places: a drive along this road puts you further than simple geography from the 21st century.

◉ Sights

Begin your Hwy 70 drive in the south in **Sweetwater**, along I-20, some 40 miles west of Abilene. Long and lonely vistas of lush ranch land await as you drive north on Hwy 70. About 55 miles north, turn west at the

T-junction with US 380 and drive 5 miles to the nearly evaporated ghost town of **Clare-mont**. About all that remains is a red stone jail, which could be a movie set.

Return east and rejoin Hwy 70. Some 40 miles of occasional rivers, scattered annuities (oil wells) and countless cattle later, you're in the modestly named hamlet of **Spur**. Most of the once-proud brick structures downtown are barely hanging on, like a chimney with bad grout. Stop into **Dixie Dog Drive-In** (216 W Hill St, Spur; mains from $4; ⊗8am-8pm) for a timeless small-town fast-food experience. The chili cheeseburger is the bomb. Or stop off at the **Turnaround Cafe** (📷806-271-3983; 202 Burlington Ave, Spur; mains $5-12; ⊗5:30am-8:30pm Tue-Sun) for top-notch diner fare.

Just another 11 miles north brings you to the seat of Dickens County: **Dickens**. Another fading burg, here you can still sense the pride of the original settlers in the massive courthouse built from carved limestone. Catch up on all the gossip at **TC's Ponderosa** (📷806-623-5260; 136 US 82, Dickens; mains from $5; ⊗7am-8pm), which is inside a gas station. Great barbecue is served up simply on Formica tables. Try the hot links and get a pickled egg and pineapple pudding for the road.

From here it is nearly 57 miles almost due north through verdant cattle and cotton country to your ultimate destination, Turkey. Pause in towns such as **Roaring Springs** in Motley County for smatterings of tiny shops that will never attract the attention of Wal-Mart.

Turkey

📷806 / POP 380

The lovely lady in city hall told us that 'people are dying too quick.' And indeed, like the flight path of its namesake bird, Turkey has been descending for decades. But amid the grizzled streets is a not-to-be-missed cultural attraction.

◎ Sights & Festivals

★**Bob Wills Museum**   MUSEUM
(📷806-423-1146; www.bobwillsday.com; cnr 6th & Lyles Sts; ⊗9-11:30am & 1-4:30pm Mon-Fri, 9am-noon Sat) FREE Bob Wills was one of the most important Texas musicians, and his life is recalled at the eponymous museum. Located in the old elementary school (which also has the tiny city hall and library), the displays cover much of Wills' adventurous life, which included a string of B-movie Westerns.

BUDDY HOLLY, A REAL LEGEND

Lubbock native Charles Hardin 'Buddy' Holley was just five years old when he won a local talent contest playing a toy violin. By the time he was a teen, Buddy became a regular performer on local radio in a band that blended country and western with rhythm and blues. But Holly (the 'e' was dropped by an early concert promoter) soon became a leading pioneer of a new kind of music – rock and roll. Together with his backup band, the Crickets, Holly drove to Clovis, New Mexico, in early 1957 to record a demo of a song called 'That'll Be the Day.' Within months, Holly had a Top 10 record to his credit, with many more hits to follow, including 'Peggy Sue,' 'Not Fade Away,' 'Maybe Baby,' 'It's So Easy,' 'Rave On,' 'Fool's Paradise' and 'Oh, Boy!'.

Buddy Holly was among the first rock performers to write his own material, and he was among the first to experiment with multitrack overdubbing and echo in the studio. An accomplished guitarist and pianist, Holly also used his voice as an instrument, employing a hiccup here and falsetto there to distinctive effect. He and the Crickets were the real deal. In Texas, they often served as a warm-up act to visiting stars (including a young Elvis Presley), and when they hit it big they were among the first white performers to perform at the legendary Apollo Theater in Harlem, New York City.

If his talents weren't enough, Holly was guaranteed immortality by dying young – he was killed in a plane crash on February 3, 1959, near Clear Lake, Iowa. (Fellow rockers JP 'The Big Bopper' Richardson and Ritchie 'La Bamba' Valens were also on board.) His legend continues to grow and his songs and style are emulated endlessly.

The Buddy Holly Story, a 1978 film that starred Gary Busey and which won an Oscar for its music, is a highly fictionalized account of his life. In a classic bit of melodrama, Holly's parents are falsely shown opposing his music career, while the mountains behind the 'Lubbock' bus station are pure Hollywood, literally.

But it's the music that survives. Wills was a major creator of a genre of music known as Western Swing, described by David Vinopal in the *All-Music Guide*. Wills reached his greatest fame in the 1940s with his band the Texas Playboys, with whom he recorded such hits as 'San Antonio Rose' and 'Faded Love.'

The museum includes lots of artifacts from the musician's life, including his fiddles, scrapbooks, movie posters and a gazillion photos. In the halls outside are haunting class photos from the adjoining high school, which closed in 1972. They tell stories of a time when the future of Turkey looked much different.

★ **Bob Wills Days** MUSIC
(☑806-423-1253; www.bobwillsday.com; ⊘late April) Turkey celebrates Wills' legacy with Bob Wills Days, when 10,000 or more people stuff themselves into Turkey for a weekend of pickin' and grinnin', with jam sessions galore. Many well-known musicians appear and jam.

✖ Eating

If Turkey's barbecue joint is closed, head west to the diner in Quitaque.

JB's Bar-B-Q BARBECUE $
(☑806-423-1512; 102 Main St; mains $7-10; ⊘11:30am-8pm) Almost miraculous! This great little barbecue joint serves up fine sausage, even as the population shrinks around it.

Quitaque

☑806 / POP 390

Quitaque has been a rival of Turkey's for decades; the latter never forgave the former for getting the town's combined schools in the 1970s. But this small town isn't doing much better than Turkey, although the beauty of Caprock Canyons brings a steady stream of travelers.

✖ Eating

Caprock Cafe CAFE $
(☑806-455-1429; www.caprockcafequitaque.com; 201 Main St; mains $6-12; ⊘6am-8pm Mon-Wed, to 9pm Thu-Sat; 🔊) It doesn't look like much, but then again you don't have much choice, so fortunately the Caprock Cafe scores with good diner fare. Lunch buffets are big, with a different special each day (chicken one day, catfish the next). Otherwise it also offers breakfasts and burgers. It's popular with Caprock Canyons campers fed up with campfire meals.

Caprock Canyons State Park & Trailway

Although it's not as well known as Palo Duro Canyon State Park, Caprock Canyons shares the same kind of stunning topography and abundant wildlife. Even the casual visitor is likely to see mule deer, roadrunners and aoudad, the North African barbary sheep transplanted to the Panhandle in the 1950s. The sunsets are stupendous.

🏃 Activities

★ **Caprock Canyons State Park Trails** HIKING
The state park has some outstanding trails. Stop at the park visitor center for a map showing trailheads and distances. For an easy trail of about 2.5 miles round-trip, follow the hikers-only Upper Canyon Trail from the South Prong tent camping area trailhead to the South Prong primitive camping area and back.

Beyond the primitive camping area, the Upper Canyon Trail becomes increasingly steep and rugged; the cliffs and bluffs are not for the foolhardy. It won't be hard to imagine what it was like for the Comanche people in their final days on the run from the US Army here in the early 1870s.

Caprock Canyons Trailways HIKING
Running through three counties from Estelline to the northeast to South Plains to the southwest, the 64-mile abandoned-railroad-bed Trailways opened in 1993. Highlights include some 50 bridges and the 742ft Clarity Tunnel, a historic railroad passage. It's popular with hikers, bikers and riders. The route runs across the plains and drops into the appropriately named Red River Valley.

Trail access points and parking lots can be found along TX 86 at Estelline, Parnell, Tampico Siding, Turkey and Quitaque. On this section, the trail runs parallel to, but a good distance from, the highway. At Quitaque, the trail swings south then west for the final 23 miles to South Plains – the portion that includes the tunnel. Access points on this part of the trail are at Monk's Crossing and South Plains.

🛏 Sleeping

Other than camping in the park, options are few: most motels are along I-27 in Tulia, Canyon and Amarillo.

Caprock Canyons
State Park Camping
CAMPGROUND **$**
(☑ 806-455-1492; https://tpwd.texas.gov/state-parks/caprock-canyons; Quitaque; sites $12-22)
Primitive campsites ($12) are available along the Trailways and in the more remote reaches of the park; get a permit from the state park before setting out. The park also has more developed campgrounds. Walk-in campsites ($12) are the most atmospheric.

Honey Flat is the park's most developed camping area, with 35 sites with water and electricity (per site $17 22). It's an easy walk to Lake Theo.

ℹ Information
Visitor Center (☑ 806-455-1492; ⊘ 8am-noon & 1 5pm Sun-Thu, 8am 6pm Fri & Sat) At the park's visitor center you can rent an audio tour for use with a vehicle or possibly arrange for a trail bike.

Palo Duro Canyon
At 120 miles long and about 5 miles wide, Palo Duro Canyon is second in size in the USA only to the Grand Canyon. The cliffs striated in yellows, reds and oranges, rock towers and other geologic oddities are a refreshing surprise amongst the seemingly endless flatness of the plains, and are worth at least a gander.

Canyon
Small yet cultured, Canyon is an interesting gem of a town. Georgia O'Keeffe once taught art at what is now West Texas A&M University, and today's campus is home to what many people figure is the best history museum in Texas – the Panhandle-Plains Historical Museum. Moreover, this is an ideal starting spot for Palo Duro Canyon State Park, one of the state's natural showpieces.

◉ Sights
★ Panhandle-Plains
Historical Museum
MUSEUM
(☑ 806-651-2244; www.panhandleplains.org; 2401 4th Ave; adult/child $10/5; ⊘ 9am-6pm Mon-Sat Jun-Aug, to 5pm Sep-May) The many ways to skin a buffalo is but one of the myriad highlights of this magnificent museum, a Texas plains must-see. You can hit the highlights in an hour or easily lose a day.

Collections and displays include the Panhandle's oil heyday as seen through

CAPROCK WINERY
About four miles southwest of the Llano Estacado winery, **CapRock Winery** (☑ 806-863-2704; www.caprockwinery.com; 408 E Woodrow Rd, south of FM 1585, Lubbock; ⊘ noon-5:30pm Tue-Thu, noon-6:30pm Fri, noon-6:30pm Sat) is worth a visit for its beautiful mission-style headquarters, a showplace both inside and out. CapRock makes about a dozen wines.

the prism of the boomtown of Borger and an old-time filling station; life-size casts of dinosaurs; the oldest assembly-line auto in the world (a 1903 Ford); world-class art from Texas painters and photographers; and the role of the buffalo in the rich cultures of Native Americans.

🛏 Sleeping
The drive south from Amarillo can be a chore at busy times, so it's better to stay at the several choices in Canyon for a visit to the park.

Buffalo Inn
MOTEL **$**
(☑ 806-655-2124; www.buffaloinncanyontx.com; 300 23rd St/US 87; r $50-80; 🅿🛜) This classic 1950s single-story motor-court is centrally located by the West Texas A&M campus. It's snappily maintained and has an authentic charm lacking in new chains. Rooms have fridges and microwaves.

Best Western Palo Duro Canyon
MOTEL **$$**
(☑ 806-655-1818; www.bestwestern.com; 2801 4th Ave; r $80-180; 🅿@🛜🅿) As tidy inside as the white paint is outside, this 51-unit motel lacks any regional charm, although the decor does pick up a few canyon colors. It's convenient to the canyon and I-27. The pool, alas, is indoors away from the balmy Texas air.

🍴 Eating
Canyon has good eats; the main drag, 23rd St, has many good locally owned options amid the chains.

La Bella Pizza
PIZZA **$**
(☑ 806-655-7666; www.labellaonline.com; 700 23rd St; mains from $7; ⊘ 11am-midnight Mon-Thu, to 1am Fri & Sat) Pizza that beats the chains is the huge draw here. College students, hungry tourists and fans of Italian food love this

place for its authentic flavors and high quality. The dining room is basic and small; you can get your pizza delivered to your motel.

Feldman's Wrong Way Diner AMERICAN $
(☑806-655-2700; www.feldmansdiner.com; 2100 N 2nd Ave; mains from $7; ⊙11am-10pm; 🚻) As the menu says, this classy diner is dedicated to anyone who has made a wrong turn, wrong decision or wandered off the beaten path. Here, at least, you'll know you've done the right thing. Steaks, catfish and burgers star, with lots of salads too. A model train circles overhead. Feldman's now has a bar.

Look for the windsock on the roof.

Palo Duro Canyon State Park

Sights

★**Palo Duro Canyon State Park** PARK
(☑806-488-2227; www.tpwd.state.tx.us; 11450 Park Rd 5; adult/child $5/free; ⊙main gate 7am-10pm, unless camping overnight) The multihued canyon was created by the Prairie Dog Town Fork of the Red River, a long name for a little river. The over 26,000 acres that make up the park attract hikers, horseback riders and mountain bikers eager for recreation, and artists and photographers drawn by the magnificent blend of color and desert light.

The gorge has sheltered and inspired people for a long time. Prehistoric Indians lived in the canyon 12,000 years ago, and Coronado may have stopped by in 1541. Palo Duro was the site of an 1874 battle between Comanche and Kiowa warriors and the US Army.

Activities

Lighthouse Trail HIKING
Palo Duro's most popular hiking trail leads to the **Lighthouse**, a hoodoo-style formation that's nearly 300ft tall. Almost all of the nearly 6-mile round-trip is flat and easily traversed. The floodplain to the southwest of the trail has perhaps the park's greatest concentration of wildlife, including aoudad sheep, white-tailed mule deer and wild turkeys.

Old West Stables HORSEBACK RIDING
(☑806-488-2180; www.oldweststables.com; 11450 Park Rd 5; rides from $40; ⊙Mar-Nov) Offers a variety of trips in Palo Duro Canyon on tame horses. The stables are about 3 miles past the park entrance.

🛏 Sleeping

The parks offers popular **campsites** (Palo Duro Canyon State Park; sites $12-26) and a few **cabins** (☑512-389-8900; Palo Duro Canyon State Park; per night $60-125). Nearby Canyon has many motels and hotels.

✕ Eating

Food options are limited in the park; bring groceries and/or a picnic from Canyon.

Palo Duro Trading Post MARKET, CAFE $
(☑806-488-2821; www.palodurotradingpost.us; 11450 Park Rd 5; mains from $7; ⊙8:30am-7:30pm Mon-Sat, 11am-7pm Sun Mar-Nov) Has supplies and burgers.

END OF THE COMANCHE TRAIL

Until 1871, the Comanches were the most feared of the Plains Indian tribes. While others had been beaten by the US Army and forced into camps and reservations, the Comanches were undefeated and had actually expanded their territory, Comancheria, which encompassed what is today everything in Texas and Oklahoma north and west of Austin. Beginning that September, cavalry led by Colonel Ranald S Mackenzie fought a series of running skirmishes with bands of Comanches in and around the Blanco Canyon (other battles had taken place in Caprock and Palo Duro Canyons). The conflict proved to be the beginning of the end for the Comanches, who lost much of their goods and wealth in addition to having the heart of their territory invaded by the army for the first time. By 1875 the last free band of Comanches had surrendered.

The pivotal battles were fought in the Blanco Canyon, which can be easily seen just 3 miles east of Crosbyton on US 82, itself 38 miles east of Lubbock. Various paved farm roads running north of here penetrate into the canyon, which remains windy and largely desolate today. As you follow the White River, try to imagine Comanches and cavalry troops eyeing each other from the valley and escarpments.

☆ Entertainment

Texas   THEATER
(☑806-655-2181; www.texas-show.com; 11450 Park Rd 5; tickets $13-31, meal adult/child $16/9; ☺8:30pm Tue-Sun early Jun–mid-Aug) Hokey, jingoistic, over-the-top, effervescent and loud are just some of the adjectives for this open-air musical show in the natural beauty of the park's Pioneer Amphitheatre. From 6pm on show nights, it offers an extra-cost barbecue dinner catered by Canyon's Feldman's Wrong Way Diner (p194).

Amarillo

☑806 / POP 197,100

Long an unavoidable stop, roughly halfway between Chicago and LA on old Route 66, Amarillo continues to figure in travel plans, simply by being the brightest light on the 543-mile stretch of I-40 between Oklahoma City, Oklahoma, and Albuquerque, New Mexico.

And though the town may seem as featureless as the surrounding landscape, there's plenty here to sate even the most attention-challenged during a road respite. Beef, the big local industry, is at the heart of Amarillo and it features in many of its attractions, including a starring role at the Big Texan Steak Ranch.

◉ Sights

Like a good steak, Amarillo is marbled with railroad tracks. Running south of town, I-40 is especially charmless. Instead, follow SE 3rd Ave from the east to SW 6th Ave through the comatose center and decaying west side to SW 6th Ave. Locally dubbed the **San Jacinto District**, the strip between Georgia St and Western St was once part of Route 66 and is Amarillo's best shopping, dining and entertainment district.

★**Cadillac Ranch**   MONUMENT
(I-40, btwn exits 60 & 62) To millions of people whizzing across the Texas Panhandle each year, the Cadillac Ranch, also known as Amarillo's 'Bumper Crop,' is the ultimate symbol of the US love affair with wheels. A salute to Route 66 and the spirit of the American road, it was created by burying, hood first, 10 Cadillacs in a wheat field outside town.

In 1974 controversial Amarillo businessperson and arts patron Stanley Marsh funded the San Francisco–based Ant Farm collective's 'monument to the rise and fall of the Cadillac tail fin.' The cars date from 1948

to 1959 – a period in which tail fins just kept getting bigger and bigger – on to 1963, when the fin vanished. Marsh relocated the cars in 1997 to a field 2 miles west of its original location due to suburban sprawl (which is again encroaching on this location).

The cars are easily spotted off the access road on the south side of I-40. The accepted practice today is to leave your own mark on the art by drawing on the disintegrating cars, which gives them an ever-changing patina. Bring spray paint in case other visitors haven't left any around.

★**American Quarter Horse
Hall of Fame & Museum**   MUSEUM
(Map p196; ☑806-376-5181; www.aqha.com; 2601 I-40 E exit 72A; adult/child $6/2; ☺9am-5pm Mon-Sat) Quarter horses, favored on the Texas range, were originally named for their prowess at galloping down early American racetracks, which were a quarter-mile long. These beautiful animals are celebrated at this visually striking museum, which fully explores their roles in ranching and racing.

★**Amarillo Livestock Auction**   MARKET
(Map p196; ☑806-373-7464; www.amarillolive stockauction.com; 100 S Manhattan St; ☺11am Mon) A slice of the real West is on display every Monday morning at the Amarillo Livestock Auction, just north of SE 3rd Ave on the city's east side. The auction is still one of the state's largest, moving more than 100,000 animals annually (from its 1970s peak of 715,000).

Once the auction starts, things happen fast: cattle are herded in through one pneumatic gate and out through another, and most animals sell within about 30 seconds. The auctions draw few tourists, but all are welcome. Grab lunch at the Stockyard Cafe (p199).

**Wonderland
Amusement Park**   AMUSEMENT PARK
(Map p196; ☑806-383-3344; www.wonder landpark.com; 2601 Dumas Dr, off US 87 north of the centre; $17-25; ☺Apr-Aug, hours vary; ♿) If plowing along sedately for hours on the bland interstate has you ready for a little more excitement, then careening through the double loops of this park's Texas Tornado roller coaster should shake you out of your lethargy. A fun local amusement park (ignoring the hideous garden-gnome mascot), Wonderland has thrill rides, family rides and a water park. Check the online calendar for specific opening days and hours.

Amarillo

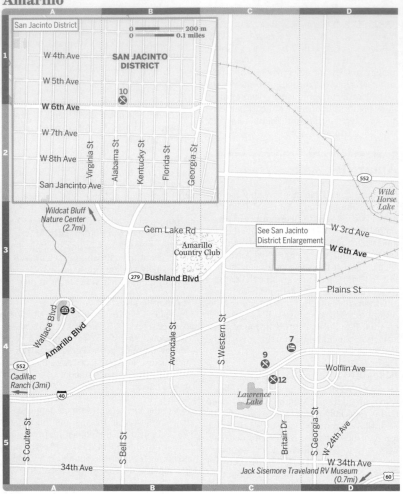

Amarillo

◉ Top Sights
1 Amarillo Livestock Auction G3
2 American Quarter Horse
  Hall of Fame &
  Museum G4

◉ Sights
3 Don Harrington Discovery
  Center A4
4 Wonderland Amusement
  Park F1

🛏 Sleeping
5 Baymont Inn & Suites Amarillo East F4
6 Best Western Santa Fe H4
7 Wyndham Garden Amarillo C4

✖ Eating
8 Crush Wine Bar & Deli G2
9 El Tejavan C4
10 Golden Light Cantina B1
11 Stockyard Cafe G3
12 Tyler's Barbeque C4

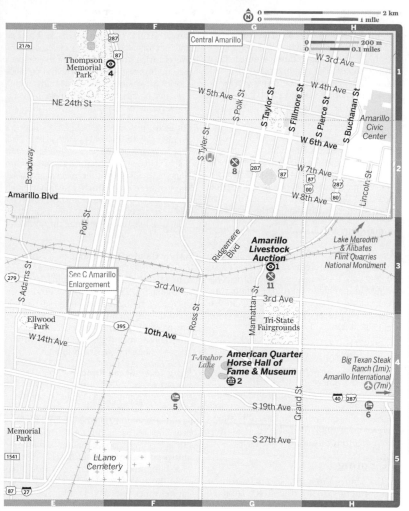

Wildcat Bluff Nature Center NATURE RESERVE
(☎806-352-6007; www.wildcatbluff.org; 2301 N Soncy Rd; adult/child $4/3; ☉dawn-dusk) Stretch those road legs at this 600-acre nature center, which has trails winding through grasslands, cottonwoods and bluffs. Spy on a prairie-dog town and try to spot a burrowing owl or porcupine while avoiding rattlesnakes and tarantulas. The center is just northwest of town, off TX 335.

Don Harrington Discovery Center MUSEUM
(Map p196; ☎806-355-9547; www.discovery centeramarillo.org; 1200 Streit Dr; adult/child $11/8; ☉9:30am-4:30pm Tue-Sat, from noon Sun; 🚻) Sadly you can't inhale any helium and talk like Donald Duck, but the lighter-than-air gas that was an Amarillo industry is honored at the Don Harrington Discovery Center. Aquariums, a planetarium and science exhibits (including a good one on birds of prey) round out a visit.

🛏 Sleeping

With the notable exception of the Big Texan Inn, most of Amarillo's motel accommodations are chains (in fact, there can't be one brand missing from the endless slew along I-40). Exits 64, 65 and 71 all have clusters.

Big Texan Inn
MOTEL **$**

(☑ 800-657-7177; www.bigtexan.com; 7700 I-40 E, exit 74; r $70-100; ✻🎧🛏🐕) The hotel part of Amarillo's star attraction has 54 rooms with fussy Old West details behind a faux heritage facade. The real highlight – besides the modest prices – is the outside pool in the shape of Texas. Should you try the huge steak challenge, even crawling across the parking lot to collapse in your room may be beyond you.

Best Western Santa Fe
MOTEL **$$**

(Map p196; ☑ 806-372-1885; www.bestwestern. com; 4600 I-40; r $80-140; 🅿✻@🎧🛏🐕) Modern motel with a large outdoor pool. Rooms are decorated with a range of greys and tans. There are indoor corridors.

Baymont Inn & Suites Amarillo East
MOTEL **$$**

(Map p196; ☑ 806-372-1425; www.hamptoninn. com; 1700 I-40 E, east of exit 71 on south side; r $60-120; ✻🎧🛏🐕) A standard outlet of the comfortable and reliable midrange chain (this was formerly a Hampton Inn). There are 116 rooms in a two-story building. Guests enjoy breakfast, a pool and a hot tub.

Wyndham Garden Amarillo
HOTEL **$$**

(Map p196; ☑ 806-358-6161; www.wyndhamhotels.com; 3100 I-40 W, near exit 68; r $100-160; ✻@🎧🛏🐕) Ignore its stark exterior (unless you're fascinated by the grain silos) and concentrate on the multitude of services offered at this chain hotel aimed at business travelers. The 263 rooms over 10 stories have numerous plush touches.

✖ Eating

At first burp, Amarillo seems awash in chain eateries along the I-40 frontage roads, but delve a little deeper to find some gems, especially along SW 6th Ave. However, don't close your eyes to everything on I-40, as Amarillo's top attraction, the Big Texan, awaits.

★ Tyler's Barbeque
BARBECUE **$**

(Map p196; ☑ 806-331-2271; http://tylersbarbeque.com; 2014 Paramount Blvd; mains $8-15; ⊙ 11am-8pm) Amarillo's favorite spot for barbecue is worth the love. The line is always long, get there early because when it sells out, it closes. The mesquite-grilled meats (the ribs and brisket are tops) are redolent with smoke. Get a seat so you can watch the west Texas sunset.

★ Golden Light Cantina
BURGERS **$**

(Map p196; ☑ 806-374-9237; www.goldenlight cafe.com; 2908 SW 6th Ave; mains $5-9; ⊙ cafe 11am-10pm, bar 4pm-2am) Classic cheeseburgers, home-cut fries, green chili stew and cold beer have sated travelers on Route 66 at this modest brick dive since 1946. On many nights there's live country and rock music in the atmospherically sweaty adjoining cantina.

El Tejavan
MEXICAN **$**

(Map p196; ☑ 806-354-2444; www.eltejavan.com; 3420 I-40 W; ⊙ 8:30am-9pm Mon-Thu, to 10pm Fri & Sat, to 4pm Sun) Enchiladas, tostadas, chili relleno and all the other usuals are here. However, here everything is just that much better. Many options include shrimp, or create your own combo plate. It may look bland on the outside, but it's all piquant on the inside, even at breakfast.

Cowboy Gelato Smokehouse
AMERICAN **$**

(☑ 806-376-5286; http://cowboygelato.com; 6103 S Coulter St; mains $5-12; ⊙ 11am-9pm Mon-Wed, to midnight Thu-Sat, 11am-3pm Sun) The Texas plains are flat as a frying pan and often just as hot. Escape the heat in this cute cafe which makes its own creamy gelatos. The recent addition of a smokehouse means that the burgers, brisket and even the pizza are smoky great.

★ Big Texan Steak Ranch
STEAK **$$**

(www.bigtexan.com; 7701 I-40 E, exit 75; mains $10-40; ⊙ 7am-10:30pm; 🎮) A classic, hokey Route 66 roadside attraction, the Big Texan made the move when I-40 opened in 1971 and has never looked back. Stretch-Cadillac limos with steer-horn hood ornaments offer free shuttles to and from area motels, marquee lights blink above, a shooting arcade pings inside the saloon, and a big, tall Tex road sign welcomes you (after taunting billboards for miles in either direction).

The legendary come-on: the 'free 72oz steak,' a devilish offer as you have to eat this enormous portion of cow plus a multitude of sides in under one hour, or you pay for the entire meal ($72). Contestants sit at a raised table to 'entertain' the other diners and you can watch anytime via a live webcam (we watched one beefy guy who started out all cocky but by the 45-minute mark was less than half done and staring glumly at the door).

Less than 10% pass the challenge, although in 2014 one ravenous lunatic (a 125lb woman named Molly Schuyler) wolfed it all down in 4 minutes 58 seconds, then ate a complete second serve by the 9:59 mark! Insane eating aside, the ranch is a fine place to eat, the steaks are excellent – and still huge. Adding to the fun are strolling cowboy troubadours, a beer garden with superb house-brewed beers and a buzzing bar. In a word, it's a hoot!

Stockyard Cafe AMERICAN **$$**
(Map p196; ☑806-374-6024; 100 S Manhattan St; mains $6-25; ☺6am-2pm Mon-Sat, to 9pm Fri) This cafe in the Amarillo Livestock Auction building is where the cattlemen sit down for some beef. The steaks are ideal – thick and perfectly churred – but most people have the plate-swamping chicken-fried steak. Follow your nose here, past corrals and railroad tracks. The dining room is no-nonsense as are the breakfasts.

Crush Wine Bar & Deli AMERICAN **$$**
(Map p196; ☑806-418-2011; www.crushdeli.com; 701 S Polk St; mains $10-33; ☺11am-11pm Mon-Thu, to 12:30am Fri & Sat) Folks in suits and skirts and cowboy boots flock here for Amarillo's best beer and wine selection plus fare that goes beyond the beefy local vibe. Salads, tapas and creative light fare are ideally enjoyed outside on the patio. Crush anchors a small nightlife district downtown.

ⓘ Information

Texas Travel Information Center (☑806-335-1441; 9700 E I-40, exit 76; ☺8am-5pm, to 6pm summer; ☺) Excellent resource, with vast amounts of info at a handy freeway rest stop

ⓘ Getting There & Away

Rick Husband Amarillo International Airport (AMA; ☑806-335-1671; http://airport.amarillo. gov; 10801 Airport Blvd) Located on the eastern edge of town, north of I-40 via exit 76. It's served by American Eagle (Dallas–Fort Worth),

DALLAS & THE PANHANDLE PLAINS AMARILLO

ROUTE 66: GET YOUR KICKS IN TEXAS

The Mother Road arrows across Texas for a mere 178 miles. The entire route has been replaced by I-40, but through frontage and access roads plus detours through towns such as Amarillo, you can recreate most of the old route.

Given the featureless landscape, one can only imagine the road ennui suffered by scores of travelers as they motored past the brown expanses. As always, there were plenty of entrepreneurs ready to offer diversions for a buck or two. Going east to west, here's some Route 66 highlights in Texas.

Follow old Route 66 which runs immediately south of I-40 from the Oklahoma border through barely changed towns such as **Shamrock**, with its restored 1930s buildings.

About 33 miles from the border, cross I-40 to the north side and the battered town of **McClean**. There, the **Devil's Rope & Route 66 Museum** (www.barbwiremuseum.com; 100 Kingsley St, McLean; ☺9am-4pm Mon-Sat Mar-Nov) **FREE** has vast barbed wire displays (where hipsters look for new tattoo patterns) and a small but homey and idiosyncratic room devoted to Route 66. The detailed map of the road in Texas is a must. Also worth a look are the moving portraits of Dust Bowl damage and the refugees from human-made environmental disaster.

You'll have to join I-40 at exit 132, but just west of here on both sides of the freeway are Route 66–themed rest stops.

The next sights will appear on the horizon long before the hamlet of **Groom** and exit 113 appear in your windshield: the famous **Leaning Water Tower** and (one of) the **World's Tallest Cross**. The former was an eye-catching gimmick by a long-gone gas station; the latter tops out at 190ft.

At exit 78 leave I-40, which runs just south of **Amarillo**, and follow SE 3rd Ave and SW 6th Ave through town. Here you'll find a plethora of Route 66 sites: the **Big Texan Steak Ranch** (p198), the historic **livestock auction** (p195) and the San Jacinto District, which still has original Route 66 businesses such as the **Golden Light Cantina** (p198).

Just west of Amarillo, after exit 62, look for the **Cadillac Ranch** (p195), where 10 road veterans have met a colorful end.

Use the old highway north of I-40 or exit 36 to reach **Vega**, an old road town that seems little changed in decades, but which still has some decent cafes. Some 14 miles west, **Adrian** clings to fame as the purported historic Route 66 midpoint, with LA and Chicago each 1139 miles distant.

Just at the New Mexico border, tiny **Glenrio** makes the moniker 'ghost town' seem lively.

WHAT THE...? RV MUSEUM

Long before today's posh gas-guzzling recreational vehicles (RVs) hit the road, laden with every convenience right down to the satellite dish, intrepid Americans looking for adventure had much simpler vehicles. This **museum** (📞 806-358-4891; www.rvmuseum.net; 4341 Canyon Dr, off I-27 south of town; ⏰ 9am-5pm Mon-Fri, to 4pm Sat) FREE at Jack Sisemore Traveland RV dealership has trailers and RVs from the 1930s to the 1970s, a time when entertainment meant watching Dad hit his head on the pint-sized door frame.

United (Houston) and Southwest (Dallas and Denver).

Greyhound (Map p196; 📞 806-374-5371; www.greyhound.com; 700 S Tyler St) Runs buses east and west on I-40 plus to major cities in Texas such as Dallas ($60, seven to nine hours, three daily).

Around Amarillo

The best sights near Amarillo are Palo Duro Canyon and the little towns along Route 66. But you can also find some natural escapes to the north.

◎ Sights & Activities

★ **Alibates Flint Quarries
National Monument** PARK
(📞 806-857-3151, 806-857-6680; www.nps.gov/alfl; Cas Johnson Rd, off TX 136, Fritch; ⏰ Contact Station 9am-4pm) FREE It's not every day you can pick up a hammer stone used to make tools 10,000 years ago or hold discarded shards of beautifully colored flint left behind by ancient peoples. But at Alibates Flint Quarries, visitors can touch the past and learn what it was like to live off the land when mammoths roamed the plains.

Tours, which are the main way to visit, involve 1.5 miles of walking. You must call to reserve these trips in advance. Otherwise, there is a short self-guided walk you can do.

**Lake Meredith National
Recreation Area** PARK
(📞 806-857-3151; www.nps.gov/lamr; visitor center 419 E Broadway St, Fritch; ⏰ 24hr) FREE Some 35 miles northeast of Amarillo, this recreation area is a result of the Sanford Dam water project on the Canadian River. It's a popular spot for boating and fishing.

Canadian

📞 806 / POP 2950

Named for the local river, Canadian has few links with the cheery country far to the north (although with locally popular Coors being owned by Molsen, you could say the convenience stores are filled with Canadian beer). Rather, it is a once-dying Texas plains town (one of dozens) that, thanks to the leadership of the local Abraham family, has uniquely saved itself by embracing tourism.

Main St – often a place to watch out for falling bricks in other small Texas towns – has been much restored; stores, cafes and a beautifully renovated movie theater are among the highlights.

Outside of town, a series of nature trails wander through the fertile countryside. In spring people come from all over to see the rather comical mating habits of the prairie chicken – antics worthy of an *Animal Planet* special.

◎ Sights

Citadelle GALLERY
(📞 806-323-8899; www.thecitadelle.org; 520 Nelson Ave; adult/child $10/free; ⏰ 11am-4pm Thu-Sat) A diverse collection of art collected around the globe and housed in a 1910 mansion. Good special exhibitions.

River Valley Pioneer Museum MUSEUM
(📞 806-323-6548; www.rivervalleymuseum.org; 118 N 2nd St; ⏰ 9am-5pm Tue-Fri) FREE This well-curated museum has exhibits that cover the history of the region, including the Kiowa, Comanche and Cheyenne tribes who once called today's Hemphill County home. You can learn about how the area was transformed by ranching and, later, oil exploration.

✖ Eating

Bucket AMERICAN $
(📞 806-323-8200; 207 S 2nd St; mains $6-9; ⏰ 7am-5pm) Diner fare is the order of the day. Good breakfasts and a long lunch menu with all the usual suspects. The front presents an old-timey facade to town. Offers baked goods like fresh bread and addictive cookies.

Houston & East Texas

Best Places to Eat

➡ Killen's Barbecue (p230)

➡ Fargo's Pit BBQ (p239)

➡ Royers Cafe (p236)

➡ Original Ninfas (p217)

➡ Buttermilk's (p243)

Best Places to Sleep

➡ Hotel ZaZa Houston (p213)

➡ Lancaster Hotel (p212)

➡ LaSalle Hotel (p238)

➡ White Oak Manor B&B (p245)

Why Go?

More down-home than Dallas, more buttoned-up than Austin, Houston has money and culture, but wears them like a good ol' country boy come to town. What's that mean? Award-winning, chef-run restaurants where ties are rarely required. Attending world-class museum exhibits followed by cheap beer at patio bars. Enclaves of attraction spread all across the state's largest – and widest – city.

When you get sick of the concrete maze of interstates, it's easy to escape. Within day-trip distance you can visit NASA and the place where Texas won its independence. Washington County entices antique hunters, history buffs and anyone who just loves beautiful, rural countryside. Further afield, northeast Texas *is* the Piney Woods, with towering forests, winding roads, natural attractions and Southern belle historic towns like Jefferson and Nacogdoches.

As you wander the back roads, keep your nose at the ready to follow the scent of superb barbecue and chicken-fried steak.

When to Go
Houston

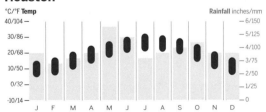

| **Mar & Apr** | **Oct** Temperatures | **Dec** Towns go all |
Mar & Apr Azaleas and bluebonnets in bloom; not-too-hot weather with lower humidity.

Oct Temperatures crawl down from summer highs; it's small-town festival time.

Dec Towns go all out for Christmas with light shows, festivals, even outdoor ice-skating.

Houston & East Texas Highlights

1 Patio Drinking (p225) Kicking back on a shady patio, drink at hand, in an atmospheric Houston bar like Porch Swing Pub.

2 Buffalo Bayou Park (p204) Exploring this newly gussied up park, which is surprisingly naturalistic, in the very heart of Houston.

3 Space Center Houston (p230) Pondering what was, what might have been and what still could be at the heart of NASA's US space program.

4 Jefferson (p244) Ghost hunting in this former riverboat town with buildings dating back to the 1840s.

5 Nacogdoches (p240) Exploring this old pioneer town on foot.

6 Caddo Lake (p246) Boating among the mysterious cypress trees on this labyrinthine lake.

7 Round Top (p235) Browsing, and maybe buying, at the enormous antiques fair or simply having a great lunch.

HOUSTON

📞 281, 713, 832 / POP 2.2 MILLION

Think laid-back, pick-up truck and boot-scooting town meets high-powered, high-cultured and high-heeled metropolis. During the day, chill out in your flip-flops, take in museums and go shopping, then hit happy hour on a leaf-shaded deck. At night, revel in culinary or cultural bliss – the restaurant and entertainment scene are renowned across the region. Here starched jeans are de rigueur in all but the very fanciest of restaurants.

Diverse residential neighborhoods and enclaves of restaurants and shops spread far and wide. Where residents of other cities talk about the weather, Houstonians talk about parking. Wealth from oil and energy companies supports luxurious shopping areas but you can also enjoy down-home fun, although don't underestimate the sauna-like summers. Don't forget that one of the town's main attractions – NASA's Space Center Houston in Clear Lake – is outside the city limits, a 30-minute drive down I-45.

History

The two most important words in Houston's history are 'oil' and 'cattle.' But the city's spectacular growth would never have happened without two others: 'air' and 'conditioning.' Until the 1930s, Houston was a sleepy regional center with a population under 100,000. Thus you'll find relatively few historic buildings here. Once air-conditioning became available on a widespread basis, the population jumped; by 1960 it numbered nearly a million.

From the 1970s through 1990s, the city's fortunes followed the price per barrel of oil: boom, then bust. The area's business base diversified to include the medical services, high-tech and space industries. Throughout the 2000s, Houston's economic growth continued, attracting a diverse, multicultural population. Over 200,000 New Orleans residents resettled in Houston after Huricane Katrina in 2005, which has added even more to the strong Creole and Cajun influences in the city.

In 2009 Annise Parker was elected as the first openly lesbian mayor of a large US city. She served three terms until 2016 when term limits prevented her from running again (she'd been hugely popular). She was replaced by Sylvester Turner, a longtime African American politician.

◎ Sights

Despite Houston's general sprawl, most of the areas of interest for visitors lie north or south of I-59 in the 10 miles between the Galleria area and the city center. The largest concentration of attractions is in the Museum District. But don't overlook downtown and the many delights of Buffalo Bayou.

Remember that shopping, eating and drinking in neighborhoods like eclectic Montrose or the historic Heights are also local attractions.

◎ Downtown

You'll see few pedestrians braving the hot downtown sidewalks as underground air-conditioned pedestrian tunnels link most downtown buildings. However there's plenty to explore at street level and along the river.

★ **Buffalo Bayou Park**   PARK
(Map p218; 📞 713-752-0314; http://buffalobayou. org; Shepherd Dr to Sabine St, btwn Allen Pkwy & Memorial Dr; ⊙ dawn-dusk most areas) This newly developed sinuous 160-acre park follows Buffalo Bayou west from downtown. There are numerous parking areas and you can walk here from many points. There are areas for exercise, contemplation, art exhibits and much more. The views back to downtown are striking. Activities here include kayak tours with Bayou City Adventures (p211) and bike rentals with Bike Barn Bayou Rental (p211).

Discovery Green   PARK
(Map p214; www.discoverygreen.com; 1500 McKinney St; ⊙ 6am-11pm; 🚻; 🚇 Convention District) Your place to frolic downtown. This 12-acre park has a lake, playground, fountains to splash in, outdoor art, restaurants and a performance space. The Green has become a hub for festivals and activities such as movies on the green, nighttime flea markets – even a Christmas-time ice rink. Check the online calendar for more.

Market Square Park   PARK
(Map p214; www.marketsquarepark.com; 301 Milam St; ⊙ 6am-11pm; 🚇 Preston) FREE You can get a real feel for old Houston from the 19th-century buildings that line two sides of the square, the historical center of downtown. A few restaurants line the square, including La Carafe (p223) in the historic 1848 Kennedy Trading Post building, and

QUIRKY HOUSTON: ART CARS & BEER CAN HOUSES

Conservative Houston has a quirky, creative streak – one the **Orange Show Center for Visionary Art** (Map p206; 713-926-6368; www.orangeshow.org; 2401 Munger St; adult/child $5/free; noon-5pm Wed-Sun Jun-Sep, shorter hours other times) fosters with a few oddball museums and one fabulous parade.

The late Jeff McKissack spent decades molding his house into a junk-art tribute to his favorite fruit. Today the giant, welded steel oranges and plastic flower art takes up a mazelike 300 sq ft at the Orange Show Center.

Meanwhile, is it a house or is it a sculpture? More than 50,000 aluminum cans cover the **Beer Can House** (Map p218; 713-926-6368; www.beercanhouse.org; 222 Malone St, off Memorial Dr; adult/child $5/free; noon-5pm Wed-Sun Jun-Sep, shorter hours other times) as siding, as edging, as wind chimes. It's worth buying a self guide booklet or taking a tour to learn more. Either way, don't miss the video on the house's history.

If you're not in town for the fabulous **Houston Art Car Parade** (p211) in April, the next best thing is to view a few of the decorated vehicles at the **Art Car Museum** (Map p206; 713-861-5526; www.artcarmuseum.com; 140 Heights Blvd; 11am-6pm Wed-Sun) **FREE**. The handful of art cars represented here are all wild examples of why you should try to be in town for the parade. Check out the quirky-cool rotating exhibits, which have included subjects such as road refuse and bone art but also serious exhibits by noted contemporary artists.

---

there's a cafe in the park. In summer the small green space plays host to concerts and outdoor movies.

Allen's Landing Park   PARK
(Map p214; 1001 Commerce St; Preston) Named after Houston's founders, Allen's Landing marks the spot on Buffalo Bayou where Houston's settlement began. So far the original wharf has been improved with concrete paths and grassy lawns that offer great walking and views. Check with Bayou City Adventures (p211) for kayak tours that take in the downtown sights.

Heritage Society at
Sam Houston Park   MUSEUM
(Map p214; 713-655-1912; www.heritagesociety. org; 1100 Bagby St; museum free, tours adult/child $15/6; museum 10am-4pm Tue-Sun, tours 10am, 11:30am, 1pm & 2:30pm; Main St Sq) **FREE** Take a free tour using your phone around the 10 historic homes and buildings that have been moved to this park. Among them, the **Yates House** (1870) is the home of a freed slave who became a prominent local preacher, and the **Old Place** (1823) a log cabin thought to be the town's oldest. Guided tours get you inside.

Montrose & Museum District

Museum-lovers, you've hit the jackpot in the area north around Hermann Park. To get full details of all 19 museums or to plot

your route, check out the Houston Museum District (www.houstonmuseumdistrict.org) website.

★ Hermann Park   PARK
(Map p218; 713-524-5876; www.hermannpark. org; Fannin St & Hermann Park Dr; 6am-11pm; Hermann Park/Rice U) This 445-acre park is home to playgrounds, a lake with paddleboats, a picturesque **Japanese Garden**, the **Hermann Park Miniature Train** (Map p218; 713-526-2183; www.hermannpark.org; 6104 Hermann Park Dr, Kinder Station, Lake Plaza; per ride $3.50; 10am-6pm; ; Hermann Park/Rice U) and the **Houston Zoo** (Map p218; 713-533-6500; www.houstonzoo.org; 6200 Hermann Park Dr; adult/child $18/14; 9am-7pm; Memorial Hermann Hospital/Houston Zoo). It offers shady walks under mature old oak trees and there are some lovely formal gardens. Don't miss the recently opened McGovern Centennial Gardens (p210).

On many nights during much of the year, you can enjoy a performance or concert for free on the lawn at the open-air Miller Outdoor Theatre (p226).

★ Houston Museum of
Natural Science   MUSEUM
(Map p218; 713-639-4629; www.hmns.org; 5555 Hermann Park Dr; adult/child $25/15, free Thu 2-5pm; 9am-5pm; ; Hermann Park/Rice U) World-class traveling exhibits – on everything from prehistoric cave paintings

HOUSTON & EAST TEXAS HOUSTON

Greater Houston

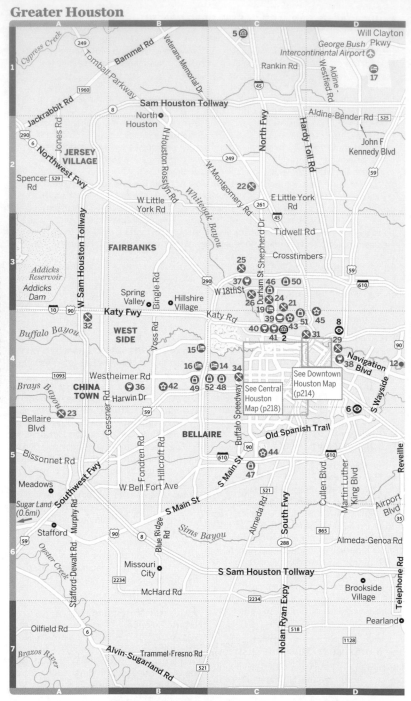

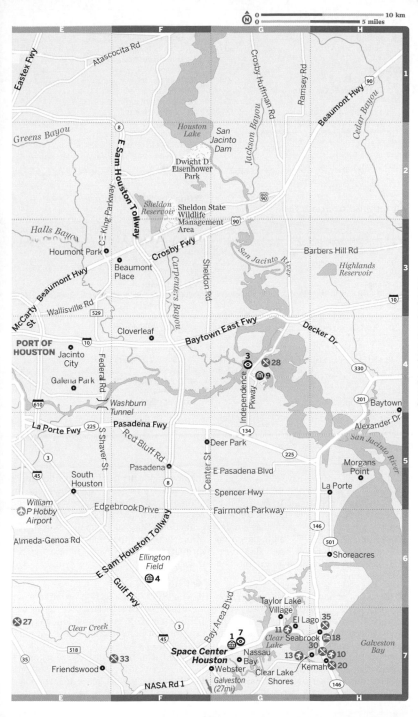

Greater Houston

to Mayan civilization – have always been a big part of the attraction at this stellar museum, the most popular in Texas. The permanent collection is no less impressive, with massive dinosaur skeletons (the curator advised on *Jurassic Park*), mummies from ancient Egypt, rare gems (like a 2000-carat blue topaz) and interactive exhibits on earth's biosphere.

★ **Menil Collection**   MUSEUM
(Map p218; ☑ 713-525-9400; www.menil.org; 1533 Sul Ross St; ⊙ 11am-7pm Wed-Sun) FREE The Menil Collection houses over 17,000 artworks and objects, including more than 10,000 works of art, sculpture and archaeological artifacts that John and Dominique de Menil collected during their lives. The modernist building, designed by Renzo Piano, houses

rotating highlights from their extraordinary collection – everything from 5000-year-old antiquities to works by Kara Walker, René Magritte and today's art stars – plus rotating exhibitions. Don't forget to also visit the Cy Twombly Gallery (p210) and the serene and meditative Rothko Chapel, annexes of the collection.

★ **Rothko Chapel**   MUSEUM
(Map p218; ☑ 713-524-9839; www.rothkochapel. org; 3900 Yupon St at Sul Ross St; ⊙ 10am-6pm) FREE A temple of contemplation, a church or brutalist architecture? The Rothko Chapel and its serene grounds is whatever you want it to be. With 14 large paintings by American abstract expressionist Mark Rothko, it's a perfect place to pause and meditate.

Walking Tour
Buffalo Bayou

START ALLEN'S LANDING PARK
END KITCHEN AT THE DUNLAVY
LENGTH 3½ MILES; THREE HOURS

To avoid the heat, do this walk in the morning. Start where Houston began at **1 Allen's Landing Park** (p205) on Buffalo Bayou. Stay at water level here and begin walking west on the south side of the muddy waters of Buffalo Bayou. Recent work has resulted in a curvaceous network of walking and biking paths along the bayou. Down here, the Houston skyline soars overhead while a vast tangle of elevated highways and bridges attest to the local love of the automobile.

After a half mile pause for a rest amid the fountains of **2 Sesquicentennial Park.** Now walk up to street level and follow Smith St southwest for three blocks until you get to an often-overlooked local landmark: **3 Tranquility Park**. Highly stylized, it is meant to evoke a sense of the moon's surface through raised features and water. Look for the plaques recalling the mission of *Apollo 11*, which was controlled just down the road at NASA.

Exit the southwest corner of the park and walk one block northwest on Walker St where you can descend steps down to the Buffalo Bayou path.

Walk generally west along the slow-moving water for about a quarter-mile until you reach the Sabine St bridge. Cross north and stop off at the **4 Water Works**, a former utility building that's the de facto headquarters of Buffalo Bayou Park and which offers refreshments, galleries, park information, bike rental and more.

Stay on the north side of the bayou and walk the curving paths west. Stop to smell the flowers at various meadows and botanical features. Pause to look back at the Houston skyline. After 1.5 miles, you'll reach the lush **5 Green Tree Nature Area**, where you can spot dozens of bird species and appreciate the original vegetation of the area.

Cross back south on the Waugh Dr Bridge and turn west. After a short distance you'll see the cool waters of the restored **6 Lost Lake**. Nearby you can get refreshments of all kinds at **7 Kitchen at The Dunlavy** (p217).

WHAT THE...?
FUNERAL MUSEUM

'Any day above ground is a good one.' That's the trademark of the **National Museum of Funeral History** (Map p206; www.nmfh.org; 415 Barren Springs Dr; adult/child \$10/7; ☺10am-4pm Mon-Fri, to 5pm Sat, noon-5pm Sun). If you've ever wanted to see a coffin collection that includes a casket made of money, literally, or one that's crab-shaped, now's your chance. Exhibits cover embalming, famous memorials and historical hearses. Halloween would seem a good time to check out the Day of the Dead festival room.

McGovern Centennial Gardens   PARK

(Map p218; ☑713-524-5876; www.hermannpark.org; off Hermann Dr, Hermann Park; ☺9am-5pm, later in summer; ☒Museum District) FREE These recently opened gardens have a spiral climbing hill that affords views of the construction cranes poking up through the skyline. It also has extensive botanical and sculpture gardens with notables such as Martin Luther King.

Holocaust Museum Houston   MUSEUM

(☑713-942-8000; www.hmh.org; 5401 Caroline St; adult/child \$12/free; ☺9am-5pm Mon-Fri, 10am-5pm Sat, noon-5pm Sun; ☒Museum District) A superbly curated and presented museum offers an in-depth education on the context, history and aftermath of not only the holocaust itself but of Nazi Germany's terrifying rise to power. Other exhibits trace the lives of Houston-connected European Jews and focus on the rescue efforts made by the Danish.

Due to damage sustained from Hurricane Harvey, the museum is operating out of a temporary site (9220 Kirby Dr) until late 2018. Call ahead before visiting.

Museum of Fine Arts, Houston   MUSEUM

(Map p218; ☑713-639-7300; www.mfah.org; 1001 Bissonnet St; adult/child \$18/free, Thu free; ☺10am-5pm Tue & Wed, to 9pm Thu, to 7pm Fri & Sat, 12:15-7pm Sun; ☒Museum District) French impressionism, the Renaissance and post-1945 European and American painting really shine in this nationally renowned palace of art, which includes major works by Picasso and Rembrandt. Across the street, admire the talents of luminaries such as Rodin and Matisse in the associated **Lillie & Hugh Roy Cullen Sculpture Garden**

(Map p218; cnr Montrose Blvd & Bissonnet St; ☺9am-10pm) FREE.

A vast new expansion to house modern art is on tap for 2019.

Cy Twombly Gallery   MUSEUM

(Map p218; ☑713-525-9450; www.menil.org; 1501 Branard St; ☺11am-7pm Wed-Sun) FREE This annex of the Menil Collection contains some of the most notable works by its namesake abstract artist. Twombly (1928–2011) first became famous in New York in the 1950s for his bold and lush works.

Contemporary Arts
Museum Houston   MUSEUM

(CAMH; Map p218; ☑713-284-8250; www.camh.org; 5216 Montrose Blvd; ☺10am-7pm Tue-Fri, to 9pm Thu, to 6pm Sat, noon-6pm Sun; ☒Museum District) FREE One of Houston's epicenters of what's cool, new and cutting edge. Immerse yourself in ongoing special exhibitions at a museum whose strength is its lack of a permanent collection.

Asia Society Texas Center   ARTS CENTER

(Map p218; ☑713-496-9901; http://asiasociety.org/texas; 1370 Southmore Blvd; building free, exhibits \$5; ☺11am-6pm Tue-Fri, 10am-6pm Sat & Sun; ☒Museum District) The contemporary architecture of the Asia Center building, complete with infinity pool and hourly misty fog, is as impressive as its changing exhibits. Check the schedule for Asian-community-related events and art exhibitions.

◉ Further Afield

Saint Arnold Brewery   BREWERY

(Map p206; ☑713-686-9494; www.saintarnold.com; 2000 Lyons Ave; tours \$10; ☺beer hall 11am-4:30pm Mon-Thu, to 10pm Fri, to 3pm Sat) The beer hall at Houston's most famous craft brewery overlooks the production area and is freely open for drinking and eating. Tours are usually offered at various times during the day.

Bayou Bend Collection & Gardens   MUSEUM

(Map p218; ☑713-639-7750; www.mfah.org; 6003 Memorial Dr; tours adult/child \$12.50/6.25, gardens only \$7.50/5; ☺10am-5pm Tue-Sat, 1-5pm Sun) The Museum of Fine Arts, Houston curates the impressive historical decorative arts collection (1600s to 1850s) displayed here. The 1928 home belonged to Ms Ima Hogg, a well-known Houston civic leader and generous philanthropist. (As the joke goes, you know you're from Houston if you can say Ima Hogg without laughing.) Tours include admission to 14 acres of gardens. It's west of downtown on the north side of Buffalo Bayou.

Lone Star Flight Museum MUSEUM
(Map p206; ☏346-708-2517; http://lsfm.org; Ellington Airport, 11551 Aerospace Ave) This museum, relocated from Galveston, where the collection was battered by Hurricane Ike in 2008, is south of Houston at the former Ellington Air Force Base. It should have opened in new $40-million hangars by the time you read this. It will feature over 25 restored warplanes, including an iconic B-17 and B-25 from WWII.

🏃 Activities

Bike Barn Bayou Rental CYCLING
(Map p218; ☏713-955-4455; http://bikebarn.com; 105 Sabine St, Buffalo Bayou Park, Water Works; rentals per hour from $9; ☺10am-dusk daily summer, weekends only other times) Buffalo Bayou Park and the surrounding areas are fine places to bike. Rent and get advice here.

👉 Tours

Texana Tours TOURS
(☏281-772-9526; www.texanatours.com; rates vary) To get to grips with Houston in just three hours, take this fascinating tour with a born-and-bred Houstonite which takes in most significant neighborhoods and offers a mine of intriguing city facts. Other tours venture further afield to some of the rural state parks and NASA. Rates vary depending on group size.

Bayou City Adventures KAYAKING
(Map p218; ☏713-538-7433; http://bayoucity adventures.org; 3324 Allen Pkwy; kayak tours from $30, ☺10am-5pm Tue-Sun) Explore Buffalo Bayou and the downtown waterways by kayak. Rentals and shuttles are available. For the uninitiated we recommend taking a kayak tour of the Houston skyline area or one further afield and more extreme. Advance reservations required.

Sam Houston Boat Tours BOATING
(Map p206; ☏713-670-2416; www.portofhouston. com; 7300 Clinton Ave; ☺tours 10:30am & 2:30pm Wed, Fri & Sat, 2:30pm Sun) FREE Sir back for 90-minute boat tours of one of the largest ports in the USA; reserve in advance. Besides huge container ships, you'll see seemingly endless chemical plants and tankers.

Segway Tours of Houston TOURS
(☏866-673-4929; http://segwaytoursofhouston. com; 2hr tour $80) Discover Houston's history or cruise through Buffalo Bayou Park on guided tours on Segways, the geeky self-balancing personal transporters. Reservations required; confirm start location when you book.

Houston Urban Adventures TOURS
(☏832-992-3179; www.houstonurbanadventures. com; tours from $35) Eclectic tour offerings include a trip through Houston's tunnel system and a downtown pub crawl. Advance reservations required.

Houston Culinary Tours FOOD & DRINK
(☏713-853-8100; www.visithoustontexas.com; tours from $180) Monthly foodie adventures are led by local chefs and food celebrities. Book well in advance.

🎉 Festivals & Events

Houston Livestock Show & Rodeo RODEO
(☏832-667-1714; www.rodeohouston.com; NRG Center, 3 NRG Pkwy; event tickets from $18; ☺Feb or Mar; 🅿Reliant Park) For three weeks beginning in late February or early March, rodeo fever takes over Houston. The barbecue cook-off is a hot seller but so are the nightly rodeos followed by big-name concerts. Buy tickets far in advance. Fairgrounds-only admission gets you access to midway rides, livestock shows, shopping and nightly dances.

It's held in the vast complex that includes Reliant Stadium and the old Astrodome. Note: animal-welfare groups say many rodeo practices are harmful for animals. Some events might be difficult for sensitive viewers.

Azalea Trail CULTURAL
(☏713-523-2483; www.riveroaksgardenclub.org; per site $10; ☺Mar) Named for the spectacular flowering shrubs in bloom at each location at this time of year. Six or more historic homes and gardens are opened for tours one weekend in March. Save money with an advance ticket good for all sites ($25).

Bayou City Art Festival ART
(☏713-521-0133; www.artcolonyassociation.org; ☺late Mar & mid-Oct) FREE Hundreds of artists sell their wares, and there's a festive array of musicians and food. This popular biannual festival takes places in Memorial Park each March, and downtown each October.

★Houston Art Car Parade PARADE
(www.thehoustonartcarparade.com; along Smith St, downtown; ☺2nd Sat Apr) Wacky, arted-out vehicles (think *Mad Max*, giant gerbils and more) hit the streets en masse at the city's

top alt event. The parade is complemented by weekend-long festivities, including concerts and a legendary ball (buy tickets well in advance).

Pride Houston   LGBT
(☑ 713-529-6979; www.pridehouston.org; ☺ mid-Jun) One of the largest LGBT parades in the southwest. Weeklong citywide events culminate in a grand parade downtown when 1000-plus participants entertain with colorful floats, costumes and music.

Juneteenth Emancipation
Celebration   CULTURAL
(http://juneteenthfest.com; Emancipation Park, 3018 Dowling St; ☺ mid-Jun) This celebration of African American culture, with plenty of gospel, jazz and blues, takes place at Emancipation Park around June 19 – the day in 1865 when word reached Texas that slaves had been emancipated.

The park marks the site where African Americans gathered to celebrate emancipation in 1865; for many years during segregation, it was the only Houston park blacks could use. It's now been beautifully restored and improved.

Fiestas Patrias   CULTURAL
(☑ 713-926-2636; www.visithoustontexas.com; ☺ Sep) This September 16 festival features a parade, a ball, street music and dance performances in celebration of Mexican Independence Day.

🛌 Sleeping

A few Houston hotels stand out, but the vast majority of sleeping spots are generic chains. Generally the further out you get, the cheaper the motel. However, this may entail spending your nights near the roar of the interstate, with long drives into town.

Accommodation-sharing and vacation-rental sites offer the best options if you want to stay close to action and avoid always having to drive – and park – your car. Stay downtown and you'll be walking distance to the Theater District, Market Sq or the light rail. Around the I-59 corridor between downtown and the Galleria, in Midtown, Montrose and the Museum District, you're well located for museums, shops and restaurants.

🛌 Downtown

⭐**Lancaster Hotel**   HISTORIC HOTEL **$$**
(Map p214; ☑ 713-228-9500; www.thelancaster.com; 701 Texas Ave; r from $120; P ❄ @ 🛜 🐾; 🚇 Preston) Original marble and old-fashioned decor make this gracious nine-story hotel feel more like London than Houston. Built in 1926, the hotel has been thoughtfully maintained through the years. A real antidote to chain drabbery.

Due to damage sustained in August 2017 from Hurricane Harvey, the hotel is closed temporarily. Call ahead before visiting.

Aloft Houston Downtown   HOTEL **$$**
(Map p214; ☑ 713-225-0200; www.alofthouston downtown.com; 820 Fannin St; r from $150;

HOUSTON FOR KIDS

Young 'uns gettin' restless? There's a great place to play right downtown, **Discovery Green** (p204). Think playgrounds, play fountains, fun art and a kid-friendly restaurant.

In the museum district, **Hermann Park** (p205) is home to playgrounds, a lake with paddleboats and the **Hermann Park Miniature Train** (p205). More than 4500 animals inhabit the semitropical, 55-acre **Houston Zoo** (p205), also in the park. Activities include wildlife talks catering to different age groups and summertime zoo sleepovers. Don't miss feeding the giraffes daily at 11am and 2pm.

Walking distance from Hermann Park you'll find the high-octane, stupendously fun **Children's Museum of Houston** (Map p218; www.cmhouston.org; 1500 Binz St; $12; ☺ 10am-6pm Tue-Sat, to 8pm Thu, noon-6pm Sun; 🚇 Museum District), where little ones can make tortillas in a Mexican village, or draw in an open-air art studio. A few blocks away, future surgeons will like checking out the huge organs on display at the interactive **Health Museum** (Map p218; ☑ 713-521-1515; www.mhms.org; 1515 Hermann Dr; adult/child $10/8; ☺ 9am-5pm Mon-Sat, to 7pm Thu, noon-5pm Sun; 🚇 Museum District).

Looking for a way to beat the summer heat? Take the kids to **Ice at the Galleria** (Map p206; ☑ 713-621-1500; www.iceatthegalleria.com; 5015 Westheimer Rd, Galleria Mall; admission $8, skate rental $3.50; ☺ 10am-5pm & 7-10pm Mon-Thu, 10am-10pm Fri, 11am-10pm Sat, noon-8pm Sun; 👶). Yes, that's right, there's an ice rink right in the center of the city's biggest mall.

P ❋ 🔊 📶; 🚇Central Station) Another hotel conversion of a historic commercial building downtown, the Aloft (a Marriott brand) has modly decorated rooms across 10 floors. It's been much remodelled over the years, so don't expect period charm, rather look for trendy design details as exemplified by the hipster motif on the delightful rooftop pool.

Sam Houston Hotel　　BOUTIQUE HOTEL **$$**
(Map p214; 📞832-200-8800; www.thesam houstonhotel.com; 1117 Prairie St; r $110-200; P ❋ @ 📶 ❄; 🚇Preston) Sleek yet low-key, the smallish rooms at this historic 1924 10-story property have a contemporary decor done in all-grey. Rooms have luxe features like plush towels, gourmet coffeemakers and more, which are a far cry from its roots as a budget hotel for traveling salesmen. It's part of the Hilton conglomerate.

Magnolia Hotel　　BOUTIQUE HOTEL **$$**
(Map p214; 📞713-221-0011; www.magnoliahotel houston.com; 1100 Texas Ave; r from $140; P ❋ @ 📶 ❄; 🚇Central Station) Layered in luxurious velvet and damask, the 314 rooms in this downtown hotel are both stylish *and* comfortable. Built in 1926, this landmark building housed the *Houston Post* newspaper and later was the US corporate offices for Shell.

Club Quarters　　HOTEL **$$**
(Map p214; 📞713-224-6400; http://clubquarters hotels.com; 720 Fannin St; r from $100; P ❋ @ 📶; 🚇Main St Sq) There are 16 floors with 382 rooms in this vintage hotel downtown. The prices are very good value and the location is excellent. Some rooms have kitchenettes.

Hotel Icon　　BOUTIQUE HOTEL **$$$**
(Map p214; 📞713-224-4266; www.hotelicon.com; 220 Main St; r from $290; P ❋ @ 📶; 🚇Preston) You can feel the history in this hotel's ornate red-and-gold lobby. Originally a landmark bank building, there is a 1911 bank-vault reception area, soaring marble columns and coffered ceilings. Take the antique elevator up to modern-chic rooms. It's part of the Marriott empire.

🛏 Midtown, Montrose & Museum District

Morty Rich Hostel　　HOSTEL **$**
(Map p218; 📞713-636-9776; www.hiusa.org/houston; 501 Lovett Blvd; dm from $32, r $85; P ❋ @ 📶 ❄; 🚇Ensemble/HCC) A lavish Montrose mansion (a previous mayor's residence) hosts this plush Hosteling Interna-

tional (HI) member. The rooms are bright and clean, with four to eight simple beds per dorm, many with en suite. There's also one private double (book well ahead). Hang out in the billiard room or cool off in the backyard pool after a hard day's sightseeing. Accessible via public transport.

⭐La Maison in Midtown　　INN **$$**
(Map p218; 📞713-529-3600; http://lamaisonmid town.com; 2800 Brazos St; r $170-230; P ❋ 📶; 🚇McGowen Station) Relaxing on the wraparound porch while taking skyline views or enjoying a breakfast feast, you'll feel the Southern hospitality at this purpose-built, urban inn. The seven rooms are individually decorated, and all have elevator access. Includes breakfast.

Palms on West Main　　B&B **$$**
(Map p218; 📞713-522-7987; www.palmsonwest main.com; 807 W Main St; r from $100; P ❋ 📶) In a lovely older neighborhood, this B&B offers three rooms in a 1914 Dutch-colonial-style home. Relax on the broad porch and enjoy the personalized hospitality of the owners. Rooms have many antiques and eclectic decor.

**Extended Stay America –
Greenway Plaza**　　MOTEL **$$**
(Map p218; 📞713-521-0060; www.extendedstay america.com; 2330 Southwest Fwy (I-59); r from $100; P ❋ 📶) A multistory, interior-access chain motel on the I-69 freeway. Nothing is a far drive, and the restaurants of Upper Kirby and those of Rice Village are just a couple miles away. Rooms are bare bones but have kitchen facilities.

⭐Hotel ZaZa Houston　　BOUTIQUE HOTEL **$$$**
(Map p218; 📞713-526-1991; www.hotelzaza.com; 5701 Main St; r from $250; P ❋ @ 📶 ❄; 🚇Museum District) Hip, flamboyant and fabulous. From the bordello-esque colors to zebra accent chairs, everything about Hotel ZaZa is good fun – and surprisingly unpretentious. Our favorite rooms are the concept suites such as the eccentric Geisha House, or the space-age 'Houston We Have a Problem.' You can't beat the location overlooking the Museum district's Hermann Park, near the tram.

La Colombe d'Or Hotel　　LUXURY HOTEL **$$$**
(Map p218; 📞713-524-7999; www.lacolombe-dor.com; 3410 Montrose Blvd; ste from $300; P ❋ 📶) Not unlike the famed Colombe d'Or in Provence (no relation), this guesthouse offers nicely designed rooms and a

Downtown Houston

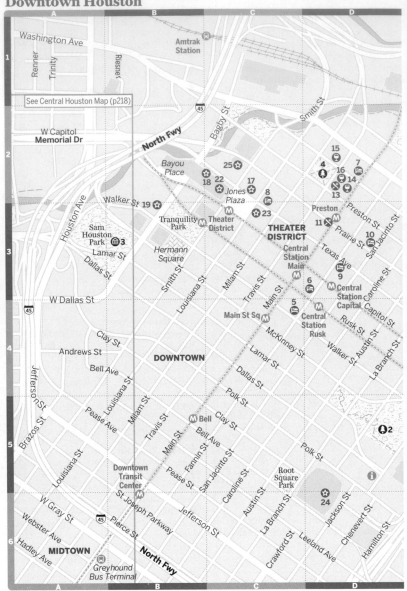

good French restaurant. Each of the five exquisite, one-bedroom suites were inspired by the colors and styles of a great artist – think Cezanne, Van Gogh, Renoir. This 1923 Montrose mansion has a museum-like feel (the art on display is conveniently for sale). There are also nine villas.

It's 1 mile west of Ensemble/HCC metrorail station.

label. It's in a glossy, glassy highrise close to the Galleria and River Oaks. Get one of the 312 rooms on a high floor for a view.

**Hotel Indigo Houston
at the Galleria**　　　　　BOUTIQUE HOTEL **$$**
(Map p206; ☑713-621-8988; www.uptown houstonhotel.com; 5160 Hidalgo St; r from $180; P✳@�widehat) Hotel Indigo is a large six-story hotel near the Galleria. It is part of Hilton's midrange Indigo brand. Rooms are bright and have small fridges.

Hotel Granduca　　　　　LUXURY HOTEL **$$$**
(Map p206; ☑713-418-1000; www.granduca houston.com; 1080 Uptown Park Blvd; r from $230;

🛏 Galleria

Hotel Derek　　　　　BOUTIQUE HOTEL **$$**
(Map p206; ☑713-961-3000; www.hotelderek.com; 2525 West Loop S; r $100-300; P✳@�widehat❄🐾) Urban chic or accessible elegance, pick your

(P ❄ @ 🛜 🏊) Expect some vague notions of Tuscan style with a Texan welcome. Graduca was inspired by a Duke's palazzo, so rooms are luxe and the pool area is a garden oasis. In Uptown Park, the hotel is close enough to the Galleria (with free transport to it), yet a bit removed from the mad traffic.

🛏 Houston Heights

Sara's Inn on the Boulevard INN $$
(Map p206; ☎713-868-1130; www.saras.com; 941 Heights Blvd; r $150-250; P ❄ @ 🛜) A 100-year-old Queen Anne Victorian feels right at home among the historic houses of the Heights. Eleven airy rooms say 'boutique hotel' more than 'frilly B&B.' The inn has a sprawling Southern porch that's been welcoming guests for three decades.

🛏 Airport

Houston Airport Marriott BUSINESS HOTEL $$
(Map p206; ☎281-443-2310; www.marriott.com; 18700 JFK Blvd; r from $180; P 🔄 @ 🛜 🏊) This 1970s concrete creation couldn't be closer to George Bush Intercontinental Airport because it's *in* George Bush Intercontinental Airport. Splash in the outdoor pool while jets roar overhead.

✖ Eating

Houston's restaurant scene is the city's most vibrant feature. Locals love to eat out and you'll find everything from comforting Tex-Mex to smokin' barbecue to inventive bistros run by top chefs. Most areas of the city have good options.

To keep track of the latest, check out the features and listings at *Texas Monthly* as well as www.thrillist.com/houston, www.houston.eater.com and http://houstonfoodblog.com.

✖ Downtown

Downtown dining is on the upswing as more hotels open in renovated office buildings. There are some excellent restaurants in the gentrifying streets of the Warehouse District or East End (EaDo) just east of the center.

★ Stanton's City Bites BURGERS $
(Map p206; ☎713-227-489; www.stantonscitybites.com; 1420 Edwards St; mains $6-12; ⊙11am-8pm Tue-Sat, to 4pm Sun; 🛜 ♿) In a town where the competition for best burger is tough, Stanton's is always on the A-list, with big, stacked juicy burgers. The chipotle option has spicy zing. Besides beer and wine, there's a range of interesting craft-made soft drinks and sodas.

Local Foods AMERICAN $
(Map p214; ☎713-227-0531; www.houstonlocalfoods.com; 420 Main St; mains $8-16; ⊙10am-8pm; 🚇Preston) It didn't take long for this collection of cafes to become a Houston institution. The downtown location serves up all the fare that's won over a legion of customers. The curried-egg-salad sandwich served on artisan-baked bread is but one of the fresh and flavorful faves. Kale and

---

ON THE GO: HOUSTON FOOD TRUCKS

Unlike in some other cities, food trucks in Houston really move. You might see the same one in two or three places on the same day. Check online for their latest locations, but they're often near bars and cafes in Montrose. The **Menil Collection** (p208) and **Museum of Fine Arts, Houston** (p210) parking lots are also frequent stopovers. Note: you'll rarely see them downtown because of parking regulations.

Oh My Gogi! (Map p218; ☎281-694-4644; www.ohmygogi.com; 5555 Morningside Dr; mains $3-8; ⊙9pm-3am Wed-Sat; 🚇Dryden/TMC) A fusion of two local cultures: try Korean barbecue tacos or kimchi quesadillas. This truck is perfectly situated for the Rice University bars.

Tacos Tierra Caliente (Map p218; ☎713-584-9359; 2003 W Alabama St; mains $2-5; ⊙8:30am-11pm Mon-Sat, to 10pm Sun) Some of Houston's best tacos in the city are served piled high from a battered food truck (try the pastor – spicy roast pork). Although there's nowhere to sit, just across the road is the West Alabama Ice House. A fine spot for a taco feast while nursing a few cold ones. At other times you can get Mexican breakfasts.

Waffle Bus (www.thewafflebus.com; mains $3-7) Waffles and waffle sandwiches, with toppings from sweet to savory (cheeseburger, smoked salmon etc). Usually open for lunch, often around the University of Houston.

quinoa are just some of healthy standards on the menu.

Treebeards   CAJUN **$**
(Map p214; http://treebeards.com; 315 Travis St; mains $8-15; ☺11am-2:30pm Mon-Fri; ☒Preston) Locals flock to this downtown chain at lunchtime to chow down on savory Cajun gumbos and crawfish étoffée, but don't discount the appeal of daily changing specials like jerk chicken and blackened catfish.

★Original Ninfas   MEXICAN **$$**
(Map p206; ☒713-228-1175; www.ninfas.com; 2704 Navigation Blvd; mains $11-25; ☺11am-10pm Mon-Fri, 10am-10pm Sat & Sun) Generations of Houstonians have come here since the 1970s for shrimp diablo, *tacos al carbon* (beef cooked over charcoal) and handmade tamales crafted with pride. Great service, seats outside and very fine salsas.

Kitchen at The Dunlavy   AMERICAN **$$**
(Map p218; ☒713-360-6477; www.thedunlavy. com; 3422 Allen Pkwy; mains $8-20; ☺7am-2pm) The creative pick for a fine breakfast, brunch or lunch amid the charms of Buffalo Bayou Park. Order at the counter and then find a table in the high-ceilinged dining rooms, where light comes from chandeliers. The menu has creative takes on upscale diner fare. Enjoy a fine coffee or drink from the bar.

Oxheart   MODERN AMERICAN **$$$**
(Map p214; ☒832-830-8592; www.oxheart houston.com; 1302 Nance St; menus $79; ☺5:30-10pm Thu-Mon) Houstonians Jeff Hu and Karen Man delight foodies and critics alike with the inventive flavor pairings on the four to seven-course tasting menus. In the ever-changing lineup you'll find dishes that are sourced locally and fresh with the seasons. You can pair your dining adventure with wines by the course for a reasonable $35.

✖ Midtown & Museum District

Midtown has up-and-coming and diverse dining options spread out around Travis and W Gray Sts.

★Lankford Grocery   BURGERS **$**
(Map p218; ☒713-522-9555; 88 Dennis St; mains $5-14; ☺7am-3pm Mon-Sat) Don't expect to be buying a jar of Tang at this old grocery store which is now dedicated to serving some of Houston's best burgers. Thick, juicy and loaded with your choice of condiments,

---

TOP BURGERS, MEXICAN & BARBECUE
••
Houston's three main food groups are all meaty, tasty and casual.

Stanton's City Bites (p216) Huge burgers served in many flavors.

Lankford Grocery (p217) The city's juiciest burgers in a down-home setting.

Original Ninfas (p217) Classic Mexican; don't miss the beef fajitas.

Hugo's (p221) Master chef Hugo Ortega's restaurant is regional Mexican at its finest.

Gatlin's BBQ (p222) Go early before the smoked brisket sells out.

Goode Co BBQ (p222) Great barbecue in an open-air barn.

---

what more could you want? The interior is shambolic but you're unlikely to notice. Regulars cheerfully razz each other while busy waiters recite the day's specials.

Get here early ahead of the lunch rush.

This Is It   SOUTHERN US **$**
(Map p218; ☒713-521-2920; http://houston thisisit.com; 2712 Blodgett St; mains $6-12; ☺7-10am & 11am-8pm Mon-Sat, 11am-6pm Sun) Soul food served cafeteria-style in the Museum District: think oxtails, ham hocks and ribs – cooked from the, well, soul. The dining room is simple and there are tables on the fenced patio.

Breakfast Klub   SOUTHERN US **$**
(Map p218; www.thebreakfastklub.com; 3711 Travis St; mains $9-16; ☺7am-2pm Mon-Fri, 8am-2pm Sat & Sun; ℗☎; ☒Ensemble/HCC) Come early; devotees line up around the block for down-home breakfast faves like fried wings 'n' waffles. Lunch hours are slightly less crazy at this coffeehouse-like eatery; choose from salads, sandwiches and soups. Coffee is great.

Tacos A Go Go   TEX-MEX **$**
(Map p218; ☒713-807-8226; http://tacosagogo. com; 3704 Main St; mains $6-10; ☺7am-10pm Mon-Thu, 8am-2am Fri & Sat, 8am-9pm Sun; ☒Ensemble/HCC) Everyone has their own favorite of the served-all-day, scrambled-egg breakfast tacos here: we like bacon, bean and potato – with jalepeño, of course. One of several Houston locations, it's a very popular late-night

Central Houston

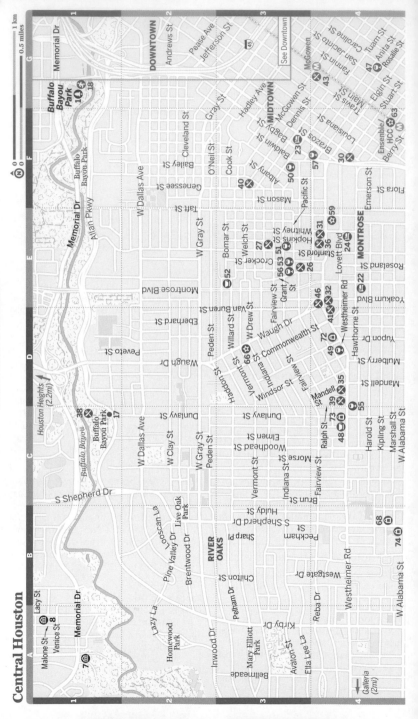

DOWNTOWN

See Downtown

MIDTOWN

Ensemble/
HCC

MONTROSE

RIVER
OAKS

Buffalo Bayou Park

Memorial Dr

Buffalo
Bayou Park

Galleria
(2mi)

Houston Heights
(2.2mi)

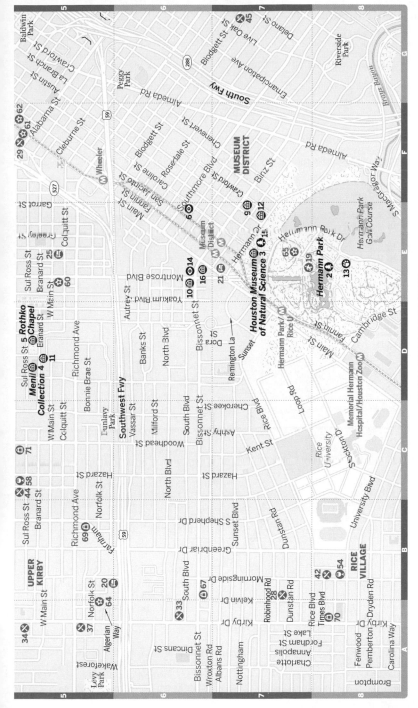

Central Houston

haunt on weekends and always a good spot for a margarita.

★ **Brennan's of Houston**   CAJUN $$$
(Map p218;   ☎713-522-9711;   www.brennans houston.com; 3300 Smith St; ⊗11am-2pm Mon-Sat, from 10am Sun, 5:30-10pm daily) The most famous name in New Orleans cooking runs this refined restaurant in Midtown. It's no mere offshoot but is a culinary temple all of its own. New Orleans flavors are blended with Texas, ingredients are uberfresh and the menu changes with the seasons. Service is excellent and the dining room elegant. Reserve in advance for a table in the beautiful courtyard.

Reef   SEAFOOD $$$
(Map p218; ☎713-526-8282; www.reefhouston. com; 2600 Travis St; lunch mains $10-30, dinner mains $20-40; ⊗11am-10pm Mon-Fri, 5-11pm Sat; ⊠McGowen) Gulf Coast seafood is creatively

prepared and served in a sleek and sophisticated dining room. Chef Bryan Caswell has won oodles of national awards for himself and his restaurant. The dining room is casual and lofty; there are tables outside. Many come just for the bar.

✗ Montrose

Mixed among the area's funky boutiques and bars, Montrose eateries (radiating out from the intersection of Westheimer and Montrose Blvd) are some of the most creative in town.

Baby Barnaby's Café
CAFE $

(Map p218; 713-522-4229; www.barnabyscafe. com; 602 Fairview St; mains $8-15; 7am-noon Mon-Fri, 8am-2pm Sat & Sun) A pint-sized outlet of the locally beloved Barnaby's Cafe chain. Breakfasts and lunches are imaginative versions of American diner classics such as hash and eggs, waffles, burgers and more. Ingredients are fresh and service is snappy. Some locations, including a larger dining room right next door, also serve dinner.

Dolce Vita
ITALIAN $$

(Map p218; 713-520-8222; www.dolcevita houston.com; 500 Westheimer Rd; mains $12-20; 5-10pm Tue-Fri, 11:30am-10pm Sat & Sun) Excellent Italian fare at great prices makes the name Dolce Vita (Sweet Life) highly appropriate! Find a romantic corner on one of two floors of this old house, or choose a table under twinkling lights on the patio. Authentic individual thin-crust pizzas come with Italian flavors like clams, fresh basil, parmesan and more.

Mala Sichuan
CHINESE $$

(Map p218; 832-767-0911; 1201 Westheimer Rd; mains $8-20; 11:30am-10:30pm;) Houston has had many influxes of people from Asia through the years and many have added to the city's culinary bounty. The family behind this dead-on authentic Sichuan restaurant serves up amazing chili dumplings, beef soup, aromatic noodles and many veggie options. Grab a table on one of the floors; service is quick. It's part of eatery-filled Montrose.

Underbelly
MODERN AMERICAN $$

(Map p218; 713-528-9800; www.underbelly-houston.com; 1100 Westheimer Rd; mains $14-40; 11am-3pm & 5-10pm Mon-Fri, 5-11pm Sat; Ensemble) Chef Chris Shepherd set out to fuse Houston's multicultural influences. He succeeds with dishes like cornbread-crusted oysters in kimchi butter and Vietnamese meatballs with gravy. Everything is sourced directly from farmers and producers. Bring a group; plates are meant for sharing. It's a 20-minute walk from Ensemble Metrorail station in the Montrose neighborhood.

El Real Tex-Mex Cafe
TEX-MEX $$

(Map p218; 713-524-1201; http://elrealtexmex. com; 1201 Westheimer Rd, to midnight Fri & Sat;) Set in a former movie theater, El Real serves up first-rate Tex-Mex, with sizzling fajitas, steaming enchiladas and fluffy soft-shelled tacos among many standout choices. Everything is top quality and there's good attention to detail, eg the kitchen roasts and grinds the spices daily. There are outdoor tables and a good bar.

Indika
INDIAN $$

(Map p218; 713-524-2170; http://indikausa.com; 516 Westheimer Rd; lunch & brunch mains $16-20, dinner mains $17-36; 11am-2pm & 6-10pm Tue-Sat, 11am-3pm Sun) Indika's alluring dining room sets the tone for the sublime Indian food, a fusion of authentic tastes and adventurous preparations, such as crabmeat samosas with papaya-ginger chutney. Great happy hour and Sunday brunch.

Baba Yega Cafe
AMERICAN $$

(Map p218; 713-522-0042; www.babayega.com; 2607 Grant St; mains $8-18; 11am-9pm Mon-Thu, to 10pm Fri & Sat, 10am-9pm Sun;) A pretty garden bungalow cafe with excellent casual fare, including towering burgers. It also has a long veggie and vegan menu, with many fresh and inventive dishes. Sunday brunch is popular, line up early.

La Grange
TEX-MEX $$

(Map p218; 832-962-4745; http://lagrange houston.com; 2517 Ralph St; mains $8-14; 4pm-midnight Mon-Wed, to 1am Thu & Fri, 11am-1am Sat & Sun) Enjoy Tex-Mex and Latin-accent flavors on good-priced mains at this frolicsome bar-restaurant. There's a big patio, shuffleboard and other diversions. It gets busy on weekends, so don't expect quick service; quintessential Houston outdoor fun.

★ Hugo's
MEXICAN $$$

(Map p218; 713-524-7744; http://hugosrestau rant.net; 1600 Westheimer Rd; lunch mains $15-22, dinner mains $23-30; 11am-10pm Mon-Thu, to 11pm Fri & Sat, 10am-9pm Sun) Chef Hugo Ortega elevates regional Mexican cooking

HOUSTON & EAST TEXAS HOUSTON

and street food to high art in this much-celebrated Montrose bodega. You can sample Oaxacan-style dishes and some well-spiced meats. Although many of the items seem familiar, the menu here is much closer to Mexico than Tex-Mex. Brunch is outstanding; the patio alluring. Book ahead for any meal.

Don't miss the opulent Sunday-brunch buffet (10am to 2:30pm).

✖ Rice Village

Rice Village's bustling shopping area near the university is home to numerous casual restaurants.

Goode Co BBQ   BARBECUE $$
(Map p218; www.goodecompany.com; 5109 Kirby Dr; plates $11-18; ⊙ 11am-10pm) Belly up to the beef brisket, smoked sausage and gallon ice teas in a big ol' barn or out back on picnic tables. Even on the hottest day, the beer is cold at this, the original location of a Houston institution.

Benjy's   MODERN AMERICAN $$$
(Map p218; ☑ 713-522-7602; www.benjys.com; 2424 Dunstan Rd; lunch & brunch $10-20, dinner mains $16-38; ⊙ 11am-9pm Sun & Mon, to 10pm Tue-Thu, to 11pm Fri & Sat) Local ingredients star at this fashionable Rice Village restaurant. Saturday and Sunday brunch is the week's highlight for many. Brunch dishes have a Southern accent while dinner is a creative medley of regional flavors from across the US.

✖ Upper Kirby, River Oaks & Galleria

North of I-59, Kirby gradually blends into the ritzy River Oak area. Houston's most ambitious restaurants (and prices) are found here and in the Galleria area.

House of Pies   AMERICAN $
(Map p218; ☑ 713-528-3816; www.houseofpies.com; 3112 Kirby Dr; mains $7-12; ⊙ 24hr) Classic diner fare served 24/7. The pies are really the thing here: banana cream, lemon ice box, buttermilk, German chocolate, wild blueberry... But the place is also a late-night breakfast hit when the bars turn food-craving masses out onto the streets.

Tiny Boxwoods   CAFE $$
(Map p206; ☑ 713-622-4224; http://tinyboxwoods.com; 3614 W Alabama; mains $10-45; ⊙ 7am-10pm Tue-Sat, 9am-2pm Sun) Set among blooming flowers in a River Oaks garden shop, this lovely cafe is a natural respite for food lovers looking for inventive fare. The breakfasts feature fresh and organic ingredients. Salads are served through the day, along with sandwiches and burgers. At night there are gourmet pizzas and casual mains with local meats and seafood. The bar is inventive.

Kata Robata Sushi & Grill   JAPANESE $$
(Map p218; ☑ 713-526-8858; http://katarobata.com; 3600 Kirby Dr; mains $9-24; ⊙ 11:30am-3pm & 5-10:30pm Mon-Fri, noon-10pm Sat & Sun) Houston's freshest sushi. Specialty rolls and super *toro* tuna (tuna belly; fatty tuna) aren't the only options that shine on this eclectic menu, which includes fusion noodle and grill dishes. We dare anyone to dislike the miso mac 'n' cheese.

✖ Houston Heights & Washingon Ave

Hubcap Grill   BURGERS $
(Map p206; ☑ 713-862-0555; http://hubcapgrill.com; 1133 W 19th St; burgers $6-10; ⊙ 11am-9pm Mon-Thur, to 10pm Fri & Sat) Maybe Hubcap is popular because everything's homemade, from the freshly formed beef patties to the site-baked buns and hand-cut fries. The choices are myriad, some unconventional such as Texas BBQ. Take shelter, order from the window and find a seat at a picnic table. Great beer list.

Gatlin's BBQ   BARBECUE $$
(Map p206; ☑ 713-869-4227; http://gatlinsbbq.com; 3510 Ella Blvd; mains $7-16; ⊙ 11am-9pm Mon-Sat) Some of Houston's best barbecue. Buy your slow-smoked brisket (the top item) and baby backs – and pulled pork, and turkey – by the pound or by the plate. But watch your timing; not only are hours limited, it sometimes sells out.

Boil House   CAJUN $$
(Map p206; ☑ 713-880-3999; www.theboilhouse.com; 606 E 11th St; meals $12-30; ⊙ 5-9pm Wed-Fri, 11am-9pm Sat & Sun) The name sums up your experience at this delightfully authentic crawfish boil joint. Order your shellfish by the pound and a steaming pile of crawfish or shrimp soon appears in a heap on your table. Start peeling and dig in. It's BYOB (Bring Your Own Bottle) and you need to get there early to claim a picnic table. The kitchen looks like a garage.

Down House
MODERN AMERICAN $$

(Map p206; ☑ 713-864-3696, http://treadsack. com/downhouse; 1801 Yale St; sandwiches $10-15, mains $12-20; ☺ 9am-11pm; 🛜) Take a break from the hip shopping of the Heights. Craft beer and creative sandwiches are on the daily menu, but so are larger evening dishes like a bone-in pork chop or shrimp and grits. If it weren't in Houston, we'd be tempted to call this a gastropub. Great beer and drinks list.

Greater Houston

Burns Original BBQ
BARBECUE $

(Map p206; ☑ 281-999-5559; 8307 1/2 De Priest St; mains $6-15; ☺ 10:30am-7:30pm Tue-Sat) Head north up past I-45, past the I-610 beltway and then drive into an unassuming neighborhood. Pass some modest homes and look for a jammed parking lot. You've found one of the best BBQ joints in Texas. Beef spare ribs, satiny brisket and pork ribs are all fall-off-the-bone tender and redolent with smoke. Grab a seat inside or out, but don't wait too long – it runs out and closes early.

Crawfish & Noodles
VIETNAMESE $

(Map p206; ☑ 281-988-8098; 11360 Bellaire Blvd; mains $6-15; ☺ 3-10pm Mon-Fri, noon-10pm Sat & Sun) Pairing Vietnamese seafood and noodles with Cajun flavors was inevitable after Vietnamese immigrants became an important part of the fishing economy along the Gulf. Out here west of the center, there are dozens of strip malls filled with all manner of Asian shops, restaurants and huge supermarkets. This simple storefront is best-known for its namesake pairing. Delish!

★ Taste of Texas
STEAK $$$

(Map p206; ☑ 713-932-6901; www.tasteoftexas. com; 10505 Katy Fwy; mains $25-60; ☺ 11am-10pm Mon-Thu, to 11pm Fri, 3-11pm Sat, 3-10pm Sun; 🅿) Welcome to Houston's favorite steakhouse. While other beef palaces start perusing Las Vegas leases at the first sign of success, this long-running gem stays true to its one location. Go to the butcher shop out back to specify how you want your steak cut. Afterward, get lost in the huge salad bar. Intimate corners contrast with the cavernous central eating space.

 ## Drinking & Nightlife

Houston's subtropical climate means that a drink on an open-air patio is practically mandatory. The Montrose neighborhood is the classic hangout, but you'll also find great outdoor spaces concentrated in Midtown, Rice Village and the Heights.

Hard-partying bars and clubs are scattered around town, but Washington Ave defines all that is hip and happening in Houston nightlife. Some of Houston's most popular dance clubs are also hot LGBT venues.

Parking is generally bad everywhere there's nightlife in Houston. Avoid driving worries by using cabs or ride-sharing services.

 ## Downtown

Radiating out from the 300 block of Main St is a good place to start looking for downtown's idiosyncratic nightlife scene.

★ Captain Foxheart's
Bad News Bar & Spirit Lodge
COCKTAIL BAR

(Map p214; ☑ 718-387-6962; 308 Main St; ☺ 5pm-2am) On restaurant-lined Main St, look for the door marked with law offices, then ascend the stairs to this elegant cocktail hideaway. Take a seat at the long polished bar, or in an armchair beneath low-lit chandeliers, and sip some of Houston's finest libations. On warm nights, the inviting terrace over the street is a perfect spot to enjoy the night air.

★ Moon Tower Inn
BEER GARDEN

(Map p206; www.damngoodfoodcoldassbeer.com; 3004 Canal St; ☺ noon-2am Mon-Sat, to midnight Sun) Moon Tower Inn is a simple shack with a huge yard strung with lights and picnic tables. It draws a lively crowd of young and old who hunker over frothy housemade microbrews plus burgers, weenies and more. It's got an edgy Warehouse District vibe.

★ La Carafe
BAR

(Map p214; ☑ 713-229-9399; 813 Congress Ave; ☺ 1pm-2am) Set in Houston's oldest building (1848), La Carafe is the most atmospheric old bar in the city. It's a warmly lit drinking den, with exposed brick, sepia photos on the walls and flickering candles. You'll also find a great jukebox and a friendly, eclectic crowd. On weekends, the upstairs bar room opens, with a 2nd-floor balcony overlooking Market Sq.

Warren's Inn
BAR

(Map p214; ☑ 713-247-9207; 307 Travis St; ☺ 11am-2am Mon-Sat, 2pm-2am Sun; 🚇 Preston) The jukebox at this lovable downtown dive bar has been officially voted the best for oldies

GAY & LESBIAN HOUSTON

Despite Houston's conservative streak, the town has a hot gay scene, which centers in Montrose.

To take the pulse on the local LGBTQ community, *OutSmart* (www.outsmartmagazine. com) is the go-to news source that also has a bar guide. Every June, the community sponsors a huge **Pride Parade** (p212).

Houston has no less than 20 gay-oriented bars and clubs. The largest and loudest is **South Beach** (Map p218; ☑ 713-529-7623; www.southbeachthenightclub.com; 810 Pacific St; cover from $15; ⊙ 9pm-2am Thu, to 4am Fri & Sat), where young guys and high-tech dance music keep things hot. **F Bar** (Map p218; www.fbarhouston.com; 202 Tuam St; ⊙ 9pm-2am Tue-Sat, 5pm-2am Sun), a 'boutique nightclub,' has a slightly more mature crowd – plus award-winning DJs. Right in Midtown, the **Houston Eagle** (Map p218; http://eaglehouston. com; 611 Hyde Park Blvd; ⊙ 9am-5am Fri & Sat, 6pm-2am Sun) dance club aims to attract the manliest of men. Theme nights are many.

With a stylish but low-key vibe and cheap drinks, **JR's Bar & Grill** (Map p218; www. jrsbarandgrill.com; 808 Pacific St; ⊙ noon-2am) consistently rates among the best in Houston – especially with reigning drag-queen champion Kofi as emcee.

Start out on the chill back patio at **Pearl Houston** (Map p206; ☑ 713-868-5337; www. pearlhouston.com; 4216 Washington Ave; ⊙ 5pm-2am Tue-Sun), a long-running – and welcoming – women's bar; after midnight when the DJ comes on, migrate to the dance floor where you can show off your moves.

in town, while the cheap drinks have been unofficially voted the stiffest.

🍷 Montrose & Midtown

Sterling House   BAR
(Map p218; ☑ 281-972-0577; http://sterlinghouse htx.com; 3015 Bagby St; ⊙ 4pm-2am Mon-Fri, noon-2am Sat & Sun) Great drinks (especially the margaritas), music and good times are the norm at this two-story house, complete with wraparound porches. There's tasty, casual fare.

Anvil Bar & Refuge   COCKTAIL BAR
(Map p218; ☑ 713-523-1622; http://anvilhouston. com; 1424 Westheimer Rd; ⊙ 4pm-2am) Housed in a 1950s-era tire store, and still with the original bare-brick walls and industrial piping, this bar has got one of the best beer selections in the city, plus some of its most eclectic cocktails. If you want to get your colleagues sozzled in style, this is the place. There's an amazing range of whiskeys.

West Alabama Ice House   BAR
(Map p218; ☑ 713-528-6874; 1919 W Alabama St; ⊙ 10am-midnight Mon-Fri, to 1am Sat, noon-midnight Sun) Texas' oldest 'ice house' (where people really used to come to get their ice; now an open-air boozer) draws the crowds, from bikers to lawyers. We think it's because of the cheap beer and huge

dog-friendly yard with picnic tables. Food trucks (barbecue, tacos) are nearby when hunger strikes.

Poison Girl   BAR
(Map p218; ☑ 713-527-9929; 1641 Westheimer Rd; ⊙ 4pm-2am) Add a festive back patio with a baby-boomer-friendly Kool Aid man statue to an arty interior with vintage pinball games and you get one very cool, dive-y bar with an eclectic crowd. Lounge outside or find a dark make-out corner inside.

13 Celsius   WINE BAR
(Map p218; ☑ 713-529-8466; www.13celsius.com; 3000 Caroline St; ⊙ 4pm-2am; 🚇 McGowen) The only bar in Houston to keep a completely temperature-controlled wine cellar has an earthy Italian *enoteca* (wine bar) feel. Knowledgeable bartenders offer guidance. There are small plates of fine meats and cheeses available.

Agora   CAFE
(Map p218; ☑ 713-526-7212; www.agorahouston. com; 1712 Westheimer Rd; ⊙ 9am-2am; 🛜) A jukebox and a vast selection of wines by the glass in a coffee shop? Yes, please. OK, so not everyone's discussing Greek philosophy here, but the student/boho vibe is indeed old school. Sit on the front patio or on the quiet 2nd-level balcony, where you can enjoy some superb people-watching.

Inversion Coffee House   CAFE
(Map p218; ☑ 713-523-4866, www.inversioncoffee house.com; 1953 Montrose Blvd; ⊙6:30am-10pm Mon-Fri, 7:30am-10pm Sat & Sun; 🔊) A great indie coffeehouse. Even if you're not in Montrose, the casual local vibe, decent baked goods and a rotation of food trucks outside make it worth a detour.

🍺 Rice Village

The tall trees along Morningside Dr provide a cool and leafy location for several pub patios. Start in the 5100 block and wander south.

Little Woodrow's   BAR
(Map p218; ☑713-521-2337; http://littlewood rows.com; 5611 Morningside Dr; ⊙3pm-2am Mon-Fri, noon-2am Sat & Sun; 🚇Dryden/TMC) You really can't get more kicked-back than a giant shaded deck with sports on the TVs and so many beers on tap. One of several around town, the Rice Village Woodrow's attracts a lively university crowd.

🍺 Houston Heights & Washington Ave

The Heights corner of White Oak and Studemont is home to great hangouts, all with great patios. Washington Ave, meanwhile, is Houston at its hippest. You'll find plenty of places to party between TC Jester and Heights Blvd: bars, sports pubs, dance clubs...

★ Porch Swing Pub   PUB
(Map p206; ☑713-880-8700; www.porchswing pub.com; 05 Heights Blvd, cnr Washington Ave; ⊙11am-2am; 🍴) One of the biggest and best patios on the Washington nightlife strip. Picnic tables are close together, so you'll get to know your neighbors as you tip back a local brew and sample classic pub grub.

McIntyre's   BAR
(Map p206; ☑713-333-5531; www.mcintyreshou ston.com; 1230 W 20th St; ⊙4pm-midnight Mon & Tue, to 2am Wed-Fri, 11am-2am Sat & Sun) It may be fairly new but this is already a classic Heights bar, given its huge patio, cheery yet juiced crowds, live music and good, cheap eats from the on-site food truck.

Onion Creek Cafe   CAFE
(Map p206; ☑713-880-0706; www.onioncreek cafe.com; 3106 White Oak Dr; ⊙7am-midnight Sun-Wed, to 2am Thu-Sat) Open for early-morning coffee and breakfast tacos through to late-night cocktails and house-smoked brisket sliders, Onion Creek is the quintessential hangout in the Heights. On weekends every table on the sprawling, tree-filled patio is taken.

☆ Entertainment

Houston's mainstream cultural heart lies downtown in the Theater District (http://downtownhouston.org/district/theater), at the intersection of Smith St and Texas Ave.

Elsewhere, especially in Midtown, you have plenty of choices for theater as well live music at clubs and concert halls, though Texas country is surprisingly scarce.

Look for event listings in widely available, and free, independent weekly *Houston Press* (www.houstonpress.com).

★ Alley Theatre   THEATER
(Map p214; ☑713-220-5700; www.alleytheatre.org; 615 Texas Ave; 🚇Central Station) Houston's top theater is fresh off a massive 2015 makeover. It offers a packed lineup of shows, large and small, many cast with its revered in-house ensemble of actors.

★ Rudyard's Pub   LIVE PERFORMANCE
(Map p218; ☑713-521-0521; www.rudyardspub. com; 2010 Waugh Dr; ⊙11:30am-2am) Offers live fare many nights, which includes comedy, poetry slams and karaoke, plus a mix of edgy and indie bands. A great selection of microbrews and good pub grub (especially the burgers) make this a great place to hang out, even when there's nothing else on. Good terrace too.

★ Match   LIVE PERFORMANCE
(Midtown Arts and Theater Center Houston; Map p218; ☑713-521-4533; https://matchouston.org; 3400 Main St; 🚇Ensemble/HCC) A performance space for more than 500 Houston cultural groups and organizations that aren't part of the big money Theater District downtown. Opened in 2017, the impressive facility has four spaces that can seat 70 to 350 people for theater, dance, music and more. There are also galleries and meeting spaces. The vibrant calendar is worth a look.

★ McGonigel's Mucky Duck   LIVE MUSIC
(Map p218; ☑713-528-5999; www.mcgonigels. com; 2425 Norfolk St; ⊙11am-2am Mon-Sat) Acoustic, Irish, folk and country performers play nightly in pubby surrounds. Concert

prices vary but Mondays (open-mike) and Wednesdays (Irish folk) are free. It's a great space with a classy supper-club look, and nicely prepared pub food.

Ensemble Theater   THEATER

(Map p218; ☑ 713-520-0055; www.ensemble houston.com; 3535 Main St; 🚇 Ensemble/HCC) Nationally renowned African American theater company.

AvantGarden   LIVE PERFORMANCE

(Map p218; ☑ 832-287-5577; www.avantgarden houston.com; 411 Westheimer Rd; ⊙ noon-6pm Sun) The center for alt-anything in Houston. This old house has a great garden patio and is host to an eclectic mix of performances, from strange theater to poetry readings to live music. On some days you can try your hand at figure modeling. There's a good bar to provide creative lubricants.

Miller Outdoor Theatre   THEATER

(Map p218; ☑ 281-373-3386; www.milleroutdoor theatre.com; 6000 Hermann Park Dr; ⊙ schedule varies mid-Mar–mid-Nov; 🚇 Hermann Park/Rice U) FREE Hermann Park's outdoor theater is a great place to lay out a blanket on a balmy night and enjoy a free concert, play or ballet.

White Oak Music Hall   LIVE MUSIC

(WOMH; Map p206; ☑ 713-237-0370; www.white oakmusichall.com; 2915 N Main St; ⊙ hours vary; 🚇 Fulton/North Central) An excellent addition to Houston's music scene, there are two indoor music venues as well as a vast open-air lawn with room for 3000. There are top local and touring musical acts.

Last Concert Cafe   LIVE MUSIC

(Map p214; ☑ 713-226-8563; www.lastconcert. com; 1403 Nance St; ⊙ 11am-10:30pm Mon & Tue, to 2am Wed-Fri, 4pm-2am Sat, 10am-10pm Sun; 🚇 UH-Downtown) For a real local original, find your way to the warehouse district northeast of downtown. After you knock on the red door (there's no sign), you can hang out at the bar or dig into cheap Tex-Mex and listen to live music (Wednesday to Saturday) by top local bands in the grassy, palm-filled backyard.

Cézanne   JAZZ

(Map p218; ☑ 832-592-7464; www.cezannejazz. com; 4100 Montrose Blvd; ⊙ 9pm-midnight Fri & Sat) Simply Houston's best place to hear jazz (just be sure to get there during its six hours of opening each week). Above the Black Labrador, this classy, intimate venue mixes

some of the best Texas and international jazz with a very cool piano bar.

AMC Dine-in Houston-8   CINEMA

(Map p214; ☑ 713-223-3456; www.amctheatres. com/movie-theatres/houston/amc-dine-in-hou ston-8; 510 Texas Ave, Bayou Place) Formerly Sundance Houston, this theater shows indie, foreign and art-house films in an upscale setting.

Hobby Center for the
Performing Arts   THEATER

(Map p214; ☑ 713-315-2525; www.thehobby center.org; 800 Bagby St; 🚇 Central Station) Home to the **Theatre Under the Stars** (TUTS; Map p214; ☑ 713-558-8887; www.tuts.com), which produces big-budget, Broadway-style musicals (actually inside and in air-conditioned comfort, despite the company's name). Also gets big-name performers on tour.

Wortham Center   THEATER

(Map p214; ☑ 832-487-7041; www.houstonfirst theaters.com; 501 Texas Ave; 🚇 Central Station) Wortham Center is a large, multivenue complex that is home to the **Houston Ballet** (☑ 713-227-2787; www.houstonballet.org; 501 Texas Ave, Wortham Center; 🚇 Central Sation) and the **Houston Grand Opera** (☑ 713-228-6737; www.houstongrandopera.org; 501 Texas Ave, Wortham Center; 🚇 Central Sation). It is also home to a range of performances, from jazz to traveling cultural troupes.

Due to damage sustained from Hurricane Harvey, the center is closed till May 2018. Call ahead before visiting.

Jones Hall for the Performing Arts THEATER

(Map p214; ☑ 713-224-7575; www.houstonfirst theaters.com; 615 Louisiana St; 🚇 Central Station) Jones Hall hosts the **Houston Symphony orchestra** (Map p214; ☑ 713-224-7575; www.houstonsymphony.org) and the **Society for the Performing Arts** (Map p214; ☑ 713-227-4772; www.spahouston.org), which brings dance troupes to town. It is also a venue for tourist performers and special events like lectures about NASA discoveries and more.

Continental Club   LIVE MUSIC

(Map p218; ☑ 713-529-9899; www.continental club.com; 3700 Main St; ⊙ 7pm-2am most nights; 🚇 Ensemble/HCC) You can't beat the top-notch rock, rockabilly and theme events at least five nights a week. It's got a good bar and patio; the performance hall has just the right atmospheric grunge and sweaty crunch.

Fitzgerald's　　　　　　　　　　LIVE MUSIC
(Map p206; www.fitzlive.com; 2706 White Oak Blvd; ☺ /pm-2am Thu-Sat) When the Fitz first opened in the late '70s everyone from Stevie Ray Vaughan to the Ramones played here. Today you might catch a grunge-rock or heavy-metal show. It's housed in an old wooden dance hall, a Heights landmark.

Firehouse Saloon　　　　　　　　LIVE MUSIC
(Map p206; ☑ 281-513-1995; www.firehouse saloon.com; 5930 Southwest Fwy, off I-69; ☺ 6pm-midnight Thu-Sat) Live Texas music with a twang. Though you can catch the odd rock or rockabilly band playing at this big barnlike place, most of the acts are pure country. It's southwest of town.

Revention Music Center　　　CONCERT VENUE
(Map p214; ☑ 713-230-1600; www.reventionmusic center.com; 520 Texas Ave, Bayou Place) This massive entertainment venue books big-name music performers and various acts that include local roller derby.

NRG Stadium　　　　　　　　　　FOOTBALL
(Map p206; www.reliantpark.com; 1 Reliant Park; ☑ Reliant Park) The **Houston Texans** (www.houstontexans.com) play at this retractable-roof stadium., which replaced the once-iconic Astrodome. As their fortunes have improved in recent years (they're doing better than the hated Dallas Cowboys), Texans' games now attract raucous crowds. The stadium namesake, NRG, is a local energy company.

Minute Maid Park　　　　　　　BASEBALL
(Map p214; ☑ 713-259-8000; 501 Crawford St; ☑ Convention District) The **Houston Astros** (http://houston.astros.mlb.com) play pro baseball right downtown. Heat-averse Houstonians enjoy the retractable roof, which allows games to be played in air-conditioned comfort. The stadium has had numerous names through the years, as corporate sponsors come and go (most want to forget the 'Enron Field' era).

Toyota Center　　　　　　　　BASKETBALL
(Map p214; www.houstontoyotacenter.com; 1510 Polk St; ☑ Convention District) Basketball fans can watch the NBA's **Houston Rockets** (www. nba.com/rockets) at this huge, modern arena which also hosts big-name concerts.

🛍 Shopping

Shopping is a top activity in Houston. In addition to the malls, you can find some interesting neighborhoods of shops.

🛍 Downtown

Chocolate Bar　　　　　　　　　　FOOD
(Map p218; ☑ 713-520-8599; www.theoriginal chocolatebar.com; 1835 W Alabama St; ☺ 10am-10pm Mon-Sat, noon-10pm Sun) Resistance is futile. The hand-crafted chocolate here – in all of its forms: bar, confection, cake, pie, ice cream – is irresistible.

Whole Earth Provision Co　SPORTS & OUTDOORS
(Map p218; ☑ 713-526-5226; www.wholeearth provision.com; 2934 S Shepherd Dr; ☺ 10am-9pm Mon-Sat, noon-7pm Sun) Along with lots of sporty shoes, clothes and gadgets for the outdoorsy set, Texas-based Whole Earth has essential travel merchandise such as guidebooks and high-tech gadgets. Has good state-park info.

🛍 Montrose & Midtown

Montrose has good shops but they're spread out: fashionistas searching for a bargain should start in the 1600 to 1800 block of Westheimer St, near Dunalavy Rd, where they'll find a mix of used- and new-clothing stores selling everything from vintage to punk to Tokyo mod.

Space Montrose　　　　GIFTS & SOUVENIRS
(Map p218; ☑ 832-649-5743; www.spacemon trose.com; 1706 Westheimer Rd; ☺ 11am-9pm Mon-Sat, to 7pm Sun) A classic indie shop that exudes the Montrose vibe; look for crafts and gifts with artistic sensibility. Everything is made by crafty people in the USA.

Buffalo Exchange　　　　　　　CLOTHING
(Map p218; ☑ 713-523-8701; www.buffaloex change.com; 2901 S Shepherd Dr; ☺ 10am-9pm Mon-Sat, 11am-8pm Sun) Houston's outlet of the nationwide chain of selective buy-sell-trade clothing stores is in chic Montrose digs. Yes, they're picky, and that's a good thing.

Silverlust Fine Jewelry　　　　JEWELRY
(Map p218; ☑ 713-520-5440; www.silverlustonline. com; 1338c Westheimer Rd; ☺ 10am-6pm Mon-Fri, to 4pm Sat) Custom designs and fabulous service are the hallmarks of this indie shop in the heart of Montrose.

Galleria

Beyond the namesake mall, 'the Galleria' refers to the whole surrounding neighborhood, which has many more shopping and dining plazas.

Galleria   MALL
(Map p206; www.simon.com; 5075 Westheimer Rd; ⊙10am-9pm) The sprawling Galleria is Texas' biggest indoor shopping center, with 2.4 million sq ft, over 400 stores, 30 restaurants, two hotels and an ice-skating rink. Just about every upscale national department and chain store you can think of is represented here, in what's ultimately a very large traditional enclosed mall that may well have already peaked.

River Oaks District   MALL
(Map p206; ☑713-904-1310; www.riveroaks district.com; 4444 Westheimer Rd; ⊙10am-7pm Mon-Sat, noon-6pm Sun) Dare we say it? The mantle for luxe shopping in Houston has moved to this outdoor, village-style mall east of the Galleria. It offers a bevy of international chains, including Brunello Cucinelli, Tom Ford, Stella McCartney, Etro, Joie and Patek Phillippe at deBoulle.

Central Market   FOOD
(Map p206; ☑713-386-1700; www.centralmarket. com; 3815 Westheimer Rd; ⊙8am-10pm) Stock up on well-priced organic and incredibly varied fresh produce at this upscale Texas grocer. Many foods are ready to eat.

Houston Heights

Funky vintage shops, eclectic homewares, antique outlets and artsy clothing boutiques concentrated along a short stretch of 19th St west of Yale St in the Heights (www.houstonheights.org). On the first Saturday of every month, 19th St takes on a carnival-like air with outdoor booths and entertainment.

The eclectic old neighborhood's bungalow homes add to the charm of shopping here, as does the odd cafe or two.

★Casa Ramirez Folkart Gallery   ART
(Map p206; ☑713-880-2420; 241 W 19th St; ⊙10am-5pm) A beautiful shop filled with vintage art and handicrafts from Mexico, plus unique items from top artisans south of the border.

Haute Dimensions   CLOTHING
(Map p206; ☑832-649-5835; www.haute-dimen sions.com; 6521 N Main St; ⊙11am-6pm Tue-Sat) Great little women's clothing store run by a fashionable mother-daughter team. Excellent recommendations, no matter your style.

Kaboom Books   BOOKS
(Map p206; ☑713-869-7600; http://kaboombooks. com; 3115 Houston Ave; ⊙noon-8pm Mon-Sat, to 6pm Sun) Everything a great neighborhood bookstore should be is exemplified by this Heights gem.

Rice Village

One of the few parts of town best explored on foot, Rice Village buzzes with a hip student energy thanks to neighboring Rice University. Though upscale chains are well represented in a mall-like plaza, many of the smart shopping options on outlying streets are one of a kind.

The area is bounded by Kirby and Morningside Drs and University and Rice Blvds.

★Chloe Dao Boutique   CLOTHING
(Map p218; ☑713-807-1565; http://chloedao.com; 6127 Kirby Dr, Rice Village; ⊙11am-7pm Mon-Sat, noon-5pm Sun) Try on *Project Runway* winner Chloe Dao's fashionable wares in this Rice Village gem that's all about local design, looking good and having fun.

★Brazos Bookstore   BOOKS
(Map p218; ☑713-523-0701; www.brazosbook store.com; 2421 Bissonnet St; ⊙11am-8pm Mon-Sat, noon-6pm Sun) Houston's top independent bookseller since 1974. Browse local titles or meet authors at their many monthly events. Excellent staff recommendations and a fine collection of books by Texans and about Texas.

River Oaks & Upper Kirby

You'll find a good mix of local stores, cute little strip malls and larger shopping areas in the upscale west side of Houston. West Alabama, between Kirby Dr and Timmon St, is a good place to look for high-end art and antiques.

Cactus Music   MUSIC
(Map p218; ☑713-526-9272; www.cactusmusic tx.com; 2110 Portsmouth St; ⊙10am-9pm Mon-Sat, noon-7pm Sun) Off Richmond Ave in Upper Kirby, Houston's original indie-music store pleases hippies, punks and country kids

alike. There are occasional performances in store.

Greater Houston

Cavender's CLOTHING
(Map p206; 713-664-8999; www.cavenders.com; 2505 S Loop West 610; 9am-9pm Mon-Sat, noon-6pm Sun) The largest local outlet for the chain of cowboy- and Western-wear superstores.

Y'Alls Texas Store GIFTS & SOUVENIRS
(281-353-6269; www.yalls.com; 216 Midway St, Spring; 10am-5pm) For bluebonnet-covered, Texasy souvenirs, check out the collection of stuff in this vintage store in the heart of the town of Spring, north of Houston.

Information

TOURIST INFOMATION

Houston Visitors Center (Map p214; 713-437-5557; www.visithoustontexas.com; 1300 Avenida de las Americas, Hilton Americas; 7am-10pm) As much a giant souvenir shop as an info center; right across from the convention center.

MEDICAL SERVICES

Memorial Hermann (713-222-2273; www.memorialhermann.org; 6411 Fannin St; 24hr) Memorial Hermann hospital is the main hospital in one of the world's largest medical complexes.

MONEY

Travelex Currency Services (713-398-6130; www.travelex.com; 5085 Westheimer Rd, Galleria; 10am-9pm Mon-Sat, 11am-7pm Sun) Offers currency-exchange services.

Getting There & Away

AIR

Houston Airport System has two airports.

George Bush Intercontinental Airport (IAH; Map p206; 281-230-3100; www.fly2houston.com/iah; 2800 N Terminal Rd, off I-59, Beltway 8 or I-45;) Located 22 miles north of the city center. It's a hub for United Airlines, with service by other major airlines to destinations worldwide. The confusing and poorly designed sprawl of gates and terminals can test the fortitude of even veteran travelers.

William P Hobby Airport (HOU; Map p206; 713-640-3000; www.fly2houston.com/hobby; 7800 Airport Blvd, off Broadway or Monroe Sts;) Located 12 miles southeast of town, Hobby Airport is smaller and more manageable than George Bush Intercontinental

Airport. It's a major hub for Southwest Airlines and has mostly domestic service.

Bus

Long-distance buses depart from the **Greyhound Bus Terminal** (Map p214; 713-759-6565; www.greyhound.com; 2121 Main St; Downtown).

TRAIN

The *Sunset Limited* stops at the **Amtrak Station** (800-872-7245; www.amtrak.com; 902 Washington Ave) three times a week en route between New Orleans and Los Angeles; Texas stops also include San Antonio and El Paso.

Getting Around

TO/FROM THE AIRPORT

SuperShuttle (800-258-3826; www.supershuttle.com) Provides regular shared ride service from both Bush ($23) and Hobby ($19) airports to hotels and addresses around town.

Bicycle

Houston B-Cycle (713-865-3662; http://houston.bcycle.com; membership 24hr $5, 7 days $15; 6am-11pm) is good for a quick jaunt about town. Find a B-Cycle station, swipe your credit card and head off on a bicycle (which you can return at other stations). The first hour is included in the membership charge. Download the useful app for full info.

CAR & MOTORCYLE

Downtown, metered streetside parking is made easier by numerous vending machines that sell timed tickets that are not site specific. Lots are plentiful, if not cheap (upwards of $25 a day).

Outside downtown, parking is usually free but can be in short supply. In fact for many Houstonians, the availability of parking is the most important consideration in picking a restaurant. Don't be put off by valet parking at restaurants and malls; if it costs at all, it's cheap, and it can be easier than finding a space.

CITY PASS

Seeing all the major sights and traveling with children? Then the City Pass (adult/child $56/46) can help you save up to 40%. With it you get admission to five major Houston attractions, including the Houston Museum of Science, the Houston Zoo, the Museum of Fine Arts, Houston, and Space Center Houston. Buy it online, at the visitor center or at attractions.

PUBLIC TRANSPORTATION

Houston's public transportation is run by **Metro** (Metropolitan Transit Authority; ☑ 713-635-4000; www.ridemetro.org; 1 way $1.25, day pass $3). Bus transit is geared toward weekday, downtown commuters. The exception are the fast and frequent trams ('Metrorail') which run on three routes, including the very useful Red Line that serves Reliant Park, the Rice University area, Hermann Park and the Museum District, Midtown and downtown.

Free **Greenlink** (☑ 713-635-4000; www.downtownhouston.org; ☉ Green Route 6:30am-6:30pm Mon-Fri, Orange Route 6:30pm-midnight Thu & Fri, 9am-midnight Sat, 9am-6pm Sun) shuttle buses run on two routes serving major sights around downtown. Buses arrive every seven to 10 minutes.

TAXI & RIDE SHARE

Taxis include **Yellow Cab** (☑ 713-236-1111; www.yellowcabhouston.com). Rates can be high and quickly add up. Uber is more reasonable.

CLEAR LAKE & AROUND

Less than 30 miles south of downtown Houston is the greater Clear Lake area, home to the very popular Space Center Houston as well as aquatic diversions of all kinds, including a fun amusement park, and some important historic sites.

To the north where Buffalo Bayou empties into the estuary that flows into the bay, you'll find the industrial town of La Porte with its vital attractions. At Clear Lake's outlet, look out for the communities of Seabrook and Kemah; the latter an entertaining waterfront village with amusements and eateries. You could definitely visit the whole area as a day trip or on the way to Galveston, but the number of things to do – and the traffic to and from Houston – makes an overnight worthwhile.

No matter your itinerary, don't miss the best barbecue in the Houston region.

◉ Sights & Activities

★ **Space Center Houston**   MUSEUM
(Map p206; ☑ 281-244-2100; http://spacecenter.org; 1601 NASA Pkwy; adult/child $30/25; ☉ 10am-5pm, later some weekends & summer) Dream of a moon landing? You can hardly get closer than at the official visitor center and theme park–esque museum next to NASA's Johnson Space Center. The 90-minute tram tour of the center itself includes the historic Mission Control (you know, the 'Houston' as in

the *Apollo 13* transmission, 'Houston, we have a problem.').

Rocket Park   HISTORIC SITE
(Map p206; ☑ 281-244-2100; 1601 Nasa Rd 1, Johnson Space Center; ☉ 9am-6pm) **FREE** It's as impressive as it is sad: a surviving example of a never-used Saturn V rocket, which took astronauts to the moon and which was the most powerful rocket ever used by the US, on its side in a building that barely encloses it near the Johnson Space Center entrance. The close confines of the structure make it hard to comprehend the 363ft height but you can still sense the incredible power and technology, which has never been matched since.

Pinky's Kayak Rental   WATER SPORTS
(Map p206; ☑ 713-510-7968; www.pinkyskayakrental.com; 4106 NASA Pkwy, El Lago; kayak rental 1hr $25, additional hours $10) Rent kayaks for Taylor Lake, which is a perfect place to paddle. Also offers kayak tours.

✖ Eating

Waterfront restaurants line the filigreed shoreline. Be sure to plot a course that includes a stop at Killen's Barbecue (p230) in Pearland, west of I-45.

★ **Killen's Barbecue**   BARBECUE $$
(Map p206; ☑ 281-485-2272; www.killensbarbecue.com; 3613 E Broadway St, Pearland; mains $9-24; ☉ 11am-8pm Tue-Thu & Sun, to 9pm Fri & Sat) This tidy wood restaurant with its grassy site and outdoor patio is a pilgrimage spot for barbecue fans. Ronnie Killen has achieved meaty nirvana with his brisket, ribs, sausages, pulled pork and more. Everything here is superb; besides the meat, even often humdrum sides like coleslaw and creamed corn (always made with fresh corn) shine.

Kemah

☑ 281, 713 / POP 2000

On the edge of Galveston Bay, Kemah waterfront is a grotesque carnival of commercialism to some, a keep-the-family-busy blessing to others. On weekends, expect to wait on traffic-clogged Hwy 146.

Kitschy souvenirs are available on the boardwalk, but more interesting are the quirky boutiques on Bradford and 6th Sts. There you can by a hand-carved pelican statue before or after you have your tarot reading or fudge.

✦ Activities

Kemah Boardwalk AMUSEMENT PARK
(Map p206; ☑281-535-8113; www.kemahboard
walk.com; 215 Kipp Ave, off Hwy 146; admission free, all-day ride pass adult/child $25/19;
◉10:30am-10pm, with seasonal variations; 🖼)
Get ready to ride: boardwalk amusements
here include a serious Ferris wheel, a roller
coaster and a tower ride among numerous
others.

The carnival-like atmosphere comes complete with step-right-up and try-your-luck
games, fun food stands and bayside dining
and drinking. If you decide to book a ride on
the Beast (adult/child $17/14), a 70ft, 70mph
jetboat, you *will* get wet.

🛏 Sleeping & Eating

Boardwalk Inn HOTEL $$$
(Map p206; ☑281-334-9880; www.kemahboard
walkinn.com; 8 Kemah Boardwalk; r $150-350;
❄🛜) Can't wait to join the melee? Stay
above the Kemah Boardwalk with a balco-
ny overlooking all the craziness. Large, sea-
side-inspired rooms (some with balconies
with views) provide plenty of space for a
family. Ask about packages, which include
all-day ride passes.

Art of Coffee CAFE $
(Map p206; ☑281-532-6371; 609 Bradford Ave;
snacks $2-5; ◉7am-8pm; 🛜) Top-notch coffee
drinks and excellent baked goods make this
a good place to recharge. The walls are lined
with art; there are seats outside.

T-Bone Tom's AMERICAN $$
(Map p206; ☑281-334-2133, http://tbonetoms.
com; 707 Hwy 146; mains $8-30; ◉dining room
11am-10pm, bar to 2am) A Kemah classic for
generations, T-Bone Tom's started smoking
meat in 1961. Now, in addition to site-made
smoked sausage, it serves steaks, seafood and
sandwiches in rustic surrounds. Tom's Backyard hosts bands and musicians Tuesday
through Sunday evenings.

Aquarium AMERICAN $$
(Map p206; ☑281-334-9010; www.aquariumres
taurants.com; 11 Kemah Boardwalk; mains $15-30;
◉11am-9pm Sun-Thu, to 10pm Fri & Sat; 🖼) The
food is fine, but you really come for the
thrill of dining surrounded by a multistory,
50,000-gallon aquarium at this chain, con-
cept restaurant.

La Porte

☑281, 713 / POP 34,900

Two of the Houston area's most historic
sights are in this industrial town southeast
of Houston. Chemical plants are more com-
mon here than shopping malls.

◉ Sights

**San Jacinto Battleground
State Historic Site** MUSEUM
(Map p206; ☑281-479-2421; www.sanjacinto-
museum.org; 3523 Hwy 134; park admission
free, attractions vary; ◉9am-6pm) A hal-
lowed site for some Texans, this 1100-
acre park is where Texas fought for – and
won – its independence in 1836. You can
learn about the battle by browsing the
excellent museum, watching the movie,
then riding nearly 500ft up to the ob-
servation deck for a look over the battle-
ground and beyond.

The exhibits and the tower all charge ad-
mission. The site itself is free and retains a
natural feel, despite the chemical plants in
the distance.

**Battleship Texas
State Historic Park** HISTORIC SITE
(Map p206; ☑281-479-2431; http://tpwd.
texas.gov/state-parks/battleship-texas; 3523
Independence Pkwy; site free, tours adult/child
$12/3; ◉9am-5pm) A quick drive from San
Jacinto park, the 1914 battleship USS *Tex-
as* served in both WWI and WWII. Now
moored next to the busy Buffalo Bayou
ship channel, the ship is open for tours
which let you see and learn about how
seamen lived and fought about 100 years
ago.

For warship buffs, it's a fascinating jour-
ney back in time. Note that the ship's hull is
in dire need of structural repair and it may
close at any time if funds can be found to
save it.

🍴 Eating

Monument Inn SEAFOOD $$
(Map p206; ☑281-479-1521; www.monumentinn.
com; 4406 Independence Pkwy S; meals $12-30;
◉11am-9pm Sun-Thu, to 10pm Fri & Sat) Right at
the ferry dock and near the parks, this large,
modern place has good Gulf seafood with
ship-channel views.

Seabrook

📖 281, 713 / POP 12,800

There's blessedly little to do here in this laid-back waterfront community on the north side of Clear Lake along the bay. Consider it a low-key place to hang your hat and enjoy some seafood.

Old Parsonage Guest Houses BUNGALOW **$$**
(Map p206; 📞 713-206-1105; www.seabrook accommodation.com; 1113 Hall St; houses $150-250) Live like a local at one of two fully furnished guesthouses for rent. Each professionally decorated cottage has two bedrooms and an equipped kitchen. Walking distance to Old Seabrook eateries and a quick drive to the Kemah Boardwalk.

Tookie's BURGERS **$**
(Map p206; 📞 281-942-9334; www.tookiesburgers. com; 1202 Bayport Blvd; mains $6-12; ⊙ 11am-10pm) Everybody's favorite burger: the thick beef patties and hand-cut onion rings have cooked up a passionate following. Tookie's is as casual as it gets, inside and out on the back patio.

★**Outriggers**
Seafood Grill & Bar SEAFOOD **$$**
(Map p206; 📞 281-474-3474; www.facebook.com/ OutriggersSeafoodGrillBar; 101 Bath St; mains $9-30) You can't beat the Gulf-caught fried shrimp and sunburnt sailor crowd here. Locals know to stake out a deckside waterfront table early on weekend afternoons to drink away the afternoon while watching the boats come and go to Galveston Bay. There's live music weekends in the downstairs bar. It's under the Kemah Bridge (Hwy 146).

Huntsville

📖 936 / POP 39,800

Thick, shady forests of tall pine trees; only 70 miles north of Houston, Huntsville feels far removed from city life. Driving I-45 north, you'll know you have found the spot when you see the humongous, 67ft-tall Sam Houston statue looming just north of exit 109.

The town is permanently associated with the Texas prison system, which is headquartered here and which operates the busiest death row in the US.

◉ Sights

Sam Houston
Memorial Museum HISTORIC SITE
(📞 936-294-1832; http://samhoustonmemorial museum.com; 1402 19th St; site free, museum

adult/child $5/3; ⊙ 9am-4:30pm Tue, from noon Sun) 🆓 Several Sam Houston–related buildings are located in a 15-acre park on the campus of Sam Houston State University, just south of downtown. The museum looks at the complex life of Houston, who won the decisive victory over Mexico at the Battle of San Jacinto, but who was also removed as Texas governor after he opposed secession for the Union at the start of the Civil War. The site includes buildings associated with Houston when he lived here.

Texas Prison Museum MUSEUM
(📞 936-295-2155; www.txprisonmuseum.org; 491 Hwy 75 N; adult/child $5/3; ⊙ 10am-5pm Mon-Sat, noon-5pm Sun) As depressing as it is fascinating, the Texas Prison Museum doesn't sugarcoat its exhibits, such as 'Old Sparky,' the electric chair once used to dispatch the condemned. Exhibits have an underlying theme of brutality, although there is little about the ongoing controversies around allegations that the state has executed innocent people in its rush to judgement.

✖ Eating

★**New Zion**
Missionary Baptist Church BARBECUE **$**
(📞 936-294-0884; 2601 Montgomery Rd; mains from $12; ⊙ 11am-6pm Thu-Sat) Well sure, you can worship God here, but most people flock to worship the incredibly good barbecue cooked in a smoky shack next to the church. All-you-can-eat plates, pork ribs, brisket, sausage and chicken are the staples. The Sunday-morning church services are gospel-singing sensations.

Farmhouse Café SOUTHERN US **$$**
(📞 936-435-1450; 1004 14th St; mains $8-20; ⊙ 11am-8.30pm Mon-Sat, to 3pm Sun; 👪) The 'meat and three' blue-plate lunch specials are Texas-hearty – this is chicken-fried steak country. Don't be put off by the strip-mall location – inside it has a friendly farmhouse feel. Choosing which kind of pie is painful, but lemon icebox or chocolate mousse are tops.

ⓘ Information

Statue Visitor Center (📞 936-291-9726; www.huntsvilletexas.com/148/Statue-Visitor-Center; 7600 Hwy 75 S, exit 109 off I-45; ⊙ 9am-5pm Mon-Fri, 11am-5pm Sat & Sun) Right at the Sam Houston statue, this very useful visitor center has regional information, including a driving tour outlining the many sites associated with the state prisons.

❶ Getting There & Away

Greyhound Station (🕿 936-295-3732; www.greyhound.com; 1000 12th St) Encapsulates some of the local human drama. This is where newly released inmates who don't have a ride home catch the bus. It's 1½ hours to Houston (one way $27).

WASHINGTON COUNTY

Have you seen those iconic photos of a lone live oak tree on a small rise overlooking an endless field of bluebonnets? It may well have been snapped in Washington County. With old courthouse squares alive with shops and cafes, frequent town festivals, and historic Texas-independence sites, you can't get more stereotypically small-town Texas than this.

Sitting equidistant from Houston and Austin (about 70 miles from either), Washington County makes an easy country escape from the city. No town is more than 40 miles from the region's main center, Brenham.

Besides history, parks and wildflowers, the region has several wineries. The Texas Bluebonnet Wine Trail (www.texasbluebonnetwinetrail.com) links them.

Brenham

🕿 979 / POP 16,200

No wonder downtown Brenham is listed on the National Register of Historic Places – it's darn cute. Wandering the atmospheric streets full of boutique and antique shops is a good day's diversion. Since 1907 this community has also been the home of Blue Bell Creameries, producer of the unofficial state ice cream of Texas. As the largest town in the region, Brenham is both a good base for exploring and a must-see destination in its own right.

❍ Sights

The visitors center offers good touring maps for downtown and the local area. Follow the 'wine trail' to visit four local wineries.

Brenham Heritage Museum   MUSEUM
(🕿 979-830-8445; www.brenhamheritagemuseum.org; 105 S Market St; adult/child $3/1; ❍10am-4pm Wed-Fri, to 5pm Sat) The local history museum is housed in a landmark 1915 building. Exhibits are well funded and include the life of a local man serving as a confederate soldier and how immigration shaped the region.

Toubin Park   PARK
(208 S Park St) Duck into Belle's Alley, between Alamo and Commerce Sts, on your downtown wanderings. There tiny Toubin Park has illustrated signs that show the story of a devastating 1866 fire. You can also see below ground to one of the private cisterns built to combat water troubles. It's off S Park St.

Pleasant Hill Winery   WINERY
(www.pleasanthillwinery.com; 1141 Salem Rd; tour free, tastings $3-10; ❍noon-5pm Fri, 11am-6pm Sat) This lovely little vineyard in the country has several well-regarded wines, including a much-lauded Blanc du Bois. Three to four tours are offered on weekends.

Blue Bell Creameries   FACTORY
(🕿 979-830-2179; www.bluebell.com; 1101 S Blue Bell Rd; ❍8am-5pm Mon-Fri; 🅿) Explore the museum-like visitors center before heading to the gift shop and ice-cream parlor (scoop $1). Oddly there are no weekend hours. Production tours have been discontinued since listeria infected its products in 2015.

Over 50 permanent and seasonal flavors are produced annually. The top-three favorites remain the same: homemade vanilla, cookies 'n' cream and Dutch chocolate.

🛏 Sleeping

⭐**Ant Street Inn**   INN $$
(🕿 979-836-7393; www.antstreetinn.com; 107 W Commerce St; r $150-300; ❇🕿) You'll get a full dose of 19th-century Texas rustic elegance

---

EAST TEXAS NATIONAL FOREST

East Texas has four large national forests, the largest being **Sam Houston National Forest** (🕿 ranger station 936-344-6205; www.fs.fed.us/texas; 394 FM 1375 W, New Waverly), covering 255 sq miles just 60 miles north of Houston between I-45 and US 59. Recreational facilities include lakes, camping and mountain-biking and hiking trails. The 128-mile **Lone Star Hiking Trail** (http://lonestartrail.org) is the longest wilderness footpath in Texas. The website has an essential trail guide that lists water sources and track sections that are closed due to washouts and other problems.

Exercise caution during deer-hunting season (November to early January; call the ranger's office for exact dates).

in the rooms of this historic inn located in a downtown building that dates from the 1890s. The 15 rooms are stylish, with plush, period decor; guests can rest in rocking chairs overlooking the back garden. Excellent breakfasts are served in the in-house cafe.

Brenham House B&B   B&B $$
(☑ 979-251-9947;   www.thebrenhamhouse.com; 705 Clinton St; r $160-230; ❋ 🛜) Multicourse, gourmet breakfasts (included) always feature a delicious bread or pastry and use organic products where possible. Five comfortable rooms in the rambling 1900s home are as gracious as your hosts. It's a short walk to downtown.

✕ Eating & Drinking

Funky Art Café   AMERICAN $
(☑ 979-836-5220; www.funkyartcafe.com; 202 W Commerce St; mains $7-12; ⊙ 11am-2pm Mon-Sat) Right downtown, you're greeted by artworks that embody the name as you enter. ('Is that a monkey or are you happy to see me?') The changing menu is equally creative, with salads, soups and sandwiches all differing from the norm.

Must Be Heaven   CAFE $
(☑ 979-830-8536; http://mustbeheaven.com; 107 W Alamo St; mains $6-10; ⊙ 8am-5pm Mon-Sat, 11am-3pm Sun) At lunch or for an afternoon snack, go for the fine sandwiches, ice-cream treats and homemade pies. There are now several more locations in the region.

★ Truth BBQ   BARBECUE $$
(☑ 979-830-0392; 2990 US 290; mains $8-18; ⊙ 11am-4pm Thu-Sun) The barbecue is superb, and that's no lie. Just be sure to show

---

SCENIC DRIVE: BEYOND WASHINGTON COUNTY

Brenham and Washington County may be the most well-known region in east central Texas, but don't stop there. Fayette and Austin Counties to the south are also riddled with small town attractions and scenic vistas. Get a good map and take to the rural roads. You'll likely make all sorts of discoveries. At the very least expect to see bucolic countryside and, in spring, bluebonnets. **Visit Brenham Texas** has lots of good route and wildflower info.

---

up during the very limited opening hours. Among the usual lineup, the brisket makes some swoon, especially when served in one of the artful sandwiches. Sides are all a cut above the norm.

Volare Italian Restaurant   ITALIAN $$
(☑ 979-836-1514;   www.volareitalianrestaurant. com; 102 Ross St; mains lunch$8-12/dinner $11-24; ⊙ 11am-2pm & 5-9:30pm Tue-Sat) Authentic rustic Italian meals are served in a lovely wooden house. Look for faves like lasagne as well as seafood and meaty mains. The wine list is excellent; the tables in the lovely garden are popular.

Brazos Valley Brewing Co   BREWERY
(☑ 979-987-1133;   http://brazosvalleybrewery.com; 201 W First St; ⊙ 5-10pm Fri, noon-8pm Sat, 1-6pm Sun) Among the excellent beers you can enjoy on the fine patio at this downtown microbrewery are a great IPA and a coffee ale.

🛍 Shopping

For many, wandering and window-shopping are the main attractions in Brenham. Start on Alamo St near the courthouse, where there are singular specialty clothing, gift and homeware stores. Antiques also abound.

ℹ Information

Visit Brenham Texas (☑ 979-836-3696; www. visitbrenhamtexas.com; 115 W Main St; ⊙ 10am-5pm Mon-Fri, to 3pm Sat) Look for the visitor center inside the 1925 Simon Theater, where you can pick up info on the entire county. Download the app, which has maps and seasonal info, such as where to see wildflowers. The visitors' guide is an excellent regional resource.

Burton

☑ 979 / POP 350

Just a hop and a skip (12 miles) from Brenham, this gem of a little town was where much of the agricultural area's cotton used to be processed. In fact, you'll see a lot of cotton iconography on signage around the area. Scenic drives in these parts include Hwy 390, which is a route that dates back to Indian times.

⊙ Sights

Burton Cotton Gin & Museum   MUSEUM
(☑ 979-289-3378; www.cottonginmuseum.org; 307 N Main St; adult/child $6/4; ⊙ 10am-4pm Tue-Sat) Learn everything and more you ever wanted to know about growing cotton locally at

this well-organized museum. Twice-daily 90 minute tours really get at the fabric of the industry.

Saddlehorn Winery WINERY
(📞979-289-3858; www.saddlehornwinery.com; 958 FM 1948 N; tasting free; ⊙11am-6pm) Two miles northeast of town, taste the Barn Red, a rich berry blend, from these ranch vineyards.

🛏 Sleeping & Eating

Inn At Indian Creek INN $$
(📞979-289-2032; www.innatindiancreek.com; 2460 Boehnemann Rd; r $150-200; ❄🖱) Two cottages on this lovely estate make for a perfect getaway. Each is equipped with a full kitchen and various luxuries. Sit on your porch and gaze out over the gently rolling hills and oak trees and revel in the silence. It's about 2 miles southwest of Burton.

★Brazos Belle Restaurant FRENCH $$
(📞979-289-2677; http://brazosbellerestaurant. com; 600 Main St; mains $12-30; ⊙5:30-8:30pm Fri & Sat, 11:30am-1:30pm Sun) Strictly for those on a weekend break, this attractive restaurant is right in the tiny center. The menu is heavily French accented and changes with the seasons. Many ingredients are grown in the kitchen garden. Due to the very limited hours, be sure to arrive with plenty of time to wait if necessary; cash only.

Round Top
📞979 / POP 100
The tiny rural outpost of Round Top has several big claims to fame. The old town square, if it's big enough to even call it that, is home to one of Texas' landmark cafes. Two times a year one of the country's top-10 antiques markets takes over not only the town, but the county for 10 days each time.

'Downtown' Round Top has a collection of small, old buildings set up to house arts and craft galleries and other small shops around a grassy, shady square. Note: almost everything in town is closed Monday and Tuesday.

⊙ Sights

Winedale Historical Complex HISTORIC SITE
(📞979-278-3530; www.cah.utexas.edu/museums/ winedale.php; 3738 FM 2714; ⊙by appointment) In the countryside 4 miles northeast of Round Top look for the Winedale historic village, part of the University of Texas at Austin.

Tours are by appointment only; the best way to see the historic homes and storefronts is when they are open for festivals throughout the year. The structures all date from the 19th century and have furnishings accurate for the era.

★☆ Festivals & Events

Shakespeare at Winedale THEATER
(📞512-471-4726; www.shakespeare-winedale. org; 3738 FM 2714, Winedale; adult/child $10/5; ⊙mid-July–mid-Aug) In summer get thee to a barn – the Shakespeare at Winedale barn, that is, where loyal fans drive for miles each summer to see University of Texas students perform Shakespeare plays in a rustic setting redolent of the Bard's more ribald comedies. Buy tickets in advance online. Besides the main season, there are limited performances other times.

★Round Top Antiques Weekends ANTIQUES
(http://antiqueweekend.com; Hwy 237, btwn Burton & La Grange; most venues free; ⊙varies by venue, usually 9am-6pm) What started out as Ms Emma Lee Turney's little antiques fair in 1968 has morphed into Round Top Antiques Weekends, encompassing more than 30 sq miles, six small towns, thousands of dealers and over 100,000 attendees. It takes place one weekend in April and one in October, but in reality events run for about 10 days each time. This is not one show, but many spread over 60 venues in vast barns and huge tents. The website is an essential resource.

🛏 Sleeping & Eating
There are a few inns and B&Bs in the area and there are numerous motels in both Brenham and La Grange, each about 16 miles away. Be sure to book far in advance for the antiques fairs.

Belle of Round Top B&B B&B $$
(📞936-521-9300; www.belleofroundtop.com; 230 Days End Lane; r $200-275; ❄🖱) Set on a hill above town, the two-story covered porches on the 1874 Belle of Round Top B&B lend it all the grace and Southern charm of an old plantation home. The five rooms are plushly furnished.

★Prairie by Rachel Ashwell B&B $$$
(📞979-836-4975; http://theprairiebyrachelashwell.com; 5808 Wagner Rd; cottages $200-500; ❄🖱) The queen of shabby chic herself designed the stylish places to sleep at Prairie

by Rachel Ashwell. Whether a king suite studio or a two-bedroom bungalow, each of the eight individual cottages is straight out of Pinterest – one surrounded by a pastoral landscape to rival any painting.

Royers Pie Haven CAFE $
(☑ 979-249-5282; https://royerspiehaven.com; 190 Henkel St; treats from $5; ⏱ 10am-4pm Wed & Sun, 8am-6pm Thu-Sat) This appealing cafe is run by the local Royers clan and is just the spot if all you want is a fine coffee drink and a slice of one of the legendary pies. Go on, have the buttermilk pie.

★ Royers Cafe AMERICAN $$
(☑ 979-249-3611; www.royersroundtopcafe.com; 105 Main St; mains $9-30; ⏱ 11am-2pm Wed, to 9pm Thu-Sat, noon-3pm Sun) This cafe is one of the finest places for down-home food in Texas. It's almost as famous for its great sandwiches (grilled shrimp BLTs) and mains (center-cut pork chops, grilled rack of lamb) as it is for its vast selection of pies. The decor is a crazy collection of memorabilia covering every inch of the old clapboard walls.

🔒 Shopping

Shops in the center are open 11am to 5pm Wednesday through Sunday year-round.

La Grange

☑ 979 / POP 4700

Technically, La Grange lies in Fayette County, 40 miles south of Brenham, but it is a key part of any tour of Washington County and beyond. Its especially large main courthouse square invites exploration of the surrounding blocks. Nearby farmlands define bucolic.

⊙ Sights

Texas Quilt Museum MUSEUM
(☑ 979-968-3104; www.texasquiltmuseum.org; 140 W Colorado St; adult/child $8/6; ⏱ 10am-4pm Thu-Sat, noon-4pm Sun) In the center, this museum was opened by the organizer of the annual Houston quilt show. Two refurbished mid-19th-century buildings make an excellent home for permanent and special exhibits. The permanent collection includes both historic and contemporary works by noted artists.

Rohan Meadery FARM
(☑ 979-249-5652; www.rohanmeadery.com; 6002 FM 2981; tastings $5; ⏱ noon-6pm Wed-Sun) The tastings of the sweet and spicy honey wines at Rohan Meadery may be for adults, but

there is a picnic area outside for families to enjoy. You can also sample seasonal juices and ciders. It's 9 miles northeast of town.

Jersey Barnyard FARM
(☑ 979-249-3406; www.texasjersey.com; 3117 Hwy 159; tours adult/child $10/8; ⏱ 10am-6pm Mon-Sat, 1-6pm Sun; 🐾) Less than 2 miles north of town you and the little ones can take a hay ride, milk a cow and otherwise learn all about family farming. A shop sells fresh dairy products produced at the farm.

🍴 Eating

Prause Market BARBECUE $
(☑ 979-968-3259; 253 W Travis St; mains from $8; ⏱ 7am-2pm Mon-Fri, to 1pm Sat) This traditional meat market has been a staple of the main square for decades. Each morning, it fires up a wood-fired brick pit and cooks up brisket, ribs and sausage. You can buy this bounty to go or get it served on a paper plate which you can take to the bare-bones dining area. Don't miss the potato salad.

Weikel's Bakery BAKERY $
(☑ 979-968-9413; http://weikels.com; 2247 W Hwy 71; treats from $2; ⏱ 5am-9pm) Be sure to stop by Weikel's Bakery for some site-baked *kolaches* (Czech-inspired rolls stuffed with sweets or savories, such as fruit jam or jalepeño sausage and cheese); it serves barbecue too. It's west of the center in a modern commercial strip.

ℹ Information

La Grange Chamber of Commerce (☑ 979-968-5756; www.lagrangetourism.com; 171 S Main St; ⏱ 9am-5pm Mon-Fri, 10am-5pm Sat, noon-5pm Sun) Has a free walking-tour brochure of the main square and other regional information.

Chappell Hill

☑ 979 / POP 600

Talk about a one-horse town. The historic area on Main St is hardly three blocks long but it has over two dozen registered historic landmarks.

Chappell Hill is known for its locally made smoked sausage, which you can pick up at any one of the barbecue joints along the highway.

Chappell Hill Lavender Farms FARM
(☑ 979-251-8114; www.chappellhilllavender.com; 2250 Dillard Rd; ⏱ 10am-2pm Thu & Fri, 9am-5pm Sat, 11am-4pm Sun Mar-Oct) FREE Eight miles northeast of town, spring smells awfully

sweet at this flower farm. Here you can picnic, roam the fields and cut your own lavender – or shop for related products in the gift shop.

Bever's Kitchen CAFE **$$**
(☑979-836-4178; www.bevers-kitchen.com; 5162 Main St; mains $7-15; ☺11am-3pm Mon-Thu, to 9pm Fri & Sat) A classic country cafe that's been packing in fans of classic country fare since 1984. On weekends a picker plays on the front porch while you eat chicken-fried steak, burgers and meatloaf or choose from dozens of perfect pies.

Washington-on-the-Brazos

☑979 / POP 100

Nicknamed 'the Birthplace of Texas,' this Washington is where Texas declared its independence from Mexico on March 2, 1836. Today you can still get a feel for the frontier in this rugged naturalistic park on the flood-carved banks of the Brazos River.

The drive here on FM 1155 from Chappell Hill to the south takes in some beautiful Brazos River Valley scenery.

Head east across the Brazos River and the topography changes to flat floodplains and agricultural fields, with Bryan-College Station 30 miles to the north. Brenham is 20 miles south; Houston, 80 miles southeast.

Bring a picnic and enjoy it on the banks of the river.

◉ Sights

★**Washington-on-the-Brazos State Historic Site** PARK
(☑936-878-2214; http://wheretexasbecametexas. org; 23400 Park Rd 12, Washington; admission free, all-site pass adult/child $9/6; ☺park 8am-7pm, visitor center 10am-5pm) This state historic site preserves and recreates parts of the original settlement that numbered 200 people in 1835. Make sure to watch the visitor center video before you take a tour of **Independence Hall** (where the Texas constitution was read) and the town-site grounds. There are several extra-cost sites here.

Park highlights include the **Star of the Republic Museum** (☑936-878-2461; www. starmuseum.org; 23200 Park Rd 12, Washington-on-the-Brazos State Historic Site; adult/child $5/3; ☺10am-5pm) which tells a glossy story of early Texas through artifacts and exhibits. **Barrington Living History Farm** (☑936-

878-2214; www.tpwd.state.tx.us; 23100 Park Rd 12; adult/child $5/3; ☺10am-4:30pm) was originally the home of the last president of the Republic of Texas. Today costumed docents, and real sheep and cows, recreate farm life in the 1850s. Demonstrations include how to cure a freshly slaughtered pig.

✖ Eating

R Place AMERICAN **$$**
(☑936-878-1925; http://rplacetexas.com; 23254 FM 1155 E; mains $6-20; ☺11am-6pm Fri & Sun, to 9pm Sat) Weekends-only, artfully tattered R Place serves sandwiches and barbecue, and Saturday night cooks up one main dish at dinner for patrons to enjoy family style. There's seating outside and very cold beer, plus a good wine list.

BRYAN–COLLEGE STATION

'Welcome to Aggieland.' Texas A&M University is the reason for being, not only for College Station but for neighboring Bryan, which was long ago subsumed into one metro area. Each school year the town's combined permanent population gets a whopping 46,000 student boost. Then all the businesses on College Station's main drag, University Blvd, really bustle.

However, even if you don't wear maroon-colored underwear (the Aggie color), you'll likely love downtown Bryan, which is walkable and lined with some excellent restaurants and bars.

◉ Sights

At 5200 acres, Texas A&M (which originally stood for Agricultural and Mechanical) is one of the nation's largest college campuses. While the buildings come off as more corporate than picturesque, the school is steeped in tradition – in fact, students claim it's more like a religion.

George Bush Presidential Library & Museum MUSEUM
(☑979-691-4000; http://bushlibrary.tamu.edu; 1000 George Bush Dr W, College Station, off FM 2818; adult/child $9/3; ☺9:30am-5pm Mon-Sat, noon-5pm Sun) Whether you agree with the former president's politics or not, it's hard not to be fascinated by this museum. Exhibits trace George HW Bush's life and career, and serve as an interesting primer

TEXAS A&M FOOTBALL – THE 12TH MAN

Who is the 12th man? Well about 30,000 fans screaming their heads off at **Kyle Field** during a home game. The tradition started in 1922 during a difficult Dixie Classic game (precursor to the Cotton Bowl). So many injuries were sustained that coach DX Bible thought he might not have enough players to finish. So former player E King Gill was pulled from the stands and suited up. At game end he was the last player standing on the sidelines, and though he never touched the ball, his willingness was well noted.

Today the student body and fans stand throughout the game to show that they are the 12th man, ready to help. And they aren't quiet about it either. Yell leaders on the field use an elaborate set of hand and body gestures to call the response-chants – which the fans know and shout.

It should be noted, however, that as much as the Aggies like to boast about 'the 12th man,' most other American universities with huge football programs have rival traditions. Texas A&M arch-rival University of Texas, for instance, has its instantly recognizable 'hook 'em horns' hand signals.

on American history from WWII through the 1990s. Although generally well-curated, exhibits could be more forthcoming on how Bush lost his reelection bid to Bill Clinton in 1992 despite having sky-high approval ratings after the first Gulf war.

Follow Bush's rise from Texas oil prospector through his virtual tour of national politics: from ambassador to the UN, to Republican National Committee (RNC) chairman, to Central Intelligence Agency (CIA) director, to becoming the 41st president. Family moments, and Barbara Bush's, contributions are also included. Interestingly, Bush had no ties to Texas A&M but rather had his facility placed here after the Aggies offered the best deal – just as his son George W Bush (the 43rd president) gave his presidential library to Southern Methodist University (SMU) in Dallas despite having no ties to that school, again after they offered the best deal. Most other presidential libraries and museums are in places with direct links to the respective president.

Texas A&M Appelt

Aggieland Visitor Center UNIVERSITY
(☑ 979-845-5851; http://visit.tamu.edu; Rudder Tower, College Station; ⊙ 8am-5pm Mon-Fri) You have to book ahead for a free walking tour offered by the visitor center. If you plan to explore the campus on your own, stop here first to pick up a map. Otherwise, how will you find the 6500lb of bronze 'Aggie' class ring at the Haynes Ring Plaza?

Kyle Field STADIUM

(☑ tickets 979-845-5129; www.aggieathletics.com; 198 Joe Routt Blvd, College Station) Over 102,000 fans pack behemoth Kyle Field for Aggie games. It's one of largest football stadiums in this football-crazed state – one notorious for successfully intimidating visiting teams (even if the Aggies actually haven't finished the season ranked number one since 1939). Although games are permanently sold out, check ticket reselling websites and you'll find tickets for sale – if you're willing to pay the price (especially as the team has been on extended stretch of mediocrity).

🛏 Sleeping

Chain motels line Hwy 6 along the eastern edge of Bryan–College Station and on University Dr. On football weekends, all lodgings sell out for a 50-mile radius.

★ LaSalle Hotel HISTORIC HOTEL $$

(☑ 979-822-2000; www.lasalle-hotel.com; 120 S Main St, Bryan; r $100-200; ❄ 🛜) This vintage hotel has come full circle: it started as a hotel in 1928, went through some tough times with the rest of downtown Bryan in the following decades but has now been reborn as a hotel again. And a fine one it is. Vintage-style rooms are spread across seven floors.

Outside on the plaza, the hotel has an open-air lounge and regular live weekend performances by bands. Best of all, the rest of downtown's delights are a short walk away.

Vineyard Court Hotel BOUTIQUE HOTEL $$

(☑ 888-846-2678; www.vineyardcourt.com; 1500 George Bush Dr E, College Station; ste $110-200; ❄ 🛜 🏊) Gurgling fountains, a wisteria arbor and a courtyard pool make this all-suite hotel feel worlds removed from school. Each room has a full kitchen. Each night there's a free wine-and-cheese happy hour and in the morning there's continental breakfast. The gardens are a real oasis.

Abigaile's Treehouse   B&B $$
(☑ 979-823-6350; www.abigailestreehouse.com; 1015 E 24th St, Bryan; r $130-200; ☒ ☎) Architecture- and design-lovers will dig the uniquely shaped Abigaile's, which does indeed resemble a tree. Four deluxe rooms look out onto leafy, manicured gardens, the Eagle's Nest has a great deck. This is a complete antidote to chain motels.

✖ Eating

College Station is all about chains and cheap-and-cheerful eateries aimed at students. By contrast, Bryan has some excellent restaurants downtown.

★ Fargo's Pit BBQ   BARBECUE $
(☑ 979-778-3662; 720 N Texas Ave, Bryan; mains $8-15; ◷ 11am-7pm Tue-Sat) Classic Texas barbecue is on offer at this dead-simple storefront. Legendary pitmaster Alan Caldwell guards his secret smoking techniques but the wonderful results are all public. Service is fast and friendly and the inevitable lines move quick. People love the brisket but the chicken is its secret achievement.

★ Village   CAFE $$
(☑ 979-703-8514; www.thevillagedowntown.com; 210 W 26th St, Bryan; mains $6-15; ◷ 8am-5pm Sun-Tue, to midnight Wed-Fri, to 2am Sat; ☎) Relaxed, artsy cafe by day (it has regular juried art shows); swinging scene by night. Local bands play weekend evenings, followed by a salsa dance party every Saturday night. Thursday is for singer-songwriters. The menu includes full breakfasts and sandwiches. Everything is sourced locally, including the beer and wine.

Madden's
Casual Gourmet   MODERN AMERICAN $$
(☑ 979-779-2558; www.pmaddenscasualgourmet. com; 202 S Bryan Ave, Bryan; lunch mains $11-15, dinner $25-30; ◷ 11am-2pm Mon-Wed, to 9pm Thu-Sat) With rustic elegance and gracious service, Madden's specializes in adventurous dishes such as a chocolate, coffee and chile-rubbed beef tenderloin with cheddar polenta, it also offers vegetarian fare. Menus change seasonally.

Veritas Wine & Bistro   FUSION $$$
(☑ 979-268-3251; www.veritaswineandbistro.com; 830 University Dr E, College Station; lunch mains

$15-20, dinner mains $25-50; ◷ 11am-2pm Mon-Sat, 5.30-9.30pm daily) There's a creative touch here, whether it's the sea bass with miso sauce or a barely seared steak, served sushi-style. Daily specials are a standout. Book the kitchen table where you can watch the chefs work their magic. This is where Aggies get their parents to take them when they're broke.

🍷 Drinking & Nightlife

★ Revolution Cafe & Bar   BAR
(☑ 979-823-4044; www.facebook.com/revolution bcs/; 211 B S Main St, Bryan; ◷ 6pm-2am Sat-Wed, from 4pm Thu & Fri) Wander down tiny Carnegie Alley on the backside of Main St and you'll discover this fabulous, offbeat bastion of alternative joy. There are tables and chairs on gravel in the courtyard. Inside, there's excellent booze and beer plus regular live music.

Dixie Chicken   BAR
(☑ 979-846-2322; www.dixiechicken.com; 307 University Dr, College Station; mains $6-10; ◷ 10am-2am) An Aggie tradition since 1974, you can't say you've seen A&M if you didn't drink at the Dixie Chicken. Burgers and pitchers of beer are the usual fare. Expect live country music and loud crowds on weekends, all under the baleful stare of some mangy taxidermied deer heads.

Proudest Monkey   BAR
(☑ 979-361-4777; http://proudestmonkey.com; 108 S Main St, Bryan; ◷ 11am-11pm Sun-Thu) This long, narrow bare-brick bar has a fine lineup of Texas microbrews, although nothing is on tap. People like to catch games here while enjoying burgers and tacos.

ℹ Information

Bryan–College Station Convention & Visitors Bureau (☑ 979-260-9898; www. experiencebcs.com; 1101 University Drive E, Ste 108, College Station; ◷ 8am-5pm Mon-Fri) The visitor bureau publishes a comprehensive guide to eating, drinking, playing and staying in Bryan–College Station, with detailed maps, too. Also available online. It has good info on visiting on football weekends.

ℹ Getting There & Away

Greyhound (☑ 800-231-2222; www.grey-hound.com; 301 E 26th St, Roy Kelly Parking Garage, Bryan; one-way to Houston from $22) Greyhound has one bus a day to Houston (2¼ hours).

NORTHEAST TEXAS

Tall pine forests in Texas? Yep. This region northeast of Houston and east of Dallas is so filled with mixed hardwood and conifer forests, in fact, that it is known as the 'Piney Woods.' And that's not all that's a bit of a surprise in this part of the state. The Northeast was the area in Texas most attached to the ways of the Old South, and subsequently affected by the Civil War. You'll find a traditional Southern influence in accents, antebellum architecture and Southern food here.

Though lacking in jaw-dropping superlatives, the gently rolling wooded terrain provides plenty of low-key thrills for nature lovers, especially around Caddo Lake. Pretty, small towns, such as Kilgore and Nacogdoches, are enough to beguile any visitor with their classic central squares and stately brick buildings. Jefferson was once a riverboat town, and is undeniably still the biggest draw in the area.

ℹ Information

The *North East Texas Visitor & Events Guide* (www.northeasttexasguide.com) is widely available at visitor centers, and is online. The Texas Historic Commission markets the region as the Texas Forest Trail Region (http://texasforesttrail.com).

Nacogdoches

📞 936 / POP 33,800

Whether Nacogdoches (nack-uh-*doe*-chuss) really is the oldest town in Texas (as it claims) might be debated, but it's definitely old. The first European settlement here dates from 1716, when a mission was established as a remote outpost of the Spanish empire. Most of the historic brick buildings on the cobblestone downtown square date to the mid-1800s. It's a great place to explore, especially as so much of town is easily walkable.

Today's town has a remarkably genteel sensibility balanced by a college-town buzz from Stephen F Austin State University. Come spring, the area's true colors show with the proliferation of azaleas.

⊙ Sights

The visitor information center (p241) has a small, free museum and provides excellent historic self-walking-tour maps both for the old town center and the Oak Grove Cemetery. Interesting antiques shops occupy many of the old storefronts on Main St.

Oak Grove Cemetery   CEMETERY
(200 N Lanana St; ⊙dawn-dusk) This historic cemetery received its first customer in 1837 and was soon the preferred resting place for a variety of early Texas pioneers. Note how early Catholics were segregated in their own area. Immediately north of the cemetery is the **Zion Hill Historic District**, which was the segregated home for Nacogdoches's African American community during much of the town's first hundred years.

Durst-Taylor House & Gardens   HOUSE
(📞936-560-4443; www.ci.nacogdoches.tx.us; 304 North St; ⊙10am-4pm Tue-Sat) **FREE** Get a sense of the simple life led by less-affluent farmers at c 1835 Durst-Taylor house. Docents grow gardens appropriate to the period here and demonstrate pioneer skills. It's an easy walk from downtown.

Ruby M. Mize Azalea Garden   GARDENS
(www.nacogdochesazaleas.com; 2107 University Dr, Stephen F Austin State University; ⊙dawn-dusk Mar) When 7000 plants bloom each spring at this botanical garden it's an explosion of colors and an azalea extravaganza. There are three different mapped routes on the 25-mile **Nacogdoches Azalea Trail** to follow plus events like home tours, plant sales and tours. Check with the visitor center to estimate when blooms will peak.

Sterne-Hoya House   HOUSE
(www.ci.nacogdoches.tx.us/departments/shmuseum.php; 211 S Lanana St; ⊙10am-4pm Tue-Sat) **FREE** The Sterne-Hoya House, built in 1830, is a good example of a refined town house of the era, and was the site of Sam Houston's baptism (sites visited by Sam Houston are the Texas equivalent of 'George Washington slept here'). It's in a genteel neighborhood just east of downtown.

Stone Fort Museum   MUSEUM
(📞936-468-2408; www.sfasu.edu/stonefort; cnr Clark & Griffith Blvds, Stephen F Austin State University; ⊙9am-5pm Mon-Sat, 1-5pm Sun) **FREE** Don Antonio Gil Y'Barbo's 1789 stone house subsequently served as a grocery store, a saloon and a fortification. Exhibits in the reconstructed 'fort' serve as an overview of east Texas history.

📖 Sleeping

Nacogdoches has several excellent B&Bs and inns that are close to the pleasures of the center. Chain motels are inconveniently located on Hwy 59, away from the action.

⭐ **Hardeman House**　　B&B $$
(📞 936-205-5280; www.hardemanhouse.com; 316 N Church St; r $100-140) What gorgeous woodwork and well-decorated rooms there are in this 1892 Victorian. Expect a warm welcome from proprietors who live here with their family. You may find it hard to leave the comfortable chairs on the wide wraparound porch. It's very central.

⭐ **Hotel Fredonia**　　BOUTIQUE HOTEL $$
(📞 936-564-1234; www.thefredonia.com; 200 N Fredonia St; r $100-200; P❄🅟🛜🏊) Enjoy mid-century style at this centrally located six-story hotel. A lavish renovation in 2017 has made this once again one of the nicest properties in the region. Ask for a cabana room out by the lushly landscaped saltwater pool.

Jones House Bed & Breakfast　　B&B $$
(📞 936-559-1487; http://thejoneshousebandb.com; 141 N Church St; r $100-150; ❄🛜) Three stories *and* a turret make this 1897 Victorian

mansion one of the town's finest. There are three spacious rooms with period furniture. The house has a dramatic corner location very close to the center.

🍴 Eating & Drinking

Butcher Boy's　　AMERICAN
(📞 936-560-1137; http://butcherboysnac.net; 603 North St; mains $7-15; ⊙10am-7pm Mon-Sat) Join the crowds queuing at the counter to place your order for great burgers, chicken-fried steak or barbecue. Options are many, try the fried okra. It's always busy and is a short walk from the center.

Banita Creek Hall　　CLUB
(📞 936-462-0000; http://banitacreekhall.com; 401 W Main St; ⊙8pm-midnight Wed-Fri, to 1am Sat) Grab a guy or gal and two-step around the floor to live local country music in a suitably sweaty hall. Wednesday night offers country-and-western dance lessons.

ℹ️ Information

Charles Bright Visitor Center (📞 936-564-7351; www.visitnacogdoches.org; 200 E Main St; ⊙9am-5pm Mon-Fri, 10am-4pm Sat, 1-4pm Sun) This remarkably thorough visitor center has information on just about any area subject

---

SIGHTS AROUND NACOGDOCHES

The rural lands around Nacogdoches are the sites of three not-to-be-missed attractions that cover a fair swath of the state's history.

Remnants of Texas' Native American past are few and far between. So the 1200-year-old ceremonial mounds at **Caddoan Mounds State Historic Site** (📞 936-858-3218; www.visitcaddomounds.com; 1649 Hwy 21 W, Alto; adult/child $4/3; ⊙8:30am-4:30pm Tue-Sun, 🚻), just 25 miles east of Nacogdoches, are a fascinating introduction. The visitor center here does a good job explaining how people lived here when the dramatic mounds were constructed. Interesting interpretive trails cover the area's history. It's a nice picnic spot too.

El Camino Real, the royal road connecting missions between Mexico City and current-day Louisiana, ran right through Nacogdoches. At **Mission Tejas State Park** (📞 park info 936-687-2394, reservations 512-389-8900; http://tpwd.texas.gov/state-parks/mission-tejas; 105 Park Rd 44, Grapeland; adult/child $2/free; ⊙8am-4pm), 32 miles east of Nacogdoches, you can see a replica of the 17th-century Mission San Francisco de los Tejas, tour the 1820s Rice Family Log Home and hike in the footsteps of Davy Crockett on a part of the road itself. The pleasant, 660-acre park also has shady, reservable campsites ($10 to $15).

Thirty-five miles north of Nacogdoches, relive the glory days of the steam engine on the **Texas State Railroad** (📞 877-726-7245; www.texasstaterr.com; Park Road 76, Rusk & 789 Park Road 70, Palatine; adult/child from $35/23; ⊙limited schedule May-Sep; 🚻). Four-hour, round-trip train rides travel through dogwood-bloom-filled forests between Rusk and Palatine. Either direction you go, the train stops long enough for a picnic lunch before returning. Some trains are pulled by steam engines; operating days are limited. There are various classes of service (we recommend the open-air cars for the views) and extra-cost thematic rides (moonlight dinner trains etc).

NATIONAL FORESTS OF THE NORTHEAST

Davy Crockett National Forest (☑936-655-2299; www.fs.usda.gov/texas; Ranger station, 18551 TX 7, Kennard) With 251 sq miles, Davy Crockett National Forest is one of the less developed forests and contains the **Ratcliff Lake Recreation Area**, and the picturesque, 20-mile **Four C National Recreation Trail** overlooking the Neches River. Canoers will dig the **Big Slough Canoe Trail**, part of a 3000-acre wilderness area which contains some of the biggest old-growth timber in Texas.

Sabine National Forest (☑409-625-1940; www.fs.usda.gov/texas; Ranger station, 5050 Hwy 21 E, Hempell) Along the Texas–Louisiana border, Sabine National Forest lines the west bank of **Toledo Bend Reservoir**, where you'll find recreational, boating and camping sites onshore. Inside the park, **Indian Mounds Recreation Site & Wilderness Area** offers several hiking trails.

Angelina National Forest (☑936-897-1068; www.fs.usda.gov/texas; Ranger station, 111 Walnut Ridge Rd, Zavalla) The Angelina National Forest has the **Sawmill Hiking Trail**, a 5½-mile-long gem along the Neches River. For the area's best boating and fishing, head to the **Sam Rayburn Reservoir**.

that might interest you, plus a small museum on local history.

ℹ Getting There & Away

Greyhound (☑800-231-2222; www.greyhound.com; 4010 South St/US 59, Sunshine Inc) Greyhound offers one bus a day to Houston (2¾ hours, from $34) from an inconvenient location 2 miles south of the center.

Tyler

☑903 / POP 100,300

Amidst the often-bland charms of northeast Texas, Tyler is a like a rose amid the, well... The city is one of the nation's centers of rose growing and it has a stunning municipal garden. It also makes a good stop if you're heading through the region.

◉ Sights

★**Tyler Municipal Rose Garden**   GARDENS
(☑903-531-1212; www.cityoftylerrosegarden.com; 420 Rose Park Dr; ⊙garden dawn-dusk, museum 8am-5pm Mon-Fri, 9am-5pm Sat, 1-5pm Sun) FREE Romantics, be prepared to swoon: home to the country's biggest domestic supply of roses, Tyler is also home to this 14-acre garden with 38,000 plants in 500 varieties. A museum on-site gives full details on roses and the history of the rose festival.

Camp Ford Historic Park   HISTORIC SITE
(☑903-592-5993; http://smithcountyhistorical society.org/camp-ford/; 6540 US Hwy 271 N; ⊙park 8am-6pm, museum 10am-4pm Tue-Fri, noon-4pm Sat) FREE Camp Ford was the

largest prisoner of war (POW) camp run by the Confederacy west of the Mississippi. Opened in 1863, it held over 5000 Union prisoners; conditions were often appalling. Outside the camp, mob-rule often prevailed. Freed African Americans were often slaughtered and burned at the stake for having 'Yankee sympathies.' The site today has interpretive trails, a reconstructed POW cabin and a small museum.

Kiepersol Estates Winery   WINERY
(☑903-894-8995; www.kiepersol.com; 3933 FM 344 E; tours & tastings $10-15; ⊙tasting room 11am-7pm Tue-Sat.) Walk the mile-long vineyard trail, have a taste or take a tour (confirm schedule in advance); located 15 miles southeast of downtown. The winery produces a range of styles, including full-bodied reds like Cabernet and Syrah. Visitors can enjoy the winery restaurant, which is open for lunch and dinner Tuesday to Saturday. It serves steaks and fresh seafood. Book in advance.

★ Festivals & Events

Azalea & Spring Flower Trail   CULTURAL
(www.visittyler.com/azaleatrail; ⊙Mar-Apr) Organized each spring, this festival of blooms is held over about two weeks, starting sometime later in March, depending on each year's peak blooming time (check the website for annual updates). Two routes totaling 10 miles are set each year and pass by the area's most spectacular public and private floral displays. On some weekend days you can buy tickets for open-air buses that cover the routes.

HOUSTON & EAST TEXAS TYLER

Texas Rose Festival   FLOWER
(www.texasrosefestival.com; ⊙ mid-Oct) Flowers are the focus of this annual festival in the 'Rose City' in the fall. There's a short parade, the crowning of a rose queen and floral displays. It's a spectacle of local pomp.

🛏 Sleeping & Eating

Rosevine Inn   B&B $$
(☑ 903-592-2221; www.rosevine.com; 415 S Vine Ave; r $130-200; P ✳ 🤙) Tyler's Rosevine Inn is a gracious brick home offering bounteous breakfasts and four comfy rooms and two suites. Enjoy the outdoor hot tub, the red barn decked out as a rec room (pool players, rejoice!) and the gardens.

**Fairfield Inn & Suites
by Marriott Tyler**   HOTEL $$
(☑ 903-561-2535; www.marriott.com; 1945 W SW Loop 323; r $100-150; P ✳ 🤙 ⚊) Standard chain hotel on the south side of town, newer than most.

⭐ **Stanley's Famous
Pit Barbecue**   BARBECUE $
(☑ 903-593-0311; http://stanleysfamous.com; 525 S Beckham Ave; mains $7-13; ⊙ 7-10am Mon-Fri, 11am-10pm Mon-Sat) Your one-stop shop for good food and drink in Tyler. Superb barbecue in all forms is served in sandwiches, on plates, in tacos and more. Top regional country, blues and rock groups plus vocalists perform on Friday and Saturday nights. Sit in the rambling dining room or out on the terrace.

Rick's on the Square   AMERICAN $$$
(☑ 903-531-2415; www.rix.com; 104 W Erwin St; lunch mains $7-12, dinner mains $20-40; ⊙ 11am-midnight Mon-Fri, 4pm-1am Sat, 10am-2pm Sun) In Tyler's somnolent old downtown, Rick's is in an old brick building and offers an upscale option for a night out. The menu is straightforward American comfort (steaks, burgers, seafood); the bar serves top-end cocktails, microbrews and good wines. On weekends, there's live music and dancing.

Canton

☑ 903 / POP 3600

Each month over 100,000 bargain hunters descend on this small town looking to buy cheap stuff at the legendary First Monday Trade Days (which actually take place the previous four days). The rest of the month,

Canton is a sleepy little town with a pleasant courthouse square and a few full-time shops offering various goods cheap.

🍴 Eating

⭐ **Buttermilk's**   AMERICAN
(☑ 903-567-3287; www.buttermilkscanton.com; 100 W Dallas St; mains $6-12; ⊙ 11am-8pm Mon-Thu, to 9pm Fri & Sat) Far above average country fare is on offer at this tidy corner brick cafe in the heart of town. The burgers are actually famous and the rest of the dishes are prepared fresh and with care (fried green beans and fried green tomatoes are among the notable sides).

🛍 Shopping

Canton First Monday Trade Days   MARKET
(☑ 903-567-6556; http://firstmondaycanton. com; ⊙ dawn-dusk) FREE First Monday Trade Days have been taking place in Canton since the 1850s. Today more than 5000 vendors gather the Thursday through Sunday before every first Monday of the month. Peak summer weekends, more than 100,000 visitors may attend this, the state's largest flea market.

Canton Dish Barn   HOMEWARES
(☑ 866-700-7323; www.cantondishbarn.com; 208 W Dallas St; ⊙ 9am-5pm) Typical of the shops that are open locally through the month is this store selling brightly colored dishes.

ℹ Information

Canton Visitor Bureau (☑ 903-567-1849; www.visitcantontx.com; 119 N Buffalo St; ⊙ 9am-5pm Mon-Fri) Has local B&B info as well as full details on the First Monday Trade Days.

**WHAT THE...?
TIGERS IN TEXAS**

Tiger Creek Wildlife Refuge (☑ 903-858-1008; www.tigercreek.org; FM 14, exit 562 off I-20; adult/child $18/14; ⊙ 10am-5pm, last entry 4pm), 13 miles north of downtown Tyler, is home to over 50 big cats that have been rescued from non-zoo captivity across the country. Tour the wooded enclosures on the ever-expanding, 30-acre-plus site and meet the lions, leopards, cougars – and tigers. It's supported by the Tiger Missing Link Foundation.

HOUSTON & EAST TEXAS CANTON

Kilgore

☑ 903 / POP 14,900

Twenty miles east of Tyler, Kilgore's old downtown recalls the kind of place you might imagine James Dean roaming around circa *Giant* movie era. An old theater, the brick front buildings and dusty streets, the oil wells rising in the distance... Indeed, many of the buildings date to the boomtown era after oil was discovered here in 1930. Check out the art-deco downtown (corner of Kilgore and E Main Sts), where several boutique Western-wear shops sport names like Calamity Jane's and Crystal Spur.

◉ Sights

World's Richest Acre Park PARK
(cnr E Main & Commerce St) Once home in the 1930s to the world's densest collection of oil derricks, this downtown park now has one of the originals plus 36 replicas.

Rangerette Showcase & Museum MUSEUM
(☑ 903-983-8265; www.rangerettes.com; 1100 Broadway; ⊗ 9am-4pm Mon-Fri) FREE Oil is not the only kind of drilling Kilgore is famous for; the town also claims bragging rights as home to the world's oldest women's precision drill teams, the Kilgore Rangerettes. These ladies – in their nifty red shirts, blue skirts and white hats and boots – perform at high-profile events. Don't skip the video at the museum, as it's your chance to see the Rockette-like, high-kicking action. Every April the Rangerettes showcase their dance talents at a variety showcase, called the Revels.

East Texas Oil Museum MUSEUM
(☑ 903-983-8295; www.easttexasoilmuseum.com; Kilgore College Campus, cnr Hwy 259 & Ross St; ⊗ 9am-5pm Tue-Sat) FREE Trace the town's boom – and bust – at the evocative East Texas Oil Museum, with vivid exhibits that do an admirable job re-creating the pre-oil discovery town. The World's Richest Acre Park has 36 re-created, light-topped oil derricks to commemorate the wells that gave this site its name. This patch of real estate yielded 2.5 million barrels of oil during a 30-year run. At the height of the boom, the number of oil wells in town numbered 1200.

✗ Eating

★ **Country Tavern** BARBECUE $$
(☑ 903-984-9954; www.countrytavern.com; 1526 FM 2767; mains $8-25; ⊗ 11am-9pm Mon-Thu, to 10pm Fri & Sat) ⌿ The Country Tavern, 5 miles west of Kilgore on Hwy 31, is known statewide for its wonderfully tender barbecued ribs and other wood-smoked meats. The nearly windowless metal building has a lot less charm than the same-colored barbecue sauce, which has a nice kick.

Jefferson

☑ 903 / POP 2100

With gracious architecture, a perfectly preserved old town, charismatic locals and a superb natural setting, Jefferson is the kind of town tourist boards dream about. Once the largest inland river port in the USA, pre–Civil War Jefferson was a mini New Orleans: the stomping grounds of a wild bunch of gamblers, riverboat men and madams. Since then, Jefferson has calmed down considerably.

The town is relatively small, but don't even think of stopping for just an afternoon. The old streets (first laid out in 1842) beg to be strolled, with a requisite stop at one of the soda fountains, of course. Then there are the antique shops to browse, historic homes to tour, ghosts to hunt... Make sure you take a boat ride on the Big Cypress Bayou, part of Caddo Lake. Jefferson's a seductive Southern belle with a checkered past – don't be surprised if you fall under her spell.

◉ Sights

The first thing to do is to take a stroll around town and soak up the vintage charms. The visitor center has a full list of all the small museums and house tours that keep irregular hours. Don't forget that Caddo Lake (p246) is only 15 miles away.

Jefferson is visitor-driven, so not everything will be open on weekdays.

Jefferson Historical Museum MUSEUM
(☑ 903-665-2775; www.jeffersonmuseum.com; 223 W Austin St; adult/child $7/3; ⊗ 9:30am-4:30pm) The three-story, 1888 brick courthouse contains interesting exhibits on early life in east Texas and the original Caddo Indian tribe. There's interesting detail on the steamboat commerce that built the area. Kids like the model trains.

Excelsior House HISTORIC SITE
(☑ 903-665-2513; http://theexcelsiorhouse.com; 211 W Austin St) FREE This central, historic hotel was built in the 1850s by a riverboat captain. Famous guests have included US

presidents Ulysses S Grant and Rutherford B Hayes, as well as poet Oscar Wilde. Ask about free daily tours of the hotel – and the ghosts.

The Grove   HOUSE
(📞 903-665-8018; www.thegrove-jefferson.com; 405 Moseley St; tour $6; ☺ tours 2pm Sat, 11am Sun) The Grove, a private home built in 1861, had reports of hauntings way back in 1882. Take an hour-long tour with owner and author Michael Whittington, who has written about Jefferson and the town's ghosts. Confirm tour times and book in advance.

Atlanta Private Railway Car   HISTORIC SITE
(📞 903-665-2513; 208 W Austin St, Excelsior House; tours $5; ☺ by appointment) Rail baron Jay Gould once offered to bring the railroad to Jefferson, but the town (inauspiciously) turned him down, deciding to bet its future on river traffic. Gould's ultraluxe private 1888 railroad car, the *Atlanta*, now sits near the center of town. Contact Excelsior House (p244) about tours, usually, but not always available 10am to 3pm.

🚶 Tours

★ **Turning Basin Riverboats Tours**   BOATING
(📞 903-665-2222; www.jeffersonbayoutours. com; 200 Bayou St; adult/child $10/5; ☺ Tue-Sat Apr-Oct) You'll hear plenty of local lore on the narrated, hour-long flat-bottom boat rides on the dramatic and scenic waters of Big Cypress Bayou. The launch point is just across Polk St bridge from downtown. Call for varying departure times, and for required reservations.

Historic Jefferson Railway   RAIL
(📞 866-398-2038; www.jeffersonrailway.com; 400 E Austin St; adult/child under 6 from $12/free; ☺ 9pm Fri, 2:30pm, 4:30pm & 9pm Sat Jun-Aug; 👶) Summer weekends, take a narrated open-air train-car ride during the day, or a ghost tour at night. Theme trains (Great Train Robbery, Halloween, Christmas) operate other weekends during the year. Most trains are pulled by steam engines.

Historic Jefferson Ghost Walk   WALKING
(📞 903-665-6289; http://jeffersonghostwalk.com; cnr Austin & Vale Sts; adult/child $15/8; ☺ 8pm Fri & Sat) Learn about the town's tragedies and legends as you walk in and among the old buildings. Ghost tours last about an hour and a half. Buy tickets at the meeting place beginning at 7:30pm tour nights.

✨ Festivals & Events

Pilgrimage Tour of Homes   CULTURAL
(www.jeffersonpilgrimage.com; adult/child $24/3; ☺ May) One weekend in May the influential local garden club hosts a home tour of historic properties. It's the event of the year, with accompanying balls, plays and a parade.

🛏 Sleeping

Jefferson boasts it's the B&B capital of Texas. Options range from one-room cabins to Victorian mansions. The visitor center lists most online.

Marshall (population 24,000) is 15 miles south and has numerous chain hotels near exits off I-10.

★ **White Oak Manor B&B**   B&B $$
(📞 903-665-8185; www.bedandbreakfastjefferson tx.com; 502 E Benners St; r $110-170; ❄ 🛜) Make yourself at home, relax on the wraparound porch or pop popcorn and watch a movie in one of three rooms at this welcoming Greek Revival house, a short walk from downtown.

Benefield House   B&B $$
(📞 903-665-9366; http://benefieldhouse.com; 1009 S Line St; r $90-150; ❄ 🛜) All the frills you'd expect of a Victorian 'painted lady.' Deep, rich colors and period-appropriate American antiques fill this Queen Anne home. Except for the king-size beds and essential air-conditioning, you might think you were back in the 1800s.

Delta Street Inn   B&B $$
(📞 903-665-2929; www.deltastreetinn.com; 206 E Delta St; r $100-150; ❄ 🛜) With the restrained mix of gorgeous English antiques and comfortable reproductions, the owners here have created the ideal B&B. This restored 1920s inn combines a classic feel with modern convenience in all five rooms. Amenities include a game room, daily treats and a coffee bar for early mornings.

Jefferson Hotel   HISTORIC HOTEL $$
(📞 903-665-2631; www.historicjeffersonhotel.com; 124 W Austin St; r $90-120; ❄ 🛜) Fans of paranormal activity are advised to stay at this historic, if dated, 25-room hotel. For example, rooms 19 and 20 have been known to freak out eye-rolling skeptics (even Stephen King is rumored to have been spooked). Furnishings are period specific; upstairs rooms have a wide porch.

✗ Eating

Jefferson has more restaurants than you'd expect for a town its size. Many are situated around Austin St in the old downtown core.

★ Kitt's Kornbread
Sandwich & Pie Bar
AMERICAN $

(☑ 903-665-0505; www.kittskornbread.com; 125 N Polk St; mains $6-12; ☉ 11am-3pm Mon-Fri, to 5pm Sat, noon-3pm Sun) Old-fashioned chicken and dumplings is the savory star at this family-run cafe. But be sure to save room for the pie. All 15 varieties are tasty, but the buttermilk pie is just 'that' much better. Oh, and as you'd surmise: the cornbread is superb, especially in sandwiches.

★ Joseph's Riverport Barbecue
BARBECUE $

(☑ 903-665-2341; 201 N Polk St; dishes $5-11; ☉ 11am-7pm Tue-Sat, to 2pm Sun) Texas barbecue done right. Order at the counter and retreat to the long wooden tables with your groaning plate of brisket, turkey breast, fried okra, plus sweet iced tea – if you can grab a space from the locals. The swamp fries combine a little of everything: french fries, brisket, peppers, cheese and more.

Five D Cattle Co
STEAK $$

(☑ 903-562-1291; http://fivedcattle.com; 9 N Main St, Avinger; mains $16-30; ☉ 4:30-8pm) Reasonable steaks and the friendly, down-home atmosphere are worth the drive 15 miles west to Avinger. Everybody knows everybody eating in here in these converted old wooden store buildings; you soon will too.

 ## Shopping

Look for antiques stores lining the western end of Austin and Lafayette Sts, and also on S Polk, S Vale and S Walnut Sts.

Jefferson General Store
GIFTS & SOUVENIRS

(☑ 903-665-8481; www.jeffersongeneralstore.com; 113 E Austin St; ☉ 9am-7pm Sun-Thu, to 10pm Fri & Sat) A kitschy delight: the old general store is crammed with an idiosyncratic array of Texas-themed souvenirs. When you're done shopping, cool off with an ice cream or soda at the counter. All manner of old-timey sweet treats are sold for takeout.

ℹ Information

Jefferson Visitor Center (☑ 903-665-3733; www.visitjeffersontexas.com; 305 E Austin St; ☉ 9am-5pm Mon-Fri, daily in summer) Helpful staff with comprehensive information; it even has a binder with pictures and descriptions of nearly every B&B or rental within a 50-mile radius.

Caddo Lake

Picture craggy, partly submerged bald cypress trees covered with low-hanging moss swaying in the breeze. Imagine floating quietly past 3ft-tall herons and egrets on labyrinthine waterways. Envision the occasional alligator eyes gliding by... You've got the scene: evocative, intoxicating and OK, we admit it, a little eerie. Texas' largest freshwater lake snakes off into narrow bayous and tributaries that cover more than 26,000 acres that are well worth exploring by boat. If you can, get up early to watch as the steam rises off the bayous.

The lake's de facto headquarters is the community of Uncertain, which is a junky meandering area of fishing shacks, tour companies, cabins, groceries, and a few casual restaurants and small cafes. For more information log onto www.caddolake.info.

Don't forget bug spray.

◉ Sights & Activities

★ Caddo Lake State Park
PARK

(☑ 903-679-3351; http://tpwd.texas.gov/stateparks/caddo-lake; 245 Park Rd 2, Karmack; adult/child $4/free, campsites $10-20, cabins $75-115; ☉ office 8am-5pm, park 24hr) Caddo Lake State Park is a good place to start your lake adventure. Take an interpretive hike through the cypress forest on the lake's western edge. Or, in summer, rent a canoe from the on-site concession, Old Port Caddo Rentals & Tours (p246). The park has some great little cabins built by the Civilian Conservation Corps (CCC) and the 46 riverside tent sites are pretty sweet.

Old Port Caddo Rentals & Tours
CANOEING

(☑ 903-431-1673; www.oldportcaddo.com; 2670 Blairs Landing Rd, Karnack; canoe rental per day $35, tours adult/child $18/10) In summer rent a canoe or enjoy an hour-long pontoon boat tour; reservations required. Tours and rentals generally April to October but confirm in advance. The dock is inside the state park area.

☞ Tours

★ Caddo Outback
Backwater Tours
BOATING

(☑ 903-789-3384; www.caddolaketours.com; 1869 Pine Island Rd; 2-person tours per hour $50) Local authorities call affable local boy John Winn when someone gets lost on the lake. You should call him too; his private, one-hour to full-day tours take you by 18ft swamp boat to places other outfitters can't reach. Ask about nighttime tours. Book in advance.

Captain Ron's Swamp Tours   BOATING
(☑ 903-679-3020; http://captronswamptours.com; 756 Pine Island Rd, Karnack; 70min tours from $15; ◷ 10am, noon, 2pm & 4pm Wed-Sun Mar-Nov) Operates tours to key parts of the lake on a 28ft-boat that seats 16.

🛏 Sleeping & Eating

Accommodation tends to be in lake cabins geared for groups here to fish and drink beer. You'll find B&Bs in Jefferson and motels in Marshall.

When you're ready for a repast, local menus feature fried catfish and other swamp seafood. There are many more choices in Jefferson.

Hodge Podge Cottages   COTTAGE $$
(☑ 903-789-3901; www.hodgepodgecottages.com; 724 Cypress Dr, Uncertain; cottages $135-175; 🛜) Offers everything from a mobile home to a regular house to a dry-docked houseboat for overnight rental on a large grassy site next to the river. Most of the 11 units sleep up to eight people and have a two-night minimum. Free canoe use included; there's a fishing pier and cleaning station.

★ Shady Glade Cafe   AMERICAN $
(☑ 903-789-2123; 510 Cypress Dr; mains $6-15; ◷ 8am-5pm) Right on the lake near the docks, this wooden restaurant is always busy with gossiping locals, many lounging around on battered chairs out front. The menu carries the usual catfish and fried pickles. Daily specials usually include several shrimp dishes. It also rents a few cabins nearby.

River Bend Restaurant   SEAFOOD $$
(☑ 903-679-9000; 211 FM 2422, Karnack; mains $18-28; ◷ 5-9pm Wed & Thu, to 10pm Fri, 11am-10pm Sat, noon-7pm Sun) Enjoy great water views from the glass-enclosed patio and a large covered deck. Catfish, chicken-fried steak, hush puppies and more lead a classic east Texas lineup of dishes.

Big Pines Lodge   SEAFOOD $$
(☑ 903-679-3655; www.bigpineslodge.com; 747 Pine Island Rd, Karnack; mains $10-22; ◷ 4-9pm Thu & Fri, 11am-9pm Sat & Sun) A 60-year-old Caddo Lake classic in a modern building

right on the river. There is multitier terrace seating outside. Most dishes are some combination of catfish and shrimp.

Carthage
☑ 903 / POP 6900

Carthage is barely a spot on the map out near the Louisiana border. But it was the birthplace of legendary cowboy singer Tex Ritter, and honors his musical legacy. The town is fairly isolated, if visiting, try to come through on a Saturday so you can catch the music show.

Texas Country Music Hall of Fame   MUSEUM
(☑ 903-693-6634; www.carthagetexas.us/hallof fame/; 310 W Panola, Carthage; adult/child $10/5; ◷ 10am-4pm Mon-Sat) Browse the exhibits about the radio and silver screen star Tex Ritter, and other legends of Texas country, then sit back and listen to them sing from the free juke box.

Country Music Hayride   CONCERT
(☑ 903-622-4390; www.thecountrymusichayride. com; Esquire Theater, 114 W Sabine St, Carthage; adult/child $6/3; ◷ 7pm Sat) An east Texas institution in the old downtown Esquire Theater. On Saturday evenings the Country Music Hayride harks back to the early days of the Grand Ol' Opry and other country variety shows. After a troubled period, the show was reborn in 2017. Check the website to confirm acts and schedules.

Edom & Ben Wheeler

The small town of Ben Wheeler (population 450; https://benwheelertx.com) is really the vision of one man, Brooks Gremmels, who grew up here many years ago. He decided to save it from the tumbleweed-like fate of many small Texas towns by buying up as much property as he could and encouraging offbeat small businesses to locate here. So far it's been a success, with buildings being restored to a 1935 look and many cafes and boutiques opening. Various folk festivals are held through the year.

Eight miles southeast, Edom (population 370, http://visitedom.com) is another small town with hints of a greater past. Linking the pair is one of those two-lane rural Texas roads that are always interesting for a drive: FM 279, which meanders along through some fecund farms.

HURRICANE HARVEY

Hurricane Harvey made landfall in Southeast Texas on August 25, 2017, bringing with it the winds of a category 4 storm and rains the region had literally never seen before. Over the course of four days, the Houston area received nearly 52 inches of rain – a record for the continental US – and the city's bayous overflowed their banks. Flooding affected much of Harris County, and the coastal towns of Rockport and Port Aransas were among those that bore the brunt of the storm winds.

Recovery efforts have been impressive and many places have been able to get up and running again remarkably quickly; some are still recovering and our listings give details on this wherever possible.

Many coastal towns in the region rely on tourism and will be keen to welcome visitors again after they've been able to recover, but before you travel, check the official government website of any city you want to visit (houstontx.gov for Houston) for updates as well as drivetexas.org for any lingering road closures.

For more tips on where to find the best of this region, see www.countylinemagazine.com.

Cute little countrified cafes are the stock and trade of the two villages.

Eating

Moore's Store BURGERS $
([☎] 903-833-5100; www.mooresstore.com; 1551 FM 279, Ben Wheeler; mains $6-15; ⊘ 11am-10pm Sun-Fri, to 1am Sat) A mix of country, blues and Cajun-music bands play Friday through Sunday night at Moore's Store, a 1933 mercantile store. The burgers and beers are popular with the weekend Harley-riding crowd

Shed Cafe SOUTHERN US $
([☎] 903-852-7791; 8337 FM 279, Edom; mains $5-24; ⊘ 6:30am-8pm Tue-Sat, to 4pm Sun & Mon) The Shed Cafe routinely wins praise for its fried chicken. The rest of the fare is filling and the dirt parking lot is usually full.

Forge PIZZA
(http://theforgebenwheeler.com; 1610 FM 279, Ben Wheeler; mains $7-18; ⊘ 8am-11pm Wed-Sat, to 9pm Sun) The Forge serves pizza (plus salads, tacos and sandwiches), and offers singer-songwriter folk music Thursday through Saturday. Wednesday is open-mike night. The cafe has a big wraparound porch. Special events through the year include barstool races.

☆ Entertainment

Old Firehouse LIVE MUSIC
([☎] 903-852-2781; www.jeffreylancephotography.com/theoldfirehouse; 8241 FM 279, Edom; ⊘ 10am-3pm Thu-Sat) You can hear acoustic music performances at this small little gallery. Confirm schedules in advance.

HOUSTON & EAST TEXAS EDOM & BEN WHEELER

Gulf Coast & South Texas

Best Places to Eat

➡ Roosevelt's at the Tarpon Inn (p275)

➡ Taco N' Madre (p290)

➡ El Meson de San Augustin (p290)

➡ Maceo Spice & Import (p260)

Best Places to Sleep

➡ Inn at Chachalaca Bend (p279)

➡ Casa de Palmas Renaissance Hotel (p287)

➡ La Posada Hotel & Suites (p290)

➡ V Boutique Hotel (p271)

Why Go?

America's 'Third Coast,' as it has dubbed itself, is a place of many contrasts. The beach-town scene of Port Aransas is a sea of calm compared with the frenetic hedonism of South Padre Island, for one. There are plenty of reminders of the state's dramatic history too, from the first shots of the Mexican-American War at the Palo Alto Battlefield National Historic Site to the long and bumpy history of the port city of Galveston.

Along the Rio Grande River, border politics affect all aspects of life. In many ways the area forms a cultural border distinct from Mexico and Texas, a unique multicultural and bilingual region that for a short time was even an independent state. The Republic of the Rio Grande may not have survived as a political entity, but this unique history still accents the towns and remote stretches from Brownsville to Laredo and beyond.

When to Go
Corpus Christi

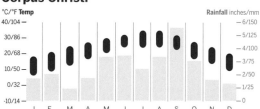

Mar Spring Break! Hordes of partying students, but also peak bird-migration season.	**Apr–May & Sep–Oct** The weather is just right and crowds are few.	**Dec–Feb** Peak 'Winter Texan' season and reasonably warm temperatures.

Gulf Coast & South Texas Highlights

1 Aransas National Wildlife Refuge (p264) Bird-watching in this coastal wetlands reserve of nearly 115,000 acres, which serve as spotting grounds for hundreds of species.

2 Brazos Bend State Park (p262) Getting up close and personal with wild alligators.

3 Bishop's Palace (p256) Gaping at what was the crowning jewel of Galveston

during the 1800s, the island's heyday as the country's second-busiest port.

4 Padre Island National Seashore (p277) Savoring 60 miles of nearly undeveloped

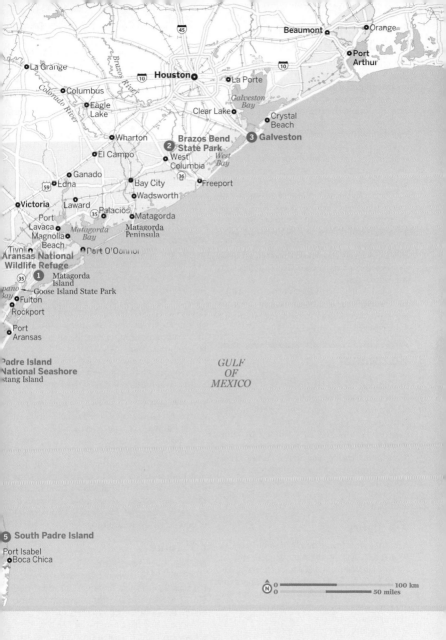

beach, less than an hour's drive from a major city and airport.

5 Sea Turtle, Inc. (p280) Working hard to restore critically endangered Kemp's ridley seaturtle populations by joining one of the summer hatchling releases on South Padrev Island.

BEAUMONT & THE GOLDEN TRIANGLE

The cities of Beaumont, Port Arthur and Orange – each roughly 20 miles apart – make up the points of the Golden Triangle in the southeasternmost corner of the state. The area has more in common culturally and environmentally with neighboring Louisiana than with the rest of Texas. Among the cypress trees, swamps and coastal wetlands, you can find natural adventures, but the rest of the area's attractions are tied to the oil-and-gas industry.

When oil gushed skyward from a site called Spindletop in 1901, it set the stage for the region's development. Some of the largest petrochemical companies in the world were founded near Port Arthur and Beaumont. The area is not always the world's prettiest, though there's a certain dystopian visual quality that appeals to some.

Spend a day or two exploring the Golden Triangle's good museums and interesting oil-related sights, plus a few more for nature-lovers and birders.

Beaumont

🕿 409 / POP 118,296

In addition to the petrochemical industry, Beaumont has developed a busy port on the Neches River that services offshore oil-drilling platforms. At local museums you can learn most everything you ever wanted to know about local oil and gas. Some money from these industries has gone to fund arts and cultural institutions. Life here largely takes place along the interstate. Downtown is pleasant but mostly quiet, apart from a block of up-scale bars.

⊙ Sights

Art Museum of Southeast Texas MUSEUM
(🕿 409-832-3432; www.amset.org; 500 Main St; ⊙ 9am-5pm Mon-Fri, from 10am Sat, from noon Sun; ⊒ 6/7/8/10) **FREE** This museum manages to pack a surprisingly diverse collection of rotating fine- and folk-art exhibits into its small display space, and the emphasis on regional artists means you're likely to make a few discoveries. Check the website to see what's on.

Spindletop & Gladys City Boomtown Museum MUSEUM
(🕿 409-880-1750; www.lamar.edu/spindletop-gladys-city; 5550 Jimmy Simmons Blvd, off US 69; adult/child $5/2; ⊙ 10am-5pm Tue-Sat, 1-5pm Sun; ⊒ 7)

Several prospectors saw promise in the Spindletop salt dome, but it took nearly a decade before an exploratory well leased by Anthony Lucas blew a fountain of oil and kicked off the Petroleum Age in the US. Almost overnight Gladys City sprang up, full of wildcat oil explorers, and soon wooden oil derricks crowded together like trees in a forest. This intriguing, open-air museum re-creates part of the original boomtown.

Though the buildings are replicas, most of the objects are 1890s and 1900s originals. A local photo studio in business at the time is to thank for much of the amazing documentation at the museum. Only one thing is missing – add 800,000 barrels of spilled oil and then you'd really know what it felt like back then.

McFaddin-Ward House HISTORIC BUILDING
(🕿 409-832-2134; www.mcfaddin-ward.org; 1906 McFaddin Ave, visitor center 1906 Calder Ave; tours $5; ⊙ 10am-2:30pm Tue-Sat, 1-3:30pm Sun; ⊒ 3) Visit this fabulous 1906 beaux-arts/colonial-revival mansion to see the excess made possible by the Spindletop oil boom. Members of the McFaddin family lived in the house until 1984; their original antique furnishings fill the lavish rooms. Tours, which start with a short film and last around an hour, are mandatory and reservations are suggested – especially on Sunday when tours of the 1st floor are free.

Gator Country WILDLIFE RESERVE
(🕿 409-794-9453; www.gatorrescue.com; 21159 FM 365, at I-10 exit 838; adult/child $15/12; ⊙ 10am-5pm) Feed the gators, photo-op with small reptiles and watch a live edutainment show put on by this local animal-rescue outfit. You may have seen the Gator Country crew in one of their roles rescuing alligators from human threats on cable-TV shows like *River Monsters* and *Gator 911*. The park is 15 miles west of downtown Beaumont.

🎧 Tours

Neches River Adventures BOATING
(🕿 409-651-5326; www.nechesriveradventures.org; 801 Main St, Beaumont Riverfront Park; adult/child $15/10; ⊙ 8am-8pm Mar-Nov) A two-hour cruise on the flat-bottomed pontoon boat *Ivory Bill* takes passengers through the Neches River ecosystem, which has more than 200 tree species, countless birds and of course alligators. Public tours depart each Saturday from the Beaumont Riverfront Park (reservations required), and charters are possible daily pending availability.

🛏 Sleeping

Beaumont lodging options are not the greatest. Chain motels and hotels are numerous on I-10, but many are outdated. The largest concentration is near the US 69/96/287 interchange. Call ahead for availability as many places were busy during the hurricane relief efforts.

Holiday Inn & Suites – Parkdale HOTEL $$
(☑409-892-3600; www.ihg.com; 7140 US 69 N, at Rte 105; r $110-140; ❄🅿🛜♨) Welcoming staff and modern rooms make this a top choice among the chain gang. The location just north of town is ideal for those heading toward the Big Thicket.

La Quinta Inn – Beaumont West HOTEL $$
(☑409-842-0002; www.laquintabeaumontwest. com; 6820 Walden Rd; r $90 120, ❄🅿🛜, 🛜4) A well-maintained iteration of the La Quinta chain with attentive staff. Amenities include microwaves and minifridges in the room, hot breakfast, and an outdoor pool and hot tub.

🍴 Eating

Visitors are a bit spoiled for choice with the wide range of restaurants in Beaumont, but stick with the Cajun/Southern/BBQ trifecta that defines so much of the Golden Triangle's cuisine and it'll be hard to go wrong.

Patillo's Bar-B-Que BARBECUE $
(☑409-833-3156; 2775 Washington Blvd; meals $8-12; ⊙10am-8pm Tue-Fri, to 4pm Mon, to 6pm Sat; ❄; 🛜8) Though the location has changed numerous times, Patillo's has been a mainstay of Beaumont's food scene since 1912. The beef links use a local southeast Texas style that's unusual and a little greasy (albeit definitely worth trying), but the ribs are classic and almost divine.

Suga's Deep South Cuisine & Jazz Bar SOUTHERN $$
(☑409-813-1808; http://sugasdeepsouth.com; 461 Bowie St; lunch & brunch $8-18, dinner mains $12-28; ⊙11am-3pm & 4-10pm Mon-Fri, 4-11pm Sat, 10:30am-3pm Sun; ❄🛜🍴; 🛜1/2/3/6/7/8/10) Set in a sleek, historic 1914 building, Suga's gives off a sexy speakeasy vibe. Southern dishes like blackened shrimp with remoulade and grits definitely speak with a Creole accent, and live performances will keep you around after dinner ends.

Floyd's Cajun Seafood CAJUN $$
(☑409-842-0686; http://floydscajunseafood.res taurant; 2290 I-10 S; lunch $9-11, dinner mains $16-29; ⊙11am-10pm Sun-Thu, to 11pm Fri & Sat; 🛜4)

All the Cajun classics, plus lots of lively fun, are available at this beloved southeast Texas chain. Expect a wait weekends, especially during spring crawfish season, and on weekdays during the popular lunch service from 11am to 2pm.

ℹ Information

Beaumont Convention & Visitors Bureau
(☑409-880-3749; www.beaumontcvb. com; 505 Willow St; ⊙8am-5pm Mon-Fri; 🛜1/2/3/5) In addition to an information office, the CVB has a great website and mobile app. Regional visitor guides can be requested online.

Ben J Rogers Regional Visitor Center
(☑409-842-0500; 5055 I-10 S; ⊙9am-5pm) Pick up a copy of the visitor guide to the entire Golden Triangle and southeast Texas at this welcome center 15 miles west of downtown Beaumont.

ℹ Getting There & Away

Amtrak Stop (☑800-872-7245; www.amtrak. com; 2555 W Cedar St) This unstaffed train platform is served by Amtrak's *Sunset Limited* service between Los Angeles and New Orleans.

Around Beaumont

Nature lovers should head out of town to explore two sprawling nature reserves.

◎ Sights

Anahuac National Wildlife Refuge WILDLIFE RESERVE
(☑409-267-3337; www.fws.gov/refuge/Anahuac; 401/ FM 563, Anahuac; ⊙park gates dawn-dusk) Of the three national wildlife refuges along the Gulf Coast from Galveston to Louisiana, the 34,000-acre Anahuac has the best access – 50 miles northwest of Galveston and 80 miles southeast of Houston – and is therefore the most popular. The main entrance is the gateway to the majority of the facility's trails and an excellent hiking/driving loop around **Shoveler Pond**.

Big Thicket National Preserve NATURE RESERVE
(☑visitor center 409-951-6700; www.nps.gov/ bith; 6102 FM 420) FREE Until the mid-19th century, Big Thicket was a dense and mysterious forest where Civil War draft dodgers hid out. Today the national preserve is the crossroads of Texas' most interesting ecosystems: where coastal plains meet desert sand dunes, and cypress swamps stand next to pine and hardwood forests. Growing here are 145 different tree and plant species, plus 20 rare and hard-to-find orchids. Entry is

CAJUN CULTURE

The Golden Triangle is also referred to as the Cajun Triangle due to the large number of Cajuns living in the area. French-speaking settlers exiled from l'Acadie (now Nova Scotia) sought refuge in adjacent southwestern Louisiana in the mid- to late 18th century (the term 'Cajun' is a corruption of 'Acadian'). In the early 20th century many Cajuns moved across the border to Beaumont and Port Arthur to find work in the oil fields.

Cajun culture is famed for its cuisine, music and spirit. Let the *bons temps roulée!* The influence is felt in Houston and towns along the coast, but nowhere more strongly than here. Don't pass up this opportunity to eat specialties such as boudin (sausage made from spicy pork and rice), seafood gumbo (a roux-based soup) and etouffée (seafood in a creamy but spicy sauce), or try the classic red beans and rice with pork sausage. On menus you'll also see po'boys (loaf sandwiches filled with such fried treats as oysters, shrimp or catfish).

Locals can't wait for crawfish season to come around. If you're in town between March and May, you have to try a crawfish boil. These small, lobsterlike shellfish (also called 'mudbugs') are dropped live into the pot simmering with spicy cayenne seasonings. Corn on the cob, new potatoes, sausage or shrimp go in too. . Make sure you wear a bib, and under no circumstances should you rub your eyes for the next few hours.

free and so is camping, though you'll need a permit from the visitor's center.

Orange

📞 409 / POP 18,595

The smallest of the Triangle cities, Orange may have been named for citrus trees that once grew here or for Dutch settlers; no one is certain. A widely scattered Cajun population lives along the secluded bayous and tributaries of the Sabine River, which forms the border with Louisiana.

Prominent 20th-century local businessman WH Stark and his philanthropic son HL Stark have greatly influenced the cultural offerings in Orange. Tour the **Stark Museum of Art** (📞 409-886-2787; http://stark culturalvenues.org; 712 Green Ave; adult/child $6/5; ⊙ 9am-5pm Tue-Sat), which has collections of native wildlife and bird art, including works by John J Audubon. Or visit the **WH Stark House** (📞 409-883-0871; http://starkculturalvenues.org; 610 W Main St; tours adult/child $6/5, no children under 10yr; ⊙ 9am-5pm Tue-Sat), a museum itself. But our favorite family-funded attraction is the **Shangri La Botanical Gardens & Nature Center** (📞 409-670-9113; http://starkcultural venues.org; 2111 W Park Ave; adult/child $6/5; ⊙ 9am-5pm Tue-Sat). Though it's not totally isolated, you can still get a good feel for the area's environment by peering through the bird blind at the heron rookery on Ruby Lake, or by taking a boat ride on Adam's Bayou.

 Eating

Old Orange Cafe AMERICAN **$**
(📞 409-883-2233; http://oldorangecafe.com; 914 Division St; dishes $8-15; ⊙ 11am-3pm Mon-Fri, 10am-2pm Sun; ⊛ 🛜) Serving up Americana classics in a restored building and decorated with historic photos of Orange, this is a place to celebrate modern cuisine and local history. It's only open for lunch, but as long as you show up before posted closing hours, it should be possible to get an order in.

ℹ Information

Texas Travel Information Center (📞 800-452-9292, 409-883-9416; www.traveltex.com; 1708 I-10 E; ⊙ 8am-6pm) If you're entering the area from the east, you'll find a state-operated Texas Travel Information Center just over the Texas–Louisiana border in Orange. It has statewide information and a nature walk over the swamp out back.

Port Arthur

📞 409 / POP 53,818

After the Spindletop oil well blew, Port Arthur prospered, growing into a pretty little town – eventually home to a young Janis Joplin and numerous other celebrities. The oil-and-gas industry is still strong here and you can't miss the refineries along Hwy 82. At night the tower lights oddly resemble a city skyline at night. Huge deep-sea drilling rigs wait in gulfside maintenance yards for their chance to get back out and continue the search. Authentic Cajun and Vietnamese food are reason enough to visit, as is the town's one great museum.

◉ Sights

Lakeshore Dr near the center of Port Arthur has good views from the tall levee and a few beautiful old homes from the region's glory days, such as **Rose Hill Manor** (☑ 409-985-7292; 100 Woodworth Blvd; ☐ 1/2) FREE and the **Pompeiian Villa** (☑ 409-983-5977; 1953 Lakeshore Dr; $2; ☺ 10am-2pm Mon-Fri; ☐ 1/2), which have managed to survive the hurricanes. The visitors bureau provides a free driving-tour map covering historic sites, as well as a booklet about birding hot spots in the region.

Museum of the Gulf Coast   MUSEUM
(☑ 409-982-7000; www.museumofthegulfcoast. org; 700 Procter St; adult/child $6/3; ☺ 9am-5pm Mon-Sat; ☐ 1/2/3/4) This is a splendid museum that covers the natural, geological and cultural history of the region from 'Jurassic to Janis Joplin.' A large section is devoted to local celebrities like Janice, who remained a hometown girl until her death in 1970. Other area musicians covered include blues great Clarence 'Gatemouth' Brown and Jiles Perry Richardson Jr, aka 'the Big Bopper.'

Don't miss the small hall devoted to the works of painter and graphic artist Robert Rauschenberg, another hometown legend.

✕ Eating

Local cuisine is dominated by two major trends: decades of immigration and a massive shrimping industry. Cajun, Vietnamese and seafood are among the best choices. Some of the best eats are in the neighborhoods of Nederland (north) and Groves (east), so it's best to have your own transport to get the most out of the food scene here.

★ Bahn Mi Deli   VIETNAMESE $
(☑ 409-548-4629; 746 9th Ave; sandwiches $3; ☺ 8am-6pm Mon-Sat, to 5pm Sun; ☐ 3/4) You'll probably pass by a couple of times before you find it. The corner-store vibe isn't immediately convincing, but after tasting one (or a few) of the traditional-style *bahn mi* sandwiches, you may just find yourself wishing you'd taken advantage of the 'buy 5 get 1 free' promo. Staff speak some English, and can help explain the menu.

There's one tiny table, but patrons will generally takeout.

Sartin's Seafood   SEAFOOD $$
(☑ 409-721-9420; www.sartins.com; 3520 Nederland Ave, Nederland; mains $10-23; ☺ 11am-9pm Mon-Thu, to 10pm Fri & Sat; ☀ ☎) Owned by an ex-daughter-in-law of the original Sartin restaurant family in Sabine Pass, this casual Nederland outlet is famous for its barbecued crabs. Those and other grilled or fried seafood, with a Cajun spice, are offered alone and in combo platters.

Larry's French Market &
Cajun Restaurant   CAJUN $$
(☑ 409-962-3381; www.larrysfrenchmarket.com; 3701 Pure Atlantic Rd/FM 366, Groves; lunch dishes $8-11, mains $10-27, buffet $30; ☺ 11am-2pm Mon-Wed, to 9pm Thu, to 10pm Fri, 5-10pm Sat) Larry's has a real Louisiana vibe. You can't get more authentic than this rustic restaurant and dance hall. During lunch the local specialties – including shrimp creole, fried crawfish, and gumbo – are served cafeteria-style. On Thursday, Friday, and Saturday nights from 5pm the hot tables turn into an incredible all-you-can-eat buffet. (There's always a menu as well.)

From Thursday to Saturday evenings the dance floor fills with dancers shuffling to upbeat Cajun two-step, swamp pop and zydeco bands. The regulars couldn't be friendlier, but get there early on weekend evenings or you'll find you're in for a long wait.

ⓘ Information

Port Arthur Convention and Visitors Bureau
(☑ 409-985-7822; www.visitportarthurtx.com; 3401 Cultural Center Dr; ☺ 8am-5pm Mon-Fri; ☐ 3/4/11) Area visitor guides are available in person, or by request online.

Galveston
☑ 409 / POP 47,743

Part genteel Southern belle, part sunburned beach bunny: Galveston Island is Houston's favorite playmate. The old gal took a pretty severe beating by hurricane Ike in 2008, but she's battled back to normal since. Sitting on a barrier island near the northern end of a 600-mile-long Texas coastline, Galveston may not have the state's favorite beaches, but there's nowhere else boasting such a beautiful combination of sun-drenched historic charms.

◉ Sights

Galveston Island is 30 miles long but no more than 3 miles wide. The two biggest attractions – the historic districts and beaches – lie at the

Galveston

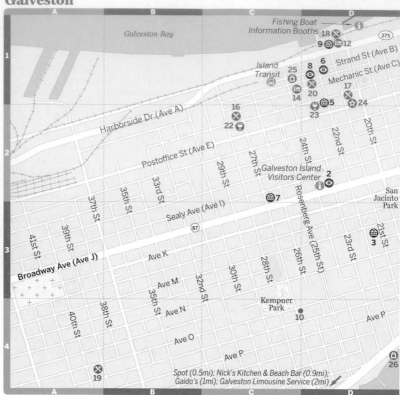

northeastern end of the island, bordered by Seawall Blvd and the gulf to the southeast and Harborside Dr and the port to the northwest. Look for the larger commercial amusement parks further west, southwest of 61st St.

A thin strip of freely accessible beaches lines Seawall Blvd. But there's more sand and services – and less concrete wall – at organized beaches. Fewer people frequent the southwestern beaches along San Luis Pass Rd, the extension of Seawall Blvd beyond town.

★ **Bishop's Palace**   HISTORIC BUILDING
(Map p256; ☑ 409-762-2475; www.galvestonhistory.org; 1402 Broadway Ave; adult/child $12/9; ⏰10am-5pm Sun-Fri, to 6pm Sat) Built between 1886 and 1893, this ornate stone mansion has hidden back stairs, false-lit stained glass and other fun features. It was constructed by the affluent entrepreneurial Gresham family, though the more colloquial name dates from the 1923 purchase of the

building by the Catholic Church when it was the home of the resident bishop for Sacred Heart Church. Self-guided audio tours of the first two floors explain the home's history, and discount coupons and tickets are widely available.

Monthly 'Basement to Attic' docent-led tours (per person $30) take in parts of the home otherwise off-limits to visitors.

Bryan Museum   MUSEUM
(Map p256; ☑ 409-632-7685; www.thebryanmuseum.org; 1315 21st St; adult/child $12/4; ⏰11am-4pm Thu-Mon) Housed in the 1895 Galveston Orphans' Home, this excellent museum displays a portion of the Bryan family's collection of historical documents and artifacts covering a range of Texas and Galveston history. After your visit, grab a drink ($2 to $6) from the gift shop and lounge around in the seating scattered across the grounds.

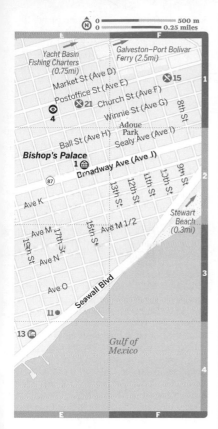

East End Historic District AREA

(Map p256; www.eastendhistoricdistrict.org; btwn 11th & 19th Sts, Mechanic St & Broadway Ave) Bordering the Strand, the residential East End Historic District has scores of pretty old houses, from simple cottages to Greek Revival mansions, some of which are often featured on the annual Historic Homes Tour (p259). A good guide and map is available on the district's website or at the erratically open visitor center on the southwest corner of 15th and E.

The East End Historical District Association sometimes hosts walking tours. Contact newwalkingtour@eastendhistoricdistrict.org for information.

East End Lagoon NATURE RESERVE

(www.eastendlagoon.org; Boddecker Dr, off Seawall Blvd; ⊙dawn-dusk) FREE The last stretch of untouched coastal prairie on Galveston's East End, this 684-acre tract has been set aside for conservation purposes and is open to visitors. Bird-watching and fishing are popular, and if it isn't flooded, there are a few small hiking trails winding through it.

Access is on Boddecker Dr, about halfway between Seawall Blvd and East Beach.

Galveston Arts Center ARTS CENTER

(Map p256; ☑409-763-2403; www.galveston artscenter.org; 2127 Strand St; ⊙11am-5pm Tue-Sat, from noon Sun) FREE Right on the Strand, this two-floor gallery showcases contemporary artwork primarily from local artists or artists focused on local themes. It also organizes Saturday **ArtWalk** (☑409-763-240; www.galveston

artscenter.org/artwalk.php; 2127 Strand St; ⏰6-9pm Sat) FREE events every four to six weeks.

Frost Bank
HISTORIC BUILDING

(Map p256; ☎409-763-1151; www.frostbank.com; 2201 Market St; ⏰9am-5pm Mon-Fri) This 1874 bank building has undergone several name changes over the years, and the name on the marquee still belongs to the 1923 'United States National Bank,' but since 2000 the name on the front has belonged to local chain Frost. Even if you don't have any business, it's worth having a look in the historic lobby.

Strand Historical District
AREA

(Map p256; btwn 25th & 20th Sts, Strand & Church Sts) Stroll the historic Strand District to get an appreciation of the city's glory days in the late 19th century. The commercial horse-drawn carriages clip-clop over historic trolley tracks and past elaborate brick facades fronting Victorian-era buildings that now contain shops and restaurants. Informative historical markers identify buildings around the district. Look for the Grand 1894 Opera House (p261), which is still in operation.

The old dock area just north off Harborside Dr has been converted to house waterfront restaurants and museums.

Galveston County Beach Pocket Parks
BEACH

(☎409-692-4455; http://galvestonparkboard.org; 11745 San Luis Pass Rd; per vehicle weekdays/weekends $12/16; ⏰9am-5pm Mar-Sep) Several long stretches of beach run by the county are found southwest of town off San Luis Pass Rd (the continuation of Seawall Blvd). Pocket Park 1, the first on the way south, is an undeveloped stretch of sand. Pocket Park 2 has showers, concessions, and umbrellas available for rent.

East Beach
BEACH

(☎409-797-5111; 1923 Boddecker Dr, off Seawall Blvd; per vehicle Mon-Fri $12, Sat & Sun $15; ⏰dawn-dusk) Also called Apffel Park, this vast expanse of hard-packed sand is at the very far northeastern end of the island. On summer weekends, it hosts live concerts and becomes one vast outdoor party (large signs proclaim 'drinking permitted').

There is beach parking for a mere 7000 cars here. Per-vehicle admission is discounted weekdays and during the off-season.

Moody Mansion & Museum
HISTORIC BUILDING

(Map p256; ☎409-762-7668; www.moodymansion. org; 2618 Broadway Ave; adult/child $10/8; ⏰tours 11am, 1pm & 3pm Mon-Fri, hourly 11am-3pm Sat & Sun) One of the grandest on the island, this home dating from 1895 still shines with the splendor of Galveston's heyday as an American boomtown. Self-guided audio tours take in 20 rooms of original family furnishings throughout the nearly 28,000-sq-ft mansion, and last about an hour. Discounted entry is available on the website.

Texas Seaport Museum & Tall Ship Elissa
MUSEUM

(Map p256; ☎409-763-1877; www.galveston history.org; Pier 22, cnr Harborside Dr & 21st St; adult/child $12/9; ⏰10am-6pm) This vast museum explains every facet of life around Galveston's port during its heyday in the 19th century. Outside, clamber aboard to tour the *Elissa*, a beautiful 1877 Scottish three-masted barque that is still seaworthy. Combination tickets with Historic Harbor Tours (p259) are available.

Moody Gardens
AMUSEMENT PARK

(☎800-582-4673; www.moodygardens.com; 1 Hope Blvd; rainforest/aquarium/all-attraction day pass $22/22/60; ⏰10am-6pm Sep-May, to 8pm Jun-Aug; ⊛) Three colorful glass pyramids form the focus of one giant entertainment complex. The Aquarium Pyramid showcases king penguins, fur seals and the largest array of sea horses in the world. The 10-story Rainforest Pyramid is a lush tropical jungle full of plants, birds, butterflies and a wonderful creepy-crawly bug exhibit. The Discovery Pyramid hosts traveling exhibits and some so-so space-related stuff.

🏃 Activities

Many stores along Seawall Blvd rent bicycles ($25 to $40 per day) and four-seater, pedal-operated surreys ($20 per hour). Both are excellent ways to roll on down the beachfront seawall path. Water-sports gear like surfboards ($45 per day) and kayaks are also usually for rent.

In the winter months, birders will have no trouble spotting waterbirds here. For a list of the area's best sites, log onto www.galveston naturetourism.org.

Fishing

Red snapper is the fish most prized by people fishing offshore from Galveston, though limits are often enforced. You have your pick of fishing charters and party boats from the information stands at Pier 19; the visitor center keeps a full list.

On the south side of the small harbor on Wharf Rd a string of **Fishing Boat Information Booths** (Map p256; Wharf Rd; ⊙6am-7pm) organize fishing trips and party boats, while the head office of the Galveston **Yacht Basin** (☑409-765-3000; http://galvestonyachtbasin.com; 715 N Holiday Dr; ⊙9am-5pm) can provide contact details for others.

Galveston Fishing Pier   FISHING
(☑409-974-4383; www.galvestonfishingpier.com; 9001 Seawall Blvd; adult/child $12/6; ⊙5am-11pm) This privately run fishing pier sells day-pass admission and rents fishing rods (each $10 and $25 deposit). For non-fishers, a one-hour entrance pass ($3) is free with a receipt from the on-site restaurant.

Tours

Numerous tours ply the island's, from haunted walks and historic homes to boat tours spotting dolphins. For a full list see the Galveston Island Visitors Center (p261) in person or online.

★Artist Boat Kayak Adventures   KAYAKING
(Map p256; ☑409-770-0722; www.artistboat.org; 2627 Ave O; per person 2/4hr tours $25/50; ⊙9am-5pm Mon-Fri) Nonprofit Eco-Art organization Artist Boat runs a number of educational programs in Galveston that meld nature and culture, most famously kayaking trips through the island's wetlands. Guides combine science and art during these creative and fascinating kayak tours of the natural sights around Galveston Island; advance reservations required. Ask about discounted tours that support the Coastal Heritage Preserve area off the West Bay.

Historic Harbor Tours   BOATING
(Map p256; ☑409-763-1877; www.galveston history.org; Pier 22, Texas Seaport Museum; adult/child $10/8; ⊙11:30am, 1pm, 2:30pm & 4pm Thu-Tue) Patrons often spot dolphins on these very reasonable, one-hour tours of the harbor, which is also filled with boats and oil rigs. Call to ensure tours are going that day.

Island Bicycle Company   WATER SPORTS, CYCLING
(Map p256; ☑409-762-2453; www.islandbicycle company.com; 1808 Seawall Blvd; ⊙9:30am-6pm Sun-Wed, to 9pm Thu-Sat) On the Seawall, Island Bicycle is a convenient choice for renting most activity gear: surreys, bicycles, surfboards, standup paddleboards, boogie boards, kayaks etc. You can even rent fishing poles ($30 per day) or metal detectors for beachcombing ($40 per day).

✦ Festivals & Events

Mardi Gras   CARNIVAL
(www.mardigrasgalveston.com; ⊙Jan/Feb/Mar) For 12 days before Ash Wednesday, Galveston does the best New Orleans impression it knows how, with parades, pageants, parties and more. At least one Sunday is dedicated to families, but the rest of the party can get a little crazy. Make lodging reservations far, far in advance.

★Historic Homes Tour   CULTURAL
(☑409-765-7834; www.galvestonhistory.org; 2228 Broadway Ave, Galveston Historical Foundation; per person $30; ⊙May) The Galveston Historical Foundation puts the island's finest privately owned old houses on display on the first two weekends in May. In addition to tours of historic homes, other events include organized evening strolls, bicycle and bus tours, and a jazz brunch.

Dickens on the Strand   CULTURAL
(☑409-765-7834; www.galvestonhistory.org; adult/child $8/5; ⊙Dec) On the first (and sometimes second) weekend in December, the historic Strand District morphs into Victorian London. Costumed jugglers and musicians take to the street as peddlers vend their old-timey wares and Queen Victoria herself makes a special appearance.

🛏 Sleeping

Rates for hotel/motel rooms vary widely from the lows of midweek winter to the highs of summer weekends. During special events, two-night stays may be required and everything books up months in advance. Because of the heat in August, sometimes late-summer rates are reasonable. The island's official website, www.galveston.com, compiles a thorough list of lodgings. Be wary of budget motels, some of which are truly dismal.

Beachcomber Inn   MOTEL $
(☑409-744-7133; www.galvestoninn.com; 2825 61st St; r $75-216; P ❄ 🛜 🛋) A block removed from the beach, this basic two-story motel provides a neat-and-clean budget break on weekdays, but weekend upcharges are generally poor value. Minifridges and microwaves in every room.

Tremont House   HERITAGE HOTEL $$
(Map p256; ☑409-763-0300; www.thetremont house.com; 2300 Mechanic St; r $143-280) Built in 1880 as the headquarters of the Leon & H Blum Company, at the time the island's largest

importer and wholesaler. Today Tremont House's luxury rooms on the edge of the Strand District often book out far in advance for weddings and events.

Harbor House BOUTIQUE HOTEL $$
(Map p256; ☑ 409-763-3321; www.harborhouse pier21.com; Pier 21, off Harborside Dr; r $159-289; ❄ 🛜 ≋) Stay among the shops and museums of the Pier 21 complex in the heart of the historic Strand District. Rustic touches accent the 42 large, comfy rooms occupying a wharfside warehouse. Rooms have good views of the harbor through smallish windows.

There's no pool, but guests can use the lovely facilities at the Hotel Galvez.

.Hotel Galvez HERITAGE HOTEL $$$
(Map p256; ☑ 409-765-7721; www.galveston.com/ galvez; 2024 Seawall Blvd; r $160-315; ❄ 🛜 ≋) Bask in palm-fringed Spanish-Colonial luxury at this 1911 historic hotel, currently managed by the Wyndham corporation. The full-service spa services – muscle-soaking milk bath or seaweed contour wraps, for example – are renowned, and the pool deck has a lovely gulf view. Ask about special package spa deals.

🍴 Eating

The dining scene is a mix of independent eateries and seafood chains from Landry's restaurant group. A cluster of the latter can be found at the waterfront Pier 21 complex off Harborside in the Strand District, while tucked back into the downtown streets are scores more small restaurants serving delicious food. This seaside city is heavy on the seafood, but classy enough to feature cuisine from across the country and around the world.

★Maceo Spice & Import CAJUN $
(Map p256; ☑ 409-763-3331; www.maceospice. com; 2706 Market St; mains $7-13; ⊙ 11am-3pm) This excellent importer and spice market also happens to serve the best muffalettas and Cajun food in town at tables crammed between the shelves. The shop stays open till 5pm, but lunch service ends at 3pm.

Mama Teresa's Flying Pizza ITALIAN $
(Map p256; ☑ 409-765-6262; www.mamateresas. com; 416 21st St; mains $10-18; ⊙ 4-10pm Tue-Thu, to 11pm Fri, 11am-11pm Sat, to 10pm Sun) A longtime institution on the Bolivar Peninsula, Mama Teresa's was pushed over to Galveston by the destruction of Hurricane Ike. It serves authentic Italian pasta and pizza, not

to mention fantastic subs and dinner plates. *Mamma mia,* is it good.

Shrimp N Stuff Downtown SEAFOOD $
(Map p256; www.shrimpnstuff.com; 216 23rd St; mains $7-15; ⊙ 10am-9pm Mon-Thu, to 10pm Fri, 7:30am-10pm Sat, to 9pm Sun; 🛜) The famous fried seafood chain has expanded, and now you can gobble up fresh seafood a short stroll from the historic Strand without trekking out all the way to the original **Ave O** (Map p256; ☑ 409-763-2805; www.shrimpnstuff.com; 3901 Ave O; mains $7-15; ⊙ 10:30am-8:30pm Sun-Thu, to 9:30pm Fri & Sat) location.

Farley Girls Cafe AMERICAN $
(Map p256; ☑ 409-497-4454; http://farleygirls. com; 801 Postoffice St; mains $10-15; ⊙ 10:30am-3pm Mon-Fri, from 8:30am Sat & Sun; 🛜) The historic building may be elegant, with fern-studded colonnades and high wood ceilings, but the tasty comfort food and counter service are down-home casual. Eclectic offerings include Hell's Kitchen fettuccine, goats' cheese and candied pecan salad, and a handful of standard-menu pizzas. At brunch (all day on weekends), it serves tasty eggs Benedict, breakfast burgers, and eggs with saucy Gouda-and-mushroom grits.

Olympia Grill SEAFOOD $$
(Map p256; ☑ 409-765-0021; www.olympia grill.com; Pier 21, off Harborside Dr; mains $11-28; ⊙ 11am-9pm Sun-Thu, to 10pm Fri & Sat) The seafood is pretty good, especially the inclusion of Greek ingredients that sets it apart from competitors in the area, but really you're here for the big back porch overlooking the channel. On breezy summer afternoons, it can be hard to drag yourself back to the Strand.

Sunflower Bakery & Cafe AMERICAN $$
(Map p256; ☑ 409-763-5500; http://thesunflower bakeryandcafe.com; 512 14th St; mains $9-18; ⊙ 7am-5pm; 🛜) Everything is made from scratch, as it should be: site-baked breads, daily made desserts and piled-high sandwiches are staples. That it also serves mouthwatering mains and runs regular lunch specials is a bonus.

Gaido's SEAFOOD $$$
(☑ 409-761-5500; www.gaidos.com; 3802 Seawall Blvd; mains $20-40; ⊙ 11am-9pm Sun-Thu, to 10pm Fri & Sat) Run by the same family since 1911, Gaido's is a local favorite in Galveston. Expect vast platters of no-compromise seafood (oh,

the oysters…) served on white tablecloths and with hushed tones. It has a more casual sister restaurant, **Nick's Kitchen & Beach Bar** (☑ 409-762-9625; http://nicksgalveston.com; 3828 Seawall Blvd; mains $11-26; ⊙ 11am 10pm Mon-Fri, to 10:30pm Sat & Sun), next door.

Drinking & Nightlife

The pedestrian-friendly Strand District provides bar-hopping potential with a couple of great old boozers and several hip new entries, along both Postoffice St and Strand St. Classic beach bars stretch out along Seawall Blvd, and tucked in the neighborhoods just behind, a few local craft breweries have been pumping out good beer.

DTO
COCKTAIL BAR

(Map p256; ☑ 409-497-2760; www.dtogalveston. com; 2701 Market St; ⊙ 4pm-2am Tue-Sun; 📶) The small porch out front definitely represents the Daiquiri Time Out ethos, but head inside to find a cocktail bar that even bartenders from Houston drive down to hang out at. If it's not busy, ask the bartenders for recommendations, including cocktails using their homemade spirits.

Proletariat
PUB

(Map p256; ☑ 409-356-9092; www.proletariat gallery.com; 2221 Market St; ⊙ 4pm-midnight Sun-Thu, to 2am Fri & Sat) This combination pub and gallery space, built into a renovated 1869 office building, has a strong selection of wine and craft beers to sip while browsing the works of local artists. It's a regular stop on weekend ArtWalk (p257) tours.

Spot
BAR

(☑ 409-621-5237; http://thespot.islandfamous. com; 3204 Seawall Blvd; ⊙ 11am-10pm Sun-Thu, to 11pm Fri & Sat) This boisterous bar complex overlooking the gulf is the best of many competitors. The huge complex has an array of rooms, including a bamboo-filled tiki bar. Head upstairs to the Sideyard for ocean breezes and lawn furniture over Astroturf. Good burgers and tacos help absorb the vast array of fancy cocktails on offer. Live music on weekends.

☆ Entertainment

Grand 1894 Opera House
THEATER

(Map p256; ☑ 409-765-1894; www.thegrand.com; 2020 Postoffice St; ⊙ box office 9am-5pm Mon-Sat) The beautifully restored 1894 Opera House well illustrates Galveston's turn-of-the-20th-century culture and wealth. Popular concerts,

broadway shows and humorous theatrical productions are still staged here. On days when there are no shows or set-up activities underway, self-guided tours are allowed. Check the website for schedules.

🛍 Shopping

★ La King's Confectionery
FOOD

(Map p256; ☑ 409-762-6100; www.lakingscon fectionery.com; 2323 Strand St; ⊙ 10am-7pm) Watch the saltwater taffy, peanut brittle and chocolates being made at this throwback to the 1920s Strand. It's an old-fashioned candy store and ice-cream parlor that will delight the young and the young at heart.

Murdoch's Bathhouse
GIFTS & SOUVENIRS

(Map p256; ☑ 409-762-7478; 2215 Seawall Blvd, at 22nd St; ⊙ 9:30am-10pm) Built in the late 1800s, destroyed in the 1900 hurricane. Rebuilt in 1901, blasted again in 1909. Repeated 1910/1915, and *again* in 2008. Murdoch's has had a tough run of it, but it remains a Galveston favorite for souvenirs, beer, and rocking chairs staring out toward the gulf – seemingly in defiance of it all.

🛈 Information

The **Galveston Island Visitors Center** (Map p256; ☑ 409-797-5144; www.galveston.com; 2328 Broadway, Ashton Villa; ⊙ 9am-5pm) is full of suggestions for things to do (and places to eat) in Galveston, plus it has details of discount passes for travelers who plan to hit the big tourist sites.

🛈 Getting There & Away

From Houston, follow I-45 southeast for 51 miles. On the island, the highway morphs into Broadway Ave and travels toward the historic districts. Turn off onto 61st St to reach Seawall Blvd.

South of the Moody Gardens area, Seawall Blvd continues down the length of the island as Sun Luis Pass Rd and then Bluewater Hwy before turning back onto the mainland in the Brazosport area. With no traffic, this interesting route adds about half an hour on the way to Rockport or Corpus Christi compared to the interstate, but given the reality of Houston traffic, this will actually be faster most of the time.

BOAT

From points east, including Beaumont and Port Arthur, the **Galveston–Port Bolivar Ferry** (☑ 409-795-2230; http://traffic.houston-transtar.org/ferrytimes; 1 Ferry Rd; ⊙ 24hr) connects the long, lonely Bolivar Peninsula to the island around the clock via TX 87. Trust us, cruising the peninsula with the waves about 300ft

beyond is a much more enjoyable experience than Houston traffic.

BUS

Scheduled buses run by **Galveston Limousine Service** (☑ 409-744-5466; www.galveston limousineservice.com; 5225 Ave U) travel to and from both Houston Hobby Airport (round-trip/one-way $80/45, one hour) and Houston Intercontinental Airport (round-trip/one-way $100/55, two hours) six times or more each day. Advance reservations are required, with discounts available online.

ℹ Getting Around

Hurricane Ike knocked the Galveston Island Trolley, run by **Island Transit** (Map p256; ☑ 409-797-3900; www.galvestontx.gov; adult/child $1/50¢), off the rails. Until this excellent link between the Strand and Seawall is restored – expected at some point in 2018 – you really need a car to get around. The island's bus service caters to commuters and students more than tourists.

CAR & MOTORCYCLE

Paid parking is enforced along the length of Seawall Blvd and much of downtown from 10am to 6pm. While visitors to downtown can use cash meters (or a number of private lots), parking along the Seawall can only be paid on the **PayByPhone** (☑ 866-234-7275; https://paybyphone.com/locations/galveston; Seawall Blvd) website or mobile app or by calling ☑ 866-234-7275.

THE COASTAL BEND

The name 'Coastal Bend' can rather amorphously apply to communities from Galveston to South Padre Island. But its heart is the rural stretch running from the southern tip of Galveston Island to Corpus Christi. Here small towns, often forgotten by time, lie next to the water at the end of long and quiet roads. Many shelter in the profusion of inlets and bays, protected by more than 100 miles of uninhabited barrier islands. The only visitors to the islands are birds, which flock here by the score.

The region just south of Galveston, the lands here are rural and often bucolic. Natural areas such as Aransas National Wildlife Refuge (p264) and Brazos Bend State Park should be your focus, along with the inviting towns of Fulton and Rockport.

West Columbia & Around

☑ 979 / POP 3905

Between 1824 and 1828, Stephen F Austin, under contract with the Mexican government, granted 297 titles to settle land in the newly acquired colony of Texas. These grantees, known as the Old Three Hundred, settled in the area between the Brazos and Colorado Rivers and were among the first legal Anglo-American immigrants to settle on Mexican land.

Settlers from across the US were among the Old Three Hundred, and many of them settled in the area that would eventually become West Columbia. Now, a small town, the Varner-Hogg Plantation and a collection of restored historic buildings attest to the former importance of the area during those frontier days.

◉ Sights

⭐ **Brazos Bend State Park**　　　STATE PARK
(☑ 979-553-5101; http://tpwd.texas.gov; 21901 FM 762, Needville; adult/child $7/free; ⊙ 8am-10pm, visitor center 8am-4:30pm, to 9:30pm Fri & Sat) Alligators. Alligators everywhere. You'll surely enjoy the diversity of wetland and forest landscapes, bird-watching, maybe even get some use out of the 37 miles of looping hiking trails, but the lingering impression for most visitors is total bayou shtick: moss-covered cypress trees and alligators all around. It's all scenic, but try to make it to the observation tower on 40-Acre Lake for a view out over the lowlands. RV and tent sites are available from $12 per night plus entrance fees.

Varner-Hogg Plantation　　　HISTORIC SITE
(☑ 979-345-4656; www.thc.texas.gov; 1702 N 13th St; adult/child $4/3; ⊙ 8am-5pm Tue-Sun) This 1824 plantation includes a grand mansion and several other historic outbuildings that can be explored. Amid beautiful pecan and magnolia trees, visitors learn about how various owners made money growing, drilling and distilling – often with slaves or indentured servants. The historical displays on-site take an honest look at this darker side of local history as well as lighter notes, including the role the plantation played in hosting Mexican general Antonio López de Santa Anna as a 'guest' after his surrender.

To see the inside of the Plantation House you'll have to join one of the tours (price included with admission) that run hourly from 9am to 11am and 1:30pm to 3:30pm. At the time of research a B&B was under development on the premises inside the 1920s 'Oil Field Cottage' – call for details.

MATAGORDA ISLAND WILDLIFE MANAGEMENT AREA

Covering 56,688 acres of barrier island and saltwater marshes, the **Matagorda Island Wildlife Management Area** (📞361-205-1510; http://tpwd.state.tx.us/matagordaisland) FREE is an undeveloped playground for wilderness lovers. You'll have to hire a boat to get over, and bring absolutely everything you need, but wild camping is allowed (even encouraged!), and you may well have the island all to yourself. There's a park office at 2200 7th St, 3rd fl, in Bay City, if you want to chat with rangers before a trip out.

Matagorda Island has no bridge connection to the mainland, no telephone, no electricity and no drinking water. It does have 80 miles of white beaches along its 38-mile length, plus almost limitless hiking possibilities. More than 320 species of bird drop by throughout the year, and deer, coyotes, raccoons, rabbits, alligators and more call it home. While you're exploring the island, keep an eye out for the 1852 lighthouse on the north end.

Most people visit just for the day. To use one of the 12 primitive camping sites, see the website. The only way out to the island is by boat across the 8 miles of Espiritu Santo Bay from Port O'Connor. Check out the local chamber of commerce website (http://port oconnorchamber.com) and look under 'Business Directory'.

Sleeping

Aycock Crews House
B&B $$

(📞979-345-6931; www.aycockcrews.com; 520 CR 703; r $125-175; ❄🌐) This three-room B&B books up often for weddings, but if you can get a reservation, it's one of the most character-filled accommodation options in an area largely dominated by chain hotels. It's named for Captain Richard Aycock, who built house in the 1870s and was the last riverboat captain and pilot to work a stern wheel paddleboat on the Brazos River opposite.

Continuing south along the river road, a number of houses bear historical markers attesting to their importance during the period when Columbia was a major river town along the Brazos.

Matagorda

Names in this area must have been hard to come by, because authorities decided to confuse everybody by christening a bay, a town, a county, a peninsula and an island with the same name – Matagorda. The tiny town, little more than a handful of stores and homes, offers a link to the peninsula (Matagorda Peninsula, not to be confused with Matagorda Island, the remote state park off Port O'Connor), a popular spot for fishing.

There are 23 miles of lonely white-sand **beaches** out here. In Matagorda buy a $10 permit at **Stanley's Market** (📞979-863-7613; http://stanleysgeneralstores.com; 725 Market St; ❄5am-10pm) or CJ's One Stop, and then drive out onto the beach and stake your claim. Note that the beach is legally a state highway with a speed limit of 20mph, and all laws still apply. If you're not in a 4x4, you'll do better to hike in.

Sights

Jetty Park
PARK

(FM 2031) FREE This small county park at the end of the road is a good alternative for groups that aren't in a vehicle that can handle the dunes. There are showers, bathrooms and picnic tables, and you can leave your car parked here while you hike down to the beach. Note that swimming is prohibited near the jetty due to strong currents.

Matagorda Bay Nature Park
PARK

(📞979-863-2603; www.lcra.org; 6430 FM 2031; ❄dawn-dusk) FREE Matagorda Bay Nature Park is a great resource with numerous programs where you can learn about the wetlands and barrier islands. Check for schedules; the guided kayak tours ($40 including kayak rental) are excellent. Camping is free, but reservations cost $6 to $7.50.

Aransas National Wildlife Refuge

For bird-watchers the 115,000-acre **Aransas National Wildlife Refuge** (📞361-286-3559; www.fws.gov/refuge/aransas; FM 2040; per person/car $3/5; ❄sunrise-sunset, visitor center 9am-4pm, Wed-Sun only Apr 15-Oct 14) is the premier site on the Texas coast, with more than 400 species having been documented here. Even people who don't carry binoculars and ornithological checklists can get caught up in the bird-spotting frenzy that peaks here every March and November and is great throughout the year. None are more famous, more followed or more watched than the whooping-cranes – among the rarest creatures in North America. About 250 survivors of this species spend summer in Canada and November to March in the refuge. Spotters and scientists come from all over the world to study the 5ft-tall birds.

The scenery alone is spectacular – the blue Aransas Bay waters are speckled with green islets ringed with white sand. Native dune grasses blow gently in the breeze while songbirds provide choral background music.

It's possible to experience the refuge from the water with Rockport-based tour operators. **Wharf Cat** (📞 361-729-4855; www.texas whoopers.com; 320 Navigation Circle, Rockport; tours adult/child from $50/25; ⊘ 10am-2pm Nov-Apr) operates boat tours Tuesday to Sunday during whooping crane season (November to April), while **Rockport Birding & Kayak Adventures** (📞 877-892-4737; www.whoopingcranetours. com; 215 N Fulton Beach Rd, Fulton; 3hr tours per person from $55; ⊘ 7:30am-4:30pm) can outfit parties for paddle tours.

Rockport & Fulton

📞 361 / POP 8766

A pedestrian-friendly waterfront, numerous worthy attractions, fishing boats plying their trade, and cute little downtown Rockport make the adjoining towns of Rockport and Fulton an enjoyable stop. The coastal road between the two makes a nice walk or bike ride, and there's information in the chamber of commerce about nature trails in the area.

The side streets between TX 35 and Aransas Bay are dotted with art galleries and curio shops, especially in the center of Rockport; the towns claim to be home to the state's highest percentage of artists.

◉ Sights

Rockport Harbor   HARBOR
Crescent-shaped Rockport Harbor is one of the prettiest on the Gulf Coast. It's lined with all manner of boats (shrimp, fishing charter, tour and pleasure craft) and a series of rustic peel-and-eat shrimp joints and bait shops.

**Fulton Mansion State
Historical Park**   HISTORIC BUILDING
(📞 361-729-0386; www.thc.texas.gov; 317 S Fulton Beach Rd, Fulton; adult/child $6/4; ⊘ 9:30am-4:30pm Tue-Sat, 12:30-4:30pm Sun) This imposing 1870s mansion comes as a surprise amid other more modern – and modest – shorefront buildings. It was built by George Fulton, who was clever with the design. On the outside, it looks like an imposing French Second Empire creation, right down to the mansard roofs. Inside those walls, however, are concrete foundations and walls more than 5in thick. Although other contemporary buildings have been blown away, the mansion has withstood several hurricanes.

An education and history center offers interactive exhibits, presentations and Victorian craft activities. Tours of the mansion itself are self-guided, but there are friendly and knowledgeable docents on hand to offer insight and answer any questions.

Rockport Center for the Arts   ARTS CENTER
(📞 361-729-5519; www.rockportartcenter.com; 902 Navigation Circle, Rockport; ⊘ 10am-4pm Tue-Sat, 1-4pm Sun) **FREE** It's worth popping into this cheery center, housed partly in a charming 1890s building, to see what's going on with the lively local arts scene. It offers painting classes, is right on the water and largely features locally sourced artwork (some of which is available for purchase).

⊙ Tours

Gone Coastal Guide Service   BIRD-WATCHING
(📞 281-832-1445; www.gonecoastaltx.com; 32 Red Oak Lane, Holiday Beach; 3hr tours per group from $300) Gone Coastal organizes airboat tours for bird-watching and wildlife-viewing through Aransas National Wildlife Refuge, Matagorda Island and more, as well as fishing and hunting trips. It doesn't accept walk-ins – call ahead to reserve a tour.

🛏 Sleeping & Eating

The Fulton waterfront by the mansion has a few modest motels plus one upscale boutique option, and there is a patch of chain hotels north of Rockport Harbor.

★**Lighthouse Inn
at Aransas Bay**   BOUTIQUE HOTEL **$$**
(📞 361-790-8439; www.lighthousetexas.com; 200 S Fulton Beach Rd, Fulton; r $149-209, ste $179-239; 🅿❄) Many of the 78 large rooms at this boutique hotel just steps from Aransas Bay have exceptional sea views, and even if yours

doesn't you can admire the seascape from a rocking chair on the large back porch. There's also a private fishing pier, for the sporty.

Due to damage sustained in August 2017 from Hurricane Harvey, Lighthouse Inn is closed temporarily. Call ahead before visiting.

Apple Dumpling Deli DELI $
(📞 361-790-8433; www.appledumplingdeli.com; 114 N Magnolia St, Rockport; mains $8-10; ⏰ 11am-3pm Mon-Sat) Don't let the rec-hall exterior deter you from this locally loved deli and cafe in downtown Rockport. The homemade ice cream is creamy and dreamy and the sandwiches on homemade bread are just the thing for picnics amid the local natural splendor.

Moondog Seaside Eatery AMERICAN $$
(📞 361-729-6200; www.facebook.com/Moondog SeasideEatery; 100 N Casterline Dr, Fulton; mains $8-24; ⏰ 11am-9pm Mon-Fri, to 10pm Sat & Sun; ❄🤙) Ask for a table out on the back deck to watch the shrimp boats coming and going as you wait for one of Moondog's huge burgers or Tex-Mex plates, or come back on weekend evenings as locals and vacationers gather here to get the night started with live music.

Due to damage sustained in 2017 from Hurricane Harvey, Moondog was operating as a food truck until repairs are completed.

Boiling Pot SEAFOOD $$
(📞 361-729-6972; 201 S Fulton Beach Rd, Fulton; meals $20; ⏰ 4-9pm Mon-Thu, 11am-9pm Fri-Sun; ❄) This is a rustic classic, and a lot of fun. Mountains of shellfish plus potatoes, sausage and corn are dumped in a pot full of boiling water, then they're dumped on your paper-covered table and you dive in (no cutlery, no crockery – bibs provided).

Latitude 28°02′ SEAFOOD $$
(📞 361-727-9009; www.latituderockport.com; 105 N Austin St, Rockport; mains $15-37; ⏰ 5-9pm Tue-Sun) The finest dining locally. Look for creative takes on seafood at this stylish little place that doubles as an art gallery. The local special, grouper, is prepared several ways; sides vary seasonally. Shrimp and oyster dishes are also excellent. Due to damage sustained from Hurricane Harvey, Latitude 28°02′ was expected to be closed till January 2018. Call ahead.

🍸 Drinking & Nightlife

Many of the waterfront eateries double as music and beer joints once the sun goes down. Even on weekends it's quiet by midnight, though, so get your party fix elsewhere on the coast.

Daily Grind CAFE
(📞 361-790-8745; http://rockportdailygrind.com; 302 S Austin St, Rockport; drinks $2-6; ⏰ 7am-3pm Tue-Sat; 🤙) Fresh ground coffee from a wide menu of styles, hot-from-the-oven bakery treats ($2-$9), and the attached fine-art photography gallery with nice prints of Texas themes. It's just a shame it closes too early for our late-afternoon cup.

ℹ Information

Rockport-Fulton Area Chamber of Commerce (📞 361-729-6445; www.rockport-fulton.org; 319 Broadway St, Rockport; ⏰ 9am-5pm Mon-Fri, 2pm Sat) This highly helpful office is across from Rockport Harbor. There's a small informative display inside that gives some insight into the ecological importance of the area.

COASTAL PLAINS

Goliad is well worth a detour from the coastal bend; it's a charming small town steeped in history. Victoria's downtown offers a nice stop on a longer itinerary, and the two clusters of chain motels offer an easy overnight in between other parts of the state. If driving, you might consider a circle route that takes in the coast one way and the plains the other.

Victoria

📞 361 / POP 62,592

Founded in 1824 by impresario Martin DeLeon, Victoria still has some 100 historic buildings near its downtown. Many have been restored by owners drawn to the deeply shaded, oak-lined streets. The Explore Victoria Visitor Center (p266) has tour information.

The picturesque DeLeon Plaza and Old Victoria County Courthouse anchor the historic downtown, with numerous restaurants and interesting old buildings an easy walk away.

👁 Sights

Old Victoria County Courthouse HISTORIC BUILDING
(📞 361-575-2762; 101 N Bridge St; ⏰ 9am-5pm Mon-Fri; ♿ green) FREE Fronting the picturesque DeLeon Plaza, the majestic granite and limestone Old Victoria County Courthouse dates from 1892 (replacing a more modest 1849 structure), when such buildings were a source of local civic pride. Short self-tours are possible via an entrance on the southern side of the building.

🛏 Sleeping

La Quinta Inn – Victoria South   HOTEL $
(☑361-703-5060; www.lq.com; 3107 S Laurent St; r $90-115; ❋ 🌐) This standard chain option on the south side of town is convenient as a base to explore the surrounding countryside.

Due to damage sustained in August 2017 from Hurricane Harvey, La Quinta Inn is closed temporarily. Call ahead before visiting.

Homewood Suites   HOTEL $$
(☑361-578-1900; http://homewoodsuites3.hilton. com; 6705 Zac Lentz Pkwy; ste $105-117; ❋ 🌐) This chain option on the north side of town is all suites, and rates include dinner on weekdays.

🍴 Eating & Drinking

The most interesting selection of restaurants centers on the downtown area, with the historic **Fossati's Delicatessen** (☑361-576-3354; 302 S Main St; mains from $5; ⊘11am-2pm Mon-Fri; 🚍green) a particular local favorite. Ask at the Explore Victoria Visitor Center for information on the 'Great Coastal Texas Barbecue Trail,' of which **Mumphord's Place** (☑361-485-1112; http://mumphordsplacebbq.com; 1202 E Juan Linn St; mains $5-11; ⊘11am-7pm Tue-Thu, to 8pm Fri, to 6pm Sat; 🚍green) is an anchor.

Huvar's Artisan Market   AMERICAN $
(☑361-576-9171; www.huvars.com; 110 W Juan Linn St; mains $9-13; ⊘8am-2pm Mon-Fri, 6-9pm Thu-Sat; 🌐 📶; 🚍green) Housed in a historic commercial building on the south side of the old town, Huvar's has a farm-to-market vibe and a hip ambience to complement the tasty coffee and food.

Dairy Treet   AMERICAN $
(☑361-573-3104; 3808 N Laurent St; meals from $5; ⊘10:30am-10pm; 🚍all routes) This local favorite is an old-time soft-serve-ice-cream joint with fresh cooked burgers and hand-dipped onion rings. It's pure Americana hanging out here on a balmy evening. When it's cold out, staff close up shop once business slows down in the evening.

Moonshine Drinkery   BAR
(☑361-489-3479; www.moonshinedrinkery.com; 103 W Santa Rosa; drinks $3-10; ⊘4pm-midnight Wed, Thu, Sun, to 2am Fri & Sat; 📶; 🚍green, gold) For a craft beer or fancy cocktail downtown, this is the go-to place, and the regular schedule of live music certainly doesn't hurt either. Try a flight of assorted moonshine flavors for a real kick.

ℹ️ Information

Explore Victoria Visitor Center (☑361-485-3116; www.explorevictoriatexas.com; 700 N Main St; ⊘8:30am-5pm Mon-Fri; 🚍green & gold) The tourist information office has details on the locally designed 'Great Coastal Texas Barbecue Trail' and 'Victoria Beyond the Grave' experiences, as well as brochures for points of interest across the region.

Goliad

☑361 / POP 1908

'Remember the Alamo!' is the verbal icon of the Texas revolution, but it should also be 'Remember Goliad!' as Goliad is where, on Palm Sunday, March 27, 1836, Mexican general Antonio López de Santa Anna ordered nearly 500 Texan prisoners shot in cold blood. The death toll was double that at the Alamo and helped inspire the Texans in their victory over Santa Anna at San Jacinto the following month.

There is a wealth of historic sites in and around the lovely town of Goliad, making this a must-see stop. It's 26 miles along US 59 from Victoria.

◉ Sights

The hub of Goliad, **Courthouse Square**, features a grand old 1894 courthouse. Among the many stately oaks on the square is one labeled the 'Hanging Tree,' for self-explanatory reasons, from a darker time in the town's past. A historical marker recalls the Regulators, 50 vigilantes who 'pursued criminals with vigor and often with cruelty' from 1868 to 1870.

Presidio La Bahia   HISTORIC SITE
(☑361-645-3752; www.presidiolabahia.org; Called Cinco de Mayo, off US 183; adult/child $4/1; ⊘9am-4:45pm) Built in 1749 by the Spanish to deter the French who were sniffing around the eastern edges of their empire, Presidio La Bahia played a role in six revolutions and wars while serving under nine different flags (including the bloody-arm Goliad flag, an early symbol of independent Texas). Texas revolutionaries seized the fort – now restored by the church – in October 1835, and renamed it 'Fort Defiance' during their occupation of the site.

🛏 Sleeping & Eating

Courthouse Sq has a few small cafes; on the second Saturday of each month Market Day lures vendors of all types.

SCENIC COASTAL DRIVE: GALVESTON TO CORPUS CHRISTI

Following the coast between Galveston and Corpus Christi is not a straightforward adventure. Roads and highways that jog in and out seem to change names and numbers with every turn. But it's worth the effort for the timeless towns and natural backwaters that see little traffic diverted from busy US 59 and US 77 inland. You can cover this route easily in a day, but if you plan on spending time in any of the nature areas and beaches, make it two.

The Route

After the upscale beach houses that extend to the southern tip of Galveston Island, the sudden lack of development after you cross the San Luis Pass bridge to the relative emptiness of Follets Island can be a pleasant surprise.

Surfside Beach, 13.5 miles southeast, is a workmanlike party town, where few pass the convenience store at the main crossroad without stopping for a case of beer.

Fans of oil refineries will appreciate the 11-mile drive inland on TX 332. Watch for signs for the delightful **Sea Center Texas** (🗹 979-292-0100; www.tpwd.state.tx.us; 302 Medical Dr, Lake Jackson; ⊙9am-4pm Tue-Sat, 1-4pm Sun; ♿) [FREE] in **Lake Jackson**.

From Lake Jackson, take FM 2004, which becomes FM 2611 when it crosses TX 36. This a lovely drive through lush lands laced with rivers and peppered with wildflowers. Turn north when you hit FM 457, go 6 miles and turn west on FM 521 for 15.5 miles to TX 60, then turn south to Matagorda and the beaches, a total of 55 miles from Lake Jackson.

From Matagorda, drive back north 9 miles to FM 521 and turn west. You make a big loop to the north around a nuclear power plant – watch out for lobsters the size of Godzilla – and after 19 miles you turn south on TX 35 for 5 miles to **Palacios**.

Continue on TX 35 for 50 miles through Port Lavaca (avoiding any temptation to detour to uninteresting Port O'Connor) until just past tiny Tivoli, where you should turn southeast on TX 239. Follow the signs for 18 miles through humdrum corn farms until you reach the wonders of **Aransas National Wildlife Refuge** (p264).

Leaving Aransas NWR, take FM 774 through a series of turns 12 miles west to TX 35. Turn south and go 13.5 miles to Lamar and the charms of **Goose Island State Park** (🗹 361-729-2858; www.tpwd.state.tx.us; 202 S Palmetto St; adult/child $5/free; ⊙8am-10pm). The park was closed temporarily following Hurricane Harvey. Call ahead before visiting.

From here, it's only 6 miles south on TX 35 to the fun twin coastal towns of Fulton and Rockport. Port Aransas, a good place to bed down, is only 20 miles beyond while Corpus Christi is 30 miles further on.

Goliad State Park Campground CAMPGROUND $
(🗹 361-645-3405; https://tpwd.texas.gov/state-parks/goliad; 108 Park Rd 6, off US 183; sites $10-25; ⊙office 8am-5pm, gates close 10pm except to overnight guests) There are well-shaded camping areas in the park, including many along the San Antonio River. Reserve in advance by calling 🗹 512-389-8900.

Due to damage sustained in August 2017 from Hurricane Harvey, some areas of the campground may not be accessible. Call ahead or check online before visiting.

★**La Bahia Restaurant** TEX-MEX $
(🗹 361-645-3900; 1877 US 183; mains $8-15; ⊙11am-9pm Tue-Thu, to 10pm Fri & Sat, to 7pm Sun) The homemade shells, fantastic salsa and delicately spiced meat here make for what may be one of the best taco plates of any Tex-Mex joint in the state. It gets busy and you may

have to wait for a table at dinner, but that's just a testament to the quality.

★**McMillan's BBQ** BARBECUE $$
(🗹 361-645-2326; 9913 US 59, Fannin; mains from $15-30; ⊙10am-3pm Mon-Wed, to 7pm Thu-Sun; ❋) Close to the Fannin battleground site, this small roadhouse is loved for its sweet and savory barbecue and especially the buttery, tender beef brisket. Though the dining room is tiny, owner/chef Louis McMillan has some big opinions on good barbecue – take time to chat with him if it isn't too busy.

ℹ Information

Goliad Chamber of Commerce (🗹 361-645-3563; www.goliadcc.org; 231 S Market St; ⊙8am-noon & 1-5pm Mon-Fri) Friendly staff, but there's not a lot of info on hand.

CORPUS CHRISTI AREA

Corpus Christi is the center of life in its namesake region and bay. Its museums and attractions can fill a day or more, while the pull of the beaches on Mustang and Padre Islands is irresistible – not to mention Port Aransas is easily the most charming beach town in Texas. But it's not all sand and sea – it can be cowboys and cattle too if you like. An easy day trip from Corpus Christi takes you to Kingsville, home of the massive King Ranch (p278) dynasty and one of the largest and oldest working ranches in the world, or further to tiny Sarita and the remnants of the once-great **Kenedy Ranch** (✆ 361-294-5751; www.kenedymuseum.org; 200 E La Parra Ave; adult/child $3/2; ⊙ 10am-4pm Tue-Sat, from noon Sun).

Corpus Christi

✆ 361 / POP 305,215

Nicknamed the 'Sparkling City by the Sea,' but known to many simply as Corpus, this city by the placid bay of the same name is a growing and vibrant place. Its attractions are worth a visit and its perpetually sunny location is beguiling.

Spaniards named the bay after the Roman Catholic holy day of Corpus Christi in 1519, when Alonzo Álvarez de Piñeda discovered its calm waters. The town established here in the early 1800s later took the name as well. Growth was slow due to yellow fever in the 19th century and a hurricane in 1919. Construction of Shoreline Blvd and the deepwater port between 1933 and 1941, combined with a boom brought on by WWII migration, caused rapid growth. Although the downtown is sleepy away from the water, the city does good business attracting large conventions and meetings at the vast American Bank Center.

⊙ Sights

Downtown Corpus lies behind Shoreline Blvd, a wide seafront boulevard that was designed by Gutzon Borglum, the sculptor of Mt Rushmore. The city plays hosts to a range of interesting museums, several nature reserves and plenty of water-sports options. Or, if you just want to hang out on the beach, there are about 131 miles of it just across the causeway on North Padre and Mustang Islands.

★ **Art Museum of South Texas**   MUSEUM
(Map p270; ✆ 361-825-3500; www.artmuseumof southtexas.org; 1902 N Shoreline Blvd; adult/child $8/free; ⊙ 11am-3pm Tue-Fri, from 10am Sat) Rotat-

ing exhibits of contemporary art are the main feature at this dramatic museum, across an art-filled plaza from the Museum of Science & History. Rotating exhibits join selections from the permanent collection of American art. It's free the first Friday of each month.

There's a limited-menu branch of Hester's Cafe (p271) inside, which can be accessed without a museum ticket.

★ **Texas State Aquarium**   AQUARIUM
(Map p270; ✆ 361-881-1230; www.texasstateaquar ium.org; 2710 N Shoreline Blvd, North Beach; adult/child $26/19; ⊙ 9am-5pm, from 10am Sun; P ⊕) You can learn about marine life along the Gulf Coast at this newly renovated space. There are three large handling tanks to get up close to sharks, jellyfish, stingrays and the like, plus exhibits covering the depth of ocean life. The daily schedule of 30-minute presentations includes everything from stingray feeding and raptor flights to otter and diving shows, which change seasonally (so inquire about timings when you arrive).

The aquarium also keeps captive dolphins, which may concern some visitors. Animal-welfare groups claim keeping dolphins in enclosed tanks is harmful for these complex animals. Weekday tickets are $2 cheaper if you buy online.

Oso Bay Wetlands Preserve   NATURE RESERVE
(http://ccparkandrec.com; Oso Bay, end of Holly Rd; ⊙ dawn to dusk) FREE Overlooking Oso Bay, this city-run nature reserve of 162 acres has 4 miles of trails to wander. The surrounding wetlands are a haven for birdlife, and volunteers at the visitor center can help identify species. The gate is open 7:30am to 7pm Monday to Saturday, but visitors that arrive outside of these times can use the walk-in entrances on Holly Rd.

K Space Contemporary   MUSEUM
(Map p270; ✆ 361-887-6834; http://kspacecontem porary.org; 415d Starr St; ⊙ 11am-5pm Wed-Sat) FREE This small space hosts contemporary-art exhibitions, which rotate every four to six weeks, with a penchant for emerging artists. The often-provocative installations are thought provoking, but themes can sometimes be mature, so check what's showing before bringing children.

Heritage Park   HISTORIC SITE
(Map p270; http://ccparkandrec.com; N Chaparral St, at Resaca St; ⊙ dawn-11pm) FREE Originally a neighborhood of old homes, Heritage Park has morphed into a theme park of old

homes. A dozen Corpus houses, from humble to grand and dating back as far as 1851, have been moved to this area bounded by Mesquite, N Chaparral, Hughes and Fitzgerald Sts. Only the central Galvan house was open to visitors at the time of writing, but they're all posted with informative historical markers that give background.

Museum of Science & History   MUSEUM
(Map p270; ☑ 361-826-4667; www.ccmuseum.com; 1900 N Chaparral St; adult/child $11/9; ⊙ 10am-5pm Tue-Sat, noon-5pm Sun; ♠) Explore Spanish shipwrecks, Texas' natural history and more at this fun museum. See how native Texas proved to be the doom of French explorer La Salle, and have a look at the peculiar gallery devoted to historical and modern firearms. There's also a huge two-story science center to get kids engaged.

Museum of Asian Cultures   MUSEUM
(Map p270; ☑ 361-882-8827; www.asiancultures-museum.org; 1809 N Chaparral St; adult/child $6/3; ⊙ 11am-5pm Tue-Sat) This small but well-curated museum is worth a look if you have an interest in art from across South and Southeast Asia, but particularly from Japan. There are some interesting masks and Kabuki figures, plus a tranquil bamboo garden. Despite the posted hours, it's often closed due to staffing shortages.

USS Lexington Museum   MUSEUM
(Map p270; ☑ 316-888-4873; www.usslexington.com; 2914 N Shoreline Blvd, North Beach; adult/child $15/10; ⊙ 9am-5pm, to 6pm Jun-Aug) Dominating the Corpus Christi bay is this 900ft-long aircraft carrier moored just north of the ship channel. The ship served in the Pacific during WWII and was finally retired in 1991. High-tech exhibits give visitors a chance to relive some wartime experiences on any of five self-guided tours. During the evening, the ship is eerily lit with blue lights that recall its WWII nickname: 'the Blue Ghost.' Admission includes a 3-D movie screening in the ship's Mega Theater.

🏃 Activities
There are a handful of beaches in or near Corpus, most notably across the harbor bridge at North Beach.

Most of the skippers who charter boats are based in Rockport or Port Aransas because it puts them closer to the gulf, but CC-based anglers can fish right off the beaches near town or on North Padre Island.

Laguna Madre, west of Padre Island, is a prized windsurfing location thanks to the unusually calm waters and the nearly constant breezes. The alphabetically shaped T and L docks downtown are home to large marinas.

Schlitterbahn Corpus Christi   WATER PARK
(☑ 361-589-4200; www.schlitterbahn.com; 14353 Commodore Dr; adult/child $40/28; ⊙ 10am-6pm weekends Apr-May, to 8pm daily May-Aug) With 18 different water attractions, an on-site resort with restaurant, and a nine-hole golf course, a family could easily spend a few days here without leaving the premises.

Wind & Wave Watersports   WATER SPORTS
(☑ 361-937-9283; www.windandwave.net; 10721 S Padre Island Dr/TX 358; ⊙ 9:30am-7pm) This is a good place to get information on local conditions. It rents boogie boards, surfboards for the terminally optimistic ($30 per day) and kayaks (from $50 per day). If you want an early start in the morning, you can drop by to pick up gear after 5pm the day before your rental starts.

🧭 Tours

Bay Cruise   BOATING
(Map p270; ☑ 361-881-8503 ext 2; https://harrisonslanding.net; Harrison's Landing, 108 Peoples St, T-Head; 1hr cruises adult/child $15/10; ⊙ sailing times vary) Frequent departures of one-hour cruises on Corpus Christi Bay in the summer, off-season Thursday to Sunday only. Options for longer trips are also available.

🎉 Festivals & Events

Buccaneer Days Festival   FESTIVAL
(☑ 361-882-3242; www.bucdays.com; 1513 N Chaparral St; ⊙ May) Held in early May, this festival celebrates the region's long history of piracy with 10 days of music and parades on the Corpus Christi waterfront.

🛏 Sleeping
You might want to opt for the beach-town charms of Port Aransas for your slumber and visit Corpus as a day trip. But there are good options near the water here, and the parks on Padre and Mustang Islands all have camping facilities.

Super 8 Motel – Bayfront   MOTEL $
(Map p270; ☑ 361-884-4815; www.wyndham-hotels.com/super-8; 411 N Shoreline Blvd; r $80-120; ❄ 🛜 🐾) No surprises at this chain offering, but you will find decent budget rooms in an excellent downtown location, smack-bang between the T-heads and the nightlife of Water

Corpus Christi

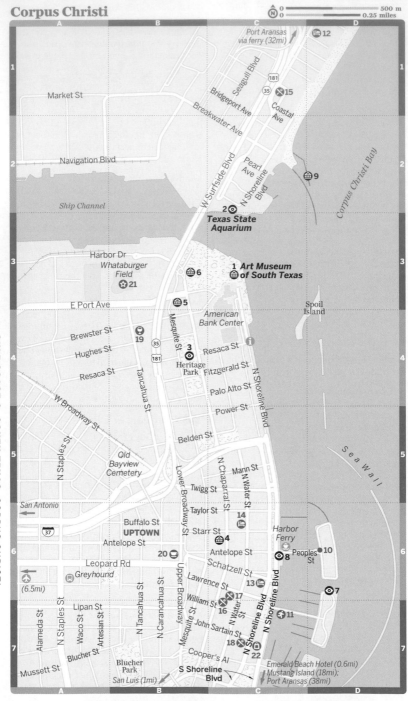

0   500 m
0   0.25 miles

Port Aransas
via ferry (32mi)

Market St

Navigation Blvd

Ship Channel

Seagull Blvd

Bridgeport Ave

Breakwater Ave

Pearl Ave

N Shoreline Blvd

W Surfside Blvd

Coastal Ave

181

35

15

12

9

Corpus Christi Bay

2
Texas State
Aquarium

Harbor Dr
Whataburger
Field

21

6

1 Art Museum
of South Texas

Spoil
Island

E Port Ave

5

Brewster St

Hughes St

Resaca St

Mesquite St

American
Bank Center

19

35

181

3
Heritage
Park

Resaca St

Fitzgerald St

Palo Alto St

Power St

N Shoreline Blvd

i

4

W Broadway St

Tancahua St

Belden St

N Staples St

Old
Bayview
Cemetery

Lower Broadway St

N Chaparral St

Mann St

N Water St

Twigg St

Taylor St

Starr St

14

Sea Wall

San Antonio

37

Buffalo St
UPTOWN

Antelope St

Leopard Rd

20

Greyhound

N Staples St

N Tancahua St

N Carancahua St

Upper Broadway

Mesquite St

4

Antelope St

Schatzell St

Lawrence St

William St

John Sartain St

Cooper's Al

16

17

18

N Water St

N Shoreline Blvd

Harbor
Ferry

8

Peoples
St

10

7

11

13

22

Alameda St

N Staples St

Waco St

Artesian St

Lipan St

Blucher St

Mussett St

Blucher
Park

San Luis (1mi)

S Shoreline
Blvd

Emerald Beach Hotel (0.6mi)
Mustang Island (18mi);
Port Aransas (38mi)

Corpus Christi

St. The pool is probably more inviting than the limpid waters across the street. Don't confuse this with the other Super 8 in town, which is off I-37 in the industrial quarter.

★**V Boutique Hotel** BOUTIQUE HOTEL **$$**
(Map p270; ☑ 361-883-9200; www.vhotelcc.com; 701 N Water St, 2nd fl; r $160-210, ste $320; P❄🛜) Adored by guests, this small hotel in the heart of downtown offers a high level of service, and you can order room service from the excellent restaurant downstairs. It has eight comfy, well-equipped rooms, all with carpeting and a subdued modern design scheme; they range in size from studios to one-bedroom loft suites. Call to book for a 10% discount.

Unless you approach from the north, it can be hard to find. It's upstairs in the 'Vietnam Restaurant' building.

Emerald Beach Hotel HOTEL **$$**
(☑ 361-883-5731; www.hotelemeraldbeach.com; 1102 S Shoreline Blvd; r $180-250; P❄@🛜🏊) Right on the water at the southern tip of downtown, the Emerald confronts you with tough choices between the sand, the hotel's two bars and its indoor pool. Most rooms have balconies, but 1st-floor rooms in the annex building open directly onto a shared walkway above the beach.

Hotel DeVille HOTEL **$$**
(Map p270; ☑ 361-882-3500; www.hoteldevilletx.com; 3500 Surfside Blvd, North Beach; r $200-230, ste $700; ❄🛜) The newest option on North Beach, this modern hotel is about 500ft from the shoreline. The massive DeVille Suite can hold up to 15 guests, but if you don't need quite that much space, there are standard kings and queens

✗ Eating

Restaurants cluster on the streets surrounding Chaparral and Water Sts downtown.

San Luis MEXICAN **$**
(☑ 361-885-0117; 2110 Laredo St; meals $5-9; ⊙6am-2pm Mon-Sat, 7am-3pm Sun) A dead-simple Mexican diner with the requisite Selena posters, San Luis serves indescribably good food. Breakfast orders start at $1.35, but even if you can't make it by 11am everything about this place is a fantastic value.

Padre Island Burger Company BURGERS **$**
(☑ 361-949-3490; www.padreislandburgercompany.com; 11878 TX-361, North Padre Island; mains $10-15; ⊙11am-10pm) One might be forgiven for mistaking this place for a dive bar, and it isn't far off after dark, but it also happens to serve up some of the best burgers in the area. Make sure to order the fries with garlic aioli. It's inside the intersection of PR 22 and TX 361 on Padre Island.

Hester's Cafe CAFE **$**
(☑ 361-885-0558; www.hesterscafe.com; 1714 S Alameda St; mains $7-12; ⊙7am-3pm Mon-Sat; 🛜) The great coffee is a given in 'too cool for brewed' Corpus, but Hester's is also much loved for its excellent breakfasts, creative salads, delicious sandwiches and quiches, and beautiful desserts. There are three branches in town, including one inside the Art Museum of South Texas (p268), but this is the coziest.

Hamlin Pharmacy and Fountain CAFE **$**
(☑ 361-853-7303; www.hamlinfg.com; 3801 S Staples St, at Hamlin Shopping Center; mains $3-9; ⊙8am-4:30pm Mon-Sat) A character-filled throwback to the days when drugstores all had lunch counters, this is the real 1960s

deal. Sit on a barstool or in a tiny booth and have a bowl plus something luscious from the soda fountain. The cook, Jesse Lerma, has been manning the grill since just a few months after the fountain opened in 1960.

Hamlin is in a vintage strip mall about 5 miles south of the marinas. The on-site bakery, with a more modern menu of items such as macarons and key lime pie, is also worth a look.

Whataburger   BURGERS $

(Map p270; ☏ 361-881-9925; www.whataburger.com; 121 N Shoreline Blvd; mains from $3; ☉24hr) Corpus Christi's own entry in the burger-chain wars, Whataburger got its start in town in 1950. This location, with its view of the marina, wears much of the 1970s orange motif found in the chain's 700 other outlets. The trademark big-diameter (and wafer-thin) burger is the locally loved fast-food choice and the 2nd floor has decent views.

Don't miss the statue of the chain's founder, Harmon Dobson.

Blackbeard's On the Beach   TEX-MEX $

(Map p270; ☏ 361-884-1030; http://blackbeards. restaurant; 3117 E Surfside Blvd, North Beach; mains $7-20; ☉11am-9pm Sun-Thu, to 10pm Fri & Sat; 🖥) On North Beach, this rollicking place serves up tasty Mexican and American cuisine with a strong seafood focus. Wash it down with cheap margaritas while sitting back for the live music, but watch out for the ghosts that are reputed to haunt the place. Oh, and if it's your birthday? Yours is on the house.

Executive Surf Club   SOUTHERN $

(Map p270; ☏ 316-884-7873; www.executivesurf club.com; 312 N Chaparral St; mains $5-12; ☉11am-11pm Sun-Thu, to midnight Fri & Sat; 🖥🖥) Dig into a burger or a chicken fried steak at your surfboard table and sip a craft brew from locally sourced Lazy Beach Brewing at this longtime Corpus Christi fave. It has a pet-friendly porch plus live music, and it's just divey enough that you can forget you're downtown.

Water Street Seafood Company   SEAFOOD $$

(Map p270; ☏361-882-8683; www.waterst marketcc.com; 314 N Chaparral St; mains $13-25; ☉11am-10pm Sun-Thu, to 11pm Fri & Sat; 🖥) Busy all week because of the huge and changing selection of fresh seafood, much of it not deep-fried, and there's a 'playa' menu for those that lean more toward the 'turf' than the surf. It also has a very popular oyster bar, big with the after-work crowd. It's the best option for higher-end fare in Corpus Christi's downtown.

🍷 Drinking & Nightlife

★**Brewster Street Icehouse**   BAR

(Map p270; ☏361-884-2739; www.brewsterstreet. net; 1724 N Tancahua St; ☉11am-2am; 🖥🖥) The perfect embodiment of the Texas icehouse. Bring the kids for a burger, friends for a beer, or wander over after a game at Whataburger Field for the live music. Thursday nights are Texas Country, but Friday to Sunday run the range of genres. The food is pretty good too, even the $8 lunch special. You're darn tootin' it's a good deal.

SELENA

Selena Quintanilla Perez, easily the most famous daughter of Corpus Christi, was almost single-handedly responsible for the crossover of Tejano music to the mainstream. She had a charismatic stage presence and, since her murder in 1995, has assumed martyr status for many. Images of her can be found in shops and restaurants all over town.

Selena was 23 when Yolanda Saldivar, the president of her fan club, shot her in the parking lot of the Days Inn near the Corpus Christi airport. At the trial prosecutors successfully argued that Saldivar shot the singing star because Selena had discovered that Saldivar was stealing Selena's money. Saldivar got life in prison.

In death, Selena's music still sells and many devotees make the pilgrimage to Corpus. Her story has been embraced by fans because it is one with which they can empathize. Selena's parents tried and failed at running a Mexican restaurant in Corpus, and it fell to their plucky daughter and her crowd-pleasing talents to save the family from ruin. Along the way, she ran afoul of her father, an authoritarian who objected to her revealing stage clothes. And she married her lead guitarist in a secret ceremony. It was great melodrama, as seen in 1997's film *Selena,* which made a star of the then relatively unknown Jennifer Lopez.

In Corpus Christi, the **Selena Memorial & Statue** (Map p270; 600 N Shoreline Blvd; ☉24hr) stands at the entrance to the Peoples St T-Head on Shoreline Blvd. But to really celebrate Selena and feel links to her life, don't miss the **Selena Museum** (☏361-289-9013; www.q-productions.com/museum.html; 5410 Leopard St; adult/child $3/1; ☉10am-4pm Mon-Fri).

Happy hour is 4pm to 6pm every day.

The icehouse was once an essential part of Texas community life, a place for neighborhoods to gather and social bonds to form. Very few still exist, and even fewer still retain the communal vibe as authentically as Brewster.

Green Light Coffee COFFEE
(Map p270; 361-434-0846; www.facebook. com/greenlightcoffeeshop; 600 Leopard St, Suite 100; 7am-4pm Mon-Fri;) We'd almost say it was trying to hard if it wasn't just. that. good. With nitro and cold brew on tap ($3) alongside more traditional espresso-based favorites ($1 to $3) and a classy minimalistic interior, this is probably the coolest coffee shop this side of Austin and Houston.

🛍 Shopping

Art Centre of Corpus Christi ART
(Map p270; 361-884-6406; www.artcentercc.org; 100 N Shoreline Blvd; 10am-4pm Tue-Sat, to 8pm Wed, 1-4pm Sun) Gallery space and studios for regional artists are housed in this grand old building downtown, which stays open late on Wednesday nights for an 'Art Market' for fine art. The Citrus Bistro inside is good for lunch (mains $8 to $10).

ℹ Information

Corpus Christi Visitor Information Center
(Map p270; 361-561-2000; www.visitcorpus christitx.org; 1400 N Shoreline Blvd; 9am-5pm Mon-Thu, to 6pm Fri-Sun) In the waterfront kiosk near the art museum.

ℹ Getting There & Away

You'll find **Corpus Christi International Airport** (CRP; 361-289-0171; www.corpuschristiairport. com; 1000 International Dr) 6 miles west of downtown at International Dr and TX 44. American Eagle serves Dallas–Fort Worth International Airport; Continental Express serves Houston's George Bush International Airport; and Southwest serves Houston's William P Hobby Airport.

Greyhound (Map p270; 361-226-4393; www. greyhound.com; 602 N Staples St; 8am-1:30am) has regular service to Houston ($25, 4½ hours), Brownsville ($14, 3½ hours), San Antonio ($20, 2½ hours) and beyond.

ℹ Getting Around

Cabs from the airport to downtown cost at least $35; most motels and hotels run shuttles.

The B (361-289-2600; www.ccrta.org; adult/ child $0.75/0.35, day pass $1.75) is the jaunty name for the local buses. Fares are cheap and buses on most routes run about 6:30am to 6.30pm, although few run on Sunday.

The most useful route for travelers is the 78 CC Beach/Bayfront services which link the downtown and marina areas with the North Beach area and runs all the way to the Southside Transit Station for transfer to Port Aransas.

In addition, The B sometimes operates a **harbor ferry** (Map p270; 361-289-2600; www.ccrta. org; Peoples St T-Head; single ride $1.50; 10am-6:30pm Wed-Mon Jun-Aug, weekends only mid-Mar–May & Sep-Nov) across the channel between the museums and the Lexington, but the future of the service was uncertain at time of writing.

Port Aransas

361 / POP 3480

On the northern tip of Mustang Island, the town of Port Aransas (Ah-*ran*-ziss), or Port A to locals, is in many ways the most appealing beach destination on the Texas coast. It is small enough that you can bike or walk everywhere, but large enough to host loads of activities and nightlife. The pace is very relaxed, and daily life is dominated by hanging out on the beach, fishing and doing nothing – perhaps followed up by a few cold drinks as the sun goes down.

This area was seriously impacted by Hurricane Harvey. Travellers are advised to call ahead before visiting.

◉ Sights

Port A makes a great base for fishing trips or beach vacations, but the prime barrier-island location also makes for good bird-watching.

Mustang Island has 18 miles of silvery white beaches on the gulf side, or it's an easy day trip to the undeveloped coastline of Padre Island National Seashore (p277).

Leonabelle Turnbull
Birding Center NATURE RESERVE
(361-749-4158; www.cityofportaransas.org; Ross Ave; dawn-dusk) FREE A short boardwalk runs through the tall grass to an observation tower with wide-open views over the nature reserve and ship channel. Local guides run a free birding tour Wednesday at 9am.

Due to damage sustained from Hurricane Harvey, the center is closed till March 2018. Call ahead before visiting.

San José Island ISLAND
( ) A privately owned island just across the ship channel from Port Aransas, known as St Jo to locals. This squat desert island, 2 miles at its widest but 21 miles long, is popular for

---

> ### ⓘ DRIVING THE BAY LOOP
>
> You can do a loop of Corpus Christi Bay in two hours without stops, assuming you can catch the Port Aransas ferry without a wait. In the south, Padre and Mustang Islands are joined to the mainland via the John F Kennedy Causeway across Laguna Madre. The causeway in turn is reached from Corpus Christi by either Ocean Dr from downtown or by TX 358 (S Padre Island Dr, often called just SPID), which links to the other highways and passes by an ocean of shopping malls. To the north over the harbor bridge and past North Beach, a car ferry links Port Aransas to TX 361, which leads to Aransas Pass where TX 35 links with US 181 and back to Corpus.

fishing and beachcombing. There are absolutely no services, so users are advised to bring over everything they require (including water). The **jetty boat** (☑361-749-5448; www.fishermanswharfporta.com; 900 Tarpon St; adult/child $12/6; ⊘7am-6pm) runs many times daily for the five-minute trip: on demand until around 10am and then regularly back and forth till 6pm.

IB Magee Beach Park   BEACH
(☑361-749-6117; www.nuecesbeachparks.com; Beach St; ⊘24hr) FREE The main access point to this county-run park is via Beach St (try to remember that). The park has rest rooms, the Horace Caldwell fishing pier and seasonal concession stands. Day use is free, but beach camping is $12 per site and developed sites are $20 to $25, payable at the pier.

Due to damage sustained from Hurricane Harvey, the park is closed till March 2018. Call ahead before visiting.

Nature Preserve
at Charlie's Pasture   NATURE RESERVE
(☑361-749-4158; www.cityofportaransas.org; Port St; ⊘dawn-dusk) FREE Over 1200 acres of nature preserve look out over the bird-filled marshes and salt flats on the east side of town. The 2-mile-return boardwalk stroll leads to several observation decks and a tower on Salt Island, from which the preserve unfolds.

🏃 Activities

There are myriad places offering water adventures and gear for surfing, kiteboarding and more. There are dozens of fishing boats offering trips and private charter; the tourist bureau has listings. Rates run from $50 to $1000 or more, depending on destination, duration and what you're trying to catch.

Horace Caldwell Fishing Pier   FISHING
(☑361-749-5333; Port Aransas Beach Rd; ⊘24hr) The pier is a one-stop shop for fishing, from gear rentals to bait and licenses. It's $2 per person to enter and another $2 per pole or net, and passes expire at 5am the following morning.

Deep Sea Headquarters   FISHING
(☑361-749-5597; www.deepseaheadquarters.com; 440 W Cotter Ave; ⊘6am-10pm) The name says it all. Daily fishing excursions are available as three-hour (adult/child $43/37), five-hour ($84/63) and eight-hour ($116) trips; all include equipment and bait.

Woody's Sports Center   BOATING
(☑361-749-6969; www.woodys-pa.com; 136 Cotter Ave; dolphin/fishing cruise from $30/45; ⊘6:30am-6pm Sun-Thu, to 8pm Fri, 6am-8pm Sat) The go-to place for arranging dolphin-watching (adult/child $30/20), kid-themed pirate tours and highly recommended fishing trips (four-hour trips adult/child $45/25, charters also available).

Island Surf Rentals   WATER SPORTS
(☑361-749-0822; www.islandsurfrentals.com; 130 East Ave G; ⊘9am-6pm Sun-Thu, to 7pm Fri, 8am-7pm Sat) Per day rentals: surfboards ($25), boogie boards ($10), bikes ($20) and kayaks ($45 to $60).

Fisherman's Wharf   BOATING
(☑361-749-5448; www.fishermanswharfporta.com; 900 Tarpon St; 5hr trip adult/child $70/35; ⊘6am-8pm) Fisherman's Wharf runs the jetty boat (p273) to San José Island as well as a daily one-hour dolphin-spotting trip at 4:30pm (either trip adult/child $12/6). It also runs five-hour fishing excursions daily from 8am to 1pm and 2pm to 7pm (adult/child $70/35).

🛏 Sleeping

There are more motel/condo rooms in Port A than there are permanent residents, so there are plenty of options and something to meet most budgets. Not surprisingly, summer weekends are when rooms are at their dearest; book in advance. Rates drop significantly in low season, but so do the crowds that make the town so much fun.

Many places were closed temporarily after Hurricane Harvey and those that weren't were busy with relief workers. Call ahead.

Amelia's Landing
MOTEL **$$**

(☑ 361-749-5572; www.ameliaslanding.com; 105 N Alister St; r $180-210; ☀ ☎ ☒) This centrally located motel has an aviation theme, with units each decorated for a different bit of flying lore (Red Baron room, Amelia Earhart room, Apollo room etc). All are loaded with amenities (fridges, DVDs, microwaves), and some have kitchens or kitchenettes. It books up early in high season.

Tarpon Inn
HISTORIC HOTEL **$$**

(☑ 361-749-5555; www.thetarponinn.com; 200 E Cotter Ave; r $126-180, ste $180-300, ☀ ☎) Dating from 1900, when the town was still called Tarpon, this charming if rickety place has been rebuilt several times after hurricanes. The lobby has more than 7000 huge silver scales from the 6ft-long namesake fish. Many rooms are small and have no TVs or phones, but do have lots of character and rocking chairs on the verandah.

Sea Shell Village
CONDO **$$**

(☑ 361-749-4294; www.seashellvillage.com; 502 East Ave G; r $165-300; ☀ ☎ ☒) These bright, colorful condo-style units are close to the beach and can each sleep two to six. Floor plans differ, but all come with kitchens or kitchenettes and are ideal for a longer stay (weekly rates available).

Dancing Dunes
CABIN **$$**

(☑ 361-749-3029; www.5dancingdunes.com; 1607 11th St; r $185-300; ☀ ☎) Five funky beach cabins around a connecting porch have two or three bedrooms each. Flotsam, jetsam and wrecked rowboats decorate the grounds and decor like a holiday episode of *Laverne & Shirley*. Guaranteed fun, with character and characters.

TurnKey

Vacation Rentals
ACCOMMODATION SERVICES **$$**

(☑ 361-221-8983; www.turnkeyvr.com/port-aransas-texas; 1115 TX 361c; rentals $100-1000) This national vacation-rental agency has an office in Port Aransas with a varied assortment of listings that run the gamut from small houses right on the beach to mass luxury homes.

✖ Eating

Port A has a great selection of restaurants, most of them casual affairs where flip-flops and swimsuit seem de rigueur. Seafood is the obvious go-to here, but there are a few humdrum places that fry up frozen fish.

While many places were affected by Hurricane Harvey, most were hoping to reopen by early 2018.

Crazy Cajun
CAJUN **$**

(☑ 361-749-5069, 303 Beach St; mains $8-20; ☺ 5-10pm Mon-Fri, from noon Sat & Sun) This lively, ramshackle eatery always packs a crowd. There is an á la carte menu, but you should probably just order the Hungry Cajun ($16), a tabletop serving of boiled sausage, shrimp, crab and veggies – all of which is plunked down on butcher paper for a messy but fun eat-with-your-hands feast.

Avery's Kitchen
CAFE **$**

(☑ 361-749-0650; 200 West Ave G; mains from $6, buffet $8; ☺ 7am-9pm) Home cookin' by chef and proprietor Avery Hernandez comes cheap, but such is the quality and the friendly vibe that crowds keep coming back. The lunch buffet is a fantastic deal, and the breakfasts get plaudits. Hours can be erratic, but it's worth making several attempts if you have to.

★ Roosevelt's at the Tarpon Inn
SEAFOOD **$$$**

(☑ 361-749-1540; www.rooseveltsatthetarponinn.com; 200 E Cotter Ave; mains $28-48; ☺ 5-10pm) The fine dining room at the Tarpon Inn is worth getting spiffed up for. Reserve a table on the verandah and settle back to enjoy a seasonal menu of seafood and steaks, simply and creatively prepared, accompanied by a couple glasses of nice wine. The space is small, so reservations are recommended.

🍸 Drinking & Nightlife

It's the quirky bars that make up so much of Port Aransas' always-summer beach-town vibe. Full of character, offbeat fun and cheap drinks; it's a great place to sling one back.

Kody's
BAR

(☑ 361-749-8226; http://kodysrestaurant.com; 2034 TX 361; ☺ 11am-2am) Somehow straddling the line between family restaurant and lively jukebox joint, Kody's is fun no matter which time of the day you visit. The food menu, mostly seafood, is actually pretty good (lunch $5 to $10, dinner $9 to $24). Order at the bar.

Shorty's Place
BAR

(☑ 361-749-8224; http://shortysportaransas.com; 823 Tarpon St; ☺ 10am-2am Mon-Sat, from noon Sun; ☎) The town's 'oldest and friendliest' watering hole is filled with real local seadogs and characters both inside and out on the battered porch. It has dartboards and pool tables, and the ceiling is adorned with hundreds of caps from around the world. You can bar-hop around the block here, by the docks, and the party seems to get started early.

GULF COAST & SOUTH TEXAS PORT ARANSAS

ℹ️ BEACH PARKING PERMITS

You can drive your vehicle right onto the sand at many points in Port Aransas and Mustang Island, and often the beaches are so packed that even a regular car will have no problem – just look to see what others are doing. At city and county beaches, you'll need a **beach** parking permit ($12). These are easily purchased at convenience stores, supermarkets and the **Port A tourist office**.

Gaff   BAR

(📞 361-749-5970; http://gotothegaff.com; 323 Beach St; ⏰ 11am-11pm Sun-Thu, to midnight Fri & Sat) Out by the beach, this ramshackle bar (drinks from $3) is perfect for anyone aspiring to arrested development. Weekend fun includes belt-sander races and chicken-poop bingo (come on bird, come on!). There's decent pizza and subs (mains $9 to $21) plus live music that includes blues and country.

The Brewery   BREWERY

(📞 361-749-2739; http://portaransasbrewery.com; 429 N Alister St; ⏰ 11am-8pm Tue-Thu, to 9pm Fri-Sun) Come for the promise of microbrews (we love the Milk Stout, and IPA lovers will be impressed by the house option), stay for the gourmet burgers and pizzas (mains $12 to $22). There's a small deck out front.

ℹ️ Information

Port Aransas Chamber of Commerce & Tourist Bureau (📞 361-749-5919; https://portaransas. org; 403 W Cotter Ave; ⏰ 9am-5pm Mon-Sat) Loans out binoculars for bird-watching.

ℹ️ Getting There & Away

A highlight of getting to Port A is the free, constantly running **ferries** (📞 361-749-2850; ⏰ 24hr) which connect with TX 361 and Aransas Pass on the mainland. The ride takes 15 minutes and the wait is usually under 10 minutes, but at busy times it can be 45 minutes or longer. The only other option is to drive south, following TX 361 for 18 miles to the edge of Corpus Christi and the turnoff for Padre Island National Seashore.

The public-transit option for Port Aransas is operated by Corpus Christi's **The B** (p273). Route 65 runs thrice each morning and afternoon (only two morning departures on Sunday) from the Southside Transfer Station in Corpus Christi to the intersection of Sandcastle and 11th Sts in Port A and back. From the final stop you can transfer to buses to Corpus Christi airport and downtown.

ℹ️ Getting Around

For San José Island, across the channel to the north of Port Aransas, the **Jetty Boat** (p273) makes regular runs throughout the day (adult/child $12/6 round-trip) from Fisherman's Wharf until 6pm.

Local shuttle 96 departs from the Cinnamon Shore neighborhood on the south edge of Port A at the top of every hour from 10am to 5pm, up to the Horace Caldwell Pier and across to the ferry landing before heading back south. Fares are 75¢ and you can flag it down anywhere on the route.

Golf carts are extremely popular among both short- and long-term residents. **Cars & Carts** (📞 361-749-1655; www.carsandcarts.com; 325 East Ave G; cart rental per hr/day $32/176; ⏰ 8am-9pm), among others, rents them out by the day or longer.

Mustang & Padre Island Beaches

The Gulf Coast here is essentially one 131-mile-long beach, including 18-mile Mustang Island and massive 113-mile North Padre Island (the second-largest island by area in the US, after New York's Long Island). The most notable sections for beachgoers are Mustang Island State Park and Padre Island National Seashore.

The rest of the beach is administered by Nueces County. There are access roads every few miles, and most have a parking area; parts of the beach are blocked off so that inattentive drivers in 4WDs can't mow you down. Sand dunes back most of the beach area. Only since the 1970s have some monstrous condo developments appeared on Mustang Island near Port Aransas; otherwise most of the sand is blissfully undeveloped.

For most of the beaches you'll need a permit to drive on the sand. However, a 6-mile stretch just north of Padre Island National Seashore is free.

Mustang Island State Park

The well-equipped **Mustang Island State Park** (📞 361-749-5246; www.tpwd.state.tx.us; 17047 TX 361; adult/child $5/free; ⏰ 7am-10pm except to overnight guests) covers 4000 acres and has 5.5 miles of beach. It is popular with surfers, but given the normally calm nature of the gulf you may have to wait for storms to see any surfable waves. Some picnic areas have shade. For anglers, there's a jetty on the north end of the park's beachfront and the visitor center sells Texas fishing licenses.

There are 300 nonreservable primitive drive-up campsites ($10) on the beach that have access to water, cold showers and rest rooms. A more formal – and reservable – camping area with individual water and electricity hookups costs $20 per night; the sites are all 50yd to 75yd from the beach.

Due to damage sustained from Hurricane Harvey, the park was due to be closed till January 2018. Call ahead before visiting.

Padre Island National Seashore

The longest stretches of undeveloped barrier island in the world, the southern part of **Padre Island** (📞361-949-8068; www.nps.gov/pais; Park Rd 22; 7-day pass per car $10; ⊙park 24hr) is administered by the National Park Service (NPS). Its main feature is 65 miles of white sand and shell beaches, backed by grassy dunes and the very salty Laguna Madre.

The island is home to all the coastal wildlife found elsewhere along the coast and then some. There's excellent birding, of course, plus numerous coyotes, white-tailed deer, sea turtles and more. It offers a delightful day's outing for anyone who wants to try a little natural beauty, or a major adventure for anyone who wants to escape civilization.

The excellent park map is free at the entrance. Besides showing the island in great detail, it has good infor about flora, fauna and activities such as fishing and beachcombing.

🎿 Activities

Park rangers advise campers and hikers of the common sense needed for a trip down the island's undeveloped south beach. Bring at least 1 gallon of water per person per day, along with sunscreen, insect repellent, good shady hats and other sensible attire. Shore fishing is permitted with a Texas state fishing license.

Bird Island Basin faces the hypersaline Laguna Madre and has been voted as one of the best windsurfing spots in North America.

Worldwinds Windsurfing   WINDSURFING
(📞361-949-7472; www.worldwinds.net; Bird Island Basin Rd, off Park Road 22; ⊙11am-6pm Apr-Sep, to 5pm Oct-Mar) Offers windsurfing lessons ($65 to $80 per lesson, two to three hours including equipment) and rental of kayaks, standup paddleboards and windsurfing gear.

🛏 Sleeping

Reservations are not accepted for any of the facilities. Aside from the paid **Bird Island Basin** (Bird Island Basin Rd, off Park Rd 22; campsite per

night $5) and **Malaquite** (off Park Rd 22; campsites $8) campgrounds, primitive camping on the beaches is free with a permit from the visitor center. Many people park their RVs and trailers along the first 5 miles of beach, but enter the sands at your own risk: a tow will run at least a few hundred dollars.

ℹ Information

Malaquite Beach Visitor Center (📞361-949-8068; www.nps.gov/pais; ⊙9am-5pm) The Malaquite Beach Visitor Center is on the beach just before the end of the paved road. It has showers, rest rooms and picnic facilities and offers excellent info. Check the schedule for interpretive walks (there's usually one at 11am along the beach).

Kingsville

📞361 / POP 26,213

King is the name of the game in this company town, which is the direct result of the fabled 825,000-acre King Ranch, an operation that stretches across four Texas counties. Former riverboat captain Richard King established the ranch in 1853 on land that others saw as a scrub-covered semidesert. King saw scrub-covered semidesert with the only natural springs for hundreds of miles. Today the ranch is bigger than Rhode Island, a state that the ranch's fences would reach if they were laid end to end.

◉ Sights

King Ranch
HISTORIC SITE

(✏ visitor center 361-592-8055; www.king-ranch. com; 2205 W TX 141; ranch tours adult/child $20/6; ⊙ 10am-4pm Mon-Sat, noon-5pm Sun) Much of the King Ranch is not open to the public. But there are 60,000 head of cattle, 400 horses and dozens of cowboys here – many fifth- and sixth-generation descendants of Kineños, who moved en masse to the ranch in the 1860s from the small Mexican town of Cruillas. Tours depart from the ranch's visitor center, which is just inside the rather modest entrance on the west side of Kingsville at the end of Santa Gertrudis Ave.

King Ranch Museum
MUSEUM

(✏ 361-595-1881; www.king-ranch.com; 405 N 6th St; adult/child $10/4; ⊙ 10am-4pm Mon-Sat, 1-5pm Sun) Housed in a renovated ice-storage house downtown, the King Ranch Museum covers the history of the ranch and the Kings. Be sure to follow the minor family dramas of the first generation, and admire the collection of historic cars and saddles. No photos.

✕ Eating

Harrel's Pharmacy
CAFE $

(✏ 361-592-3355; www.harrels.com; 204 E Kleberg Ave; mains from $5; ⊙ 8am-5pm Mon-Fri, to 3pm Sat) Besides capsules with cold and flu remedies and a slew of knickknacks, this pharmacy serves up a time capsule in the form of an authentic soda fountain that hasn't changed in decades. The hash browns at breakfast are real, the burgers juicy and cheap, and the soda sweet and tasty.

King Ranch Saddle Shop
GIFTS & SOUVENIRS

(✏ 877-282-5777; www.krsaddleshop.com; 201 E Kleberg Ave; ⊙ 10am-6pm Mon-Sat) The upmarket King Ranch Saddle Shop has expensive clothing, gear and souvenirs branded with the distinctive King Ranch 'Running W' logo, which looks like a squiggly snake.

ⓘ Information

Kingsville Visitor Center (✏ 361-592-8516; www.kingsvilletexas.com; 1501 N Hwy 77, at Corral Ave; ⊙ 9am-5pm Mon-Fri, 10am-2pm Sat) Right at the freeway exit on the north side of town.

LOWER GULF COAST

Palm trees and hot humid weather are but one sign you've hit the subtropical southern Gulf Coast. Ribbons of traffic zipping along TX 100 to South Padre Island mean that you've come within the gravitational force of the state's favorite beach party town. Slow down a bit on the way to Padre, and you'll find pleasant natural surprises at Laguna Atascosa National Wildlife Reserve and learn the interesting history of gateway town Port Isabel.

Port Isabel

📞 956 / POP 5006

In the days before inexpensive hurricane insurance made South Padre Island (SPI) viable as a town, Port Isabel was the focus of life near the southern end of Texas. Records show that Spaniards and pirates both made frequent landfalls here in the 16th, 17th and 18th centuries. From 1872 it was the hub for more-reputable steamship landings as the terminus of the Rio Grande Railroad, and nearby Brazos Island was the major shipping point for ferrying goods in and out of South Texas until the deep-water port at Brownsville was opened in 1936.

Today Port Isabel is a scenic stop just before South Padre Island. Its small old town covers the waterfront for a couple of blocks on either side of the base of the TX 100 Queen Isabella Causeway.

◉ Sights

The three main sights are all within easy walking distance of each other and the small historic district. You can buy combined tickets for all three (adult/child $9/free).

Treasures of the Gulf Museum
MUSEUM

(✏ 956-943-7602; http://portisabelmuseums.com; 317 E Railroad Ave; adult/child $4/free; ⊙ 10am-4pm Tue-Sat) Sunken treasure! That's the focus of this fun museum, which has artifacts from three Spanish galleons that went down nearby in 1554. It does a good job of telling the stories of the hapless crews and passengers and the perils of travel in the sailing age.

Port Isabel Historical Museum
MUSEUM

(✏ 956-943-7602; http://portisabelmuseums.com; 317 E Railroad Ave; adult/child $4/free; ⊙ 10am-4pm Tue-Sat) Built (in 1899) sturdily of bricks to resist storms, the home of the history museum served at various times as the town's railroad station, post office and general store. It now houses a large collection of artifacts from the 1846–48

GULF COAST & SOUTH TEXAS PORT ISABEL

LOS FRESNOS & LAGUNA ATASCOSA NATIONAL WILDLIFE REFUGE

There's one great reason to head along TX 100, the South Padre Island road, and three compelling reasons to linger in Los Fresnos.

Laguna Atascosa National Wildlife Refuge (☑956-748-3607; www.fws.gov; 22688 Buena Vista Rd; per vehicle $3; ☺gates dawn-dusk, visitor center 8am-4pm) is a bird-watching wonderland, with more confirmed species than any other property in the country.

In between trips to the reserve fill up on authentic Mexican food at **Elva's Mexican Restaurant** (☑956-233-1533; 719 W Ocean Blvd; mains $5-10; ☺6am-3pm Mon-Sat, to 2pm Sun), do some shopping at the uniquely strange **Bobz World** (☑956-233-2353; www.bobzworld.com; 36451 TX 100; ☺9am-7pm Mon-Fri, to 8pm Sat & Sun), or spend a night in what is effectively a private nature reserve at one of the best B&Bs on the Gulf Coast: the **Inn at Chachalaca Bend**.

Where to Stay

Inn at Chachalaca Bend (☑956-233-1180; www.chachalaca.com; 36298 Chachalaca Bend; r $160-180, lodge $300) Tucked away into a quiet corner of nowhere, the five private rooms (half of which open onto the wraparound shared balcony on the 2nd floor) and inviting common area would look magnificent if it weren't for the standalone lodge building – three stories. It also has a fireplace, a private library, and an observation tower surveying the surrounding forest.

Adolph Thomae Jr County Park (☑956-748-2044; www.cameroncountyparks.com; 37844 Marshall Hutts Rd, Rio Hondo; campsites $30, tent sites w/out hookups $15; ☺gate 5:30am-10pm) Barely inside the northwestern edge of Laguna Atascosa NWR, this small county campsite is the only place at which camping is officially allowed within the reserve. The peaceful sites on the banks of Arroyo Colorado aren't half bad, and you could hike in from here to the park's west lake trail if you put your mind to it.

Mexican-American War, and smaller displays on regional and local history. You'll find it one block south of TX 100, near the lighthouse.

Port Isabel Lighthouse HISTORIC BUILDING
(☑956-943-7602; http://portisabellighthouse.com; 414 E Queen Isabella Blvd/TX 100; adult/child $4/free; ☺9am-5pm) The Port Isabel Lighthouse was built between 1852 and 1853. A climb up its 70 steps yields great views of the surrounding area, SPI and the gulf. It is also the source of local tourist info. At the time of research, the entire exhibition space was being renovated and replanned.

Eating

The waterfront is predictably lined with popular seafood joints and bars with decks overlooking the water, but for the best food around look a few blocks inland.

★**Joe's Oyster Bar Restaurant** SEAFOOD $
(☑956-943-4501; 207 E Maxan St; mains $7-14; ☺11am-7pm) Ask for recommendations on where to eat in Port Isabel, and this combination fishmonger and restaurant is the most common suggestion by far. It makes a mean po'boy sandwich, the oysters are renowned, and you can get anything to go for picnics or packed fresh for cooking later in the condo.

Manuel's Restaurant MEXICAN $
(☑956-943-1655; 313 E Maxan St; mains from $5; ☺7am-2pm Tue-Sun) The steady 'patting' sound you hear comes from the ladies in the back room making flour tortillas. Everything is dead simple here, including the decor, but the classic Mexican fare is excellent and the ambience casual. Get a side of avocado with anything you order, including the *heuvos* at breakfast.

South Padre Island

☑956 / POP 2816

Covering the southern 5 miles of South Padre Island, the town of South Padre Island (SPI) works hard to exploit its sunny climate. The water is warm for much of the year, the beaches are clean and the laid-back locals are ready to welcome every tourist who crosses the 2.5-mile Queen Isabella Causeway from the mainland (the permanent population is augmented by 10,000 or more visitors at any given time, more in peak periods).

January and February, when the weather can be either balmy or a bit chilly, are the quietest months to visit SPI (though still popular with Winter Texans). The busiest and most expensive periods are spring break (all of March except the first week) and summer, when the moderating gulf breezes make the shore more tolerable than the sweltering inland areas, and the normally chill vibe turns into hedonistic party central for unending weeks at a time.

⊙ Sights

★ Sea Turtle, Inc
WILDLIFE RESERVE

(📞956-761-4511; www.seaturtleinc.com; 6617 Padre Blvd; suggested donation adult/child $4/2; ⊙10am-4pm Tue-Sun, to 5pm Jun-Aug) No, you can't handle the sea turtles. But you can see rescued turtles and learn firsthand about the slow rebirth of critically endangered Kemp's ridley turtle populations. The center serves as a hospital for injured animals, runs educational programs for the public and releases young turtles once they're old enough to face the world on their own. To find out when hatchlings will be released – generally at sunrise in summer – call the Hatchling Hotline (📞956-433-5735).

South Padre Island
Birding & Nature Center
NATURE RESERVE

(📞956-761-6801; www.southpadreislandbirding. com; 6801 Padre Blvd; adult/child $6/3; ⊙9am-5pm) Part of the World Birding Center, this 50-acre nature preserve has boardwalks through the dunes, bird blinds, spotting towers and much more. Learn the differences between a dune meadow, a salt marsh and an intertidal flat in the flashy exhibit hall. Look for butterflies, egrets, alligators, turtles, crabs and much more. There's a blackboard out front listing recent sightings at the reserve. While the visitor center is only open during office hours, ticketed guests can access the boardwalks from dawn to dusk.

You can also access some of the site for free from a boardwalk at the SPI Convention Center (📞956-761-3000; www.sopadre.com; 7355 Padre Blvd) just to the north.

University of Texas Rio Grande Valley –
Coastal Studies Laboratory
AQUARIUM

(📞956-761-2644; www.utrgv.edu/csl; 100 Marine Lab Dr, Isla Blanca Park; ⊙1:30-4:30pm Mon-Fri) FREE This small working lab is open for self-guided tours of its small fish tanks and various wall displays. If you can get past its meager utilitarian charms, you'll find lots of information about local marine life. Entrance is free, but you will have to pay the Isla Blanca (p283) entry fee to access the facility.

Activities

There are so many activities on SPI that you may be exhausted before you start...if you ever do.

Fishing

More than 50 fishing boats leave from the piers on the lagoon.To find a guide and/ or boat charter, it's best to just wander the docks and talk to the skippers to find one who seems in sync with what you want. Contact Isla Cruises if you're in a hurry and want to reserve in advance. Group trips start at $40. You may catch flounder or speckled trout close to SPI. Longer trips head into the deep waters of the gulf for prime game fish.

Horseback Riding
South Padre Island
Adventures
HORSEBACK RIDING

(📞956-415-0526; www.horsesonthebeach.com; Padre Blvd, North End; 1hr rides from $40; ⊙8:30am-6:30pm May-Sep; ⊕) This adventure center is best known for its horseback rides on the beach ($40 to $80), but there are also ziplines and a petting zoo. It's all the way north on Park Rd 100, just before it dead ends into the dunes, about 10 miles from the end of the causeway.

Water Sports

You'll find outfits offering parasailing and other rides over and on the water along the beaches in the developed part of SPI. The lagoon side is renowned for wind-powered water sports like windsurfing. There are dozens of operators; two of the best (offering lessons and rental) are Windsurf, Inc (📞956-761-1434; http://southpadre-kiteboarding. com; 224 W Carolyn St) and Windsurf the Boatyard (Map p282; 📞956-561-4189; www. windsurftheboatyard.com; 206 W Dolphin St; ⊙9am-6pm).

Tours

Isla Cruises
BOATING

(Map p282; 📞956-761-4752; www.islatours.com; 1 Padre Blvd; tours from $10; ⊙8am-8pm) Isla Cruises offers daily 1½-hour boat tours to see dolphins or sunsets, and four-/eight-hour fishing trips ($20/95), including bait and tackle. You can bring your own beer on board.

🛏 Sleeping

SPI is a varied mix of beach overdevelopment, charming cottages and long stretches of empty sand. Options to bed down are myriad, but without advance reservations you may be be stuck bedless during spring break and on busy weekends. Of course, you can always claim a patch of sand on the north end of the island.

Flamingo Inn   MOTEL $
(Map p282; ☑ 956-761-3377; www.flamingo-spi.com; 3408 Padre Blvd; r $80-100, ste $130; ❄ 🛜 🏊) The first impression screams chain motel, but the managers live on-site and there are quirks (like the colonnaded hot-tub suites) that make it more beach-bum chic. It has a pool and free breakfast, and it's a block from the beach. All 29 rooms have fridges, coffee pots and microwaves.

Isla Blanca County Park
Campground   CAMPGROUND $
(☑ 956-761-5494; http://cameroncountyparks.com; 33174 Park Rd 100; tent sites $15, sites with amenities from $25; 🛜) Popular because of its proximity to the action, this park has a variety of camping facilities including sites with beach views. Long-term rates are available. Reservations may only be made for stays of seven or more days. Check in at the small building on the right before reaching the entrance gate.

★ Palms Resort   MOTEL $$
(Map p282; ☑ 956-761-1316; www.palmsresortcafe.com; 3616 Gulf Blvd; r $150-230; ❄ 🛜 🏊) This friendly two-story motel has a great location beside the grass-covered dunes on the gulf, and while the rooms themselves don't have waterfront views the excellent alfresco beachfront restaurant/bar has nothing but. Units are large and tidy with ceramic-tile floors, fridges and microwaves.

Tiki Condominium Hotel   RESORT $$
(☑ 956-761-2694; https://thetikispi.com; 6608 Padre Blvd; r $130-340; ❄ 🛜 🏊 🐾) This Polynesian-themed veteran turns up the tiki clichés at the north end of developed SPI. Units have full kitchens and range in size from one to three bedrooms, but even on the furthest block you're never more than 10 minutes from the beach and even less from the two swimming pools. Two-night minimum. Pet friendly, for a fee ($75).

Wanna Wanna Inn   MOTEL $$
(Map p282; ☑ 956-761-7677; www.wannawanna.com; 5100 Gulf Blvd; r $100-225; ❄ 🛜) Much re-

modeled, the low-rise Wanna Wanna has 15 rooms, some with excellent views of the gulf from its beachfront location. Most units have microwaves and fridges, but there's one unit with a kitchenette. The beachside bar (p283) is fun.

🍴 Eating

Except for the peak periods, SPI closes early. Unless noted otherwise, plan on dining by 9pm. Condo dwellers will find plenty of markets for all those essential foods you'd never eat at home, but for a broader selection it's either Blue Marlin Supermarket (p284) or a trip across the causeway to the grocery stores of Port Isabel.

Grapevine Cafe and Coffeehouse   CAFE $
(Map p282; ☑ 956-761-8463; 100 E Swordfish St, Suite A; mains $5-12; ⏰ 7am-3pm Fri-Sun, from 7:30am Mon-Tue & Thu; 🌱) Tasty fresh coffee ($2-$5) is backed up by a reliable menu of American and Tex-Mex breakfast and lunch dishes, ranging from eggs Benedict to huevos rancheros, with a decent number of gluten-free and vegetarian choices.

Daddy's Seafood & Cajun Kitchen   CAJUN $
(Map p282; ☑ 956-761-1975; www.daddysrestaurant.com; 1808 Padre Blvd; mains $8-26; ⏰ 11am-10pm) It's not exactly Cajun spicy, but it certainly has Cajun flavor. Order big with the Cajun mixup: a mess of shrimp, crawfish, sausage, potatoes

South Padre Island

and corn all boiled up together. Lunch specials for $10 are also popular.

Sea Ranch SEAFOOD $$
(Map p282; ☎ 956-761-1314; http://searanchrestau rant.com; 1 Padre Blvd; mains $20-32; ☺ 5-9pm Sun-Thu, to 10pm Fri & Sat) A little classier than the beach-bum standard on SPI, Sea Ranch has an impressive menu of wild-caught seafood and Angus steaks. It overlooks the harbor and has an elegant vibe. It doesn't take reservations, but it's worth the wait.

Pier 19 SEAFOOD $$
(Map p282; ☎ 956-761-7437; www.pier19.us; 1 Padre Blvd; mains $9-27; ☺ 7am-11pm; 🛜) On a pier jutting far out along the water, this rambling eatery has a huge menu of fried seafood, burgers, ceviche, fish tacos, po'boys and much more. If you're just looking for a sundowner, head to the bar all the way out at the end for postcard views.

Blackbeard's SEAFOOD $$
(Map p282; ☎ 956-761-2962; www.blackbeardsspi. com; 103 E Saturn Lane; mains $7-25; ☺ 11:30am-10pm Sun-Thu, to 11pm Fri & Sat) It's been dishing

South Padre Island

✦ Activities, Courses & Tours

🛏 Sleeping

✗ Eating

⊕ Drinking & Nightlife

🛍 Shopping

out seafood in SPI since 1978, and while the large servings and quality speak for themselves, the huge outdoor terrace certainly isn't hurting its cause. Blackbeard's is popular, and you might have to wait, but luckily there's an on-site bar to help you pass the time.

 Drinking & Nightlife

★**Padre Island
Brewing Company**   MICROBREWERY
(Map p282; ☑956-761-9585; www.pibrewingcompany.com; 3400 Padre Blvd; ⊙11:30am-10pm, to 11pm Fri & Sat) Although it's not on the beach, this microbrewery is well worth a visit for its changing lineup of local brews. The sampler ($7) is 6oz pours of all five on tap, or if you've already picked a favorite the pitchers are $12.75. Burgers, pizzas and other bar food

are popular, and there's a full seafood menu to choose from. Mains are $10 to $26.

Wanna-Wanna Beach Bar & Grill   BAR
(Map p282; ☑956-761-7677; www.wannawanna.com; 5100 Gulf Blvd, Beach Access 19; ⊙11am-10:30pm) A picture-perfect cliché of the laid-back beach bar and restaurant. Lounge barefoot in plastic chairs on the shaded deck and take in the surf and sights. Burgers and other basics ($6 to $14) go down easy, but nothing competes with the large cold drinks. It's tucked out back of the Wanna Wanna Inn (p281).

Louie's Backyard   CLUB
(Map p282; ☑956-761-6406; www.lbyspi.com; 2305 Laguna Blvd; ⊙4pm-2am Mon-Fri, from 11:30am Sat & Sun) Spring-break central, Louie's serves

---

BEACH GUIDE

South Padre Island (SPI) is plump with beaches, but there are great variations along the 34 miles of bright white, hard-packed gulf sand. You can enjoy the company of a few thousand of your best friends you haven't met yet, go for a drive, get lost in the dunes, or shed virtually everything far from another soul.

SPI's spine, Padre Blvd, extends 12 miles from the south to a point where the pavement literally ends at a wall of sand. Within the city limits, roughly the area south of the SPI Convention Center, there are 23 free beach-access points between the condos, motels and houses that line the sand. These have very limited parking and seldom have toilets.

North of here it gets increasingly undeveloped and there are several access points where you can drive your vehicle out onto the sand, sometimes for a fee. On summer weekends, many of these areas are tailgating paradises.

Need an umbrella to shade you from the energetic sun and some beach loungers to rest your weary bones? Most beach-access points have vendors that will rent you gear. Among the largest is **Beach Service** (Map p282; ☑956-761-5622; www.padrebeachservice.com; 120 East Atol, inside Charlie's Hideaway; rentals from $30; ⊙10am-6pm Mar-Nov), with 20 locations. You can reserve in advance (vital on busy weekends) or have your gear delivered.

Isla Blanca County Park (☑956-761-5494; http://cameroncountyparks.com; 33174 Park Rd 100; per vehicle $10; ⊙24hr) Just south of the causeway, this county park is the most popular beach on SPI thanks to various concessions and facilities.

Andy Bowie County Park (Beach Access 2; ☑956-761-3704; www.cameroncountyparks.com; 7300 Park Rd 100; per car $10; ⊙dawn-dusk) Across from (SPI) Convention Center, this pleasant beach park is surrounded by condo and hotel developments. It has a shaded picnic building with views and real toilets and is 5.5 miles north of Isla Blanca. Beach Access 2 has all the facilities (and entrance fees), but continue to Beach Access 3 and 4 for undeveloped but free access.

Edwin King Atwood County Park (Beach Access 5; www.cameroncountyparks.com; 27159 Park Rd 100; per car $10; ⊙dawn-dusk) Two miles north of Bowie, signed as Beach Access 5, Atwood sports towering sand dunes backing the beach. This is a beautiful, unspoiled area with nothing but long views of the horizon and a couple of toilets. Keep an eye out for vehicles accessing the beach here.

North End (Park Rd 100, North End; ⊙24hr) Padre Blvd ends 12 miles north of Isla Blanca. North of here there's 20 miles of empty sand and dunes all the way to Port Mansfield Pass. Nude sunbathers, anglers, bird-watchers and other outdoorsy types can find a sandy acre to call their own; vehicles can drive on the beach, but be wary of soft sand.

a mere 3000 to 4000 every night. There are multiple stages, big-name rappers, a dance floor overlooking the water, cheap booze and bar snacks, and a minimalist dress code that allows for just about anything. There's also a full buffet and menu, but for food you'll usually do better elsewhere.

Boomerang Billy's Beach Bar & Grill BAR
(Map p282; ☑ 956-761-2831; www.boomerangbillys beachbar.com; 2612 Gulf Blvd; ⊙11am-late) Billy's is behind the shambolic Surf Motel and is one of the few bars right on the sand on the gulf side. 'Mellow' sounds a bit too energetic for this ultimate crash pad. On weekend afternoons, listen to the talented singing of Leslie Blasing, who belts her tunes out over the sand.

Coconuts BAR
(Map p282; ☑ 956-761-4218; www.coconutsspi.com; 2301 Laguna Blvd; ⊙10am-2am) The clichés start with the thatched roof over the deck, but that doesn't stop the mixed crowd of tourists and locals from cutting loose from before the sun sets until well after midnight. Live music rocks the house.

Blue Marlin Supermarket MARKET
(Map p282; ☑ 956-761-4966; 2912 Padre Blvd; ⊙7:30am-10pm) For self-catering, this is the best choice on the island and prices are similar to the mainland.

 Shopping

Paragraphs BOOKS
(☑ 956-433-5057; http://paragraphsonspi.blogspot. com; 5505 Padre Blvd; ⊙10am-5pm Mon-Fri, to 4pm Sat, noon-4pm Sun; �📶) An excellent indie bookstore with a nice patio and a pet-friendly vibe. The collection in store is eclectic, but it can special-order or locate hard-to-find titles upon request.

ℹ Information

South Padre Island Convention & Visitors Bureau (Map p282; ☑ 956-761-4412; www. spichamber.com; 610 Padre Blvd; ⊙9am-5pm) Lots of island insight and a small museum display on the history of the island and region.

ℹ Getting There & Away

If you can get out to SPI, you won't necessarily need a car. The developed area is fairly compact, easy for walking or cycling, and there's a shuttle around the island and across the causeway to Port Isabel and onward to Brownsville airport.

SPI cab companies include **BB's Taxi** (Map p282; ☑ 956-761-1111; www.bbstaxi.com; 104 E Ling St), charging $60 to Brownsville airport, $80 to Harlingen airport, and $150 to McAllen airport.

ℹ Getting Around

The **Wave** (☑ 956-761-1025; www.spadre.com/ thewave.htm; ⊙7am-9pm), a shuttle service, serves the island as far north as the convention center and all the way south to Isla Blanca County Park and over the causeway to Port Isabel. Buses on all three routes run every 30 to 60 minutes. Flag down the shuttles anywhere on the routes and they'll let you hop on.

South Padre Island Route Heads north from city hall on Padre Blvd to the convention center, returning south via Gulf Blvd to the entrance of Isla Blanca County Park before looping back around.

Port Isabel Route Starts at the Las Palmas shopping center on the intersection of TX 100 and TX 48 on the western side of Port Isabel, and runs the full length of Padre Blvd to the convention center.

Laguna Heights Route Runs from the community of Laguna Heights, 2 miles west of Las Palmas on TX 100, through Port Isabel and across the causeway to the La Copa Beach Hotel on SPI.

From Las Palmas shopping center, it's also possible to connect to Brownsville's MetroConnect blue line and transfer onward to the city's airport shuttle (daily pass $5).

If public transport isn't frequent enough for you, rental services such as **Rental+ Plus** (☑ 956-772-1111; 2300 Padre Blvd) offer bikes, scooters and superpopular golf carts by the hour or day.

RIO GRANDE VALLEY

The semitropical southern border area of Texas is much wetter than the arid west, thanks to the moisture-laden winds off the Gulf of Mexico. This lush environment is perfect for farming; much of the winter produce sold in the USA comes from Texas.

The temperate winter climate attracts hordes of migratory creatures. A breed known as 'Winter Texans' – American retirees from the north – arrives in flocks, as do more than 500 species of bird, who in turn attract bird-watchers to scores of natural spots.

The valley begins at the mouth of the Rio Grande, which meets the gulf in vast palm-studded wetlands, lagoons and remote beaches.

Heading west up the valley most of the land is given over to farming until the area around McAllen, at which point the gulf winds diminish and the land becomes increasingly arid and the population thins.

Brownsville

📱956 / POP 175,023

Brownsville's counterpart across the Rio Grande, the Mexican town of Matamoros, grew to prominence in the 1820s as the Mexican port closest to then-booming New Orleans. After the Mexican-American War (1846–48), American merchants and traders thought it wise to cross the Rio Grande to Texas, where they established Brownsville in 1849. The town was named for Major Jacob Brown, the US commander of Fort Taylor (later renamed Fort Brown), who died during a Mexican raid in 1846.

During the rest of the 19th century, the fast-growing town was filled with ornate brick structures that drew their architectural inspiration from Mexico and New Orleans. Many survive today and help make Brownsville an atmospheric stop. Its authentic and slightly gritty culture make it excellent as a day trip from South Padre Island or a stop on a longer Rio Grande Valley itinerary.

◉ Sights

One of the best things you can do in Brownsville is simply go wandering around the downtown area. Streets such as E Washington and E Elizabeth are still busy with the kinds of small shops that once lined main streets across the USA, although ironically, most of the customers now are day-trippers from Mexico.

Downtown Brownsville still has dozens of 19th-century buildings, many of which are slowly moldering away. Be sure to get a copy of the excellent *Guide to Historic Brownsville* at the museums or at the Brownsville Convention & Visitors Bureau (p286). This free brochure details the city's heritage and has several excellent walking tours, any of which can be visited on a one-hour stroll.

★ **Sabal Palm Sanctuary**   NATURE RESERVE
(📱956-541-8034; www.sabalpalmsanctuary.org; 8435 Sabal Palm Grove Rd; adult/child $5/3; ⊙7am-5pm Thu-Tue) The only palm tree native to Texas grows at this 557-acre sanctuary, operated by a foundation for the National Audubon Society. It sits in a bend of the Rio Grande River with one of the few groves never to have been plowed up. It's a lush, beautiful and peaceful place with excellent nature hikes.

Galeria 409   ART
(📱956-455-3599; 409 E 13th St; ⊙noon-5pm Thu-Sat) Founded by artist Mark Clark to showcase local talent, this small gallery hosts rotating exhibits on important local issues (border communities, especially) and more whimsical themes. The building is a historic structure, completely renovated by Mark. Ask about the grisly accidents that have befallen previous occupants.

Historic Brownsville Museum   MUSEUM
(📱956-548-1313; www.brownsvillemuseum.org; 641 E Madison St; adult/child $4/2; ⊙10am-4pm Tue-Fri, to 2pm Sat) Housed in the grand Spanish Colonial–style 1928 Southern Pacific Railroad Depot, this small museum houses historical artifacts and photography. In the annex is an 1872 steam locomotive that once ran the route between Brownsville and Port Isabel. The museum is part of the Mitte Cultural District.

Fort Brown   HISTORIC SITE
(📱956-882-8200; www.utrgv.edu; 80 Gorgas St, off International Blvd; ⊙dawn-dusk) [FREE] This former US army outpost, dating from 1846, is named for Jacob Brown, who died here that year fighting the Mexicans. Flooding forced an 1868 relocation to the site, where several buildings still stand. They have been restored and are now used by the shared campus of University of Texas at Brownsville and Texas Southmost College. It's still possible to see the 1868 post hospital (now Gorgas Hall), 1882 chapel, 1904 commissary and the 1850 Neale Home. Historical markers detail the background of each.

Brownsville Heritage Complex   HISTORIC SITE
(📱956-541-5560; www.brownsvillehistory.org; 1325 E Washington St; adult/child $4/2; ⊙10am-4pm Tue-Sat) The 1851 home of Brownsville founder Charles Stillman, and later the Mexican Consulate in Brownsville, is part of the Brownsville Heritage Complex. Next door, in the main museum building, a reconstruction of the historic Crixell Saloon is the centerpiece of displays that recount the history of Brownsville. This is a good place to learn about the downtown area.

🛏 Sleeping

Most motels are along I-69E as it enters town. Unless you are getting an early start for bird-watching you might want to stay amid the beachy charms of South Padre Island, an easy 28 miles northeast, and visit Brownsville as a day trip.

Holiday Inn Express   HOTEL $$
(📱956-550-0666; www.hiexpress.com; 1985 N Expwy, exit US 77/83 at Ruben Torres Sr Blvd; r $90-129;

GULF COAST & SOUTH TEXAS BROWNSVILLE

) A fairly standard iteration of the comfortable chain, the HI has 74 rooms across three floors with inside corridors. The pool is outside near young palms. Guests enjoy a large breakfast buffet (included in price).

🍴 Eating & Drinking

El Ultimo Taco Taqueria   MEXICAN $
(☏ 956-554-7663; 938 N Expwy; menu items $1-6; ⊙ 11am-3am Sun-Thu, to 4am Fri & Sat) Tacos, flautas, tostadas and beans. That's it. Yet they're so good they've been voted the best tacos in the Rio Grande Valley several times, and the small dining room and large patio aren't enough to hold the crowds, meaning there's often a wait. For a real treat, ask for the special charro beans.

Vermillion   TEX-MEX $
(☏ 956-542-9893; www.thevermillion.com; 115 Paredes Line Rd; mains $8-14; ⊙ 11am-10:30pm Sun-Wed, to 11:30pm Thu-Sat) Though a restaurant has operated on this very spot since the Vermillion family relocated here in 1934, things have gone a bit upscale from the original burger stand. Both the Tex (sublime chicken-fried steak) and the Mex (excellent fajita nachos) are good.

El Hueso de Fraile   CAFE, BAR
(☏ 956-579-5776; www.brownsvillecafe.com/; 837 E Elizabeth St, Suite D; ⊙ 11am-2am Mon-Sat, 5pm-2am Sun; 🛜) This combination cafe-bar and Latin American-folklore preservation center has local artists' work for sale and daily live performances from 8:30pm. It tries to be a lot of things, but they all come off pretty well, especially the 70 or more craft beers and specialty coffees. Check the website for performance information.

🛍 Shopping

Mercado Juarez   ARTS & CRAFTS
(☏ 956-346-3171; 1008 E Elizabeth St; ⊙ 9am-6pm) Housed in the former Majestic Theater, this small market is full of color from across the border. Clothing, pottery and other crafts sold by vendors from Matamoros and beyond are convenient for those who won't be making the trip to Mexico themselves.

ℹ Information

Brownsville Convention & Visitors Bureau
(☏ 956-546-3721; www.brownsville.org; 650 Ruben M Torres Sr Blvd; ⊙ 8am-5pm Mon-Fri) On the west side of US 77/83, this excellent source of information on the entire area is perhaps the most enthusiastic local ambassador we've met in South Texas.

ℹ Getting There & Away

Brownsville lies at the southern end of I-69E, which together with the remnants of US 77 forms the spine of the southern Gulf Coast. The full-day drive from here to somewhere like Dallas, 545 miles to the north, reinforces just how big Texas is.
Brownsville South Padre Island International Airport (BRO; ☏ 956-542-4373; www.flybrownsville.com; 700 Amelia Earhart Drive), 4 miles east of downtown, has service on American Eagle to Dallas–Fort Worth and on United Express to Houston. From the airport to South Padre Island the free **Island Airport Shuttle** (☏ 956-542-4373; www.flybrownsville.com/172/Island-Airport-Shuttle; 700 Amelia Earhart Dr; ⊙ 6am-8pm) is the best deal in town, connecting

---

ℹ DAY TRIPS TO MEXICO: SHOULD YOU VISIT?

Time was when no visit to the Rio Grande Valley was complete without a jaunt across the border into one of the towns such as Nuevo Laredo, which is twinned with Laredo on the US side. Good and cheap Mexican food (and tequila), mariachis, cheap souvenirs as well as cut-rate dental work and prescription drugs were just some of the lures. Plus there was the thrill of entering a different culture, just by strolling across a bridge spanning the Rio Grande.

In recent year, however, lurid headlines caused by the carnage of Mexico's drug wars have put a big question mark over border-town day trips. Although tourists are not targets, fear of getting caught up in the violence is a real concern. Meanwhile, businesses that have delighted generations of Americans (or simply sold them cheap pharmaceuticals) have suffered greatly.

Should you visit? The best answer is to ask locally on the Texas side of the border; conditions change constantly. No matter what, you'll probably be safest visiting during the day. You can also check with the US State Department (http:\\travel.state.gov) for travel advisories. While across the border, look out for images of La Sante Muerte (Holy Death), an iconic figure of a skeleton with a scythe dressed in robes. It's the symbol of a fast-growing religious cult popular with the gangs, and is indicative of their presence in the area.

with the island's Wave shuttle on the Port Isabel route for transfer onto the island.

Greyhound (🖉 956-546-7171; www.greyhound. com; 755 International Blvd, Suite H; ⊙ 4am-midnight) has a station just three blocks west of the Gateway International Bridge. There is frequent service to McAllen ($6, 70 minutes) and several buses daily to Corpus Christi and beyond ($18, 3½ hours). Buses also fan out across Mexico from the sister station across the border.

Around Brownsville

At first glimpse little more than a long stretch of dry lifeless prairie marsh, the region surrounding Brownsville plays an important conservation role and has also been the home to surprising historic firsts and lasts. These wetlands play host to a multitude of bird species such as brown pelicans, aplomado falcons and mangrove warblers, and even serve as nesting grounds for the critically endangered Kemp's ridley sea turtle.

In earlier times they also hosted two noteworthy battles, and it was here that the opening salvos of the Mexican-American War and the final shots of the US Civil War were fired. Not shabby for a bit of empty prairie marsh.

◉ Sights

Boca Chica Beach
BEACH
(🖉 956-784-7500; www.fws.gov; TX 4, south end; ⊙ dawn-dusk) FREE Hugging the border just above where the Rio Grande empties into the gulf, Boca Chica is a rarely visited 10,680-acre wilderness very literally at the end of the road. SpaceX's proposed launch site nearby may change all that, and will certainly have some impact on access, but for now it's a peaceful slice of sand dunes away from the world.

Palo Alto Battlefield
National Historic Site
HISTORIC SITE
(🖉 956-541-2785, ext 233; www.nps.gov/paal; 7200 Paredes Line Rd; ⊙ 8am-5pm) FREE On May 8, 1846, General Zachary Taylor and his troops defeated a larger Mexican army on this site in the first major battle of the Mexican-American War. The visitor center does an excellent job of putting the battle into context: were the Americans invaders or defenders? The result is a surprisingly evocative and moody place.

Resaca de la Palma State Park
STATE PARK
(🖉 956-350-2920; http://tpwd.texas.gov; 1000 New Carmen Rd, off US 281; adult/child $4/free; ⊙ park 7am-10pm daily, visitor center 8am-5pm Wed-Sun) Part of the World Birding Center, this new

1200-acre park surrounds 4 miles of *resaca* (oxbow lakes), which are ideal for birds and their spotters. Trails wander through this semitropical landscape making this a lovely – and bug-filled – stop, even if your interest in birds is flighty. Alternatively, trams leave hourly for a 2.75-mile loop trip through the reserve.

McAllen

🖉 956 / POP 129,877

McAllen is not only near the Mexican border, but also a natural border. To the east are the lush green lands of the Rio Grande Valley, with farms, palm trees and fast-sprouting population. To the west is the beginning of the Chihuahuan Desert, where the land becomes more barren and the climate increasingly arid.

McAllen is the center of two Texas industries: grapefruits and Winter Texans. The former are picked when ripe and juicy and, increasingly for the region's tourism industry, the latter are as well.

Although McAllen may be a little short on attractions, its hotels and restaurants make it a good base for exploring the natural delights of the surrounding area, including the many sites of the World Birding Center.

◉ Sights

Museum of South Texas History
MUSEUM
(🖉 956-383-6911; www.mosthistory.org; 121 E McIntyre St, Edinburg; adult/child $7/4; ⊙ 10am-5pm Tue-Sat, 1-5pm Sun) The Museum of South Texas History covers transborder history with interactive multimedia exhibits that take visitors through frontier ranch houses and on board the steamboats that once plied the Rio Grande. The museum is housed partially in the 1910 Hidalgo County Courthouse in Edinburg, 7 miles north of McAllen.

🛏 Sleeping

La Copa Inn
MOTEL $
(🖉 956-686-1741; www.lacopamcallen.com; 2000 S 10th St; r $64-73; ❋ 🛜 🞩) A modest motel that is part of a small local chain, the La Copa is an older 150-room motel that's had a faux Spanish makeover. It's clean and good value.

★ Casa de Palmas
Renaissance Hotel
HISTORIC HOTEL $$
(🖉 956-631-1101; www.marriott.com; 101 N Main St; r $156-205; ❋ @ 🛜 🞩) Dating from 1918 and lovingly restored, the elegant but not pretentious

Casa de Palmas is the classiest place in town. Right downtown, the 165 rooms surround a beautiful central courtyard and pool, and are managed by upscale Marriott.

✖ Eating & Drinking

In this city that sees itself as a bridge between cultures, it should be no surprise that Mexican and Tex-Mex cuisine exist in equal measure, often in the same restaurant. There are alternatives, but why bother when the quality is this good?

Ms G's Tacos n' More   MEXICAN $
(☑956-668-8226;   www.msgstacosnmore.com; 2263 Pecan Blvd; mains from $3; ☺6:30am-8pm Mon-Fri, 7am-3pm Sat) Ms G herself arrives every morning at 4:30am to make the region's best flour tortillas for her deceptively simple tacos. Options are numerous, but you'll never go wrong with chorizo and potato, especially at three for $4. There's no indoor seating, so either picnic or grab it from the drive-through and keep on going.

Costa Messa   TEX-MEX $$
(☑956-618-5449; www.costamessargv.com; 1621 N 11th St; mains from $8; ☺11am-10pm) With a menu that straddles the border between Mexican and Tex-Mex, this slightly formal place is a great option to test the waters of the Rio Grande's culinary mélange. The fiery guacamole is not to be missed.

Patio on Guerra   STEAK $$$
(☑956-661-9100; www.patioonguerra.com; 116 S 17th St; mains $18-48; ☺11am-11pm Mon-Thu, to 2am Fri, 5pm-2am Sat) At the top of a small nightlife district in the historic district, the Patio is popular for after work happy-hour drinks from the huge wine list that boasts more than 130 options. Diners can choose from quality steaks or more exotic meats like quail and kangaroo, all served on the restaurant's namesake patio. There's live entertainment most nights.

Grain to Glass   BAR
(☑956-322-3315; https://graintoglass.com; 5921 N 23rd St; ☺4pm-midnight Mon-Thu, to 2am Fri, noon-2am Sat, to midnight Sun) With around 30 craft brews on tap at any given time (and more in bottles), Grain to Glass has made a mission of bringing the beer revolution to the Rio Grande Valley. It's very much a local pub, and the owners even claim their mothers designed the extensive food menu, but we never made it past those endless shining taps to find out.

Roosevelt's at 7   BAR
(☑956-928-1994; 821 N Main St; ☺11am-2am, from 1pm Sat & Sun; ☏) In a land where miserable watery domestic beers rule, the over 40 taps here are like a vision, a glorious vision. On the edge of a modest arts district, Roo's has a large patio with a pool table and lots of casual food, like excellent pizza, sandwiches and salads.

☆ Entertainment

Cine El Rey   PERFORMING ARTS
(☑956-278-0626; www.cineelrey.org; 311 S 17th St) An anchor of the 17th St nightlife district, the historic Cine El Rey has transitioned from from the Spanish-language films of the past to genre-crossing live music and stand-up comedy.

ℹ Information

McAllen Convention & Visitors Bureau (CVB; ☑956-682-2871; www.visitmcallen.com; 1200 Ash Ave; ☺8am-5pm Mon-Fri) Just off US Business 83, the CVB is focused on business rather than tourist needs.

ℹ Getting There & Away

McAllen is a great base for exploring the Rio Grande Valley as it's right at the intersection of two interstates and the upper valley's main highway.

Busy **McAllen Miller International Airport** (MFE; ☑956-681-1500; www.mcallenairport.com; 2500 S Bicentennial Blvd) is just south of US 83, off S 10th St. American flies to Dallas–Fort Worth, United serves Houston, Allegiant goes to Las Vegas, and Aeromar runs a route to Mexico City.

Greyhound (☑956-686-5479; www.greyhound. com; 1501 W US Business 83; ☺5am-midnight) has frequent service to Brownsville ($5, 75 minutes) and San Antonio ($29, 4½ hours), and other points in Texas. There's one bus daily up the valley to Laredo ($23, 3½ hours).

Around McAllen

There are a number of natural sights along the Rio Grande Valley near McAllen that are reason enough to make McAllen your base, though you'll need your own vehicle to make the most of the area.

◉ Sights & Activities

La Sal del Rey Reserve   NATURE RESERVE
(☑956-784-7500; www.fws.gov; off TX 186, Edinburg; ☺dawn-dusk) **FREE** The 530-acre La Sal del Rey (Salt of the King) derives its name from a colonial Spanish law that awarded 20% of all harvest to the Crown. At this hypersaline

lake, atop an estimated 4 million tons of salt, that amounted to a lot for the king. The 1-mile trail walk from the parking lot to the lakebed is great for ground animals like javelina and bobcat, but the real draw is bird-watching at the water's edge.

From McAllen take I-69C north to TX 186, then turn west. The reserve entrance is a small parking lot on the left after 10.6 miles.

Santa Ana
National Wildlife Refuge
NATURE RESERVE

(☑ 956-787-3079; www.fws.gov; FM 907, off US 281; per vehicle $5; ◷ dawn dusk, visitor center 8am-4pm) A self-proclaimed birder's paradise, this 2088-acre refuge is one of the valley's most beautiful spots. Lakes, wetlands and subtropical thorny forest combine for a peaceful setting where the only noises come from birds. The refuge is the seasonal home to almost 400 bird species, and hundreds of butterfly species have been spotted here as well. Handouts at the visitor center include an 11-page guide of likely local species, and that doesn't even include the nonavian wildlife native to the area.

Bentsen-Rio Grande Valley
State Park
OUTDOORS

(☑ 956-584-9156; www.tpwd.state.tx.us; 2800 S Bentsen Palm Dr; adult/child $5/free; ◷ park 7am-10pm, center 8am-5pm) Spot some 300 or more bird species in this serene 760-acre park, which is headquarters for the World Birding Center network. Much of the park surrounds *resacas*, water-filled former river channels that support lush foliage, and upon which several excellent bird blinds have been built. The visitor center has excellent trail guides and many bird books, and can rent binoculars. Inquire about special programs like bird walks and tram tours.

The site is good for bikes (per day $5 to $12), which make getting to key attractions, like the 1.8-mile Rio Grande loop trail, easy. The park's 10 widely spaced tent sites (per site $12) rarely fill up and have water. Surrounded by thorny brush and shaded by trees, the pastoral experience is described as 'waking up with the birds.'

To get here, take the Bentsen Palm Dr (FM 2062) exit off US 83, 3 miles west of Mission, and drive south till it dead ends at the park.

🛏 Sleeping

Alamo Inn
B&B $

(☑ 956-782-9912; www.alamoinnbnb.com; 801 Main St, Alamo; ste $75-85; ❄🕾) A brilliant find, especially for for birders. This historic inn is lovingly operated by a local couple with tons of tips on local sights and attractions. They self-identify with the birder crowd, and therefore know all the best local spots. The inn is 7 miles east of McAllen along Business US 83/E Center Ave.

Laredo
☑ 956 / POP 236,091

Even more than other Texas border towns, Laredo has always been tightly entwined with its sister city to the south, the fittingly named Nuevo Laredo (New Laredo). News stories of drug violence and tight border controls have severely crimped a place where Mexico and the US seemed to blend the most seamlessly even just a decade ago.

While the border situation remains unsettled, Laredo makes for a good stop on any Rio Grande itinerary. The city's old downtown is evocative and has three good museum spaces, and the historic architecture alone makes exploring worthwhile. And in many ways, starting with the strong Hispanic culture, Laredo's like a trip south of the border without the customs inspection.

◉ Sights

Laredo's oldest quarter occupies a compact area on the Rio Grande's north bank between the international bridges. Religious and historical significance abound, and it's the most pleasant section of the city to explore on foot.

Republic of the Rio Grande Museum
MUSEUM

(☑ 956-727-3480; http://webbheritage.org; 1005 Zaragoza St; $?; ◷ 9am-4pm Tue-Sat) Housed in the 1840 capitol of the short-lived Republic of the Rio Grande, this excellent museum brings that turbulent period to life with displays about the confused political climate of the time and items from everyday life. The oldest part of the building dates to the 1830s.

San Agustín Plaza
HISTORIC SITE

Parts of this downtown plaza, the oldest in Laredo, date from 1767. The streets surrounding it are cobblestoned and lined with ancient oaks where you can escape the sun and often listen to music with locals relaxing on the park's benches. For details about the historic buildings throughout downtown, pick up a copy of the brochure *Heritage Walking Tour of Historic Laredo* at the **Laredo Convention & Visitors Bureau** (CVB; ☑ 956-794-1712; www.visitlaredo.com; 501 San

Agustín Ave, at Lincoln St; ⊘9am-5pm Mon-Fri) or at area hotels.

🛏 Sleeping

Most of Laredo's lodgings are on San Bernardo and Santa Ursala Aves, which run parallel to the I-35 through downtown to the border.

Rialto Hotel   HISTORIC HOTEL $
(✆956-725-1800; www.therialtohotel.com; 1219 Matamoros St; r $50-70) Starting life in 1925 as a car dealership and later office space, this historic downtown building is now run as a boutique hotel. The atmosphere feels a little clinical at times, but rooms are clean and the 1st-floor restaurant serves a killer Mexican breakfast.

★**La Posada Hotel & Suites** HISTORIC HOTEL $$
(✆956-722-1701; www.laposada.com; 1000 Zaragoza St, San Agustín Plaza; r $110-200; ❄@🛜🏊🐕) Far and away the nicest choice in Laredo, this hacienda-style hotel occupies a complex of buildings dating from 1916 (originally a high school). The stylish rooms surround two large pools and gardens; the deeply shaded courtyard verandahs are a world away from the city outside. Some rooms have patios overlooking the river and border area.

🍴 Eating & Drinking

Mexican-food fans will want to stay multiple nights here. Laredo has everything from upscale Mexican fusion to hole-in-the-wall taquerias, and the base level for quality is exceptionally high. Don't waste a single meal on mediocre food.

★**Taco N' Madre**   MEXICAN $
(✆956-791-8226; www.tacon-madre.com; 119 E Saunders St; mains $6-12; ⊘9am-11pm) These are, without hyperbole, some of the best tacos we've ever eaten. The meat is juicy and perfectly seasoned, the tortillas fresh, the salsa piquant without being overbearing. Two or three is a reasonable meal, but good luck tearing yourself away before consuming double that. Cash only.

There are 12 locations across Laredo, but the hole-in-the-wall atmosphere on Saunders only adds to the appeal.

★**El Meson de San Augustin**   MEXICAN $
(✆956-712-9009; www.elmesondesanagustin.com; 908 Grant St; mains $6-11; ⊘11am-4:30pm Mon-Sat) Six days a week, superb food pours forth from this tiny, ubernondescript family-run restaurant just off the historic square. Walk through the barely marked door and be immersed in a wonderland of home-style Mexican cooking. Menus are mostly in Spanish, but staff are happy to help translate.

Palenque Grill   MEXICAN $$$
(✆956-728-1272; www.palenquegrill.com; 4615 San Bernardo Ave; mains $18-40; ⊘11am-midnight Sun-Wed, to 1am Thu, to 2am Fri & Sat; ❄🛜🍴) The upscale chain of the Taco Palenque empire features an airy main dining room and a huge terrace. The menu is ambitious and features a broad range of regional cuisine from across Mexico. From the moment the chips, salsa and toppings arrive with your menus, you'll know something delicious is about to happen.

ⓘ Information

Texas Travel Information Center (✆956-417-4728; www.txdot.gov; I-35 & US 83 exit 18; ⊘8am-5pm) About 16 miles north of Laredo, this comprehensive info center is a showpiece and worthy of a stop just for the Southwestern architecture and gardens.

ⓘ Getting There & Away

Laredo International Airport (LRD; ✆956-795-2000; www.ci.laredo.tx.us/airport; 5210 Bob Bullock Loop) has regular service by American Eagle and United Express to their respective hubs at Dallas–Fort Worth and Houston and twice-weekly service on Allegiant to Las Vegas. The airport is off Bob Bullock Loop, 1.2 miles north of US 59 on the town's northeast side.

Greyhound (✆956-723-4324; www.greyhound.com; 610 Salinas Ave; ⊘24hr) operates from downtown. It offers frequent service to San Antonio ($14, three hours) and Houston ($18, six to eight hours), plus once daily down the Rio Grande Valley to McAllen ($25, 3½ hours). To get to Eagle Pass, you'll have to transfer via San Antonio.

To Nuevo Laredo there are two bridges, one an extension of I-35 and the other a continuation of Convent Ave. Both are open 24 hours.

For self-drivers, I-35 makes an easy trip of the 135 miles to San Antonio and US 83 runs parallel to the border en route to Eagle Pass. From the end of US 59 in town, it's long 313-mile drive to make it all the way to Houston.

Big Bend & West Texas

Best Places to Eat

➡ Reata (p313)

➡ Starlight Theater (p303)

➡ Crave Kitchen & Bar (p323)

➡ L&J Cafe (p323)

➡ Cattleman's Steakhouse (p323)

Best Places to Sleep

➡ Indian Lodge (p307)

➡ Holland Hotel (p312)

➡ La Posada Milagro (p302)

➡ El Cosmico (p309)

➡ Hotel Indigo (p320)

Why Go?

Welcome to the land of wide open spaces. Along I-10 there's not much to look at – just scrub brush and lots of sky – but dip below the interstate and you'll find vistas that are as captivating as they are endless. Sometimes the rugged terrain looks like the backdrop in an old Western movie; other times it looks like an alien landscape, with huge rock formations jutting suddenly out of the desert.

But what is there to do? Plenty. Exploring an enormous national park that's nearly the size of Rhode Island. Stopping in small towns that will surprise you with minimalist art, planet-watching parties or fascinating ghost-town ruins. Checking out the new microbreweries in a reenergized El Paso. Chatting with friendly locals whenever the mood strikes you. And letting the delicious slowness of west Texas get thoroughly under your skin.

When to Go
El Paso

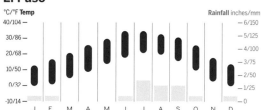

Jan & Feb Don't worry about winter weather – the desert is moderate and dry.

Mar–May Prime time: temperatures are still cool and wildflowers are in bloom.

Jul & Aug If you can take the heat, you'll avoid a lot of the crowds.

Big Bend & West Texas Highlights

1 Big Bend National Park (p293) Getting up early to hike a leafy trail to a big view in the Chisos Mountains.

2 Chinati Foundation Museum (p308) Stepping into a historic artillery shed in Marfa for a scenic collision of art, architecture and the west Texas plains.

3 Davis Mountains State Park (p305) Watching the setting sun change the sky's color in every direction from the summit of Skyline Drive.

4 Starlight Theatre (p303) Enjoying music, margaritas and mixing with the locals in Terlingua ghost town.

5 Scenic Drive (p318) Observing the twinkling city lights of two border towns on a lofty evening drive in El Paso.

6 Hoodoos Trail (p304) Savoring the view of the Rio Grande, Mexico and the amazing rock foundations in Big Bend Ranch State Park.

7 McDonald Observatory (p305) Joining a late-night stargazing party in remote Fort Davis.

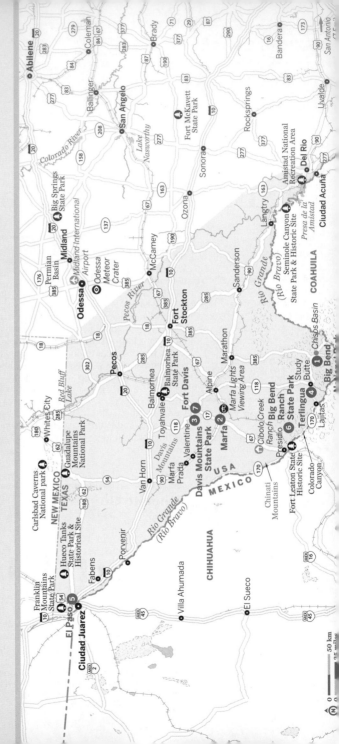

BIG BEND NATIONAL PARK

Everyone knows Texas is huge. But you can't really appreciate just how big it is until you visit this **national park** (✆432-477-2251; www. nps.gov/bibe; US Hwy 385, Panther Junction; 7-day pass per vehicle $25), which is almost the same size as Rhode Island. When you're traversing Big Bend's 1252 sq miles, you come to appreciate what 'big' really means. It's a land of incredible diversity, vast enough to allow a lifetime of discovery, yet laced with enough well-placed roads and trails to permit short-term visitors to see a lot in two to three days.

Big Bend has one area – the Chisos Basin – that absorbs the overwhelming crunch of traffic. The **Chisos Mountains** are beautiful, and no trip here would be complete without an excursion into the high country. But any visit to Big Bend should also include time in the **Chihuahuan Desert**, home to curious creatures and adaptable plants, and along the **Rio Grande**, a watery border between the US and Mexico.

When to Go

➜ Most travelers consider spring and fall the best times to visit Big Bend National Park.

➜ Spring means moderate temperatures and lots of wildflowers (and lots of people). Fall is also quite pleasant, especially for white-water rafting.

➜ Summer (June through August) is hot, with typical daytime temperatures around 100°F (38°C); late summer can be rainy.

➜ Winter is relatively mild, although temperatures in the Chisos can fall below freezing and Basin Rd typically closes two or three times, sometimes for several days. The snow is never too deep for hiking.

➜ In every season it's wise to layer your clothes in the morning and peel off top layers as you warm up.

Orientation

Park headquarters and the main visitor center (p301) are at Panther Junction, which is on the main road 29 miles south of the Persimmon Gap entrance and 22 miles east of the Maverick entrance (near Study Butte). A **gas station** (✆432-477-2294; Panther Junction; ☺convenience store 7am-6:30pm May-Sep, 8am-5:30pm Jun-Aug, pumps 24hr) here offers fuel, repairs and a small stock of snacks and beverages.

From Panther Junction, it's a (relatively) short 10-mile drive to the Chisos Basin. Sharp curves and steep grades make Chisos Basin Rd unsuitable for recreational vehicles longer than 24ft and trailers longer than 20ft.

Another major road leads 20 miles southeast to Rio Grande Village, where you can find the only other **fuel pumps** (✆432-477-2293; Rio Grande Village; ☺8am-7pm Oct-May, to 5pm Jun-Sep) within the park (good to know because you're a long way from anywhere).

The other principal road, the 30-mile Ross Maxwell Scenic Dr, takes off from the main park road west of Panther Junction.

Geology

For millions of years, Big Bend lay at the bottom of the sea, part of a trough that extended into what is now Arkansas and Oklahoma. Over time, the sea became shallower and eventually disappeared, leaving a wondrous fossil record of marine life and beds of limestone, both thick (the Sierra del Carmen and Santa Elena formations) and thin (the Boquillas formation). Once the sea was gone, the dinosaurs took over; Big Bend was especially favored by pterosaurs, the largest flying creatures ever (with a wingspan of 35ft or more).

About 65 million years ago, the Cenozoic era began, and tectonic forces produced the Rocky Mountains and the Sierra Madre. Volcanic activity followed, spreading ash and lava over thousands of miles in the region. Increased tensions in the earth's crust created faulting, dropping the central portion of the park while further elevating the Chisos Mountains. Meanwhile, the Rio Grande carved the great canyons that define the river today.

◉ Sights

Fossil Discovery Exhibit   MUSEUM
(www.nps.gov/bibe) As you look out at the desert from the pavilion that houses the park's newest exhibit, it's hard to imagine that a shallow sea once covered much of Texas, followed by a swampy coast. Fossils and displays spotlight the amazing range of plants and animals that thrived here over the last 130 million years – the teeth on the sea-dwelling Xiphactinus, which looks like an overgrown piranha, is the stuff of nightmares. Local dinosaurs get plenty of attention too.

The exhibit is 17 miles south of the Persimmon Gap Visitor Center (p301), near Mile 9 on the main park road.

Big Bend National Park

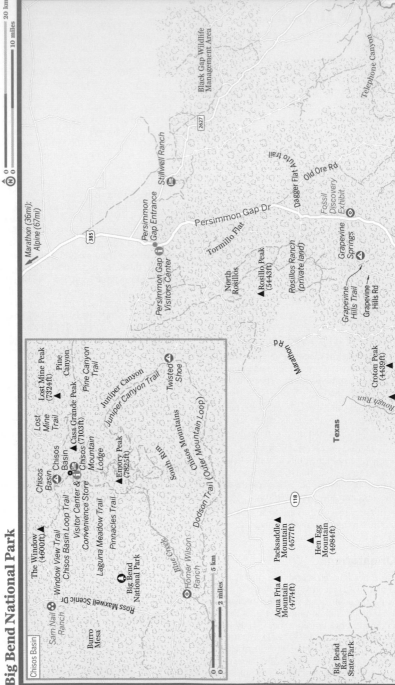

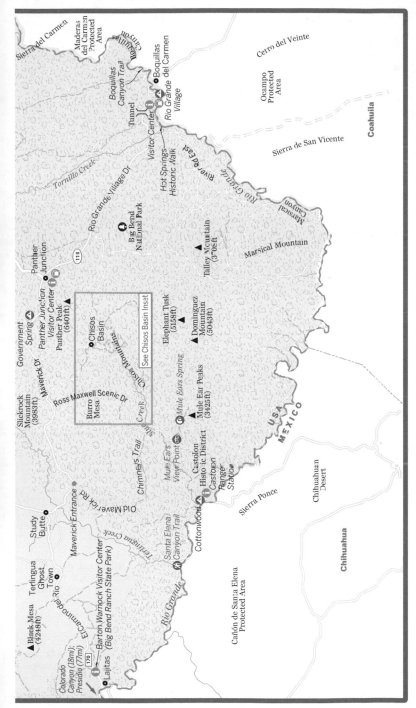

HIKING IN BIG BEND

With more than 150 miles of trails to explore, it's no wonder hiking is big in Big Bend. Here are some of the most popular hikes; get specifics from any of the visitor centers. Distances are round-trip.

Chisos Mountains Hikes

Window View Trail (0.3 miles) The absolute lowest amount of commitment is this short trail that leaves from behind Chisos Basin's **convenience store** (p298). It's paved and wheelchair-accessible – perfect for nonhikers or for anyone who wants to watch the sunset over the Window.

Chisos Basin Loop Trail (1.8 miles) Also leaving from the Chisos Basin store, this trail offers nice views of the basin and a relatively large amount of shade provided by the Mexican piñons and alligator junipers.

Window Trail (5.6 miles) This popular trail has a great payoff: after descending into scrub brush, you enter a shady canyon and scramble around on some rocks, then the trail suddenly ends with a narrowed pass and a 200ft drop-off. Leave from the **campground** (p298) trailhead to shave more than a mile off the hike. The return is steep and unshaded; this trail is best done in the morning.

Lost Mine Trail (4.8 miles) Another really popular trail, this one is all about views, which just get better and better as you climb over 1000ft in elevation. If you're not up for the full climb (which ends with a series of switchbacks), you can get a pretty good payoff with impressive views just 1 mile in.

Emory Peak (9 miles) Sturdy hikers can bag the highest peak at Big Bend. Begin on the Pinnacles Trail at the Chisos Basin Trailhead. At the junction at 3.5 miles, take the Emory Peak Trail, a 1-mile trail to the summit. Be prepared to climb at the finish: it ends with a short scramble up a sheer rock wall.

South Rim (13 to 14.5 miles) Many serious hikers say this is their favorite trek, mainly because of the view at the end: from the South Rim, the vista includes Santa Elena Canyon and the Sierra del Carmen. Consult with the visitor center for your best plan of attack.

Castolon Historic District HISTORIC SITE
(www.nps.gov/bibe; ⊙ visitor center 10am–noon & 1-4pm Nov-Apr) Dwarfed by the looming Sierra Ponce, the Castolon Compound buildings date from 1920. A half-mile historic stroll offers a brief look at frontier life. Start at the famous **La Harmonia Store**, which is a mainstay for locals on both sides of the river as well as an ice-cream-vending oasis for tourists. There is a park **visitor center** in the building, where you can pay the entrance fee, pick up permits and check out the exhibits.

Sam Nail Ranch RUINS, HISTORIC SITE
(www.nps.gov/bibe; Ross Maxwell Scenic Dr) A short walk from the Ross Maxwell Scenic Drive, just five minutes or so in, you'll find the ruins of the Sam Nail Ranch. Nail arrived in 1909 and raised cattle, sheep and goats here, leaving in 1946. The windmill still pumps for no one's benefit, and the ruins of the adobe house and the shed can feel vaguely haunted, especially at dusk.

 Activities

Scenic Drives

Big Bend National Park has 110 miles of paved road and 150 miles of dirt road, and scenic driving is easily the park's most popular activity. Booklets describing the parks paved roads ($1.95) and backroads ($3.95) are available at the Panther Junction visitor center (p301), and are also for sale online at www.bigbendbookstore.org.

Maverick Drive The 23-mile stretch between the west entrance and park headquarters is notable for its desert scenery and wildlife. Just west of Basin Junction, a side trip on the gravel Grapevine Hills Rd leads to fields of oddly shaped, highly eroded boulders.

Ross Maxwell Scenic Drive This 30-mile route leaves Maverick Dr midway between the west entrance and park headquarters. The Chisos Mountains provide a grand panorama, and the big payoff is the view

Desert Hikes

Grapevine Hills Trail (2.2 miles) The highlight of this fascinating desert hike near Panther Junction is Balanced Rock, a much-photographed formation of three acrobatic boulders that form an inverted-triangle 'window.' After hiking almost a mile in, you'll climb 0.25 miles over some rocks to reach the window.

Mule Ears Spring (3.8 miles) Bring your hat for this pretty desert hike that crosses several arroyos before leading you to a small spring, a rock corral and a small adobe house.

Chimneys (4.8 miles) With no shade, the sun can be brutal, but the trail is mercifully flat. Your reward is rock formations and Native American pictographs and petroglyphs.

Riverside Hikes

Rio Grande Village Nature Trail (0.75 miles) Beginning at campsite 18 at the **Rio Grande Village campground** (p299), the trail passes through dense vegetation before emerging in the desert for a view of the Rio Grande. This is a good short trail for birding and photography.

Hot Springs Historic Walk (0.75 miles) On the way to the hot springs – a stone tub brimming with 105°F (41°C) spring water at the river's edge – you'll pass historic buildings and Native American pictographs painted on rock walls.

Boquillas Canyon Trail (1.4 miles) After a short climb, you'll descend a sandy path to the river. Leave time to play on the sand slide and enjoy the sunlight dancing on the canyon walls.

Santa Elena Canyon Trail (1.6 miles) At the end of Ross Maxwell Scenic Dr (a long drive from most of the park) is a short trail into a photogenic river canyon. You start by crossing Terlingua Creek, which could be wet or muddy, so plan accordingly.

of Santa Elena Canyon and its 1500ft sheer rock walls.

Rio Grande Village Drive This 21-mile drive leads from park headquarters toward the Sierra del Carmen range, running through the park toward Mexico. The best time to take this drive is at sunrise or sunset, when the mountains glow brilliantly with different hues.

Backpacking

Big Bend's primitive backpacking routes range from well-traveled desert washes to the truly challenging limestone uplifts of Mesa de Anguila and the Dead Horse Mountains. Rangers say that because of the constantly changing trail and spring conditions, it's pretty much impossible to plan an extended backpacking trip before you actually get to the park. What you can do instead is figure out how much time you have and the distance you'd like to cover – based on that information, park staff will help you plot a trip. Many trails require use of topographical maps and a compass.

Backcountry camping requires a permit ($12). In the Chisos Mountains, 42 designated campsites are available along various trails. Open-zone camping is available outside the mountain area. Pick your zone and find your ideal spot; just stay at least a half-mile from a road and 100yd from trails, historic and archaeological sites, dry creek beds, springs and cliff edges.

Bird-Watching

Over 450 bird species have been spotted in the park; prime sites include Rio Grande Valley, the Sam Nail Ranch, the Chisos Basin and Castolon near Santa Elena Canyon. The Big Bend region may be best known for its **peregrine falcons**, which, while still endangered, have been making a comeback. The current number of peregrine-falcon nests is not known, but there are some within the park.

Among other Big Bend bird celebrities, the Colima warbler has its only US nesting spot in the Chisos Mountains, where it lives from mid-April through mid-September. More common Big Bend species include golden eagles, cactus wrens, ravens, Mexican jays, roadrunners, acorn woodpeckers, canyon towhees and a whole bunch of warblers and hummingbirds.

River Trips

The Rio Grande has earned its place among the top North American river trips for both rafting and canoeing. Rapids up to class IV alternate with calm stretches that are perfect for wildlife-viewing, photography and just plain relaxation.

Trips on the river can range from several hours to several days. **Boquillas Canyon** is the longest and most tranquil of the park's three canyons and is best for intermediate to advanced boaters and canoeists with camping skills. **Colorado Canyon** is just upriver from the park and, depending on the water level, has lots of white water. **Mariscal Canyon** is noted for its beauty and isolation, and **Santa Elena Canyon** is a classic float featuring the class IV Rock Slide rapid.

Guided floats cost about $145 per person per day ($79 for a half-day), including all meals and gear (except a sleeping bag for overnighters). The following companies have been in business a long time and have solid reputations:

➡ **Big Bend River Tours** (☑ 432-371-3033, 800-545-4240; www.bigbendrivertours.com;

THE STARS AT NIGHT ARE INDEED BIG & BRIGHT

Big Bend has taken major steps to reduce light pollution in the last few years, installing LED lights and retrofitting outdoor light sources on more than 280 buildings and in other developed areas. These steps make it easier to see stars in the night sky. The International Dark Sky Association awarded the park a gold-tier certification in 2012, and the park shares the honor with only a dozen or so other parks worldwide.

Check the *Paisano*, the park's seasonal newspaper, for a list of celestial events, from solstices to meteor showers, that may occur during your visit. Evening ranger talks may cover night skies, with a telescope provided for celestial viewing.

23331 FM 170; half-/full day river trip $75/135) Offers saddle-paddle tours with half a day each rowing and horseback riding.

➡ **Desert Sports** (☑ 432-371-2727, 888-989-6900; www.desertsportstx.com; 22937 Rte 170; full-day river trip $225) Tops with bikers for its bike-canoe combo trips.

➡ **Far Flung Adventures** Puts together fun outings, such as wine-tasting river trips.

Want to go it alone? Any of the above companies will rent you equipment and provide shuttle service. Just remember to obtain your free permit, required for day and overnight use on sections of the river overseen by the park, at Panther Junction visitor center (p301) within 24 hours before putting in. Permits for the lower canyons of the Rio Grande are available at the Persimmon Gap visitor center (p301).

☞ Tours

Far Flung Adventures   CANOEING, HIKING
(☑ 432-371-2633; www.bigbendfarflung.com; FM 170, Terlingua; half-/full day $79/145) Far Flung does it all when it comes to guided adventures, offering paddling tours, hiking trips and Jeep and ATV excursions. Also rents out canoes and Jeeps.

🛏 Sleeping

Tent campers or smaller RVs that don't require hookups can use the three main campgrounds; some take reservations but some are first-come, first-served. Sites typically fill up during spring break, Thanksgiving and Christmas. There are also primitive roadside campsites in the backcountry.

There are only three pet-friendly rooms in the Chisos Mountain Lodge complex, and they are found in the cottages, which book out two years in advance.

Chisos Basin Campground   CAMPGROUND $
(☑ 877-444-6777; www.nps.gov/bibe; tent & RV sites $14) The most centrally located of the main campgrounds, this 60-site place has stone shelters and picnic tables, with bathroom facilities nearby. It's located right near the Chisos Lodge Restaurant (p299) and the **Basin Store** (☑ 432-477-2291; ⊙ 7am-9pm), as well as several popular trails. Twenty-six sites are available for advance reservations from November 15 through May at www.recreation.gov; the rest are first-come, first-served.

Both tents and RV are allowed at the campsite but trailers over 20ft and RVs over

24ft are not recommended. The road to the campground is narrow and winding, and the campsites are small. No hookups but there is a dump station.

Cottonwood Campground CAMPGROUND $
(www.nps.gov/bibe; tent sites $14) Set beneath cottonwood trees near Castolon, the 24-site Cottonwood Campground provides a subdued and shady environment along the river with no generators or idling vehicles to ruin the ambience. No hookups and no dump station. Pit toilets and water are available. No reservations.

**Rio Grande Village RV
Campground** CAMPGROUND $
(☑ 432-477-2293, 877-386-4383; www.nps.gov/bibe; RV sites per 2 people $33, per extra person $3) If you have a larger RV, Rio Grande Village is the only facility with hookups within the park. (Trailers over 25ft have trouble navigating the winding roads down into the Chisos Basin.) Twenty sites can be reserved and five are first-come, first-served. This campground is run by Forever Resorts. Call for a reservation.

**Rio Grande Village
Campground** CAMPGROUND $
(☑ 877-444-6777; www.nps.gov/bibe; campsites $14) On the southeastern edge of the park, this campground offers 100 sites with water and flush toilets. Generators may only be used from 8am to 8pm; mercifully, there is also a no-generator zone available. Forty-three sites can be reserved in advance from November 15 though April 15 at www.recreation.gov.

Chisos Mountain Lodge MOTEL $$
(☑ 432-477-2291, 877-386-4383; www.chisosmountainslodge.com; lodge & motel r $147-151, cottages $166; P❄🤶) Run by concessionaire Forever Resorts, the four lodging options in Chisos Basin (collectively known as the Chisos Mountain Lodge) get good, if not great, marks. You can do better if you stay outside the national park, but the scenery here is a lot better, and it's nice to not have to drive 45 minutes to rest after your hike.

The lodge offers four overnight options. Roosevelt Stone Cottages are the choice accommodations in the park. Each has three double beds and sleeps six people semi-comfortably. Cottages have microwaves and minifridges but no air-conditioning; three are pet friendly. There are only five of these cottages, though, so they're hard to come by.

Casa Grande Lodge, the Rio Grande Motel and Emory Peak Lodge have modest, motel-style rooms with microwaves, mini-fridges and good views (aside from Emory Peak Lodge) of the basin and surrounding mountains; rooms in the Casa Grande Lodge have balconies. Most rooms come with two double beds; some have a king or one double and one single. No TVs or telephones. Also, there's no cell-phone coverage here, though there is free wi-fi in the public common areas. You'll find air-conditioning in the Casa Grande Lodge and the Rio Grand Motel.

Reservations are a must, but there are often cancellations.

✖ Eating

Run by concessionaire Forever Resorts, the Chisos Lodge Restaurant is the only full-service restaurant in the park. It offers breakfast, lunch and dinner and has a small bar. Otherwise, bring your own food or buy snacks and basic groceries at one of the park convenience stores. For more restaurant options head to Study Butte/Terlingua.

Chisos Lodge Restaurant AMERICAN $$
(Lodge Dining Room; www.chisosmountainlodge.com; Chisos Mountain Lodge; lunch $7-12, dinner $10-22; ⊙ 7-10am, 11am-4pm & 5-8pm) Talk about a captive audience: it's a 45-minute drive to the nearest other restaurants (in Study Butte and Terlingua). Still, the food (enchiladas, burgers, vegetable wraps, fish tacos) here is decent, and the views over the Chisos Basin are sublime.

🔒 Shopping

Snacks, camping supplies, cold beer, suntan lotion, sun hats and even some souvenirs can all be found at the Chisos Basin Convenience Store right next to the visitor center (p301). It also has an ATM. You can find a similar selection at the **Rio Grande Village Store** (☑ 432-477-2293; www.chisosmountainslodge.com; ⊙ 8am-7pm Oct-May, to 5pm Jun-Sep; 🤶) and in the **La Harmonia** (☑ 432-477-2222; www.chisosmountainslodge.com; ⊙ 9am-5pm Sep-May, 10am-4pm Jun-Aug) store at Castolon.

ℹ Information

DANGERS & ANNOYANCES

Big Bend National Park is one of the most remote spots in North America, set amid wild country with all kinds of potential hazards. It's not an inherently dangerous place, but you should take precautions.
➤ Don't underestimate the heat; this is the desert, after all. Drink lots of water, and take plenty with you when you hike.

WORTH A TRIP

ROCK ART ALONG THE RIO GRANDE

Although humans visited the Rio Grande region 12,000 years ago, they were wanderers, hunting the mammoth and bison that once lived here in abundance. By 7000 years ago, the climate had changed it into the arid desert it is today, and a new culture appeared. Although these people lived amid harsh conditions, they possessed a creative spark and produced a distinctive style of art seen only along the Lower Pecos River, Devils River and Rio Grande. It has come to be known as the **Pecos River Style**.

The defining characteristic of Pecos River Style art is a towering shaman who usually holds an *atlatl,* or ancient spear, in his hand. According to rock-art expert Solveig Turpin, 'The figure may be headless or crowned with antlers, feline ears, radiant hair or horns. The body is rectangular, often tapering to stubby legs...the shaman can be surrounded by miniature replicas of itself, sometimes inverted as if falling from the sky, or herds of deer, often pierced by spears.'

The best pictograph sites are along the Rio Grande just downriver from the Pecos confluence. These sites are east of Big Bend, off US 90 between Del Rio and Langtry. Here is a summary of recommended sites:

Amistad National Recreation Area (☑ 830-775-7491; www.nps.gov/amis; 9685 US 90 W; ⊙ visitor center 8am-4:30pm) **FREE** **Panther Cave** and **Parida Cave** are the most well-known sites for rock art here. Both are most easily reached by boat and thus not easily accessed by casual day-trippers. Unfortunately, boats can no longer be rented at the Amistad marinas.

Seminole Canyon State Park & Historic Area (☑ 432-292-4464; www.tpwd.texas.gov; off US 90, Comstock; adult/child under 13yr $3/free; ⊙ visitor center 8am-4:30pm) Pictographs line the wall of **Fate Bell Shelter**, a cave dwelling accessed by a guided hike at the state park Wednesdays through Sundays. Various rock-art styles are on display in **Presa Canyon**, seen by guided hikes offered in the spring and fall. After a 3-mile hike, visitors can see Panther Cave – and its namesake rock-art panther – from a canyon-top viewpoint that sits across Seminole Canyon in the Amistad recreation area.

White Shaman Preserve Guides with the **Rock Art Foundation** (☑ 210-357-1910; www.rockart.org; 42535 W US Hwy 90; ⊙ 12:30pm Sat Sep-May) **FREE** , part of San Antonio's Witte Museum, lead 90-minute tours to this pictograph site, which depicts the flight of a shaman to the spirit world. Check the website for tour dates and registration details and directions.

→ To protect against sunburn, wear a hat, sunscreen, long pants and a long-sleeved shirt.

→ Do your hiking early in the morning or in the evening, not at midday when the unrelenting sun turns Big Bend into one giant oven.

→ The poisonous snakes and tarantulas here won't attack unless provoked. Simple rule of thumb? Don't provoke them. Most snakes keep a low profile in daylight, when you're unlikely to see them. Night hikers should stay on the trail and carry a flashlight.

→ Big Bend's scorpions are not deadly, but you should still get prompt attention if you're stung. Shake out boots or shoes before putting them on.

EMERGENCY & MEDICAL SERVICES

Big Bend is no place to get seriously injured or gravely ill. The closest hospital is in Alpine, 108 miles from Panther Junction. However, the nonprofit **Terlingua Fire & EMS** (☑ 432-371-2536; www.facebook.com/terlinguafireems; 23250 FM 170) has a first-aid station that's 26 miles west of Panther Junction, where trained paramedics can offer some assistance.

MAPS

Readily available at the entrances and visitor centers, the free National Park Service (NPS) *Big Bend* map is adequate for most visitors to the park. You'll also find summaries and mileage information about popular trails in the *Paisano*, the free park newspaper. The visitor centers also sell trail guides.

Serious backpackers or anyone looking to hike the less developed trails will want to pick up a topographic map at the visitor centers or bookstores in the gateway towns.

MONEY

This is one of the few parts of the country where you can drive a couple of hours and not find a bank. There are, however, ATMs at the convenience stores in **Chisos Basin** (p298), **Rio Grande Village** (p299) and the **Panther Junction gas station** (p293).

TOURIST INFORMATION

In addition to the park headquarters and visitor center at **Panther Junction** (Main Visitor Center; ☑ 432-477-1158; www.nps.gov/bibe; ☺ 9am-5pm), visitor centers are found in **Chisos Basin** (☑ 432-477-2264; www.nps.gov/bibe; ☺ 8:30am-noon & 1-4pm) and at **Persimmon Gap** (☑ 432-477-2393; www.nps.gov/bibe; ☺ 9-11:30am & 12:30-4pm). There are also seasonal visitor centers open November through April at **Castolon** (☑ 432-477-2222; www.nps.gov/bibe; ☺ 10am-noon & 1-4pm Nov-Apr) and the **Rio Grande Village** (☑ 432 477 2271; www nps gov/bibe; ☺ 8:30am-4pm Nov-Apr).

Find out how to make the most of your visit from park rangers, and check bulletin boards for a list of upcoming interpretive activities. You'll also find a variety of free leaflets on special-interest topics, including biological diversity, hiking and backpacking, geology, archaeology and dinosaurs.

ⓘ Getting There & Away

There is no public transportation to, from or within the park. The closest buses and trains run through Alpine, 108 miles northwest of Panther Junction. The nearest major airports are 230 miles northeast in Midland and 325 miles northwest in **El Paso** (p327).

You'll find gas at the service stations at **Panther Junction** (p293) and **Rio Grande Village** (p293).

Please note that the border patrol has checkpoints for vehicles coming from Big Bend. If you're not a US citizen, presenting your passport will help avoid delays (ie prove you're not coming from Mexico).

WEST OF BIG BEND NATIONAL PARK

Small towns. Ghost towns. Towns that aren't even really towns. Throw in lots of dust and a scorching summer heat that dries out the stream of visitors until it's just a trickle.

This isn't everyone's idea of a dream vacation – but if you can't relax out here, then you just plain can't relax. Whatever concerns you in your everyday life is likely to melt away (along with anything you leave in your car). With rugged natural beauty and some offbeat destinations, it is easy to see why this unlikely corner of the country is actually fueled almost entirely by tourism.

Terlingua & Study Butte

☑ 432 / POP 291

A former mining boomtown in the late 19th and early 20th centuries, Terlingua went bust when the cinnabar mines closed down in the 1940s. The town dried up and blew away like a tumbleweed, earning Terlingua its ghost-town status.

Slowly the area has repopulated, thanks in large part to its proximity to Big Bend National Park: it supplies housing for park employees, and businesses and services for visitors. Many of the old adobes have been reclaimed by river guides, artists and others who relish the solitude of the backcountry.

People here talk about Terlingua, Study Butte (*stoo*-dee *byoot*) and Terlingua ghost town as if they're three different towns, but the only real town here is Terlingua; the other two are just areas of it. Addresses are loose here: have patience if you're using a GPS, but really, the town's not that big.

◉ Sights & Activities

There's not a lot to see 'round here, except some stone **ruins** and an old **cemetery** from the early 1900s. Many of the ruins are on private land, so remember: 'uninhabited' does not equal 'open to the public.'

The cemetery, however, is open to visitors, and it's one of the most fascinating final resting places in the US. No manicured lawns or tasteful headstones here: these graves are piled high with local rocks that reflect the style of the nearby ruins.

For many locals and laid-back travelers, the main activity in Terlingua is sitting on the porch of the Terlingua Trading Co (p303), drinking a beer and shooting the breeze while watching the sunset – an activity we highly recommend. Pick up a brochure on the **walking tour** of historic Terlingua here.

For more active types, Terlingua sits amid prime **mountain-biking** territory. Desert Sports (p298) provides rental bikes, along with advice on the best places to ride. It also offers raft, canoe, bike and combo trips throughout the Big Bend area.

There are some well-run stables at the Lajitas Golf Resort & Spa (p302) that are open to local visitors whether they're staying at the resort or not. The **Lajitas Equestrian Center** offers horseback trail rides by the hour, as well as sunset rides.

ORIENTATION

Study Butte refers to a cluster of buildings on Hwy 118 outside the west gate of Big Bend. One mile up the road, where Hwy 118 meets FM 170, are a bank and post office; head west on FM 170 for more of the town's business district. Keep going for 5 more miles to reach the historic area called the **Terlingua ghost town**, where you'll find old ruins and new businesses built on top of old ruins.

Big Bend & Lajitas Stables HORSEBACK RIDING
(☑ 432-371-3064, 800-887-4331; www.lajitasstables. com; Hwy 118 & FM 170; ☺ rides from Big Bend $45-100, from Lajitas $75-120; 🏇) Offers trips ranging from one hour to a full day from stables in both Study Butte and Lajitas. Kids six and up can ride. The saddle/paddle trip from Lajitas includes a morning horseback ride, followed by lunch, then an afternoon river paddle ($195). Also offers overnight trips.

🛏 Sleeping

You might think lodging would be inexpensive out here – quite the opposite. Expect to pay a little more than you think you ought to.

BJ's RV Park CAMPGROUND $
(☑ 432-371-2259; www.bjrvpark.com; FM 170; tent/ RV sites $20/28; 🛜🐕) Sure, it's dry and dusty – the whole town is dry and dusty. At least it has showers. This utilitarian but welcoming park, 5 miles west of Hwy 118, provides a handy alternative when everything's full up in Big Bend. The grassy lawn has a few tent sites.

Big Bend
Resort & Adventures MOTEL, CAMPGROUND $
(☑ 432-371-2218, reservations 877-386-4383; www. bigbendresortadventures.com; 53623 Hwy 118, at FM 170 junction; tent sites $18, RV sites $34-39, r $89-110; 🛜🐕) Run by Forever Resorts, this place has all sorts of sleeping options, including serviceable motel rooms in the Motor Inn and Mission Lodge, duplex units ($189), a 3-bedroom house ($398), tent camping and RV sites. Rooms in the Mission Lodge were being revamped at the time of writing.

La Posada Milagro INN $$
(☑ 432-371-3044; www.laposadamilagro.net; 100 Milagro Rd; r $195-210; ❄🛜🐕) Built on top of and even incorporating some of the adobe ruins in the historic ghost town, this guesthouse pulls off the amazing feat of providing stylish rooms that blend in perfectly with the surroundings. The decor is west-Texas chic, and there's a nice patio for enjoying the cool evenings.

Pet fee is $20 per stay.

Big Bend Holiday Hotel HOTEL $$
(☑ 432-203-6929; www.bigbendholidayhotel. com; r $130, ste $160-195, houses $200-250, Perry Mansion $245; 🛜) Near the famous Starlight Theatre and Terlingua Trading Co are a variety of lodging options managed by Big Bend Holiday Hotel, many done up in ranch-style decor with a Spanish influence. For the most part they're fairly fancy for a ghost town, but without putting on airs.

Under the same management company you'll find suites, a house and the two surprisingly nice bedrooms in the ruins of the old Perry Mansion. Let 'em know what you want and they'll make you feel right at home.

Lajitas Golf Resort & Spa RESORT $$$
(☑ 432-424-5000; www.lajitasgolfresort.com; Rte 170; r/ste/cottages from $219/319/399; 🐕❄🛜🏊🐕) About a 30-minute drive west from the junction in Terlingua, what used to be small-town Texas got bought up and revamped into a swanky destination. Choose from a range of different experiences, from motel rooms to condos to RV camps. Among the nicest are rooms in the high-ceilinged Officers' Quarters, a complex modeled after the original at Fort Davis.

The resort has a pool, lighted tennis courts and an 18-hole golf course called Black Jack's Crossing.

🍴 Eating

The settings and locals can be a little quirky, but our advice? Just go with it. If you're game for the unexpected, you'll find good food, good folks and likely some good drinking.

Espresso...Y Poco Mas CAFE $
(☑ 432-371-3044; www.laposadamilagro.net; 100 Milagro Rd; snacks $5-7; ☺ 7:30am-2pm; 🛜) We love this friendly little walk-up counter at La Posada Milagro (p302), where you can find pastries, breakfast burritos, lunches and what might just be the best iced coffee in all of west Texas.

The cafe incorporates stone ruins for an authentic ghost-town feel, and the shady patio is a great place to soak up the ambience, make new friends, fuel yourself up and use the wi-fi.

★ Starlight Theatre
AMERICAN $$

([phone] 432-371-3400; www.thestarlighttheatre.com; 631 Ivey Rd; mains $10-27; [hours] 5pm-midnight Sun-Fri, to 1am Sat) You'd think a ghost town would be dead at night (pardon the pun), but the Starlight Theater keeps things lively. This former movie theater fell into roofless disrepair (thus the 'starlight') before being converted into a restaurant. The menu features steaks and wild game, plus a few burgers and sandwiches. There's live music nearly every night in spring and fall.

If there's no entertainment inside, there's usually someone strumming a guitar outside on the porch. To get there, take Hwy 170 to the turnoff for the ghost town and follow the road to the end.

DB's Rustic Iron BBQ
BARBECUE $$

([phone] 432-210-3457; www.rusticironbbq.com; 23270 FM 170; sandwiches $10, plates $14-17; [hours] 11am-6pm Thu-Sun) You might get a helping of pit-master poetry from personable owner Don 'DB' Baucham if business is slow and you're from out of town. Poetry or not, if you're hankering for some fine smoked brisket or sausage, pull over for this roadside food truck. Settle in at a table under the canopy.

La Kiva Restaurant & Bar
BARBECUE $$

([phone] 432-371-2250; www.la-kiva.com; 23220 FM 170; mains lunch $14-20, dinner $12-26; [hours] 11am-2pm & 5-10pm, bar open later) Talk about your underground restaurants. This quirky place specializing in barbecue and grilled meat is literally right underground – just look at those rock walls. There's frequent live music, and happy hour is from 5pm to 6pm, when the house margaritas are $3.50. Buns, bread and pizza dough are all homemade. This place is worth checking out.

Although the kitchen closes at 2pm (lunch) and 10pm (dinner), the bar is open until 3pm (after lunch) daily, until midnight Sunday through Friday and until 1am Saturday. It's about 3 miles west of Hwy 118.

🔒 Shopping

Terlingua Trading Co
GIFTS & SOUVENIRS

([phone] 432-371-2234; http://terlinguatradingco.homestead.com; 100 Ivey St; [hours] 10am-9pm) This store in Terlingua ghost town has great gifts, from hot sauces and wines to an impressive selection of books. Pick up a brochure on the **walking tour** of historic Terlingua, or buy a beer inside the store and hang out on the porch with locals at sunset.

ℹ️ Information

Big Bend Chamber of Commerce ([phone] 432-317-3949; www.bigbendchamberofcommerce.org) Visit for more information on the area.

West Texas National Bank ([phone] 432-371-2211; www.wtnb.com; [hours] 8:30-11am & 2-4:30pm Mon-Wed & Fri, 8:30-11am & 2-6pm Thu) At the junction of Hwy 118 and FM 170; has a 24-hour ATM.

Big Bend Ranch State Park & Around

The 486-sq-mile **Big Bend Ranch State Park** ([phone] 432-358-4444; http://tpwd.texas.gov; off Rte 170; adult Nov-Apr/May-Oct $5/3, child under 13yr free) sprawls across the desert between Lajitas and Presidio, reaching north from the Rio Grande into some of the wildest country in North America. As massive as it is, this former ranch is one of the best-kept secrets in Big Bend country. It's full of notable features, most prominently the **Solitario**, a geological formation that sprang up 36 million years ago in a volcanic explosion. The resulting caldera measures 8 miles east to west and 9 miles north to south.

The scenic River Road (p305) ribbons across the park beside the Rio Grande on FM 170. Short hiking trails between FM 170 and the river work well for day-trippers who want to stretch their legs and explore a bit

---

THE CHAMPIONS OF CHILI

Every November, Terlingua is invaded by thousands of visitors with a hankering for homemade chili. This is no small-town festival: the **Terlingua Chili Cookoff** is such a big deal that they actually have *two* events to accommodate the hundreds of entrants.

International Chili Championship (CASI; www.casichili.net/terlingua.html; Terlingua; $40; [hours] Nov) Held by the Chili Appreciation Society International.

Original Terlingua International Frank X Tolbert-Wick Fowler Championship Chili Cookoff (www.abowlofred.com; Terlingua; $40; [hours] Nov) Less competitive and more like a big, delicious party.

Don't expect to enjoy quality time with the locals during these events, though; they mostly go into hiding.

of the striking scenery. Rugged hiking and mountain-biking trails crisscross the backcountry.

Since the park has few facilities and few visitors, you should come prepared. If you're headed into the backcountry, bring a good map, spare tires, a full tank of gas, a gallon of water per day per person, sunscreen, a hat, mosquito repellent and a well-stocked first-aid kit.

◎ Sights

Barton Warnock
Visitor Center   VISITOR CENTER
(☑432-424-3327; http://tpwd.texas.gov; FM 170; adult Nov-Apr/May-Oct $5/3, child under 13yr free; ⊙8am-4:30pm) If you stop at only one Chihuahuan Desert exhibit in Big Bend country, make it this one, at the eastern entrance of Big Bend Ranch State Park (p303), 1 mile east of Lajitas on FM 170. This education center is staffed by some of the most knowledgeable folks in the region, and the renovated interpretive center holds a trove of information about the history, natural history and archaeology of the diverse Big Bend region. There's also a 2-acre **desert garden**.

Tee Pees Picnic Area   PICNIC AREA
(http://tpwd.texas.gov) For a leisurely lunch and a few photographs, plan to stop at this striking picnic area. You'll know when you see it – those tipis are hard to miss.

Fort Leaton
State Historic Site   VISITOR CENTER, FORTRESS
(☑432-229-3613; http://tpwd.texas.gov; FM 170 E, Presidio; adult Nov-Apr/May-Oct $5/3, child under 13yr free; ⊙8am-4:30pm Thu-Mon) This restored adobe fortress doubles as the western entrance and **visitor center** for Big Bend Ranch State Park (p303), 4 miles southeast of Presidio. Look for exhibits about history and archaeology on-site. You can get backpacking, camping and river-use permits here.

---

❶ BRINGING YOUR DOG
....
Dogs are not permitted in most of the park. They are allowed on two trails along FM 170 – Closed Canyon and Hoodoos – and within 1.4 miles of a campsite, but they must be on a leash that's 6ft long or less.

☂ Activities

Closed Canyon Trail   HIKING
(http://tpwd.texas.gov; FM 170; ▣) About halfway down the River Road, an easy hike leads through a sandy wash to a towering slot canyon. Because of long drop-offs within in the canyon, you won't be able to make it all the way to the Rio Grande, but the steep and narrow rock walls soaring above you are an impressive sight. Round-trip distance is about 1.4 miles.

Hoodoos Trail   HIKING
(http://tpwd.texas.gov; FM 170; ▣) A 1.1-mile loop trail leads to a small grove of **hoodoos** – crumbly and soft rock formations of mudstone or tuff, typically topped by a harder capstone. Take one look and you'll see why they're also known as 'goblins'. A short spur trail ends at a lofty **viewpoint** sweeping in the the Rio Grande, Mexico and rolling mountains. Impressive indeed.

★☆ Festivals & Events

Chihuahuan Desert Bike Fest   CYCLING
(☑432-371-2727; https://bikefest.desertsportstx.com; Big Bend Ranch State Park; ⊙Feb) More than 500 mountain bikers converge on the rugged trails of Big Bend Ranch State Park (p303) each February for three days of rides across the backcountry, plus a lot of socializing.

❶ Information

Sauceda Ranger Station (☑432-358-4444; http://tpwd.texas.gov; 1900 Sauceda Ranch Rd; ⊙8am-6pm) In the park interior, this outpost requires a 27-mile drive up a dirt road and may not be easy to access. Check the park website for GPS coordinates and maps.

CENTRAL WEST TEXAS

The small towns of west Texas have become more than just the gateway to Big Bend National Park. Fort Davis, Marfa, Alpine and Marathon have a sprawling, easy-going charm and plenty of ways to keep a road-tripper entertained. Art enthusiasts will enjoy the galleries and museums in Marfa, while outdoor adventurers can hike and camp in the Davis Mountains, where stargazing at McDonald Observatory is highly recommended. And if you're fond of quirky sights, bars and lodging, well, this region has got you covered. From mystery lights to a white-buffalo bar to tipis, it's all just a bit offbeat.

Fort Davis & Davis Mountains

☑ 432 / POP 1250 (FORT DAVIS)

More than 5000ft above sea level, Fort Davis has an altitudinal advantage over the rest of Texas, both in terms of elevation and the cooler weather it offers. That makes it a popular oasis during the summer, when west Texans head toward the mountains to escape the searing desert heat. The area is part of both the Chihuahuan Desert and the Davis Mountains, giving it a unique setting where wide-open spaces are suddenly pierced by rock formations springing from the earth.

As for the town itself, it sprang up near the actual fort of the same name, built in 1854 to protect the pioneers and gold rushers who were heading out west from the attacks of Comanche and Apache warriors. The town retains an Old West feel befitting its history.

◉ Sights

★ **McDonald Observatory**   OBSERVATORY
(☑ 432-426-3640; www.mcdonaldobservatory.org; 3640 Dark Sky Dr; day pass adult/child 6-12yr/under 6yr $8/7/free; ☺ visitor center 10am-5:30pm; ♿) Free from the light pollution of big cities, the middle of west Texas has some of the clearest and darkest skies in North America, making it the perfect spot for an observatory. Some of the world's biggest telescopes are here, perched on the peak of **Mt Locke** (6791ft) and so enormous you can spot them from miles away. The popular star parties (p306) help you see the night sky in a whole new way.

A day pass gets you a **guided tour** (held at 11am and 2pm) that includes close-up peeks at (but not through) the 8.75ft Harlan J Smith Telescope and the 36ft Hobby-Eberly Telescope, as well as a solar viewing, where you get to stare at the sun without scorching your eyeballs. Tours last about 2½ hours. Make sure to call ahead: reservations are required for all programs (including star parties).

The observatory is 19 miles northwest of Fort Davis. Allow 30 minutes to drive from town.

**Davis Mountains
State Park**   STATE PARK, VIEWPOINT
(☑ 432-426-3337; www.tpwd.state.tx.us; Hwy 118; adult/child under 13yr $6/free) The majestic sunrises and sunsets at this remote park rival any we've seen – and we've seen plenty. This wonderful place is just a few miles northwest

WORTH A TRIP: RIVER ROAD

West of Lajitas, **Route 170** (also known as the River Road, or El Camino del Rio in Spanish) hugs the Rio Grande through some of the most spectacular and remote scenery in Big Bend country. Relatively few Big Bend visitors experience this driving adventure, even though it can be navigated in any vehicle with good brakes. Strap in and hold on: you have the Rio Grande on one side and geological formations all around, and at one point there's a 15% grade – the maximum allowable. Stop for easy and scenic short hikes and overlooks along the way.

When you reach Presidio, head north on US 67 to get to Marfa. If you plan to go back the way you came, travel at least as far as **Colorado Canyon** (20 miles from Lajitas) for the best scenery.

of Fort Davis on Hwy 118, set amid the most extensive mountain range in Texas. Hiking, mountain biking, horseback riding (BYO horse) and stargazing are all big attractions here, as is bird-watching. (You can pick up a bird checklist from park headquarters).

In daylight, you can check out the surrounding area and neighboring mountain ranges. Before sunset, drive or hike (2.6 miles one way) to the overlook at the top of **Skyline Drive**. Sufficiently moved? Continue down to the **CCC overlook** for a colorful twilight panorama. After it gets dark – and boy, does it get dark – you can test your knowledge of the constellations.

Overnighters can camp within the park or bunk down at Indian Lodge (p307).

**Fort Davis National
Historic Site**   HISTORIC SITE
(☑ 432-426-3224; www.nps.gov/foda; Hwy 17; adult/child under 16yr $7/free; ☺ 8am-5pm; ♿) A remarkably well-preserved frontier military post with an impressive backdrop at the foot of **Sleeping Lion Mountain**, Fort Davis was established in 1854 and abandoned in 1891. More than 20 buildings remain – five of them restored with period furnishings – as well as 100 or so ruins.

It's easy to picture the fort as it was in 1880, especially with bugle calls sounding in the background. It's even easier in summer, when interpreters dressed in period clothing are on hand to describe life at the fort.

A STAR-STUDDED EVENT

On Tuesday, Friday and Saturday nights, about half an hour after sunset, **Mc-Donald Observatory** (p305) shows off its favorite planets, galaxies and globular clusters at its popular **star parties** (adult/child $12/8), where professional astronomers guide you in some heavy-duty stargazing. Using ridiculously powerful laser pointers, they give you a tour of the night sky, and you'll get to use some of the telescopes to play planetary Peeping Tom.

Remember: it gets cold up there at night, even in the summer, so wear layers you don't think you'll need – lest you find yourself plunking down $35 for a hoodie from the gift shop.

The fort is strategically located at the foot of Sleeping Lion Mountain and **Hospital Canyon**. The site serves as the trailhead for several hikes, ranging from the 1-mile **Tall Grass Loop** to the more ambitious 3-mile trek to Davis Mountains State Park (p305). Ask for a trail map in the fort's **visitor center**, where there's also an engaging museum.

Rattlers & Reptiles   MUSEUM
(☑ 432-426-2465; 1600 N State St; adult/child under 10yr $4/1; ⊙ 10am-dark) Snakes, spiders, scorpions...all the things you should check your boots for before you put them on can be seen on display at this funky little museum. Sure, the critters on display give some people the willies, but better to run into them here than out on the trail – or worse yet, in your tent.

**Chihuahuan Desert
Nature Center**   NATURE RESERVE
(☑ 432-364-2499; www.cdri.org; 43869 Hwy 118; adult/child under 13yr $6/free; ⊙ 9am-5pm Mon-Sat year-round, plus 12:30-5:30pm Sun Apr-Oct) Four miles south of town, the Chihuahuan Desert Nature Center exhibits the region's flora in gardens and on trails. Take a 2-mile hike down into a canyon, watch butterflies flitting around wildflower gardens, check out a permanent exhibit on mining or visit the cactus greenhouse.

🏃 Activities

Scenic Drive
Pack the kids into the car – or hop on your bikes – and head out for 75 miles of paved splendor on this scenic drive through the Davis Mountains. First you go up, up, up...then you come down, down, down. The countryside is so gorgeous, it's no wonder this is considered one of the most scenic drives in the US. It's also tops among cyclists – at least, the ones who can handle the climb.

Head out on Hwy 118 northwest from town, then turn left on Hwy 166, which loops you back to town. Or go the opposite route; both afford equally appealing views, although the former is better in the morning so you're not driving/riding into the sun, while the latter is better in the afternoon. Without stops, it should take about two hours. Get gas before you leave, as well as snacks and water.

Cycling
Fort Davis is one of Texas' best areas for road cycling. In addition to the Scenic Drive, which is as challenging as it is dramatic, there's some nice, gentle terrain just outside of town for casual cyclists. Unfortunately, there's no place in town that rents bikes, so you'll have to bring your own, either from home or from another town. Your best bet for a road-bike rental is El Paso.

Horseback Riding
Prude Ranch   HORSEBACK RIDING
(☑ 432-426-3202; www.prude-ranch.com; Hwy 118; 1hr rides $30, half-day rides with lunch $110; ⊙ Mon-Sat) Looking for a short horseback ride through the Davis Mountains? Consider Prude Ranch, which began life as a cattle ranch 100 years ago. One-hour rides begin at 9:30am, 11am, 1:30pm and 3pm. The ranch is 6 miles northwest of town.

🛏 Sleeping

**Davis Mountains State Park
Campground**   CAMPGROUND $
(☑ park office 432-426-3337, reservations 512-389-8900; www.tpwd.texas.gov; Hwy 118; tent sites $8-15, RV sites $20-25) Pitch your tent here and the stargazing can go on till the wee hours. The campsites are in a lush, tree-shaded environment and include picnic tables and grills. Backcountry camping and RV hookups are also available.

Stone Village Tourist Camp   MOTEL $
(☑ 432-426-3941; www.stonevillagetouristcamp. com; 509 N State St; camp r $39, motel r $78-108, ste $108; P 🗔 🕿) This renovated motel is a fun little bargain. The 14 regular rooms are cheery and comfortable, and the six camp

rooms are perfect for the budget traveler. Located in the former garages, they have concrete floors, stone walls, a roof, electricity, a sink and even wi-fi. The only catch? One end of the room has a screen and privacy curtain instead of a wall.

If you're looking for more room, inquire about a suite.

★ Indian Lodge
INN $$

(✔ lodge 432-426-3254, reservations 512-389-8982; www.tpwd.texas.gov; Hwy 118; r $95-125, ste 135-$150; P ❄ 🎧 🖳) Located inside Davis Mountains State Park (p305), this historic, 39-room inn is actually its own separate state park. Built by the Civilian Conservation Corps in the 1930s, it has 18in-thick adobe walls, hand-carved cedar furniture and ceilings of pine viga and *latilla* that give it the look of a Southwestern pueblo – that is, one with a swimming pool and gift shop. Reserve early.

The comfortable and surprisingly spacious guest rooms are good value, and the sunrises from the upper rooms are amazing (room 121, whoa!). Check for movie nights in the assembly room (where wi-fi is also more reliable). The fare at the on-site Black Bear Restaurant (p307) is typically quite good.

Veranda Historic Inn
B&B $$

(✔ 888-383-2847; www.theveranda.com; 210 Court Ave; r $115-145; ❄ 🎧) Set a short stroll from the town center, this charming B&B has 10 antique-filled rooms and suites set in an 1883 adobe building. The oldest hotel in west Texas (hence the 'historic' namesake), it has a shaded porch and pretty gardens – fine spots for a sundowner.

Hotel Limpia
HOTEL $$

(✔ 432-426-3237, 800-662-5517; www.hotellimpia. com; 101 Memorial Sq; r $95-125, ste $129-149; P 🔄 🎧 🖳) Built in 1912, this historic hotel leans heavily on antiques and floral prints – Victorian meets Old West, like the womenfolk came along and gussied up the place. There are few finer places to kick back than on the rocking chairs on the back porch. Also offers suites in a ranch-style building, plus budget rooms just across the street.

✕ Eating & Drinking

Local liquor laws mean you can't order an adult beverage with your dinner, but almost every place in town is cheerfully Bring Your Own Bottle (BYOB), with the exception of the Black Bear Restaurant, where it's forbidden. The Blue Mountain Bistro is the only option listed here with a full bar.

Stone Village Market
MARKET, SANDWICHES $

(✔ 432-426-2226; www.stonevillagetouristcamp. com; 509 N State St; sandwiches $5-6; ☺ 7am-7pm; 🎧) Looking for the perfect sandwich for your sunset picnic? Then step up to the deli counter at this welcoming market for the touted cranberry-almond chicken salad. There are plenty of snacks and drinks in the surrounding market to round out your meal.

Black Bear Restaurant
AMERICAN $$

(✔ 432-477-2291; www.tpwd.texas.gov; 16453 Park Rd 3, Indian Lodge; breakfast & lunch $7-12; ☺ 7am-2pm Wed-Sun) What could have been a perfunctory restaurant at the Indian Lodge within Davis Mountains State Park is actually a more-than-decent dining option. Look for burgers, BLT sandwiches, chicken-fried steak, burritos, soup and salad on the menu. At press time, the restaurant was serving only breakfast and lunch, with dinner not scheduled for the foreseeable future.

In the past, we were lucky enough to enjoy a weekend breakfast buffet that was laden with hot, delicious treats (adult/child $11/5; available Sundays and on busy Saturdays). More biscuits and gravy? Yes, please!

Blue Mountain Bistro
AMERICAN $$

(✔ 432-426-3244; www.blue-mountain-bistro.com; 101 Memorial Sq; mains $12-32; ☺ 5-8pm Sun-Tue, to 9pm Fri & Sat, 7:30-10am Sat & Sun) Fort Davis' only upscale eatery serves up hearty bistro fare in the evening (mountain trout, steak

---

DETOUR: BALMORHEA STATE PARK
....

Austin doesn't have a state monopoly on refreshing, spring-fed swimming pools – just check out beloved and popular **Balmorhea State Park** (✔ 432-375-2370; www.tpwd.texas.gov; Hwy 17; adult/child under 13yr $7/free; ☺ 8am-7:30pm or sunset), which has been drawing those in search of a refreshing swim since the 1930s, when it was built by the Civilian Conservation Corps. The pool covers 1.75 acres – making it the largest spring-fed swimming facility in the US. It's 25ft deep and about 75°F (24°C) year-round. Note that there's no lifeguard on duty.

You'll find the park in Toyahvale, 5 miles south of the town of Balmorhea (*bal*-mo-ray), which is just off I-10.

and fries, and at least one vegetarian option). Blue Mountain also has the only full bar in Jeff Davis County – and it stays open later than the restaurant. Good to know when a six-pack from the grocery store just won't do.

Fort Davis Drug Store AMERICAN $$
(📞432-426-3929; www.fortdavisdrugstore.net; 113 N State St; breakfast $6-10, dinner $7-19; ⊙7:30am-7:30pm Sun-Fri; 🛜🅿) Part diner, part old-fashioned soda fountain – but no 1950s nostalgia here. The theme is pure cowboy, with corrugated metal, big wooden chairs and lots of saddles providing the backdrop. Dine on country-style breakfasts, diner-style lunches and full mains at dinner. But whatever you do, save room for a banana split (or at least a milkshake).

❶ Information

On Sunday, this sleepy little town takes a full day of rest; most of the businesses are closed till Monday.

Jeff Davis County Library (📞432-426-3802; https://fortdavislibrary.ploud.net; 100 Memorial Sq; ⊙10am-6pm Mon-Fri, to 2pm Sat; 🛜) Hook up to free wi-fi or use one of the computers at the Jeff Davis County Library, housed in the former county jail between the town square and the courthouse.

Fort Davis Chamber of Commerce (📞432-426-3015; www.fortdavis.com; 4 Memorial Sq; ⊙10am-3pm Mon-Fri) Visit the Fort Davis Chamber of Commerce at the junction of Hwys 118 and 17.

Marfa
📞432 / POP 1981

The New York art scene collides with west Texas cowboy culture and Border Patrol formality in tiny, dusty Marfa, where the factions seem to coexist without conflict as they go about their lives. Maybe it's the mysterious Marfa Mystery Lights that keep the vibe more quirky than antagonistic.

Founded in the 1880s, Marfa's major cultural hallmarks date from the latter part of the 20th century. Its first taste of fame came when Rock Hudson, Elizabeth Taylor and James Dean arrived to film the 1956 film *Giant;* it's since served as a film location for *There Will Be Blood* and *No Country for Old Men.*

As for those New Yorkers: Marfa is a pilgrimage destination for art-lovers, thanks to one of the world's largest installations of minimalist art, which has attracted galleries, quirky lodging options and interesting

restaurants. The US Border Patrol has a headquarters here and has noticeably expanded its presence in recent years.

◎ Sights

★Chinati Foundation Museum MUSEUM
(📞432-729-4362; www.chinati.org; 1 Calvary Row; adult/student Full Collection Tour $25/10, Selections Tour $20/10; ⊙by guided tour 10am & 2pm Wed-Sun) As you step inside the historic artillery shed, with its enormous windows, sweeping desert views and sun-dappled aluminum boxes, the Marfa hoopla suddenly makes sense. Artist Donald Judd single-handedly put Marfa on the art-world map when he created this museum on the site of a former army post. The grounds and abandoned buildings now house one of the world's largest permanent installations of minimalist art. The whole place is an immersive, breathtaking blend of art, architecture and landscape.

Dedicated art enthusiasts will most enjoy the **Full Collection Tour**, which takes up most of the day, but the 2½-hour **Selections Tour** should satisfy most visitors; it spotlights the works of the foundation's four founding artists, including Robert Irwin, whose latest work for the museum, a window-lined structure on the site of a former army hospital, opened in 2016.

If you don't have time for a tour, at least check out Judd's 15 works in concrete spread across the plain just east of the visitor center. These works are open to the public free of charge from 9am to 4:30pm Wednesday through Sunday (check in at the front office before heading out).

Ballroom Marfa GALLERY
(📞432-729-3600; www.ballroommarfa.org; 108 E San Antonio St; suggested donation $5; ⊙10am-6pm Wed-Sat, to 3pm Sun) FREE Be sure to find out what's happening at Ballroom Marfa, a nonprofit art space located in a former dance hall. The focus is on offbeat, interesting projects, including film installations and excellent monthly concerts.

Judd Foundation HOUSE
(📞432-729-4406; www.juddfoundation.org; 104 S Highland Ave; tours adult/student $25/12.50; ⊙office 9am-5pm) The Judd Foundation maintains and preserves the living and work spaces of minimalist artist Donald Judd, who founded the Chinati Foundation Museum. Two tours of these private spaces are offered: the **Block Tour** (11am daily plus 4:30pm Thursday to Sunday) explores his

residence, three studios (which hold early works) and his library; the **Studios Tour** (2pm Thursday to Saturday) takes in studios that display furniture by the artist and his paintings from the 1950s and '60s.

Marfa Mystery Lights
Viewing Area VIEWPOINT
(Hwy 90) Ghost lights, mystery lights...call them what you want, but the **Marfa Lights** that flicker beneath the Chinati Mountains have captured the imagination of many a traveler over the decades. On many nights, the mystery seems to be whether you're actually just seeing car headlights in the distance. Try your luck at this viewing area about 9 miles east of Marfa on Hwy 90/67.

Once there, look to the south and find the red blinking light. That's where you will (or won't) see the lights doing their ghostly thing. This phenomenon is best enjoyed if you can channel your inner preteen (all the better if you actually are a preteen) and simply choose to believe that something really exciting has just happened.

But then again there are convincing-enough accounts of mysterious lights that appear and disappear on the horizon – accounts that go all the way back to before there was such a thing as cars. The cowboy who first reported seeing them in 1883 thought they were Apache signal fires.

⭐✪ Festivals & Events

Every May or June, Marfa puts on the **Marfa Film Festival** (www.marfafilmfestival.com; ☺May/Jun), screening features and shorts – including some of the Texas-centric movies that have used Marfa as a filming location.

El Cosmico also throws a variety of events throughout the year, from live-music performances to politically themed gatherings. Check its calendar online to see what's brewing.

🛏 Sleeping

⭐**El Cosmico** CAMPGROUND $
(☑432-729-1950; www.elcosmico.com; 802 S Highland Ave; tent sites per person $30, safari tents $95, tipis & yurts $165, trailers $165-210; 🅿🛜🐾) One of the funkiest choices in all of Texas, where you can sleep in a stylishly converted travel trailer, tipi, safari tent or even a yurt. It's not for everyone: the grounds are dry and dusty, you might have to shower outdoors, and there's no air-conditioning (luckily, it's cool at night). But when else can you sleep in a tipi?

The cool, colorful community lounge and the hammock grove make particularly pleasant common areas, and the eclectic gift store is a recommended Marfa shopping spot. Our tip? Bring a flashlight. Pet fee is $10 per night.

Hotel Paisano HOTEL $$
(☑432-729-3669; www.hotelpaisano.com; 207 N Highland Ave; d $100-150, ste $160-260; ❄@🛜♨🐾) Marfa's historic hotel has a unique claim to fame: it's where the cast of the movie *Giant* stayed. The comfy rooms are nicely designed, and the whole place does has a dignified charm. The best rooms have a fireplace and a private terrace. There's a first-rate restaurant, a snazzy covered pool and a touch of taxidermy for good measure.

The James Dean room, where they say the legendary actor slept, is only $169 per night. Bringing Fido? It's $20 per pet per night.

Thunderbird BOUTIQUE HOTEL $$
(☑877-729-1984; www.thunderbirdmarfa.com; 601 W San Antonio St; r $160-190; ❄🛜♨) Fresh from an extensive revamp, this classic 1950s motel welcomes guests with rooms that are hip and minimalist. The grounds and common areas are as cool as the desert air at night. All rooms have queen beds and a few have an extra daybed. No TVs.

⭐**Hotel St George** BOUTIQUE HOTEL $$$
(☑432-729-3700; www.marfasaintgeorge.com; 105 S Highland Ave; r from $260; ❄@🐾) In a town with a thing for minimalist cubes, this one is

our favorite. The design-minded digs, which opened in 2016, are the brainchild of local resident and Chinati Foundation board member Tim Crowley. Details and decor reflect fine artisanship, regional history and Marfa-sourced creativity, from the eye-catching art to the spare but inviting Marfa Book Company (p311), which relocated here.

On-site, the Bar St John bustles beside the lobby, while Laventure lures diners with its innovative American fare. Pets are $30 per day.

Cibolo Creek Ranch
RANCH $$$

(☑432-229-3737; www.cibolocreekranch.com; US 67; r/ste from $370/745; ☻❋☎☲) Now famous as the remote but luxurious ranch where US Supreme Court Justice Antonin Scalia died in 2016, this is where to stay if you *really* want to get away. Marfa is the closest town, but it's still a 45-minute drive from there – one reason the ranch has its own chef. Activities offered include fishing, wildlife photography and mountain biking.

 Eating

Restaurant schedules tend to be fickle around here, so call ahead to double-check hours (or be prepared to be flexible). Restaurants can be closed for seemingly no reason, even on days they're typically supposed to be open. You can pick up a very helpful listing of weekly restaurant hours at the visitor center.

I LOVE...MARFA

Marfa is showing up on-screen again, this time as the backdrop for director Jill Soloway's *I Love Dick*, an Amazon Prime production based on the 1997 novel of the same name by feminist writer Chris Kraus. The show had a single-episode premiere in 2016, complete with mysterious object-of-obsession Dick riding into downtown Marfa on horseback.

The show tracks the shenanigans of a high-strung New York City filmmaker who follows her husband to Marfa after he accepts a writing fellowship at the prestigious but fictional institute that anchors the quirky town. It's social commentary, satire and an engaging story rolled into one. With shots of wide plains and skies, sun-baked neighborhoods and the old-time downtown, plus sounds of the passing train, Marfa is practically a character in the story – the most stable and likable one, it seems.

The bar at the Hotel St George (p309) serves breakfast and lunch daily.

Food Shark
FOOD TRUCK $

(www.foodsharkmarfa.com; 909 W San Antonio St; mains $6-9; ☻noon-3pm Fri-Sun) See that battered old food trailer near the main road through town? If you do, that means Food Shark is open for business. If you're lucky enough to catch it, you'll find incredibly fresh Greek salad and the specialty, the Marfalafel. Daily specials are excellent, and sell out early.

Marfa Burrito
MEXICAN $

(☑325-514-8675; 515 S Highland Ave; burritos $5; ☻6am-2pm) Across the US you can usually assume that a restaurant serves good grub if you see police eating inside. In Marfa, the predictor of goodness is the Border Patrol, and you'll find them chowing down (along with everyone else in town) at this simple place, where big burritos earn high praise. Look for the hand-painted sign outside. Cash only.

Stellina
ITALIAN $

(☑432-729-2030; www.stellinamarfa.com; 103 N Highland Ave; small plates $5-9, mains $10-16; ☻5pm-late) The current Marfa 'in' place, this intimate but convivial restaurant is drawing stylish crowds with its rustic Italian dishes and innovative vegetable starters, which tend to come come pickled, roasted or fried. The long central bar anchors the place, and though it might look impossibly crowded, the hard-working staff keeps service flowing with skill.

Get Go
MARKET $

(☑432-729-3339; www.thegetgomarfa.com; 208 S Dean St; ☻9am-9pm) This fancy-pants grocer caters to the highly developed palates of Marfa's sophisticated world travelers. One must have access to Nicolas Feuillatte champagne, organic goat-milk yogurt and yerba maté tea when one is traveling in the desert, *n'est ce pas?* All kidding aside, it's kind of amazing what wonderful treats you can find in the aisles of this small-town shop.

Squeeze Marfa
CAFE $

(☑432-729-4500; www.squeezemarfa.com; 215 N Highland Ave; mains $8-12; ☻8am-3pm Tue-Sun; ☎) This cute little cafe across from the courthouse serves fresh and healthy breakfasts, lunches and smoothies ($4), all the better to enjoy on the narrow, shady patio. Service can be leisurely, but hey, it's Marfa, what else you gotta do? The address is on Highland, but the entrance is on Lincoln.

Cochineal
AMERICAN $$$

(☑ 432-729-3300; www.cochinealmarfa.com; 107 W San Antonio St; small plates $9-12, mains $22-42; ☺ 5:30-10pm) Foodies flock to this stylish but minimalist eatery (with outdoor courtyard) for a changing menu that showcases high-quality organic ingredients. Portions are generous, so don't be afraid to share a few small plates – maybe along the lines of brisket tacos, oyster-mushroom risotto or housemade ramen with duck breast – in lieu of a full dinner. Reservations are recommended.

Great cocktails (try the tequila old-fashioned), and a decent wine selection too.

🍷 Drinking & Nightlife

Planet Marfa
BAR

(☑ 432-386-5099; 200 S Abbott St; ☺ 2pm-midnight Fri & Sun, to 1am Sun mid-Mar–Nov) Marfa-style nightlife is epitomized in this wonderfully funky open-air bar that's officially open on weekends from spring break to Thanksgiving. There's usually live music at night, and shelters are scattered about to protect you from the elements. If you're lucky, someone will save you a spot inside the tipi.

Lost Horse
BAR

(☑ 432-729-4499; www.losthorsesaloon.com; 306 E San Antonio St; ☺ 4pm-midnight Sun-Fri, to 1am Sat) Follow the crack of pool balls and the crooning of a solitary country-and-western singer to find this atmospheric cowboy bar on the main strip. It has saddles, skulls and taxidermy, and an eye-patch-wearing owner named Ty Mitchell. Thirsty folk shouldn't miss this Texas classic writ large.

Capri
COCKTAIL BAR

(☑ 432-729-1984; www.thunderbirdmarfa.com; 601 W San Antonio St; ☺ noon-midnight) For a civilized drink, step into the cool confines of this new cocktail bar that's part of the revamped Thunderbird motel complex, where you'll find the Chinati crowd having a postwork tipple. Inviting patio, too. The service vibe can be a bit too-cool-for-school, but just keep drinking that hibiscus margarita and it won't matter anymore.

🛍 Shopping

Marfa Book Company
BOOKS

(☑ 432-729-3700; www.marfabookco.com; 105 S Highland Ave; ☺ 9am-8pm) A book-lover's oasis in desolate West Texas, Marfa Book Company stocks art books, guidebooks and a large selection of Texas literature. Located on the 1st floor of the Hotel St George (p309).

Freda
ARTS & CRAFTS

(☑ 432-729-2000; www.shop-freda.com; 207 S Highland Ave; ☺ noon-6pm Wed-Sun) This tiny shop sells locally made art, jewelry and apothecary items like salves and serums.

ℹ Information

Marfa Visitors Center (☑ 432-729-4772; www.visitmarfa.com; 302 S Highland Ave; ☺ 8am-5pm Mon-Fri, 10am-4pm Sat & Sun except event weekends) Lots of great information on galleries, restaurants and local attractions. The restaurant handout, with detailed opening hours for all the eateries in town, is superhelpful, especially if you're visiting during the off-season, or on a Monday or Tuesday (p312).

Marfa Public Library (☑ 432-729-4631; www.marfapubliclibrary.org; 115 E Oak St; ☺ 9am-5pm Mon-Wed & Fri, to 6pm Thu, 10am-2pm Sat; 🛜) Free wi-fi and internet access

ℹ Getting There & Away

There's an airport in Marfa, but you can't catch a flight there unless you actually charter one. The closest commercial airports are 156 miles away at **Midland** and 190 miles away at **El Paso** (p327).

You can, however, catch a Greyhound. The **bus station** (☑ 432-729-1992; 1412 Berlin St) is on Berlin St, just west of downtown. For train service, Amtrak serves nearby Alpine (26 miles away).

Alpine

☑ 432 / POP 5952

Packed tight with hotels and eateries, plus residents who are pretty darn friendly, Alpine works well as a base camp for regional exploring. Centrally located between Fort Davis, Marfa and Marathon, Alpine is about a half-hour drive from any of them. And it's not just a geographical hub: it's the seat of Brewster County and the biggest of the four towns, offering services and amenities the others don't.

As the only city in the area with more than 5000 people, it also has the area's sole four-year college and its only modern hospital. Plus it serves as a transportation center, with Amtrak and Greyhound stations in the heart of downtown.

US 90 through downtown splits into two one-way thoroughfares. Avenue E rolls west while traffic on Holland Ave runs east.

⦿ Sights

Museum of the Big Bend
MUSEUM

(☑ 432-837-8143; www.museumofthebigbend.com; 400 N Harrison St; donations accepted; ☺ 9am-5pm Tue-Sat, 1-5pm Sun) FREE On the campus

WHEN TO GO

Yep, it's small. Go 1 mile in any direction from the center of town, and you've just left town. Also, Marfa is on its own schedule, which is pretty much made up according to whim. Plan on coming late in the week or on a weekend, because more than half the places you'll want to visit are closed early in the week. To repeat: do *not* visit on a Monday or Tuesday.

of **Sul Ross State University**, this little museum is a great place to delve into the past, with exhibits on marine fossils (a warm shallow sea covered Big Bend 135 million years ago), Native American pictographs, Spanish missionaries, Mexican pioneers, buffalo soldiers (the nickname for the African American soldiers who fought in the Civil War) and – of course – cowboys, with a full-scale chuck wagon on display.

The multimedia museum is designed for maximum visual appeal, incorporating broad and impressive re-creations rather than cases full of relics. Reading is kept to a minimum, but, when called for, the beautifully designed signage draws you right in.

Hancock Hill
VIEWPOINT

(E Ave B) Behind Sul Ross State University, a trail leads up the dusty slopes of Hancock Hill. There are fine views of the area and some curious artifacts here – including a battered school desk that some uni students dragged up in 1981. To reach it, head uphill to the first rock pile and follow the trail to the right; it's about a 20-minute walk. For more information and directions, visit www.sulross.edu/page/1077/desk.

🌄 Tours

Teri Smith Rock Hunts
OUTDOORS

(☑ 432-837-2451; www.terismithrockhunts.com) Teri Smith, who owns Antelope Lodge, leads weekly rock hunts on various local ranches – you might find agate, jasper, calcite, petrified wood or fossils. The ranches charge various fees for entry ($10 to $50), plus there's a required membership with the Rollin' Rock Club ($10 to $16) or an approved Texas rock club. Details on the website. No summer trips.

✹✷ Festivals & Events

Cowboy Poetry Gathering
CULTURAL

(☑ 432-837-2326; www.texascowboypoetry.com; ☉ Feb/Mar) Preserving the oral tradition of the American West, the annual Cowboy Poetry Gathering is held every year in late February or early March. This down-home event takes over most of town, from university classrooms to Kokernot Park. Poetry recitations, gun-twirling pistolero demonstrations and chuck-wagon breakfasts are just some of the activities on hand.

🛏 Sleeping

You must book hotel rooms several months in advance if you plan on attending the Cowboy Poetry Gathering (p312). Visit the website of the Alpine Chamber of Commerce (www.alpinetexas.com) for more lodging options.

Antelope Lodge
CABIN $

(☑ 432-837-2451; www.antelopelodge.com; 2310 W Hwy 90; s $53-75, d $58-80, ste $105-130; 🅿 ❄ 🛜 🐾) You'd think from the name you were getting a hunting lodge, but it's nothing like that. Rustic stucco cottages with Spanish-tile roofs – each one holding two guest rooms – sit sprinkled about a shady lawn. There's a casual, pleasant vibe, and the rooms have kitchenettes. Ask the geologically minded owner about her guided rock hunts.

Pets cost $15 per night per pet.

★ Holland Hotel
HISTORIC HOTEL $$

(☑ 432-837-2800; www.thehollandhoteltexas.com; 209 W Holland Ave; r $150-225, ste $170-250; 🅿 ❄ 🛜 🐾) Built in 1928, this beautifully renovated Spanish Colonial building has elegantly furnished rooms set with carved wood furniture, Western-style artwork and sleek modern bathrooms. The lobby, with its stuffed leather chairs and wood-beamed ceiling, is a classy place to unwind; there's a good high-end restaurant, the Century Bar & Grill, attached. Solo traveler on a budget? Try the tiny 'Nina's Room' ($95).

Fair warning: the train tracks run right by here, so wear the provided earplugs or risk being awoken by a friendly *woo-woo* in the night. A bonus: you can use the swimming pool at the Holland's sister property, the Maverick Inn.

Maverick Inn
MOTEL $$

(☑ 432-837-0628; www.themaverickinn.com; 1200 E Holland Ave; r $120-150; 🅿 ❄ 🛜 🐾 🐾) Maverick road-trippers will feel right at home at this retro motel that's been smartly renovated with luxury bedding and flat-screen TVs. Rooms have Texas-style furnishings and terracotta floors, and the pool looks mighty nice after a hot, dusty day. You can also borrow a guitar or peruse Texas coffee-table books in the lobby. We like your attitude, Maverick Inn.

The pet fee is $25 per pet per stay.

Eating

Alicia's Burrito Place
MEXICAN $

(☑432-837-2802; 708 E Gallego Ave; mains $5-12; ☉9am-3pm Mon, 8am-3pm Tue-Sun) Alicia's is known for its quick and hot breakfast burritos: eggs, bacon and the like get rolled up in a portable meal you can eat with your hands – known to cure a hangover or two in their time. The Mexican cheeseburger is also a favorite. Drive-through service is available. Cash only.

Reata
STEAK $$

(☑432-837-9232; www.reata.net; 203 N 5th St; lunch $10-15, dinner $13-40; ☉11:30am-2pm & 5-10pm Mon-Sat) Named after the ranch in the movie *Giant,* Reata turns on the upscale ranch-style charm – at least in the front dining room, where the serious diners go. Step back into the lively bar area or onto the shady patio for a completely different vibe, where you can feel free to nibble your way around the menu and enjoy a margarita.

Century Bar & Grill
AMERICAN $$

(☑432-837-1922; www.thecenturybarandgrill.com; 209 W Holland Ave; mains $13-34; ☉5-9pm Tue-Thu, to 10pm Fri & Sat, 11am-2pm & 5-9pm Sun) Located inside the Holland Hotel (p312), this place has the same vibe as the rest of the building: historic but fashionable, like a ranch done in dark woods with splashy touches. The excellent food – American, but leaning toward Texan – is a nice addition to the Alpine dining line-up. Good bar scene too. Reservations recommended.

Drinking & Nightlife

Big Bend Brewing Co
MICROBREWERY

(☑432-837-3700; www.bigbendbrewing.com; 3401 W Hwy 90; ☉tap room 4-6pm Wed-Fri, 1-6pm Sat) The taproom is bare bones at this microbrewery on the outskirts of town, but with picnic tables inside and out, chatty beer drinkers all around and wide-open views of the western landscape, you'll hardly notice the lack of frills. Its flagship Tejas lager is an easy-drinking end to your epic afternoon.

☆ Entertainment

Harry's Tinaja
LIVE MUSIC

(☑432-837-5060; 412 E Holland Ave; ☉noon-2am) This locals' watering hole is fun, a little divey and occasionally even boisterous. You're likely to find friendly old-timers hanging out and telling stories till the wee hours, but if not, there's also a pool table and sometimes there's live music. Posted hours are to 2am, but if you find it closed, it's 'cause no one showed up that night.

Be forewarned, solo-traveling women – you will get chatted up here.

Railroad Blues
LIVE MUSIC

(☑432-837-3103; www.railroadblues.com; 504 W Holland Ave; ☉4pm-2am Mon-Sat) This is the place to go in Alpine for live music and the biggest beer selection in Big Bend Country. The club has hosted an impressive list of musicians, and sometimes draws Austin-based bands heading west on tour. If you'd rather just enjoy some friendly conversation, hit up happy hour (4pm to 7pm).

Open Sundays on holiday weekends and for the Super Bowl.

Shopping

Front Street Books
BOOKS

(☑432-837-3360; www.fsbooks.com; 121 E Holland Ave; ☉9am-6pm Mon-Fri, 10am-6pm Sat, 1-6pm Sun) The best bookstore in town is open daily and has a smart selection of new, used and out-of-print titles, as well as a good selection of regionally themed books. With a surprising number of well-known authors living in the area, this bookstore has some pretty big-city book signings, too. The helpful staff are what indie bookstores are all about.

Kiowa Gallery
ARTS & CRAFTS

(☑432-837-3067; 105 E Holland Ave; ☉10am-5pm Tue-Fri, 10:30am-5pm Sat) Paintings, folk art, cool crafts and jewelry fill this space, floor to ceiling. Offerings range from real art to just fun stuff to hang on the wall, all with a uniquely 'west Texas' take on things.

ℹ Information

INTERNET ACCESS

Alpine Public Library (☑432-837-2621; www.alpinepubliclibrary.org; 805 W Ave E; ☉9:30am-6pm Tue, Thu, Fri, to 9pm Wed, 10am-2pm Sat; 🛜) Free internet access.

MEDICAL SERVICES

Big Bend Regional Medical Center (☑432-837-3447; www.bigbendhealthcare.com; 2600

Hwy 118 N) One of the region's state-of-the-art hospitals, offering basic care and a 24-hour emergency room.

MONEY

Fort Davis State Bank (☑ 432-837-1888; www.fdsb.com; 1102 E Holland Ave; ⊘ ATM 24hr, lobby 9am-3pm Mon-Fri, drive-through service 8am-5:30pm Mon-Thu, to 6pm Fri, 9am-noon Sat) A 24-hour ATM service near Sul Ross State University.

West Texas National Bank (☑ 432-837-3375; www.wtnb.com; 101 E Ave E; ⊘ ATM 24hr, lobby 9am-3pm Mon-Fri, drive-through service 7:30am-6pm Mon-Fri, 9am-noon Sat) A 24-hour ATM service right in the middle of town.

POST

Alpine Post Office (☑ 432-837-9565; www.usps.com; 901 W Holland Ave; ⊘ 8am-4pm Mon-Fri, 10am-1pm Sat)

TOURIST INFORMATION

Alpine Chamber of Commerce (☑ 432-837-2326; www.alpinetexas.com; 106 N 3rd St; ⊘ 9am-5pm Mon-Fri, to 2pm Sat) Alpine's Main St organization has put together a *Historic Walking Tour* brochure featuring 44 stops in the downtown area. Pick up a copy at the chamber of commerce.

❶ Getting There & Away

There are no scheduled flights round these parts, but Alpine's airport, north of town along Hwy 118, can accommodate charter flights.

Greyhound (☑ 432-837-5497; www.greyhound.com; KCS Quick Stop, 2305 E Hwy 90; ⊘ 6am-10pm) offers bus service to and from El Paso and San Antonio, with a transfer in Fort Stockton. Buy tickets online or at the convenience store where the bus stops.

Rental cars are available from **Alpine Auto Rental** (☑ 432-837-3463; www.alpineautorental.com; 2501 E Hwy 90; ⊘ 8am-6pm Mon-Sat).

Amtrak's *Texas Eagle* and *Sunset Limited* routes stop at the **train station** (☑ 800-872-7245; www.amtrak.com; 102 W Holland Ave). Service frequently runs late, so it's important to call Amtrak to get an update before setting out. Check the website for prices and schedules.

Marathon

☑ 432 / POP 430

This tiny railroad town has two claims to fame. First, it's the closest town to Big Bend's north entrance, providing a last chance to fill up your car and your stomach before immersing yourself in the park. And it's got the Gage Hotel, a true Texas treasure that's

a worthwhile reason to stay awhile – or at least overnight.

Just don't show up and say 'Mar-a-*thon*' like it's a race. If you want to fit in 'round these parts you've got to say 'Mar-a-*thun*' – and it helps if you're wearing a hat and give a friendly nod each time you say it.

◉ Sights

Target Marathon   LANDMARK
(Hwy 90) At some point in early 2016, a tiny cinderblock shack on US 90 morphed into Target Marathon, complete with the Target bull's-eye. There's nothing here except a sly nod to Prada Marfa (p309), itself a sly nod to commercialism and art. We think. Whatever it symbolizes, guerrilla art in the middle of nowhere is always fun for a selfie.

The building is on the south side of the highway beside the railroad tracks, about 15 miles west of Marathon, midway to Alpine. It could disappear at any time, but for now it's easy to spot.

✷ Festivals & Events

Marathon2Marathon   SPORTS
(www.marathon2marathon.net; ⊘ Oct) Pronunciation aside, with a name like Marathon, this was bound to happen. This race is a 26.2-mile run through the desert from Alpine to Marathon, and it's a qualifying race for the Boston Marathon (which after west Texas should be a cinch). Runners and spectators alike mark the occasion with a street festival.

⛏ Sleeping

Marathon Motel & RV Park   CABIN $
(☑ 432-386-4241;   www.marathonmotel.com; 701 US Hwy 90; r $80-130, tent/RV sites $15/35; ✴ ☎ ☎) A lot of places in Texas seem to have their claim to fame: for this renovated 1940s motel, it's that it was used as a filming location in the Wim Wenders movie *Paris, Texas*. The cabins are rustic but cute, and a lovely central courtyard surrounded by an adobe wall makes a nice place to hang out.

Gage Hotel   HISTORIC HOTEL $$$
(☑ 432-386-4205; www.gagehotel.com; 102 NW 1st St/Hwy 90; r $229-279; ✴ @ ☎ ☎) This Old West hotel has a fabulous style that's matched only by its love of taxidermy. Each room at this property is individually (though similarly) decorated with Native American blankets, cowboy gear and leather accents. The original building was

designed by Henry Trost and built in 1927, while the Los Portales annex has more expensive rooms that surround the lovely pool.

Room 10 is rumored to be haunted, and you might hear a whispering ghost hunter or two in the hallway early in the evening (although at this price point that shouldn't be happening?). Our slumber in room 10 was disappointingly ghost-free.

✖ Eating

French Co Grocer   MARKET $
(✐432-386-4522;   www.frenchcogrocer.com; 206 N Ave D; sandwiches $5-6, pizzas $9-18; ⊙7:30am-9pm Mon-Fri, from 8am Sat, from 9am Sun; ⊚) Stock up on picnic supplies for the road or enjoy them at the tables outside at this charming little grocery store – formerly the WM French General Merchandise store, established in 1900. It also stocks toothbrushes, fresh-baked cookies, wine, cookout necessities, hats – things you might need if, oh, say, you were about to go camp in a remote national park.

12 Gage   AMERICAN, FUSION $$$
(✐432-386-4205; www.gagehotel.com; 101 US 90 W; mains $21-45; ⊙6-9pm Sun-Thu, to 10pm Fri & Sat) In a ranch-fabulous setting, the 12 Gage serves a seasonal menu of creative fusion fare, with underlying Western themes (meaning meat). Think Moroccan-spiced lamb chops, sriracha-braised osso buco and Texas quail with Italian prosciutto and tomato-mushroom risotto cakes. Cowskin-covered chairs, chandeliers made of horns and a modicum of taxidermy add to the atmosphere, which is remarkably elegant.

🍺 Drinking & Nightlife

V6 Coffee Bar   COFFEE
(✐432-386-4205; www.gagehotel.com; 109 NE 1st St; ⊙7am-5pm) Whoa! The nitro iced coffee here is really darn good. Mix it up right and you'll be set for your drive to the national park down the road. Nice service too, and the place shines with a modern but inviting interior. Run by the Gage Hotel, but a few steps away, the shop also sells sandwiches and cookies.

White Buffalo Bar   BAR
(✐432-386-4205; www.gagehotel.com; 102 NW 1st St; ⊙4pm-midnight Sun-Thu, 3pm-2am Fri & Sat) Guess what's on the wall of this upscale bar located in the Gage Hotel (p314)? Not just taxidermy but *rare* taxidermy. Enjoy a margarita and just try to ignore the glassy stare of the enormous white buffalo. You might catch live music on the patio.

ℹ Information

Marathon Chamber of Commerce (www.visitmarathontexas.com; 105 Hwy 90 W) Check the website for local information. There's also a small information kiosk at the intersections of US 90 and US 385.

ℹ Getting There & Away

There is no public transportation to Marathon. Amtrak serves Alpine, which is 32 miles west on Hwy 90.

EL PASO

📞915 / POP 681,824

El Paso has found its cool. Long considered a sleepy western town (it's as far west as you can get in Texas), El Paso moseyed along, keeping its head low while dangerous Ciudad Juarez (just over the Rio Grande) grabbed headlines to the south and New Mexico grabbed tourists to the north. But no more.

A sleek new hotel has opened downtown, luring locals back to the city's core for socializing and dining. A streetcar line linking downtown and the University of Texas at El Paso (UTEP) is under construction. The new Montecillo entertainment and residential district to the west is booming. The city even has a new baseball team, the El Paso Chihuahuas. And the ultimate arbiter of cool? The city's first microbrewery opened in 2015.

Outdoorsy types have it made here: there's cycling and hiking in the largest urban park in the US, and the nearby Hueco Tanks State Park (p317) is ideal for wintertime rock climbing. Prefer the indoors? The city's top museums are free. Best of all is the hospitality of the locals, which makes this city of nearly 700,000 feel a whole lot smaller.

History

Native Americans had already settled the El Paso area for thousands of years when Spanish explorers first arrived in the 1530s. What is now the Mexican city of Juárez was founded in 1659 as 'El Paso del Norte,' but it wasn't until 1827 that the first permanent settlements were established on the northern banks of the Rio Grande on the site of what is today El Paso.

By 1873, El Paso had been incorporated as a Texas city. The Southern Pacific Railroad came to town in 1881, bringing with it gunfighters like John Wesley Hardin and kicking off El Paso's 'Wild West' era.

In 1911 the Mexican Revolution, led by Pancho Villa, sent many Mexicans fleeing from Juárez to safety in El Paso, but it also stirred up controversy over the precise location of the US–Mexico border. The Chamizal Convention of 1963 settled it once and for all, and the two cities sit on opposite banks of the Rio Grande, together but separate.

⊙ Sights

⊙ Downtown

★ El Paso Museum of Art   MUSEUM
(Map p324; ☑ 915-212-0300; www.elpasoart museum.org; 1 Arts Festival Plaza; ⊕ 9am-5pm Tue-Sat, to 9pm Thu, noon-5pm Sun) FREE This thoroughly enjoyable museum is in a former Greyhound station. They'd want us to brag about their Italian *Madonna and Child* (c 1200), but the Southwestern art is terrific, and the engaging modern pieces round out the collection nicely. All this *and* it's free? Well done, El Paso, well done.

El Paso Holocaust Museum   MUSEUM
(Map p324; ☑ 915-351-0048; www.elpasoholo caustmuseum.org; 715 N Oregon St; ⊕ 9am-5pm Tue-Fri, 1-5pm Sat & Sun) FREE It may seem a little incongruous in a predominately Hispanic town, but the Holocaust Museum is as much a surprise inside as out for its thoughtful and moving exhibits, which are imaginatively presented for maximum impact.

LOS MURALES STREET ART

They're not always mentioned in guidebooks – maybe because they're primarily in the poorest areas of town – but Los Murales, the street murals of El Paso, are perhaps the city's preeminent cultural treasure. Of the more than 100 murals in the city, the greatest concentrations are south of downtown between Paisano Dr and the Border Hwy, and north of Paisano Dr near Douglass Elementary School. There are also more than 40 murals painted on the freeway columns around Durazno Ave between Copia and Raynolds Sts. Stop by the downtown **visitor center** (p327) for a map.

Magoffin Home   HISTORIC BUILDING
(Map p324; ☑ 915-533-5147; www.visitmagoffin home.com; 1120 Magoffin Ave; adult/child 6-18yr/ child 5yr & under $4/3/free; ⊕ 9am-5pm Tue-Sat, noon-5pm Sun) One of Texas' best-kept secrets, this El Paso landmark was built in 1875 for Joseph Magoffin, an early El Paso politician and businessman. With 4ft-thick adobe walls and many original furnishings, the home is a fine example of the Southwest territorial style of architecture prevalent during the late 19th century. Self-guided and guided tours are available (check the website for guided tour times, which vary daily).

⊙ North

Franklin Mountains State Park   PARK
(Map p318; ☑ 915-566-6441; www.tpwd.texas.gov; 1331 McKelligon Canyon Rd; adult/child under 13yr $5/free; ⊕ visitor center 8am-4pm Mon-Fri, Tom Mays Unit 8am-5pm May–mid-Sep, 8am-5pm Mon-Fri, 6:30am-8pm Sat & Sun Apr–mid-Sep) At over 24,000 acres, this is the largest urban park in the US. It's a quick escape from the city to the home of ringtail cats, coyotes and countless other smaller animals and reptiles. There's excellent **mountain biking** and **hiking** here, with **North Franklin Peak** (7192ft) looming overhead.

Head to the **visitor center** (Map p318; ☑ 915-566-6441; www.tpwd.texas.gov; 1331 McKelligon Canyon Rd; ⊕ 8am-4pm) to get a basic park map, written descriptions of the hiking trails, mountain-bike trail maps, or route maps of the 17 different **rock-climbing** routes. (The visitor center will be relocating in 2018, so confirm the location before setting out.) You'll find most of the trails in the Tom Mays Unit of the park, which is east of the I-10 off Transmountain Rd.

Wyler Aerial Tramway   CABLE CAR, VIEWPOINT
(Map p318; ☑ 915-566-6622; www.tpwd.texas.gov; 1700 McKinley Ave; adult/child under 13yr $8/4; ⊕ noon-7pm Fri & Sat, 10am-5pm Sun) Sure, you'd feel a sense of accomplishment if you hiked to the top of the Franklin Mountains. We're not suggesting you take the easy way out (or are we?), but it only takes about four minutes to the top via this gondola system. After gliding 2600ft and gaining 940ft in elevation, you'll reach the viewing platform on top of **Ranger Peak** (5632ft), where you'll enjoy spectacular views of Texas, New Mexico and Mexico.

For maximum enjoyment, bring binoculars and a jacket – maybe even a picnic to enjoy at the top (but leave alcohol and glass bottles at home). Call ahead to make sure the gondola is not closed due to high winds.

First Armored Division & Fort Bliss Museum   MUSEUM

(Map p318; ☑ 915-568-4512; www.bliss.army.mil/museum; Bldg 1735 Marshall Rd; ☺ 9am-4pm Mon-Fri, 10am-3pm Sat) FREE As the largest air-defense training center in the Western world, **Fort Bliss** consumes much of the desert northeast of El Paso, and trains troops from all the NATO-allied nations. The museum's collection depicts the history of the fort from 1849 to the present. The big draw inside and out of this 50,000-sq-ft space? The big artillery, from missiles to tanks.

Currently, you can only enter the fort with a Visitor's Pass, issued after you provide a valid, US approved form of ID (driver's license, passport, state ID etc). Your best bet for an entry gate is the Buffalo Soldier Gate off Airway Blvd. The museum is next to the commissary. Call the museum if you run into any problems entering the fort.

◉ East

Hueco Tanks State Park & Historical Site   PARK

(☑ park 915-857-1135, reservations 512-389-8911; www.tpwd.texas.gov; 6900 Hueco Tanks Rd No 1/FM 2775; adult/child under 13yr $7/free; ☺ 8am-6pm Mon-Thu, 7am-7pm Fri-Sun May-Sep, 8am-6pm Oct-Apr) About 32 miles east of El Paso, this 860-acre park contains three small granite mountains that are pocked with depressions (*hueco* is Spanish for 'hollow') that hold rainwater, creating an oasis in the barren desert. The area has attracted humans for as long as 10,000 years, as evidenced by a chipped stone spear point found at the site. Park staff estimate there are more than 2000 **pictographs** here, some dating back 5000 years.

To minimize human impact, a daily visitor quota is enforced: make reservations up to 90 days in advance to gain entry. At park headquarters you'll find a small gift shop, an interpretive center and 20 campsites ($12 to $16). You can explore the North Mountain area by yourself, but to hike deeper into the park – where the more interesting pictographs are – you must reserve and join one of the pictograph, birding or bouldering/hiking **guided tours** (☑ 915-849-6684), which run Wednesday through Sunday when guides are available. Before camping

---

❶ WHAT TIME IS IT?

When it comes to time zones, El Paso sides with New Mexico, conforming to Mountain Time rather than Central Time like the rest of Texas. Confusing? Occasionally, if you're telling someone in neighboring Van Horn or Fort Stockton what time you'll meet them, be sure to add on the extra hour you'll lose just by leaving El Paso.

---

or taking a self-guided tour, visitors much watch the park orientation video.

If you're into **rock climbing**, chances are you already know about Hueco Tanks, which ranks among the world's top climbing destinations during winter months (October through early April), when other prime climbs become inaccessible. In summer, however, the desert sun generally makes the rocks too hot to handle.

El Paso Zoo   ZOO

(Map p318; ☑ 915-212-0966; www.elpasozoo.org; 4001 E Paisano Dr; adult/child 3-12yr/senior $12/7.50/9; ☺ 9:30am-5pm, last admission 4pm) Home to a large number of endangered animals, including the Asian elephant, Sumatran orangutan, Malayan tiger and the rare Amur leopard. All told, more than 670 animals represent 231 species, all packed into 35 acres. You can catch a free-flight bird show in the new Wildlife Amphitheater, which added 4000 sq ft for housing birds, mammals, reptiles and invertebrates.

Overall, it's not the biggest or most impressive zoo you've ever seen, but it's worth a visit. And it's mercifully shady for both the animals and you.

◉ West

National Border Patrol Museum   MUSEUM

(☑ 915-759-6060; www.borderpatrolmuseum.com; 4315 Transmountain Rd; ☺ 9am-5pm Tue-Sat) FREE This small but informative museum spotlights the history and activities of the US Border Patrol, which was originally funded in 1924, three days after Congress passed the *National Origins Act,* a law that severely limited immigration based on country-of-origin quotas. The collection of tools and vehicles used to cross the border and elude capture is fascinating, from ladders to boats to motorized hanggliders.

Greater El Paso

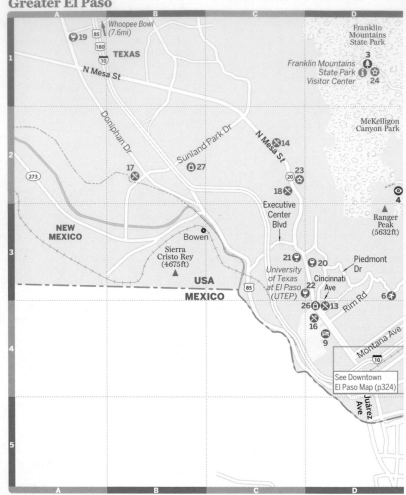

El Paso Museum of Archaeology MUSEUM
(📞915-755-4332; http://archaeology.elpasotexas. gov; 4301 Transmountain Rd; ⊙9am-5pm Tue-Sat) **FREE** The dioramas depicting the lives of the region's ancient peoples aren't particularly illuminating, but the baskets, pottery and hunting tools created by their Native American descendants are worth a look. The centuries-old effigy pots – complete with faces – are especially cool.

Outside you'll find a **desert garden** and 15 miles of **nature trails**. But be careful where you step – rattlesnakes and unexploded ordnance are posted hazards!

🏃 Activities

Scenic Drive SCENIC DRIVE
(Map p318) Popular at night for city-lights viewing, Scenic Dr offers great views of El Paso, Juárez and the surrounding mountains. Take N Mesa St to Kerbey Ave (across from the university), head east till it becomes Rim Rd, then turn right on Scenic Dr. En route, keep an eye out for little **Murchison Park** (4222ft), a fine spot for sunrises.

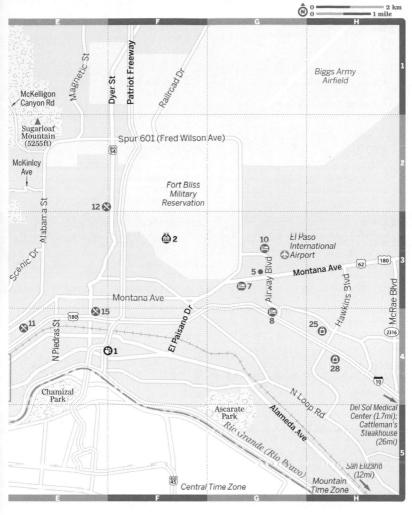

👉 Tours

Crazy Cat Cyclery CYCLING
(Map p318; ☑ 915-772-9666; www.crazycatcyclery.
com; 6625 Montana Ave; full-day bike rental $30-
45; ⊙9am-7pm Mon-Sat, to 5pm Sun) The best
source of local cycling information and
equipment. Some of the city's best mountain biking is five minutes away, and staff
will point you in the right direction and sell
you a map if you'd like one. They also offer
scheduled group rides led by enthusiastic
cyclists.

Border Sights Tours TOURS
(☑ 915-533-5454; www.bordersights-tours-of-elpaso.
com; adult/child under 19yr $50/23) Tours of the
city, the Mission Trail (p321) and more, as
well as specialty tours (for extra charge) like
wine-tasting – all north of the border. Pickup
at your location available.

🎊 Festivals & Events

Viva El Paso! CULTURAL
(☑ 915-231-1165; www.viva-ep.org; ⊙Jun-Aug)
Singing! Dancing! History! Exclamation
points! For a lively introduction to local
history, head for Viva El Paso!, an outdoor

Greater El Paso

theatrical extravaganza held Friday and Saturday nights, and on a couple of Sundays, every summer in McKelligon Canyon Park's amphitheater (p326).

Sun City Music Festival MUSIC
(www.facebook.com/suncitymusicfestival; Ascarate Park; ⊙ Sep) More than 20,000 fans of electronic dance music – and wild costumes – head to Ascarate Park in early September for this two-day festival with three stages. Recent headliners include Skrillex and the Chainsmokers.

Sun Bowl College Football Classic SPORTS
(☑915-533-4416, 800-915-2695; www.sunbowl. org; 2701 Sun Bowl Dr; ⊙ Dec) Takes place the last week in December at Sun Bowl Stadium, with many pregame events held throughout the holiday season.

🛏 Sleeping

Almost every hotel in El Paso is a chain; you'll need to cross into New Mexico to find a B&B. Budget motels mainly cluster on N Mesa St around the university and on Montana Ave near the airport and Fort Bliss.

Most of the top-end hotels cater to business clients. This makes weekday stays at these places rather pricey, but most offer good deals Friday through Sunday.

🛏 Downtown

Gardner Hotel HOTEL, HOSTEL $
(Map p324; ☑915-532-3661; www.gardnerhotel. com; 311 E Franklin Ave; r $63-70; 🛜) Fresh from a makeover on *Hotel Impossible* in 2016, El Paso's oldest continually operating hotel has a newfound cool. But don't worry history fans, it probably hasn't changed too much since John Dillinger stayed here in the 1930s (hint: room 221 is where the outlaw slept).

The basic rooms are carpeted and fan-cooled only, but the lobby, with its leather armchairs and historical mementos, is a fine place to unwind. The Gardner also has hostel-style dorm rooms (from $25).

Hotel Indigo BOUTIQUE HOTEL $$
(Map p324; ☑915-532-5200; www.ihg.com; 325 N Kansas St; r from $196; P🕸@🛜🏊🐾) Downtown El Paso has a new spring in its step, thanks in part to this 2016 hotel. From young business travelers passing through to locals sipping cocktails in the glossy bar, the Indigo has become a destination itself. Modern but inviting rooms start above the 5th floor – home to the lobby, the bar and the pool – so views are big.

There's also an on-site restaurant, the Downtowner.

Holiday Inn Express
El Paso – Central
HOTEL **$$**

(Map p324; 915-544-3333; www.hiexpress.com; 409 E Missouri Ave; r $114-131; [P][⊜][@][⊚][≋][※]) Sure, it's wedged between a freeway and train tracks, but it still manages to be surprisingly quiet and calm inside. The rooms are cheerful and up to date, and breakfast is included. Pet fee is $25 per stay.

Doubletree El Paso Downtown
HOTEL **$$**

(Map p324; 915-532-8733; http://double tree.hilton.com; 600 N El Paso St; r from $199; [P][⊗][⊚][≅]) The former International Hotel is one of the nicer places downtown. The rooms are luxuriously smart, with pleasing color palettes and all the little niceties you could want.

East West

Hilton Garden Inn
HOTEL **$$**

(Map p318; 915-351-2121; www.hiltongardeninn. com; 111 W University Ave; r $149-199; [P][※][@][⊚][≋]) Opened at the edge of UTEP, the Garden Inn was built to blend with campus architecture. So, of course, it resembles a Bhutanese *dzong* (religious fortress) – what else? (Architects thought the style would fit the desert-mountain landscape.)

The interior, however, is more 'nice chain hotel' than 'exotic monastery.'

Casa de Suenos
B&B **$$**

(575-874-9166; www.casaofdreams.com; 405 Mountain Vista Rd S, La Union, NM; r $104-110; [⊜][⊚]) El Paso may not have a bed and breakfast, but New Mexico does, and it's just 20 miles from downtown. The decor is uber-Southwestern, but it's a serene retreat from the city. Breakfast is included.

East

Coral Motel
MOTEL **$**

(Map p318; 915-772-3263; www.coralmotel.net; 6420 Montana Ave; r $45-55; [P][※][⊚]) Anyone who loves 1950s roadside nostalgia will feel right at home at this friendly little motel, replete with Spanish-style barrel-tile roof and *Jetsons*-esque sign. Rooms are simple – white cinder-block walls, floral bedspreads and dated bathrooms – but you can't beat the price.

Hampton Inn & Suites
El Paso – Airport
HOTEL **$$**

(Map p318; 915-771-6644; http://hamptoninn. hilton.com; 6635 Gateway Blvd; r/ste $189/199; [P][※][@][⊚][≋]) Beside the I-10 and close to the airport, this place is busy. But cordial

---

EXPLORING THE MISSION TRAIL

Ready for some local history? This 9-mile trail links two mission churches and a presidio chapel, all of which are on the National Register of Historic Places. Privately owned by the Catholic Diocese, they're not always as visitor friendly as you might like, but you can arrange a tour or get more information from the **Mission Valley Visitors Information Center** (http://visitelpasomissiontrail.com; 9065 Alameda Ave; ⊙9am-4pm Mon-Fri, to 3pm Sat & Sun; ⊚).

The best known of the three is **Mission Ysleta** (915-859-9848; www.ysletamission. org; 131 S Zaragoza Rd; ⊙7am-4pm Mon-Sat) **FREE**, Texas' oldest continually active parish. Although the original structure from 1682 is long gone, the current church, built from adobe bricks, clay and straw, dates back to 1851, and a beautiful, silver-domed **bell tower** was added in the 1880s.

Two miles from Ysleta is **Socorro Mission** (915-859-7718; http://visitelpasomission trail.com; 328 S Nevarez Rd; ⊙10am-4pm Mon-Fri, 9am-6pm Sat, 9am-1pm Sun) **FREE**. Originally built in 1681 by the Piro tribe of Native Americans, who later assimilated into the Tiguas, the church was repeatedly rebuilt after Rio Grande flooding. Although the outside is fairly plain, the inside has some impressive decorative touches, including beautifully hand-painted **roof beams** rescued from the 18th-century mission.

The last stop is the **presidio chapel of San Elizario** (915-851-2333; http://visitel pasomissiontrail.com; 1556 San Elizario Rd, San Elizario; ⊙7am-9:30am Mon-Fri, open for Mass Sat & Sun) **FREE**, with roots tracing back to a nearby military fort which was established for the Spanish government in 1684. Today, peaceful San Elizario, a city about 20 miles southeast of downtown El Paso, is notable for its 1882 church and the adjacent town plaza, where Juan de Oñate issued his 1598 proclamation claiming the region for Spain.

staff keep the ship sailing skillfully – with friendly reminders to enjoy the complimentary happy hour with alcoholic beverages and snacks (Monday to Thursday 5pm to 7:30pm). Spacious rooms boast a classically modern style. Extended stay? Suites with kitchens are available, plus there's a laundry on-site. Breakfast is included.

Wyndham El Paso Airport HOTEL $$

(Map p318; 915-778-4241; www.wyndham hotels.com; 2027 Airway Blvd; r $122-135, ste $140-243; P💺🐕@🛜❄🏊🏋) Late arrival? Early departure? Staying 600ft from the airport has its advantages. But this place has more to offer than just proximity: it also has the biggest and best hotel pool in town – complete with a lofty corkscrew water slide!

Pet fee is $25 per stay.

✖ Eating

El Paso has dozens of good Mexican restaurants (the red enchiladas are especially renowned); it's also known for steakhouses.

Lots of buzzy new restaurants and bars are opening in the Montecillo district in west El Paso, about 4 miles north of UTEP via N Mesa St (a fairly easy stop if you're driving from New Mexico on the I-10).

✖ Downtown

H&H Coffee Shop MEXICAN $

(Map p324; 915-533-1144; 701 E Yandell Dr; breakfast mains $5-9, lunch $4-9; ⊙7am-3pm Mon-Sat) It doesn't look like much, but sometimes good things come in weird packages. This hole-in-the-wall – which, curiously, is attached to a car wash – is a well-known breakfast hangout that's authentic El Paso and draws a mix of folks. The car wash is open until 4pm, Monday to Saturday.

Craft & Social AMERICAN $

(Map p324; 915-219-7141; www.craftandsocial. com; 305 E Franklin St; mains $10-12; ⊙11am-10pm Mon-Wed, to 11pm Thu & Fri, 3-11pm Sat, 1-9pm Sun, bar open later Mon-Sat) A welcome addition to El Paso, Craft & Social whips up high-end sandwiches (featuring ingredients such as oven-roasted chicken, Brie and roasted red peppers), artisanal cheese and smoked-meat platters, and zesty salads. All go nicely with craft brews from Belgium, Germany and the USA.

It's an appealing, anytime sort of place, with bar stools, communal tables, a few armchairs and sidewalk seating.

G&R Restaurant MEXICAN $

(Map p324; 915-546-9343; www.grrelp.com; 401 E Nevada Ave; mains $3-11; ⊙8am-8pm Mon-Thu, to 9pm Fri & Sat) Family-owned since 1960, G&R is a local favorite. The colonial-style dining room is fun and colorful – all the better to enjoy the authentic and superaffordable enchiladas, rellenos and burritos.

Green Ingredient VEGETARIAN $$

(Map p324; 915-298-1010; www.greeningre dienteatery.com; 201 E Main St; breakfast & lunch mains $7-19, dinner $9-19; ⊙8am-4pm Mon-Thu, to 8pm Fri) 🌿 Yes, you can find quality vegan and vegetarian fare in the land of cowboys and beef. You just have to walk into the depths of a downtown bank building to find it. Step inside this small but airy place for pancakes and omelets in the morning, salads and sandwiches at lunch and smoothies all day.

Tabla TAPAS $$

(Map p324; 915-533-8935; www.tabla-ep.com; 115 Durango St; small plates $6-28; ⊙11am-10pm Mon-Thu, to 11pm Fri & Sat) Get ready to share all sorts of awesomeness. The small plates here fuse Spanish classics with the flavors of the Southwest in mouthwatering combos like smoked duck with red mole, flank steak with chimichurri, and pork-confit sliders. Tabla is set in a beautifully converted brick warehouse with tall ceilings and an open kitchen.

Cafe Central AMERICAN $$$

(Map p324; 915-545-2233; www.cafecentral. com; 109 N Oregon St; mains lunch $13-15, dinner $20-50; ⊙11am-11pm Mon-Wed, to 2am Thu-Sat) If you've got someone to impress – prices be damned – this is *the* place to go. It's the kind of place where, if you drop your napkin, someone will have picked it up, folded it and handed it back to you before you even notice. The seasonal cuisine is solid, and the small, elegant dining room attracts El Paso's finest patrons.

✖ North

Chicos Tacos MEXICAN $

(Map p318; 3401 Dyer St; tacos $3-5; ⊙9am-midnight) With two locations, Chicos Tacos specializes in its namesake fare – with lots of garlic. Expect a crowd at this fast-food joint from about 10pm to midnight, when El Pasoans citywide experience a collective craving. Crispy rolled tacos, swimming in tomato salsa and shredded cheese, are the specialty.

West

Crisostomo MEXICAN $
(Map p318; www.burritocrisostomo.com; 5658 N Mesa St; burritos $1.25-3.25; ⊙7am-9pm Mon-Fri, to 8pm Sat, to 4pm Sun) What do you do when you run a hugely popular burrito joint in Juárez but your customers stop crossing over to see you? You cross over to them. This Mexican favorite has three locations this side of the border, serving up tasty, filling and inexpensive burritos and quesadillas.

★Crave Kitchen & Bar AMERICAN $$
(Map p318; ☑915-351-3677; www.cravekitchen andbar.com; 300 Cincinnati Ave; breakfast mains $8-18, lunch & dinner $9-28; ⊙7am-11pm Mon-Sat, to 6pm Sun) Winning extra points for style – from the cool sign to the cutlery hanging from the ceiling – this hip little eatery serves up creative comfort food: green-chile mac 'n' cheese, juicy burgers with sweet-potato waffle fries and decadent breakfasts. Lots of craft-beer choices on the menu too. There are several locations across town, including one on the **east side** (☑915-594-7971; www.cravekitchenandbar.com; 11990 Rojas Dr; breakfast mains $8-18, lunch & dinner $9-28; ⊙7am-11pm Mon-Sat, to 6pm Sun).

Geogeske AMERICAN $$
(G2; Map p318; ☑915-544-4242; www.g2geo geske.com; 2701 Stanton St; mains $10-35; ⊙11am-10pm Mon-Thu, to 11pm Fri & Sat) It's hard to describe the strip-mall location: Pleasingly neutral? Not at all strip-mally? No matter, the food is the draw here, both in quality and variety, with everything from sandwiches to Chilean sea bass on the menu. And it's located right on the up-coming trolley line (p328).

Rib Hut BARBECUE $$
(Map p318; ☑915-532-7427; www.ribhutep.com; 2612 N Mesa St; mains $8-24; ⊙11am-10pm Mon-Sat, noon-9pm Sun) Go all Neanderthal-like and join the UTEP crowd over a serious plate of ribs in this funky little A-frame building with typical campus-adjacent decor. Wednesday night is packed for rib night, when ribs are $2.29 each.

State Line BARBECUE $$
(Map p318; ☑915-581-3371; www.countyline.com/ StateLine.html; 1222 Sunland Park Dr; mains lunch $10-35, dinner $14-35; ⊙11:30am-9:30pm Mon-Thu, to 10pm Fri & Sat, to 9pm Sun) Vegetarians, plug your ears: it's hard to say what we like better, the groovy roadhouse-style decor, or the mounds and mounds of delicious, steaming brisket, sausage and ribs.

Stonewood
Modern American Grill STEAK $$$
(Map p318; ☑915-584-2914; www.stonewoodsteak. com; 4935 N Mesa St; mains lunch $12-36, dinner $13-55; ⊙restaurant 11am-11pm, bar to 2am) This stylish venture from the team behind the popular Crave Kitchen & Bar dispels the myth that a quality steakhouse has to look like a wood-paneled man cave. With its welcoming vibe, sleek central bar, high ceiling and open kitchen – where the steaks are cut in-house and grilled over pecan wood – this place works well for date nights and girl-friend gatherings.

East

★L&J Cafe MEXICAN $
(Map p318; ☑915-566-8418; www.landjcafe.com; 3622 E Missouri Ave; mains $8-11; ⊙9am-9pm Sun-Wed, to 10pm Thu-Sat) One of El Paso's best-loved Mexican joints, L&J serves up delicious tacos, fajitas and famous green-chile chicken enchiladas – plus a legendary menudo (tripe stew) on weekends. It's next to the historic Concordia cemetery, and at first glance looks a bit divey. Don't be de-terred: it's been open since 1927, and the inside is much more inviting.

Amigos MEXICAN $
(Map p318; ☑915-533-0155; 2000 Montana Ave; mains $8-11; ⊙6:30am-3pm Mon, to 8pm Tue-Fri, 7am-8pm Sat & Sun) This sunny spot on Mon-tana is a reliable favorite that will jolt your taste buds from their ennui. The friendly owner can let you know which dishes re-ally bring on the *fuego* (fire), or help you pick something suited for a more moderate palate.

★Cattleman's Steakhouse STEAK $$$
(☑915-544-3200; www.cattlemansranch.com; Indian Cliffs Ranch; mains $30-50; ⊙5-10pm Mon-Fri, 12:30-10pm Sat, 12:30-9pm Sun; ▣) This place is 20 miles east of the city, but local folks would probably drive 200 miles to eat here – the food is good and the scenery is even better. Portions are huge, and for just $6 extra you can share a main and gain full access to the family-style sides.

Come early and wander around the grounds of Indian Cliffs Ranch, where you'll see everything from bunnies to buffa-lo waiting for you in their pens, then catch the sunset either before or after your meal.

Downtown El Paso

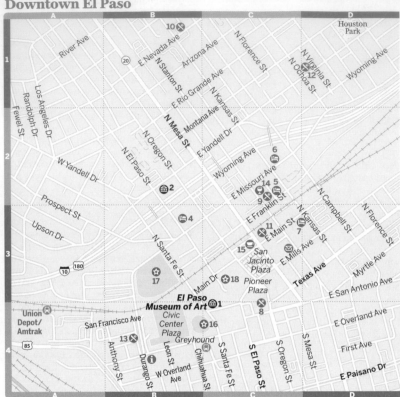

Downtown El Paso

To get there, exit the I-10 at Fabens, then follow the signs to 4.7 miles northeast of the interstate.

🍷 Drinking & Nightlife

The biggest drinking news in El Paso is its new craft-beer craze. The city's first microbrewery opened in 2015, and two more

Thursdays and so much more. Don't miss the back patio: it's a nice spot to chill.

West

★ Hillside Coffee & Donut   COFFEE

(Map p318; ☑ 915-474-3453; www.facebook.com/HillsideCoffee; 4935 N Mesa St; ⊙6am-10pm Sun-Wed, to midnight Thu-Sat) We don't know whether to recommend this place for the iced coffee, the gourmet doughnuts or the welcoming service. How about all three? If you're in west El Paso and need a jolt – from caffeine, sugar or a bright, buzzing locale – stop here. The barista's helpful friendliness almost made us cry, as if we'd encountered a unicorn or something.

It's in the new Montecillo development.

Ode Brewing Co   MICROBREWERY

(Map p318; ☑ 915-351-4377; www.odebrewingco.com; 3233 N Mesa St; ⊙11am-11pm Sun-Wed, to midnight Thu-Sat) The craft-beer scene has been slow to ignite in El Paso, but with the opening of the city's first three microbreweries – all since 2015 – we dare say the scene is on fire. Or maybe smoldering nicely? Ode was first on the scene and keeps drawing imbibers with its easy-drinking ales and lagers. The patio is darn nice too.

The gourmet pub grub on the menu has a decadently global spin: the poutine duck-fat fries are covered with green-chile sausage gravy.

Hoppy Monk   BAR

(Map p318; ☑ 915-307-3263; www.thehoppymonk.com; 4141 N Mesa St; ⊙3pm-midnight Mon-Wed, to 2am Thu, 11am-2am Fri & Sat, 10am-midnight Sun) We love this place off N Mesa St on the west side, not just for its beer selection, which is voluminous and includes – no surprise – some great Belgians, but for its nice patio and better-than-usual pub food.

Hope & Anchor   BAR

(Map p318; ☑ 915-533-8010; www.hopeandanchorelpaso.com; 4012 N Mesa St; ⊙3pm-2am Mon-Sat, 4pm-2am Sun) Too crowded inside? That's OK, we were heading to the beautiful patio to enjoy the nice weather anyway. This is a great place to unwind – and it's just down the road from the Hoppy Monk. Pub crawl, anyone?

Tin Man Filling Station – Montecillo   CRAFT BEER

(Map p318; www.facebook.com/tinmanep; 4935 N Mesa St; ⊙noon-midnight Sun-Wed, to 2am Fri &

---

quickly followed. Since the scene is still fresh and the market far from saturated, it's a great time to see what the new brewers are up to and check out the shiny new tap rooms and production facilities.

Downtown

Coffee Box   COFFEE

(Map p324; www.elpasocoffeebox.com; 401 N Mesa St; ⊙6:30am-10pm Mon-Fri, 8am-10pm Sat, 8am-8pm Sun; 🛜) Housed inside two metal freight containers stacked on top of one another, this eye-catching – and narrow – coffee shop across from San Jacinto Plaza sells fantastic iced coffees. Pastries and macaroons are also on offer if you need a snack.

Briar Patch/Hyde Patio Bar   GAY

(Map p324; ☑ 915-577-9555; www.facebook.com/BriaratHyde; 508 N Stanton St; ⊙2pm-2am) You can keep your calendar full at this place: Trivia Mondays, Karaoke Tuesdays, Latin

Sat) The bar stools are made from brightly painted kegs at this tiny and hip bar (and growler-filling station), which serves only Texas craft beers. The flagship location is at 2301 N Zaragosa St.

Aceitunas BAR
(Map p318; ☎ 915-845-2277; www.aceitunas beergarden.com; 5200 Doniphan Dr; ⏱4pm-2am Wed & Thu, 3pm-2am Fri & Sat, plus 3pm-2am Sun Apr-Sep) A unique spot in El Paso, this open-air beer garden is a great place to wind down after a long day – the folks here are some of the friendliest you will meet. Extra points for its signature T-shirt: 'The liver is evil and must be punished!'.

☆ Entertainment

El Paso has a lively fine-arts scene and plenty going on in the bars and nightclubs too. If you ask around, you can find live music almost any night of the week.

To learn what's going on in town, check the the *El Paso Times* events calendar (http://events.elpasotimes.com) or pick up a copy of the free weekly *What's Up* (www.whatsuppub.com).

Abraham Chávez Theatre THEATER
(Map p324; ☎ 915-534-0609; www.elpasolive.com; 1 Civic Center Plaza) The sombrero-shaped Abraham Chávez Theatre is host to most of El Paso's major performing organizations – including **El Paso Symphony Orchestra** (Map p324; ☎ 915-532-3776; www.epso.org), **Showtime! El Paso** (Map p324; ☎ 915-544-2022; www.showtimeelpaso.com) and **El Paso Opera Company** (☎ 915-581-5534; www.epopera.org) – and many touring concerts and plays.

McKelligon Canyon Amphitheater LIVE PERFORMANCE
(Map p318; McKelligon Canyon Rd) The Viva El Paso! (p319) musical plays here on Friday and Saturday nights, and a handful of Sundays, from June though August.

Plaza Theatre THEATER
(Map p324; ☎ 915-534-0633; www.theplaza theatre.org; 125 Pioneer Plaza) This elaborate theater under the stars is all indoors: pinpoint lights replicate celestial bodies, and vines cling to faux Spanish courtyard walls. Also home to a 1071-pipe Wurlitzer organ. Plays, concerts and shows are staged at this 1930 downtown landmark.

Alamo Drafthouse CINEMA
(Map p318; ☎ 915-845-7469; www.drafthouse.com/el-paso; 250 E Montecillo Dr) The popular Austin theater chain recently opened in west El Paso in the mixed-use Montecillo development. Come for craft beer, good food and a top-quality movie-viewing experience.

El Paso Chihuahuas BASEBALL
(Map p324; www.epchihuahuas.com; Southwest University Park, 1 Ballpark Plaza) The new **Southwest University Park stadium** (www.southwestuniversitypark.com) downtown is the home of the the the El Paso Chihuahuas, one of the best-named baseball teams out there. The Chihuahuas, who started playing in 2014, are the Triple-A affiliate of the San Diego Padres. The season runs from April through August.

🛍 Shopping

Like most major US cities, El Paso has its share of big shopping malls. **Cielo Vista Mall** (Map p318; ☎ 915-779-7070; www.simon.com/mall/cielo-vista; 8401 Gateway Blvd W; ⏱10am-9pm Mon-Sat, noon-6pm Sun) is located off I-10 on the east side; **Sunland Park Mall** (Map p318; www.sunlandparkmall.com; 750 Sunland Park Dr; ⏱10am-9pm Mon-Sat, noon-6pm Sun) is the major westside shopping center. Savvy shoppers can hunt for deals at the **Outlet Shoppes at El Paso** (☎ 915-877-3208; www.theoutlet-shoppesatelpaso.com; 7051 S Desert Blvd, Canutillo; ⏱10am-9pm Mon-Sat, to 7pm Sun), 20 minutes northwest of town on I-10.

So El Paso GIFTS & SOUVENIRS
(Map p318; ☎ 915-777-0803; www.soelpaso.com; 2717 N Stanton Dr; ⏱10am-6pm Mon-Fri, to 4pm Sat) We shouldn't have sampled that jalapeño-bacon jam – now we want to buy a jar. The jalapeño-pecan brittle was darn

good too. The free samples will get you at this welcoming shop, run by a 4th-generation El Pasoan, that specializes in all things El Paso. You'll find everything from cowboy socks to Day of the Dead trinkets, Christmas ornaments and edible treats.

Paradigm Texas GIFTS & SOUVENIRS, HOMEWARES
(Map p318; 915-544-7000; www.paradigm texas.com; 10am-6pm Mon-Fri, to 5pm Sat) The home decor, accessories and gifts at this thoughtfully curated shop have impeccable style, but the offerings tend to share a sense of fun that keeps the place from taking itself too seriously. Browse through everything from adult pop-up books and mini-cocktail kits to bright, hand-crafted towels and colorful Sugarfina candies.

Whoopee Bowl ANTIQUES
(915-886-2855; 9010 N Desert Blvd, Canutillo; 10am-5pm Mon-Sat) This isn't the kind of antique store where you find Chippendale furniture or a rare Fabergé egg. It's the kind of place where you pull up your Dodge Ram to haul home an enormous fiberglass chicken or a wooden cigar-store Indian. Sure, there are smaller items, but the real fun is exploring the huge front yard full of ridiculous treasures.

Located on the I-10 access road just before the New Mexico border.

El Paso Connection HOMEWARES
(915-852-0898; 14301 Gateway Blvd; 9am-5pm) This sprawling place east of town is made up of several showrooms and warehouses crowded with antique and imported goods, such as lampshades made from cowhide and large pieces of Southwestern-motif furniture.

Tony Lama Factory Store SHOES
(Map p318; 915-772-4327; www.tonylama.com; 7156 Gateway Blvd E; 9am-8pm Mon-Sat, noon-5pm Sun) A local outlet center for classic cowboy and Western footwear off the I-10, with everything from work boots to fancy going-dancing boots.

ⓘ Information

DANGERS & ANNOYANCES

El Paso is among the safest cities of its size in the US, thanks in part to Operation Hold the Line, an effort to crack down on illegal immigration. Green-and-white Border Patrol vehicles are highly visible all along the El Paso side of the Rio Grande, and the police presence has had the side effect of quelling crime.

NOT QUITE SOUTH-OF-THE-BORDER SHOPPING

Feel like you're missing out on south-of-the-border bargains? For an experience not altogether unlike shopping in Juárez, Mexico, head to the **Golden Horseshoe** area between Stanton and El Paso Sts and San Antonio Ave in downtown El Paso, where cheap clothing, jewelry and housewares abound. It's fairly scruffy, but it avoids the danger of crossing the border. (This area is also known as the Downtown Shopping District, which sounds a bit less fun.)

Crossing over into Mexico is a different story. While El Paso is one of the safest cities, Juárez has become one of the most dangerous, due to gruesome violence – some of it random – resulting from drug wars. For now, just say no.

EMERGENCY

El Paso Police (911, nonemergency 915-832-4400; 911 N Raynor St)

Del Sol Medical Center (915-595-9000; www.laspalmasdelsolhealthcare.com; 10301 Gateway Blvd W) Provides 24-hour acute care and emergency services on the east side.

Providence Memorial Hospital (915-577-6011; www.thehospitalsofprovidence.com; 2001 N Oregon St) Westside hospital with a 24-hour emergency room.

INTERNET ACCESS

El Paso Public Library (915-212-7323; www.elpasolibrary.org; 501 N Oregon St; 10am-7pm Mon-Thu, 11am-6pm Fri, 10am-6pm Sat, noon-6pm Sun;) Free internet access. Check the website for additional branches.

POST

Post Office (Map p324; 915-532-8824; www.usps.com; 219 E Mills Ave; 8:30am-5pm Mon-Fri, to noon Sat)

TOURIST INFORMATION

El Paso Visitor Center (Map p324; 915-534-0661; www.visitelpaso.com; 400 W San Antonio St; 9am-4pm Mon-Fri, to 2pm Sat) Stocks racks and racks of brochures, and the staff is quite helpful. It also has a well-populated website for planning.

ⓘ Getting There & Away

AIR

El Paso International Airport (ELP; Map p318; 915-212-0330; www.elpasointernational

airport.com; 6701 Convair Rd; 🕿) is 8 miles northeast of downtown El Paso.

Southwest Airlines is the biggest carrier at El Paso International. Other airlines include American Airlines, Delta, United and Allegiant.

BUS

The terminal for **Greyhound** (Map p324; 📞915-532-5095; www.greyhound.com; 200 W San Antonio Ave) is four blocks from the center of downtown.

CAR & MOTORCYCLE

El Paso is on the I-10 just 12 miles from the New Mexico border, but a long day's drive or more from any other major city in Texas. Stay on I-10 eastbound for San Antonio or Houston; I-20, the route to Fort Worth and Dallas, leaves I-10 about 150 miles east of El Paso.

The only other major highways are Hwy 54, which runs north to I-40, and Hwy 62/180, the route to Guadalupe Mountains and Carlsbad Caverns National Parks and eventually to Lubbock.

TRAIN

You can catch Amtrak at **Union Depot** (📞800-872-7245; www.amtrak.com; 700 W San Francisco Ave), which serves both the *Texas Eagle,* which runs from Los Angeles to Chicago with stops in San Antonio, Austin and Dallas, and the *Sunset Limited,* which runs from Los Angeles to New Orleans with stops in San Antonio and Houston. Check the website for fares and schedules.

❶ Getting Around

TO/FROM THE AIRPORT

El Paso International Airport is accessible by bus, taxi and shuttles. The last Sun Metro airport bus from downtown currently leaves at 7:30pm Monday to Friday, 8:15pm on Saturday and 6:15pm on Sunday.

BUS

Sun Metro (📞915-212-3333; www.sunmetro. net; single fare adult/child 6-18yr $1.50/1, day pass $3.50, exact change required) is El Paso's bus service, operating more than 60 routes citywide. Check the website for current route maps and schedules.

Transfers are free but should be requested when you board your original bus.

STREETCAR

In the near future, exploring the city without a car will get easier: new streetcar lines connecting downtown and UTEP are under construction. For the project, the city is refurbishing six streetcars that were in use before the trolley system stopped running here in 1974. They should be up and running in 2018 and will be equipped with air-conditioning, wi-fi and wheelchair ramps.

TAXI & RIDE SHARE

Look for taxi stands at the airport and the Greyhound and Amtrak depots. Rates are $1.65 at flag fall, $2.25 each additional mile. We've been warned about unscrupulous cabbies charging extortionate rates downtown, so double-check rates before boarding and make sure the meter's on.

Border Taxi (📞915-533-4245; www.border-taxi. com)

Yellow Cab (📞915-532-9999; www.yellow cabelpaso.com)

Uber (www.uber.com) and Lyft (www.lyft.com) are both available here.

GUADALUPE MOUNTAINS NATIONAL PARK

We won't go so far as to call it Texas' best-kept secret, but even many Texans aren't aware of the **Guadalupe Mountains National Park** (📞915-828-3251; www.nps.gov/gumo; US Hwy 62/180; 7-day pass adult/child under 16yr $5/free; ⊙visitor center 8am-4:30pm). It's just this side of the Texas–New Mexico state line and a long drive from practically everywhere in the state.

Despite its low profile, it's a Texas high spot, both literally and figuratively. At 8749ft, Guadalupe Peak is the highest point in the Lone Star State. The fall foliage in McKittrick Canyon is the best in west Texas, and more than half the park is a federally designated wilderness area.

The NPS has deliberately curbed development to keep the park wild. There are no restaurants or indoor accommodations and only a smattering of services and programs (so plan ahead to keep your gas tank full and your cooler stocked). There are also no paved roads within the park, so whatever you want to see, you're going to have get there on foot. But the hiking and high-country splendor are top-notch.

History

Until the mid-19th century, the Guadalupe Mountains were used exclusively by Mescalero Apaches, who hunted and camped in the area. Members of this tribe, who called themselves Nde, became the hunted starting in 1849, when the US Army began a ruthless 30-year campaign to drive them from the area. The mid-19th century also marked the brief tenure of the Butterfield Overland Mail

WORTH A TRIP: CARLSBAD CAVERNS

If you've made it all the way out to the Guadalupe Mountains, you're not too far from another excellent natural attraction: **Carlsbad Caverns National Park** (☎575-785-2232, bat info 505-785-3012; www.nps.gov/cave; Carlsbad Cavern Hwy; adult/child $10/free; ⊙caves 8:30am-5pm late May-early Sep, to 3:30pm early Sep-late May; ♿). Although over the border in New Mexico, it's only 40 miles from the Guadalupe Mountains National Park, making it closer than, well, almost everything else in the state of Texas.

Cave entrance fees are good for three days and get you access to the one-hour **self-guided tour** of the Big Room, the seventh-largest cave chamber in the world. There are additional fees, and reservations are required, for six different **ranger-led tours**, including the King's Palace and the Hall of the White Giant. Please note that each of the guided tours has an age limit of anywhere from four to 12 years, depending on difficulty (of the route, not the child), so plan accordingly if you're traveling with a little one.

BIG BEND & WEST TEXAS GUADALUPE MOUNTAINS NATIONAL PARK

Route. Guadalupe Mountains National Park was established in 1972.

Geology

A geologist's dream, Guadalupe Mountains National Park sits amid the world's most extensive exposed fossil reef. In fact, the mountains contain the world's best example of a 260- to 270-million-year-old exposed rock layer, the **Guadalupian Global Stratotype**.

The reef began to grow 250 million years ago, when an immense tropical ocean covered parts of Texas, New Mexico and Mexico. Over a period of five million years, lime-secreting marine organisms built the horseshoe-shaped reef to a length of 400 miles. After the sea evaporated, the reef was buried in sediment for millions more years, until a mountain-building geological uplift revealed part of it as the Guadalupe Mountains.

◎ Sights

Pinery
HISTORIC SITE

Check out the ruins of a Butterfield Overland Mail stagecoach stop via an easy and wheelchair-accessible 0.75-mile round-trip trail leading from the Pine Springs Visitor Center (p330); the ruins are fragile and climbing on them is forbidden. Despite its remote location, the Pinery is the only remaining Butterfield station ruin standing close to a major highway. If you're not up for a walk, there's a pull-off further east along US Hwy 62/180.

Frijole Ranch & Museum
MUSEUM

(www.nps.gov/gumo; ⊙usually open 8am-4:30pm) **FREE** This museum about 2 miles northeast of the Pine Springs Visitor Center has historical exhibits inside an old ranch house that

give some good insight into what it must have been like to live in such a remote location. A tiny one-room schoolhouse nearby might just make your kids appreciate how good they've got it. Staffed intermittently.

🏃 Activities

Interpretive programs are held on summer evenings in the Pine Springs campground amphitheater, as well as several times a week during the spring. Topics depend on the rangers' interests, but they have included everything from stargazing to geology (p329).

Bird-watchers flock to the park, especially McKittrick Canyon, for excellent viewing opportunities. There are no formal programs, but a checklist of the park's 260 species is available at the Pine Springs Visitor Center (p330).

Although many park trails are open to **horseback riding**, no horses are available in or near the park, and no overnight pack trips are permitted. For people bringing their own horses, corrals and campsites are available at Dog Canyon and Frijole Ranch; reserve them by calling the visitor center up to two months in advance.

Hiking

With more than 80 miles of trails and no real designated scenic drives through the park, Guadalupe Mountains National Park is a hiker's oasis, with trails ranging from short nature walks to strenuous climbs. To find the hike that's right for you, enquire at the visitor center (p330), but here are a few good ones to get you started:

➡ **McKittrick Canyon Trail** (www.nps.gov/gumo; ⊙8am-6pm Apr-Oct, to 4:30pm Nov-Mar) is among the park's most popular trails, and deservedly so. The 6.8-mile round-trip is level and scenic any time of year, though especially so in the fall. The **Pratt Cabin** (4.8 miles round-trip) is a highlight. The cabin was built in 1932 by petroleum geologist Wallace Pratt, who later donated the land to the NPS; it remains furnished as the Pratt family left it. Big Adirondack chairs beckon on the porch, and picnic tables and rest rooms make this a good lunch spot.

➡ Want to stand on the highest spot in Texas? Needless to say, you'll have to work for it on the 8.5-mile round-trip hike up Guadalupe Peak (8749ft). No rock climbing is necessary, but there's a 3000ft elevation gain, so go easy if you've just driven in from the lowlands.

➡ If you're looking for something a little easier, try the Smith Spring Trail starting at Frijole Ranch (p329). This path, shaded by Texas madrone and alligator juniper, is a perfect spot for getting out of the desert heat without too much exertion. The 2.3-mile loop takes you to Manzanita Spring and gradually climbs up to the refreshing Smith Spring, both precious watering holes for wildlife.

Be aware that the weather can be unpredictable out here. Thunderstorms are likely on summer afternoons, and winds frequently blow 40mph to 50mph in spring and early summer.

🛏 Sleeping

If you want to stay in the area, there aren't a lot of options. You can camp in the park and bring your own food. Aaaaand...that's it.

If camping doesn't appeal and you want to spend more than a day exploring the park, you can drive 45 minutes to Whites City, NM, a resort town with over 100 motel rooms and two RV parks.

Guadalupe Mountains Campgrounds CAMPGROUND $
(☑ 915-828-3251; www.nps.gov/gumo; tent & RV sites $8) The park's campgrounds are first-come, first-served – unless you have a group

of 10 or more, in which case you can reserve a group camping spot up to 60 days in advance (for $3 per person). Campsites fill up during spring break, and several nights a week in the summer, although visitors arriving by early afternoon will usually find a site.

The most convenient campgrounds are at Pine Springs, right along Hwy 62/180 near the visitor center; if it looks full, look for the 'campground host' sign for directions to overflow spots.

If all the sites are full, RVs are permitted to park overnight at the nearby state-highway picnic areas.

ℹ Information

DANGERS & ANNOYANCES

➡ Dehydration is the park's main danger. Carry and drink plenty of water – the park recommends one gallon per person per day.

➡ If you're camping, keep your tent flaps closed to keep out snakes, scorpions and desert centipedes. (Five rattlesnake species live in the park, but rangers say no one has ever been bitten in the park's almost 50-year history.)

TOURIST INFORMATION

Information, restrooms and drinking water are available at the **Pine Springs Visitor Center** (☑ 915-828-3251; www.nps.gov/gumo; ⊙ 8am-4:30pm). You'll also find water, restrooms and outdoor exhibits in McKittrick Canyon; the Dog Canyon Ranger Station has information, restrooms and water.

You can also visit the park website to download a map of the park before you visit.

ℹ Getting There & Away

Guadalupe Mountains National Park is on Hwy 62/180, 110 miles east of El Paso and 55 miles southwest of Carlsbad, NM. The closest gas stations are 35 miles in either direction on Hwy 62/180 and the closest services are in Whites City, NM, 45 minutes northeast of the park entrance on Hwy 62/180.

Understand
Texas

Texas Today

Oil set the pace for the state's early development, but modern Texas is diversified and constantly evolving. The economy has been one of the strongest in the nation for the last decade, and by most economic indicators it remains so. But so too is the population growing – quickly. Demographics seem to be shifting toward a young majority fueled by transplants both domestic and international, and immigration reform is as hot a topic as they come.

Best on Film

The Alamo (1960) John Wayne's epic masterpiece, mostly filmed near Austin.

Friday Night Lights (2004) The ups and downs of high-school football define the social scenes of much of small-town Texas. Later adapted for TV.

Giant (1956) The life of an oil and ranching family, starring Elizabeth Taylor, Rock Hudson and James Dean.

There Will Be Blood (2007) Though set in California, this depiction of early-era oil explorers was filmed in part near Marfa.

Best in Print

Lone Star: A History of Texas and the Texans (TR Fehrenbach; 2007) Comprehensive history of the state and people.

Lone Star Literature (ed Don Graham; 2006) Anthology of Texas works, far-reaching and diverse.

In a Narrow Grave (Larry McMurtry; 2001) Classic essays on Texas from the renowned local author.

The Longhorns (J Frank Dobie; 1980) Legends and history of the iconic Texas cattle breed and ranching in the region.

Looking for Texas (Rick Vanderpool; 2000) Follows the author's 20,500-mile journey photographing the word 'Texas' across the state.

Conservative–Liberal Divide

Texas is a red state with a blue heart. During the 2016 presidential election – as in every election since 1976 – the state's 38 electoral votes were cast for Republican candidates. Looking county by county, the notable and consistent exceptions to the red-state rule are Travis County (Austin) and Harris County (urban Houston). There is also a liberal majority in the growing Mexican American–dominated counties along the rural southwestern border in the Rio Grande Valley.

Republicans have dominated the Texas state legislature and the governor's office for more than 10 years. Governor Rick Perry led the charge until his 2016 presidential run, and Greg Abbott has pushed forward with conservative policies since his transition to that role.

Of the divisive conservative/liberal topics that regularly resurface, the ground seems to continue shifting on one: same-sex marriage rights. Most cities and counties have established marriage-equality laws at the local level in line with US Supreme Court rulings, but rural Irion County continues to refuse to recognize same-sex unions; the Texas Supreme Court began to hear cases in early 2017 that could once again put limits on these rights in defiance of national norms.

The Economy & Oil

Historically oil and gas exploration and production was the only factor in the success or failure of Texas fortunes. But the boom-and-bust cycle of the 1980s taught the state a thing or two about diversifying. Today the Texas economy is based on numerous breadwinners, including a strong tech sector around Austin and a large biomedical industry in Houston. Oil no longer tops the list.

During the global recession and slow national recovery, the Texas economy continued to expand, with an average growth rate of 3.1% (compared to the nation's 1.6%); the absence of income tax, low average housing prices and strong consumer-protection laws spared residents from the worst of the national slump. Texas is continually near the top of private-sector job creation and near the bottom of the 10 largest states in unemployment rate. The mood continues to be justifiably upbeat about the future.

Population Growth

Texas has been the fastest-growing state in the USA during the 2000s, adding nearly eight million people during the first 16 years of the decade. According to the US Census Bureau, five of the country's 11 fastest growing cities are in Texas. While some of the population growth is attributable to the strong economy and domestic immigration, a portion is due to natural increase. A shrinking and aging Anglo (ie Caucasian) population and a growing and young Hispanic one has meant a marked demographic change, especially in urban areas. The Texas State Data Center measured a minority-majority first in 2005, and estimates a demographic shift to a Hispanic majority will happen no later than 2035.

And that's only discussing the population that's been counted. Undocumented immigrants in Texas, mostly Hispanic, number approximately 1.68 million according to the Department of Homeland Security. Three Texas cities are among the top 10 US population centers for unauthorized immigrants. Many provide manual labor as a part of the Texas workforce. Critics argue that the population is a drag on state resources, such as social services for the poor and tuition assistance. Immigration reformers cite the United States' historical tradition of welcoming all. With no solution in sight and a shifting population, the only thing certain in Texas is change.

POPULATION: **27,862,596**

AREA: **268,597 SQ MILES**

GROSS STATE PRODUCT (GSP): **1.638 BILLION**

UNEMPLOYMENT: **4.2%**

if Texas were 100 people

77 would be white
13 would be African American
6 would be Asian
1 would be Native American
3 would be Other

belief systems
(% of population)

77 Christian
1 Jewish
1 Muslim
1 Buddhist
20 other

population per sq mile

USA   TEXAS   DALLAS COUNTY

† ≈ 85 people

History

The Lone Star State was a cultural and political hotbed from the start, with six flags belonging to different colonial powers – and temporarily an independent Texas – before joining the USA. Perhaps because of this, legend looms large in Texas history. Mention the Alamo or the JFK assassination and you're bound to hear a variety of tales told, a mix of fact and exaggerated fiction. Not surprising, really, in a state where the history is as iconic as it is actual.

In the Beginning

The word 'Texas' goes back to 1691. Spanish explorers found the native Caddo people so friendly that they began to call their new territory *tejas* ('tay-has'), a corruption of the Caddo word for 'friend.'

Texas hasn't always been Texas. Or Mexico, for that matter. Or the United States, or Spain, or France, or any of the six flags that once flew over this epic state in its eight changes of sovereignty (which doesn't even include the little Republic of the Rio Grande). The earliest evidence of humans in what is now Texas exists in the *llano estacado* ('staked plain') section of Texas and New Mexico. Little is known about the various indigenous peoples, but by the time the first Europeans arrived in the 16th century, several distinct groups of Native Americans were settled in the region. One of these tribes, the Caddo people, still figures strongly as a namesake and cultural influence in east Texas, where the Caddo Mounds State Historic Site commemorates their unique history.

Spanish Acquisition

Spanish explorers first arrived in Texas territory during the 1500s, mapping the gulf coast and searching for gold. During one failed incursion, Cabeza de Vaca and his Moroccan-born slave Esteban (likely the first non-native person of color to explore the New World) were stranded and held by the Karankawa people. His diaries spurred on exploration for years to come.

By the mid-17th century, the Spaniards' tack was more 'please read this pamphlet' than 'take me to the riches.' The conquistadores had triumphed in lands from Florida through present-day Mexico and beyond. Spain set about constructing a series of *misións* (missions) and *presidios* (forts) to convert the Native Americans to Christianity and,

TIMELINE	Prehistory	c 1400 BC	1539
	More than 16 species of dinosaurs roamed the future Texas landscape until they became extinct, more than 65 million years ago.	The Caddo people establish a sedentary society, based on agriculture, in east Texas. They construct ceremonial mounds outside present-day Nacogdoches.	Half of those on Franciscan friar Marcos de Niza's greed-fueled expedition die during tribal attacks. The friar flees back to Mexico – hastily claiming the ground he'd covered for Spain, of course.

not incidentally, into Spanish subjects. The earliest mission constructed in Texas was in the 1680s, near what is now El Paso.

The French Threat

Meanwhile, the French were also sniffing around North America. In the 1680s, they laid claim to the territory they called Louisiana and to a piece of east Texas. This hardly amused the Spanish, who constructed Mission San Francisco de los Tejas, outside present-day Nacogdoches (the site is a state park today), and other fortifications. Due to disease, hostile native attacks and Spanish settlement, French 'rule' in the east dissipated a scant five years later.

Mission Impossible

In 1718 the Spanish began building missions and forts in south-central Texas to reduce the distances crossed by supply trains. Mission San Antonio de Valero, which later became known as the Alamo, and sites along the present-day Mission Trail were constructed around this time. In 1731 the settlement of Villa de Bexar was established by Spanish colonists imported from the Canary Islands, and a civil government was set up in the area. The Spanish Governor's Palace still lies at the heart of San Antonio.

More than 30 missions were eventually built here. During the heyday of the missions, from 1745 to 1775, they became successful enough to attract the rather unpleasant attention of Apache and Comanche tribespeople. While the missionaries and native tribes who lived within the system learned to defend themselves against physical attack, the failure of the Spanish colonial system itself was a major factor in the missions' eventual undoing.

Mexican Independence

Concurrent with the American, French and Spanish squabbling over North America at the end of the 18th century, a growing movement in Mexico sought freedom from Spain. Sporadic fighting took place from 1810 until 1821, when Spain agreed to Mexican independence. An opportunistic soldier named Antonio López de Santa Anna eventually helped establish a Mexican Republic, of which he was elected president in 1833.

Americans Horn In

Before 1820, settlers moving to Texas from the USA were mainly relocated Native Americans, who were being forcibly removed from newly acquired US territories in the southeast.

The first large group of Anglo American settlers in Texas arrived as the result of a deal brokered by Moses Austin. He negotiated for the Spanish government to allow him and 400 families from the USA to move into central Texas but he died before the move could begin. His son, Stephen

---

East Texas cypress trees are hundreds of years old. The moss that hangs off them was nicknamed 'Spanish Beards' by early French settlers in an attempt to insult their Spanish rivals.

HISTORY SPANISH ACQUISITION

Newly independent Mexico administratively grouped Texas with the Mexican state of Coahuila To the north, Mexico included much of what is now Southwestern USA.

1598	1718	1800	1810
Spanish explorer Juan de Oñate stopped to feast with Native Americans on the banks of the Rio Grande. Some Texans believe it to be the first real Thanksgiving.	The Mission San Antonio de Valero, aka the Alamo, is founded in present-day San Antonio.	Napoléon Bonaparte forces the Spanish to cede Louisiana to France. Yet three years later France turns around and sells the entire Louisiana Territory to the USA for $15 million.	Miguel Hidalgo y Costilla, parish priest of the town of Dolores, issues his now-famous call to rebellion, the Grito de Dolores, demanding 'death to bad government.'

Fuller Austin, who is credited in Texas folklore as the 'Father of Texas,' carried out his father's plans in 1821, attracting more than 5000 Americans and creating a bustling trade with Mexico.

The word 'Texian' was coined to describe the region's residents, who were beginning to form a separate identity. By 1830, with more than 30,000 settlers in the Texas territory, the situation was becoming, well, revolting. In that year, a Mexican decree banned further American settlement and limited the importation of slaves; however, unauthorized immigrants from the US continued to do both. Around that time, political unrest in Mexico led to the imposition of martial law and banning of weapons in many Mexican territories, including Texas.

Texas War for Independence

Stephen F Austin traveled to Mexico City to plead the settlers' case for independence, but was arrested and detained. William B Travis led a group of hot-headed Texians who'd rather fight than allow more Mexican troops to arrive. Armed skirmishes throughout 1835 sparked the Texas War for Independence, which officially ran from September 30, 1835, to April 21, 1836.

In December 1835, at the outbreak of war, Texian troops (composed of Americans, Mexicans and a fair number of English, Irish, Scottish, German and other European settlers) captured San Antonio, and occupied and further fortified the Alamo.

Remember the Alamo!

'You may all go to hell, and I will go to Texas.' – Davy Crockett, 1835

It's hard to tell the story of the Battle of the Alamo. There's hot debate about the number of defenders and of Mexican troops and casualties, among many other details. Objective, first-hand accounts have been, to date, impossible to find.

It is generally agreed that on February 23, 1836, Mexican general Antonio López de Santa Anna led anywhere from 2500 to 5000 Mexican troops in an attack against the Alamo. The 160 or so men inside the fortress included James Bowie (of Bowie-knife fame), who was in command of the Alamo until pneumonia rendered him too sick; William B Travis, who took command of the troops after Bowie's incapacity; and perhaps most famous of all, David Crockett, called 'Davy' by everyone. Crockett, a three-time US congressman from Tennessee with infamous taste in headgear, first gained fame as a frontiersman and then for his public arguments with President Andrew Jackson over the latter's murderous campaigns of Native American 'removal' in the southeastern USA. Less well known were Bowie's and Travis' African American slaves, who fought alongside their masters during the battle and were two of the only male survivors.

The Six (Count 'Em) Flags of Texas

Spanish *1519–1685; 1690–1821*

French *1685–90*

Mexican *1821–36*

Republic of Texas *1836–45*

United States *1845–61*

Confederate States *1861–65*

United States *1865–*

1819	1825	1836	1836
The USA acquires Florida in exchange for Spanish control over Texas; the USA will control all territory east of it.	The first skirmish in the Texas War for Independence takes place on October 2, when Texians raise a flag daring Mexican troops to 'Come and take it' (their cannon, that is).	The Battle of the Alamo begins on February 28 and lasts for 13 days.	On April 21, Sam Houston's Texian army wins a decisive battle against Mexican General Santa Anna. Texas becomes a republic.

Travis dispatched a now-famous letter to other revolutionaries pleading for reinforcements, saying that his men would not stand down under any circumstances – his call was for 'Victory or death.' Because of slow communications, the only reinforcements that arrived in time were a group of about 30 men from Gonzales, Texas, bringing the total number of Alamo defenders up to 189 – at least according to literature from the Daughters of the Republic of Texas (DRT), which lists the names of all but one, an unidentified African American man.

Santa Anna's troops pounded the Alamo for 13 days before retaking it. Mexican losses were devastating; estimates run as low as 1000 and as high as 2000. When the Alamo was finally recaptured, the advancing troops executed almost all of the surviving defenders. The few who were spared, mostly women, children and slaves, were interrogated and released.

Remember Goliad

Colonel James Fannin and more than 400 volunteers who had set out too late to assist at the Alamo encountered Mexican troops north of Goliad. After a daylong battle, the Texians surrendered and were taken to the *presidio*, which was occupied by the Mexican army. On March 27, Palm Sunday, Santa Anna ordered between 300 and 350 prisoners shot – a death toll about twice the number lost at the Alamo. The two events, instantly labeled 'massacres' by Texians, galvanized the troops, who continued fighting under the rallying cry of 'Remember the Alamo! Remember Goliad!'

Perhaps as a result of losses suffered and supplies spent at the battles of the Alamo and Goliad, Santa Anna's troops simply were not prepared when, on April 21, they ran into troops commanded by Samuel Houston. The Texian general was a former major general in Tennessee's militia and an 'Indian fighter' under US general (later president) Andrew Jackson. At the Battle of San Jacinto, outside modern-day Houston, Santa Anna's forces were finally and completely routed. Texas' war for independence was won.

The Lone Star Republic

The 54 delegates who gathered at Washington-on-the-Brazos on March 1, 1836, literally wrote the Texas Declaration of Independence overnight – while the Alamo was under siege. Though Texas declared itself a 'a free and independent republic,' neither the USA nor Mexico recognized it as such. In its early years the new republic's main business was forging trade and political ties, and trying hard to establish a government and a capital city.

In 1839 the central Texas village of Waterloo was renamed Austin, in honor of Stephen F, and the capital established there. That same year, the Republic of Texas' policy toward the Native Americans who lived within its borders changed drastically, and a ruthless and thorough

Alamo Movies

The Immortal Alamo *(1911)*
Silent film.

The Alamo *(1960)*
John Wayne directed and starred.

The Alamo: Thirteen Days to Glory *(1987)* Starring Brian Keith.

The Alamo *(2004)*
Starring Dennis Quaid.

El Camino Real was a trail between Mexico and Louisiana that was well traveled by the Spanish, and later by incoming US settlers. Historical markers along 34 miles of northeast Texas' Hwy 21, outside Alto, mark part of the route.

1846	1848	1850s	1900
Texas' annexation by the USA leads directly to the Mexican-American War, a total rout in which US troops capture Mexico City from Santa Anna.	At the end of the Mexican-American War, Mexico cedes modern Texas, California, Utah, Colorado and most of New Mexico and Arizona to the USA.	Dallas gets artsy: a group of French artists and intellectuals prove instrumental in the early settlement of Dallas in the 1850s.	The (first) Great Storm hits populous Galveston Island, killing an estimated 6000 to 8000 people the night of September 8.

Until 1839 the city of Austin was called Waterloo. (It's still the name of Austin's best-known music shop, Waterloo Records.)

campaign of removal began, leading to an increase in raiding parties. The turn of the decade was also marred by continual harassment from Mexican troops in the south.

President Sam Houston and the republic lobbied Washington for annexation as a territory in order to gain assistance in settling both the border dispute with Mexico and issues with Native Americans. A country for less than 10 years, Texas was annexed to the USA during a state constitutional convention in 1845.

Civil War & Reconstruction

The US Civil War (1861–65) was brought on by a number of issues, including states' rights, but standing in the foreground was the moral and economic debate over slavery. Settlers poured into Texas from slave-owning states in the South, but then-Governor Sam Houston was firmly against the South-favored secession. Popular opinion and a referendum defeated him, and he was forced to resign.

Texas seceded from the USA and joined the Confederate States of America on March 16, 1861. Aside from providing an estimated 80,000 troops, Texas' role in the Civil War was mainly one of supplying food to the Confederate war machine. Even if Texas soil did not play a large part in the war, the wounds ran incredibly deep for years afterward.

President Andrew Johnson, the Southerner and former slaveholder who succeeded Lincoln, devised a Reconstruction plan. While his plan granted many concessions, it was absolutely firm that the states' constitutions ratify the 13th Amendment, abolishing slavery, before re-admittance. The Texas Constitution of 1866, hastily drawn up to assure re-admittance to the Union, granted African Americans some measure of civil rights, but it did not give them the right to vote until martial law imposed it. Hyper-restrictive Black Codes, later to be expanded to what became known as Jim Crow laws, were introduced, making it illegal for African Americans to be unemployed, restricting freedom of movement and segregating much of Southern life into white and African American camps.

The first barbed fence, then known as 'thorny wire', was patented by Michael Kelley in 1868. The Devil's Rope Museum in McLean today recognizes 2000 types of barbed wire. Learn more on the *99% Invisible* podcast episode on barbed wire at http://99percentinvisible.org/episode/devils-rope.

On the Cattle Trail

During the Civil War, the Confederate forces' need for food had increased Texas cattle production. Ranching in Texas became an enormous business, and cattle drives – the herding of up to 200,000 head of longhorn steers northward – were born.

Of all the trails that ran through Texas, the evocatively named Goodnight-Loving Trail to Pueblo and Denver, Colorado, and Cheyenne, Wyoming, and the Sedalia Trail to Sedalia, Missouri, are the most famous. But it was the Chisholm Trail – through San Antonio to Abilene, Kansas, at the western terminus of the Kansas Pacific Railroad – that spurred the

1909	1913	WWI	1920s
After being jailed for six weeks at Fort Sam Houston, Apache leader Goyathlay (aka Geronimo) dies a prisoner of war. The US military has still not repatriated his remains.	Mexican revolutionary Pancho Villa is a darling of the American media, portrayed as a dashing freedom fighter. Eventually, the US turns against him and Villa is mysteriously assassinated in 1923.	Four major military bases are established in Texas for training – Camp Travis (San Antonio), Camp Logan (Houston), Camp MacArthur (Waco) and Camp Bowie (Fort Worth).	Twenty-eight bars and two breweries line the party-hearty streets of Brenham, Texas. Prohibition comes to town, the bars close, and the parties go underground.

business of bringing Texas cattle to market. By 1873 the railroad had reached Fort Worth, and cattle could also be transported the newfangled way.

Though immortalized in many old Western movies, the cattle-drive days barely lasted two decades. By the early 1880s, with the invention of barbed wire, fences stretched across much of Texas. Disputes naturally arose. In 1883 Texas banned the cutting of fences, legislating a new way of life throughout the state. (In Austin it's still illegal to carry and conceal wire cutters in your pocket.) The Texas Rangers, once mere border guards, were reinstated as a state police force to enforce the new law. This was, effectively, the end of what most of us think of as the cowboy era.

Black Gold

As early as 1866, oil wells were striking in east Texas. At the time, oil was being put to a number of uses, including the sealing of dirt roads. But speculators bet that oil, found in sufficient supply, could replace coal as an energy mainstay.

Everything changed on January 10, 1901, when a drilling site at Spindletop, east of Houston in Beaumont, pierced a salt dome, setting forth a gusher of oil so powerful that it took days to bring it under control. Spindletop began producing an estimated 80,000 barrels of oil per day. As automobiles and railroads turned to the oil industry for fuel, discoveries of 'black gold' financed the construction of much of modern Texas.

San Antonio's early-20th-century growth was also due to the military; Fort Sam Houston was joined by Kelly Air Force Base, now the nation's oldest air force base, in 1917, followed by Lackland, Randolph and Brooks Air Force Bases.

In 1517 Alonzo Avarez de Piñeda mapped the coast of the Gulf of Mexico from Florida to Mexico, creating the first cartographic record of present-day Texas. He camped at the mouth of the Rio Grande (which he called the 'river of palms'), but is believed to have never actually stepped foot in what is now modern Texas.

HISTORY BLACK GOLD

BRENHAM RECONSTRUCTION BARBECUE

On the eve of WWI, the central Texas town of Brenham was heavily German and Czech; kids of different heritages all studied German in school. Then the Ku Klux Klan rode into town, tarring and feathering those of German descent, beating up prominent town businesspeople and torching the German newspaper print shop. People began avoiding the mean streets of Brenham, and city-center businesses withered.

City leaders decided to solve the problem Texas-style: by throwing a giant barbecue to which they would invite all sides. On the day of the festivities, October 29, 1923, more than 12,000 people (over half the county) – German speakers, African Americans, Czechs, Mexicans, you name it – gathered at the firefighters' park to eat smoked meat cooked over giant pits, plus German potato salad and peach cobbler with Brenham Creameries' (later Blue Bell) ice cream. Soon after that the KKK – at least in Brenham – disbanded.

1939	WWII	1963	1960s
If you build it, the tourists will come: WPA workers build 17,000ft of walkways and two bridges on the river in downtown San Antonio for a massive project named the Paseo Del Rio (aka River Walk).	The government creates a dozen new military bases and activates more than 40 airfields in Texas.	On November 22, as his motorcade passes by, President John F Kennedy is fatally shot from a 6th-floor window in the Book Depository in Dallas.	LBJ administration sees the USA through the invasion of North Vietnam, civil protest at home and 'the Great Society,' an unprecedented flurry of social legislation.

The Great Depression

Following the end of WWI in 1918, Texas' economic machine, as well as the nation's, was humming right along. The surge in private automobiles made for an enormous Texas oil boom, and people were dancing the Charleston in the streets.

Then, on Black Thursday, October 24, 1929, the New York Stock Exchange hiccuped and the bottom fell out of the economy. The crash, the result of unchecked Wall Street trading practices, led the US and the world into the Great Depression. Northern Texas was part of the region that became known as the 'dust bowl,' as former farmland was destroyed by overuse and lack of rain. Increased oil production caused a market glut that further depressed prices.

As part of Roosevelt's New Deal, the Works Progress Administration (WPA) and Civilian Conservation Corps (CCC) were created. The WPA sent armies of workers to construct buildings, roads, dams, trails and housing. The CCC worked to restore state and national parks. The cabins and other lodging in state parks such as Caddo Lake and Davis Mountain date from this time.

WWII & Postwar

New Deal or not, some felt what the country really needed to break out of the Depression was a good war. The Japanese attack on Pearl Harbor, Hawaii, on December 7, 1941, finally brought the USA into the fighting that had been going on throughout the world since 1939.

The Texas war machine was brought back to full capacity. With the activation of all its bases, the creation of more than a dozen new ones and more than 40 airfields, Texas became a major preparing ground for WWII soldiers – almost 1.5 million were trained in the state.

The economic prosperity in the USA after WWII was unprecedented. The wartime economy had created a powerhouse, and when the fighting stopped in 1945, industry didn't want to stop with it. For the next 15 years, the US economy surged, fueled by low consumer credit rates and a defense-based economy that plowed money into manufacturing military hardware (as well as ever more automobiles and household appliances). Most people were feeling pretty good. So good, in fact, that a whole passel of Texans was born in this period: the baby boomers.

1960s

Native son Lyndon Baines Johnson was from Stonewall, east of Austin, in south-central Texas. Johnson, affectionately known as LBJ, had a well-deserved reputation for being a hard-nosed Southern Democrat. He was as stubborn as a barn full of mules, as dirty a political fighter as he needed to be, and fiercely loyal to Texas in the fight for pork-barrel

Germans introduced Texas to something for which we can all be grateful: Texas barbecue. The method of smoke-curing meats for storage in such a way that it remained soft and tender has its origins, locals say, in local German shops.

NASA's space shuttle fleet – *Columbia, Challenger, Discovery, Atlantis* and *Endeavour* – flew a total of 135 missions between 1979 and July 2011.

1969	1978	1970s	1984
Neil Armstrong transmits the first words from the surface of the moon: 'Houston, the Eagle has landed,' on July 20.	*Dallas,* the prime-time soap opera following the oil-rich Ewing clan, premieres to an adoring audience. Fans storm the real Southfork Ranch.	Gas prices quadruple. Texans – who are the biggest domestic oil supplier and have many of the nation's largest refineries – profit and profit some more.	PC revolutionary Michael Dell creates a little computer company from his University of Texas dorm room. (The billions come later.)

government contracts. As majority leader of the US Senate, Johnson accepted the vice-presidential nomination in 1960.

On November 22, 1963, President John Fitzgerald Kennedy and Vice President Johnson rode in separate open limousines through downtown Dallas. At 12:30pm, JFK was shot. Texas governor John M Connally, riding in the seat in front of the president, was also injured by gunfire. The president died at 1pm; Connally survived. Later that day, as Kennedy's body was being transported to Washington, DC, Vice President Johnson took the oath of office aboard Air Force One, the presidential airplane, with Jacqueline Kennedy standing at his side. LBJ defeated Barry Goldwater in the presidential election of 1964, and his administration oversaw some of the USA's most tumultuous, tragic and socially catalyzing events, including the Vietnam War and Civil Rights Movement.

Texas produces 36% of the oil in the US. If it were an independent country, it would be the sixth-largest oil producer in the world.

Boom then Bust

The energy crisis in the 1970s brought Sultan-of-Bruneian wealth to Texas. The crisis began when members of the Organization of the Petroleum Exporting Countries (OPEC) imposed a major reduction in oil sales to the USA and its allies to punish the country for its pro-Israel policy. Texans found themselves the biggest domestic suppliers of oil, and laughed all the way to the bank.

The oil shortage created a class of nouveaux riches, who played the part as if they had been supplied by central casting. Newly wealthy Texans bought British titles outright from debt-ridden members of the British aristocracy, creating legions of Lady Jane Billy Bobs and Duke Zachary Jims. Ranches became practically passé in the move to bigger and better spreads for oil barons, who also built skyscrapers, hotels, casinos and pleasure domes. The original *Dallas,* a prime-time soap opera following the high jinks of that wacky, oil-rich Ewing clan, premiered in 1978 and showed off Texas excess for all the world, which lapped it up.

HOUSTON & THE SPACE RACE

One of the first things Johnson did upon election as vice president was to work on instituting well-funded federal programs back home in Texas. The most notable of these was the relocation of National Aeronautics and Space Administration (NASA) Mission Control from Florida to Texas. At the time, the Mercury space missions were just getting under way. As the 'space race' between the USA and the USSR heated up, the forward-thinking vice president realized the enormous financial potential. He lobbied congress mercilessly and in 1961 was victorious. Although launches continued to leave from Cape Canaveral, Mission Control and the astronaut training program were moved to the Manned Space Flight Center (now, cozily enough, called the Johnson Space Center) outside Houston.

1990	1993	Late 1990s	2000
Ann Richards, a Democrat, becomes Texas' first woman governor to be elected in her own right.	Federal agents storm the Branch Davidian compound outside Waco. Cult leader David Koresh and 85 of his followers, along with four law-enforcement officers, are killed.	The dot-com boom hits. Laid-back college town and capital Austin becomes a hotbed for technology companies, earning the nickname 'Silicon Hills.'	On November 2, Texas Governor George W Bush becomes the second George Bush to be elected president of the United States.

Texas History Resources

....

Texas State Historical Association (www.tshaonline.org)

Lonestar Junction (www.lsjunction.com)

Daughters of the Republic of Texas (www.drtl.org)

Texas Almanac (www.texas almanac.com)

By the close of the energy crisis, the country had developed new sources of oil (mainly in Texas and Central and South America, as well as in Alaska) and new types of energy (nuclear, hydroelectric and others that had existed for years, but had yet to be put to large-scale use).

When Iran ceased sales to the US in 1979, other oil producing nations flooded the market. As OPEC argued, oil prices halved; by 1986, it was down to a paltry $10 a barrel, and Texas was hurting. Oil extraction and exploration became unprofitable. Downtown Houston became little more than a ghost town, with unoccupied office towers filling the streets in what looked like a postapocalyptic nightmare.

During the 1990s the Texas economy diversified. Trade with Mexico began booming with the 1994 passage of the North American Free Trade Agreement (NAFTA). Technology was another big story in the 1990s; Austin, with its highly educated populace, became a powerhouse of high-tech companies and innovation.

Double Feature: The George Bushes

Though originally from Massachusetts, Republican George HW Bush (the senior) moved his young family to west Texas in 1948, where he worked in the oil industry. By the 1960s he had turned to politics, representing a Houston district in the House of Representatives before he later became CIA director and Ronald Reagan's vice president in 1981. He ran and won one term as president in 1988.

His son George W Bush grew up in Midland and Houston. He'd worked on others' campaigns, as a business owner in oil and gas exploration and production, and as managing partner of the Texas Rangers baseball team, but he'd never held public office before winning the Texas governorship in 1994 and again in 1998.

Recent Texas Governors

Greg Abbott (2015 to present)

....

Rick Perry (2000–15)

....

George W Bush (1995–2000)

....

Ann Richards (1991–95)

....

Bill Clemens (1987–91)

....

Mark White (1983–87)

In January 2001, Bush junior became only the second son in American history (after John Quincy Adams in 1824) to follow his father to the White House. The election was a bitterly contested one involving recounted votes in Florida and a landmark Supreme Court case. In the end, although Al Gore received more popular votes than Bush, he lost by electoral votes. Bush defied his critics by winning the presidency again in 2004.

Not All That Long Ago

Those still involved in the oil industries had long joked: 'Lord, give me just one more boom and I promise I won't piss it away.' Crude-oil prices rose dramatically in the early 2000s, and it looked like their dreams just may have come true. Texas took a hit along with the rest of the nation during the global economic crisis, but the state economy remained strong.

2008	2011	2013	2017
On September 1, Hurricane Ike makes landfall at Galveston, devastating the island and knocking out power in parts of Houston for 21 days.	NASA's Mission Control at Johnson Space Center in Houston guides the last space-shuttle launch before decommissioning the spacecraft.	On April 17, 2013, a fertilizer plant explosion kills 15 and wounds at least 160, devastating the tiny town of West, Texas (population 2800).	Wildfires in the Texas Panhandle burn over 500,000 acres of land near Amarillo.

Life in Texas

There are about as many ways to live in this giant state as there are fleas on a farm dog. Sure, pickup trucks, cowboy boots and country songs are a part of the puzzle, but so are *quinceañeras* (15th-birthday, coming-of-age parties) and Tejano-*conjunto* music. That said, a few constants remain: faith, family and Friday-night football all still run deep to the heart of Texas.

Who Are Texans?

Texan First

'Don't mess with Texas' was the bumper-sticker slogan of a famous anti-litter campaign, but the sentiment speaks volumes about the fiercely in-dependent spirit of Texas. After all, this is the only state in the union that was once its own republic – and locals from Longview to Laredo won't let you forget it. Texans, in general, are mighty patriotic and proud to be Americans, but they are Texans first.

Why, you say? Maybe it's leftover cowboy cockiness. Or maybe it's because Texas is as big as a country. As a sovereign nation, the state's economy would be the 10th largest in the world, and one of the few that kept on growing during the global recession. Fifty-four of the top Fortune 500 companies call Texas home; Houston is the nation's second busiest port; the state has one of the top-10 lowest costs of living... If all this sounds like bravado, it is. And as they say here, 'it ain't braggin'' if it's true.' Newcomers may find the home-state pride equal parts obnox-ious and endearing, but locals (and quite a few recent transplants, too) wouldn't have it any other way.

Talkin' Texan

Howdy, y'all... Say that to a single person and they'll know you ain't from around here, are ya. 'Y'all' is a conjunction of 'you' and 'all', making it plural. Everybody knows that.

The way Texans talk is mighty particular, and it ain't to be mistaken with any old Georgia boy's drawl. Linguists who study this say the accent's influences draw from the Lower South (Louisiana, Alabama) and South Midland (Tennessee, Kentucky) dialects, mixed in with Mexican Spanish and Central European influences.

What's all that mumbo-jumbo mean? It's a Southern accent, sure 'nough, but it's not quite as lilting (some might say as mushy) as those in the Deep South (though you hear that a bit in East Texas). The main sound characteristic is the flattened vowels, which is what makes 'right' sound 'raht', as in 'I'll be *raht 'chere* when you get back.' There's also a tendency to elongate words. We know some who can stretch an af-firmative *yea-a-as* into mighty near three syllables. And that's another thing: here two-word adjectives and verbs are used to add emphasis: *fixin' to* (intending or about to), *might oughtta* (maybe should), *cotton to* (take a liking to).

But it's not just about the *way* Texans say thangs, it's *what* they say. Though usage might be fading a bit, colorful metaphors and similes

Funny Names for Texas Towns
Happy
Utopia
Bobo
Earth
Paris
Bacon
Turkey
Notrees
Cut and Shoot

still spice up conversations. This author's personal favorite is when her 95-year-old mother-in-law says something is 'so soft it makes her ass laugh.' A few more fun ones (avert your eyes if you're easily offended):

⇒ *More nervous than a cat in a room fulla rockin' chairs*

⇒ *Hotter than a jalapeño fart*

⇒ *Purdy (pretty) as a speckled pup*

⇒ *Slicker 'n owl sheee-it*

⇒ *He was on that like white on rice*

⇒ *She was hit with the ugly stick*

⇒ *This ain't my first rodeo*

⇒ *Dance with the one that brung ya*

Regional Differences

All inadequate, of course, but it is possible to make some vast generalizations about the different personalities you'll find in the cities and regions around the state.

If Texas is a 'Whole Other Country,' as the tourist board claims, then Austin is another country within that country. The progressive politics and creative inhabitants of the capital city are just way too far out there for many Texans. Hippies moved in during the 1970s and their legacy lives on: living green is not an idea here, it's a way of life. Even the dot-com people who came next were totally cool. Today, the high-tech workforce pool (and favorable tax structures) continues to attract employers like Facebook and eBay. Downtown especially, the population is youngish, hip, athletically outdoorsy and probably has the highest number of tattoos per capita. People who live in other cities are likely to admit Austin's a great place to visit, they just don't want to live there, but Austinites are more than OK with that.

In the Big D you'll find more shoppers and socialites – it's the see-and-be-seen set of the Texas crowd. But it's not all show. Dallas is sixth on the list of cities that house the most billionaires (with a 'B') in the world – 21 live in Dallas, to be exact. That's not to say people aren't friendly – this *is* Texas, after all. Folks here will smile and call you sweetie-pie along with the best of 'em. Thankfully the big hair and rhinestone-studded-style days passed with the '80s (ok, the '90s). This is the new *Dallas,* complete with a new TV show.

In Dallas the money's new, and everyone flaunts it. In Houston the money's old, and nobody gives a damn. This is the kind of town where the guy in old cowboy boots drinking a Lone Star at the bar might be an oil-company millionaire. (Or he might just be a guy in old cowboy boots.) Wearing jeans to a fancy restaurant is not frowned upon as long as they're starched. Although completely casual, Houston retains a strong conservative streak. Even though the city has a large gay and lesbian population and an annual Pride Parade, you're unlikely to see much PDA on the street.

San Antonio is probably the most Tex-Mexican of the bunch, and locals are proud of their Hispanic art and culture. Townwide fiestas (festivals) are common, and you can hear mariachis on the River Walk nightly. These festivities are just a natural outgrowth of the warm, extended-family get-togethers that happen every weekend all around town. If you're lucky enough to be invited, you'll be calling the matriarch *abeula* ('grandmother,' or a term for a beloved older woman) before long.

El Paso is closer to California than to east Texas, and it shows. In many ways the residents (and the food) have a lot more in common with New Mexico than with the Texas Hill Country heartland.

Texas Cultural Guides

Kinky Friedman's Guide to Texas Etiquette (Kinky Friedman; 2001)

Just a Guy: Notes from a Blue Collar Life (Bill Engvall; 2007)

There's Nothing in the Middle of the Road but Yellow Stripes & Dead Armadillos (Jim Hightower; 1997)

Fixin' to be Texan (Helen Bryant; 1998)

If a Texan passes you on a country road, they'll likely raise a few fingers off the steering wheel in greeting or give a nod of their head. That's driving code for 'Howdy,' so nod back and smile.

West Texans, in general, are a rural lot. Living with that blazing sun and desert drought isn't easy. It's a hardy, well-tanned soul that chooses such an isolated life; that's probably why there's a certain stubborn, determined-to-go-my-own-way spirit here. Artists and outdoorsy folks are drawn to outposts such as Marfa and Fort Davis.

Weather is a big topic of conversation in Texas. When it rains a lot, it can be a *gully-washer*, a *toad-strangler* or *turd-floater*. But until it rains like *a cow pissin' on a flat rock*, it's hardly coming down at all.

Ethnic Identities

Hispanic

According to the census bureau, just under 40% of Texas' population is of Hispanic descent. But that statistic is misleading, and not just because everyone might not have been counted. Tex-Mex is a way of life here. Mexican culture, foods and traditions are inexorably interwoven in the Texas tapestry – whether people are conscious of it or not. Office workers order out breakfast *taquitos* (tacos) for breakfast, Spanglish peppers everyone's conversations and schoolkids study 'the first Thanksgiving,' when Don Juan de Oñate and 500 followers broke bread with Native Americans on the banks of the Rio Grande in 1598.

Understandably, the Hispanic influence is more pronounced the further south you get. But there are pockets in any city where it's no trouble at all to get around if you don't speak English. Unfortunately, the state's prosperity has not extended evenly to all quarters. Texas has the highest proportion of minimum-wage workers in the USA, and the lowest percentage of citizens who hold a high-school diploma. Areas of the state with the highest numbers of Hispanics are often the poorest. Bringing family members in other countries over officially is a complicated process that can take years and years. It's not uncommon to hear of those who hired 'coyotes,' the often exploitative 'guides' who help some circumvent the system.

European

Of the many European immigrant groups that arrived at the turn of the 20th century, it's the Germans and the Czechs that have had the longest-lasting cultural affects on the state. Most settled in Hill Country and central-east Texas counties like Washington, where today you can see signs asking *Jak sa maš?* (How are you?) A surprising number of residents still speak the language of their forebears. Both the small-town dance halls and meat-market barbecue that Texas is famous for grew out of traditions these Europeans brought with them. Local festivals in central areas celebrate the polka and favorite foods, such as sausage and *kolache* (sweet-bread pastries stuffed with savories or sweets).

Asian

Although making up only between 4% and 7% of any city's population, Asian immigration to urban Texas has been increasing, especially from Vietnam. Houston has the largest melting pot, with Korean neighborhoods and a 'Little India,' in addition to large Vietnamese and Chinese communities. This has meant an expanded array of authentic foods have entered the local lexicon. Don't be surprised when a *bánh mì* (Vietnamese sandwich) food truck pulls up next to you.

Native American

There's a notable absence of Native Americans in Texas. The small population is a result of several factors, including disease. But much of it can be attributed to the mass exile way back during the end of the Republic of Texas and beginning of statehood. There are three state-recognized tribes with reservations in Texas. The Alabama-Coushatta Reservation, and its casino, is in east Texas, near Livingston. The Ysleta del Sur Pueblo have their reservation outside El Paso, and the Kickapoo Tribe occupies

In smaller Texas towns, traffic still comes to a halt for funeral processions – even on the highway. Follow locals' lead and pull off to the side.

land in southwest Texas, near Eagle Pass. Of the east Texas tribe whose language gave Texas its name, the Caddo Indians, only a dozen or so native speakers remain.

Lifestyle

So you want to know about life in Texas? Pull on some boots, get in the truck, cruise the farm-to-market (FM) back roads, eat hole-in-the-wall barbecue, jump in a swimming hole, buy someone a beer, sweet-talk your waiter, burn your tongue with salsa, witness the madness of a high-school football game, say 'ma'am' to young girls and old ladies alike, wave to a stranger, curse in Spanish and two-step all night in a honky-tonk. In other words, live it.

Recreation

Texas is a work-hard, play-hard kind of state. Kicking back is serious business around here. Come weekend, you'll usually find folks in the great outdoors: off at their hunting camp, attending their tyke's football game, throwin' some meat on the pit (which could be any kind of barbecue, even a gas grill) or just rockin' on the neighbor's porch.

In the summer heat, water plays a big role – anyone who can get to some usually does. Lakes fill with recreational boaters and swimmers, and those who are close enough to hit the beaches do so. Rivers seem to hold a special place in Texan hearts. Many a Texan grew up floating in an inner-tube down the Guadalupe, or the Frio, or the Comal, or the San Marcos... Whether riding over mild white water, shoes flying, kids squealing, or drifting peacefully for hours with beer in the cooler bobbing next to you, it's a big party – one that's not to be missed if you can help it. Locals don't even worry if the river's not running, they'll set their camp chair – or their bottoms – down in the water and stay a spell anyway.

Based on old Texas law, it's still illegal to shoot a buffalo from the 2nd story of a hotel. It's also illegal to milk a stranger's cow.

Hunting & Gun Ownership

Yes, there are a lot of guns in Texas. And no, Texas gun laws are not especially strident. Beyond saying that, it's hard to pin down many specifics about gun ownership in the state. Wild guestimates conclude that there are about 51 million guns here, for a population of 26 million. Most owners here firmly believe that they have a right to protect their property and those they love; that having a gun, and knowing how to use it, is not just a crime deterrent, but a crime stopper.

Not to mention that hunting is as much a Texas tradition as the pickup truck. Boys get their first pellet guns at eight or 10, and they're accompanying their fathers on dove and deer hunts soon after. Girls are more than welcome to come along if they want to. Gun owning is a way of life in Texas, and despite increasing gun-control legislation in other states, that's not something likely to change any time soon.

Though not enforced, according to the Texas Bill of Rights, one must acknowledge the existence of a supreme being before being able to hold public office.

Religion

Texas is considered to be the 'buckle' in the Bible Belt – a swath of states across the Southern USA associated with conservative Protestantism and evangelical Christianity. Roughly 56% of the population claims some religious affiliation. Surprisingly, Catholicism is actually the largest denomination, due to the significant Hispanic population.

The evidence is in the good number of churches you'll see as you drive along. Lubbock is rumored to have the highest number per capita in the US, but that's hard to pin down. Abilene has three Christian universities in a town of 122,300 people. In Houston, charismatic church leader Joel Osteen bought out the former Rockets basketball stadium when his

Lakewood Church needed to expand (that's 16,300 seats filled twice on Sunday).

In east Texas, this also means many of the counties are 'dry' – you can order drinks in restaurants, but you can't buy liquor at stores there. And nowhere in the state can you buy beer before noon on a Sunday. Go out to a restaurant for lunch that day and you'll find all the tables full with families come straight from church in their Sunday best.

Culture
Literature

Writing has deep roots in Texas. In the 1880s, famed short-story writer William Sidney Porter, whose pen name was O Henry, lived and wrote in a Victorian cottage in Austin that's now the O Henry Museum. Born in 1890, Pulitzer Prize–winning novelist Katherine Anne Porter, who grew up in Kyle, won critical acclaim for her penetrating short stories.

There are hundreds of notable Texan writers, and more are coming up all the time. We've listed a sampling of the best that Texas has to offer to give you an overview. An honorable mention goes to vampire-tale author Anne Rice, who was born in Texas but writes about and lives in New Orleans.

Larry McMurtry (b 1936) The Wichita Falls–born icon whose many Texas-set books and screenplays have entered into the realm of legend. *Lonesome Dove*, *The Last Picture Show* and *Terms of Endearment* are just a few of his novels.

Sandra Cisneros (b 1954) A San Antonio resident who grew up straddling the Mexican-American cultural line. Her first novel, *House on Mango Street*, is a must-read.

The Searchers (directed by John Ford, 1956) is one of the finest roles ever for John Wayne – the ultimate silver-screen cowboy. A pioneer family is murdered on their Texas ranch, and their daughter Natalie Wood is kidnapped, setting off a decade-long search by her uncle, played by the Duke.

ICONIC TEXAS FILMS

Giant (1956) This film's as sprawling as the King Ranch that was its inspiration. Elizabeth Taylor, Rock Hudson and James Dean are superb in this big-ticket yarn tracing the life of an oil and ranching family.

The Last Picture Show (1971) This engaging film is based on a Larry McMurtry novel that follows the coming of age of two high-school football players in a deader-than-dirt small Texas town in the 1950s.

The Thin Blue Line (1988) Director Errol Morris' powerful documentary tells the story of Randall Adams, who was given a life prison sentence for murdering a Dallas policeman but who turned out to be innocent. The film got Adams released – no small feat – and captured the confession of the real killer.

El Mariachi (1992) Robert Rodriguez' little movie shot on the Texas–Mexico border for $7000 became an icon for film-school students everywhere when it was shown across the USA. It is a charming fable about an unlucky traveling mariachi.

Hands on a Hard Body (1997) SR Bindler's hilarious documentary follows four sleep-deprived contestants as they vie to win a new Nissan hardbody pickup truck.

Hope Floats (1998) Sandra Bullock and Harry Connick Jr play former school mates falling in love when she returns to her small Texas hometown after a messy divorce. Does a good job showcasing life in little Smithville.

Friday Night Lights (2004) Predating the TV series, the movie is based on Buzz Bissinger's true story about the role the local Permian Panthers High School football team played in uplifting the depressed west Texas town of Odessa.

No Country for Old Men (2007) Cormac McCarthy's bleak Western landscapes meet the Coen Brothers' morbid humor in this rapturously terrifying flick. It's a harrowing, tightly paced film about a welder in west Texas who finds a bundle of drug money and decides to keep it. (Guess what? *Bad* idea.)

LIFE IN TEXAS CULTURE

James A Michener (1907–97) A Texas transplant, Michener is known for his epic fictionalized histories of regions and countries, including, of course, *Texas*.

Molly Ivins (1944–2007) Nobody beat syndicated columnist Molly Ivins on pure acerbic wit and the exposure of Texasisms big and small. Her books were even better; start with *Molly Ivins Can't Say That, Can She?*

Cormac McCarthy (b 1933) El Paso–born McCarthy has written numerous brooding, dark and masterfully crafted novels. *All the Pretty Horses* won the US National Book Award.

Mary Karr (b 1955) Known for her best-selling, shoot-from-the-hip memoir *The Liar's Club,* which brought her gritty Texas girlhood to vivid life. *Cherry* was the follow-up.

James Lee Burke (b 1936) Best known for his series of Dave Robicheaux detective novels, such as *Purple Cane Road.* Burke also wrote *Two for Texas,* a historical novel covering the Texas War for Independence.

Rick Riordan (b 1964) His page-turning thrillers have wonderfully twisted plots; look for *The Devil Went Down to Austin, The Last King of Texas* or *The Widower's Two-Step.*

On the Big & Little Screen

Hundreds and hundreds of films have been shot in Texas, including cult favorites *Dazed and Confused* and *Office Space,* and the original slasher flick, *Texas Chainsaw Massacre.*

In recent years Austin's filmmaking scene has blossomed into an industry spearheaded by directors Richard Linklater, Robert Rodriguez and Quentin Tarantino, and actor Sandra Bullock, all of whom either live or own property in Austin. Of the state's many film festivals, the town boasts two of the heavy hitters: the Austin Film Festival (p70) in October and the South by Southwest (SXSW) Film Festival (p70) in March.

Any number of TV shows have included Texas in some capacity, including *Reba, King of the Hill, The Client List* and even *Storage Wars Texas,* a reality show on A&E. But *Dallas* (1978–89) is undoubtedly the most recognized Texas TV show of all times. The soap opera resumed in 2012 as the new *Dallas* for three additional seasons, continuing to follow filthy-rich oil family the Ewings. Several original cast members returned; unfortunately, Larry Hagman (who played Ewing scion 'JR') passed away during the filming of the second series.

Stars from Texas

Carol Burnett

Patrick Swayze

Jennifer Love Hewitt

Eva Longoria

Jamie Foxx

Matthew McConaughey

Renee Zellweger

Steve Martin

Tommy Lee Jones

Summer Glau

THE COWBOYS

Perhaps no other figure in literary or cinematic history has been so romanticized as the cowboy. The image has become a symbol of the freedom of wide open spaces and the industrious and untamable nature of the people of Texas themselves.

Mexican *vaqueros* (wranglers) brought their methods to Texas and passed them on. The cowboys caught calves using a rope called a lariat (from the Spanish *la reata*), and imprinted them for identification using the heated-iron design of the owner's brand. When the cowboys got bored they strengthened their skills by competing with one another – events that have evolved into the rodeos held all over the state come springtime.

But it's the cattle drive (p338) that most captured the cinematographer's vision of Texas. Around the end of the Civil War, cowboys would herd thousands of cattle up the Chisholm Trail to Kansas City railroads. The pack was led by a scout and the chuckwagon, the field kitchen used to prepare food in advance of the arrival of the herd. To filter the dust, cowboys used bandanna handkerchiefs tied over their noses and mouths.

While horses would be changed in relays along the trail, the cowboy always kept his own masterfully crafted saddle. By the 1880s the railroads had come to Fort Worth and most of the land was fenced. Cattle-driving was a hardscrabble life, one that didn't last more than a couple of decades, but the cowboy legacy in Texas endures today.

Coming in a close second for illustrating iconic Texas stereotypes is *Friday Night Lights* (2006–11), based on the film and the book of the same name. It was originally based on life and football in the small west-Texas town of Odessa. Though garnering critical acclaim and cult-like status in-state, it was never universally popular and was canceled. You can still catch it on iTunes and Netflix.

Music Scene

Country-and-western crooners dusty from the trail, western-swing artists mixing it up, outlaws creating their own kind of music – whatever subgenre of country you want to discuss, you can bet it ties back to Texas. That's not to say there aren't rockers from the Lone Star State, of course: Austin has long been a hub of the alternative scene and Tejano still gets some play in the south.

Early Cowboy Country

The musical roots for country and western trace back to Anglo-Irish folk songs. But it was the singing cowboys of the silver screen that first brought the sound to national attention in North America. Classic singers like Gene Autry and Tex Ritter, both Texas-born boys, first played the musical hero on radio shows in the 1930s, then on TV; combined they also starred in more than 100 movies.

About the same time, Bob Wills was playing his violin at ranch dances in west Texas. He learned frontier-style fiddlin' from his granddad and jazzy blues from African American workers in the cotton fields. He mixed that with other sounds he heard around – mariachi, Tejano, polka – and the result was western swing, a Texas original. 'San Antonio Rose' became the signature song of his band, the Texas Playboys. This enduring new style of country music continues to be popular today.

Music Museums

Tex Ritter's Texas Country Music Hall of Fame (p247)

Bob Wills Museum (p191)

Buddy Holly Center (p188)

Museum of the Gulf Coast (p255)

The Classics

The 1950s and '60s saw the emergence of Nashville and the Grand Ole Opry as an epicenter of the country sound, which included everything from ballads to rockabilly, an offshoot of western swing. Some of the classics in country music from this era had Texas connections: Earnest Tubbs, Jim Reeves, Buck Owens, Johnny Horton, Lefty Frizzell, Johnny Rodriguez, George Jones, Don Williams, Ray Price, Roger Miller and Willie Nelson, among others. The latter three toured Texas' small clubs and honky-tonks together for many years; country-music variety hours were also all the rage on television at the time. (If you look online, you can find photos of a young, straight-laced, short-haired Willie Nelson from back then.) Even if all the stars weren't from Texas, many were crooning about it: Marty Robbins' bittersweet 'El Paso' is perhaps the most classic country ballad of all time.

Outlaw Country & Austin's Influence

Whether it was Willie Nelson leaving Nashville or the Armadillo World Headquarters club opening that had more influence on what happened next in Texas country is hard to say. But either way, it had to do with Austin.

The Armadillo of the 1970s was a hippie haven. The club's owners included Eddie Wilson, former band manager for Shiva's Head Band, and Jim Franklin, a local muralist and poster artist. They created a place that quickly became known as a counterculture hangout, a bar frequented by bikers, cowboys, hippies and college kids alike. They played a wide variety of music, but it was here that Texas singer-songwriters pioneered what would be called 'outlaw country.'

Willie had come home to Texas looking for more creative freedom than Nashville allowed. He, Waylon Jennings and Kris Kristofferson started writing music that mixed softer, traditional Nashville country with blues and rock, rhythms reminiscent of honky-tonks' early days. Though there was an edge to the music, the term 'outlaw' had a lot more to do with the singers' personal lives than with the music.

Tunes such as 'Luckenbach, Texas' and 'Mammas, Don't Let Your Babies Grow Up to be Cowboys' forced the industry to take notice. Musicians and bands who had been hard-pressed to find an audience for their country-rock songs began to flock to the Armadillo. Acts like Asleep at the Wheel and Kinky Friedman regularly played to packed crowds. In 1976, *Austin City Limits*, a live Texas public-radio music program that's still on the air, debuted with Willie Nelson playing on the first episode.

Though the Armadillo as it was closed its doors in the 1980s, **Threadgill's World Headquarters** (512-472-9304; www.threadgills.com; 301 W Riverside Dr; mains $8-15; 11am-10pm Mon-Thu, to 10:30pm Fri, 10am-10:30pm Sat, to 9:30pm Sun) restaurant, opened in 1996 in a building next door, continues to book live acts five nights a week.

Loosely based on a now-defunct bar in a Houston suburb called Gilley's, John Travolta's *Urban Cowboy* (1980) struck a chord across the nation (though Texans often heard a dissonant note, claiming it was a caricature of local culture). For the next few years there were country-and-western bars with mechanical bulls all across the country.

MUSIC SCENE OUTLAW COUNTRY & AUSTIN'S INFLUENCE

Popular Country & George Strait

Little did the San Marcos college band Ace in the Hole know that when they hired George Strait as lead singer in 1981 they'd be launching a superstar. At the time of writing, Strait has had 45 number-one hit singles on *Billboard* – the most of any country musician. But he didn't stop there, releasing a 40th album. His signature neotraditional sound, and those starched Wrangler jeans and boots, are the reason for much of his success. George Strait is a real cowboy: one with a ranch, one who participates in team-roping events. In fact, what started as a little family affair with him and his brother Buddy catchin' calves has morphed into the **George Strait Team Roping Classic** (www.gstrc.com) in San Antonio, during which more than 650 teams compete for $700,000 in prizes.

Not just George Strait, but numerous country artists from Texas have garnered popular, mainstream country success from the 1980s to today. Perhaps you've heard a few of their names: the Gatlin Brothers, Barbara Mandrell, Kenny Rogers, Tanya Tucker, Reba McEntire, Brooks & Dunn (well, OK, one of them), Leanne Rimes, Dixie Chicks, Blake Shelton, Miranda Lambert... Should we go on? Of the up-and-

TEXAS COUNTRY TOP 10

New San Antonio Rose Bob Wills & His Texas Playboys

Luckenbach, Texas Waylon Jennings

On the Road Again Willie Nelson

Amarillo by Morning George Strait

What I Like about Texas Jerry Jeff Walker & Gary P Nunn

Miles and Miles of Texas Asleep at the Wheel

El Paso Marty Robbins

Waltz Across Texas Ernest Tubbs

Corpus Christi Bay Robert Earl Keen

God Blessed Texas Little Texas

ROCK IN TEXAS

There are those who say that Lubbock-born Buddy Holly invented rock and roll. While that may be stretching the truth more than a little, it's true that Texan musicians have been at the forefront of rock since its inception.

Other notable Lone Star rockers you may have heard of include Roy Orbison, Roky Erickson of the 13th Floor Elevators, Janis Joplin, ZZ Top, the Steve Miller Band, the Fabulous Thunderbirds and the Butthole Surfers. Possibly the biggest name to come out of Texas these days is Houston-born rock-pop diva Beyoncé, who has won an armful of Grammys with her 3½-octave range.

Texas also has proven a hotbed for indie-rock talent, and the best place to see it – other than every night of the week at clubs throughout Austin, Denton and Dallas – is at the SXSW and Austin City Limits festivals. Austin-based alternative bands that have achieved some success include Spoon and White Denim. For more on the current scene, check out http://austin.thedelimagazine.com.

comers, Morgan Frazier, a John Lennon Songwriter Contest winner, is one to watch – at 19 she's already played the Grand Ole Opry several times.

Texas Country Today

Meanwhile, back at the ranch... Texas continued producing singer-songwriters who didn't quite fit the Nashville country mold. Following close behind Waylon and Willie were artists like David Allen Coe, Lyle Lovett, Jimmie Dale Gilmore, Robert Earl Keen, Lucinda Williams, Rodney Crowell and Jerry Jeff Walker (admittedly a transplant).

And yet another subgenre was created. When you hear someone talking about 'Texas country,' they're talking about a sound as well as describing the fact that the musicians hail from the state. Think of it as a progressive continuation of the outlaw phase. Radio stations across the state host daily or weekly Texas-country hours; some have even changed their format to be all Texas country, all the time.

Dance Halls & Honky Tonks

Czech and German immigrants brought more than barbecue to the central part of the state when they arrived in the late 1800s: they also brought their tradition of dance halls. At one time there may have been thousands of cavernous wooden dance halls in the country, but few remain today.

Though they originally hosted polka bands, today they're all country. Most are old, but some, like Cheatham St Warehouse (p121), are newer, or made from metal. The well-known Gruene Hall (p120), outside San Antonio, is one of the oldest dance halls in Texas. But many halls are in tiny towns too small to mention, or perhaps hold dances only once a month – for example, **Twin Sisters Dance Hall** (www.twin sistersdancehall.com) in Blanco. If you're interested, it's worth searching out venue info and schedules on dance hall websites. (Hint: Schroeder Hall, Kendalia and Anhalt are classics, but not always open.)

Honky-tonks may be a bit more like bars than dance halls, but many have that same great old-timey Texas feel to them, Broken Spoke (p83) in Austin being the perfect example. You'll find these in towns and cities rather than way out in the country; they may be anything from a tiny basement bar to a huge *Urban Cowboy*–esque nightclub like Billy Bob's (p168) in Fort Worth. Bandera has several. We love the ones that are in old grocery stores or other businesses, such as John T Floore's Country Store (p113) and **Coupland Inn** (www. couplanddancehall.com).

When you're ready to head out two-stepping, what music will you be hearing? The clubs and halls in and around Austin and Hill Country especially have an incredible array of talent to choose from. Some of the old-timers occasionally still play in the area, so you may catch Willie Nelson or Ray Price if you're lucky. Cornell Hurd, the Derailers and Dale Watson are all great country crooners with tunes you can boot-scoot to. Mickey & the Motor Cars have a primarily Americana, rockabilly sound. And we love the bluesy-rock sensibility that Kelly Willis brings to her shows, usually performed with her husband, Bruce Robison.

More information:

➡ *Dance Halls & Last Calls: A History of Texas Country Music* (Geronimo Treviño III; 2002)

➡ Texas Dance Hall Preservation Inc (www.texasdancehall.org)

➡ Honky Tonk Texas, USA (www.honkytonktx.com/dancehalls)

Football!

What's the official religion in the state of Texas? Football. The word alone will incite passion, a smile and plenty of opinions in many Texans. Boys in Texas are raised to play when they're barely out of the cradle. And come game day – any game, at any level – all else is set aside to watch and, often, to party.

High-School Football

If you are in Texas on a Friday night from September to November, you should absolutely attend a high-school football game. HG Bissinger's book about Odessa, *Friday Night Lights,* and the subsequent movie and TV series, nail it. Texas high-school ball takes on mythic proportions and meanings, especially in small towns. At stake in games are local pride, reputations and other intangibles that fuel the mania. The team's quarterback is the local hero, every bit as popular as a mayor when things are going well.

Increasingly, 16- to 19-year-olds are expected to be facsimiles of the pros. Roughly 40,000 fans attended the most watched game of the Texas State High School Championships in 2016, held in the Dallas Cowboys' AT&T Stadium. Following local teams from across the state is not hard to do given the numerous websites on the subject; many games are now also televised each weekend.

Austin is home to Texas Roller Derby (www.txrd. com), five teams of tough athletes who also know how to put on a fun and flashy show.

How seriously games are taken can be seen by the trappings that surround them. Coaches are not as well paid here as in the pros, but they definitely do better than regular teachers. Then there are legions of students supporting the team's effort: assistants and trainers; varsity cheerleaders who ascend to the squad through competitions as ruthless as those on the field; vast marching bands; dancing and drill teams; honor guards for the flags; and many more. That's not to mention the enthusiastic parents who cheer, scream and raise more and more money.

For more information, try these websites:

Dave Campbell's Texas Football (www.texasfootball.com)
Texas High School Football (www.texashsfootball.com)
Texas Preps Football (www.txprepsfootball.com)

College Games

High-school games are great, but college football really makes Texas tick. Graduates are unfailingly loyal to their alma mater, but many rabid fans have never set one foot, academic or otherwise, on their favorite team's campus. State-school rivalries go back decades. The bitterest contest in Texas college football? Hands down, it's the University of Texas (UT) Longhorns and the Texas A&M Aggies. Next is the University of Oklahoma Sooners and the UT Longhorns. As the reorganization of the conferences that determine what teams play each other threatened to end some long-held series, lawmakers intervened. Yes, the classic Thanksgiving morning UT versus A&M football game got the state legislature's attention – it's that important.

OH, THERE ARE OTHER SPORTS?

Contrary to appearances, Texas does have all the same sports available as any other state. Soccer is quite a common activity for young boys and girls first taking to a field, but playing becomes less common as multisport athletes age and specialize in a more popular game. Softball, baseball and basketball are all played in intramural and school leagues.

On the national level, Dallas' Texas Rangers and the Houston Astros baseball teams have nice stadiums and draw some crowds. The National Hockey League (NHL) Dallas Stars ice hockey team draws less of a crowd, but there's still some turnout.

The Houston Rockets and Dallas Mavericks, pro National Basketball Association (NBA) teams, hold their own in terms of attendance and fan base, but Texans really go crazy for the San Antonio Spurs, a basketball team that has won five NBA championships – one of only five teams in the league to have done so.

In Major League Soccer, FC Dallas and the Houston Dynamo represent their respective cities. Houston won the league twice in 2006 and 2007, and neither have claimed the MLS Cup since, though FC Dallas did win the Supporters Shield in 2010 and 2016 for the best regular-season record in the league.

Each school has an elaborate set of traditions surrounding the game. UT fans 'bleed orange,' in reference to the school colors. A&M has 'yell' instead of 'cheer' leaders, who stir up massive noise in the stands with call-and-response chants that everybody knows. Various incarnations of the Texas Tech Red Raiders' primary mascot, the Masked Rider, have been galloping into the stadium (on real horseback) since 1954.

College football's not just fun and games, either: it's an industry. UT head coach Tom Herman's salary is a cool $5 million (plus incentives), putting him in a tie for the position of the country's 6th-highest paid coach with rival Kevin Sumlin of A&M. The rationale given for such salaries is that a successful team brings in huge revenue for the university. Needless to say, a coach's performance is a hot topic all season.

National Football League Teams & Tailgating

The Dallas Cowboys are the most famous football team not only in Texas but probably the entire USA. No one seems to mind that their glory days may have been in the 1980s, though.

Houston still mourns the loss of their original National Football League (NFL) team, the Oilers (now the Tennessee Titans), back in 1996. The city got a new team in 2000, the Texans, which continues to grow in popularity. When the Texans made the playoffs for the first time in 2011, it helped residents outside Houston find some interest in the team.

Tailgating, the practice of partying in the parking lot before kickoff, is almost a requirement before game attendance. Heck, some people tailgate and then watch the game on satellite TVs *in* the parking lot. Though this pregame party takes place nationwide, Texans do it up big. Expect to see pop-up 12ft-by-12ft awnings and guys painted in team colors kicking back in comfortable camp chairs next to a spread of food worthy of a top catering company. Preparations may be the most elaborate at pro games, but college fans get in on the act too. Though most college stadiums do not sell beer, they allow it – on game day only – out in the parking lot and at campus picnic spots nearby.

Land & Wildlife

Let the Texas landscape surprise you. No less than 35 ecoregions exist here, and not one of them is called 'hot and flat as a pancake'. (Though perhaps the northern Panhandle Plains should be...) In any case, contrary to stereotypes, white-sand beaches, soaring pine forests and snowcapped mountains are all part of the picture. Indigenous birds, mammals and alligators outnumber the head of cattle here. All told, the natural attractions are a major reason to visit Texas.

The Land

Texas, as everyone here will tell you, is big. The second-largest state in the US has an area of more than 268,000 sq miles. While that's less than half the size of Alaska, Texas is larger than all of Germany, the UK, Ireland, Belgium and the Netherlands combined. But those Western movies lie: Texas is not all dry desert, tumbleweeds and oil wells. In fact, with the natural boundaries of the Gulf of Mexico at the east and the Rio Grande at the west and south, Texas ranks as the eighth-largest state for total water area.

Texas Parks & Wildlife (www.tpwd.state.tx.us) is an incredible resource for information on land use and wildlife in Texas. Their downloadable Young Naturalist series is recommended for kiddos.

Within each major natural region of Texas there's a remarkable range of terrain. In northeast Texas, the Piney Woods is the southwestern edge of the southern coniferous forest belt and is characterized by a mix of pine and hardwood growth. The Gulf Coastal Plains, which run along the coast from Port Arthur to Brownsville, contain bays, lagoons, sandy barrier islands, saltwater marshes and flat grasslands. In the furthest southern reaches, palm trees grow here naturally.

Verdant hills and meandering rivers make up central Hill Country, which is part of the Edward Plateau, a limestone karst region. The southern Texas plains, from Hill Country south to the Rio Grande Valley, is brush country, with scrubby vegetation and abundant prickly-pear cacti. Spreading north of Austin there are several regions of prairies and plains. The land in the Panhandle is the highest and driest of these. Tablelands spread east of Lubbock and Amarillo, containing red rock canyons, badlands and mesas.

In west Texas, the basin-and-range terrain is home to the Guadalupe Mountains, with elevations of more than 8000ft, as well as Chihuahuan desert lands. South of the Guadalupe Mountains, the Big Bend region follows the Rio Grande through dramatic canyons and sheer walls beyond the Chisos Mountains.

National & State Parks

Texas has two national parks, Big Bend and Guadalupe Mountains, as well as 14 national preserves (www.nps.gov), 55 state-park properties (www.tpwd.state.tx.us) and four state forests. Oil drilling and natural-gas exploration is allowed, but managed, in some of the natural preserves and on public lands. As well as providing opportunities for recreational activities, many of the preserves offer interpretive activities and educational programs.

Environmental Diversity

Texas' sheer size and environmental diversity mean that it's home to a startling array of wildlife: over 5000 species of plant, 600 different birds (more than any other state) and 142 mammal species are found here.

Fauna

To the eternal shame of early settlers, American bison, or buffalo, were hunted to the brink of extinction and today exist only in remnant populations. These days, the two most famous Texas animals are the armadillo and longhorn steer, respectively the state's official smallest and largest mammals. The armadillo, whose bony carapace is unique among mammals, resembles an armored vehicle. Many homeowners are annoyed when the armadillo digs up their lawns in its search for grubs. Speeding drivers are a hazard for the armadillo, which you may first encounter as an inevitable sight on a long Texas drive: roadkill. Deer are also populous – and potential road dangers – in Hill Country.

Once the most common mammals found in west Texas, another (unofficial) mascot of the state is the black-tailed prairie dog essentially a fat, friendly squirrel that lives off prairie grasses. Highly sociable, prairie dogs live in large colonies called 'towns' and hibernate in winter. Natural and human-caused environmental changes have vastly reduced their population over the years, but protected prairie-dog towns can be found in west Texas and the Panhandle Plains.

It's a big old mammal party in Big Bend: a whopping 75 species call the region home. The black bear, all but gone from the region by the mid-20th century, made an amazing comeback about 20 years ago; more than 200 sightings are now reported in a typical year, most in the national park's Chisos Mountains. Mountain lions (sometimes called panthers)

STRIKIN' IT RICH

The most exciting geological aspect of Texas is why there's oil. The sticky black stuff sits beneath Texas, southern Mississippi and Alabama, and Louisiana; there is heaps of it under the Gulf of Mexico near all these states, as well as the Mexican states of Tamaulipas, Veracruz and Tabasco – all areas surrounding the huge sedimentary basin that forms the Gulf of Mexico.

Evolving for more than 100 million years, the basin consists of a thick sequence of sedimentary rocks. As the sedimentary material makes its way deeper into the earth, it's subjected to a great deal of pressure and heat – enough to convert much of the organic debris (the remains of plants and animals that are always part of sedimentary material) into petroleum. You know, to refine for gasoline, to fill up those ubiquitous Texas trucks needed to traverse these great distances... See, every issue here comes back, inexorably, to the land.

Petroleum flows freely, but tends to collect into large masses that migrate into traps – so named because rocks or other impermeable materials catch the oil – where it forms pools. Pools are what oil explorers are after. Under Texas, salt domes (which are just what they sound like) act as traps; when they're pierced, oil that has been trapped beneath gushes forth. That's what happened when early 1900s prospectors first struck oil at Spindle Top in Beaumont, and at the World's Richest Half Acre in Kilgore. Gushers, however, are rare these days, as oil exploration has become extremely sophisticated.

More recently it's the Eagle Ford shale, found south of Hill Country, that's making news. This late Cretaceous rock formation is mineral-rich, with oil and gas deposits. The high percentage of carbonate makes the formation more brittle, and therefore responsive to hydraulic fracturing (aka 'fracking'), which is used to extract it. This somewhat controversial process is fueling a growing economy in once-moribund south-central Texas.

are seen fairly rarely, but about two dozen live in the Chisos. And that blur you just saw streaking across the desert? It's probably a jackrabbit – Big Bend's full of the critters.

Bats

Thirty-one species of bat – those blind flying mammals that populate horror movies, Halloween decorations and attics – call Texas home. But bats are actually Texans' friends: they eat large amounts of mosquitoes and insects nightly, and rarely bother humans.

You'll hear references to 'Mexican free-tailed bats' – these are the ones you'll see streaming out from caves and from underneath the Congress Ave Bridge in Austin just before dusk. This is actually a migratory subspecies of Brazilian free-tailed bats *(Tadarida brasiliensis)*.

The endangered Mexican long-nosed bat has its only US home in the Chisos Mountains, where it summers. A total of 20 bat species live at Big Bend, ranking it top among national parks in bat diversity.

Texas' official flying mammal is the Mexican free-tailed bat. For a list of the best places to spot them, download the Texas Parks & Wildlife's bat-watching brochure at www.tpwd.state.tx.us/publications.

Birds

An image in many a traditional and blues song, the mockingbird – a long-tailed gray bird that can mimic other birds' songs – is the official bird of Texas.

Texas has more than 600 documented bird species – over 75% of all species reported in the US. Several on that list are threatened species. The endangered golden-cheeked warbler, which exclusively nests in central Texas, is best identified by the male's distinctive song heard during late spring. Delisted, but still protected, bald eagles nest in the eastern part of the state from October to July, and overwinter in the Panhandle Plains and central-east Texas. Aransas Pass on the Gulf Coast is the wintering home to the endangered whooping crane, the tallest bird in North America – males approach 5ft in height and have a 7ft wingspan.

More than 50% of species spotted in Texas are just passing through. The Central Flyway for annual bird migrations cuts right through Texas. Some avian navigators use this path to commute from the Arctic Circle all the way down to Patagonia. Spring migration starts as early as February, when ospreys are seen in great numbers near Houston, and continues through May. Fall migration runs roughly from September through November.

Shorebirds and water fowl – roseate spoonbill, ibis, heron, egret and, of course, ducks and geese – can commonly be found in coastal areas year-round, though their numbers increase come winter.

Dolphins & Fish

You don't have to drag the kids to SeaWorld in San Antonio to spot dolphins. Several species of dolphin call the Gulf of Mexico home, including rough-toothed, common, bottle-nosed, striped, pantropical, Atlantic spotted and Risso's dolphins. Take a boat ride along the coast and you'll likely see them playing in your wake.

Game fish are common throughout the state, especially bass and trout, and sport fishing is very popular in the gulf. Most of the Big Bend region's native fish are tiny. One species, the Big Bend mosquito fish, lives in only one pond inside Big Bend National Park and nowhere else in the world. At one time, the population sadly had dwindled to two males and one female.

Arachnophobes, beware: tarantulas are common in rural Texas, as are scorpions – 11 species of stinging scorpion live in the Big Bend region. Spot one? Give it plenty of room.

American Alligators

The name 'alligator' derives from the Spanish *el lagarto* (the lizard), and you'll find these reptiles in east Texas swamps and along the Gulf Coast.

They are usually (but not exclusively) found in fresh water: shallow lakes, marshes, swamps, rivers, creeks, ponds and human-made canals. Caddo Lake, Brazos Bend State Park and Anahuac National Wildlife Refuge are three likely places to catch a sighting.

Gators are carnivorous: even hatchlings eat insects, frogs, small fish, snails and the like. But they prefer prey that can be swallowed whole, such as fish, birds and snakes. Cold-blooded gators are warm-weather fans and are rarely active when the temperature dips below 68°F (20°C) – cold comfort to anyone who likes to swim the bayous come winter. Their metabolism slows considerably in cold weather, but they can die when the temperature is more than 100°F (38°C). To cool themselves, they sit on riverbanks or in the shade with their mouths wide open, which dissipates heat.

Horror movies aside, alligators generally eat only when they're hungry, not as a punitive measure – unless they're feeling attacked.

Snakes

There are snakes in Texas – hundreds of varieties of 'em. Thankfully the vast majority are not harmful. When walking through tall grass anywhere, especially in Big Bend, do keep an eye and ear out for the 11 poisonous kinds of rattlers. The very common western diamondback is the most dangerous; they can grow to be 8ft long, and have a big, heavy, brownish body marked with dark (almost black) diamond shapes, set off by yellowish white borders. Look where you're going and listen up: they usually rattle before they attack.

The coral snake's poison is the most potent of any North American snake. It looks very pretty – a slim body with sections of black and red divided by thin, orange-yellow stripes – and it can easily be mistaken for the harmless scarlet king snake. To tell them apart, remember this cheerful little rhyme: 'Red on yellow, kill a fellow; red on black, friend for Jack.' Fortunately, the coral snake is very shy and generally nocturnal, and on the whole it rarely bites people.

When traveling in high-risk areas, such as Big Bend or any place where there are tall grasses or shrubs, you can reduce the risk of being bitten by using basic common sense: wear boots and long pants, for example.

Flora

Wildflowers

Wildflowers are to Texas what fall foliage is to Vermont: a way of life. Wildflower tourism is so entrenched in the state that highway and local visitor centers can help you plan entire trips around watching them bloom. So what's the best time to see the crimsons and the blues in all their glory? Die-hard wildflower enthusiasts would tell you that the time to see the best and widest range is from mid-March to mid-April, when roadsides and fields throughout central and west Texas, and especially the Hill Country, become explosions of color – blankets of wonderful reds, rusts, yellows and blue. For more on finding spring sightings, search http://texas.wildflowersightings.org.

A sighting of Texas' official state flower, the bluebonnet, means that spring has officially sprung. While this wildflower, the name of which derives from its small, blue, bonnet-shaped petals, comes in several species of North American lupine, the most beloved and iconic in Texas culture is the *Lupinus texensis* – that's right, the Texas bluebonnet. Other beloved wildflower species include Indian blankets, also known as firewheels, the petals of which possess a red-orange-yellow pattern that looks almost woven. Indian paintbrushes share the same palette, but are shorter and often grow in

Field Guides

Birds of Texas (Keith Arnold; 2007)

Texas Wildflowers (Campbell & Lynne Loughmiller; 2006)

Trees of Texas (Stan Tekiela; 2009)

Animal Tracks of Texas (Ian Sheldon; 2000)

TEXAS GOES GREEN

Austin has led the way toward a greener future for Texas. The environmentally progressive city has garnered national and international awards for its initiatives, including the Green Building Program, which offers practical workshops on sustainable construction practices. Numerous private grassroots groups such as Save Our Springs Alliance – protector of the the Edwards Aquifer zone and the endangered Barton Springs salamander – act as watchdogs restraining overdevelopment.

Even the city government is getting green. Bike lanes and carbon-neutral buses have been around seemingly forever. Since 2000, all new municipal buildings in Austin have been built to Leadership in Energy & Environmental Design (LEED) standards. As of 2012, municipal departments buy 100% of their energy from renewable sources through GreenChoice.

Buying local, home-growing veggies and shopping at farmers markets have long been traditions with many Austin residents. But today we're seeing environmentally dedicated mixed-use, green communities pop up – complete with community gardens and green space, recycled art and green-energy use. We could go on, and on...

Austin may be leading the way, but other Texas towns are following suit. Houston constructed and continues to expand its light-rail system. Bike-sharing stations number 21 in town, and the Bikeways program is developing shared and single-use bike lanes. Dallas has likewise undertaken development of an extensive bikeway system. Several new gardens and green spaces have opened in that city. And all new municipal buildings (and those larger than 10,000 sq ft) are held to silver LEED standards, including the Perot Museum of Nature & Science that opened in 2012. For the SUV- and 1-ton-pickup-loving populace, it ain't always easy being green. But cities have made a start.

fields of bluebonnets. Mexican hats, which belong to the sunflower family and do resemble nodding sombreros, are easily found growing alongside highways. The pink-blossomed buttercups have a blush of yellow at the center.

Bluebonnet Festivals

Burnet (www.bluebonnetfestival.org)

Chappel Hill (www.chappellhill museum.org)

Ennis (www.visitennis.org)

La Vernia (www.lavernialions.org)

Flower-crazed tourists make the epic drive to Big Bend region specifically to see the wildflowers. The blooms peak early March to April in the lowlands and May to July in the Chisos Mountains, but it's possible to find flowers year-round; there's often a second bloom in late summer after the season's heavy rains. The Big Bend bluebonnet, a 2ft-tall relative of the Texas state flower, blooms from December through June in the lowlands. Other varieties you may see include prickly poppy, sweet William, snapdragon, cardinal flower, silverleaf, bracted paintbrush, rock nettle and desert verbena.

Desert Plants

The creosote bush is among the most prevalent desert species in Texas, with dark-green leaves and a 30ft taproot that searches for underground water. The ocotillo, sometimes called coachwhip, is a woody shrub with long, slender wands that produce scarlet flowers. Lechuguilla, a fibrous-spined agave, is unique to the Chihuahuan Desert and may grow 15ft tall. Candelilla has long been used by the area's indigenous people to produce wax.

Prickly pear is the most common kind of cactus, with several varieties: Engelman, purple-tinged, brown-spine and blind (so-called because it looks like it has no thorns – but it does, so beware). Other cactus species include fishhook, cholla, claret cup, rainbow, eagle's claw and strawberry pitaya. After spring rains, look for claret cup and other cacti in Big Bend to be in brilliant bloom.

(One species you won't find is the saguaro cactus, which – although often used by New York City ad agencies as a symbol for west Texas – is actually found in the Sonoran Desert of Arizona.)

Survival Guide

Directory A–Z

Accommodations

Rates are highest during summer high season and school holidays, but an event in town can send prices soaring.

Hotels Chain hotels and motels rule the state, but you'll find worthwhile historic hotels and boutique properties in larger cities.

B&Bs The best are family-run, with involved owners who love to chat about the area.

Camping The most scenic sites are found in state and national parks

Hostels There are very few in Texas. Most are in Austin and Houston.

Ranches Head to Bandera for horseback rides included in your stay.

Amenities

Beverages Midrange motels and hotels may have microwaves and small refrigerators in the rooms. Top-end properties usually stock the minibar with miniature liquor bottles and pricey snacks – check the price list before popping open a bottle.

Internet Wired or wireless internet is almost always available at lodgings. In top-end hotels, expect to pay from $14 per day, or it may be included in the resort fee; elsewhere, it's free.

Nonsmoking/smoking Unless otherwise noted, all lodgings we list offer at least some nonsmoking rooms. More and more hotels and motels are going completely smoke-free. B&Bs never allow smoking in the building itself, and some may not even allow smoking outside on the porch or in the garden.

Parking In the downtown core of major cities, you'll pay $17 to $40 per night for parking; otherwise it is usually freely available.

B&Bs

Texas B&Bs are not super-casual or cost-effective. These are traditionally well-established businesses, not just a spare room in someone's home. They might be in rambling old houses or newer and purpose-built. Owners usually live on-site, but in separated quarters (though some have professional innkeepers that sleep away).

Communal breakfasts are served at a set hour, at a big dining table, allowing guests to get to know one another and compare travel notes. But this is not always the case. Breakfast may be delivered to your door, or weekdays it might just be a gift certificate to a local restaurant or a light continental breakfast. Off-site innkeepers will generally provide the requisite restaurant recommendations but may be scarce outside breakfast and check-in hours.

In addition to some sort of breakfast, amenities often include baked goods in the afternoons and beverage stations available all day. Most B&Bs have common areas for guests to gather. Private, en suite bathrooms are the rule rather than the exception. Each B&B has its own policies, but almost all prohibit smoking, pets and children under the age of 12. Cancellations of less than a week may forfeit one night's room cost and two-day stays may be required.

Camping & Holiday Parks

Tent site rates range from $10 to $25 per night. Most campgrounds are set up for recreational vehicles (RVs), with electricity and water at sites ($20 to $60 per night). Facilities almost always include water, toilets and showers. Private campgrounds may have clubrooms, pools and internet access.

SLEEPING PRICE RANGES

The following prices refer to a room with a bathroom; rates do not include a 6% occupancy tax or any city taxes (up to an additional 7%).

$ less than $100

$$ $100–$250

$$$ more than $250

Hostels

The Texas hostel network is very small. Austin has several good ones, and Houston has four. Check www.hostelz. com to see if any others have popped up.

Hotels

Chain hotels and motels rule the state; relatively few places are independently owned.

HISTORIC HOTELS

Texas has some excellent historic hotels. Two of the best are the **Menger** (Map p98; ☑800-345-9285, 210-223-4361; www.mengerhotel.com; 204 Alamo Plaza; r from $176; P🐾😺) in San Antonio and the **Driskill** (Map p62; ☑512-439-1234; www.driskillhotel. com; 604 Brazos St; r/ste from $299/419; P@😺) in Austin. You'll also find a few out in the far-west Texas towns of Fort Davis and Marathon.

BARE-BONES BASIC

➡ Chains such as Motel 6, Red Roof Inn, Econo Lodge.

➡ Synthetic comforters, fake-veneer furnishings: expect that they'll all look oddly similar.

➡ Hard to find nice ones under $70 a night.

MIDRANGE

➡ Brands include La Quinta, Best Western, Hilton Garden Suites, Marriott Courtyard.

➡ From $100 to $169 per night.

➡ Changeable comforters and coffeemakers are usually standard.

➡ Rarely have an on-site restaurant.

TOP END

➡ Four Seasons, Westin, St Regis etc

➡ Boutique hotels in Houston, Dallas and San Antonio fall into this category.

➡ Stylish surrounds, posh public areas.

➡ Numerous dining and drinking outlets on-site.

➡ Rates start at $250; some basic amenities (eg internet) may cost extra.

Lodges

In national parks, accommodations are limited to either camping or park lodges operating as a concession. Lodges are often rustic-looking but usually quite comfortable inside. Restaurants are on the premises and tour services are often available.

Lodge rooms in national parks are not cheap, with most rooms going for close to $150 for a double during the high season, but they are your only option if you want to stay inside the park without camping. If you are coming during the high season, make a reservation months in advance.

Big Bend National Park has a lodge, but Guadalupe Mountains National Park does not.

Motels

Motels with $70 rooms are found mostly in small towns along major highways and near the airports and outlying interstate loops in major cities. Rooms are usually small, and although a minimal level of cleanliness is maintained, expect scuffed walls, thin towels, old furniture and strange noises from your shower. Even these rooms normally have a private bathroom, air-conditioning and a TV. The cheapest budget places may not accept reservations, but at least phone from the road to see what's available.

All of the national chain motels accept reservations by phone or online. Chains like Red Roof Inn, Travelodge and Econo Lodge are typically just a few dollars more than your basic Motel 6, which costs from around $70 per night. At

the slightly more expensive Super 8 Motels and Days Inns, expect firmer beds and free continental breakfast. Stepping up, chains in the $100-to-$169 range have more spacious rooms, indoor swimming pools and other niceties; La Quinta is a major player in this category, as are Ramada Inn, Best Western, Hampton Inn, Marriott-owned Fairfield Inn and some Holiday Inn properties.

Ranches

Guest ranches, also called dude ranches, can be fun places to stay, but they are few and far between. The exception is in the countryside around Bandera, west of San Antonio, where a dozen or more dude ranches offer horseback riding and cowboy activities as part of the daily rate, which also includes full board (from $120 per person, per day). For more information, log on to www. banderacowboycapital.com or contact the **Bandera County Convention & Visitors Bureau** (CVB; ☑830-796-3045; www.banderacowboycapital.com; 126 Hwy 16; ⊙9am-5pm Mon-Fri, 10am-3pm Sat).

Guest ranches elsewhere may provide you an opportunity to interact with animals, or they may just be a pretty place to stay in the country.

Resorts

➡ Generally located in ideal landscapes such as the Hill Country.

➡ A few may be found in cities.

➡ Enhanced grounds and facilities may include several pools, trails or sports options.

➡ Resort fee of $32 to $40 per night.

BOOK YOUR STAY ONLINE

For more accommodations reviews by Lonely Planet authors, check out http://lonelyplanet.com/hotels/. You'll find independent reviews, as well as recommendations on the best places to stay. Best of all, you can book online.

Discounts

AAA Membership in the American Automobile Association provides access to hotel-room discounts, and some reduced admission as well as roadside assistance.

Seniors If you are over the age of 65, discount rates on hotel rooms and attractions may be available. Having an American Association of Retired Persons (AARP) card is not usually required.

Students An International Student Identity Card (ISIC) or official school ID card often gets you discounts on admission to museums and other attractions.

Electricity

120V/60Hz

Food

Dinner reservations are essential at all top-end ($$$) restaurants in our listings. Smoking is not allowed indoors at most restaurants in Texas (though in some places it may be OK on the patio).

Insurance

Taking out a travel-insurance policy to cover medical problems and other issues is a good idea in the USA, where some privately run hospitals refuse care without evidence of insurance and costs can be far higher than in most developed nations. These policies are offered by travel agencies, your airline and others. Different policies cover different circumstances, so always check the fine print, especially if you're planning on undertaking any risky outdoor activities.

Worldwide travel insurance is available at www.lonely planet.com/bookings. You can buy, extend and claim online anytime – even if you're already on the road.

Internet Access

Free wi-fi service for your smartphone, laptop or tablet is extremely common in restaurants, bars, shopping centers and many other public places. Airports usually have hot spots, but it's not always free. Most hotels have wi-fi in the lobbies and wired or wi-fi access in the rooms.

Not traveling with your own device makes finding access trickier. Your best bet is the local library (free), or a copy center like FedEx Office (from $7 per hour).

Legal Matters

Aside from it being against the law to milk a stranger's cow or shoot a buffalo from any 2nd-story hotel window, the laws in Texas are similar to the rest of the US.

➡ If you are arrested, you are assumed innocent until proven guilty; you have a right to make one phone call and you will be assigned an attorney if you cannot afford one.

➡ It's illegal to possess controlled substances and to drive under the influence (more than .08% blood-alcohol level).

➡ Possession or consumption of alcohol is prohibited for anyone under 21.

➡ No Texas counties permit sales before noon on Sunday, and some Texas counties ban alcohol sales entirely.

➡ Note that driving speed limits are often strictly enforced, especially in small towns trying to make their budget. There is no provision for on-the-spot fine payment (so don't offer!).

LGBT Travelers

Texas is generally conservative. The larger cities have gay, lesbian, bisexual and transgender communities, but outside of Pride days and Austin in general, you won't see sexual identities being flaunted. In rural areas, displays of affection may draw negative attention from locals; we advise not trying it.

Resources

Gay & Lesbian Yellow Pages (www.glyp.com) Phone directories to Austin, Dallas, Galveston, Houston and San Antonio.

National Gay & Lesbian Task Force (www.thetaskforce.org) Advocacy group with great national news coverage.

This Week in Texas (www.thisweekintexas.com) Statewide publication with business directories and bar guide.

Maps

As phone and tablet GPS become more widely used, maps become less necessary, but in rural areas and some small towns in Texas these

---

EATING PRICE RANGES

The following price ranges refer to a standard main course. Tips and taxes are not included.

$ less than $15

$$ $15–$25

$$$ more than $25

GPS options are not always reliable. Maps are available at bookstores and at gas stations; you can order ahead of time at Texas Map Store (www.texasmapstore.com). Helpful maps include the following:

Delorme Texas State Atlas & Gazetteer Detailed atlas, good for rural roads.

Mapsco Indexed city maps covering all the main Texas towns.

Texas Official Travel Map Available free at many visitor centers and tourist offices across the state.

Money

ATMs are widely available. Credit cards are widely accepted, and generally required for reservations and car rentals. Tipping is essential – not optional.

ATMs

➡ Common everywhere: airports, banks, grocery stores, malls, gas station convenience stores, etc.

➡ Both your bank and the ATM you use will typically charge a small fee for each transaction (from $1.50 up to 5%).

➡ Local ATMs must display fees; check how much your bank charges before you leave home.

Credit Cards

➡ MasterCard or Visa are accepted at most places of business in Texas. A few eateries and shops take cash only.

➡ American Express, Discover and other major cards are less universal, but still widely accepted.

➡ A credit card is usually required to rent a car, make hotel reservations and purchase advance tickets for transportation.

Money Changers

The US dollar ($) is divided into 100 cents (¢). Coins come in denominations of

1¢ (penny), 5¢ (nickel), 10¢ (dime) and 25¢ (quarter). Quarters are the most commonly used coins in vending machines, toll booths and some parking meters, so it can be handy to have a stash of them. Bills (banknotes) come in $1, $2, $5, $10, $20, $50 and $100 denominations – $2 bills are rare, but perfectly legal. In smaller places, cashing $100 can be difficult. Carry some small bills, especially for tips.

Tipping

Tipping is not optional. Service employees make minimum wage and rely on tips.

Bars 15% to 20%, at least $1 per round.

Hotel $10 to $20 for concierges if they do a lot for you; $5 per stay for housekeeping is nice, though not as widely expected as other tips.

Restaurants 15% to 20%, depending on level of service.

Taxi drivers 10% to 15% of the fare.

Traveler's Checks

Traveler's checks from American Express or Thomas Cook offer protection from theft or loss, but they have fallen out of use in the US. Some places may not accept the checks at all, forcing you to exchange them in a bank. Using a mix of ATM withdrawals and some cash is easier.

Newspapers Major daily newspapers include the Austin-American Statesman (www.statesman.com), Dallas Morning News (www.dallasnews.com), Houston Chronicle (www.chron.com) and San Antonio Express-News (www.mysanantonio.com).

Magazines Texas Monthly (www.texasmonthly.com), Texas Highways (www.texashighways.com) and Texas Parks & Wildlife (www.tpwmagazine.com).

Radio National Public Radio stations in Austin (90.5FM), Dallas (90.1FM), Houston (88.7FM) and San Antonio (89.1FM) play local music and offer tips on local cultural events.

Opening Hours

Individual opening hours are listed in reviews; below are generalities. Sight and activity hours vary throughout the year and may decrease during the shoulder and low seasons.

Banks 9am–5pm Monday to Friday

Cafes 7am–8pm

Nightclubs 8pm–2am

Restaurants 11am–2pm and 5pm–10pm, or often all day

Shops 9am–6pm Monday to Saturday, 11am–6pm Sunday

Post

Postal service in the US is generally reliable and fast. Up-to-date information on rates and office locations can be found on the USPS (www.usps.com) website.

Public Holidays

Banks, schools, and government offices (including post offices) are closed on major holidays. Public holidays that fall on a weekend are often observed on the following Monday.

New Year's Day January 1

Confederate Heroes' Day January 19

Martin Luther King Jr Day Third Monday in January

President's Day Third Monday in February

BORDER PATROL CHECKPOINTS

The US Border Patrol claims the ability to operate immigration checkpoints within a zone of 100 miles from any international border, including the Texas Gulf Coast and Rio Grande border with Mexico. Travelers should be prepared to answer questions concerning their citizenship, and to show travel documents if requested.

Texas Independence Day March 2

Easter Sunday March/April (varies)

Memorial Day Last Monday in May

Independence Day July 4

Labor Day First Monday in September

Columbus Day Second Monday in October

Veterans Day November 11

Thanksgiving Fourth Thursday in November

Christmas Day December 25

Safe Travel

➡ Travel, including solo travel, is generally safe in Texas. As anywhere you should exercise more vigilance in large cities than in rural areas.

➡ Along the border with Mexico, the large law-enforcement presence is more indicative of federal policy priorities than any reason for individual travelers to fear for safety.

Guns

➡ Texas does allow personal gun ownership, including the permitted carrying of concealed hand guns, and around one in three residents exercises the right (in line with national averages).

➡ You will see signs forbidding firearms in some public places, and that will likely be your closest encounter with a gun.

➡ In Texas metro areas, as in all big cities, there are some neighborhoods that are less safe than others. Exercise a normal amount of caution. Aggravated theft (with the use of a weapon) is not common.

Recreational Hazards

In wilderness areas the consequences of a getting lost or having an accident can be very serious. Off of main trails, always travel with a hiking partner. Even on established routes, if going it alone inform someone of your destination and expected return – at the very least leaving a note in your car.

MOSQUITOES

Year-round in the great outdoors you may see mosquitoes that deserve inclusion in the Texas boast that 'everything is bigger here.' The best way to combat these bugs is to keep yourself covered (wear long sleeves, long pants, hats, and shoes rather than sandals) or apply a good insect repellent. (Repellents containing DEET are the best, but children under two should not be exposed to DEET and children aged two to 12 years should not be allowed to use repellent containing more than a 10% solution.)

JELLYFISH

Jellyfish can be present year-round in the mild waters of the Gulf of Mexico. Two varieties pack powerful stings: sea nettle, which is translucent and has tentacles attached to the edge of its bell-shaped central mass; and the Portuguese man-of-war, not actually a jellyfish but often confused for one, which looks like a translucent blue balloon with long black tentacles dangling from the center. Do not touch either of these – even if you see a dead one lying on the beach.

If you are stung, a mixture of supermarket-bought vinegar and unseasoned meat tenderizer can ease the pain. For serious reactions, seek medical attention.

Telephone

Cell Phones

Local prepaid SIM cards are widely available, though network reception can be spotty in rural areas. Only foreign phones that operate on tri- or quad-band frequencies will work in the USA.

Pay Phones & Phone Cards

With the prevalence of cell phones, pay phones have become hard to find. Airports and some gas stations may have them. Coins may sometimes be used.

For long-distance and international calls, whether at a pay phone or on a hotel's land line, use a prepaid phone card, which are sold at gas-station convenience stores and some supermarkets.

Phone Codes

In many areas, local calls have moved to a 10-digit calling system. This means you must dial the area code even when making a local call.

Country code 🖉1

International dialing code 🖉011

International Calls

For international operator assistance, dial 🖉0. The operator can provide specific rate information and tell you which time periods are the cheapest for calling. To make an international call direct, dial 🖉011, then the foreign country code, followed by the area code and the phone number. (An exception is to Canada, where you dial 🖉1 + area code + number. International rates apply to Canada.)

Time

Central Standard Time Most of Texas is an hour behind New York (Eastern time), two hours ahead of Los Angeles (Pacific time) and five hours behind Greenwich Mean Time (GMT).

Daylight savings time In effect in the US from early spring to late fall; clocks 'spring forward' one hour in March and 'fall back' one hour in November.

Mountain Standard Time El Paso and Hudspeth Counties in far-west Texas are one hour behind Central Standard Time, and six behind GMT.

Tourist Information

Larger cities and towns have tourist information centers run by local convention and visitor bureaus. In smaller towns, local chambers of commerce often perform the same functions.

The *Texas State Travel Guide* (www.traveltexas.com) is a comprehensive glossy guidebook that lists almost every city and town in the state, issued by the state tourism board. You can request one online, where most of the information is also posted, or at the Texas Travel Centers located on major interstates near the state line.

Travelers with Disabilities

Download Lonely Planet's free Accessible Travel guides from http://lptravel.to/Accessible Travel.

Communication

Braille Many ATMs and elevators have instructions in braille.

Telephone Companies are required to provide relay operators for the hearing impaired.

Public Spaces & Accessibility

Guide dogs May legally be brought into restaurants, hotels and other businesses.

Lodging Most hotels and motels have rooms set aside for guests with disabilities.

Public buildings Hotels, restaurants, theaters, museums etc are required by the *Americans with Disabilities Act* (ADA) to be wheelchair-accessible and have accessible restroom facilities

Road crossings In major cities at main intersections there are audible crossing signals, as well as dropped curbs at busier roadway intersections.

RESOURCES
→ Access-able Travel Source (www.access-able.com)
→ Mobility International USA (www.miusa.org)
→ Society for Accessible Travel & Hospitality (www.sath.org)

Transportation

Note that in general public transportation is not extensive or overly useful in Texas.

Airlines Will provide assistance for connecting, boarding and deplaning the flight, but you need to request when making your reservation.

Parking Disabled-parking sites with blue-colored demarcation are by permit only.

Public Transportation Both buses and trains must have wheelchair access available.

Standard car-rental companies Some standard companies have hand-controlled vehicles or vans with wheelchair lifts by reservation.

Wheelchair Accessible Vans (www.txwheelchairvans.com) Hires out vans in several Texas cities.

Visas

Visas are not required for citizens of Visa Waiver Program countries, but you must request travel authorization from the Electronic System for Travel Authorization at least 72 hours in advance. Visitors not eligible for the program will require a B-2 tourism visa in advance of their arrival.

Tourism & Visitor (B-2) Visa Applications

All foreign visitors who need to obtain a temporary visitor visa (B-2) must do so from a US consulate or embassy abroad. Consult that embassy's web-

site for forms and procedures, which vary by country. In general:

→ Your passport must be valid for at least six months longer than your intended stay in the USA.

→ You will need to make an appointment, and likely have an interview.

→ You'll need to submit a recent photo (2in by 2in) with the application.

→ There is a $160 processing fee, which is sometimes required in advance.

Visa Waiver Program

Currently, under the US Visa Waiver Program (VWP), visas are not required for citizens of 38 countries, including the UK, Australia, New Zealand, EU countries, South Korea and Japan. VWP regulations state the following:

→ You must have an e-Passport with electronic chip.

→ Visa waiver is good for 90 days, no extensions.

→ VWP visitors must register only with the Electronic System for Travel Authorization (ESTA; https://esta.cbp.dhs.gov) at least 72 hours before their trip begins. Once approved, ESTA registration is valid for up to two years.

→ If you don't meet any of these requirements, even if your passport if from one of the listed countries, you'll need a visa to enter the USA.

→ Note that though not a part of the VWP, citizens from Canada do not require a visa for 90-day stays.

More Information

Note that visa rules change frequently and travelers should always double-check current requirements at the Department of State (http://travel.state.gov/visa), where downloadable forms are also available.

Transportation

GETTING THERE & AWAY

Most travelers arrive in Texas by air or by car. Flights, cars and tours can be booked online at lonelyplanet.com/bookings.

Air

Unless you live in or near Texas, flying to the region and then renting a car is the most time-efficient travel option. Entering Texas as your first port of call in the US is fairly easy; there are just a few points to consider:

Customs If you're arriving from outside the USA, you must clear customs and immigration at the first airport where you land. Retrieve your luggage and return it to the belt after customs, even if it is checked through to Texas.

Digital registration Almost all international visitors will be digitally photographed and have their electronic (inkless) finger-prints scanned upon entry to the country; it takes just a minute.

Exemptions Currently many Canadian visitors, children under 14 and seniors over 79 are exempt from digital registration; for details contact the US Department of Homeland Security (DHS; www.dhs.gov).

Prohibitions The Transportation Security Administration (TSA; www.tsa.gov) prohibits pocketknives, as well as liquids and gels, on airplanes (unless the latter are stored in 3oz or smaller bottles placed inside a quart-sized, clear-plastic zip-top bag). Check the website for additional, ever-changing prohibitions.

Airports & Airlines

The main international gateways to Texas are **Dallas-Fort Worth International Airport** (DFW; ☑972-973-3112; www.dfwairport.com; 2400 Aviation Dr), which is American Airlines' hub, and Houston's **George Bush Intercontinental Airport** (IAH; Map p206; ☑281-230-3100; www.fly2houston.com/iah; 2800 N Terminal Rd, off I-59, Beltway 8 or I-45; ☎), the hub for United Airlines. **San Antonio International** (SAT; ☑210-207-3433; www.san antonio.gov/sat; 9800 Airport Blvd), **Austin-Bergstrom International** (AUS; www.austintexas.gov/airport) and **El Paso International** (ELP; Map p318; ☑915-212-0330; www.elpasointernationalairport.com; 6701 Convair Rd; ☎) have flights to and from Mexico and a limited number of other international destinations.

Numerous domestic airlines have flights to the major international airports. Additionally, **Dallas Love Field** (DAL; Map p142; ☑214-670-6080; www.dallas-lovefield.com; 8008 Herb Kelleher Way) and Houston's **William P Hobby Airport** (HOU; Map p206; ☑713-640-3000; www.fly2 houston.com/hobby; 7800 Airport Blvd, off Broadway or Monroe Sts; ☎) service numerous destinations throughout the US, primarily as hubs for Southwest Airlines.

CLIMATE CHANGE & TRAVEL

Every form of transport that relies on carbon-based fuel generates CO_2, the main cause of human-induced climate change. Modern travel is dependent on airplanes, which might use less fuel per mile per person than most cars but travel much greater distances. The altitude at which aircraft emit gases (including CO_2) and particles also contributes to their climate change impact. Many websites offer 'carbon calculators' that allow people to estimate the carbon emissions generated by their journey and, for those who wish to do so, to offset the impact of the greenhouse gases emitted with contributions to portfolios of climate-friendly initiatives throughout the world. Lonely Planet offsets the carbon footprint of all staff and author travel.

Land

Border Crossings

There are 24 official crossing points along the Texas–Mexico border; most of them are open 24 hours daily. US Customs & Border Protection (http://apps.cbp.gov/bwt) lists open hours, and estimated border waiting times for drivers.

If you are not a Mexican national, arriving from down south (whether to cross the Texas–Mexico border or not) is a serious question, given gang violence in recent years. Check with the US State Department (http://travel.state.gov/travel) for travel advisories. If you should decide to day-trip into Mexico, be aware of the following:

International taxis You may find international taxis near border crossings. Fares are from $10 to $30 – bargaining is expected.

Mexican tourism permit (*forma migratoria para turista*, or FMT) Required unless you are staying within the border zone (about 15 miles in) and not staying more than 72 hours.

Motor vehicles Taking a vehicle into Mexico is not advised, but if you do, you must obtain Mexican motor insurance and a temporary vehicle-importation permit; look for booths at crossings. Bridge tolls cost $3 per vehicle.

Passports Everyone, even US tourists visiting Mexico on a day trip, must carry a passport to enter the US.

Returning A stop at US Customs is required; be prepared to state your nationality and declare any purchases made in Mexico. Note that it is not legal to bring back many prescription drugs.

Walking Most people crossing into Mexico for a day trip from Texas walk across the bridge (most of the Mexican cities are a few steps from the Rio Grande); bridge tolls cost $1 per pedestrian.

Bus

Greyhound (www.greyhound.com), the nationwide bus company, has reduced its services considerably but still runs cross-country.

➡ Buses are generally comfortable and safe, but they are slow and do not always represent a substantial cost savings over advance airfares or car rental.

➡ Fixed routes stop in major cities only, and not always in the best part of town.

➡ For best fares reserve tickets online at least two weeks in advance or more, and travel at off-peak hours.

➡ Reduced carbon emissions are a benefit to bus riding.

Car & Motorcycle

Interstate 35 runs south from Oklahoma into the Dallas–Fort Worth metro area. The transcontinental interstate for the southern USA is I-10, and it runs from Florida to California, passing through much of Texas. Across the north of the state, I-20 serves much the same function.

Train

Amtrak (www.amtrak.com) provides two cross-country passenger services that stop in a several cities across Texas. Services are fairly comfortable, even in the reclining coach seats, and dining or snack cars are available. However, the trains run at a slow speed, with frequent service delays and late arrivals, and tickets are not always reasonably priced; booking as far in advance as possible helps. The two cross-country services are as follows:

Sunset Limited Runs three times a week between New Orleans and Los Angeles, stopping in Beaumont, Houston, San Antonio, Del Rio, Sanderson, Alpine and El Paso.

Texas Eagle Travels between Los Angeles and Chicago, stopping daily in 17 Texas cities including Dallas, Fort Worth, Austin, San Antonio and El Paso.

Sea

Cruise ships to Mexico and the Caribbean depart from the **Texas Cruise Ship Terminal** (2502 Harborside Dr) in Galveston.

GETTING AROUND

The best way to see the state is to rent a car and drive, but distances add up if you're not staying in one or two regions. To cover more ground in a shorter time, you can fly.

Air Connections between major cities and smaller airports across the state and region.

Bicycle Limited special facilities within largest cities, very little outside.

Bus Extremely limited outside big cities; not comprehensive even within.

Car Easy to rent at any airport, at in-town locations and even in suburbia.

Train Limited service on two routes through the state.

Air

Airlines in Texas

American Airlines, Southwest and United all operate flights to regional airports within Texas. Book in advance for the best deals; signing up for

---

TRAVELING IN TEXAS BORDERLANDS

Note that the US Border Patrol maintains several checkpoints at scattered locations throughout the Texas interior. If you are traveling within 100 miles of the border, be sure to carry your international passport or domestic driver's license/photo ID with you. You may be asked to pull over and produce it.

airlines' online weekly sales newsletters can be helpful.

American (☑800-433-7300; www.aa.com) Destinations include Abilene, Amarillo, Austin, Beaumont, Brownsville, College Station, Corpus Christi, Dallas, El Paso, Houston, Killeen, Longview, Lubbock, McAllen, Midland, San Antonio, Tyler and Waco.

Southwest (☑800-435-9792; www.southwest.com) Services to Austin, Corpus Christi, Dallas, El Paso, Harlingen, Houston, Midland and San Antonio.

United (☑800-864-8331; www.united.com) Routes include Amarillo, Austin, Beaumont, Brownsville, College Station, Corpus Christi, Dallas, El Paso, Harlingen, Houston, Killeen, Laredo, Lubbock, McAllen, Midland, San Antonio and Waco.

Bicycle

Cycling is a feasible way of getting around within some regions, but remember that Texas is spread out and cities are connected by major interstates, so traveling from city to city on a bike is trickier and separate bike lines are few and far between. There are bicycle-rental shops in most major cities, but the rates for each 24 hours can be as high as renting a car. If you're planning on cycling the whole time, it would pay to bring your bike with you from home.

Bicycles can be transported by air. Your best bet is to disassemble or partially disassemble them and put them in a bike bag or box. You may have to remove the pedals and front tire so that it fits in your box or bag. Check all this with the airline well in advance, preferably before you pay for your ticket. Be aware that some airlines will welcome bicycles, while others will treat them as an undesirable nuisance and do everything possible to discourage them.

Greyhound buses will accept bicycles as checked baggage for a fee. Amtrak usually accepts bicycles as

part of regularly checked baggage, although a carrying case is required and a nominal fee may be charged on smaller trains.

Cyclists should carry plenty of water and refill at every opportunity. Spare parts are widely available and repair shops are numerous, but it's still important to be able to do basic mechanical work, like fixing a flat, yourself.

Roadside Hazards

On the two-lane highways of rural Texas, folks often drive on the shoulder of the road. Some do it just because they plan to turn soon, even though 'soon' may be 5 miles down the road. Some drivers do it out of courtesy to faster drivers, creating an impromptu passing lane. Whatever the reason, bicyclists and pedestrians traveling on smaller roads would do very well to stay aware and watch out for shoulder drivers.

Boat

Two 24-hour ferry crossings make life a little easier for travelers in Texas. From Galveston to the Bolivar Peninsula, a 30-minute trip forms the missing link of TX 87. At Aransas Pass, a five-minute ride connects across to Port Aransas.

Bus

Greyhound (www.greyhound.com)is the main company serving Texas. Bus travel generally has a cost edge over flying, but not necessarily over car rental if booked ahead. Greyhound has eliminated services to smaller communities it once served, so your only real option is busing it between big cities. Service is slow and you will still need a car to get around in most towns in Texas – making it quite inconvenient to arrive in town by bus.

Car & Motorcycle

Having a car during at least some portion of your trip is all but a necessity. Texans love their vehicles and most cities are well spread out as a result. Public transportation is limited even within big metro areas – and it's nonexistent in small towns.

Crime In metro areas do not leave valuables in sight on the car seat; petty theft does happen.

Exiting Highways in-state may come together for a while and branch off each other; note that exits are not always on the right.

Interstates Posted speed limits may be as much as 85mph, and traffic can move even faster. Lanes multiply in cities; don't be surprised to find yourself in traffic that is 12 lanes across.

Rural roads Posted speed limits are often still high (as much as 70mph) on rural roads. Some locals like this, and will pass you going a million miles an hour, whizzing past trailer homes. Others will take their sweet time no matter what the speed limit; be prepared to slow down if you get stuck behind a slow driver.

Rush hour From 7am to 9am and 4:30pm to 6:30pm; major city driving is to be avoided at these hours. Also expect a mini lunch rush between noon and 1:30pm.

Size Matters Pick-up trucks and sport-utility vehicles (SUVs) dominate in Texas; if driving a compact, get used to being the smallest thing on the road.

Automobile Associations

American Automobile Association (AAA; www.aaa.com) membership provides emergency roadside service in the event of an accident, breakdown, running out of fuel or locking your keys in the car.

➡ Consider joining if you plan on doing a lot of driving in the USA.

➡ Membership also provides access to hotel discounts.

➡ Car-rental programs may offer alternative roadside assistance plans.

➡ AAA has reciprocal agreements; members of some foreign auto clubs are entitled to local services. Check in advance and bring your membership card.

Driver's License

Texas has reciprocity agreements with 83 countries, meaning your driver's license is likely good in Texas if you plan to stay less than a year.

➡ Some of the countries included are Canada, Mexico, the UK, most of Europe, Australia, New Zealand, Japan and South Korea.

➡ To make sure your country is on the reciprocal list, check the Texas Department of Public Safety's webpage (www.dps.texas.gov/Driverlicense/reciprocity.htm), or contact their office at ☑512-424-2600.

➡ It never hurts to carry an International Driving Permit (IDP) in addition to your domestic license; for foreign nationals not on the list, this is a must. IDPs are available from your local automobile association and are usually valid one year.

Fuel & Spare Parts

Gas stations They're everywhere, and usually open 24 hours. Pay at the pump with a credit card or pay in advance with cash.

Rental-Car problems In the event of a mechanical problem or breakdown in a rental car, contact the rental agency immediately (the number is likely on the key chain); they will be able to help.

Roadside assistance Having an automobile association membership or other roadside assistance can be a big help with minor problems.

Service stations Full automotive service is not generally available at gas stations. If you need an oil change or to fix a flat, national chains such as Jiffy Lube (www.jiffylube.com) and Discount

Tire (www.discounttire.com) are widely represented in Texas.

Insurance

Note that in Texas (as well as the US as a whole) you must have liability insurance for any car you drive, at a minimum.

➡ Liability insurance means that you won't have to pay for damages if you hit someone.

➡ If you're renting a car, the liability insurance is called Loss/Damage Waiver (LDW), or Collision/Damage Waiver (CDW), and is not included in rates.

➡ If you have your own private vehicle insurance elsewhere in the US, it may extend to vehicles you rent; ask ahead and bring your insurance card.

➡ In some cases, your major credit card may offer insurance coverage if you reserve and pay for the rental with that card.

➡ When you rent a car, adding LDW coverage ($10 to $25 per day extra) will always be offered as an option.

➡ Uninsured motorists in Texas account for less than 13% of drivers. Note that LDW does not cover damages and medical injuries caused by the uninsured, but your personal policy might. You can add supplemental Personal Accident Insurance to your rental if you are concerned.

Rental

All major car-rental companies in the USA have offices throughout Texas. Airports are the most common rental location, but city and suburban offices also exist.

➡ In general, reserve as far ahead as possible for the best rates. But if price is a big concern, keep checking for sales afterwards. Bookings are usually changeable without fees.

➡ Rates for a compact to midsize car generally range from $25 to $45 per day, and $170 to $250 per week.

➡ Note that in addition to the base rate, there will be heaps of local, state and airport concession taxes (15% to 20%), most companies now quote the total, tax-included price online.

➡ Weekend-only rentals can be supercheap ($5 to $20 per day).

➡ Unlimited mileage is usually included, but check to be sure. (Have we mentioned Texas is big?)

➡ Consolidators like Hotwire (www.hotwire.com) and Priceline (www.priceline.com) can sometimes save you money, especially if you're willing to accept whatever rental company they choose.

➡ Car Rental Express (www.carrentalexpress.com) is a clearing house for independent car-rental agencies; note that there aren't many in Texas and they're usually off-airport.

➡ If you plan to drop off the car somewhere other than where you picked it up, be aware that additional fees can be hefty ($100 or more).

➡ Enterprise (www.enterprise.com) has the most suburban locations in Texas.

AGE & CREDIT REQUIREMENTS

➡ Most rental agencies require that you have a major credit card in your own name, both for reserving ahead and at the counter.

➡ Some companies require operators to be at least 25 years old; those allowing 18- to 25-year-olds to drive charge high supplemental fees.

➡ Some companies will allow a spouse to legally drive a rental without paying the second driver fee (from $25).

Road Rules

➡ Drive on the right side of the road and pass on the left.

➡ Right turn on a red light is permitted after a full stop unless signs indicate otherwise. Speed limits are posted and enforced.

➡ Unless otherwise posted, speed limits are 70mph daytime, 65mph nighttime on interstates and freeways.

➡ Speed limits in cities and towns vary (25mph to 55mph).

➡ School zones have strictly enforced speed limits as low as 15mph during school hours – and using mobile phones while driving in these zones can mean big fines.

➡ Speeding fines are expensive – as much as $165 for between 1mph and 5mph over in Houston. That said, driving 5mph over the speed limit on highways is common.

➡ Driving while intoxicated (defined as not having the normal use of faculties, or .08% blood-alcohol level) is illegal; penalties are severe, starting with a minimum 72-hour confinement.

➡ Texas requires the use of seat belts for drivers and front-seat passengers. Child safety seats are also required for those under eight years old or 4ft 9in.

➡ Texas requires motorcycle riders under age 21 to wear helmets; over age 21 it is not required if a rider has completed a safety training course or has medical-

insurance coverage (greater than $10,000) that includes motorcycle accidents. Police cannot stop a helmetless rider solely to see if they qualify for exemption.

ACCIDENTS DO HAPPEN

If you get in a fender bender, take the following steps:

➡ Do not drive away. Move your car out of traffic lanes, but remain at the scene; otherwise you may spend some time in the local jail.

➡ Call ☑911 to reach the police (and an ambulance, if needed); provide as much specific information as possible (your location, if there are any injuries involved etc).

➡ Get the other driver's name, address, license number, license-plate number and insurance information. Be prepared to provide similar documentation.

➡ Tell your story to the police. It's your right under the law to have a lawyer present when answering questions, but unless a death is involved, cases where this is necessary are rare.

➡ Texas state laws permits law enforcement officers to conduct an alcohol breathalyzer test if they

suspect a driver to be intoxicated. If you take the option not to, you'll almost certainly find yourself with an automatic suspension of your driving privileges.

➡ If you're driving a rental car, call the rental company promptly.

Local Transportation

Local public transportation – including buses, light rail and trains – is available only in major cities, and even then it is not always comprehensive or traveler friendly. Operating hours differ from city to city, but in general services run from about 6am to 10pm. Basic fares average between $1.25 and $2.

Austin Buses can be handy for getting around downtown and to S Congress Ave; the light rail primarily heads out of town toward the suburbs.

Dallas Light-rail connects several downtown stops with outlying suburbs; the McKinney Ave Trolley is great for traveling between uptown and downtown. Weekdays, Trinity Express trains connect Dallas with Fort Worth.

Houston Has a limited light-rail system, good for connecting from downtown to museums, but not for going further; buses are not very useful here, or easy to navigate.

San Antonio Five 'street car' (a bus-like trolley) routes cater to city visitors, connecting all major downtown sights (Alamo, Market Square and more).

Train

Amtrak (www.amtrak.com) has two national routes, the *Texas Eagle* and the *Sunset Limited*, that connect through Texas towns. Unless you just love the romance of train travel and want to take your time getting places, the service is fairly impractical. Scheduled arrivals may be in the middle of the night and service is often late.

DRINKING & DRIVING

➡ The drinking age in the US is 21, and you need an ID (driver's license or other identification with your photograph and date of birth on it) to prove your age. Undercover agents from the Texas Alcoholic Beverage Commission may pose as employees or consumers in shops that sell alcohol, trawling for underage buyers.

➡ You could incur stiff fines, jail time and penalties if caught driving under the influence of alcohol. Statewide the blood-alcohol limit is 0.08%, which is likely to be reached after just two 12oz bottles of beer for a 135lb woman, or three for a 175lb man.

➡ If you're younger than 21 years old it is illegal to drive after you have consumed *any* alcohol – zero tolerance.

➡ Roads near notorious bars may be watched. During holidays and special events, roadblocks are sometimes set up to check for (and deter) drunk drivers.

Behind the Scenes

SEND US YOUR FEEDBACK

We love to hear from travelers – your comments keep us on our toes and help make our books better. Our well-traveled team reads every word on what you loved or loathed about this book. Although we cannot reply individually to your submissions, we always guarantee that your feedback goes straight to the appropriate authors, in time for the next edition. Each person who sends us information is thanked in the next edition – the most useful submissions are rewarded with a selection of digital PDF chapters.

Visit **lonelyplanet.com/contact** to submit your updates and suggestions or to ask for help. Our award-winning website also features inspirational travel stories, news and discussions.

Note: We may edit, reproduce and incorporate your comments in Lonely Planet products such as guidebooks, websites and digital products, so let us know if you don't want your comments reproduced or your name acknowledged. For a copy of our privacy policy visit lonelyplanet.com/privacy.

OUR READERS

Many thanks to the travelers who used the last edition and wrote to us with helpful hints, useful advice and interesting anecdotes: Alice Fontaine, Deborah McKeown, Hunter Oates, Jerry Peill, Larry Abbott, Paul Labic, Sain Alizada, Servanne Huerre, Shannon Leahy

WRITER THANKS
Amy C Balfour

Thank you for your Austin recommendations and hospitality: Chris McCray, Doug Kilday, Ken Wiles and family, John Apperson and Amanda Bachman. For fine party throwing and fierce BBQ opinions, thanks to the Austin W&L crew and their families: Jenny Stratton, Anna Salas, Kelly Rogers, Lucy Anderson, Bitsy and David Young, Chris Casey and John Pipkin. Thank you Paul and Crystal Sadler for the San Antonio and West Texas tips. To Mary, Ron and Gina in Drip, can we do it again? In West Texas, an appreciative shout out to Jenny Moore, Michelle Cromer, Anne Mitchell, and Anne and Keene Haywood. With help from Mariella Krause, Jeff Kelsey, Melissa Reid and Sarah Bunn. Finally, thanks to Alex Howard for entrusting me with this awesome assignment and cheers to my talented cowriters Stephen Lioy and Ryan Ver Berkmoes.

Stephen Lioy

Many thanks to many people, but specifically to the following. Aileen for the thousand tips, Anthony for the copilot miles and company, Jess and Kevin for always being there, Kalli and Tonie for helping me enjoy inefficiency, Shane for tips and time and sometimes beer, Cindy/Payton/Pres for being so bad at Catan, Dav and Nan and UpChuck for the very many nights and meals and help, and Jack for being Jack. *Hey Tonie...you wanna be frieeeeeends?*

Ryan Ver Berkmoes

Like the seasons of a Texas bluebonnet, life can go full circle. In 1997, *Texas* was the second book I ever did for Lonely Planet. And now here's *Texas* again after 20 years. Happily this time around I didn't have the worst meal of my life in Nacogdoches. Fond thanks to those many people who were so helpful two decades ago and again this time. And fond love to Alexis Ver Berkmoes, who is proof that as some things fade away, other things just get better.

ACKNOWLEDGEMENTS

Climate map data adapted from Peel MC, Finlayson BL & McMahon TA (2007) 'Updated World Map of the Köppen-Geiger Climate Classification', Hydrology and Earth System Sciences, 11, 163344.

Cover photograph: Guadalupe Mountains National Park. Tim Fitzharris, Getty©

THIS BOOK

This 5th edition of Lonely Planet's *Texas* guidebook was researched and written by Amy C Balfour, Stephen Lioy and Ryan Ver Berkmoes. The previous edition was written by Ryan, Lisa Dunford and Mariella Krause. This guidebook was produced by the following:

Destination Editor
Alexander Howard

Product Editor Joel Cotterell

Senior Cartographer
Alison Lyall

Book Designer Clara Monitto

Assisting Editors Janet Austin, James Bainbridge, Michelle Coxall, Bruce Evans, Carly Hall, Ali Lemer, Charlotte Orr, Simon Williamson

Assisting Cartographers

Corey Hutchison, James Leversha

Cover Researcher
Brendan Dempsey-Spencer

Thanks to Dora Ball, Evan Godt, Mark Griffiths, Kate Mathews, Catherine Naghten, Martine Power, Alison Ridgway, Tom Stainer

Thanks to researcher Michael Clark for his post-hurricane updates.

Index

Map Legend

Sights
- Beach
- Bird Sanctuary
- Buddhist
- Castle/Palace
- Christian
- Confucian
- Hindu
- Islamic
- Jain
- Jewish
- Monument
- Museum/Gallery/Historic Building
- Ruin
- Shinto
- Sikh
- Taoist
- Winery/Vineyard
- Zoo/Wildlife Sanctuary
- Other Sight

Activities, Courses & Tours
- Bodysurfing
- Diving
- Canoeing/Kayaking
- Course/Tour
- Sento Hot Baths/Onsen
- Skiing
- Snorkeling
- Surfing
- Swimming/Pool
- Walking
- Windsurfing
- Other Activity

Sleeping
- Sleeping
- Camping

Eating
- Eating

Drinking & Nightlife
- Drinking & Nightlife
- Cafe

Entertainment
- Entertainment

Shopping
- Shopping

Information
- Bank
- Embassy/Consulate
- Hospital/Medical
- Internet
- Police
- Post Office
- Telephone
- Toilet
- Tourist Information
- Other Information

Geographic
- Beach
- Gate
- Hut/Shelter
- Lighthouse
- Lookout
- Mountain/Volcano
- Oasis
- Park
- Pass
- Picnic Area
- Waterfall

Population
- Capital (National)
- Capital (State/Province)
- City/Large Town
- Town/Village

Transport
- Airport
- BART station
- Border crossing
- Boston T station
- Bus
- Cable car/Funicular
- Cycling
- Ferry
- Metro/Muni station
- Monorail
- Parking
- Petrol station
- Subway/SkyTrain station
- Taxi
- Train station/Railway
- Tram
- Underground station
- Other Transport

Note: Not all symbols displayed above appear on the maps in this book

Routes
- Tollway
- Freeway
- Primary
- Secondary
- Tertiary
- Lane
- Unsealed road
- Road under construction
- Plaza/Mall
- Steps
- Tunnel
- Pedestrian overpass
- Walking Tour
- Walking Tour detour
- Path/Walking Trail

Boundaries
- International
- State/Province
- Disputed
- Regional/Suburb
- Marine Park
- Cliff
- Wall

Hydrography
- River, Creek
- Intermittent River
- Canal
- Water
- Dry/Salt/Intermittent Lake
- Reef

Areas
- Airport/Runway
- Beach/Desert
- Cemetery (Christian)
- Cemetery (Other)
- Glacier
- Mudflat
- Park/Forest
- Sight (Building)
- Sportsground
- Swamp/Mangrove

OUR STORY

A beat-up old car, a few dollars in the pocket and a sense of adventure. In 1972 that's all Tony and Maureen Wheeler needed for the trip of a lifetime – across Europe and Asia overland to Australia. It took several months, and at the end – broke but inspired – they sat at their kitchen table writing and stapling together their first travel guide, *Across Asia on the Cheap*. Within a week they'd sold 1500 copies. Lonely Planet was born.

Today, Lonely Planet has offices in Franklin, London, Melbourne, Oakland, Dublin, Beijing and Delhi, with more than 600 staff and writers. We share Tony's belief that 'a great guidebook should do three things: inform, educate and amuse'.

OUR WRITERS

Amy C Balfour

Amy practiced law in Virginia before moving to Los Angeles to try to break in as a screenwriter. After a stint as a writer's assistant on *Law & Order*, she jumped into freelance writing, focusing on travel, food and the outdoors. Amy has hiked, biked and paddled across the United States. She recently crisscrossed Texas in search of the region's best barbecue and outdoor attractions. Books authored or coauthored include *USA, Eastern USA, New Orleans, Florida & the South's Best Trips, New England's Best Trips, Arizona, Hawaii, Los Angeles Encounter* and *California*. Her stories have appeared in *Backpacker, Sierra, Southern Living* and *Women's Health*.

Stephen Lioy

Stephen Lioy is a photographer, writer, hiker and travel blogger based in Central Asia. A 'once in a lifetime' Eurotrip and post-university move to China set the stage for what would eventually become a seminomadic lifestyle based on sharing his experiences with would-be travelers and helping provide that initial push out of comfort zones and into all that the planet has to offer. Follow Stephen's travels at www.monkboughtlunch.com or see his photography at www.stephenlioy.com.

Ryan Ver Berkmoes

Ryan has written more than 110 guidebooks for Lonely Planet. He grew up in Santa Cruz, California, which he left at age 17 for college in the Midwest, where he first discovered snow. All joy of this novelty soon wore off. Since then he has been traveling the world, both for pleasure and for work – which are often indistinguishable. He has covered everything from wars to bars. He definitely prefers the latter. Ryan calls New York City home.

Published by Lonely Planet Global Limited
CRN 554153
5th edition – Feb 2018
ISBN 978 1 78657 343 8
© Lonely Planet 2018   Photographs © as indicated 2018
10 9 8 7 6 5 4 3 2 1
Printed in Singapore